CW00687649

ADVENTISTICA

# Studies in Adventist History and Theology – New Series

Series Editors:
Johannes Hartlapp, Daniel Heinz,
Stefan Höschele, Rolf J. Pöhler

PUBLISHED BY
THE INSTITUTE OF ADVENTIST STUDIES
OF FRIEDENSAU ADVENTIST UNIVERSITY

Volume 2

# Contours of European Adventism

## Issues in the History of the Denomination on the Old Continent

Stefan Höschele & Chigemezi N. Wogu
Editors

THEOLOGISCHE
HOCHSCHULE
FRIEDENSAU

ADVENTISTICA
Studies in Adventist History and Theology – New Series
Editors: Johannes Hartlapp, Daniel Heinz, Stefan Höschele, Rolf J. Pöhler

Volume 2
Contours of European Adventism:
Issues in the History of the Denomination on the Old Continent

Book Editors: Stefan Höschele and Chigemezi Nnadozie Wogu
Layout: Chigemezi Nnadozie Wogu
Copy Editor: Jonquil Hole

Cover © rasani.design Leipzig

© 2020 Institute of Adventist Studies
Friedensau Adventist University
39291 Möckern-Friedensau, Germany
Internet: www.thh-friedensau.de
E-mail: ias@thh-friedensau.de

Printed by: Books on Demand GmbH
In de Tarpen 42, 22848 Norderstedt, Germany

ISBN: 978-3-935480-53-6

# Contents

# Stefan Höschele and Chigemezi Nnadozie Wogu

## Introduction

According to a Congolese proverb, "a single bracelet does not jingle." It is the tinkling of several bracelets that brings attention and admiration to them and to the wearer. This insight can be applied to Seventh-day Adventism in Europe: How does one best speak about the history and commonalities of this denomination on the Old Continent? We suggest by "jingling" various types of Adventism in Europe – national, regional, local – so as to evince the peculiarities, beauty, and challenges of the Adventist movement in Europe. An important step in doing so was achieved during the Third International Symposium of the Institute of Adventist Studies at Friedensau Adventist University, held on April 23–26, 2018. The event was entitled *Contours of European Adventism: Issues in the History of the Denomination on the Old Continent.* This jingling of Adventisms from several European countries brought together scholars to present unique faces and facets of this religious movement in Europe.

European Adventism has a rich heritage of diversity and unity: significant mission advance in some areas, the molding of peculiar local traditions, and the formation of regional and transnational networks. It is here that the 19th century American religion founded by the church's pioneers first translated their identity into a multiplicity of cultural and religious contexts. Thus Adventist history in Europe is replete with instances in which this movement had to face new realities and renegotiate its stance vis-à-vis society at large, other religious and cultural communities, and their own denominational tradition.

The background of this volume, and of the symposium during which the papers were presented, is a global research and publication project, the *Encyclopedia of Seventh-day Adventists* (ESDA). In 2015, the international Seventh-day Adventist Church launched the plan to publish about 10,000 articles with a focus on denominational history. Biographies, regional articles, and information on institutions, organizational entities, special events, and key publications and other phenomena are all to inform the public about what Adventists stand for, where they came from, how their movement was shaped, and what challenges they face. Another category of articles to be expected in 2020, when the ESDA will go online, will deal with special issues that the denomination faced in particular regions of the world or in general.

The editors of this volume are both involved in organizing and preparing articles for publication in two of the three church regions that comprise European countries (the so-called Inter-European and Euro-Asia Divisions). When we discussed the issues that need to be researched for the ESDA project, we quickly realized that they largely relate to Europe as a whole continent, not only to one or the other division (church region). From this insight arose the idea to utilize the biennial Adventist Studies symposia in Friedensau to bring together scholars who will write on these themes. This book is a product of this idea.

Of course, these topics could not all be treated in the same way. Some articles contribute to an understanding of particular epochs or present case studies regarding a particular country or region of Europe. This is in line with previous Adventist historiography, which has mostly focused on individual countries so far. Moreover, with regard to the themes that authors engage with here, a large variety of previous publications exists: much has already been written about some aspects of European Adventism (e.g., some important leaders and their contributions), but very little about many others. This book offers an attempt to look at European Adventism *as a whole* and to derive insights from the jingling that its facets produce.

Many of the issues that Adventism faced in Europe resemble those that emerging religious movements experience everywhere; others reflect peculiarly Adventist experiences. The contributions in part I of the book address the denomination's missionary activities and its spread with many hindrances and challenges (*Valentine; Namoradze; Činčala*), unforeseen forces and dynamics (*Lawson*), the learning experience that Adventists had to undergo in a context that differed from their North American cradle, which resulted in significant variety (*Valentine* and *Lawson* again; *Wogu; Stefánsson*), and the developments that led to further expansion beyond the continent (*Öster*).

Part II of the volume contains accounts of some of the most upsetting phases in European Adventist history. While the five contributions by *Neagu, Zaitsev, Balcar, Modoran,* and *Heinz* all focus on particular countries, periods, and individuals,* the overall picture that they paint is that of a marginal church that underwent strains, persecution, and violent attacks almost unheard of in today's Europe. While these accounts mainly come from the eastern part of the continent, they indicate that a denomination such as the SDA Church – with its non-violent ethos and strict and minority-type lifestyle – is voluntarily vulnerable when its environment chooses to oppress people of faith. The fact that congregations and even organizations have survived in spite of abundant state-sponsored persecution demonstrates how much religious convictions can mean to humans in general and to Seventh-day Adventists in particular.

The last part (III) portrays stories and presents reflections of increasingly less troubled encounters. There are today probably hardly any anti-European church leaders (*Bruinsma*), and although the Adventist relationship to their national or regional community generally remains an open question rather than a case of well-reflected belonging (*Pearson*), Adventists have been able to grow in terms of developing a mature stance vis-à-vis the state in some respects (*Rimoldi*). In one case, an Adventist politician has even been instrumental in initiating an entirely new party

---

* Because of the variety of authors, transliteration from Cyrillic script has not been done in the same manner throughout this book; this also includes the bibliography at the end of this volume.

brand (the Animal Welfare parties); it was a privilege and a highlight of the symposium to listen to Marianne *Thieme*, one of the founders and main forces of the Dutch Party for the Animals (Partij voor de Dieren). Her speech has also been included in this volume. The checkered history of Adventist relations to the dominant churches and other minority denominations (*Höschele; Sauvagnat*) also reveals a process of growth in encountering the Other: Adventists have persistently clung to their principles while steadily learning where cooperation with other movements and organizations is actually demanded by their very faith.

Some of the special features that this book presents must also be mentioned here. One is the opening chapter (*Fortin*), which reflects on European Adventism from an American perspective. We requested the author viz. presenter to explicitly speak and write from an etic (outsider's) viewpoint to enrich the otherwise somewhat self-contained European discourse. The second is the *first comprehensive bibliography of Seventh-day Adventism in Europe*. We would like to thank the two compilers, Jón Hjörleifur *Stefánsson* and Eudritch *Jean*, as well as Daniel *Heinz*, who supported the two, in a special way. This bibliography will continue growing in the future (and it will also be found on the web pages of the Institute of Adventist Studies at Friedensau). However, the fact that it is now available indicates, to us, that the study of Adventism in Europe has (finally!) reached a stage of maturation.

Hardly any academic publication of the present format – an edited volume – will be so comprehensive that readers find all they are looking for. This book is also far from perfect; some of its limitations arise from the theme (which does not necessitate an overall history of European Adventism). Another bracelet that is missing almost completely in the jingling of topics is theology: indirectly, European Adventists have contributed much to Adventist theological thinking, mainly in the 1970s and 1980s, when the continent produced many leading theologians who would ultimately work in America. However, the fact that little explicitly contextual theology has been done in the Adventist denomination so far also implies that European Adventists have not frequently developed their theological thinking as a consciously contextual Adventist project.

Two other missing aspects are reflections on church practices and on Ellen White. On the side of practices, Sabbath-keeping patterns and Sabbath challenges, worship, and the tremendous Adventist social and welfare activities would all provide much interesting research material. With regard to the denomination's prophet and her relationship to Europe, a presentation topic was suggested to potential contributors, but will have to be dealt with at a later time. Ellen White's travels in Europe have been chronicled very well, yet the symposium would have been an opportunity to reflect on how Europe impacted White's ministry in the latter part of the 1880s and beyond – and, indirectly, the denomination as a whole. Certainly these reflections will be offered by scholars at a later time.

We would like to close with words of gratitude – first of all, to God, our Creator and Redeemer, who initiated the denomination to which we belong and which we love and enjoy researching. Together with Jón H. Stefánsson (from Iceland), Eudritch

Jean (from Haiti), and Daniel Heinz (originally from Austria), we (Stefan Höschele, from Germany, and Chigemezi Nnadozie Wogu, from Nigeria) just finished a thoroughly enjoyable and interculturally enriching ESDA project year together. Reflecting and working on Adventism in Europe in manifold ways was an experience that we will always hold dear in our memory. Special thanks to Professor Rolf Pöhler, Director of the Institute of Adventist Studies, who happily postponed the symposium which had already been conceived for 2018 to 2020. Our gratitude to Jonquil Hole, former fellow ESDA editor of the TED (Trans-European) region, is so great that we can hardly express it! She volunteered to copy edit the funny English of people coming from more than a dozen non-English speaking countries and did all of it so cheerfully – we ask the Lord to give us a double portion of this spirit! Thank you very much as well to Dr David Trim and Dr Dragoslava Santrač, who are in charge of the worldwide ESDA project. Your cooperation, support, and leadership in this project, which have also catalyzed this book, have been exemplary, and we will always remain grateful to you.

We would like to end this introduction in a modest way – by requesting the reader to read Rolf *Pöhler*'s conclusion, which is entitled, "Bringing the Treasures into the City of God." If the present volume can contribute to treasuring both Adventism at large and its European variety, and thus to foster the unity of the Spirit in an amazingly diverse global denomination, then our efforts shall not have been in vain.

*Denis Fortin*

# Some Reflections on European Adventist Contributions to the Wider Church

Abstract

The Seventh-day Adventist Church in Europe is a unique form of Adventism and the contributions it makes to worldwide Adventism are numerous and very important. To a large extent, European Adventism has understood that Christianity is bigger than the Seventh-day Adventist Church and that its message is a complement to what other churches teach. Ellen White was the first one to articulate this concept in Europe, to affirm what Adventists have in common with other Christians. European Adventism has been shaped by what it means to be a small religious minority in a secular and often anti-religious society and this has shaped profoundly forms of evangelism, and relationships with other Christians and government authorities. There are challenges ahead and the future may be uncertain. Yet, European Adventist contributions to Christianity, to Adventism and to the world are beneficial and needed as a prophetic voice to speak to the rest of the Seventh-day Adventist Church and make significant contributions in understanding the denomination's relationship with society and other Christian churches.

It is a daunting task for a non-European person from North America to assess the contours of European Adventism and to provide some reflections on its contributions to the wider Seventh-day Adventist Church. European Adventism is so diverse, with so much cultural, religious, political and social diversity that in doing such an assessment one runs the risk of being too general or even irrelevant.

Nonetheless, as one looks over the history of Adventist accomplishments and challenges in Europe in the last few generations, there are a few reflections that can be considered.

## Ellen White in Europe (1885–1887) and Contextual Relevance

Even though it happened 130 years ago, Ellen White's visit to Europe between 1885 and 1887 is still a historical event that is highly valued among European Seventh-day Adventists – although one that has dimmed in significance with the passage of time.

Ellen White's visit to Europe certainly had a significant impact on the beginning of the Adventist church here, but it had an impact on her as well. For one thing, it is her visit to Europe that impressed upon her the need for her books to be translated into many other languages. And it also impressed on her the need to be relevant to the people of the different traditions and religious heritage of Europe.

While in Europe, some church members asked for permission to translate some of her books, in particular, volume 4 of the series *The Spirit of Prophecy*, which was also sub-titled, *The Great Controversy*. She agreed to this, but not before preparing an updated edition of *The Great Controversy*. Her visit to various countries and her learning more about the history of the Protestant Reformation in many places encouraged her to expand the book thus making it more relevant to Europeans as well.

Thus after her visit was completed, she added or changed a number of chapters to *The Great Controversy*. The chapters on the history of the Reformation in Bohemia (Huss and Jerome), in Switzerland (Zwingli), in France, the Netherlands and Scandinavia, and the Pilgrim Fathers to America were added and the two chapters on the later English Reformers and the Bible and the French Revolution were greatly expanded and reshaped.

Her visit to Europe helped Ellen White understand the importance of relevance and that reaching out to other people groups needed to be done with care and intelligence. Her expansion and changes to *The Great Controversy* helped European Adventists understand that the Adventist message was to be rooted in the workings of God's providence in the history of Christianity in Europe and that this Adventist message was not intrinsically an American message, but a worldwide message that had its origins in Europe a long time before William Miller began to preach it. God had been working in the hearts and minds of European Christians to focus them on the truths of God's word a long time before he worked on the hearts and minds of Miller and his followers in the nineteenth century.[1]

Ellen White understood the need for relevance and for the religious and social contextualization of the Adventist message in a very diverse European context. Although her thoughts were spoken many generations ago, what she said nonetheless set the stage for the formation of a very unique form of Adventism. And today, 130 years after her visit, European Adventism is now making a unique contribution to the worldwide Seventh-day Adventist Church. After a brief review of the relationship of the church to society and culture, this paper offers several reflections on the distinctive contributions of European Adventism.

## Relationship of the Church to Society and Culture

That the church influences culture and that culture influences the church is a well-known factor in the religious experience of Christians and should not be a surprising fact in any discussion of the social development of a new church or religious group.

---

1   One could be tempted to digress and talk of some intriguing aspects of the European translations of *The Great Controversy*, in particular the added chapter on the Reformation in Spain found only in the Spanish edition or how the French translation was done. These two historical contributions are fascinating and provide some stimulating points of discussion about Ellen White's inspiration. See Denis Fortin, "La Réforme en France et l'influence de Calvin dans l'interprétation de l'histoire du protestantisme chez Ellen White," *SERVIR – Revue adventiste de théologie* 1 (Fall 2017): 71–86.

A century ago, European historians and sociologists Ernst Troeltsch and Max Weber and, in the United States, H. Richard Niebuhr and, more recently, Peter Berger, studied this phenomenon and attempted to map out how a new religious group develops during its first four or five generations as it relates to society and culture.[2] Their findings led to the formulation of a typology of development of new religious groups from sect to church over a period of a few generations which H. Richard Niebuhr aptly applied to the American context.

This typology argues that during the first generation of a new religious movement, people join this movement by a conscious decision to leave the world (or something) in order to embrace a new community. This new group articulates together a system of beliefs which emphasizes what is different from the religious groups they are leaving. The differences in beliefs and behavior matter much more than what they have in common with their society and culture. In this first generation, the sectarian impulse is primary and strong – this new group has a special understanding of itself, of the world in which it operates, and of the future it seeks. No one else around them seems to have what they have.

The second generation of people are born in the movement and within this religious community. In distinction from the first generation there is less of a need to make a decision to join the movement or to leave something behind. Since the basic distinctive beliefs of this movement are already established, the second generation is asked to accept them by faith for the cohesion of the group. And usually the second generation complies fairly well in this process of nurture and enculturation into the philosophy and doctrines of the movement.

When we get to the third generation, the movement begins to establish institutions to solidify the movement. Education and training become more important. The older generations tend to exhort the younger generation to live by the group's standards of beliefs and behavior which are seen as a demonstration of faithfulness to the group. The sectarian impulse is less of a natural part of the DNA of this third generation.

By the time we get to the fourth and successive generations, the institutional growth of the movement is now primary. There is an increased need of well-trained administrators who will assure the growth of the movement. But at the same time the group seeks to become relevant to the society and the culture in which it lives. Its institutions need recognition. The sectarian impulse of the first generations has been replaced with the belonging impulse. By then, the sect has become a church; the movement has morphed into an institution.

---

2    The seminal works of these authors are still influential today. Ernst Troeltsch, *The Social Teachings of the Christian Churches*, trans. by Olive Wyon, 2 vols. (New York: Harper & Row, 1960); Max Weber, *The Protestant Ethics and the Spirit of Capitalism*, trans. by Talcott Parsons (New York: Scribner, 1958); H. Richard Niebuhr, *The Social Sources of Denominationalism* (New York: Henry Holt and Co., 1929); Peter Berger, *The Sacred Canopy: Elements of a Sociological Study of Religion* (Garden City: NJ: Doubleday, 1967).

During the last century, European Adventism has learned many lessons in this process of development from sect to church, and from movement to institution, many lessons that could benefit the rest of the church elsewhere in the world. Much of American Adventism is unaware of this sociological phenomenon that has also affected how it now operates in its own world and culture.

These lessons we learn from European Adventism were first suggested and introduced by Ellen White during her visit to Europe and were then incorporated to some extent over a period of some decades into a European Adventist perspective on the world and Christianity.

## European Adventist Perspective on the World and Christianity

The reflections offered here begin with the participation in the World Missionary Conference of 1910. Church historians look at the World Missionary Conference in Edinburgh, Scotland, in 1910 as the historical marker for the beginning of the modern ecumenical movement. That summer, 1200 delegates from many missionary societies met in Scotland to learn from each other how to do better missionary work in the various non-Christian cultures and countries where so many Protestant denominations labored. Seventh-day Adventists were invited to participate and three official delegates attended along with three observers. The delegates were W. A. Spicer, secretary of the General Conference, L. R. Conradi, president of the European Division, and W. J. Fitzgerald, president of the British Union.[3]

During the conference, Christians of very different faiths found that uninhibited discussions could be carried on in an atmosphere of fellowship deepened by prayer. And that is why it is said to be the birthplace of the ecumenical movement. Their doctrinal and theological differences could be clearly stated and discussed without abandoning them.

Overall, Seventh-day Adventist representatives felt the conference was a positive influence and a fulfilment of a sign of the end of time: to preach the gospel to all the world before Jesus' second coming (Matthew 24:14). In fact, Spicer saw the Protestant missionary movement of the nineteenth century as a continuation of the Protestant Reformation.

> This great gathering is of the deepest interest to us, as a sign that the day of the Lord is at hand. Here is focused a mighty movement that comes in the providence of God to prepare the way for the closing work of the gospel. ... But the sure word of prophecy also foretold the world-wide spreading abroad of the light of that Word in the days just before the coming of the Lord. And the great missionary movement of the nineteenth century

3    W. A. Spicer published two reports in the *Review and Herald*: "Notes from the Edinburgh Missionary Conference," *The Advent Review and Sabbath Herald* (July 21, 1910): 9–10, and "More Notes from the World's Missionary Congress," *The Advent Review and Sabbath Herald* (August 11, 1910): 11–12.

came as the complement and the successor of the Reformation movement. The Reformation gave the blessed Word again to the world. In the modern missionary movement we see the Lord breaking down all barriers, opening all lands, and putting that Word into the tongues of all tribes and peoples.[4]

What is remarkable in Spicer's assessment of the conference is that in 1910 Seventh-day Adventists understood that Protestant denominations all over the world were *together* indeed preaching the gospel of Jesus to cultures that had no knowledge of the biblical God and salvation. Seventh-day Adventists believed that they were thus uniting their efforts with Anglicans, Lutherans, Methodists, Presbyterians, Mennonites, Baptists, and many others to proclaim the saving gospel of Jesus. What is also remarkable is that in 1910 Seventh-day Adventists knew that they were not able to fulfill the prediction of Matthew 24:14 by themselves and that God was using all Christians in all denominational missionary societies to do this. What is to be noted as well is that church leaders in 1910 understood the Seventh-day Adventist message as a supplement to what other Protestant churches offered – they did not see the Adventist message as replacing what other churches taught. In other words, they did not see their denomination, which was then a very small fragment of the universal Christian church, as the only church entity being blessed by God.[5]

In many sectors of Adventism today, church members no longer think like this, and many evangelists and preachers, in order to convince others to join Adventism and to convince church members to give money to their ministries, say that only Adventists teach the biblical gospel and that other Protestant denominations do not. This situation is a most unfortunate assessment of the reality, one that is overly sectarian and misguided. There are likely many Adventists in Europe who think and articulate their position regarding other Christians churches in similar ways. But, presumably this is not a dominant view among European Adventists. The following section offers three sets of reflections on the contributions of European Adventism to the wider Seventh-day Adventist Church – these thoughts are also given in the context of the development from sect to church and from movement to institution presented earlier.

## Relationships to Other European Christians

First, a few more thoughts on relationships to other European Christians. Repeatedly during her two years in Europe, Ellen White emphasized that the best way to reach out to other Christians in Europe was not to attack them, as it was so commonly done in the United States at the time, but to seek to establish good relationships with them. In her communications to pastors she emphasized that the Adventist message should adopt a Christological frame of interpretation to "present truth as it is in

---

4    Spicer, "Notes from the Edinburgh Missionary Conference," 9.
5    In 1910, the Seventh-day Adventist membership was a little over 100,000 baptized members.

Jesus," as she repeatedly emphasized, and that evangelism should not seek to tear down what others believe but to begin with what we have in common.[6]

Clearly, Ellen White had moved away from a strict sectarian impulse of the first two Adventist generations to become more attuned to what is common between all Christians, a characteristic of later generations in a new movement. In part, her remarks were typical of the leader of a church, and less of a sect, seeking to establish itself in the world. In her expansion of *The Great Controversy* in 1888, after her visit to Europe, Ellen White demonstrated this principle and showed how the Adventist message had common roots with other European movements. In his reflections on the contributions of the Edinburgh World Missionary Conference in 1910, Spicer had understood this as well.

During the last century, European Adventism has undergone many changes in its development from a little known sect to become a better established church in many countries. Some of these changes were made with poise and planning, other changes came about through the tragedies of wars and schisms, some other changes came about in periods of conflicts, persecution and harassment from government authorities. But through it all European Adventism has remained an important witness of the gospel of Jesus Christ and of a particular end-time message that must be heard, a message that supplements what Christianity has missed or forgotten. European Adventism has remained much closer to the original Adventist view that the Adventist message is to supplement what other churches are teaching, not to be a replacement of what others teach.

The denominational affiliations are for the sake of mission and spiritual growth within the family of God. Belonging to any church entity does not automatically save anyone. The denomination's statement of Fundament Beliefs on the concept of the remnant and its mission states in part that every Christian believer is invited to join Adventists and have a personal part in the worldwide witness symbolized by the three angels of Revelation 14, not in order to be saved but to join together in proclaiming the soon Second Coming of Jesus.

Typical American evangelism techniques have stressed highly cognitive insights, knowledge and values, at times supplemented with sophisticated mathematical and historical facts in the interpretation of prophecies. Most receptive to this approach are naturally Protestants. In the early years of its development in Europe, much of its evangelism was directed at Protestants – to Reformed Protestants in Switzerland, Mennonites and Lutherans in Russia, Lutherans in Norway, Sweden, Denmark, Iceland and Germany, to other Sabbatarians in Romania, and to Waldensians in northern Italy. These Protestant groups were more receptive and more easily convinced of the Seventh-day Adventist message.

The success of the early years of evangelism in Europe was due in part to Conradi's insightful efforts in affirming that the basic tenets of Adventist beliefs were not of

6    Ellen G. White, *Historical Sketches of Foreign Missions of the Seventh-day Adventists* (Basel: Imprimerie Polyglotte, 1886), 283; Ellen G. White to Albert Vuilleumier, letter 23, 1885.

American origin but were in harmony with long-held beliefs agreed to by the churches of the Reformation, even some beliefs going even further back in time to early Christianity.[7] In fact, Adventism wished to say to all European Christians, that the Reformation was not really completed and that more biblical truths were still to be rediscovered and reaffirmed – in particular, the truths about the state of the dead, the Sabbath and the Second Coming of Jesus.

With this approach, connecting the Adventist message with the Reformation, or with some older European movements such as the Waldenses or John Wycliffe, was a crucial insight – the Adventist message is not really an American and sectarian movement, but it is one willed of God embracing the Protestant Reformation and its precursors. This is really what Ellen White had already affirmed indirectly in her book *The Great Controversy*, an understanding that Conradi used to strengthen Adventist identity in Europe and give it its own unique individuality. That connecting link with the churches of the Reformation sustained Adventism and allowed it to establish itself in many European regions. It gave it some credibility in the eyes of local populations and it appeared to be less a sect and more like a free church. Although it never shed its American connection or affinities, it could at least strongly affirm its European religious ancestry.

I have often heard some people in the United States, even some church leaders, describe European Adventism as too similar to Lutheranism or Calvinism in ethos, values and beliefs. It is a fair assessment to say that European Adventism has affinities with Lutheranism and Reformed life and thought because Adventist heritage, ancestry and core beliefs are also part of Lutheran and Reformed heritage. What is not recognized or realized on the other side of the Atlantic, however, is the extent to which Adventism in the United States is currently reflecting the ethos and culture of Protestant Evangelical churches and even American fundamentalism, a trend that one should be critical of.

The counter part of the overt connection with European Protestantism, however, is that Adventist evangelism would prove fairly adequate to reach Europe's Protestant believers with its public lectures and books on biblical prophecies, but would not be so well equipped to reach Roman Catholics and Eastern Orthodox. In fact, the earliest attempts at reaching Roman Catholics tended to be extremely pejorative, antagonistic and aggressive. Ellen White noted this trend and made some fairly strong remarks against it. Addressing a strong letter to Daniel Bourdeau, a French Canadian whose father had converted to Protestantism in southern Quebec in the early nineteenth century, and who now worked in French speaking areas of Europe, Ellen White told him in no uncertain terms that his approach to Roman Catholics was faulty and needlessly aggressive.

---

7    Daniel Heinz, "Ludwig Richard Conradi," in *Heirs of the Reformation: The Story of Seventh-day Adventists in Europe,* eds. Hugh Dunton et al. (Grantham, England: Stanborough Press, 1997), 114–115.

> Be cautious in your labors ... not to assail the prejudices of the people too strongly. There should be no going out of the way to attack other denominations; for it only creates a combative spirit and closes ears and hearts to the entrance of the truth. We have our work to do, which is not to tear down but to build up. We are to repair the breach that has been made in the law of God. It is the nobler work to build up, to present the truth in its force and power and let it cut its way through prejudice and reveal error in contrast with truth. There is danger that our ministers will say too much against the Catholics and provoke against themselves the strongest prejudices of that church.[8]

And to pastors assembled in Basel, Switzerland, in March 1887, she also gave strong counsels regarding their methods of evangelism toward Catholics and Protestants.

> We should not upon entering a place build up unnecessary barriers between us and other denominations, especially the Catholics, so that they shall think we are their avowed enemies. We should not create a prejudice in their minds unnecessarily, by making a raid upon them. There are many among the Catholics who live up to the light they have far better than many who claim to believe present truth, and God will just as surely test and prove them as He has tested and proved us. And just according to their willingness to stand the testing, of whatever character it may be, will be their accountability before God. From that which God has shown me, a great number will be saved from among the Catholics. There has been but little done for them except to make them appear in the worst light.[9]

These counsels were helpful and European Adventism moved away from a form of evangelism that unfortunately has long persisted in the United States. It is therefore a natural development that over time many Seventh-day Adventists in Europe began to reach out to other Christians with a friendlier approach and sought to build good interchurch relationships with other churches and local Christian educational institutions. Seventh-day Adventists are Protestants and share the same history and theological foundations with other Christian churches, and should enjoy good relationships with others. This has certainly been the reality for many of the denominational colleges and universities.

This development has also manifested itself when some segments of the denomination joined some local or national church councils, as happened in France with the Fédération protestante de France,[10] or in Finland with the Finnish Ecumenical

8    Ellen G. White to Daniel T. Bourdeau, letter 39, 1887, published in *Evangelism* (Hagerstown, MD: Review and Herald, 1946), 574.

9    Manuscript 14, 1887, talk given at Basel, Switzerland, March 7, 1887, published in *Evangelism*, 573–574.

10   The Seventh-day Adventist Church in France is a member of the Fédération protestante de France. See "Les Membres de la Fédération Protestante" (http://www.protestants.org/index.php?id=78, November 29, 2018).

Council,[11] or in Estonia with the Estonian Council of Churches[12] – to name only a few.[13]

Being part of such councils should not be perceived as a mark of apostasy as it is portrayed in the United States, but as an active attempt at witnessing positively and in an environment of respect and genuine friendship with other Christians who also belong to the universal Church of Christ. Europe is facing a far different environment for the preservation of Christianity that American Adventists do not understand nor have the capacity to understand. Secularism and anti-church and anti-religious sentiments in Europe have reached a level that requires concerted efforts among all Christians to uphold the gospel of Jesus Christ and to show together that it is a viable option in the world in which we live. For the most part, European Adventists have understood this far better than Adventists in America. As the world progressively becomes more secular and resistant to religious ideas, European Adventism has something important to share about its experience with other Christians groups in a most secular and anti-religious and suspicious context.

## Experience with Wars and Social Upheavals

The next set of reflections would like to focus on the European Adventist experience with wars and social upheavals.

For generations now, European Adventism has had to navigate the stormy waters of numerous political and social events that have regularly threatened its survival, endangered the lives of many members and thus created an attitude of caution and an outlook of vigilance.

In the last century, almost all European countries had to cope with the difficult impacts of the Great War (or World War I), then World War II, and then Communism. During these periods of intense difficulties, church members, churches and institutions had to cope with untold sacrifices, with economic hardships, with difficult living conditions, with displacements, with lack of employment, with lack of respect and harassment from authorities, and with an uncertain future. It seems that every so often, perhaps every decade, a crisis irrupts somewhere on the continent that

11   The Seventh-day Adventist Church in Finland is an associate member of the Finnish Ecumenical Council. See "Finnish Ecumenical Council" (http://www.oikoumene.org/en/member-churches/europe/finland/fec, November 29, 2018).

12   The Seventh-day Adventist Church in Estonia is a member of the Estonian Council of Churches. See "Estonian Council of Churches" (http://www.oikoumene.org/en/member-churches/europe/estonia/ecc, November 28, 2018).

13   To my knowledge, many European Seventh-day Adventist conferences or unions belong to their respective national council of churches either as full member or guest/observer: the Netherlands (Council of Churches in the Netherlands), Sweden (Christian Council of Sweden), Switzerland (National Ecumenical Council), Belgium (Comité interecclésial de Bruxelles), the Czech Republic (Ekumenická rada církví v České republice), Slovakia (Ekumenická rada cirkví v Slovenskej republike), England (Churches Together in England), and Germany (Arbeitsgemeinschaft christlicher Kirchen in Deutschland).

has the potential of spreading into a wider regional conflict. This seems to be life in Europe. It is a reality that very few American Adventists know anything about and have never experienced.

Hence, it is a hard-learned experience that is now part of European Adventist culture and ethos to be cautious and prudent toward government authorities and social and political trends, and to be carefully aware of how others perceive Adventists. There is a real constant danger, socially, politically and religiously, of being perceived as anti-anything. To be known as anti-Catholic or anti-Protestant, as anti-Communist or anti-Labour or anti-Social Democracy, may be detrimental in the future and may have some fatal consequences.

European Adventism has learned to cope with the threat of possible retribution. Churches in countries with former communist governments suffered similar kinds of retributions and some still do. Church members were harassed and persecuted and Church buildings and institutions were confiscated. The magnitude of this impact is significant although it is hard to measure adequately. Seeking peaceable relationships with the national and local governments has led church leaders to temper their social activism for fear of being on the wrong side if social and political conditions were to change. Of course, this has also caused some accommodations with some governments that we have come to regret.

Adventists in Europe have experienced what it means to be a small religious minority and how to manage this reality. They have learned that although the Seventh-day Adventist Church is a free church in European society, it is not free to speak against any and all churches or against any political movement or political leader – which is something American Adventists have not had to learn. From my perspective, European Adventism has thus learned the importance of being friendly toward others and thus to avoid creating needless polarization with other Christians or society. This approach has allowed Adventists to live peaceably and to be a good social and religious influence. Ellen White emphasized this 130 years ago that Adventists should present the truth to others "as it is in Jesus" and to not be antagonistic or aggressive toward other Christians. In this context as well, it is even more commendable that a good number of conferences and unions belong to councils of churches. Christians in Europe have learned that social and political conditions do not always favor religious faith and mutual support and witness is a necessary part of survival and growth.

It is remarkable that wherever Seventh-day Adventists have had educational and health institutions that have made it a goal to reach out and offer activities or services to benefit the local populations, these institutions have often experienced a better treatment from local authorities when social upheavals threatened these communities. When Adventists are perceived to benefit society and their neighbors, when their social and spiritual outreach enhances the lives of others, institutions and church members are more likely to be protected from dangerous harm.

One other crucial development that has happened to European Adventism because of experiences with wars and social unrest is the strong non-combatant and at time pacifist position taken in relation to participation in military organizations. In

America, the traditional non-combatant position is superficial now, not really committed to, and there are numerous young people who serve in active military units, carry weapons, and serve in war zones. Many also serve in part time state militia units. The European Adventist commitment to non-combatancy and pacifism is to be noted and gratefully praised.

## Institutional Growth and Decline

A last set of reflections focuses on how European Adventism has learned to cope with its institutional growth and decline.

There is something quite paradoxical about Seventh-day Adventist theology and practice. On the one hand, Adventism teaches that the Second Coming of Christ is very soon and from the perspective of a premillennialist eschatology insists that the eschaton will witness the total destruction of this world. Adventist eschatology claims that all the kingdoms of this world will one day soon be destroyed and the earth will lie dormant for a thousand years until it is recreated to become the abode of God and the redeemed for eternity. On the other hand, Adventism is one of the most successful religious groups in the establishment and operation of long-term institutions. In tension with its eschatology, the denomination is committed to the promotion of health, education, and social and personal welfare.

Since the 1860s, the first decade of its official organization, Seventh-day Adventists have not only extended an efficient organizational structure in almost all parts of the world, but concomitant with this is also the impulse to establish schools, health clinics and hospitals, and publishing houses wherever they were financially strong enough to do so. So, while Adventist eschatology leans toward the soon cataclysmic end of the world, the church is certainly committed as well to establishing a significant Adventist "kingdom" on earth. But one has to quickly add that Adventists need to remember that their health, temperance, education and social welfare activities are integral aspects and functions of the mission of the church to proclaim a saving message to a dying world in dire need of hope. In a sense, Adventist eschatology drives its missiology and its institutionalism.

Nonetheless, from the early years of existing as an organization, Adventism rapidly embarked on an intentional and conscious process of institutionalization that would quickly place the sectarian movement on a path toward an institutional church. It did not take very long for Seventh-day Adventists to become focused on institutional growth and therefore on how they were perceived by society. In fact, success was measured from an institutional growth perspective. Very rapidly leaders began to count the number of baptisms and membership numbers to monitor church growth, the number of schools established and the number of students enrolled, the number of health institutions established, and the number of publishing houses built and the number of books published and sold. The drive for institutional growth was strong and intentional. And it was all facilitated by a strong and unwavering belief in faithfully giving tithes and offerings. Faithfulness in stewardship was an unmistakable blessing of God on the movement and institutional church.

Yet another simultaneous blessing was stability and permanence. Wherever an institution was established, whether it was a school or a publishing house, the church became more stable and permanent. Colleges and universities have provided stability and growth in the geographical areas where they are located, whether it be at Friedensau, or near Bracknell, Cernica, Darmstadt, Florence, Geneva, Valencia, or Zaoksky. The same happened where a health institution or a retirement community is situated. Adventists build an institution, employees live nearby, and they begin to establish satellite churches. The local Adventist population grows and church members establish relationships with the community.

By the time two or three generations have lived in this geographical area, there are many church members who occupy various positions in the local community and sometimes small secondary businesses or enterprises are established. In this context, institutions greatly benefit the local community and conversely institutions receive respect and are required to reach a certain level or standard of operation. Naturally, church members will be careful not to antagonize the local population. Furthermore, the Adventist emphasis on education has always created a well-educated membership. Within a couple generations in any Adventist community, membership tends to reach a higher level of professional occupations. Institutional growth leads to repressing the sectarian impulse of one's heritage and replaces it with the desire to be perceived as a respectable religious community.

In counterpoint, because Adventism has tended to measure success in terms of institutional growth, a lack of long-term institutions may lead to the instability of the church in some countries. This is more obvious when after repeated attempts Adventists have not been able to establish even a small school. So the church struggles to remain alive. This appears to be the case of the Adventist church in Greece, for example.

And there is also failure. Since Adventists have interpreted success through the lenses of institutional growth, there is a heavy feeling of discouragement when an institution closes. The closing of the Skodsborg Sanitarium in Denmark in 1992 was a major setback for this small Adventist community. The same happened repeatedly through the years in other countries when an elementary or secondary school or seminary had to be closed for lack of financial or personnel resources to maintain an adequate institution.

Is it possible that the drive to establish institutions in a small country with a small membership was often too hasty, without adequate financial resources to sustain them long term? The impulse to duplicate American Adventism and its drive for institution building was not beneficial or advantageous in many European countries where the membership was small, where evangelism was more difficult (or more often openly intolerant of Adventist views), where numerous political and social events created huge economic disadvantages for the small membership. A challenge still facing European Adventism is to understand how to measure success without this institutional drive. Is it even possible? Is it necessary to measure success? Or do Adventists need to be faithful witnesses of the gospel of Jesus and invite others to also be disciples of Jesus in preparation for his second coming? European Adventism has much to share with the rest of the Adventist Church, particularly with those in the West, about experience with the growth and decline of institutions, and with respected institutions in synergy with their local communities.

## Conclusion

As a foreigner and observer of European Adventism from far away, my perceptions may be limited in their value and accuracy. Nonetheless I would like to say in conclusion that the Adventist Church in Europe is a unique form of Adventism and the contributions it makes to worldwide Adventism are numerous and very important. The European Adventist experience and understanding of Adventism within its context is as valid as that of Adventism in India, Brazil or Nigeria.

To a large extent, European Adventism has understood that Christianity is bigger than the Seventh-day Adventist Church and that the Adventist message is a complement to what other churches teach. Ellen White was the first one to articulate this concept in Europe. To affirm openly and positively what the denomination has in common with other Christians is part of Adventist witness and thus provides friendlier opportunities to share with others what is to be offered in preparation for the Second Coming of Christ. European Adventism has learned that Adventism should not be in competition with other Christian organizations but with them raise the banner of Christ and invite a secular population to accept Jesus as their Savior, the only Savior this world can hope for. That is a positive and beautiful contribution.

European Adventism has learned the hard way what it means to be a small religious minority in a secular and often anti-religious society. This has shaped profoundly its approach to evangelism, to relationships with other Christians and government authorities, and has taught members how to be a witness of Jesus Christ in what is often a hostile environment. Adventists in Europe demonstrate in simple ways what it means to be a disciple of Jesus. That is also a positive and needed contribution to the worldwide Seventh-day Adventist Church.

Like in America, the Seventh-day Adventist Church in Europe is facing challenges to its institutions. Many of the denomination's institutions are well respected. What has been learned from these experiences is a rich source of knowledge and a contribution that other Adventists could benefit from.

There certainly are challenges ahead and for many church members, the future maybe uncertain at times. Yet the European Adventist witness and contributions to Christianity, to Adventism and to the world are beneficial and needed. European Adventism can be a prophetic voice to speak to the rest of the Seventh-day Adventist

Church and make significant contributions in understanding the Church's relationship with society and other Christian churches. The rest of the Church awaits this
witness and one need not be shy about it.

# PART I

# MISSION
# AND THE DIVERSITY
# OF ADVENTISM IN EUROPE

*Gilbert Valentine*

# J. N. Andrews and the "Success" of the European Mission

Abstract

Vigorous public criticism was voiced by General Conference leaders in the late 1870s about the wisdom and the effectiveness of the particular mission strategies adopted by John Andrews in undertaking his mission to Europe. He was challenged over why he had not followed the tried and tested "American Model" for his mission. Leadership was troubled that results were coming too slowly, that the operation was too expensive and that the mission had not become self-sustaining quickly enough. Andrews vigorously defended the approach he had adopted given the particular socio-cultural and financial situation he faced. Circumstances on the ground and experience led him to conclude that the "American Model" was not an appropriate fit for the situation he confronted. Thus he had not followed it. Ironically, recent interpreters have faulted Andrews on the assumption that he had followed it. This paper will explore the background of the General Conference criticism of Andrews' mission to Europe, Andrews' defense, the subsequent "audit" conducted by the General Conference and the results of the audit. It will also explore how the publication of the audit's positive assessment stands in tension with Ellen White's last letter to Andrews and how this has resulted in contrasting assessments of John Andrews' legacy to Adventist mission.

The three-man General Conference Committee which convened in Battle Creek for ten days in mid-1877 was deeply worried about the financial and missionary challenges of the church. Although calls were opening up everywhere across the United States for evangelistic laborers (forty evangelistic tents were to be in operation across seventeen states during the forthcoming summer) the General Conference (GC) was heavily in debt and the nation-wide financial depression was steadily worsening. Church income was seriously shrinking. Every church entity was plunging deeper into debt including the young European Mission begun just two-and-a-half years earlier in late-1874. Europe, in fact, had become an unexpected heavy drain on church resources. The committee had thus taken "an anxious interest" in the Swiss-based Mission. It was not going in the direction they had anticipated nor was it producing the results they expected. Why was it not meeting with success? And why was John Andrews not doing what the GC leaders expected of him? "More than ever" the GC Committee asserted, "*their* influence should be felt in directing the important work there [emphasis mine]." More control was needed from Battle Creek.

The Committee wrote up its assessment and published it on the main editorial page of the *Review* of June 7, 1877. Primarily the work of James White, it was a highly critical public report on the European mission and on John Andrews' leadership of it.[1] It was not the first time John Andrews had been publicly criticized in the *Review* by his sharp-tongued, acerbic, and authoritarian president, James White.[2]

This paper will explore the background and impact of James White's criticism of Andrews' mission to Europe and Andrews' energetic defense. It will also consider the subsequent "audit" conducted by the General Conference after James White's death, an audit which exonerated and lauded Andrews and his mission. It will also explore the publication of the conclusions of the audit, the subsequent fallout and its implications for assessing John Andrews' legacy to Adventist mission.

## A Highly Critical Report

"We are becoming terribly anxious about the mission in Europe," read the General Conference Committee report.[3] It was not a ringing vote of confidence in John Andrews. The Committee appeared to have become worried primarily about the slow progress being made in the Francophone arena and by the fact that Andrews appeared to be too tightly tied to editorial work and routine magazine production processes. Why was he doing this rather than going out running evangelistic tent campaigns? They knew he was very skilled in both. The committee was also disturbed by the high level of investment that the European mission was requiring. Andrews had frequently requested further funding – sometimes desperately because the system of spend first and be reimbursed later frequently broke down. The mission was simply not becoming self-sustaining quickly enough. They had been pained to learn, for example, that Charles and Mary, Andrews' children, had been kept from their school studies in order to help their father. They had heard that the children were doing

---

1    "Our European Missions," *The Advent Review and Sabbath Herald* (June 7, 1877): 180.
2    John Andrews had frequently been the subject of James White's public and sometimes quite caustic criticism in the *Review*. See for example, "Publications in Other Languages," *The Advent Review and Herald* (November 12, 1872): 173. "Adelia P Van Horn," *The Advent Review and Herald* (November 12, 1872): 173. 176. Also *The Advent Review and Sabbath Herald* (December 27, 1871). This criticism eventually ate away at his self-confidence and proved counter-productive to the cause because it dissuaded Andrews and his senior colleagues from being willing to help reduce White's work overload. Ellen White rebuked James White for these public attacks even as she also sought to encourage Andrews, George Butler and others to take more responsibility. The dysfunctional dynamics that disrupted senior denominational leadership in 1873 and in the years immediately following provide part of the background to the criticism of Andrews. These issues and much of the discussion in this paper draws on the author's forthcoming biography of John Nevins Andrews to be published by Pacific Press.
3    Although the report was signed by the committee comprising S. N Haskell, D. M. Canright and James White, the authorial style is clearly that of James White. "Our European Missions," *The Advent Review and Herald* (June 7, 1877): 180.

such work as folding papers. From afar this looked terrible; much worse than it actually was.[4]

According to his Battle Creek critics Andrews should have started his work in a village somewhere, not in a city like Basel. The church in America had begun in villages, "humbly," and at much less cost, they reasoned. Furthermore, Andrews should not have started with a monthly paper. A paper published occasionally, three or four times a year (like James White's early *Present Truth*) would have been better than shutting himself up wholly to printing. He should have been content to leave the translation and printing "imperfectly done," and not worry about grammar, spelling or other literary mistakes, they argued.

Moreover, the French-speaking Canadian Daniel Bourdeau, who had been sent across eighteen months earlier to help him, should not have gone into France to do his evangelistic work. (He had taken himself there against Andrews' advice.) He should have stayed in Switzerland to help Andrews get that work on to a self-sustaining basis more quickly. Bourdeau should now be brought back. The workers in Europe had "a model" to follow, claimed the committee: they should copy the way the church had developed successfully in America. That model had "secured growing strength and numbers and means to the cause at every step." Why did the missionaries to Basel not follow it? "The work in Europe, in order to prosper, must copy after the American model."[5] Does not the General Conference Committee have a responsibility to prescribe the form the work should take that would "best advance and build up the cause"? The implication was that Andrews should obey! The Committee had seen this responsibility as justification for the sharp public criticisms the report proceeded to offer. The criticisms were the kind of second guessing – the public airing of his "mistakes" in the *Review* – that John Andrews had experienced numerous times before and feared so much, even as he took on the project of the mission to Europe.[6]

---

4    The folding took only one day a month and was a family enterprise. The lack of schooling was a result of a lack of money rather than the press of work. Andrews received no regular salary from the GC and all travel, educational, health and living expenses of his children he had to meet from his own pocket.

5    Ibid. The tone of the report was biting, reflecting some frustration on the part of the GC President. While speaking of Andrews as "our beloved brother," the report used exaggerated expressions and patronizing comparisons which clearly indicate frustration and a lack of confidence in Andrews' decision making. For example, the report made such arguments as: James White could have started the *Review* in Boston or New York, if he had wanted the magazine to have prestige, but he did not – he went to a small village to start. The report feared that Andrews would too easily place means in the hand of "utter strangers" on the basis of "mere correspondence." The target of this expression was Dr Ribton of Naples, Italy, whom the Battle Creek brethren had not been able to meet in person. The committee apparently overlooked that Andrews had spent a month in Ribton's home and had baptized him in the Naples bay.

6    Andrews received a circular letter form of the report after it had been published in the *Review*.

The "American model" that James White wanted implemented was one that was primarily rural based, focused on small villages and avoiding large urban centers. It involved numerous preachers engaged in local tent evangelism with revival-style, doctrinal decision-making meetings and house-to-house circulation of tracts and magazines by local volunteer workers. These would develop into full-time or part-time colporteurs nurtured by a tract and missionary society. White was thinking of his preaching around the small villages of rural New England and New York and his deliberate avoidance of cities like Boston and New York City.

## Andrews' Reply

Andrews must have winced when he read the GC committee's report in the *Review* and absorbed its tone, knowing also that the whole church was reading it at the same time. The report carried exaggerated expressions and conveyed a patronizing attitude. He could have been excused perhaps for feeling somewhat abused. He replied promptly to James White, the primary author, with vigor. He acknowledged that the committee's ideals were valid, such as "the necessity of preaching as well as printing." That was "true and right," and Andrews' strategy included this. In fact he had been doing just that for some time already.[7] The missionary editor pushed back hard against the criticisms. "There are difficulties in my way of which you can have little idea till you visit Europe," he replied to his armchair critics who claimed to know better about things from the other side of an ocean. While respectful and careful to convey a submissive tone, he asserted "our situation in Switzerland has been very different from what you suppose. It has been almost wholly different from what I expected to find." He recounted the rationale for the monthly editions of the magazine and gave the reasons for special concern when it came to insisting on linguistic precision in publication. He needed to guard against "ridiculousness" in print. Did they really want him to "ruin" the paper and their own reputation?[8] The paper was being read by "well-educated people." He could move back out to a village if they insisted but if left to his local judgment of the situation, he would need to get as "clear a light as I thought I had with respect to moving to Basel" in the first place, he asserted. He had seen the clear leading and providence of God in this but maybe he had erred on the matter if they said so.

Two months later Andrews was even more assertive in his pushback. In order to be able to publish a paper in Europe using commercial presses, the missionaries were

---

7    J. N. Andrews to James White, June 19, 1877, Ellen G. White Estate – General Conference (EGWE-GC). He had appointments for preaching up in Tramelan and Le Locle that very weekend. J. N. Andrews to James White, June 22, 1877, EGWE-GC.
8    James White was listed on the masthead as lead editor. Publishing in French with its range of diacritical markings was not so simple as publishing in English – a dimension that James White did not seem to appreciate.

"absolutely obliged to live in a city."[9] And on the matter of his associate, he was not sure it was such a good idea to bring back Bourdeau from France to Switzerland given that the French-speaking preacher had now made a breakthrough and had won some educated and highly skilled converts. Andrews would recall him if they said so but he begged for "a little time for reflection." He also confessed that he was sorry now that he had related some of the humorous cultural particulars about daily life around him and in his house such as the Swiss custom of infrequent clothes-washing and their family activity of folding papers. Such anecdotes apparently were "not under-stood." It seems that they only "made me appear in an unfavorable light," and he thus resolved to desist of speaking of such things.[10] The overall thrust of Andrews' reply to his critics was that he was doing absolutely the very best he could, given the less-than-ideal financial circumstances, the unexpected non-availability of national personnel and a very different socio-cultural setting. He was stretching himself thin (literally!) to meet the expectations of his brethren and his expectations of himself.

On the same day that he replied personally to James White, Andrews also wrote a public defense of his work for the *Review*. He did not take issue with the specific criticisms on mission strategy to avoid appearing as if he was taking a polemical or adversarial stance. But he did explain what he was doing and why. He spoke of the situation where if a foreigner tries to speak conversationally in French they are readily pardoned for mistakes but they are "*not pardoned if they write for the public*."[11] He stated that since the paper had been able to establish its pattern and had survived for twelve months he would, with careful planning, be able to spend more time, (several days each week) in preaching. But the reality was that producing *Les Signes des Temps* was not quite the same as producing the Californian *Signs* or the *Review* in Michigan, which could be managed somewhat remotely and allow for field preaching at the same time.[12] "I must beg the friends in America to have all patience possible," he wrote. "You justly look for progress in the work in Europe. Your anxiety that we who are here should accomplish something for the cause of God is great, I know; but if you knew our anxiety, you would be satisfied that we are not in ease in Zion."[13]

Erich Baumgartner in a 2010 study has critiqued Andrews' leadership and his approach to the European mission rather harshly. He sees the example of sacrifice as the only really lasting value in Andrews' mission. I believe Baumgartner has erred in two important ways in making his assessment. First, he seems to have misread the sources which led him to think that Andrews believed "the only way to establish the work in Europe was to copy the model of the church in America." In fact it was quite the opposite. Andrews was criticized by the General Conference because he did *not*

---

9    "Our Situation and Prospects," *The Advent Review and Sabbath Herald* (November 22, 1877): 64.
10   Ibid.
11   "Our Work in Europe," *The Advent Review and Sabbath Herald* (July 12, 1877): 20.
12   Andrews knew how that worked since he had managed his short time as editor of the *Review* that way.
13   Ibid.

follow the "American Model."[14] Second, Baumgartner's negative assessment of Andrews seems to be based largely on his adoption of Ellen White's critical letters of Andrews as the primary interpretive lens through which to view Andrews as a person and as a leader. This body of letters has been read by many. Andrews' responses to the letters also need to be considered as well as other relevant contextual documents. The body of letters from Ellen White arises out of a very complex context of time and place and cannot be read uncritically. A more extensive discussion of these issues can be found in Appendix I.

It is true, as Baumgartner notes, that initially Andrews struggled with culture shock after his arrival in Switzerland and communicated to his new parishioners the idea that he thought American values, customs and culture were superior. This created serious barriers between him and his parishioners in the first eighteen months.[15] The problem was exacerbated by his New England "plain speaking" pastoral style that utilized blunt, judgmental language in addressing pastoral problems. This was

---

14   Erich Baumgartner, "Charisma and Contextualization: Leadership Lessons from the Emerging Adventist Church in Central Europe, 1864–1914," in *Parochialism, Pluralism, and Contextualization: Challenges to Adventist Mission in Europe (19ᵗʰ–21ˢᵗ Centuries)*, eds. David J. B. Trim and Daniel Heinz (Frankfurt: Peter Lang, 2010), 67. Daniel Heinz also critiques Andrews for "overemphasizing the publishing work" and prematurely adopting "the American model of literature evangelism." This critique could be more nuanced in light of a more careful study of the economic circumstances facing Andrews on his arrival in Switzerland and given Andrews' limitations as an expatriate. Both Matteson and Conradi were returning nationals for whom culture and language were not the same barriers as they were to Andrews. Conradi found much of his success in working with German immigrant communities in different countries which again minimized the cultural barriers to an American religion. This strategy was not available to Andrews. See Daniel Heinz, "The Development of Seventh-day Adventist Missionary Dynamic in Europe: Assessing the Contributions of Michael B. Czechowski, John N. Andrews, and Ludwig R. Conradi," ibid, 55.

15   Andrews acknowledged that he wanted to change things and to do so quickly. "I tried prudently, but faithfully to change or correct various things," he reported, "but found it was like ploughing upon a rock. I grieved those that I tried to correct, but produced no change." Faced with this resistance Andrews unwittingly stepped even deeper into the quagmire of cross-cultural misunderstanding. He construed the resistance as evidence of "backsliding" and spiritual declension. He thought he understood their situation and that to a large extent it was "the natural result of the unfortunate things they have had to encounter" as the fallout from Czechowski's misdeeds among them. He saw them as being in "a very low state as to the spirit of the work," with "no burden upon their souls." But it was still what in America was called "backsliding," and this condition he knew called for a particular kind of medicine. Andrews thus drew upon the tried and true resources of his New England heritage of "plain speaking." He found to his loss, however, that in this place "the work of reproof was quite unknown, and wholly misunderstood." In fact it gave offense. Writing to James and Ellen White sometime later and looking back on his experience he observed, Europeans were "little acquainted with reproofs or anything of the kind." Rather, "what I said by way of reproving faults was taken as though prompted by ill will and fault finding on my part." J. N. Andrews to James White and Ellen G. White June 8, 187[5], EGWE-GC. This letter has been filed as June 8, 1878 but several lines of internal evidence suggest that it should be dated 1875.

not Andrews' natural pastoral style but one that he had felt obliged to adopt under the tutelage of James and Ellen White. He had often been critiqued by both for not taking a more confrontational "plain speech" approach to parishioners and fellow workers. Andrews quickly found that this approach did not work in Europe. It was not culturally appropriate. But he had largely worked through that problem and by mid-1877 (the time of James White's critical report) he was becoming much more culturally adapted to Europe.[16] The focus Andrews gave to the work of the magazine as the keystone of his evangelistic strategy was not because he thought it was the only way or that he must do it because that was how it was done in America. The decision to focus on publishing was taken because of the strong cultural barriers to public tent or hall evangelism, the non-availability of national helpers and an awareness of his own limitations with the spoken language. He was an expatriate with limited language skill, not a fluent returning national like John Matteson or Ludwig Conradi. After close consultation with his Swiss parishioners and with their strong advice, an evangelistic magazine seemed the best way forward given the specific circumstances he found himself in.

## Changed Circumstances Force Adjustments to Andrews' Mission Strategy

Andrews' initial strategic approach to his mission in Europe had called for reliance on national helpers who would give their full time to working with him, serving as evangelistic associates and as translators. Andrews was apparently counting on the availability of the senior elder of the group of Swiss churches, Albert Vuilleumier, and his younger relative Adémar Vuilleumier, together with the Swiss-German, Jakob Erzberger, to engage with him in local evangelistic preaching. (Erzberger had returned to Switzerland from Battle Creek twelve months previously. Adémar returned with Andrews in October 1874 after two years of ministerial and language training at Battle Creek.) To Andrew's great dismay, for several reasons this plan quickly fell apart. As he explained confidentially to members of the General Conference Committee eight or nine months after his arrival in Neuchatel, he had arrived in Switzerland too late to prevent the leading Swiss Vuilleumier family from entering with other church members into a major industrial initiative to re-establish and/or expand their watchmaking business. They had invested more than 50,000 Francs in

---

16  If Andrews had been able to benefit from attending a mission institute prior to his departure from America, he perhaps would have avoided some of the hazards of cross-cultural communication and culture shock that confront new missionaries. Such sensitizing and training considered essential for missionaries today, however, were still 100 years in the future. The university in Berrien Springs, Michigan, that now honors Andrews' memory specializes in such training. But for Andrews in 1874 it was inevitable that this transplanted New Englander would be ensnared by at least some of the pitfalls new missionaries encounter when they leave their own culture to share the gospel in a new one. Andrews would have to learn the hard way – and he did.

a large three-story, stand-alone, stone house and stable with an attached vineyard of two acres. With an additional borrowed 10,000 Francs they planned to turn the cluster of buildings into a Watchmaking factory and winery. They had no more than 30% of the needed capital from their own funds which they used for the deposit. They had then borrowed funds from other church members to make up the difference for the purchase. This project completely tied up church members' assets – "nearly all the money in the hands of our brethren," – funds that Andrews had hoped to leverage for local mission programs, salaries, publishing and other evangelistic enterprises. The large industrial investment totally absorbed the energy and the time of Albert Vuilleumier and members of his extended family and created acute financial stress for everyone around the Sabbath-keeping community as the families struggled to make the new business venture a success. Commitment to church growth and outreach though aspirational was simply not forthcoming.

Andrews was sure that Albert Vuilleumier should have been devoting himself to ministry, not running a watch factory and overseeing a small winery. Furthermore, Andrews felt familiar enough with the implications of the extended severe economic depression that had begun in 1873 (what became known as the long depression) and the changing technology in watchmaking taking place in America, to know that the new enterprise could not be made to work successfully. He told them that in his opinion their business decision was not a good one. He foresaw bankruptcy at the end of the road.[17] Because agreements had been entered into but final papers had not been signed, Andrews tried to intervene. "I tried to get them out of it on the ground that they could not raise the money. But I could not move them," he later recounted.[18] He had arrived in Switzerland a few months too late. And the cost was great.[19] Five years later, as predicted by Andrews, the watchmaking enterprise ended in bankruptcy. The result, reported Andrews, was that "the brother whose [ministerial] gift would have been so valuable to me as a helper in the cause of God has lost five years' time and a large sum of money."[20]

Andrews' attempt to intervene in the Vuilleumier family's business plans so soon after his arrival in their midst and his efforts to persuade the Swiss Sabbath-keepers to abandon their watchmaking business decision, created huge tensions and misunderstandings. These actions seriously crippled his influence with them for a

17   J. N. Andrews to the General "Conference Committee, [June] 1875, EGWE-GC. He had become familiar with the industry in America through selling substantial quantities of watches on behalf of the Swiss believers. See *The Advent Review and Sabbath Herald* (January 3, 1871): 24; "The Swiss Watches," *The Advent Review and Sabbath Herald* (Jan 14, 1873): 40.

18   J. N. Andrews in an incomplete letter written to an anticipated Committee of the *Review*, December 29, 1879, EGWE-GC. This letter relates essentially the same story Andrews tells in his 1875 report but in an abbreviated form.

19   An argument can be made that if Andrews had arrived earlier in Switzerland the business venture could have been averted. Andrews' delay in leaving for Switzerland was occasioned by procrastination on the part of James and Ellen White and fall-out over the conflict that the unwell James perceived between himself and Andrews.

20   Ibid.

long period afterwards.[21] Whether a different outcome would have been achieved if Andrews had taken time to establish a trusting and respected pastoral relationship with them before intervening is impossible to know. But it seems reasonable to assume that there may have been a greater chance that the fateful decision could have been successfully averted if he had arrived on the scene in Switzerland earlier.[22]

Another delicate personnel crisis confronted the newly arrived missionary in the person of Jakob Erzberger. The Swiss-German Erzberger, who had for a time been mentored by Andrews at his home in Rochester, N. Y. in 1873 and who had then been ordained at a camp meeting in Massachusetts, had undertaken his visit to America sponsored by the Swiss Sabbath-keepers. According to Andrews they "had expended considerable money" on his education. After his study he had come back to labor among them and engage in evangelism. Andrews discovered, much to his chagrin, that the young preacher had fallen out with the Swiss Sabbath-keepers, had become discouraged, left ministry and had moved 126 kilometers east to Basel on the German border. Andrews is discreet about the problem Erzberger had fallen into but his case was "very unfortunate and very difficult to help." As Andrews saw it, not only was the confidence of the brethren in him destroyed, but he had their ill will, and they felt very decided to let him entirely alone." Erzberger was as unyielding as the watchmakers, leading Andrews to observe that "the firmness of Europeans is not controlled by reason as often as I wish it was; so it is in many cases of nothing but obstinacy."[23] The new missionary reeled from his culture shock.

For the next "many weeks" Andrews worked intensively with Erzberger, visiting Basel repeatedly in an effort to reclaim him for ministry. He had "wholly despaired

---

21  It is possible that the offense Andrews gave by his unsuccessful intervention was still a matter of spiritual concern that was resolved only in the last months of Andrews' life. "There is reason to hope," he wrote just a few months before his premature death in 1883, that his old Swiss friends would "fully put away the old difficulties. This takes an immense load off from my heart." "Omens for Good," *The Advent Review and Sabbath Herald* (January 2, 1878): 9. The matter also concerned financial difficulties related to the bankruptcy of the Vuilleumier watchmaking business. Andrews had lent the family money and when the business collapsed it proved awkward for Andrews. The collapse of the business also involved lawsuits among the church members and between family members causing a great deal of stress and ill-feeling. See Jean Vuilleumier *Diary* (JVD), January 4, 6, February 22, 29, March 11, 24, June 17, 18, 1880 and April 28, 1883, Archives Historiques de l'Adventisme Francophone, Campus Adventiste du Salève, Collonges-sous-Salève, France (AHLF). The problem of the offense given also related to the free use of table wine among the Swiss families which Andrews had initially tried to address in a heavy-handed way and which custom continued to prevail among them. See JVD, October, 23, 1883, AHLF.

22  It is a serious question as to whether the delay in sending Andrews to Europe helped create the problem he faced when he arrived there. The procrastination in sending him was occasioned by reticence on the part of the seriously ill James White who saw Andrews as a threat to his leadership. The "leadership" crisis of 1873 generated out of the difficulties of White's autocratic, dogmatic, and easily offended temperament caused great tension among his colleagues in the leadership team and damaged the reputation of Andrews.

23  Ibid.

of success" but then eventually at the turn of 1875 "there came a great break."
Erzberger "took such action as the Spirit of God signally witnessed to and such as
gave him the confidence and the affections of every one," back in the hills above Lake
Neuchatel. Andrews, who had been greatly discouraged, felt that this was "a first special token" of God's mercy, and a very great mercy it was."[24] The turnaround came
just in time, for developments in Germany were demanding attention and Andrews
would very soon need a good German-speaking pastor-evangelist. Furthermore, Andrews desperately needed some indication of God's blessing and signs of success to
counter the frustration and deep discouragements he was experiencing in Neuchatel.

## Problematic Financial Policies for Mission

The watchmaking enterprise severely limited the ability of other Swiss church members to support the general mission work thus obliging Andrews repeatedly to go cap-
in-hand to the General Conference for funding, a "situation" that "has been in the
highest degree painful to me," he noted. Andrews' lack of ability to develop an adequately self-supported mission seriously dented his credibility with Battle Creek leaders, ready as ever to second-guess his decision making. And there was a very high
personal cost to Andrews for, rightly or wrongly, it led him to skimp on his own
expenses in food and lodging in order to make ends meet, with dire consequences to
his health. With his immunity compromised, a severe bout of pneumonia set upon
Andrews on Sabbath morning, January 13, 1877, that almost took his life. Though
his health reform principles inclined him to refuse to take any medicine, he consented
to call "one of the best physicians in the city." The doctor attended him seven times
during the crisis. At his lowest point during an extended spasm of coughing that he
could not control, he feared that he would choke to death. During several days of
delirium, days that were "blank in my memory," he reported, he was not at all aware
that Albert Vuilleumier had come from Neuchatel to pray for him.

After two weeks Andrews began to recover but he was not back into full harness
for another six weeks with magazine copy way behind schedule. It took many weeks
after that to get the magazine fully back on track.[25] The episode frightened his colleagues in Battle Creek and it had frightened Andrews.

Looking around for something to blame for in the episode, other than the fact
that contagion permeated the community, Andrews identified what he supposed
might be the cause. He was receiving no regular salary from the General Conference
and given the financial crisis, the Swiss churches were not able to sustain him. He
was obliged to sustain himself as well as the Bourdeau family. He acknowledged that
he had been cutting corners on food intake for himself and his family although it was

---

24   J. N. Andrews to the General Conference Committee, [June] 1875, EGWE-GC.
25   J. N. Andrews to James White, June 22, 1877, EGWE-GC. When the business went bank-
      rupt, apparently the law-suits between church members and family members generated much
      suspicion, divided families and considerable ill-feeling. See JVD, April 28, 1883, AHLF.

out of necessity, he noted. He could see no other way to make ends meet. "I have felt constrained to use great economy in the matter of our food," he explained to James White later in what he hoped would be a strictly confidential letter. The family had been trying to live on a two-meal a day, vegetarian, "health reform plan" and that was difficult in Europe even when money was available. When money dried up it was still more difficult.

> We have lived upon baker's [white] bread, graham pudding, potatoes and occasionally a cabbage. We have bought milk and butter sufficient for the cooking. We have used almost no fruit at all. We bought a few cherries and a very few grapes; and perhaps have laid out one dollar and a half in apples. [26]

The apples were tasteless and purchasing more fruit was simply beyond their means. Andrews pled with White not to censure him "sharply" for he had "confessed" to God and family and now to White, recognizing he had not acted wisely. But when faced with the difficult choice of paying for house rent, paper for the magazine, tracts, fuel, essential help for the Bourdeau family and food for himself when the money did not go far enough and when he could not borrow from anyone, the budget for the food was the easiest to trim back on – only temporarily of course. More revealingly, Andrews confessed that he himself was frightened. "I have feared that the brethren in America would think that our mission would cost more than it came to." He was in a no-win situation.

In the future, he confessed to White, he would not trim the food budget. He would try and employ Louis Aufranc, a recent Swiss convert, for a greater share of his time to reduce the pressure on himself. But there was one solution that he thought only James White could solve for him. Would the General Conference grant him a set salary! As things were in Switzerland, he had "no way of earning money," by which he meant the extra moonlighting income by which James White was able to double or triple his own ministerial salary. When money was sent from America for "the publication of the paper," he explained, he regarded it as "very sacred money." Taking it to use for his personal expenses made him feel "as David did in eating the shewbread" – allowed only in extreme necessity. He thus felt guilty when from time to time he had had been forced to use money intended for publishing work on his own expenses. He argued that this policy placed him "in a false position and one that is very painful." He did not want to have to decide himself what proportion of the

---

26  Some details of his account of their circumstances come from a follow-up letter he dictated two days later. Andrews acknowledged that their cook was "about the poorest cook that I ever had knowledge of." She was apparently an eighteen-year old orphan girl who had lost her job when she became a Sabbath-keeper and Andrews had offered to provide accommodation for her if she would do the housekeeping and cooking. That had not worked out successfully. Ironically, at this same time Andrews had been asked to write out a testimonial piece on Health Reform for the *Health Reformer* journal that White was trying to rejuvenate. J. N. Andrews to James White, February 8, 1876, EGWE-GC.

funds was personal for food, fuel and clothes etc., and what proportion was for publishing. Would it not be much better for the General Conference to designate what was his "pay" – he did not want a large sum. Just give him whatever was thought proper and then allow him "to have one quarter of a year's pay in advance." Remittances and the mail system thus far had been too unreliable for the system of "spend and claim" to work properly. If this could be done it would "place him on his feet," meaning it would enable him to plan, and he would be free from "embarrassment." He did not want to suggest that he was blaming anyone else for his predicament and accepted that the "fault" was perhaps his own sensitivity about these things, but it was an awareness of the super-high expectations placed upon him by the whole church that further heightened his anxiety. Once he had commenced the paper, he explained, "my anxiety to make it worthy of so sacred a cause, has been inexpressible."[27] He pled that "prompt action" be taken on his request.

The financial policy of spend first and be reimbursed later by James White necessitated reliance on his personal assets. But the initial operating fund drawn from his personal capital shrank and sometimes there were long delays in being reimbursed. It was a perilous situation. Furthermore, James White held tight control in the area of finance and tended to meticulously monitor all expenses and Church monies. This was both a function of his own business temperament and also because the flow of church funding was still so heavily dependent on his own personal fundraising ability and his entrepreneurial spirit. The lack of a formal policy framework for delegating the processing of expense claims at the General Conference to some other treasury official points to the micro-management style of White's leadership at work and the demeaning of those who had to report to him. The church was still a long way from working with annual budgets (such were not adopted until 1895).

For whatever reason, the brethren in Battle Creek decided that they could not comply with Andrews' suggested revised compensation arrangements. White's letter of reply on the matter is not extant. Perhaps the leaders feared losing control of expenses or perhaps they saw a danger in creating a sense of dependency of the Swiss brethren on the General Conference. At any rate, instead of granting Andrews' request for a more regular salary plan, they forwarded a money order to cover the expenses Andrews had already incurred. With it they sent additional privately donated monies for Andrews' personal expenses – somewhat to his embarrassment perhaps because he now felt ashamed of needing such help. Three months later, Andrews found himself backing up and explaining that he had "no disposition to find fault with the existing arrangement." He would therefore live with "the matter as it is," without a regular salary and he would continue to give a good account of the means used.[28]

27    Ibid.
28    J. N. Andrews to James White, May 26, 1877, EGWE-GC.

## Socio-cultural and Language Barriers

As Pietro Copiz has pointed out, in the denomination over time, John Andrews' vaunted linguistic ability developed legendary and mythic qualities.[29] The reality was very much less. Andrews' unexpected difficulty in mastering spoken French actually proved to be an major barrier to implementing his plan for evangelism given the non-availability of local workers. He found the task of learning a foreign language as an adult much more challenging than he had imagined. He did not become fluent enough to preach in French for two or three years after arrival and then was able to do so only with an understanding congregation. He did not feel really comfortable speaking to a sophisticated public audience of native speakers even after that. His expatriate status as an American using broken and heavily accented French set him at a distinct disadvantage. He was, however, able to develop a reasonably high level of skill in written French, and his translation and copy-editing prowess became an important strength. In proof-reading skill he exceeded even local language specialists like Louis Aufranc.

The cultural barriers to public evangelism and the intense local hostilities to such meetings, generated by the unique church-state relationships in Europe that Andrews had not encountered before in America eventually persuaded him of the limited value of such a confrontational approach to evangelism in Europe. In discussion with his Swiss advisors he became persuaded that given their over-committed circumstances, his limited skills and his abilities, a regular monthly magazine would be the best way of reaching across the barriers if it could be supplemented by personal contact through visitation and follow-up meetings. It would enable him to reach across local town cultural barriers and across national barriers to reach French speaking people groups elsewhere.

## Hedging the Criticism

James White learned from the pushback that his harsh public criticism had not only injured the feelings of his missionary colleagues but had also damaged the confidence of church members in their work. It seems that word had gotten around that the General Conference was to send an auditor to Europe to check on the wayward missionaries. In an editorial White tried to undo some of the damage and to assure Andrews, and his fellows, of the church's support. "It is right, that they should feel that they have the moral support of their American brethren," he editorialized. "Full and frank expression of our confidence and love has been made and still should be. We know these men." He added, "Our assurances of the confidence of the whole American army of brethren can hardly be stronger than they have been." On the other hand he noted, "these dear brethren should rest in Christ, and in the confidence of

---

29  Pietro Copiz, "The Linguist," in *J. N. Andrews: The Man and the Mission*, ed. Harry Leonard (Berrien Springs, MI: Andrews University Press, 1984), 165.

their brethren. They feel deeply and must guard against over-sensitiveness. And in order to succeed the missionaries must have confidence in their brethren." In reality, the question really was whether the brethren would have confidence in Andrews. White seems to have read correctly the sense of annoyance, resistance and even right-eous indignation in Andrews' vigorous response to the General Conference Commit-tee's doubts and "great concern."

Did White also sense a glimmer of disdain expressed for the armchair critics? Coping with such open criticism as had been offered in the *Review* was difficult. Accepting benignly, the second-guessing of decisions from the other side of the ocean and a completely different world, was easier said than done.[30] Andrews had found Europe to be very different. Could there not be a different way for the GC President to offer advice? Andrews was sure that White would think differently if only he could experience the culture and the frustration for himself. This broadening out into world-wide mission clearly presented a steep learning curve for the church and for its leaders. But how to be able to see for themselves was a problem. What was needed was an audit.

## Auditing Mission: William Ings (1878) and Stephen Haskell (1882)

The first attempt at an audit of the European Mission was made by sending out more helpers. John Andrews had found it necessary to adjust to the fact that James White and his committee at the General Conference did not trust his judgement in mission affairs or his strategy for mission when William Ings and his wife arrived in Basel from Battle Creek in early 1878. Ings was an accounting clerk from the Battle Creek publishing house. Andrews told twenty-three year old Willie White who at the time was deputizing for his ill and dysfunctional father, that though the Ings' visit had not been officially designated as an audit, nevertheless, Andrews clearly understood that an audit was a hidden agenda of the new arrivals. Ings' "confidential" correspondence with W. C. White during his stay in Basel plainly confirms Andrews' suspicion. But to Andrews' pleasant surprise, while Ings made some observations about efficiency to W. C. White, he affirmed, in essence, that he probably would not have done anything differently to what Andrews had done. His report was largely favorable. As a mono-lingual expat, he could not himself add anything to Andrews' mission team beyond what the missionary was already doing or trying to do although Ings did benefit from a wife who could speak German. Thus Ings went on to England, his homeland, to try his literature evangelism approach there. He found the same cultural barriers there and the same lack of easy numerous baptisms that Andrews had encountered. In fact he found it worse. This first unofficial audit seemed to allay some fears.

Eighteen months later during the darkest days of the "financial hard times" in December, 1879, church leadership in Battle Creek again looked for ways to cut costs

30   "Our European Missionaries," 68.

and find ways of achieving more rapid growth rates for its investment in mission and they considered sending out another audit team.[31] Both James and Ellen at this time, almost in a state of panic over the escalating debt, called for contraction in mission. They proposed shuttering the work in Europe and removing the headquarters to England. Ellen White believed that the message would find a more ready response there given the English language medium and the more intellectual tradition. How could the inherent intellectual power of the Adventist message be resisted, was the idea.[32] Her expectation proved to be mistaken. In the meantime the proposed closure hurt Andrews badly. He prepared extensive documentation defending the location, the francophone work and his magazine and provided an in-depth justification of all of his expenses and his decision-making.[33]

As it turned out, the financial stresses, institutional mismanagement in California in the publishing work on the part of Edson White, and the ill-health of James White resulted in the postponement of the proposed audit. Andrews would later recall the devastating emotional impact this proposal to close down his work had on him in lengthy discussions that Jean Vuilleumier recorded in his diary in 1883. The twenty-year old Jean could not record the incident Andrews related without shedding tears of his own.[34]

The death of James White in July 1881 introduced a time of major adjustment and transition in the church. At the General Conference session in October that year action was again taken to undertake an audit of the European mission. George Butler, now the new GC President, explained the decision in the *Review*, putting a glossy spin on the announcement. The need had been contemplated for several years, he said, for "leading brethren" at the General Conference to "become acquainted with the state of things in Europe in order to cooperate to the best advantage" with the missionaries there.[35] By mid-1882 such a visit could be postponed no longer. Haskell would be the auditor and would travel in company with a Brother J. W. Gardner and his wife from California. Gardner had previously travelled extensively on the

31  The "financial hard times" occurred during the long and deep economic recession from 1873 to 1881.
32  Ellen G. White to W. C. White and Mary White, February 11, 1879, EGWE-GC.
33  "Financial Report of the European Mission," October 20, 1879. General Conference Archives, Silver Spring MD (GCAr). J. N. Andrews to S. N. Haskell, December 23, 1879; J. N. Andrews to W. C. White, December 27, 1879, EGWE-GC. J. N. Andrews, Untitled Manuscript, December 29, 1879. Andrews University Center for Adventist Research, Berrien Springs, MI (AUCAR).
34  Vuilleumier spoke of the prospect as giving Andrews "a painful blow, a deadly blow. He looked back, replayed all the sacrifices he had made, thought of the death of his girl, about his work, his sleepless times, about his worries to get the work done deciphering the European terrain; ... the unspeakable anxieties, the agonizing prayers ... When I listened to him telling me this my heart was painfully torn and more than once tears shot from my eyes." JVD, May 6, 1883, AHLF.
35  "Eld. Haskell's Trip to Europe," *The Advent Review and Sabbath Herald* (May 16, 1882): 313.

Continent and "was familiar with the customs and languages of Central and Northern Europe." Butler argued that Gardener's assistance to Haskell would make the inspection tour much more profitable. At some point during the European tour an on-location European Council would gather all the overseas workers and local Swiss lay leaders to exchange experiences, share ideas and strategize together concerning the best means of outreach. The party left New York on May 13 bound for the UK.

Haskell and his travelling companions were away from the United States journeying through seven different countries of Europe for a total of five and a half months. Beginning in England, where they spent a week with John Loughborough and his small team, they journeyed to France, on to Switzerland, north to Norway and Sweden, back to Holland and Germany for the briefest of their numerous visits, down to Italy and then back again to Switzerland, across to England and then home by November 3. Haskell did not let the grass grow under his feet. He was a quick study and a person of action. After his first week he was informing *Review* readers that it had become quite apparent to him "that the publishing work is the right arm of our strength." He had seen already that "more can be accomplished by scattering reading matter, and filling such openings as the providence of God may indicate from time to time than by making such efforts as are put forth in America."[36] And this assessment was made before his visit to Basel and his meeting with Andrews and the Swiss brethren! Along the way he took time to study people, the way they lived, and their interests. He made an effort to absorb the local culture.

Haskell made Basel the hub of his European travels, returning three times to the city for varying lengths of time. On his first visit he found Andrews feeble but stable. Andrews was frustrated because he was not strong enough even to accompany Haskell on his local travels among the believers in Switzerland, but this was probably for the best anyway in that it enabled Haskell to gain a perspective of his own. He travelled in Switzerland in the company of James Erzberger, spent a weekend at Adémar Vuilleumier's home in Chaux-de-Fonds and stayed with the believers in Tramelan after taking a meeting that went until almost midnight. Then he spent a month visiting Scandinavia, Germany and Italy checking out both Torre Pellice and the Naples church that Dr. Ribton had established after his baptism by Andrews three years previously. Haskell returned to Switzerland for the Swiss annual conference in early September at Tramelan. He convened the first European-wide Council in Basel shortly afterwards on the weekend of September 15–17, 1882.

Haskell's report was very positive. One of the earliest recommendations that Haskell urged on his brethren back in Battle Creek was the need for a larger and more convenient home for the extended Andrews family. It was essential to have a place large enough to accommodate the people, the printing rooms and to have a hall for meetings, he argued. Securing a location away from the tramlines that created so much distracting noise and away from markets and stables to a place where the air was less fetid was also a necessity even though it might cost considerably more. Before he left Switzerland he had negotiated just such a relocation, obtaining a property with echoes of Ravenswood in Southampton. Andrews was grateful.[37]

As Haskell progressed through Europe and reported his findings to George Butler and to the *Review*, his observations tended to confirm the oft-repeated story Andrews had been telling his armchair critics for the previous six years. As Andrews read the reports he must have felt vindicated concerning most of the decisions he had felt obliged to make considering the circumstances he had found himself in. In an important sense, Haskell found himself defending Andrews and vindicating his course before his critics although only once did he do so in a direct and personal way. "The results already accomplished through the efforts of Eld. Andrews are in some respects truly marvelous," Haskell wrote in mid-July.[38] He affirmed the need for localization. Repeatedly he asserted that for Europe, publishing a regularly-issued periodical rather than tracts was a much more effective mission strategy. "It is evident that more can be accomplished in Europe by publications than by the living preacher," although, of course, they could not alone suffice, he asserted.[39] Furthermore, the papers needed to be published locally in order to reflect local issues and idioms. It was "impossible for a paper published in America to fully meet the wants of the European people," or even if it was published in England, he pointed out. Furthermore, Haskell acknowledged that he had "never realized the magnitude of the work, and how much can be accomplished with little expense."[40] The work in Europe should be enlarged, not retrenched. This was a direct riposte to the late James White.[41]

Haskell noted the problematic limitations that characterized the present mission outreach. In the past two years Andrews' health and his lack of editorial resources had prevented him both from visiting his local churches adequately and from following up interested readers with public and personal labor. Andrews knew this. Haskell noted that the preacher-editor had been "confined to his bed more than half of the time for a long period." *Les Signes* had done "a noble work," he reported. It had certainly gained in stature and in circulation. It was now being cited in numerous other religious journals and the Swiss Sabbath keepers had determined to increase its circulation by investing in paid advertisements for the journal in prominent daily newspapers.[42] Erzberger had been successful in the field among German speakers but

---

37  "Bro. Haskell's Visit to Europe," *The Advent Review and Sabbath Herald* (November 14, 1882): 712, 713. The new house was a large rented property in a location that "gave an abundance of sunlight and good air," and faced "no apparent danger that these will ever be shut out by other buildings." It would also make a good purchase for the future.

38  "What is Wanted in Europe," *The Advent Review and Sabbath Herald* (July 18, 1882): 456.

39  Ibid. "First give the paper then tracts, pamphlets and books," he explained, had been the experience of "every live Tract Society." Haskell's investigation apparently looked beyond just the Adventist experience and embraced the study of other missionary organizations.

40  Ibid.

41  "From Europe," *The Advent Review and Sabbath Herald* (August 1, 1882): 488.

42  "The Conferences at Tramelan and Bale," *The Advent Review and Sabbath Herald* (October 10, 1882): 632.

there had been weakness in the francophone work.[43] Haskell had not been able to travel in France visiting churches or any of the many *Les Signes* readers scattered across 45 of the 86 departments into which France was divided administratively. But Haskell did read some of the large number of letters from the numerous scattered Sabbath keepers that Andrews kept on file. In Italy in August, Haskell and Gardner engaged in day-long Bible studies with villagers in Torre Pellice. This had necessitated double translation across three languages back and forth. "I never saw people try harder to understand," he told Butler as his own understanding of the difficulties of language barriers, national histories and cultural differences appreciably deepened.[44] In both Torre Pellice and in Naples Haskell and Gardner were surprised to find more Sabbath keepers and Sabbath keeping groups among readers of *Les Signes* than even Andrews had learned of.[45]

What would have been of deep and genuine encouragement to Andrews was the message that Haskell took back to Battle Creek with him after the Swiss Conference and the European Council. Andrews had been well enough to attend both of these meetings although his speaking had needed to be restricted. Haskell had learned during his tour that things were indeed different in Europe and that the "American Model" would not work without major adaptation. Strategies for evangelism had to be adapted and localized to suit the European context. "It is very different here in the Old World from what it is in America."[46] A. A. Johns, an American pastor working in England and a participant at the Council expressed it clearly when he said that there were "peculiar circumstances by which our missionaries are surrounded," and "many difficulties that they have to surmount, which are known only to those who have labored in a foreign land."[47] In January, 1883 Haskell reiterated the theme again. "But few in America have been able to realize the difficulties under which those labor who go to Europe from this country," he noted for *Review* readers.[48] Andrews felt at last that they were being understood. Arguing as they had done that their situation could not be fully understood by those who sat in judgment in offices in Battle Creek was not simply a weak excuse. Circumstances on the ground were genuinely different. Andrews, Loughborough and Matteson were helping the Adventist church learn how to do mission and how to benefit from the trial and error process,

43   These details are based on Haskell's reports found in, "From Europe," 448 and "The European Mission," *The Advent Review and Herald* (August 29, 1882): 552.
44   S. N. Haskell to G. I. Butler, August 15, 1882 cited in "Notes from Italy," *The Advent Review and Sabbath Herald* (September 10, 1882): 601.
45   "Bro. Haskell's Visit to Europe," 713.
46   "The Work in England," 409.
47   "General Meeting at Bale, Switzerland," *The Advent Review and Sabbath Herald* (October 17, 1882): 648.
48   "Omens for Good," 9. In this report Haskell explained, tongue-in-cheek, that Andrews' former accommodation was "comparatively comfortable," if "many things were different." He then went on to list the deafening noise from the tram lines, the fertilizer smells from the neighbor's yard, the fact that the house was overcrowded and that it had no room for public meetings.

and church leaders were now, finally, also learning how to encourage them. The opportunities provided by the European Council provided a much needed larger perspective.

## Vindication

Six months after Haskell's return to the US his favorable audit assessment of Andrews work was formalized into a major report in a special supplement to the *Review*. It is not unreasonable to imagine that Andrews would have been encouraged and humbled by what he read in the eight-page *Review Supplement* that arrived in May 1883.[49] Butler, Haskell and James Fargo, as the three members of the General Conference Executive Committee jointly authored long articles in this important publication focused on reviewing the status of the church and its deeply indebted institutions. The *Supplement* presented a kind of stock-taking or a state of the church report now that James White was gone. The Committee set out possible goals and strategies for resolving a number of pressing issues including the overwhelming financial threat. The supplement devoted a substantial section to an analysis and review of Adventism's short mission history and its prospects for the future. The authors had developed a well-reasoned rationale for both an expanded mission in Europe and in England and they had identified the acute need for additional funding. The section on Europe reflected thoughtfully on the unique difficulties Andrews and his fellow missionaries had faced and then expressed a deeply affirming tribute and warm commendation. Andrews had accomplished a "most noble work" in establishing the Central European mission in spite of his physical weakness. The Committee then expressed deep appreciation for his leadership. It was a striking vindication given the criticism and suspicion of an earlier period. "We regard this mission as already a great success," they wrote.[50] That did not mean that there was not much more to be accomplished. But Andrews had worked "under the greatest difficulties" and "to the utmost of his strength," and he had "accomplished a vast amount of good under such circumstances that most men would have felt they could do nothing." An "excellent impression" had been made by the French paper.[51]

The *Review Supplement* also cleared the air on the matter of the financial suspicions. "We consider the money used in this mission well spent, and firmly believe the advantages thus gained to the cause are worth far more than the cost." The Executive Committee reported that it had closely studied the Mission's financial reports in the light of the conditions in the Swiss mission and in the light of the expectations that had been held for Andrews. They wanted *Review* readers to clearly understand

49   There is no documentation that demonstrates he read the supplement but in view of the fact that he was still having his own articles published in the *Review* it is reasonable to assume that he saw it.

50   *The Advent Review and Sabbath Herald Supplement* (May 1, 1883): 3–4. Baumgartner seems to be unaware of this publication.

51   Ibid.

that not all the church money had been paid to the missionaries as salary remuneration. Apparently some in the church had thought that that was happening. The report described Andrews' expenses and defended them as legitimate. Committee members went so far, in fact, as to suggest that there was "more danger that too great economy has been used, and that our missionaries have suffered, than that they have fared too well." "Our people will need no assurances from us," they continued, "that this beloved pioneer, who has labored so long and so faithfully in this cause, and who has almost given life itself for this mission, has not squandered the money raised for it. He has given for it more than any money can buy. It has cost him more than all the money given for the mission by our people could repay." There is no record of Andrews' reaction to the report but if he was still acting according to character, he would have offered a prayer of thanksgiving and if his advanced consumptive-impaired breathing had let him, he should have been able to sleep soundly.

The *Supplement* report also defended Loughborough's difficult English Mission, noting that while there had been some disappointment that "greater results" had not been attained, there was nothing that should discourage the church or cause it to lose hope. Again the writers of the report reflected a much more nuanced understanding of the unique challenges posed in introducing Adventism to "Old England" and expressed gratitude for the labors of Loughborough. The report would have been read by those in the know as a subtle push back against the criticisms of James White and his committee and perhaps also the veiled suspicions expressed by W. C. White to Ings in 1878. Those who were close to John Andrews would have understood it this way. Because of this subtle political edge, the *Supplement* report becomes a politically important document and it is important for the assessment of Andrews. It reflects something of the long conflict between James White and John Andrews and the perceived threat that Andrews was to James White. The document also seems to have constituted an important part of the context of a very critical letter Ellen White would finish writing to John Andrews a month later.

## The Challenge of Assessment – Success or Not

Clearly, the Haskell Audit and the publishing of the *Review Supplement* in May 1883 sought to address the criticism that Andrews had not properly followed the "American Model" in his mission strategy for Europe and to put this criticism to rest. Whether from the perspective of 2018, Andrews' Mission to Europe should be considered a success or not, is not the question this paper addresses. The question is whether the church, at the end of Andrews' life, could affirm his mission as having been successful. The report of the GC Committee in the *Review Supplement* answered this question in the affirmative in glowing and highly appreciative terms. What has caused the question of the "success" of his mission to linger these many years, however, as if it is a question still unanswered is the highly critical letter Ellen White wrote to John Andrews as he was on his deathbed. He received it when he was already but a skeleton just three months before consumption finally took his life.

Grady Smoot reads Ellen White's last letter to Andrews as "the most severe rebuke," that Ellen White ever wrote to her colleague. Daniel Augsburger says that "she scolded Andrews severely." Pietro Copiz notes that for later readers, who know that Andrews was on his deathbed, the language may appear "unnecessarily harsh, almost pitiless."[52] Ellen White appears not to have known how near death Andrews was. Andrews himself took the letter as a "severe rebuke." In truth these scholarly assessments seem diplomatically mild descriptions of the content of the letter. The letter could be seen as a devastating critique of Andrews as a person, his personality, scholarly temperament and of the way he had done his work in Europe.

The thirteen pages of the letter, which were written in a stream-of-consciousness and somewhat circular style, begin by reproving Andrews severely for not marrying again before he returned to Europe, a theme Ellen White came back to repeatedly in various ways. Angeline, his wife, who had died in 1872, had been the subject of disease and death and, according to White, he had been wrong to hug the grief for Angeline to his bosom. White asserted that he dwelt too much upon himself and his sufferings, many of which had been self-imposed, wrought by his over-conscientiousness. He was inclined to follow impressions and a conviction that these were the voice of God. He had magnified his afflictions and did this to draw sympathy to himself. This, she asserted, was unnecessary and unhelpful. It was a "birthright" problem that he had carried all through the years since his friendship with the Stevens family back in Paris, Maine, and it was a species of selfishness. Ellen White wrote that he had failed in the education of his son Charles. He had given him an education that had been too narrow and limiting. Andrews had sacrificed his own happiness because he considered that his brethren had not come up to his ideals of duty. He had given his own money to aid others when it had not been called for. He had been too parsimonious and deprived his family unnecessarily. She took the position that money from the General Conference had not been deliberately withheld.[53] Andrews worshiped intellect and gave preference to others whom he thought of as educated. He had exercised poor judgment, for example, in his relationship to Dr. Ribton of Naples.[54] Ellen White said, with a stretched hyperbole echoing that of the Biblical prophets, that

---

52    Grady Smoot, "Andrews' Role in Seventh-day Adventist History," in *John Nevins Andrews: The Man and the Mission*, 5; Daniel Augsburger, "The Adventist Colony at Basel during the Andrews Years," ibid., 341; Copiz, "Some Financial Aspects of Andrews' Mission to Europe," ibid., 326.

53    Comments about the lack of promptness in the sending of remittances appear to be a defense of James and W. C. White. W. C. White had explained to Matteson in 1879, for example, that at times there had been "delays and blunders" in settling accounts and that the failure to promptly send remittances was because the executive committee had been scattered and had "no head since father's sickness." During that time, the business had been "partly done by one member and partly by another." W. C. White to John G. Matteson, July 24, 1879, EGWE-GC. Whatever the reason, missionaries in the field were without funds.

54    Andrews felt he had been used by Ribton. He had apologized and absorbed the expense. The matter could not be undone.

nine-tenths of his problems had been born of his imagination which had been diseased.[55] God did not decree that he should die. The letter was a long and uncomfortable critique and must have been almost as difficult for the newly arrived president, Buel Whitney, to read to Andrews as it was for Andrews to hear.

It was also a letter that had been difficult for Ellen White to write and she had made several attempts to do so beginning in March.[56] The versions she had written earlier she did not feel she could send. She knew her colleague's "temperament" was "peculiar" and she did not know he would be able to receive what she said if it conflicted with his ideas. Clearly she felt uncomfortable with the way she was saying things and also probably with some of the content but she somehow felt burdened to write about certain things and knew she could "not feel free until I do write them."

Before settling on the letter she finally sent, Ellen White had talked of the material or read some of it to her son Willie. William and Jennie Ings also knew of what she was writing or had read some of her attempts.[57] But she was still not sure of herself and she told Willie that she wished she had found opportunity to talk further with both Stephen Haskell and with Bro. Gardner since they had returned from Europe. In this she had been unsuccessful.[58] Clearly she was still unsure of herself in some things and the letter was written with an awareness that further consultation and information would have been helpful.[59] There are clear points of tension between this letter and the published May report of the General Conference Committee.

---

55   As Abraham Heschel points out, Old Testament prophets would often deliver their powerful prophetic message with hyperbole or gross overstatement that should not be judged by statistical or mathematical exactitude. They were concerned with "the meaning of facts." Heschel, *The Prophets* (Peabody, MA: Prince Press, 1999), 14.

56   One short discarded version is dated March 17. Another is dated March 29. On June 11 Ellen White reported to her son that on Sabbath June 9, she had been strengthened to write thirteen pages to Elder J. N. Andrews – a third version. "Brother Whitney seems to be so long getting off. I feared that he might not get the light for him, therefore I wrote him again and this did not seem to injure me." Ellen G. White to W. C. White, June 11, 1883, EGWE-GC. This indicates that one purpose of the letter was to give guidance to Andrews' successor and time constraints imposed themselves on the situation making it less than an ideal communication. Which letter Whitney actually read to Andrews is not clear. Andrews speaks of it being in three parts and none of the extant versions have this format.

57   Ellen G. White to W. C. White, June 11, 1883, EGWE-GC.

58   Part of her letter apparently related to reports of an unwarranted strong influence of Anna Oyer over John Andrews that had been communicated to Ellen White through J. W. Gardner. The report it seems, had originated with Jean Vuilleumier in conversations he had had with Gardner in Le Locle during the time of the audit. His diary reveals that he regretted deeply making the comments to Gardner as soon as he had uttered them, felt they were wrong and misleading and that a "demon" had taken possession of him. His speaking badly of her had caused great distress. He later confessed his wrong understanding and his wrong doing to Anna Oyer herself. JVD, June 24, 1883, AHLF. The diary helps provide an important context for some of the content of Ellen White's letter.

59   Ellen G. White to Buel L. Whitney, March 30, 1883, EGWE-GC. To what extent did her own recent bereavement and the need to protect James' reputation as a leader also shape the

Andrews received the letter with his characteristic submissiveness. For him, letters from Ellen White such as this carried evidence of the prophetic charisma. If, as many biblical scholars have pointed out, the purpose of the prophetic voice in a community is to bring about change and give guidance for the life of the believer going forward, it might be asked what purpose did this letter serve other than inflicting pain? As a very ill man on his deathbed in late July 1883 without hope of recovery, what change was Andrews able to make in his marital status, in how he should educate his son or even at that stage in life how he might change his "peculiar" scholarly temperament? It has been seen as a very troubling letter. Can an understanding of the wider context help in our understanding of it?

Perhaps this last letter to Andrews should be read more as a cry of anguish in the pattern of an agonized scriptural lament over what might have been than as a prophetic call. At this stage in his life, Andrews was not in a position to change anything or do anything other than seek forgiveness and find refuge in the grace of God. A lament sees ideals not achieved. The prophetic perspective also points to ideals for the sake of others who follow, though they too would have to adapt ideals to uncomfortable messy realities in the pursuit of mission. Another perspective might suggest that the letter should be seen more as a prophetic voice speaking directly to the ideals that should generally guide mission. The realities on the ground had, in many cases, prompted Andrews to make less than ideal choices but the only place that missionaries live is in the real world and a number of the things that Ellen White describes as to what should have been done, people could not do because of circumstances. But the prophetic call to ideals is still important and this perhaps would have been helpful for the other reader in Andrews' bedchamber at the time Andrews heard it read. The only other person to benefit from the reading of this letter was Whitney and perhaps the holding out of the spiritual ideals of mission was important for him as he too would have to grapple with the realities of time and place in the difficult world of the less than ideal. Clearly the latter part of the letter seems to be addressed as much to Whitney as he approached the task of leadership as it was to Andrews.[60]

Andrews' sense of inadequacy and his lack of confidence in his decision-making evidence a low sense of self-esteem that seemed to grow worse with time. This problem he seems not to have been able to overcome. His seeking of emotional support from others in what Ellen White saw as inappropriate ways she perceived as a danger to himself and the church. Yet, Ellen White's own diaries and letters are similarly full

way she expressed her counsel to Andrews? In some subconscious way, did the letter reflect the underlying paradoxical cooperative-competitive tension that had always seemed to characterize the relationship between the two men?

60    Whitney led the work in Europe for only four years until he suffered intestinal ailments brought on by the complexities and stresses of work circumstances in Europe and he returned to America in the fall of 1887. He died of mesenteric consumption a few months later. "The Decease of Eld B. L. Whitney," *The Advent Review and Sabbath Herald* (April 17, 1888): 248. See also "Whitney," *Lake Union Herald* (December 22, 1936): 10. *Seventh-day Adventist Encyclopedia* ed., Don F. Neufeld (Washington DC: Review and Herald, 1976), 1607.

of complaints about her health with long public accounts of how she and her husband had suffered and sacrificed. They also seemed to be designed to provoke sympathy and support for their lonely stands for what she saw as truth and right. Did she recognize these dimensions of temperament and their associated dangers in herself and was she therefore more keenly aware of them also in Andrews? Did the frequent public criticism from her husband actually help Andrews to overcome the weakness or tend to make the problem worse?

And finally, how much of the last letter Ellen White wrote to Andrews was a subtle, perhaps subconscious defense of her husband? The favorable reports of Andrews in Haskell's reports at the General Conference session and his public vindication in the *Review Supplement* clearly implied a correction of misunderstandings and a subtle if not intended criticism of her husband and his treatment of Andrews. To what extent did her sense of a need to push back against these implications form part of the heaviness and the weight Ellen White felt she could not be free from until she had written?

## Conclusion: An Assessment

When Buel Whitney, Andrews' successor, sent to the *Review* editor brief details of Andrews' death and a report on the funeral, he did not intend his notice to be taken as a tribute to the fallen leader's life and work. He felt there were people better qualified for that writing task and he was sure that, by the time he sent in his funeral notice, "a fitting tribute" had probably already been offered.[61] But the pen of the best tribute writer available, Uriah Smith, was not in fact able to provide "a fitting tribute." His pen was tightly constrained by a number of factors. What kind of tribute could one write in view of Ellen White's last letter to the pioneer? But more important Andrews had made a prior request to Smith laying him under obligation to not make a fuss? This circumstance seems to have prevented a fully adequate assessment of Andrews' life ever since. In particular, was the mission to Europe a success or not? Could it have been carried out differently, more effectively, given the circumstances encountered? Had Andrews been a helpful leader? If Daniel Bourdeau had learned of the "severe rebuke" testimony read to Andrews in his last illness, it seems that others would also know of the scalding the Elder had received on his deathbed?[62] How many did is not clear. But how could one safely say much against such a backdrop?

---

61    "Death of Eld. J. N. Andrews," *The Advent Review and Sabbath Herald* (November 27, 1883): 730.
62    Andrews had briefly "mentioned his testimony which was read to him by Bro. Whitney, his writing to you and to Bro. Butler etc." D. T. Bourdeau to Ellen G. White, September 20, 1883, EGWE-GC. How much beyond this surface information was known by Bourdeau and others is uncertain.

Two years previously, in 1881, James White had been honored in the *Review* with numerous tributes from colleagues and deep expressions of gratitude. Appreciative observations on his major accomplishments and contributions to the church and discrete but respectful references to his distinctive, problematic authoritarian temperament and its weaknesses appeared for several weeks. For Andrews, by contrast, there was little more than a very subdued one-column statement giving some essential biographical details and facts about his family background and connections along with a brief reference to his major writings. It was an extended obituary, not a tribute.

Uriah Smith explained that some months previously Andrews had written to his brother-in-law, solemnly charging him that if and when their worst fears might be realized and he receive notice of his demise in foreign service, "no words of eulogy should appear in the paper." Andrews' reason was that he was fearful that Smith's "high regard" for him would "constrain you to say what I do not merit and what ought not to be said." In the tradition of William Carey of Serampore in India ("a wretched poor and helpless worm") Andrews was aware that even "his best acts" were tainted by "some trace of selfishness in them" and he had been "lacking in love toward God and man."[63] Smith felt that he had no choice, therefore, but to respect "the wishes of our dear brother" and restrain the comments that the esteem and love the church felt for the leader, "would naturally dictate."[64] And how much could he say without being perceived as undermining the authority of James White's widow? As he wrote out what he felt he could safely say, he felt that compliance with Andrews' request was "less difficult" because the works that the scholar-evangelist had left behind were "ample testimony" to "his efficiency and faithfulness" to the cause.

It has been difficult, ever since, for students of Adventist history to feel comfortable attempting an assessment of the contributions made to the church through the life and work of John Nevins Andrews. Letters of negative assessment – sent as private cautions and testimonies – are now public and have been widely read. Even in his own day they had been circulated around wide circles of leaders. Andrews' replies, his explanations, his correction of some things, his reports of changes made in response have not been generally available. Thus the negative communications have shaped perceptions and challenged assessments.[65] How are we to understand things in the larger perspective and in the light of history?

63   J. N. Andrews to US, Apr. 24, 1883, CAR. The Baptist founder of the modern missionary movement had insisted that the epitaph on his 1834 tombstone in the Serampore cemetery read, "A wretched, poor, and helpless worm on thy kind arms I fall." Andrews asked that his private, confidential note be also shared with J. H. Waggoner in California.

64   "The Death of Eld. Andrews," *The Advent Review and Sabbath Herald* (October 30, 1883): 680.

65   Papers read at the J. N. Andrews sesquicentennial celebrations at Andrews University July 20–21, 1979 all illustrate sensitive attempts to find a positive but balanced assessment in the light of the negative testimonies. See Roy E. Graham, "J. N. Andrews and Dedication," Joseph G. Smoot, "J.N. Andrews and the Bible," and Gottfried Oosterwal, "The Legacy of J. N. Andrews," AU, CAR.

Clearly Andrews was a pioneer who helped shape the church profoundly in manifold ways. His ground-breaking service in mission in Europe helped shape and establish the future of Adventist work across national and cultural boundaries; and, as he himself learned with difficulty how to adapt to local circumstance in the cause of mission, so he helped the church to learn as well. With Butler and Haskell, we may agree that that accomplishment was a success.

\*\*\*

## Appendix: A Critique of Erich Baumgartner's Critique of J. N. Andrews and His Mission

In 1999 at a Conference at Newbold College in England, Erich Baumgartner offered an assessment of John Andrews' mission leadership in a comparative study of the leadership of Andrews, Michael Czechowski and Ludwig Conradi and their contribution to Adventist mission in Europe. The paper, later published as an article "Charisma and Contextualization: Leadership Lessons from the Emerging Adventist Church in Central Europe, 1864–1914," offers a very negative assessment.[66] The assessment betrays a serious misunderstanding of the role of John Andrews and his contribution to Adventist Mission in Europe. This misunderstanding undervalues his contribution, seeing it primarily only as an example. Andrews "became a legend of dedication and missionary sacrifice" that still inspires Adventists "who are willing to forgive his weaknesses." He never overcame the tremendous obstacles he faced, failed to win the trust of the people around him and failed to "energize them to pursue the vision of a missionary church."[67] This assessment misreads the sources, and seems manifestly unjust to the missionary's memory. Two major mistaken assumptions underlie this inadequate assessment of John Andrews' contribution to Adventist mission.

The first fundamental mistaken assumption is that Andrews sought to rigidly follow the "American model" of mission and that this was ill-advised, inappropriate and ultimately unsuccessful. Baumgartner writes, "In Andrews' mind, the only way to establish the work in Europe was to copy the model of the church in America. This proved to be a fatal problem for Andrews' leadership and resulted in a buildup of tension between him and the Swiss believers that he never could fully overcome."[68] "Loyal to what he understood to be the American model, he faithfully labored till his

---

66  *Parochialism, Pluralism, and Contextualization: Challenges to Adventist Mission in Europe (19th–21st Centuries)*, eds. David Trim and Daniel Heinz (Frankfurt: Peter Lang, 2010), 63–81.

67  Ibid., 80.

68  Ibid., 67.

strength finally gave out."[69] As noted in the text, quite the opposite occurred. Andrews did not follow the "American Model."

A closer study of the documents from the period reveal that the General Conference Committee criticized Andrews sharply because, in their opinion, he was *not* in fact implementing the "American model" and that the reason for his failure to quickly establish a self-sustaining status for his mission was because of this failure to follow the model. The term "American model" was James White's term and he used it to describe the way he had successfully established early Adventism.[70] Andrews' mistake, alleged White's Committee, was that he was not following this pattern. Andrews acknowledged that he was not and could not follow the model. He defended himself against the criticism because experience in Europe was teaching him that different circumstances and a different culture meant that a different approach was indeed called for. Andrews' strategy had been adopted in order to adjust to the unique local circumstances on the ground that he faced and in order to meet local needs, taking into account the extremely limited resources available to him in Switzerland, including his own skills and limitations.

The second major mistaken assumption that Baumgartner makes in interpreting Andrews and his mission is that Ellen White's May 1883 critique of Andrews' temperament, and his ministry and numerous other critical letters can be uncritically relied on as an adequate interpretive screen for understanding Andrews.[71] These important and critical documents need to be considered in the wider context of the long complex relationship of John Andrews to both James and Ellen White and in the setting of James and Ellen White's inadequate understanding of the situation on the ground in Europe. A closer reading of these documents in the context of a broader range of sources, including John Andrews' own correspondence with the Whites, the correspondence of colleagues and diary sources suggests that the situation was much more complex. Such a reading requires a much more nuanced and sympathetic understanding than Baumgartner provides. Baumgartner seems not to be aware, for example, of the *Review Supplement* of May 1883 authored largely by Haskell and Butler which provides a very different assessment of Andrews' situation and of the "success" of his work.[72]

These two major weaknesses in the approach to the assessment of Andrews' leadership and mission tend to create a less than comprehensive perspective on John Andrews' experience in Europe. A wider context taking into account Andrews' own records and substantial newly available documentary sources suggest the need for a reappraisal in some key areas.

---

69   Ibid., 80.
70   "Our European Missions," 180.
71   See Baumgartner, 70–71.
72   G. I. Butler to B. L. Whitney, April 18, 1883, AHLF; *Review Supplement* (May 1, 1883): 3, 4.

## Unexpected Limited Resources Necessitate a Changed Strategy

John Andrews arrived in Neuchatel in late October 1874 just after the influential Vuilleumier families headed up by Albert had invested heavily in a new development of their watchmaking industry. This involved heavy financial commitments which tied up financial resources of their relatives and other church members. Andrews arrived too late to prevent this. The decision had large ramifications. Albert, the senior elder of the cluster of churches around Neuchatel, had been expected to lead out in evangelistic ministry. The industrial investment deprived Andrews of the personnel resources he was counting on for local evangelism (neither Albert nor his nephew Ademar, who had been trained in ministry for two years in America were able to commit to ministry). The decision also prevented access to critical financial resources from the Sabbatarians. In the important early stages of mission, funding available to Andrews was thus severely restricted, forcing him to rely on his own personal resources. The industrial investment eventually went bankrupt and involved unpleasant legal proceedings and a rupture in relationships apparently between church members.[73]

The restricted funding also meant that Andrews was obliged to rely much more heavily on General Conference funding than originally anticipated – a situation that aggravated relationships with the General Conference which had very high expectations of an early achievement of self-sustaining status for the mission. Andrews did not receive any salary from the General Conference. Nor did his helper, Daniel Bordeau. Local Systematic Benevolence funding was used primarily for the support of the Swiss-German pastor, James Erzberger and his mission activities.

Baumgartner suggests that the journal, *Les Signes des Temps,* was "a mixed blessing at best" and that "Andrews' perfectionism led him to exclude most of his coworkers from contributing to the success of the journal."[74] This assessment overlooks the much more positive 1883 assessment by Haskell and the General Conference itself. Andrews' choices were limited. Neither Bordeau nor Aufranc were blessed with a concern for carefulness or accuracy in writing or copy editing.[75] Publishing in French with its range of diacritical markings was not so simple as publishing in English – a dimension that James White never appreciated. Andrews judged his readership to be educated in such matters and that to ignore the issue posed the risk of the publishers being exposed to printing "ridiculousness." The choice to launch a magazine and to go monthly was a decision influenced heavily by the Swiss brethren who were sensitive to the cultural location and by the dictates of the local postal system. Such matters had to do with reputation and economic logistics. The choice to go with an

---

73   The financial troubles also apparently involved the loss of personal funds Andrews had extended to the family during the difficulties. See JVD, January 6, March 24, 1880, April 28, 1883, AHLF.
74   Baumgartner, 69.
75   Andrews' assessment of this is confirmed by Jean Vuilleumier, JVD, July 25, 1883, AHLF.

obviously American format for the magazine (large paper matching the *Review*) rather than the more economic and culturally sensitive European format was a decision made by James White not Andrews. A recognition of the complexities of the situation that Andrews found himself in and his limited range of options led Haskell's audit team in 1883 to judge that the magazine in fact had a powerful ministry and had made a major contribution to the success of the mission. They heartily endorsed the approach, and wanted it extended to include a German magazine. "Thousands of copies of our paper are going forth every month to enlighten minds dwelling [in?] darkness … An excellent impression has already been made by the French paper … We must have a German paper there in the near future."[76]

As Pietro Copiz has pointed out, there has developed a substantial mythology about Andrews' linguistic skills. The impact of Andrews' inability to quickly master conversational French has been underappreciated. It took him almost three years to acquire a level of fluency sufficient for him to preach in a public evangelistic setting in French. This limited his options during the early stages of mission. But the evidence is clear that as he developed fluency he did engage in substantial preaching both publicly and in local churches, joining in outreach and church planting with both Bourdeau and Erzberger. As an expatriate, however, he was never fully comfortable in the medium. In his later years the tuberculosis that he contracted prevented him from extensive engagement.

The argument that more preaching would have made for quicker results can be made, as it was by the advisors from Battle Creek, but this needs to be qualified by other evidence. Daniel Bourdeau's preaching in French and in France produced results very slowly against much hostility and opposition. John Loughborough and William Ings in England with their heavy emphasis on preaching, lengthy evangelistic series and intensive literature distribution produced far fewer results and more slowly than Andrews. Anti-Americanism and the culture of Europe was much more resistant to an American religion than many understood.[77] The situation was simply much more complex than either Ellen White or James White realized.

Any comparison that is made between the leadership of Andrews and Conradi based on perceived results of the work of the two men needs to be qualified by numerous dissimilarities between the two. Andrews, for example, was an expatriate, and already aging when he began his work. Furthermore he had had no previous cross-cultural experience. He struggled with culture shock, (without the benefit of prior sensitization as is now provided missionaries), but did adjust to his new culture. At

---

76  "Bro. Andrews has done most noble work there in his weakness, and those seeds of truth which have been so thoroughly watered with tears, will spring up in many hearts." *Review Supplement*, 3.

77  "It is no small matter to introduce a new doctrine so unpopular as ours . . . into old established communities, where the customs of society are fixed, where there is a prejudice against American ideas, and where the mass of the people are so poor as in Europe. It is especially difficult where the missionaries are natives of other lands, speak another language, and everything has to be learned." *Review Supplement*, 2.

the first he was "extremely critical" of Europeans, as Baumgartner observes.[78] This, however, did not last as Andrews adapted to the situation and realized that the New England tradition of "plain speaking" and of "rebuke and reproof" and the language of revivalism with its judgmental concepts of "backsliding" and the need for "reconversion" did not work in Europe. This cultural disparity long nurtured in him by James and Ellen White was a disadvantage. Apart from significant differences in temperament, Conradi had been born in Germany, was seventeen years younger than Andrews and had spent the first seventeen years of his life in Germany and had benefited from a long formal Catholic education before emigrating to the United States. He was naturally fluent in several languages and had significant cross-cultural experience. Converted to Adventism in Iowa in 1878 and educated at Battle Creek College, he had not been long influenced by interactions with James White or irreparably shaped by the American revivalist and confrontational tradition, and he was thus able to more readily adapt to a more culturally sensitive evangelistic methodology. Furthermore, when Conradi returned to Europe in 1886, it was as a national returning, not as an expatriate and he had the support of an established local organization with salary and budget resources able to support him from the outset.

The numerous personal letters from Ellen White addressed to John Andrews that Baumgartner uses as a primary filter for understanding John Andrews do provide helpful insights into his life and philosophy. Baumgartner notes that Ellen White was "very unhappy about his philosophy of work and life."[79] To accept this perspective as a kind of final verdict or even as the dominant interpretive lens without a careful understanding of "time and place" and without a careful study of John Andrews' response to the criticism is to misunderstand the correspondence and the person they are addressed to. This correspondence needs to be sensitively interpreted in the context of the distinctive temperament of her mildly bi-polar husband, his autocratic leadership style and the conflicted attitudes that James White developed towards Andrews, his closest working loyal associate. Ellen White feared that her husband's unreasonable, harsh criticism of Andrews (and two or three other colleagues) had irreparably intimidated them, destroying their self-confidence and their ability to think and act for themselves. On many occasions, for the survivability of the Advent cause Ellen White felt called to defend her husband in spite of his dominant, highly effective and yet at the same time damaging leadership style. Submission was the only alternative for associates like Andrews. It is also necessary to consider the role of a defense of her husband's posthumous reputation, as a possible factor in Ellen White's last negative interaction with Andrews in the letter sent to him on his deathbed.

The complicated nature of the long complex relationship between the Andrews, Stevens and White families also needs to be factored into the interpretive schema when seeking to understand the correspondence between Ellen White and John Andrews. The relationship was characterized by misunderstandings, offenses given, long

78   Baumgartner, 70.
79   Ibid.

memories and carried grudges. A careful consideration of such context would result in a more comprehensive and nuanced understanding of Andrews and a more balanced assessment of the "success" of Andrews' mission to Europe.

Andrews was a pathfinder, learning as he went how to succeed in cross-cultural mission. In the process one of his significant contributions was that he helped his church to learn how to be successful in mission – even in a difficult field like Europe.

Yvonne Johansson Öster

# Early Adventist Missions from Scandinavia

## Abstract

Scandinavian missionaries to foreign fields were sent out by the Seventh-day Adventist Church as early as the 1890s, in spite of low membership numbers. This paper addresses several major questions arising from these missionary ventures: What were the influences promoting these decisions? Why did these non-colonial countries have such a deep interest in supplying totally unknown countries and hitherto closed fields with well-trained young people and a ceaseless stream of support? What impact did the general Christian involvement in foreign mission have? What about the Adventist health education at Skodsborg School of Physiotherapy? In addition, what influence did the mission centre in Hamburg have, through L. R. Conradi's European General Conference? Were there any special characteristics singling out Scandinavian missionaries from others? What about the women in mission service? Finally, the paper asks whether it is possible to trace lasting insights from Scandinavian missionaries that could be applied in today's context.

The three Scandinavian countries were an early target of Adventist Foreign Mission. The Danish-American Baptist preacher who had become an Adventist pioneer, John Gottlieb Matteson, arrived in Denmark in 1877, proceeded to Kristiania (Oslo) Norway, and ended in Stockholm, Sweden, in 1885. He was also the host of Ellen G. White on her Scandinavian visits (1885–1887). Matteson had already started a Danish-Norwegian paper entitled *"Advent-Tidende"* in the USA. The fact that he had insisted on a paper for those Danes and Norwegians who did not have such a command of English as to benefit from Adventist literature, boosted Adventism in these countries. [1] James Saywer, an American, teaching Swedish immigrant children, started a paper in Swedish: *Svensk Adventhärold.* [2] Although leadership in Battle Creek were skeptical – when in America, you speak English – no one could foresee how significantly these publications were to impact the expansion of Adventist mission in Scandinavia.

When Matteson arrived in Scandinavia, he started colporteur work and evangelism schools in the three countries. Soon after the small beginnings of the three conferences in the 1880s, membership expanded considerably, even though migration became a drainage: Sabbath freedom, educational possibilities and work as well as

---

1   John Matteson, *Mattesons Lif og Advent bevaegelsens Begyndelse blandt Skandinaverne* (Nebraska: International Publishing Association, 1908); this is Matteson's autobiography.
2   *Svenska Sjundedags Adventisternas Historia* (Np: Swedish SDA Department in North America, 1928).

land was so much more attractive when going west. Sweden was a land of stark poverty and enforced strict dissenter laws in the 19th century, and it had an overwhelming class hierarchy. Between 1850 and 1920 one million Swedes left their country, i.e. one fourth of the then population. Yet Swedish immigration into America became a powerful tool in spreading Adventism; the same dynamics worked for Denmark and Norway. At the time no one could foresee what immigration into the United States would mean to the expansion of mission in and from Scandinavia.

## Influences Advancing Foreign Mission from Scandinavia

Without a formal European mission organization within the Adventist church, it is difficult to understand where the great growth in interest for foreign mission originated even before mission schools had been properly established in Scandinavia. In Sweden this was largely due to the impact of the great spiritual awakening in the 19th century. The most remarkable factors of these spiritual revival times were the following: (1) the child speakers in the 1840s,[3] (2) the spread of revival into all layers of society, even into the royal court; Ellen White noticed this when she preached in Stockholm 1885–1887.[4] (3) Moreover, mission-mindedness evolved into the formation of free churches but also numerous mission societies that emphasized the need to warn people "in the heathen countries" of the soon return of Jesus Christ. Thus, preaching the Second Coming of Jesus Christ was not a monopoly of Adventists. Adventist prophetic interpretation, though, was unique.

China was in the focus of several of these mission societies both in the Lutheran state church and in the expanding free churches. In Sweden the China Inland Mission was represented through the Swedish American Frederic Fransson's fiery appeals for China. He had two unique ideas: (1) that the poor farm hand or house maid could better adapt to China; and (2) that women were the most fitting to be sent as a spear heads into new territories. All the revival groups included women as preachers, Bible teachers and colporteurs[5] which implied that this was a plausible idea. In comparison to other Christian Protestant Free Churches, Adventists in Northern Europe were thus actually relatively late in sending out missionaries to foreign fields.

## *Early Adventist Educational Institutions in Scandinavia*

Eventually, mission schools replaced the colporteur's courses at Copenhagen, Denmark in 1889, and at Nyhyttan, Sweden in 1898. In the assembly hall at Nyhyttan Mission school,[6] there was a huge world map with the caption "Go ye into all the

---

3    See for instance LeRoy E. Froom, *The Prophetic Faith of Our Fathers*, vol. 3 (Maryland: Review and Herald, 1946), 671–686.
4    Ellen G. White diary, Stockholm, June 23–28,1887, "Third visit to Sweden," 2–3, Ms 35, 1887.
5    This goes for the SDA church in Sweden as well already in the early years of the 1900's.
6    1898 to1932 when the school moved to Ekebyholm, its present site.

world and preach the gospel to every creature."[7] This appeal fit the mood of the time very well, and it was taken very seriously indeed. The foremost goal of these schools was to foster capable workers for the church and its manifold needs within the ministry as well as administration and health work. Yet the focus on foreign mission also increased significantly during the first decades of the 20th century.[8]

In 1898 the most important Adventist institution aiming at foreign mission opened north of Copenhagen: the Skodsborg School of Physiotherapy. It was connected with Skodsborg Badesanatorium, under the leadership of Dr Carl Ottosen, a disciple of Dr John Harvey Kellogg in Battle Creek, Michigan. But for the training from Skodsborg, the number of Scandinavian missionaries would not have grown to such a great extent. Skodsborg became the Battle Creek of Northern Europe. The students came from all over Scandinavia, Iceland, Finland and the Baltic. In the pre WWII years almost all Scandinavian missionary couples had taken the four-year training for physiotherapy at Skodsborg. Most of them had in addition to that a basis in a Mission school in their own country. These facts made them able to preach, teach and heal as part of their encounter with all the unforeseen demands of pioneer mission. This goes, in most cases, for both men and women. In addition, Union College in Nebraska, USA, became a nursery of Scandinavian missionaries, as many immigrants or their children attended the Scandinavian departments there.[9]

## The European General Conference and Ludwig Richard Conradi

Ludwig Conradi initiated the European General Conference or, as it was later referred to, the European Division. Besides Matteson and Ottosen, he was the third strong man with great influence on the first decades of Nordic Adventism. After all, Hamburg was closer to Scandinavia than Battle Creek or Washington, D.C. Conradi was a constant guest speaker at various conferences, his last visit occurring in 1929.[10] There is no doubt that his inspiring stories from Russia ignited interest in the young listeners very early on. Conradi opened the eyes to a wider concept and understanding of mission. His 1940 obituary in *Skodsborgersamfundet* said:

> Pastor Conradi ... was one of the church's most important and courageous pioneers in Europe and one of those who by his experience and influence was a great supporter of Skodsborg in his time. We older folks remember vividly L. R. Conradi's fiery speeches and appeals to work in the Africa mission.[11]

7  In English!
8  In total around 90 missionaries were sent out from Sweden alone during the 20th century, average membership around 3000.
9  For instance, J.P. Anderson to China, V. Toppenberg to East Africa.
10 In Sweden 1901 to 1903,1906 to1914,1916,1920,1922,1929
11 *Skodsborgersamfundet*, 1940, 31(my translation from Danish to English). On the other hand, there was no understanding for his stand on bearing weapons in WWI, nor of his views on

The earlier concept of what may be called mission was "mission anywhere". Thus the less reached parts of Sweden were also called mission fields, e.g. *Norrländska mis-sionsfältet* (The Northern Mission field in Sweden). It was actually not until Scandinavia itself was not considered a mission field that the stream of young members started a movement to serve in foreign missions. Although Swedish Adventist missionaries served in Mainland China as early as the end of the 1890s, the first missionaries to be sent out from Sweden left in 1907 for Ethiopia/Eritrea via Hamburg.[12] This long tradition did not peter out until the end of the 1990s.[13]

## The Early Swallows

Before the turn of the century in 1900, six missionaries from Sweden left – of a membership of ca 700. Among them, two went to Iceland, two to Finland, and one to China.[14] None of them left under the auspices of the Foreign Mission Board in the US.

David Östlund sailed to Iceland in 1897 on commission by the Danish Conference. Originally one of the charter members of the Örebro church, he had attended the Union school at Frydenstrand in North Jutland, and trained as a printer in Oslo, where he also had studied German, English and Greek. After five weeks in Iceland he preached in Icelandic; he was a true linguistic genius. Östlund soon published a magazine entitled *Fraekorn* ("The Seed") at his own expense, where he wrote extensively on biblical subjects. He was also heavily engaged in the temperance movement. Östlund gained a keen understanding of the spiritual climate in Iceland, still marked by many heathen beliefs stemming from the sagas and Viking times.[15] The first baptism took place in 1900; the first church was organized in Reykjavik in 1906. Things evidently took time.

From Örebro, too, Olof Johnson, the conference leader, brought two Bible workers, Matilda Lindgren and Augusta Larsson to Helsingfors (Helsinki) in 1892. Evangelism was difficult as Finland was under tsarist rule until 1917. Mission prohibition was hampering: no public meetings, no distribution of literature or tracts; Siberia was

---

Ellen G. White. Here the Swedish-American influence superseded Conradi's skepticism to the prophet; generally, the Swedes believed her messages.

12  Gösta Wiklander, *Julius Persson: En son av Värmland och Långbanshyttan som blev Afri-kamissionär 1907* (Stockholm : SDA media, 2007), 5.

13  In the 1970s and 1980s both regular missionaries as well as short time volunteers, sponsored by state aid organizations, served in various projects. There was also a strong student missionary recruitment during the last three decades of the 1900s.

14  Olof Johnson is not counted here; he was responsible for the Swedish Conference as well. Erik Pilquist's wife-to-be, Ida Gran, was only connected to Adventism after their marriage in China.

15  Iceland was christianized in the year 1000 as a consequence of a democratic vote on the Allthing, the diet (Parliament) of the free men.

the terminal station if these rules were violated. Johnson rented a flat; it was permitted to invite others to private worship in one's home, which was done. He soon left to oversee the work in Sweden, so the two women took over. Poverty was striking; many urchins lived in the streets. Mathilda and Augusta started a children's ministry, and soon their social conscience and work for the small ones bore fruit.[16] A church was organized in 1893 with six men and six women being the first members.

China was the destination of Erik Pilquist,[17] one of the two deacons elected among the charter members of Örebro in 1885. He left for America in 1886, and from there for China in 1891, together with 34 other young Swedish American Christians. They had been inspired by Fredrik Fransson who recruited young Swedes for the China Inland Mission in 1891, 1892 and 1893. His wife-to-be, Ida Gran, came out to China in 1893. Both Erik and Ida hailed from a very poor background; he was from a small mining village north of Örebro, she came from the worst Dicken's style slum in the south of Stockholm. They learnt to live, eat and dress as Chinese and to speak Mandarin. As to strategies of surviving poverty, they knew them from home.

By the time Erik reconnected to the Adventist Church after 1897,[18] his wife Ida had fully absorbed the Adventist message. Ida was fluent in Mandarin and trained in teaching and preaching for Chinese women. After they had left Ningsia in the North, they connected with the British and Foreign Bible Society.[19] In 1899 en route to Sweden, they visited Battle Creek, a visit that had far-reaching implications on Adventist mission: it was there that Erik pleaded for medical missionaries to China, and six answered the call.[20] He also convinced Jakob Nelson Anderson, a Danish pastor from Wisconsin, to go to China. Anderson was the one who conducted the first Adventist baptism in Mainland China in 1903 and led the mission during the first years.[21] The Pilquists had prepared these first six people for baptism although they were not yet employed by the church.[22]

16  Ragnar Svensson, "Sjundedags Adventistsamfundet i Finland 1892–1972," 4–5.

17  Lawrence Onsager, "On Fire for China: The Story of Erik Pilquist, Pioneer Adventist Missionary to China," Paper presented at the conference "Reflection on Adventism in China and Asia," October 30-31, 2014, Hong Kong Adventist College.

18  E. Pilquist to editor Emil Åhrén, *Missionären*, 1897.

19  See Onsager, "On Fire for China."

20  Drs Miller and Selmons in addition to two nurses, Carrie Erickson and Charlotte Simpson; see Raymond S. Moore, *China Doctor: The Life Story of Harry Willis Miller* (Idaho: Pacific Press, 1969), 26.

21  Erik Pilquist wrote a very poetical account to Emil Åhrén, published in *Missionären*, (Autumn 1903).

22  Ibid.

## First Official Adventist Missionaries Sent from Scandinavia before 1914

In 1907 Julius Persson,[23] an experienced preacher, and Per Lindegren, a physiotherapist from Skodsborg, left Sweden via Hamburg for Asmara in the then Ethiopia. In 1909 Valdemar Toppenberg from Denmark but then based at Union College, Nebraska, arrived in Eritrea as well. Abyssinia (today's Ethiopia) was a country they could not enter, but Eritrea was open, so Asmara became the first place of Scandinavian Adventist mission establishment.[24] Ethiopia was to become the special target of Scandinavian foreign mission and it remained so until 1975.[25]

Toppenberg and Persson were soon directed to today's Tanzania.[26] It was not until the beginning of the 1920s that Toppenberg succeeded in establishing an Adventist mission in Ethiopia. Although the outbreak of World War I put a halt to mission work in Eastern Africa, Scandinavian missionaries were still sent out during the war years 1914–1918. Ole Grundset (Norwegian) and Bernhard Pedersen (Danish) were asked to start up a mission in Manchuria. Aaron Larson (Swedish-American) got the task of opening up an orphanage in Greece in the wake of the Armenian genocide after the armistice. However, compared to the great numbers of American missionaries during the first decades of the 20th century, Scandinavians were few in number. Yet their contributions were often that of resilient ground breakers in unentered territories. This is also true for the interwar period i.e. the years between 1920 and 1940.

## A Non-Colonial Heritage

Scandinavians all came from countries with relatively small population, with languages which few others could speak. They had no influence on world politics. They were no colonial power. These facts were to impact their attitudes to doing mission. They had to learn the dominant colonial language, the vernacular, and possibly even several tribal tongues. If nothing else keeps one humble, this will do, verbal communication being the most important of all mission skills.

Oscar Olsson, who went to Persia (Iran) as a teacher in 1926, wrote the following which represents more than his personal perspective:

> When you arrive in the mission field, you feel the pressing necessity to learn the vernacular as quickly as possible…if you don't go to depths in learning a language so that you

23   Julius Persson had studied at Nyhyttan and Friedensau, he might have been known to Conradi.
24   L. Conradi had done the survey of Eastern Africa and led the mission enterprises from Hamburg.
25   Hamburg was the port of departure for several Scandinavian missionaries in the 1920s as it was the site of the European General Conference.
26   Then Tanganyika-German East Africa.

can enjoy its literature, you will soon forget it. It is a remarkable thing how you become tied to a people when you know their language. When you have learned Turkish, the Turk is no stranger to you.[27]

However, the great contribution to truly make the gospel understood was made when songs were translated. Erik Pilquist in China as well as decades later Ruben Bergström in North Cameroun printed a hymnal on the basis of well-known hymns, as in fact Matteson had done as well, when he first arrived Denmark in 1877.

## Types of Outreach and a Scandinavian Legacy?

Were there any common denominators in methods even if the early Scandinavian Adventist missionaries had different points of departure? Three examples will serve as illustrations.

(1) Erik and Ida Pilquist in China 1891–1911, stressed teaching, preaching and distributing the Bible, to arouse interest. They practiced spreading the gospel trough training young boys as well as women to spread the Bible and its messages. Theirs was the task to reach the unreached.

(2) Nils Zerne and his family arrived in Syria in 1923; they stayed in the Middle East until 1937. He led the mission between 1923 and 1929. The church at large was scattered and devastated after World War I and the Armenian genocide in particular. " [w]hen he [Zerne] arrived in Beirut in 1923, he vigorously set out to *reconstruct* the work and *reorganize* the church using the few faithful members as the nucleus."[28] His method? "At the first opportunity he set out to *regroup* the scattered members and began to *nourish them spiritually.*"[29] This led to church members "ardently sharing their God-given faith with their fellow-citizen."[30] Thus, again one can see a two-way communication. Nils Zerne quickly learnt Arabic and used it for the rest of his life.

(3) Ruben and Hanna Bergström in North Cameroun 1931–1966.[31] There is reason to believe that without the clinic run by Hanna, the spreading of the gospel would not have happened. Healing the sick broke down prejudice against the white strangers as this was old slave-trade country. Local people were involved in building the mission. After some years, Ruben started a special school for evangelists. When their studies were finished, they were sent out to the villages with a kit of tools. But every month they convened at the main station to get and give feed-back as well as

---

27   Oscar Olson, *Ungdomens Budbärare*, 1930 (my translation from Swedish). Oscar Olson had to learn both Farsi and Tatari (similar to Turkish), which was spoken in the northwestern part of Iran.

28   Manough Nazirian, *The Seventh-day Adventist Church in Lebanon 1897–1997* (Beirut: The East Mediterranean Field of Seventh-day Adventists, 1999), 15.

29   Ibid.

30   Ibid., 48.

31   Hanna died in 1953. Ruben remarried physiotherapist Elisabeth Heilskov-Jonasson in 1956.

being consolidated in their faith, task and calling. This was indeed a strengthening factor of success.

Besides the keen interest in learning languages, Scandinavians lacked a hierarchical culture from their home churches. There was also in the currents of early 20$^{th}$ century a keen interest in the exotic, in conquering the unknown. To Christians this translated into foreign mission. Together these facts seem to have fostered great interest in the foreign cultures and people that the missionaries encountered. Thus letters sent home not only reported about the overthrowing of heathen customs and souls won for Christ but also contained detailed descriptions of the very different cultures Scandinavian missionaries met. Actually this was what they often wrote home about. As quite a few had a long-time commitment to one place or one country, they grew less interested in imposing their own Scandinavian culture on the people they were to serve. In some cases, as in North Cameroon and Uganda, a written language had to be created.[32] Could one then say that Scandinavians were more open to adapting to the context they met rather than imposing their own culture including their own Scandinavian Adventism? Now living former missionaries in Northern Europe tend to think so, but here research gives no definite answer.

## Did an Ideal Method Exist?

To illustrate a near-ideal method practised, a British source (themselves in Ethiopia six years in the late 1960s) mentions Erik and Borghild Palm.[33]The Palms [34]arrived in Ethiopia in 1933,worked in the isolated northern station of Debra Tabor, were taken captives during the Italian invasion, and returned in 1946 to build up the station in Debra Tabor as well as Kuyera College. Erik was a good builder and musician; both were Skodsborg physiotherapists, and stayed until their retirement in 1970. They were constantly sent to plant new mission stations. According to a fellow missionary from Britain,

> Their understanding of the pantheistic people where they worked in the South (in Abonza) showed personal insight into the culture, background, and the social needs of the people. They introduced Christianity in such a way that people could identify it as a way of life that allowed the people to want to embrace it, better their quality of life within the confines of the area they lived. Unlike other missionaries who introduced a new form of music, using Amharic translations of American gospel songs, they used local language, local style of music and put their Christian ethic into the songs in such way that it made sense to the people. The sentiment of many of the tradition Western hymns is based on a Western way of life. Was the above due to the fact that the Palms were Swedish or that they possessed insight most of us never considered? What effect did Erik's prisoner of war

---

32   In the 1930s.
33   Sherard and Sheila Wilson, UK, in Ethiopia in the 1960s. From my observation, they acquired good understanding of both language and culture. They also had an open attitude to expatriates from other Christian traditions than their own.
34   Erik Palm was Swedish, Borghild née Stokkan Norwegian – they met at Skodsborg.

experience, which he would never speak about, have on his work? Then we had other missionary teachers…they taught as if they were teaching Europeans/Americans, not realizing that the material they were teaching to students in the Western world was not familiar in the Developing world. [35]

In all honesty it is hard to identify any specific Scandinavian method that was more apt even if most persons interviewed believed there was. Rather it seems as if these were personal attitudes. However, most missionaries did stress the importance of language as a way to access people's thoughts and ideas. Without knowing the vernacular, there was evidently not much of a chance of adapting to the context presented. Could strong individuals really transcend their own cultural heritage to the benefit of a new and different culture? Was it easier if one came from a small Scandinavian country rather than from the USA, the cradle and headquarters of Adventism? Was national prestige involved?

Scandinavians as well as other Europeans had had to live with the American context of Adventism, not seldom expressed as a demand rather than a possibility. In pioneer missions both these cultural legacies – the American and the European – had to face the very different reality of Ethiopia in the 1920s or North Cameroon in the 1930s. Regardless of national background, a necessary detachment from one's own home context was necessary. If you came with no ambition to transplant a Scandinavian or American concept of living this surely was an asset opening up to the possibilities present. This did not mean to omit in any way the transformation of lives that the Gospel of Jesus Christ brought, nor the deep changing results of healthier lives and the possibilities of education that mission brought. Rather it was the old rule: To be present in the present seems to have permeated the thinking – and doing – of earliest Scandinavian missionaries, especially those who stayed on for many years.

## Women

Already in the 19th century, foreign mission was attractive to single Swedish women. It was an opportunity for a professional life without the normal gender restrictions at home. In the Protestant tradition, women did not become nuns, but for many single women to serve as a missionary meant the choice of celibacy – and the freedom from fear of dying during childbirth. It meant being somebody in one's own right, but it also implied the loss of the social status and togetherness connected with having a family.

In the Adventist denomination there was no specific policy as to the status of a future missionary in the early 1900s. But after World War I the habit-turned-policy was never to call a young single man, only married men and their families. Single women on the other hand received calls throughout the 1900s. A Danish nurse in her mid-thirties quoted a wise General Conference man saying: "It's a crime to send

35 E-mail from Sheila Wilson to Yvonne Öster, March 2018.

young girls to the mission field."[36] Yet to quote a Norwegian mission leader at the same time: "A woman can be sent to an isolated station, a man cannot endure it."[37] In this he agreed with Frederik Fransson. According to him, women were the best to be sent to unentered fields; they were less offensive – and less expensive as well!

Scandinavian Adventism in the 20th century was a family affair. Many had shared school days at Skodsborg. That also provided single women with a context of social life when in the mission field, as was the case in Ethiopia. However to consider forming a family with national men or have a courtship was indeed not encouraged.[38] The rule was then clear: in such a case the young woman had to be put on permanent leave.

Tragedies occurred; some young women left after a short time, some left the church forever. The cost of mission might have been much greater than any official triumphant baptismal reports may tell. What about the wives in isolated pioneer stations? How did church administration actually regard them? The couples who left in the 1920s and 1930s were all newly married.[39] They were put in places where the access to medical care was absent. Miscarriages occurred (because of malaria and other reasons), babies died, children died, young wives died.

The professionalism of missionary wives was always considered in the call forwarded to their husbands (or fiancés). In the *Advent Survey*[40] this is very evident.[41] The expected contributions from the wives was paramount, and work they did indeed. The statistics however of, for example, the Dogba station,[42] in the 1930s report, show only two missionaries, and only two salaries are paid. Actually there were two couples![43] In these reports the married women missionaries were non-existent (even if in this case they were professionals, a nurse and a midwife). If one believes that this was a matter of the 1930s, facts prove the opposite. Just to mention one of several similar cases: In 1976, Jengre Hospital, North Nigeria, desperately needed a new medical doctor, preferably a pediatrician, and one from Sweden was found. But it was her husband who got the call; she was shocked.[44]

This long-lived policy in the church of head-of-household salaries was a riddle to Scandinavians. The discriminating view of married women, even those professionally qualified, was both incomprehensible and utterly condescending. A discriminating system like this not only affected the expatriate women; it also affected local employees. Dr Børge Schantz, in a leading position in Lebanon the 1970s,

---

36  Else Schantz in Debra Tabor, Ethiopia, 1964. She had arrived in Ethiopia 23 years old.
37  Pastor Odd Jordal in Ethiopia commenting on nurse Alice Lind in the new clinic in Abonza, 1964.
38  Or with non-Adventist expatriates for that matter.
39  This was also the case after WWII.
40  The official magazine of the Northern European Division 1927-1942.
41  For instance, the Bergströms and the Rösts in North Cameroon 1931 onwards.
42  In North Cameroun.
43  *Advent Survey*, 1932 onwards.
44  Interview with Dr Inger Karlman, Binfield, UK, March 3, 2016.

discovered to his horror that the teachers in the church schools were salaried according to gender even with the same educational background. He changed that and caused quite a bit of anger on the part of his American superior![45]

On the theological side: it is significant that Scandinavian women from Ida Pilquist onwards used to preach, to teach the Bible, to write, and to administer mission affairs with the same skills and audacity as men. That legacy is still valid.

## Applications

When reviewing 125 years of Scandinavian Adventist missionaries' pursuits, certain aspects stand out: commitment, resilience, creativity, sensitivity as to context, and practical skills. The pioneer generation was brought up in a non-industrial home surrounding. One had to make do with things that were available and translate needs into what was feasible. Early and long-time Scandinavian missionaries taught commitment in seemingly impossible mission challenges. However, they were no saints even if the home based considered them to be and expected them to remain so. Conflicts and power struggles occurred in all sorts of ways. It is no doubt difficult when saints gather.

So what about applications for today? Should we offer lessons in Arabic and Somali at local churches in our European congregations in the big city? In-depth study of the Qur'an viewed in an Adventist context? Tackling the so-called honour culture, child marriages and FGM in our European midst? I suggest that the crucial implication of the Scandinavian Adventist missionary story is total commitment to the beliefs that Jesus himself came to save the world. He chose all kinds of instruments for his mission. Some were sometimes odd and still are. That is the mark of a fearless and resilient missionary, true to the calling of the Lord.

---

45 Email from Iris Schantz to Yvonne J. Oster, March 20, 2018. In the other cases some do not want to be identified.

*Sergo Namoradze*

# The Emergence and Development of Adventist Mission in Georgia

### Abstract

Traditionally, Georgia is known as an Eastern Orthodox country, where Christianity became the state religion from early centuries. Since then, Christianity has profoundly shaped the culture, history and worldview of this ancient nation. Protestant groups emerged onto the scene a few centuries ago and paved the way for Adventist mission. The Seventh-day Adventist Church today looks back to more than a century in this country. Nevertheless, the Adventist historical account has never been documented, except for a few mentions by researchers whose reports are framed in the perspective of the Russian empire and Soviet Union. The history of SDA mission in Georgia is intertwined with devotion and determination as well as the tragic life stories of those pioneers, among whom were native church members, missionaries and ministers not so well-known to these days. Proper discernment of Adventist history in Georgia would help recapture the mission from the prism of local cultural and historical viewpoints, and, hence, strategize outreach according to the context.

Adventism came to Georgia over 110 years ago and today is represented by 368 church members. However, so far the historical account of the Seventh-day Adventist Church in this country is fragmented because no written document was produced that would reassemble the events and important individuals of the past in chronological order.[1] This research presents the attempt to recollect the historical account based on primary and secondary sources that were available to the author, such as documents, photos, artifacts etc. The in-depth interviews with participants of the study who lived during the time of the early development, or who knew individuals who shaped the history of Adventism in Georgia, significantly shed light on the study.[2]

---

1  This contribution is condensed from my dissertation. See Sergo Namoradze, "Church Growth Theory and the Development of the Seventh-day Adventist Church Mission in Georgia: A Case Study" (PhD diss., Adventist International Institute of Advanced Studies, 2018).

2  The interviewees gave permission to the author to use their names. These in-depth interviews with Pastor Panchenko, Mrs. Glazova, and Mr. Dragan are to be considered most valuable information, as well as the interview with Konstance Mayevskaya, who personally knew Pastor Kote Karalashvili.

Georgia, also known as the "cradle of wine"[3] is mentioned in many ancient documents. These documents record the great development and influence of the kingdoms of Kolkha and Iberia (western and eastern kingdoms of Georgia respectively) that later were united under King Bagrat III in the 10th century.[4] Christianity was introduced from a very early period and became the national religion in the 4th century.[5] Since then Georgian Orthodoxy has permeated every sphere of life, thus safeguarding national identity, history and tradition. Melton and Bauman correctly assert, "As various conquerors (most of whom were Muslims) moved through Georgia, the struggle for independence became largely identified as a struggle for the defense of Orthodoxy, since many clerical and laypersons died as martyrs for their Orthodox faith."[6]

## Protestants in Georgia

Despite the dominance of the Georgian Orthodox Church, by the end of the 19th century the first Protestants had settled in Georgia. Initially, Protestantism was not brought to the Caucasus by the endeavor of Western home-based missionaries as happened in other parts of the world. Rather it was brought by German settlers, who were mostly adherents of the Lutheran creed and pietistic spirituality. The settlers never intended to evangelize the local people but pursued economic purposes supported by the Russian imperial powers.[7] Among the German settlers there were also groups inclined to apocalyptic religious notions, which used to create tension between the settlers and the authorities.[8]

Notably, Protestant settlements did not make any significant missionary progress in terms of converting locals to the Protestant faith. In this regard, Songulašvili asserts, "Contact and potential evangelism were also inhibited by the fact that the

---

3    D. D. Kacharava, G. T. Kvirkvelia, and J. Chi, *Wine, Worship, and Sacrifice: The Golden Graves of Ancient Vani* (Princeton, NJ: Institute for the Study of the Ancient World, 2008), 23; R. G. Suny, *The Making of the Georgian Nation* (Bloomington, IN: Indiana University Press, 1988), 11.

4    M. Chkhartishvili, *On Georgian Identity and Culture: Nine International Presentations* (Tbilisi, Georgia: Publishing House Universal, 2009), 17.

5    I. V. Bondyrev, Z. Davitashvili, and V. P. Singh, *The Geography of Georgia: Problems and Perspectives* (Basel, Switzerland: Springer International, 2015), 37; A. Mikaberidze, *Historical Dictionary of Georgia* (Lanham, MD: Scarecrow, 2007), 89; s.v. "Georgia."; B. A. West, "Georgia," *Encyclopedia of the Peoples of Asia and Oceania* (New York, NY: Facts on File, 2009), 37.

6    J. G. Melton and M. Baumann, "Georgia," *Religions of the World: A Comprehensive Encyclopedia of Beliefs and Practices* (Santa Barbara, CA: ABC-CLIO, 2010), 1192.

7    T. Kopaleishvili, *Protestant Churches in Georgia* (Batumi, Georgia: Shota Rustaveli State University of Batumi, 2014), 30, 34, 40.

8    Kopaleishvili, *Protestant Churches in Georgia*, 42, 43.

German settlers never learned the local languages."[9] Even when the governor asked the Lutheran pastors to attempt a mission work among mountain tribes, the pastors hesitantly rejected the offer understanding that there was not much they could do due to being unprepared.[10] The settlers refrained from mingling with the locals; and were even forbidden to marry someone from outside their country and faith.[11]

Later developments of the Protestant Church in Transcaucasia were linked to the so-called Russian revivalist religious groups such as the Dukhobori, Malakan, Subotniki, and the old rule Orthodox.[12] They were persecuted by the imperial powers and forcefully relocated to the countries of Transcaucasia.[13] This religious persecution and exile significantly furthered the Protestant faith in the region.[14] Although they did not belong to the European Protestant branches (but were rooted in Russian Orthodoxy), they were still inclined to the Protestant style of worship and Bible reading.[15]

These groups did not succeed in communicating the gospel to the locals either – perhaps also mainly because of the language factor. Johann Gerhard Oncken, who was one of the most influential leaders of the Baptist movement in Europe, underscored the importance of knowing local languages as the channels of communication in Georgia: "It is very desirable that any missionary appointed to labor in this district should not only understand the Russian language, but also be conversant with Armenian, Georgian and Turkish."[16] Thus, these minor religious groups have disappeared, or are disappearing in Georgia, because they did not succeed in communicating the gospel to Georgians not only because of the language barrier but also due to their Russian ethnic background, which made Georgians think that conversion implied an identity change.

9     M. Songulašvili, *Evangelical Christian Baptists of Georgia: The History and Transformation of a Free Church Tradition* (Waco, TX: Baylor University Press, 2015), 33.
10    Songulašvili, *Evangelical Christian Baptists of Georgia*, 33, 34.
11    R. Maisuradze, *German Religious Separatism and Lutherans in Georgia* (Tbilisi, Georgia: TSU, 1990), 21.
12    D. Buachidze, *Religious Confessions and Denominations in Lithuania and Georgia (Comparative Analysis): Cultural, Historical and Theoretical Issue of XIX (Conference Materials)* (Tbilisi, Georgia: TSU, 2004) 34; F. Coene, *The Caucasus: An Introduction. London* (NY: Routledge, 2010); R. Topchishvili, ed., *Ethnography/Ethnology of Georgia* (Tbilisi, Georgia: Universali, 2010), 44.
13    A. U. Grigorenko, *Eschatology, Millenarism, Adventism: The History and Modernity* (St. Petersburg, Russia: Evropeiski Dom, 2004), 11, 12; E. V. Zaitsev, *История Церкви АСД* [*The History of the Adventist Church*]] (Zaokski, Russia: Istochnik Zhizni, 2008), 93–99.
14    Songulašvili, *Evangelical Christian Baptists of Georgia*, 40, 41.
15    Kopaleishvili, *Protestant Churches in Georgia*, 99–101.
16    Songulašvili, *Evangelical Christian Baptists of Georgia*, 78.

Over time, several branches emerged within the Molokans. One of these branches was called *Subotniki*.[17] They observed the Sabbath and followed some Jewish customs, including the prohibition of certain foods listed in the OT. Despite the fact there is no direct historical evidence, it still can be assumed that these believers had the potential of serving as a bridge toward acceptance of Adventism by other branches of Molokans. Thus, although German colonists and Russian essentialists (Russian originated Protestant groups) apparently did not convert anyone from the local population (Georgians, Armenians, and Azeri), they paved the way for Western Protestantism, which in turn attracted the indigenous nations of Transcaucasia, including the Georgian population.

## The Beginning of Adventism in Georgia

One of the first known Christian missionaries in Georgia, who actively preached about Second Advent and thus could be regarded as the precursor of Adventism in this country was Joseph Wolff (1795–1862).[18] However, even before his arrival, the Adventist message had reached Georgia through Russian emigrants in the United States, who sent letters and brochures about Adventism to their relatives.

Dr Vagram Pampaian, the first official Seventh-day Adventist missionary in Georgia, was an American medical doctor with an Armenian background. He arrived in Tbilisi with his wife and brother in 1904.[19] Being fluent in Armenian and Turkish, he spent around two years in Tbilisi giving out pamphlets and working with the people who spoke these languages. It was known that they even attempted to study the local language, i.e. Georgian. However, in 1906, they moved to Armenia and then to Turkey to continue the work among the Armenians there.[20] As a result of his mission endeavor, he converted five people but managed to baptize only one because of persecution from the clerical authorities.[21]

At that time, in Sukhumi, West Georgia, Pastor Tsirat, who was not yet an ordained Adventist minister, began colporteur ministry. As a result of this work, in

---

17   D. O. Yunak, "Возвожу очи мои к горам. История Церкви Адвентистов Седьмого Дня в Закавказье" ["Lift My Eyes to the Hill: The SDA History in Transcaucasia"] (Tula, Unpublished manuscript, 2012); E. V. Zaitsev, *The History of the Adventist Church*, 82.

18   Heinrich J. Löbsack, Великое Адвентистское Движение и Адвентисты Седьмого Дня в России [*The Great Advent Movement and Seventh-day Adventists in Russia*] (2nd ed.) (Rostov, Russia: Caucasus Union Mission of SDA, 2006 [1st ed. 1918]), 152; Yunak, "Lift My Eyes to the Hill," 10, 11; Zaitsev, *The History of the Adventist Church*, 113.

19   Daniel Heinz et al., *Photochronic of Adventist Church in Tsarist Russia-USSR-UIP in 1882–2012* (original title in transliteration: *Fotochronika Cerkvi Adventistov Sed'mogo Dnja: V Carskoj Rossii - SSSR - SNG (1882-2012 gody)*; Charkov: European Archives of History of SDA, 2012), 11, 12; Zaitsev, *The History of the Adventist Church*, 214.

20   Yunak, "Lift My Eyes to the Hill," 83.

21   Ibid., 84.

1906, six people of German origin were converted.[22] In 1911, he was sent for mission work in Tibilis. He stayed there until the spring of 1912.[23]

## Albert Ozols (1878–1916): Experience of Resistance in Hospitable Georgia

Pastor Albert Ozols, a talented young man of Latvian origin and a medical doctor, was the person who contributed most in terms of church planting in Tbilisi. Upon conversion, he went to study in Germany and graduated from Friedensau Mission Seminary. Although fluent in German and Russian, he was aware of the importance of learning the local language in the mission field; hence, he studied Persian.[24] He arrived in Tbilisi, Georgia in 1907.[25] His earliest missionary endeavor in Georgia among German-speaking population and Latvians was fruitful. Upon arrival in Tibilis, he organized evangelistic seminars that were attended by an average of over 45 people.[26] Yet, success was not without sacrifice; in 1907–1908, the missionary work faced difficulties because of resistance by the local population and suspicion from government authorities. However, at the end of the same year, there were 23 church members in Tibilis.[27]

Between 1908 and 1909, Pastor Heinrich Löbsack visited Tbilisi and conducted evangelistic meetings. Recalling the event, he wrote, "Here we see how Europe encounters Asia. In spreading the Good News, this city in Transcaucasia has the same importance as Jerusalem had for spreading the Gospel during the life of our Savior."[28] In the same document, he recalls that in 1909, Pastor Conradi visited Tbilisi twice in order to meet Dr Pampaian and discuss the work among Armenians.[29] In 1912, the Caucasian Conference was divided into two parts because of the difficulty in visitation. This division made Transcaucasia into a separate mission field of eight

---

22  See Heinz et al., *Photochronic of Adventist Church in Tsarist Russia*, 10; Löbsack, *The Great Advent Movement* and *Seventh-day Adventists in Russia*, 228, 229; and Zaitsev, *The History of the Adventist Church*, 214.

23  Daniel Heinz et al., *Souls under the Altar*, 2nd ed. (original title in Russian: *Duši pod žertvennikom: Kniga pamjati Cerkvi Christian Adventistov Sed'mogo Dnja, posvjaščennaja žertvam religioznych repressij vo vremena Carskoj Rossii i Sovetskogo Sojuza, 1886–1986 gody*), Charkov: European Archives of History of Seventh-day Adventists, 2015), 166.

24  Zaitsev, *The History of the Adventist Church*, 214.

25  Heinz et al., *Photochronic of Adventist Church in Tsarist Russia*, 10; Löbsack, *The Great Advent Movement*, 11.

26  Yunak, "Lift My Eyes to the Hill," 27–28.

27  Ibid., 83.

28  Ibid., 85–86.

29  Ibid., 85.

congregations with 226 members under the leadership of Pastor Ozols.[30] This decision was finalized on January 1, 1914 when the Transcaucasia Mission Field was attached to the European Division.[31]

The activities of Pastor Ozols irritated the local clerical authorities, who asked help of the police to get rid of him. As a result, not only Pastor Ozols but also other Adventist missionaries were arrested and jailed.[32] One of the reports of Pastor Ozols is preserved in "Maslina"[33] where he recollects,

> Regarding the indigenous tribes, our field is very diverse. Near the Black Sea in *Kutaisi gubernia* (region in west Georgia), we witness the revival among Mingrelians and Georgians. I was able to baptize one brother who was willing to be baptized since spring, after his registration of exit from the state church. We went to visit his relatives, who observed the Sabbath, but were still registered members of the state church. After we went there, someone informed the local priest that Adventists came to that village. The priest came and ordered the local authority to arrest us. The local authority saw that we were innocent but could not do anything to free us because of the fear of the priest.[34]

This account presents the significant fact that Georgians were converted into Adventism as early as 1913. Yet in 1914, Pastor Ozols was arrested and sent to Siberia. On his way to exile, as a medical doctor, he treated patients among the prisoners. One day in 1916, he contracted a deadly disease and at the age of 38, the man with a "golden heart" died.[35]

## Adventism in Georgia under the Leadership of Pastor Galajev, 1925–1939

Taking place on October 8–10, 1925, the first constituency meeting in the Transcaucasia Mission Field marked the beginning of a new period of Georgian Adventism. Due to the lack of finances, only 20 delegates were able to attend the meeting. According to Yunak, Georgians, Armenians, Russians, and Germans were represented. At the meeting, Pastor Alexei Galajev was elected chair of the committee to oversee Transcaucasia.[36] He was an ethnic Armenian and probably one of the most

---

30  Löbsack, *The Great Advent Movement*, 285; Yunak, "Lift My Eyes to the Hill," 216

31  Yunak, "Lift My Eyes to the Hill," 217.

32  Ibid., 83–85.

33  Since 1905 the "Maslina" magazine began to be published in Russian, where various topics and first hand mission reports were covered.

34  As cited in Yunak, "Lift My Eyes to the Hill," 30.

35  Heinz et al., "Souls Under the Altar," 55; Löbsack, *The Great Advent Movement*, 296; Zaitsev, *The History of the Adventist Church*, 238.

36  Yunak, "Lift My Eyes to the Hill," 90–93. Yunak is a major historian of Adventism in several regions of the former Soviet Union. While further primary sources apparently do not exist, his account appears reliable.

capable person for this position as far as cultural sensitivity was concerned.[37] According to Pastor Panchenko, Pastor Galajev had spent his childhood in Tbilisi, Georgia, before his parents moved to Rostov, Russia.[38]

Hence, it should be assumed that he could understand the Georgian language, and presumably this is one of the reasons for his successful ministry in the region. Galajev was able to replant the church in Georgia with the help of other ministers. Yet the 10-year gap (since the arrest of Pastor Ozols in 1914 and his arrival in 1925) significantly affected the Tbilisi Adventist Church, weakening its influence and reducing its size. Panchenko in this regard asserts, "All our old members, with whom I worked, confirmed that Galajev replanted the church and was eventually arrested here. They remembered him well."[39]

Yunak (2012) makes an important comment about the new Bible worker hired in 1926 who was Georgian as is apparent from his last name – Shavadze.[40] This was the first mention of a Georgian last name among all the ministers who worked in Georgia. There was no other mention about this person later, by any additional document, or a photo that would help trace his origins and the story of his conversion. However, having a Georgian among the Bible workers was an important breakthrough. It may lead to the conclusion that there were a number of Georgian converts as early as the 1920s or even before.

Pastor Galadjev's arrest in 1939 was the start of an 18-year gap leaving Georgia without any leader or minister. This gap lasted until 1957, when Pastor Pavel Panchenko was commissioned to Tbilisi from Rostov. Not much is known about what happened from 1939 to 1957, except that [a?] few ministers from the neighboring countries visited the Adventist congregation in Tbilisi from time to time. This second gap heavily affected the Adventist mission to Georgians.

## Filling the Gap: Laity in Charge

The time between the arrest of Galajev in 1939 and the arrival in Tbilisi of Panchenko in 1957 became a significant period in terms of the development of the Adventist mission in Georgia. Not much is known about this period, except that the lay members did not give up and took charge of the work. In this regard, the interview with Mr Nikolai Dragan unfolded unknown pages of Adventist history in Georgia. Dragan was an elderly member to the Adventist Church in Tbilisi and as an eyewitness recalled the story of his mother's conversion to Adventism in the 1940s. After his mother's conversion, their house became the underground headquarters for the Adventist mission in the region.

37  Zhukaluk, *Remember Your Mentors (The History of SDA by Individuals)* (Kiev, Ukraine: Dzherelo Zhitia, 1999), 56.
38  P. G. Panchenko, *Look Who Are You the Called!* (Nizhni Novgorod: Diatlovi Gori, 2007), 1.
39  Ibid.
40  Yunak, "Lift My Eyes to the Hill," 91.

Dragan recalls that as a child, he would often see two strangers, men who had a distinct accent[41] and whose clothes were different from the locals. He called them "Sibiriaki" (from Siberia) because of the thick coats and hats they wore. They would come late to their house and leave very early in order not to be seen by anyone. For several years in their basement, unknown people would type something using a lot of paper.[42] Gradually, the persecution of his mother was intensified. Dragan recalled that he was very afraid because his mother would always warn him not to tell anybody that there were people worshipping in their basement. Nevertheless, around the 1960s, persecutions against her became more severe, prompting her to sell her house and leave Georgia.[43]

## Unknown Georgian Adventist Ministers

Since little has been known about the history of Adventism in Georgia so far, it has been generally accepted that the first Georgian speaking Adventist ministers emerged in the mid-1990s, when the first students from Georgia enrolled in Zaokski Theological Seminary, the Adventist educational institution in Russia. However, the interview with Mrs Levich (née Mayevskaya) and the personal documents she presented reveal that the existence of Georgian ministers can be traced back to a period at least 100 years earlier.

The reconstructed chronology of the ministers working in Georgia includes the following: in 1911, Pastors Tsirat and Ozols were in Tbilisi, who might have given Bible studies to Kote Karalashvili and conducted his baptismal service in Baku in 1911. In 1917, when the Russian revolution took place, he was 22 years old. Georgia's short-lived independence lasted until 1921, when the Red Army invaded the country. Perhaps at this time, Karalashvili – still a young man of 26 years – decided to escape and reached Siberia in order to exercise his faith freely. Perhaps this decision to be closer to an Adventist community was made after the detention of Pastor Ozols in 1914.

Mrs Mayevskaya recollects that he would often mention Tbilisi. He studied at the Orthodox seminary, where one of his fellow students was none else but Joseph Jugashvili (Stalin). Interestingly, both of them were dismissed from that seminary for distinct reasons: Karalashvili for his inclination to Adventism, which eventually made him a pastor, and Joseph Jugashvili (Stalin) for his inclination to revolutionary ideas, which eventually made him the brutal leader of the atheist country called the Soviet Union.[44]

There could actually be other Georgian ministers who have not been documented. For instance, the graduation pictorial of Harbin Bible School in China of

41   Dragan, in-depth interview, Tbilisi, Georgia, 2016, Folder 13, 14.
42   Dragan, in-depth interview, Tbilisi, Georgia, 2016, Folder 13, 4, 5.
43   Dragan, in-depth interview, Tbilisi, Georgia, 2016, Folder 13, 7, 14.
44   Mayevskaya, in-depth interview via Skype, Australia, Sydney, Folder 16, 3.

the year 1925[45] depicted faces of the graduates, where along with Karalashvili, there was someone by the name Matikashvili, who was apparently a young Georgian minister and a graduate from the same school. However, so far no written or oral evidence was found about this person that could tell elements of his life story.

## Pastor Panchenko: Mission Impossible (1957–1959)

January 20, 1957, marked a new beginning for Adventists in Georgia. On this date, Pastor Panchenko arrived in the capital[46] and became the pastor of Tbilisi Adventist Church.[47] Notably, one year prior to his arrival, a group of young people from Rostov, inspired by Pastor Pavel Matsanov, decided to go for a mission trip in Transcaucasia in order to encourage the members who were scattered and dispersed without leaders.[48] Perhaps the reports from this trip inspired Matsanov to send someone to Georgia. This was how Matsanov recalled the trip to Georgia about 50 years later:

> From Batumi, we arrived at the capital of sunny Georgia, Tbilisi. … We were accommodated at a very convenient, nice apartment and treated with a lot of food on the table. …. When we took our seats before the worship and bowed our heads for prayer, many of those who gathered with us began to cry for the unexpressed pain accumulated in their hearts because of the many years of loneliness and persecution.[49]

Notably, two very important things are highlighted here, loneliness and persecution, which were the major internal and external challenges of Adventists in Georgia, respectively. The Tbilisi Adventist Church, after experiencing 18 years of persecution and without any minister or missionary, was gradually devastated both physically and emotionally.

At first, the members were cautious about accepting the young man as their new leader because of the fear that the KGB might have installed an agent under the cover of an Adventist leader.[50] Later, he was fully recognized as a leader of the church, but the threat of being infiltrated by KGB agents was real: some KGB agents were present in the church and some were among the baptized members, too.[51]

In 1957, the first baptism in Tbilisi Adventist Church after so many years of stagnation coincided with the second visitation of the leaders from Caucasia and Transcaucasia, Pastors Peter Kulakov and Pavel Matsanov.[52] Indeed, it was a great event for the church, especially because the leaders visited them during a baptismal

---

45  From the personal photo collection of Mrs Mayevskaya.
46  Panchenko, *Look Who Are You the Called!*, 7.
47  Yunak, "Lift My Eyes to the Hill," 107
48  See A. G. Matsanov and P. A. Matsanova, *Through the Thorny Path* (Kaliningrad: Iantarni Skaz, 1995), 114.
49  Ibid., 115.
50  Panchenko, *Look Who Are You the Called!*, 9–10.
51  Ibid., 16.
52  Matsanov and Matsanova, *Through the Thorny Path*, 112, 118, 124.

ceremony. The baptism occurred in Lisis Lake up in the mountains. It was interesting how Pastor Panchenko describes the unexpected incident, which occurred during the baptismal service there:

> We arrived at the place that we had chosen and prepared ahead of time. ... Brother Kulakov stepped into the water. At this moment, something happened that made us worry. From across the lake the engine of the boat started and a group of police officers headed toward us. .... Now when the police officers were approaching, we became nervous. ... My heart sank when I looked at the aged pastor, who experienced so much grief and torment, and I wondered what would happen. I prayed to God as I had never prayed before and asked for protection for this hour. .... When the pastor gave a sign to start the baptism, one after the other, the candidates entered the water. .... The police looked and were extremely puzzled since they did not understand what was going on. In addition, when the last church member came out from the water, the engine of the boat moored and the police officers left, which I believed was due to divine intervention.[53]

## Withstanding the Persecution: The Power of the Laity

Glazova Luba was one of those who were baptized by Kulakov on August 26, 1957.[54] From an interview with her, several significant details can be highlighted about the mission and outreach to the Adventist Church in Tbilisi before, during, and after Panchenko's ministry. Her house became the place of religious services during the persecution that erupted after the detention of Pastor Galajev. The mother of Mrs Glazova became one of the most active leaders. Later, her religious activity was noticed by KGB, who murdered one of her daughters under mysterious circumstances.[55]

Mrs Glazova recalls the instance when KGB officers unexpectedly came to their house during the Sabbath worship. By coincidence, Pastors Kulakov and Panchenko were leading the worship at that moment. Sisters Vera and Luba Glazova engaged in an argument with KGB officers, while Pastor Kulakov tried to calm them down. Vera said, "We are not doing anything wrong, we praise God here."[56] But Pastor Kulakov asked her not to argue; and she finally cooled the conversation.

The next day both sisters were called to the KGB office for further interrogation. Vera would often say, "I don't know how to live"[57] because external persecution from the KGB and the persecution from her own husband made her life miserable.[58] As a result, both of them were fired from their respective jobs.[59] Sadly, soon thereafter

---

53   Panchenko, *Look Who Are You the Called!*, 53.
54   Glazova, in-depth interview, Tbilisi, Georgia, 2016, Folder 14, 1.
55   Ibid., 5.
56   Ibid., 17.
57   Ibid., 10.
58   Ibid., 10
59   Ibid., 18.

Vera Glazova (the sister of Mrs Glazova) disappeared from her house at night, and was found dead after four days in the river Mtkvari in Tbilisi.

1959 saw the rise of persecutions instigated by the leader of the Soviet Union, Nikita Khrushchev. Many religious workers were deported from the cities of their ministry in Caucasus and Transcaucasia, causing Christians to suffer again. Panchenko recollects the day of his arrest and the closing down of the Tbilisi congregation:

> One of the Sabbaths during the sermon, two individuals entered the hall of our worship. One was in uniform, the other was dressed casually, the third stopped at the entrance, and the fourth (as we later found) was guarding at the gate. We were surrounded, but it was clear that nobody was going to run away. Those two (one in uniform and another in casual clothes) approached the pulpit and stood by both of my sides. The one casually dressed requested my documents, it was clear he is from *Osobi Otdel* (the special department of KGB). After he was convinced that my documents are errorless, he asked if I had the permit for conducting the worship. I was prepared for this question, because. . . in those days there was a small brochure color blue, which contained the speech of Nikita Khrushchev during his visit in India. In his speech, Khrushchev underlined the freedom of religion in USSR. Therefore, when I was asked for a permit to conduct the worship, I pulled that brochure out from the pulpit, opened the page where I highlighted the excerpt from the speech and read it aloud, "In the Soviet Union, believers can conduct their worships without any prior permit from the governmental entities." The one who was asking for the permit remained speechless for a few seconds, and did not know what to do. They were shocked. Then, the one in casual dress came back to his mind, snatched the brochure from my hand and said, 'It is not written for you. You are arrested, follow us.' The police officer grabbed my hand in order to take me out. I freed my hand and addressed the congregation, 'Let's end the worship with a prayer!' Everybody stood up. … When I finished the prayer, I stepped down from the pulpit and headed toward the exit. Sisters began to cry. One sister who had a heart condition fainted, everybody was worried. I stopped at the door for a second, but the police officers kicked me from the back.[60]

Most of those who were present still remembered the arrest of Pastor Galajev, and this déjà-vu made them worry a lot for both the pastor, and the church, because they knew what consequences this may have entailed. Within 72 hours in 1959, Panchenko and his three small children were deported from Georgia.[61] Unfortunately, the ensuing 18-year gap left the Tbilisi Adventist church without a leader again and caused it to almost disappear.

60  Panchenko, *Look Who Are You the Called!*, 55–56. Emphasis in original; Panchenko, in-depth interview, Tbilisi, Georgia, 2016, Folder 15, 35.
61  Zhukaluk, *Remember Your Mentors*, 178

## New Beginning of the Church and the End of Soviet Regime in Georgia

The Adventist Church in Georgia was re-established in 1977 and has continued to flourish. Two ministers arrived in Tbilisi at the time: the Dreiling family from Armenia and the Lagutov family from Azerbaijan. They began to replant the church, and worship resumed at Glazova's house. Toward the end of the 1980s, the Soviet system began to fall apart, and religious interest could no more be suppressed by the civil powers.

The Seventh-day Adventist members gave a large amount of their savings in order to buy a lot and build a church at Lotkini.[62] Brethren from Belorussia and nearby countries volunteered to help putting up the church because the Tbilisi congregation still consisted of mostly elderly women. The small group grew rapidly and in 1980 they were able to obtain the registration from the government and started building the church, utilizing the land that had been purchased a few years earlier. By the end of 1990, there were 73 church members in Tbilisi, with a few Georgian converts among them. In Sukhumi, there were 69 members in the same year, who were mostly from the Russian-speaking population.[63]

## Insights and Assessment

From the beginning, Protestants (both German and Russian) were ethnically, linguistically, and culturally alien to the local population, which prevented them from significant communication and inclusion into the social network of the local people. The same is true with Adventists. From the very beginning, the first Adventist ministers and missionaries in Georgia faced not only persecution as an impediment to their mission endeavor but also the challenge of communication in various languages as the country is rich with various ethnic minorities living side by side with the Georgian population.

Despite these unfavorable circumstances, Adventist activities in Georgia were promising, which is evident from several written sources. For instance, Löbsack wrote quite early, "We are greatly hoping for the development of the work in Tbilisi."[64] Other records say, "We witness a revival among Mingrelians and Georgians."[65]

The fact of the conversion of Kote Karalashvili in 1911 leads to the conclusion that Georgians were responsive to Adventist the message at the dawn of Adventism even before the 20s. Pastor Yulius Teodor Betkher, who was the chairman of the Russian Union between 1907 and 1913, after visiting Georgia was so excited how

---

62  Glazova, in-depth interview, Tbilisi, Georgia, 2016, Folder 14, 23–27
63  Yunak, "Lift My Eyes to the Hill," 121.
64  Ibid., 86, cited from appendix to "Maslina" (February 1909): 19, 20.
65  Yunak, "Lift My Eyes to the Hill," 30, cited from appendix to "Maslina" (March 1913): 46–48.

the "work is also advancing among Georgians" that he made the comment: "In future we will have printed materials in this language."[66] Sadly, the first Adventist Georgian literature was published almost a century later.

Matsanov, while visiting Tbilisi in the mid-1950s, underscored two essential hindrances of the Adventist congregations: "Many years of loneliness and persecution in their hearts accumulated so much unexpressed pain."[67] Loneliness as an internal factor and persecution as an external factor significantly prevented the church from growing during several periods of the Adventist history in Georgia. Nevertheless, despite decades of struggles with identity issues, persecution and many other unfavorable circumstances, the Seventh-day Adventist church in Georgia managed to continue its existence through the selfless life of its ministers and members. However, the low growth rate during recent years demands a re-thinking and re-modeling of the Adventist mission strategy in Georgia in the future.

66  Yunak, "Lift My Eyes to the Hill," 90, cited from appendix to "Maslina" (June 1913): 107, 108.
67  Matsanov and Matsanova, *Through the Thorny Path*, 115.

*Chigemezi Nnadozie Wogu*

# Scripture, Traditions and Contexts: European Adventist Approaches to Contextualization

## Abstract

The contextual nature of theology can hardly be overemphasized. However, when does theology truly become contextual? In this paper, some approaches of European Adventists were placed on a schema of Scripture, tradition and context as developed by Stephen Bevans. It was found that although the first indigenous Adventist missionaries to Europe largely approached cross-cultural mission through a model that did not take the European context very seriously, as the denomination progressed, other models that sought to balance the elements of Scripture, tradition and context were developed and used in and out of Europe.

This paper adopts a historical perspective that analyzes academic works of Adventist theologians/historians and missiologists to identify European Adventist approaches to cross-cultural adaptation. To pursue this task, contextualization as a theological and missiological theme is presented to pave the way for understanding some (historical) approaches to contextualization in European Adventism. Using applied insights from Stephen Bevans' Models of Contextual Theology, the paper shows that although the first missionaries to Europe largely approached cross-cultural mission through a model that did not take European context seriously, as the denomination progressed, other models were developed and used in and out of Europe. Because this is the first published attempt to understand European Adventist approaches to contextualization, several examples have been chosen: Michal B. Czechowski, Ludwig R. Conradi, Ernst Kotz, Aimé Girou and Erich W. Bethmann. While these may not be fully representative of Europe, they do portray the major trends that can be observed in the Adventist story on the Old Continent.

## Contextualization: Theology and Mission of Gospel Applicability

There is no unanimously agreed upon term for doing contextual theology. The terms accommodation, inculturation, indigenization are all used to describe the process of making the gospel culturally relevant. For this chapter, contextualization, a broader term, is preferred. Contextualization may be defined as

> an attempt to communicate the message of the person, works, Word, and will of God in
> a way that is faithful to God's revelation, especially as it is put forth in the teachings of

Holy Scripture, and that is meaningful to respondents in their respective cultural and existential context.[1]

In the framework of the following analysis, "the teachings" in the definition above is seen as (1) Scripture and (2) the way Scripture has been taught in history (thus, the Christian tradition and, more specifically, key traditions of a denomination). These two elements in addition to (3) context are the *loci theologici* of contextual theologizing.

The need for contextualization can hardly be overemphasized. This need – to make the gospel relevant in every new culture – hinges on 1 Corinthians 9:19–23, 25, the *locus classicus* for contextualization. Biblical examples of God adapting his message to fit a particular context abound. Arthur Glasser argues, "the most striking evidence of contextualization in the Old Testament is the manner in which God deliberately and repeatedly shaped the disclosure of himself to this people by using the widely known, ancient phenomenon of [the] covenant."[2]

This covenant comes to life with the incarnation of Jesus in the New Testament. In the incarnation, God was not only "at home in specific segments of social reality"; his greatest self-revelation "took place within all of the particularities of a specific time and culture."[3] It is this example that Paul follows to adapt his actions to different cultural and religious settings (1 Cor 9:19–23). According to Paul, he did this for the sake of the gospel with the sole aim of soul winning.

Nevertheless, the missionary task of contextualizing the gospel in a specific environment remains a perplexing endeavour. This perplexity results from the sought-for balance of (1) faithfulness to the gospel and its meaningfulness and (2) cultural particularity coupled with cultural relativity. Consequently, contextualization theorist Dean Flemming concludes that since God values all cultures, "our articulation of the gospel must be culture-specific but not culture bound."[4]

In attempt to hold to both sides of this tension, missiologists have approached contextualization from different angles: theological, missiological or methodological. For example, in Robert J. Schreiter's seminal work *Constructing Local Theologies*, there are three approaches (translation, adaptation and contextual) viz. models that suggest "not only a relationship between a cultural context and theology, but also something about the relation between theology and the community

1    David. J. Hesselgrave and Edward Rommen, *Contextualization: Meanings, Methods, and Models* (Pasadena, CA: William Carey Library, 2000), 200.

2    Arthur F. Glasser, "Old Testament Contextualization: Revelation and Its Environment," in *The Word among Us: Contextualizing Theology for Mission Today*, ed. Dean S. Gilliland (Eugene, OR: Wipf and Stock, 2002), 40.

3    Andrew F. Walls, *The Missionary Movement in Christian History: Studies in the Transmission of Faith* (Maryknoll, NY: Orbis, 1996), xvii; Timothy C. Tennent, *Invitation to World Missions: A Trinitarian Missiology for the Twenty-First Century* (Grand Rapids, MI: Kregel, 2010), 325.

4    Dean Flemming, *Contextualization in the New Testament: Patterns for Theology and Mission* (Downers Grove, IL: InterVarsity Press, 2005), 138.

in which it takes place."[5] Steven B. Bevans' work,[6] the leading study in contextual theology, is a proposal to the theological audience based on a "systematic reflection on the nature of Christian theology into different models of contextual theology."[7] Bevans identified six models in his seminal analysis: (1) translation, (2) anthropological, (3) praxis, (4) synthetic, (5) transcendental, and (6) countercultural.

These models represent ways of doing theology and thus imply a distinct starting point as well as theological presuppositions. The conceptualization of these models emerges out of the various ways theologians combine the three sources of theology, i.e. the elements of Scripture, tradition and context (culture, history, contemporary thought forms). While these elements are what makes theology really contextual, when placed on a map, the models represent patterns of thought across a wide spectrum.

The *countercultural* model is the most conservative for its tendency to recognize the importance of context and at the same time, it distrusts its sanctity and "revelational" power. The *translation* model puts more emphasis on Scripture and tradition than on context. The *synthetic* model attempts a balance, while the *praxis* model focuses on the importance of social change in articulating theology. The most radical is the *anthropological* model, which places more emphasis on culture change than on Scripture and tradition, while the *transcendental* model's focus is not on the content of theologizing but on the subject who is theologizing.[8] In the following analysis, Bevans' models will serve as a heuristic device.

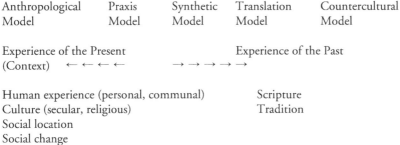

Transcendental
Model


Anthropological     Praxis          Synthetic    Translation    Countercultural
Model               Model           Model        Model          Model

Experience of the Present                    Experience of the Past
(Context)   ← ← ← ←              → → → → →

Human experience (personal, communal)        Scripture
Culture (secular, religious)                 Tradition
Social location
Social change

**Fig. 1 Bevans's Contextual Mapping**

5    Robert J. Schreiter, *Constructing Local Theologies* (Maryknoll, NY: Orbis, 1985), 6.
6    Stephen B. Bevans, *Models of Contextual Theology: Faith and Cultures* (Maryknoll, NY: Orbis, 2002, revised).
7    Angie Pears, *Doing Contextual Theology* (London: Routledge, 2010), 20.
8    Bevans, *Models of Contextual Theology*, 31–32.

## Contextualization: General Adventism

Adventists were late to the realm of contextual theological reflections. For Adventists, at least to the early 20th century, there was only one true form of Christianity – Seventh-day Adventism. Because Adventist Christianity was seen as essentially supracultural, every other religious expression was by and large considered "false religion". Since many elements of traditional cultures were viewed as being in tension with the gospel, contextualization would have meant dilution of truth.[9]

It is only recently that issues of theology vis-à-vis culture began to be considered seriously. Understandably, this is the outcome of the denomination's confrontation with a diversity of cultural expressions during cross-cultural encounters. Such encounters have also enabled Adventist leaders to understand the vast extent of cultural diversity among members. Recently, the church released a document that describes contextualization as "the intentional and discriminating attempt to communicate the gospel message in a culturally meaningful way."[10]

While the document strongly affirms the upholding of Fundamental Beliefs, local expressions of Adventism are encouraged.[11] This indicates that Adventism can become truly a church for all nations, tribes, tongues, and peoples.[12] Furthermore, a close look at this new awareness of the necessity of contextualization has led to the conclusion that some official documents such as the 28 Fundamental Beliefs, the *Church Manual*, and the traditional Baptismal Vows were framed in the context of relationship to other Christians.[13]

Generally, an emphasis on the denomination's doctrinal points has influenced Adventist contextual approaches. Owen McIntyre notes that Adventist theology earlier favoured a redemption-centred approach over a creation-centred approach.[14] Nevertheless, a creation-centred approach later influenced Adventist contextual theological thinking. For instance, the use of holistic models for mission theologizing epitomizes Adventists' ingenuity in using holism to understand the nature of humanity, its context and its need.

---

9    Cf. the insights in Stefan Höschele, *Christian Remnant—African Folk Church: Seventh-Day Adventism in Tanzania, 1903–1980* (Leiden: Brill, 2007), 264–270.

10   *Statements, Guidelines and Other Documents* (Silver Spring, MD: General Conference of the Seventh-day Adventist Church Communication Department, 2010), 149.

11   Ibid.

12   Insight from Stefan Höschele, *From the End of the World to the Ends of the Earth: The Development of Seventh-day Adventist Missiology* (Nürnberg: VTR, 2004), 59.

13   See for example the statement on "Fundamental beliefs and Preparation for Baptism," in *Adventist Responses to Cross-Cultural Mission*, vol. 1, ed. Bruce Bauer (Berrien Springs, MI: Department of World Mission, Andrews University, 2006), 174–175. There is a second volume (2007) of the same title. See also the official statements about Fundamental Beliefs, and Baptismal Vows in "Guidelines for Global Mission," Statements, Guidelines and Other Documents, 145–150.

14   Owen McIntyre, "Seventh-Day Adventist Approaches to Contextualization of Theology," *Mission Studies* 16.2 (1999): 132.

Moreover, other theologically-centred themes like Christology and pneumatology, anthropology and salvation history have also been embraced. Interestingly, these focus points appear as the starting points in Adventist theology.[15] Following this thought, elsewhere, I have identified some models used by Adventists for contextualization. Models like translation, structural holism, Holy Spirit Praxis, Mission Dei and trialogue appeal to some Adventist missiologists.[16] These models are evidence of the production of local Adventist theologies. Although Adventist scholars borrowed insights from non-Adventists in their contextual reflections and constructions, they were consistent in preserving their own eschatological and apocalyptic framework.

On the European side, doing theology in mission at first followed the general Adventist principle of rejecting culture. At the same time, a few historical instances reveal that this was not always the case. The examples in this paper reveal that European Adventists were more concerned with communication of God's word, identification with cultural and contextual issues and the adaptation of Adventist denominational tradition than the rest of their Adventist counterparts.

## Contextualization: Adventism in and out of Multi-Cultural Europe

Before Adventism – an originally North American revival movement – crossed the Atlantic, Christian Europe, aside from the presence of numerous languages and cultural diversity, had its own unique theological traditions. Traditions of the great Reformation movement of the 16th century, Pietism, Anabaptists and Seventh-day Baptists had long been established in the Old Continent. In addition, there were close alliances between established churches and the state. This alliance not only provided protection for the major churches, it hampered the development of new religious movements or free churches. Hence, anyone bringing a new "theology" to Europe had to be aware of this context.

However, the first Adventist missionaries in Europe, who themselves were Europeans, largely failed to do deliberate theological contextualization; one can see this in the cases of Michel B. Czechowski and Jakob Erzberger. Contrastingly, when Ludwig R. Conradi came to Europe, he took the cultural context very seriously, especially in his home country Germany. Aimé Girou's approach closes follows this line of thought. Later, one of Conradi's students, Ernst Kotz, who was sent to Africa, proved to be one of the most sensitive Adventist missionaries in cross-cultural contexts. Finally, the work of Erich Bethmann, a successful missionary to Muslims, developed something like a synthesis of the approaches of the aforementioned individuals. The following models unveil details of this story.

---

15  See Ministerial Association of Seventh-day Adventists, *Seventh-day Adventist Believe: A Biblical Exposition of Fundamental Doctrines* (Boise, ID: Pacific Press, 2005).

16  See Chigemezi-Nnadozie Wogu, "Constructs in Contexts: Models of Contextualizing Adventist Theology," *International Bulletin of Mission Research* 43.2 (2019): 146–158.

## Transplantation (Semi-countercultural) Model

Transplantation, in the language of Bevans, is adapting a message to a context without taking cultural dynamics into consideration. Thus, the foreign cultural garb of such a message is still visible. This transplantation model was essentially what the first missionaries (official and non-official) from North America followed when they brought the Adventist message to Europe.[17] For instance, when Czechowski came to Europe, he "too readily transferred the American experience into the European scene"[18] taking note of the cultural context. He "did" Adventism in Europe just as it was done in America by using the same outreach methods of tent meetings, open air preaching, and publishing.[19] Interestingly, through his zeal and limited experience, this self-willed missionary was so successful that in four years, he saw about 50 believers joining his movement. His aim was to establish a European Adventist Church independent of the American movement. Despite his initial success, eventually, the financial strains of maintaining a press, combined with his lack of honesty regarding his denominational background and limited sensitivity to the socio-cultural context, "the task of transplanting the American model to Europe proved too difficult for a one-man mission."[20] According to Pfeiffer it was "premature to adopt the American model in all its aspects as early as Czechowski did."[21] This model seems to be what Jakob Erzberger used when he came back to his native country of Switzerland. Unfortunately, he was not well received by his own brethren: he tried to implement the ideas he had internalized in a very different socio-cultural group into Swiss society.[22]

## Adaptation Model

This is also called the "translation model" in Bevans. Here, for the sake of clarity, I will call it "adaptation model" and discuss the translation model later. According to Daniel Heinz[23] and Erich W. Baumgartner,[24] Ludwig R. Conradi (1856–1939)

---

17  Baldur Ed. Pfeiffer, *The European Seventh-day Adventist Mission in the Middle East, 1879–1939* (Frankfurt: Peter Lang, 1978),19–25.

18  Ibid., 21.

19  For example, the weekly *L'Evangile Eternel* reflected in context and purpose the American *Review and Herald*.

20  Pfeiffer, *The European Seventh-day Adventist Mission in the Middle East*, 22.

21  Ibid.

22  Ibid.

23  Daniel Heinz, "The Development of Seventh-day Adventist Missionary Dynamic in Europe: Assessing the Contributions of Michael B. Czechowski, John N. Andrews, and Ludwig R. Conradi," in *Parochialism, Pluralism and Contextualization: Challenges to Adventist Mission in Europe (19th–21st Centuries)*, eds. David J. B. Trim and Daniel Heinz (Frankfurt am Main: Peter Lang, 2010), 51–62.

24  Erich W. Baumgartner, "Charisma and Contextualization: Leadership Lessons from Emerging Adventist Church in Central Europe, 1864–1914," in *Parochialism, Pluralism and Contextualization*, 63–82.

adapted and acculturated Adventism into the European context in his career as a pastor, leader, and missionary. When Conradi came back to Europe, he studied the situation and noticed that there were deep-rooted prejudices against the Adventist message in the Old Continent. He then sought to demonstrate the compatibility of the Adventist faith with various Protestant traditions in Europe.[25] Conradi did this by establishing explicit connections with the religious and cultural background, e.g. Adventist roots in the pietistic movement. In this light, he developed a three-fold approach that involved the use of (1) literature evangelism, (2) the public work of a pastor, and (3) Bible studies in small groups after the pattern of the Pietistic tradition.

Baumgartner elaborates: "Conradi adapted the Pietist model of meetings and developed a contextualized message. For him, the Adventist message was rooted in a historic Adventism in Europe that preceded American Adventism."[26] He did this by emphasizing the European pioneers of the biblical messages of righteousness by faith and biblical prophecy.[27] In addition, as Heinz affirms,

> Conradi attempted repeatedly to demonstrate the place of Adventist apocalypticism in the history of theology; . . . he liked to show that long before the emergence of the Millerite movement, students of scripture in Europe had preached the idea of an imminent Second Advent and that this concept had achieved great prominence with the Reformers.[28]

Moreover, Conradi's publications had a distinct European flavour in content, style and layout. His approach also focused more on colporteur work and the lecture format instead of public preaching. Conradi's approach resulted in such great success for Adventism in Europe that within a few years (ca.1870–1910) of its implementation the growth rate of the church in Europe exceeded the growth rate of the church in the United States.

## Translation Model

Ernst Kotz may be considered the finest Adventist missiological thinker before World War I. He was a self-made ethnologist who had a fascinating interest in the traditional life of the Pare of Tanzania.[29] It is not surprising, then, that he wrote the first anthropological work ever written by an Adventist. As director of the Adventist work in Pare, he took on much of the early translation work into Pare as his responsibility. Stefan Höschele has noted that the beginning of publications in Southern Pare is synonymous to the name Kotz. He published a Pare grammar manual, a small hymnal, a primer for use in schools, a translation of the gospel of Matthew and

25  Daniel Heinz, *Ludwig Richard Conradi: Missionar, Evangelist und Organisator der Siebenten-Tags-Adventisten in Europa* (Frankfurt am Main: Peter Lang, 1998), 61, 121.
26  Baumgartner, "Charisma and Contextualization," 78.
27  Ibid.
28  Heinz, "The Development," 57.
29  Höschele, *Christian Remnant*, 265.

participated in a translation project for the NT.[30] But how did he translate the gospel into Pare?

An article published in *Ministry* much later provides some insights into this realm. Bearing in mind that Kotz had learnt the Pare language, Kotz seems to have followed the guidelines of the American, British and German Bible societies in taking the original Greek as the basis for translation. In the process of translating, he avoided the danger of injecting his private or denominational interpretation into the text.[31]

Bevans's translation model explains Kotz's approach further. According to Bevans, the translation model is concerned with the essential message of Christianity. In this model, experts speak of "a gospel as core," which is supra-cultural or supra-contextual. In addition, practitioners are not concerned with a mere literal word-for-word translation. Rather, they advocate a functional approach to translation.[32] This is what Charles Kraft refers to as dynamic equivalence. Dynamic equivalence translation is an idiomatic approach to translation where communication and meaningfulness are favoured over word-for-word translation. To theologize with dynamic equivalence is an attempt at a transculturation of theological truth within the language of the hearers so that they can properly understand the true relevance of the message.[33]

Kotz, as translator, endeavored to be faithful to both the original author and the message of the gospel in order to communicate the intended impact that the message was to have upon the original readers.[34] Taking social and cultural change into perspective, he also strived to theologically translate biblical principles that were against some traditional practices. At the same time, he developed principles of health and education for the people in all areas of life.[35]

30  References to the following publications are found in Höschele, *Christian Remnant*, 84: the grammar– E. Kotz, *Grammatik des Chasu in Deutsch-Ostafrika (Pare-Gebirge)* (Berlin: Reimer, 1909; 2ᵈ ed.: Farnborough: Gregg, 1964); the primer: Missionare der S.T. Adventisten in Süd-Pare, *Fibeli ya Chasu* (Hamburg: International Traktgesellschaft, 1910); the hymnal: *Malumbo a Mtaso: 55 Geistliche Lieder in der Sprache der Vaasu[Vapare])* (Hamburg: International Traktgesellschaft, 1910), and the gospel of Matthew: *Bible—NT—Matthew—Asu (Mburi Yedi Yakwe Mateo: Das Evangelium Matthäus in der Sprache der Vaasu [Vapare])*, transl. by Missionare der S.T. Adventisten in Süd-Pare (Hamburg: International Traktgesellschaft, 1910).

31  See Ernst Kotz, "Problems of Bible Translation," *Ministry* (April 1933): 16–17.

32  Bevans, *Models of Contextual Theology*, 38–39.

33  Charles Kraft, *Christianity in Culture: A Study in Dynamic Biblical Theologizing in Cross-Cultural Perspective* (Maryknoll, NY: Orbis, 1975), 297.

34  Ibid., 271–272.

35  Hubert Kazmierczak, "Die interkulturelle Begegnung der Missionare der deutschen Advent-Missionsgesellschaft e.V. unter besonderer Berücksichtigung des Missionars Ernst Kotz im Lichte der gegenwärtigen Missionstheologie" (Diplom thesis, Theologisches Seminar Marienhöhe, 1988), 65.

## Semi-anthropological Model

Kotz did not accept everything in the Pare culture. In fact, Höschele concludes that Kotz regarded Pare culture as corrupted in many respects.[36] Yet interestingly, Kotz was not against all practices of the Pare. Rather, his writings and mission work reveal a sympathetic attitude towards traditional culture. He advocated respect for Africans as equals and even believed that one can learn something from them.[37] His critical appreciation of traditional culture, therefore, led him to identify some good elements in the Pare people. When racism was the rule at the heyday of colonial Christianity, Kotz argued in his writings that an African could either be a poet or philosopher. At the time when missionaries saw everything in traditional culture as heathen, he commented that missionaries were not to be in haste to "extinguish all heathenism with a Boniface zeal."[38] His concern, therefore, was to identify elements that could be cultivated. Hence, he researched the Pare life cycle, law, traditional economy and religion, in a bid to understand the good elements of this Tanzanian traditional culture.

One example was his use of Pare proverbs. In them he recognized a "meditation on the deepest questions of human life" and the attempt to fathom the reality and the relationship of man.[39] Through traditional stories, sayings and proverbs, he not only found a way into the Pare worldview, he used the proverbs in his preaching, writing and translation.[40]

Another example is his view on bridewealth (the price paid to a bride's parents before the marriage ceremony). Among the Pare, the practice was very popular. Although Kotz did not fully accept the practice – he even mistook European marriage custom as the Christian view, Höschele concludes, Kotz "was magnanimous enough to concede that other models had their own rights."[41] Hence, "he supported the custom with the rationale that it prevented divorce, and he was persuaded that it had no dishonoring character. His two main concerns were the function of the practice in traditional society and harmony in the church."[42]

According to Bevans, the primary concern of the anthropological model is "the establishment of or preservation of cultural identity by a person of Christian faith."[43] This model is anthropological in two ways. First, this model centers on the value and goodness of the human person. Secondly, the model makes use of insights from the

---

36  Höschele, *Christian Remnant*, 267.
37  Ibid., 265–266. See also an excellent article by Kotz: "A Narrow Way of Thinking," *Signs of the Times*, (October 31, 1933): 13–14.
38  Höschele, *Christian Remnant*, 266.
39  Kazmierczak, "Die interkulturelle Begegnung der Missionare," 66.
40  Ernst Kotz, Sklaven, 123–148. What he did with the proverbs in mission still remains unexplored to a large extent.
41  Höschele, *Christian Remnant*, 303.
42  Ibid., 302.
43  Bevans, *Models of Contextual Theology*, 54.

social science of anthropology to understand more clearly "the web of human relationships and meanings that make up human culture and in which God is present, offering life, healing and wholeness."[44]

Kotz's ideas do not entirely fit into the anthropological model. His was not a full anthropological model because of his careful attitude to cultural issues. Based on the insight that Kotz had earlier done anthropological studies under Berlin's ethnologist Felix von Luschan, this paper posits that it was in study and sympathetic identity with the Pare culture that Kotz found the concepts and symbols needed for articulating the faith of the Pare people. Kotz believed that a time might come when, among the Pare "everything has become new, and still the people will not have lost their identity in language and character. Only the ugly and the mean have had to cede."[45] In this vein, Höschele concludes, "he envisioned a transformation of culture through a Christian remnant of converted individuals. By imagining an African Adventist folk church, he went beyond the missionary model within which his denomination often operated."[46]

## Semi-synthetic Model

A synthesis of the approaches of Conradi and Kotz is seen in the writings of Erich W. Bethmann. Bethmann's approach does not entirely fit the synthetic model. Nevertheless, it can be seen as a semi-synthesis of the translation, anthropological and transcendental models.

The synthetic model is a synthesis of other models. Bevans views it as the middle-of-the-road model because it attempts to balance the translation, anthropological and even praxis models. In the continuum of Bevans' map, this approach is at the center, i.e. midway between placing emphasis on the present (social change, culture, context, experience) and the experience of the past (Scripture and tradition).[47] Thus, the model keeps the integrity of Scripture and tradition while taking the context seriously. The concern of this model is the need for continual dialogue that attempts to hold Gospel, culture, tradition and culture change together in a creative tension. Practitioners of this approach would argue that every context has elements that are unique to it and are held in common with others. Hence, there is need to be in dialogue for the purpose of enriching each other.[48]

According to Pfeiffer, Bethmann was one of the few Adventists to penetrate the mind of Islam at a deeper level.[49] Born in Berlin, he went to the School of Oriental Studies, became fluent in Arabic and for 20 years worked as a missionary in various

---

44  Ibid., 55.
45  Kotz, Sklaven, 182.
46  Stefan Höschele, "Kotz, Ernst," in *Dictionary of African Christian Biography*, accessed, April 9, 2018, https://dacb.org/stories/tanzania/kotz-ernst.
47  Bevans, *Models of Contextual Theology*, 88.
48  Ibid., 88–90.
49  Pfeiffer, *The European Seventh-day Adventist Mission in the Middle East*, 88.

parts of the Middle East (mainly Egypt, Jordan and Iraq). As a missionary, he was mostly concerned about building a bridge to Islam.[50] He took Mohammed seriously by focusing on the Islamic prophet's spiritual experience and socio-cultural context.[51] Bethmann reasoned that Mohammed was a child of his time and product of his context. Thus, Mohammed's way of doing things was not far removed from the context. As a mystic and Arab, Mohammed had internalized his religion and culture. Since ideologies surrounding the ideal prophet already existed in this context, Mohammed's people considered his rise to prophethood as authentic.

Here the principles of the translation and anthropological models are found in Bethmann's thought. He argued that it is impossible to depart from the socio-religious structure of Islam (a world in and by itself) while doing mission among Muslims. For example, it is impractical to translate Christian literature made in the West into Arabic. For Muslims to understand the literature, it has to be rewritten by those well immersed in Islamic thought so as not to repel the reader from the onset.[52] Here the dynamic-equivalence principle of translation as well as sympathy for host culture is demonstrated.

A slight diversion will be adequate at this point. This caveat is for the sake of giving another example on the use of the dynamic-equivalence principle. While serving as a missionary among Catholic believers in Spain, Girou, a former Catholic, believed that Catholics needed to be reached in their own religious, cultural and social context.[53] For example, Girou reported that he employed the Catholic expression of "Our Lord Jesus Christ" or "Our Savior Jesus Christ" whenever he spoke of Christ. On the person of Mary, he concluded: "Catholics will not speak of Mary, the mother of the Lord, without saying: 'The holy virgin Mary' or at least 'The virgin Mary.' The word 'virgin' sounds very sweet to their ears; and if it is not used by the speaker, he is soon known as an apostate."[54] He even argued that "Singing and praying, as well as the use of the words "brethren and sisters," "are all right in their proper time and place, but not in a lecture delivered to Catholics."[55]

Furthermore, in the works of Bethmann, a personal approach to Islam is favored, where friendliness, hospitality, authentic spirituality and cultural identity is preferred over an institutionalized one. Although it may take time to have numerical results, Bethmann claimed that identifying with the experiences and sufferings of Muslims

---

50  This was the main idea in his influential book *Bridge to Islam: A Study of Religious Forces of Islam and Christianity in the Near East* (Nashville, Tennessee: Southern Publishing Association, 1950).

51  See Erich Bethmann, "Studien über den Islam," *Adventbote* (March 15, 1936): 187–190, cf. Pfeiffer, *The European Seventh-day Adventist Mission in the Middle East*, 90.

52  Bethmann, *Bridge to Islam*, 248.

53  "I believe we must be Jews with the Jews, and Greeks with the Greeks, in order to save them. And we must also adapt our methods to the Catholic background and way of thinking in order to help bring Catholics nearer to the Saviour they love, but know so little. See A. J. Girou, "Effective Approach to the Catholics," *Ministry* (September 1937): 4.

54  A. J. Girou, "Effective Approach to the Catholics," 14.

55  Girou, "Effective Approach to the Catholics," 4.

may be the way to their heart as well as a bridge to establishing their faith. He further demonstrated how the mystic aspirations of Mohammed, i.e. the desire to replace elements that hindered the religious experience of Arabs becoming a "higher religion"[56] should be taken seriously.[57] This can be done by emphasizing the full power of Christ's spiritual message to Muslims because "spiritual power leaves its influence even if the results are not immediate." [58]

In part, this way of thinking mirrors the transcendental model, where the focus is the practitioner's religious experience and the power of faith to transcend culture. It is by a reflection of one's experience that one can learn to understand the source of spiritual power needed for witness.[59] For Bethmann this spiritual power is contained in the Bible, i.e. "the Word of Prophecy."[60] By taking scriptural revelation as the Word of prophecy, Christians can help Muslims see the fundamental difference in the conception of the inspiration of the Qur'an and the Bible. Quoting 2 Peter 1:19–21,[61] Bethmann demonstrated how God revealed himself through the prophetic word, actions and principles of Christ. He concluded that it is through Christ that Islam can gain that spiritual power it is most lacking.[62]

## (European Adventist) Contextualization: An Appraisal

If contextualization is making the gospel contextually relevant in a specific context which entails the adequate balance of Scripture, tradition and context (S-t-c) during the process of theologizing; based on Bevans' map vis-à-vis the S-t-c elements, on which axis do European Adventists stand? Czechowski's transplantation model was more concerned with translating Adventism to Europe. His approach was a very conservative one, focusing mainly on Adventist tradition while Scripture and Context were given little attention. This may be due to his concern to create a type of European Adventism in the Old World. His zeal and lack of proper reflection on his context forced him to transplant the American type of Adventism to Europe. Hence, his approach seems closer to the countercultural model.

Conradi's adaptation is an in-between model that takes Scripture, tradition and context seriously. However, more emphasis was placed on scripture and the general

---

56   Pfeiffer, The European Seventh-day Adventist Mission in the Middle East, 90–91.

57   Bethmann, *Bridge to Islam, 176.*

58   Ibid., 254.

59   Bevans, *Models of Contextual Theology,* 103–107.

60   Bethmann, Bridge to Islam, 252.

61   "We also have the prophetic message as something completely reliable, and you will do well to pay attention to it, as to a light shining in a dark place, until the day dawns and the morning star rises in your hearts. Above all, you must understand that no prophecy of Scripture came about by the prophet's own interpretation of things. For prophecy never had its origin in the human will, but prophets, though human, spoke from God as they were carried along by the Holy Spirit." NIV).

62   Bethmann, *Bridge to Islam,* 254.

Christian tradition. Conradi was intelligent not to do away with what mattered among Christians. This was what made his approach favourable to the German context and then wider European society. Kotz's translation and anthropological models imply taking Scripture and Adventist tradition seriously, but his sympathy for culture and willingness to identify with contextual issues of social change and experience gives him an upper hand on the whole discourse of contextual theologizing. His study of anthropology may have contributed to this type of divergence in his own approaches. Girou's dynamic-equivalence theologizing among Catholics is astounding. Doing theology the way he avowed by using important Catholic elements without bias is a vivid example of being a "Jew" to the "Jews" and "Gentile" to the "Gentiles". Bethmann, finally, seemed to have a balanced view, just like the synthesis model balances the S-t-c elements.

## Conclusion

This paper has attempted to demonstrate how some European Adventists approached contextualization based on Stephen Bevans' contextual models. With four examples, it is shown here that European Adventists were concerned with how to make the gospel contextually relevant in and out of Europe. However, these individual case studies cannot be used as a general lens for viewing European missionizing.

From the foregoing, although the approaches presented do not fully fit Bevans' map, they clearly show that contextualization even among European Adventists has a wide spectrum. Not all these attempts were conscious contextual thinking. Each missionary did theology according to his personality, education or presuppositions. This illustrates the fact that theology is indeed contextual. Although some of their approaches may be wanting when placed on the S-t-c schema, Bevans himself has opined that there is no one best approach. A specific model or two may be used based on the context or as the need arises. Nevertheless, it is fair to conclude that contextual theologizing needs to be faithful first to Scripture, and then to tradition and context. It is then that theology becomes truly contextual.

In this vein, this paper has demonstrated that Adventist missionaries have been able to develop a significant range of contextual approaches, not only in terms of actual thought, but also with regard to "method" and types or reasoning. This happened in spite of Adventism generally presenting itself as theologically homogeneous.

*Petr Činčala*

# European Adventist Ways of Reaching Secular People for Christ: Need-oriented Evangelism and Mission Outreach (1995–present)

Abstract

This paper describes a phenomenon that emerged in European Adventism in the 1990s, which can be described as need-oriented, life-style, or organic evangelism. This type of evangelism is connected with the church planting movement and mission to reach secular, un-churched people. Although this movement has not became mainstream in European Adventism, it certainly deserves attention because it offers a valid, biblically rooted, and yet culturally relevant alternative mission approach in European territories where the Seventh-day Adventist Church is plateauing or declining.[1]

It is no secret that Adventist church attendance is dropping in some parts of the world. As one can see in the appendix, this is true of many of the European Seventh-day Adventist Unions; most of these Unions are experiencing a plateau or a decline in church membership, with only a few minor exceptions.

Until the last ten years of the previous century, Adventism in many European countries "mainly reached fellow Christians. But the number of converts dwindled, because many were leaving church all together."[2] While some conferences took part in NET '96, with others joining for NET '98 or NET '99, the results were not as anticipated or hoped. Additionally, a lot of effort was placed into translating and "subtitling the tapes, but the effects were minimal."[3]

## The Missionary Nature of the Church

The innovative mission methods discussed in this paper may be contested by some, but welcomed by others. These reactions, as well as theological perspectives and an emphasis outline, will be discussed in this section. In Matthew 28:18–20, the passage

---

1   Disclaimer: The author of this article has been personally involved in this type evangelism on a local scale for an extensive period of a time. For that reason, only a description of this evangelism is provided, not a critique. Due to limited space and scope, this article is far from providing exhaustive information related to the topic. The time frame described in this article is limited to the period of personal involvement and observation of the author, as well as the period of provided testimonies of eyewitnesses.

2   Rudy Dingjan, e-mail to author, January 31, 2018.

3   Ibid.

known as the Great Commission, Jesus instructs his disciples to "go and make disciples of all nations, baptizing them in the name of the Father and of the Son and of the Holy Spirit, and teaching them to obey everything I have commanded you" (NIV). These verses serve as a Biblical mandate for mission and outreach.

Yet, one might ask, is mission essential to the Church? And if so, why? Emil Brunner argued that, "the Church exists by mission as a fire does by burning. Mission is not merely the application of theology taught in a classroom. Mission lies at the core of theology, and within the very character and action of God himself."[4] If mission and outreach comprise the very essence of God's character, then this is a topic that needs our utmost attention if we claim to be his followers.

This crucial role of mission justifies the development of a holistic mission to lost people, as well as validating the existence of church.[5] Mission is more than evangelism, and is deeper than merely a social responsibility. In view of Jesus' Great Commission, proclaiming the gospel is an essential part of mission, with the ultimate objective being that of making disciples.[6] Yet "Christian existence is essentially and fundamentally social in nature,"[7] as well. The reality of the church reflects the reality of the triune God. Just as the three divine persons exist in community within the godhead, so the church coexists as a community. The Christian Church is a community "whose inner dynamic reflects God's inner reality."[8]

So how does the church reflect the Godhead's loving teamwork in reaching out to lost people? Ellen G. White, one of the founders of the Seventh-day Adventist Church, explains it this way: "Christ's method alone will give true success in reaching the people. The Saviour mingled with men as one who desired their good. He showed His sympathy for them, ministered to their needs, and won their confidence. Then He bade them, 'Follow Me.'"[9] Christ's example of living in community with others, as well as bringing them to discipleship, is the strongest example of living out the Great Commission that can be found. Jesus not only sent his disciples on mission, but he lived out that mission in his everyday life.

## The Changing Context

In light of the burst of religiosity that followed the fall of communism (as well as other factors) in Central and Eastern Europe in the 1990s, it was clear that religion did not die out as some scholars had anticipated it would. Sociologists such as Peter

---

4    Emil Brunner, *The Word and the World* (New York: Charles Scribner's Sons, 1931), 108.
5    Russell C. Burrill, "Recovering an Adventist Approach to the Life and Mission of the Local Church" (D.Min. diss., Fuller Theological Seminary, 1997), 6.
6    David Burnett, *The Healing of the Nations: The Biblical Basis of the Mission of God* (Carlisle, England: Paternoster Press, 1996), 137.
7    Richard Rice, *Believing, Behaving, Belonging* (Roseville, CA: Association of Adventist Forums, 2002), 29.
8    Ibid., 31.
9    Ellen G. White, *Ministry of Healing* (Mountain View, CA: Pacific Press, 1909), 143.

Berger openly admit that they made a mistake in assuming that secularization would cause the death of religion. Berger confessed, "Our underlying argument was that secularization and modernity go hand in hand. With more modernization comes more secularization. It wasn't crazy theory. There was some evidence for it. But I think it's basically wrong. Most of the world today is certainly not secular. It's very religious."[10]

With this in mind, and in response to the given situation and to the biblical mandate found in Matthew 28, a new vision for mission outreach following Jesus' method was needed that included the following key presuppositions: (1) Evangelism is not an event; it is a relational process that includes application in everyday life. (2) The emphasis of the message and methods need to be framed in a plausible manner, in a language that is understandable and relevant to a given context. (3) Evangelism starts with addressing people's perceived needs and is presented to them in culturally relevant forms.

Applying Jesus' method brings these assumptions to life. When we apply the qualities that E. G. White attributes to Jesus, we find that "mingling" practically looks like spending extended time with un-churched people in the community. When she refers to "desiring people's good," we learn that this requires that the primary motive of our interactions is to make people's lives better. When she speaks of "showing sympathy," she is describing treating people with altruistic loving-kindness. The desired fruit of such a Christ-like lifestyle is winning people's confidence. This is how the soil is prepared. Once this has been done, then the invitation to meet Jesus can logically follow.

## The Beginnings of Need-Oriented Evangelism among Europeans in the 1990s

This section is limited to the memories and experiences of the author, as well as the sources that were used for this study. When Peter Roennfeldt became the Trans-European Division (TED) church growth director in 1995, he brought with him previous experience from Australia. Right from the start, he began to promote church planting to reach secular communities. The immediate response, however, was not so positive; some of the excuses – although legitimate – were lack of finances and lack of experienced people for such church planting ventures. Only after taking groups of people to see and taste this approach, which had been implemented in secular Australia, did Adventist leaders in Europe take this approach seriously.[11]

By 1998, there were young adult teams attempting to plant churches in cities located in Denmark, England, and a few other European countries; their goal was to

---

10  Peter Berger, "Epistemological Modesty: An Interview with Peter Berger," *Christian Century* (1997): 114.
11  Rudy Dingjan, e-mail from author, January 31, 2018.

reach people who did not go to church. Soon after, potential teams from other Unions (the Netherlands and Czecho-Slovakia, for example) were able to see the benefit of these so-called "café churches," and decided to try something similar.

As the need for mobilizing and equipping increased, the TED, as well as some unions, organized training events. In 2001, a ten-day church planting field school was organized under the leadership of Peter Roennfeldt in Himmerlandsgården, Denmark. Forty-five attendants came from the UK, Germany, Scandinavian countries, and the Netherlands. The experience was spiritually inspiring and motivating for mission. A similar conference was organized in 2002, this time meeting at the Swedish Ekebyholm School; this meeting lasted one week and included about 120 participants. In 2003, almost 300 participants gathered for a church planting training in Turku, Finland, with 70 participants from the Netherland Union alone.[12]

From that time on, the European Adventist church-planting movement grew. For a number of years, there were division-wide, as well as national, church planting events. Participants from both the TED and the then Euro-African Division (EUD) Unions were involved. In 2003, the SEEDS conference at Friedensau Adventist University, Germany, was organized to train people in new ways of evangelism. Church planters exchanged information and techniques to the benefit of all. In 2005, over 800 attended the Church Planters Exchange at Friedensau – but by 2011 the numbers began to wane, and when another conference took place at Friedensau, including people from across the TED and some from the EUD, it drew only 250 participants.[13]

While the initiative was growing across Europe, from 2004 to 2012, those in the Czecho-Slovakian Union Conference interested in church planting attended quarterly meetings (called "Planting"); pastors and lay leaders alike were welcome. Teams involved or interested in church planting met in meetings called "Incubator" (later called "Launch-pad") twice a year between 2004 and 2013. There was also training provided for the administrators and leaders of the CS Union and its local conferences. They participated in training called "Matrix Training & Coaching" in 2005–2007 held mostly in Sweden, which was designed to prepare the leadership for a strategic church planting movement.[14] Church members in the Czecho-Slovakian Union were also mobilized through annual weekend seminars (held by invited guests, mostly from TED) to think outside of the box and to fulfil the Great Commission. Evangelism was introduced as a way of life – a way to build "church" (defined as a fellowship of believers) outside the church buildings; the goal was that each church that would

---

12   Ibid.
13   Roennfeldt had left Europe – but there were more important reasons for the decline, including the attempt to treat East, West and Central Europe as homogenous, the unease of church administrators with a movement beyond their administrative controls, etc.
14   Martin Veselý, Skype interview with author, March 19, 2018.

bring forth another church. Church members across all age groups were invited to participate.[15]

The Netherlands Union Conference has been active in church planting since the 1990s; they continued to be active in planting churches even when the church planting movement lacked vibrancy in other countries, including when the initial planting wave had passed in other countries. In 2008, the Dutch started their Great Commission festivals on the Union campsite with 300 participants attending, including a mix of church planters and mission-minded church members. In 2009, there was a festival in Slovenia with participants from around the TED and beyond with about 400 participants. Then in 2010, the Dutch church planting festival was held during Ascension Holiday with around 400 participants. In 2012, 2015, and 2017, such church-planting gatherings were held in the Netherlands with 200, 250, and 85 mission-minded participants, respectively. In 2014, another division-wide training event was held in Hungary with 350 participants.[16] As you can see, a passion for mission and church planning was spreading. At each of these events, people met to worship God, pray together, listen, share testimonies, brainstorm, as well as gain inspiration and encouragement.

## Churches Planted

The Adventist News Network at the Church Headquarters in Washington D.C. reported on this growing movement in 2003, sharing that "the Café Church in Copenhagen, Denmark, begun in 1998, grew out of a youth church-planting movement in the country."[17] In this project, people met for worship in a popular café which presented a relaxed, cozy environment. What started in a small basement room grew until it needed a new space. A new space was then found, and worship was held in a church auditorium as a second worship service in the afternoon.

Denmark was not the only country to institute these café churches; another 2003 report on this church-planting movement was from the Netherlands and focused on the "'Uni&K' ([pronounced] unique) café-style church organized with the young

---

15 Despite the mobilization within the Czecho-Slovakian Union Conference on all levels (incl. that of administrators), the support of the movement by the Union Conference as well as all three local Conferences shifted, cooled down and stopped after personnel changes in leadership.

16 The movement in Hungary had reached a peak around 2004 with about 2,000 people attending – but fell away quickly when brought under administrative control. Peter Roennfeldt, e-mail to author, April 23, 2018.

17 Wendi Rogers and Ray Dabrowski, "Denmark: Copenhagen's Café Church Becomes a New Home for Many," Adventist News Network, March 31, 2003, accessed April 15, 2018, https://news.adventist.org/en/all-news/news/go/2003-03-31/denmark-copenhagens -cafe-church-becomes-a-new-home-for-many.

adults of Utrecht."[18] The Dutch Union leaders expressed their support for different kinds of church growth experiments. During this time, several other café churches were planted throughout Europe,[19] "in response to the changing needs of a 'post-Christian' society" across the continent.[20] In 2009, the Seventh-day Adventist Church in Paris witnessed the grand opening of House of Hope, a spiritual and cultural center; this church served as another example of a church opened to society at large.[21] These same types of community churches were planted across European countries – in England,[22] the Netherlands,[23] the Czech Republic,[24] Finland,[25] Spain,[26] and a few others.[27]

As a result of this church-planting initiative and mobilization, a number of churches were planted, and the Seventh-day Adventist Church in general grew in its ability to cope with the changing society in a more positive way. Not all participants of the conferences became church-planters, but they understood evangelism and the concept of church in a new way. Hundreds of church members were trained and became aware of mission work among secular people.

However, the report of successful new churches bringing previously un-churched people to Christ would not be honest or complete if failures were omitted. Some of the newly planted churches decided to become traditional churches, discontinuing their involvement with community-based, need-oriented evangelism. Others completely dissolved due to conflict, lack of personnel, sickness, or stress. A number of

18  ANR/ANN Staff, "Netherlands: Café Church Draws Young Adherents," Adventist News Network, June 9, 2003, accessed April 15, 2018, https://news.adventist.org/en/all-news/news/go/2003-06-09/netherlands-café-church-draws-young-adherents.

19  Such as Café Seed Helsinki in 2001, accessed March 24, 2018, http://www.seedinternational.fi, or Cottage Back Café Church in Scunthorpe, North England in 2004, http://www.cafechurch.com; https://www.andrews.edu/library/car/cardigital/Periodi-cals/Messenger_British_Union/2004/2004_18_19.pdf.

20  ANR/ANN Staff, "Netherlands: Café Church Draws Young Adherents," Adventist News Network, June 9, 2003, accessed April 15, 2018, https://news.adventist.org/en/all-news/news/go/2003-06-09/netherlands-café-church-draws-young-adherents.

21  Jean-Paul Barquon, "In France, Adventist "House of Hope" Opens," Adventist World, March 25, 2015, accessed April 15, 2018, https://archives.adventistworld.org/2010/febru-ary/in-france-adventist-house-of-hope-opens.html.

22  Examples include, London Live: www.londonliveatnottinghill.com; The Watering Hole: www.thewateringhole.org.uk; The Church: www.thechurch.nu; The Ark: www.Rivenhallark.co.uk; Red Hill: redhill.adventistchurch.org.uk; Burnt Oak: burntoak.adventistchurch.org.uk.

23  Between 2001 and 2017, about 10 church plants were organized into local churches; a number of church plants are active across the Netherlands Union of Churches.

24  Examples include Trinity: www.trinityhk.cz; Restart: https://www.facebook.com/restartuj; Port Znojmo: www.portznojmo.cz.

25  An example is Seed International Church: http://www.seedinternational.fi.

26  An example is Cero Church, Madrid: http://iglesiacero.es.

27  This list is not exhaustive in listing all of the new churches initiatives aimed at winning secular people for Christ in the period; it merely captures bits and pieces.

small groups (made up of potential church planting teams) were formed, but then fell apart for lack of support from their local churches and/or their conferences. Moreover, the financial, as well as moral, support of the Divisions, Unions, and Conferences differed significantly due to a divergence in vision, priorities, budget, and personnel.

## Community Based Project Activities (Centers of Influence)

While the previous section focused on church planting, we now turn our attention to the various ways in which European Seventh-day Adventist believers have been involved in need-based mission work with secular people in recent years. This has been done through shops, volunteer centers, cultural engagement, psycho-social help, music/bands, civic campaigns, and other original, unique initiatives. Five projects are listed below as examples. It should be noted that there are many other projects of a similar nature; it is simply beyond the scope of this paper to list all European Adventist mission initiatives.

### *Happy Hand, Copenhagen, Danish Union of Churches*

What does a charity shop have to do with evangelism? Actually, quite a lot![28] In the case of Happy Hand, located in Copenhagen, not only is money earned given to projects that support those in need, but the shop also provides a place where people who would not go to church can sit, relax, and have free coffee or tea in a Christian environment. While in this setting, they can (and do) inquire about Jesus and ask for prayer. Some people come regularly. In the corner of the shop, there is a box with scripture notes and blank notecards; people write down their prayer requests and put them into the box, knowing full well that someone will be praying for them.

Once a month, people are invited to attend a "Spiritual Wellness" meeting. At other times, they are asked to help to feed the homeless in the streets. People working in the shop may not belong to any church, yet they are learning about the love of God.[29] According to one of the project leaders, "Happy Hand is a great way of doing mission in a natural and easy way."[30]

28  Other projects of this type is ADRA Charity shops in the Czech Republic, https://www.adra.cz/dobrovolnictvi/frydekmistek/charitativni-obchody/frydek--mistek, which are connected with volunteer centers helping seniors, handicapped people, those lonely, ill or socially disadvantaged children; see https://www.adra.cz/dobrovolnictvi. Similar projects can be found in collaboration with ADRA Germany.

29  There are also other similar projects allowing people to come and relax. For example, "Auf Augenhöhe" (for more see www.auf-augenhoehe-ev.de) is a small center led by a volunteer lay person in a rural small town called Neugersdorf in Northern German Union Conference. Weekly Café Cocos meetings happen in the area with higher average age population and yet most of the 30 attendants every week are younger than 35 years. Libuše Wietrichowká Jelínková, in discussion with the author, April 22, 2018.

30  Berit Elkjær, e-mail message to author, March 22, 2018.

## PRESENCE Kulturlounge, Frankfurt, South German Union

PRESENCE Kulturlounge is a recently-established (2014) initiative led by a Seventh-day Adventist pastor. This initiative conducts weekly or bi-weekly activities (sometimes through weekends), which are organized in a rented room; these activities allow people to engage in various topics of interest.[31] The major themes of their activities are: (1) Experiencing culture – for example, observing art, watching movies, discussing cultural topics. (2) Intercultural presentations – different cultures are featured, and presentations include cooking, singing, and dancing. (3) Reflecting on worldviews – people with different worldviews are invited to share their views, whether Buddhists, Muslims or Christians. The goal is to expand people's perspectives and overcome prejudices. (4) Experiencing spirituality – this includes Bible readings (specifically the books of Job, Psalms, and Isaiah) with corresponding music. The goal is to allow people to experience the text existentially and also in a setting of cultural events.

This initiative is run by several people (both SDA and non-SDA) with a typical attendance of 15–20 people at events; 10% of attendees are considered "regulars." Relationships and friendships have been formed, leading to the opportunity for deeper reflection. Recently a Bible study group has formed as a result of this mission project.[32]

## Lebensschule, Gera, North German Union

In 1998, the pastor of local SDA church started to hold public presentations about emotional health and social issues (i.e. depression, behavioral issues, psychological problems, etc.). A few years later, a "School of Life" was formed. Regular attenders wanted to meet more than once a month and so a kind of "secular church" started. Later, some other interest-based activities were implemented (vegetarian cooking class, fitness center, etc.). Several people became interested in spiritual matters; thus, faith-based studies (Bible courses) were offered. As a result of this, the local church became strongly involved. Later, a conference for mission-minded leaders and lay people was conducted in Gera for people from German-speaking Europe. Through training activities, this "School of Life" has become an avenue for other city churches to be involved in mission.[33] Thus, the concept has been taken to and applied in other settings as well.

---

31  Another project of similar nature is "Basement" in Prague, http://www.basement30.cz.
32  Mahary Simret, in discussion with the author, April 13, 2018.
33  "Eine Langzeitaufgabe," *Adventisten Heute* (February 2017): 20–21, accessed April 15, 2018, https://advent-verlag.de/media/pdf/cc/85/21/AH-2017-02.pdf; "Das Leben lernen," *Adventisten Heute* (June 2012): 11–12, accessed April 15, 2018, https://advent-verlag.de/media/pdf/84/e3/5c/AH-2012-06.pdf. See also http://offenetueren.org. By mid-2018, Lebensschule projects had been started in about 50 Adventist churches in Germany. See Lebensschule, accessed August 20, 2018, http://www.forum-lebensschule.eu/orte.

## Gospel Generation Choir, Liberec, Czecho-Slovakian Union

The Gospel Generation Choir[34] is just one among a number of similar choirs that were organized throughout Europe as part of Adventist outreach to secular, non-churched people. This choir started in 2007 with just about seven singers, who thought that singing gospel songs in the style of the movie "Sister Act" was a fun idea, and would help them improve their English-speaking skills. Over the last eleven years, the Gospel Generation Choir has grown into one of the largest Gospel choirs in the Czech Republic.[35] Now, the children of the original members are joining the choir as they enter their adolescent years.

Although most of the choir members claim to be "atheists," they do not mind embracing the spiritual Gospel songs in English (as a second language). The choir sings in public spaces, including church buildings on various occasions. The singers and countless people around them have experienced God's presence and have learned more about his providence. The choir forms a circle and prays before each performance, and often also during rehearsals, where they also have a sacred moment of listening to a brief reflection on Scripture.[36]

## National Marriage Week, Europe

The Family Ministries Department of the Seventh-day Adventist Church in the Trans European Division organizes a Christian Home and Marriage week every February.[37] This week coincides with a National Marriage week project, originally initiated by a Christian group in England in 1996 and since 2007 has been spreading across Europe.[38] Marriage Week (which is conveniently tied to Valentine's Day, also

34  Other projects of similar nature are Croydon SDA Gospel Choir in South London, UK: http://croydonsdagospelchoir.co.uk; Maranatha Gospel Choir in Prague, the Czech Republic: http://www.mgospel.cz/en.

35  See the website gospel.centrumgenerace.cz. The choir is made of two rehearsing groups practicing in two cities, altogether with over 100 active singers. This choir has inspired starting several other choirs (Matylda a Tylda: https://www.facebook.com/matyldaliberec/; Izerina: http://www.centrumjablonec.cz/cs/spolkovy-dum/soubor-izerina; Glass Gospel Choir: http://centrum-andilek.cz/glass-gospel-zelezny-brod). For a sample of the singing, see "Lord You Are Holy: Gospel Generation with Medgine Picard," accessed March 24, 2019, https://www.youtube.com/watch?v=CZzOwxwv1vc.

36  Petr Činčala, "Witnessing in the Czech Republic: Not 'Business as Usual'," *Adventist World* (September 2014): 20–21.

37  See Family Ministries, accessed March 24, 2019, https://family.adventist.org/christian-home-and-marriage-week.

38  The National Marriage Week campaign (which occurs every year from February 7-14) not only started in Europe, but is currently run in the following European countries: Albania, Austria, Bulgaria, Croatia, Czech Republic, Germany, Hungary, Ireland, Italy, Netherlands, Poland, Romania, Slovakia, Switzerland, Ukraine, UK. See Marriage Week International, accessed March 24, 2019, http://www.marriage-weekinternational.com.

in February) draws together various media outlets, businesses, government organizations, faith groups, and anyone else who values and cares about healthy marriages.

Thus, mission-minded local churches, non-profit organizations, and individuals take the opportunity of getting involved in building healthy, strong marriages from within and from outside of local churches. The need for overcoming marriage crises, solving marriage problems, and the like, creates a platform for support groups, connecting and helping each other. It also provides an opportunity for pastors, Christian marriage counselors, and lay people to be present and minister in the community for the rest of the year. This campaign has become particularly fruitful for the Seventh-day Adventist Church in the Czecho-Slovakian Union. Thus the Marriage Week is not just in-house mission, but a nationwide public campaign. People are invited to various events to celebrate healthy marriages. The national coordinator of this initiative is a Seventh-day Adventist pastor who helps to organize the national marriage week launching press conference in collaboration with senators and congressmen.[39]

## Characteristics of the European Need Oriented Evangelism and Mission Outreach

Traditionally the Seventh-day Adventist Church conducts evangelism primarily through public evangelism campaigns, which are often preceded by felt-needs seminars. This is typically done over a period of a few months. People who attend the seminars or meetings are visited in their homes, and generally engage in Bible studies as part of their preparation for baptism. These people are normally familiar with Christian faith, as many of them grew up going to church or have previously attended a church of other denomination.

The European need-oriented evangelism described in this paper is different in that it is geared towards the majority of people who have not been raised in church, do not know the Christian God, and are unfamiliar with faith in him. They are, therefore, often biased towards and/or sceptical about the Christian church and would not go to a church on their own. Just as everyone has specific needs and interests, so do these people, and they are open to socializing with those who share the same needs or interests. Need-oriented evangelism is a life-long process that involves socializing, meeting a person's needs, and building relationships of trust. The ultimate goal is to help people experience and get to know the loving triune God – directly or indirectly.

This whole process strongly relies on the Holy Spirit, who grows the desire for God and his truth in people's hearts. This may take a few months for some, but for others, it may take years. In some cases, people stay halfway involved, never committing to baptism or joining the local church. The primary goal, however, is not to get people into the church as soon as possible, but rather to meet them where they are,

39   See www.tydenmanzelstvi.cz.

walking side by side with them on the journey of life. The soil of their hearts needs to be carefully cultivated as the seeds of the Gospel are sown.

The following are the common characteristics of the Adventist European need-oriented evangelism, which has been developing since the 1990s:

*Lifestyle.* Evangelism, namely mission, becomes an integral part of everyday life. However, it is a lifestyle usually requiring a believer to leave his or her comfort zone.

*Intentional process.* There is a saying, "If two do the same, it is not the same thing." The difference comes with the mindset, with the motivation of heart, with intention, and patience – and without rushing things.

*Holism.* The difference comes with making God a natural part of the (evangelistic) life-style. Secular and sacred are no longer separated; people can meet God before they even know it. Such a holistic life-style approach makes a good bridge for people to appreciate the holistic Adventist message later.

*Prayer.* When people get into trouble, they pray. Even secular European people will – in most cases – not mind if someone prays for them or even with them.

*Spiritual authority.* Once trust is built, such persons are open to having their "pastor," someone they look up to, talk with them when they are in difficult times or when they need counsel or prayer.

*Stories.* People are overwhelmed by information every day, and any additional information may be burdensome. However, stories from life and from the Bible – presented in a variety of ways, including media – stir their imagination and feelings.

*Art and music.* Art and music are an important part of worshipping God and experiencing spirituality. Uplifting music and art need to connect with people and bring the gospel truth to them in a way that makes sense to them.

*Interpersonal attachment.* People in general are hungry for relationships, longing for love and harmony. Jesus' method, then, is tailor-made for secular Europeans.

How does one measure the success of church planting as well as community based projects and activities? As a key leader of the Adventist church planting movement in the Netherlands, Rudy Dingjan, puts it,

> The fruit is a growing network, a mass, around the church planting team. We don't evaluate church plants by the number of baptisms, but by the number of people that become friends and attend and also lead out in activities.

> We try to encourage the unique preaching of God's character through the SDA doctrines. God's character comes out best in the SDA doctrines, making it obvious to long for Jesus' coming, as we shall see Him like He is. So also to those who are already committed Christians we have an important message to bring. [40]

---

40   Rudy Dingjan, e-mail message to author, April 5, 2018.

## Conclusion

This paper described the "what, why and how" of contemporary European Adventist need-oriented evangelism along with a brief account of its recent history. It also explored two wings of such mission enterprise, i.e. church planting and community involvement. For more receptive and open Europeans, attending a café church may be the answer. Others may need to approach the church at their own pace and the ministries described above may just be the bridges they need. Winning secular European people will not happen by simply making worship more entertaining and fancy. To connect with people is the key. "We need ministries in which we can mingle with them and let them taste Kingdom life."[41]

***

## Appendix: Annual Growth Rate of Selected European SDA Unions, 1990–2005[42]

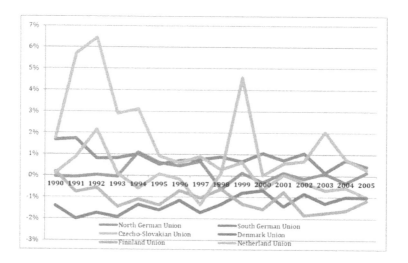

41   Ibid.
42   Data from ASTR, "General Conference (World Church Statistics)," 2018, accessed April 15, 2018, www.adventiststatistics.org. A color version of this graph is available online at the institute website (www.thh-friedensau.de/en/research/institute/school-of-theology/institute-for-adventist-studies).

Ronald Lawson

# Immigrant Influx: The Impact of Large Numbers from the Global South on Seventh-day Adventism in England, France, and the Netherlands

Abstract

In the decades since shortly after World War II, Christianity has grown rapidly in the Global South, while it has declined in most of the Global North, especially in Europe. These trends also impacted Adventism, but with one notable exception: its total membership did not decline in some countries because of an influx of Adventist immigrants, especially from the Global South. However, the newcomers made a considerable impact on the Adventist church in those countries, as the immigrants took over first local churches and then also the judicatories, and many indigenous members disappeared since they no longer recognized the church they had known earlier. This article explores the dynamics of change and the current situations in Britain, Northern France, and the Netherlands.

The center of Christianity moved slowly but surely during the twentieth century – from the Global North to the Global South, so that the majority of Christians today are nonwhite.[1] However, this "Southernized Christianity" has not confined its impact to the Global South: the patterns of international migration have shifted in recent decades, bringing increasing numbers of Christian immigrants from Africa, Asia, the Caribbean, and Latin America to parts of the Global North. The influx has inevitably impacted congregations and denominations in the receiving countries.[2]

This article examines the changing face of Seventh-day Adventism in Britain, France, and the Netherlands. Immigrants from the Caribbean were the first to migrate in large numbers and to become numerically dominant in urban areas. This pattern parallels that found by the author in New York and other urban centers in

---

1    Phillip Jenkins, *The Next Christendom: The Coming of Global Christianity* (New York: Oxford University Press).

2    Danielle Koning, "Messengers of Truth: Evangelism by a Ghanaian Seventh-day Adventist church in the Netherlands," Paper presented at the Annual Meeting of the Society for the Scientific Study of Religion, 2007; Ronald Lawson, "From American Church to Immigrant Church: The Changing Face of Seventh-day Adventism in Metropolitan New York," *Sociology of Religion,* 59.4 (1998): 329–351; Ronald Lawson, "When Immigrants Take Over: The Changing Face of Seventh-day Adventism in England, France, and Canada," Paper presented at the Annual Meeting of the Association for the Sociology of Religion, Washington, D.C., 2000.

the U.S. and Canada.[3] The paper examines the extent and dynamics of change, and sets out to answer three questions: why have the number of immigrant Adventists increased so dramatically?, to what extent have the sources of the immigrants to each country changed over time?, and what has been the impact of the influx of immigrants on the Adventist churches in these countries? The analysis utilizes and develops "secularization" theory as presented by Cragun and Lawson[4] and incorporating also "strictness" theory as expounded originally by Kelley and updated by Iannacone.[5]

## Background

Seventh-day Adventists trace their roots to the Millerite Movement during the early 1840s, which attracted upwards of 50,000 followers in the American Northeast. When the prediction of Baptist lay-preacher, William Miller, that Christ would return on October 22, 1844 proved false, his movement shattered. One fragment, guided by a young visionary, Ellen White, reinterpreted the prophecy: the pre-advent judgment had begun in heaven on that day. However, Christ's return remained imminent, and it became the Adventists' God-given task to warn the world to prepare for that event. They took this responsibility seriously, and are now active in 215 countries. The Adventist Church passed the milestone of 20 million baptized members in 2016, and has been doubling its world membership about every 10 to 12 years in recent decades.

Adventism's recent growth has been primarily, and increasingly, in the Global South, where the bulk of its membership is now clustered. Table 1 compares the growth rates in the Global North and Global South from 1960 to 2016. The membership growth in the Global South between 1960 and 1995 was 996%, compared with 123% in the Global North: during this time the proportion of the world membership located in the Global North increased from 55.5% to 86.0%. Between 1995 and 2016 membership growth in the Global South was 143.3% as compared with 27.0% in the Global North. At the end of 2016, 92.2% of world membership was located in the Global South. Most of the growth in recent decades has occurred in

3   Ronald Lawson, "Internal Political Fallout from the Emergence of an Immigrant Majority: The Impact of the Transformation of Seventh-day Adventism in Metropolitan New York," *Review of Religious Research* 41.1 (Fall 1999): 21–47; Lawson, "From American Church to Immigrant Church: The Changing Face of Seventh-day Adventism in Metropolitan New York," 329–351, 1998; Lawson, "When Immigrants Take Over: The Changing Face of Seventh-day Adventism in England, France, and Canada."

4   Ryan T. Cragun and Ronald Lawson, "The Secular Transition: The Worldwide Growth of Mormons, Jehovah's Witnesses and Seventh-day Adventists;" *Sociology of Religion*, 71.3 (2010): 349–373.

5   Dean Kelley, *Why Conservative Churches are Growing* (New York: Harper and Row, 1972); Laurence R. Iannaccone, "Why Strict Churches are Strong," *American Journal of Sociology* 99 (March 1994): 1180–1211.

Africa, Latin America, the Caribbean, and parts of Asia. Growth in Europe, North America, and Australia and New Zealand has lagged.[6]

TABLE 1
SEVENTH-DAY ADVENTIST MEMBERSHIP, DEVELOPED vs DEVELOPING WORLDS: 1960, 1995, 2016

|  | 1960 | % | 1995 | % | Increase | 2016 | % | Increase |
|---|---|---|---|---|---|---|---|---|
| Developed World[a] | 553,592 | 44.5% | 1,234,037 | 14.0% | 122.9% | 1,567,689 | 7.8 | 27.0% |
| Developing World[b] | 691,533 | 55.5% | 7,578,518 | 86.0% | 995.9% | 18,441,810 | 92.2 | 143.3% |
| World Totals | 1,245,125 |  | 8,812,555 |  | 607.8% | 20,009,499 |  | 127.1% |

[a]North America, Europe, Australia, New Zealand.
[b]The rest of the world.
Sources: General Conference 1961, 1996, 2017

In earlier published papers I examined the impact of "new immigrants" on the face of Adventism in Metropolitan New York between 1968, when new immigration laws took effect, and 1996. In 1968, Adventists there were almost entirely Caucasian (59.6%) and African-American (40%). However, by 1996 only 2.7% were Caucasians and 8.0% African-Americans: almost 90% were "new immigrants". The three largest groups, making up 83.8% of the membership, were West Indians and Guyanese (46.8%), Hispanics, where the largest group was Dominican (18.9%), and Haitians (17.1%).[7] This paper focuses on Britain (where the impact of an influx of Adventists from the Caribbean was first experienced), France, and the Netherlands.

## Research Methods

The research reported here is part of a large study of Seventh-day Adventism, which has included over 4,000 in-depth interviews with Adventist administrators, teachers, hospital personnel, pastors, students, and leading laypersons in 60 countries in all 13 divisions of the world church. This paper draws on interviews with church officials and members of both the immigrant and indigenous groups in all three countries in 1989, 1997, 2014 and 2018; I also paid special attention to these issues in the Netherlands in 2001, when I was invited to speak to gatherings of the laity, pastors, and the administration on how best to address the tensions that emerge as the number of immigrant members moves towards majority status. I have also drawn on official

6    The change of usage from "Developed World" to "Global North" is confusing because Australia and New Zealand are not located in the North, but are developed countries.
7    Lawson, "From American Church to Immigrant Church: The Changing Face of Seventh-day Adventism in Metropolitan New York," 329–351.

church statistics and reports in all three countries, and on other studies where available.[8]

Because I was traveling in order to interview church personnel, I had to use statistics provided by Church leaders, supplemented when available by official Church studies (such as that in England reported by Anthony in 1980),[9] rather than gather them painstakingly from every congregation as I had in New York, where I lived for several decades. The European data concerning the racial and ethnic composition of the membership are therefore not as precise as those collected in New York. I learned that because church leaders were concerned about the racial/ethnic distribution of their members, and talked about this among themselves, they were usually able to answer questions about the current membership distribution at the time I interviewed them. However, because the Adventist statistical reporting system did not require them to gather or report such statistics, their knowledge of changes in such distributions over time was usually vague. The fact that I had asked about such distributions several times over the years therefore proved to be valuable. Although I was usually given estimates rather than official statistics, the evidence of dramatic changes in the composition of the membership, and of the impact of these on both congregations and church judicatories, was nevertheless compelling.

## Theory

Since the 1950s the countries of the Developed World have become increasingly secular, so that the proportion of the population who have actively participated in the Mainline Churches there has declined steadily. However, participation in the more sectarian groups such as Mormons, Adventists, Witnesses, and Pentecostals continued to increase there for several decades. In 1972, Kelley asked why conservative religious groups in the USA had retained an active, committed membership rather than losing both fervor and members as the mainline liberal churches had.[10] He attributed this to the cost of membership in such groups. Here his definition of "conservative group" was in fact akin to what those sociologists who use church-sect theory define as sectarian: proclaiming an exclusive truth, with a closed, comprehensive, and eternal doctrine; insisting on adherence to a distinctive lifestyle; condemning dissenters and repudiating the "world"; and often embracing eccentric behaviors that isolate them and attract ridicule and persecution – in short, they exist in high tension with society.[11]

---

8    Note that since I follow an agreement with the Human Subjects Committee at my university to promise all interview subjects both anonymity and confidentiality, I do not reference quotes or information obtained from such sources.

9    M.L. Anthony, "Unto the Perfect Day: A Survey of Church Growth among Seventh-day Adventists in the United Kingdom and Eire During the Period 1940–1980," British Union of Seventh-day Adventists, 1980.

10   Kelley, *Why Conservative Churches are Growing.*

11   Ibid., 78–84.

In 1994, Iannaccone pointed out that in the 20 years since Kelley had published his thesis some of the so-called small sects in the USA had surpassed some of the mainline churches in size. He set out to clarify the mechanisms at work. He argued that the social costs of such distinctiveness screen out free riders, helping to retain the group's intensity since they discourage those who are not really serious from joining or encourage any present to exit. Consequently, the overall levels of commitment and participation, as measured in attendance, giving, and internal ties, increased. Outside participation by members was reduced either because it was prohibited, penalized, or inhibited as a result of expected stigmatizing behavior. Isolating the group from society in turn increased the value of its internal solidary benefits such as internal status, collective assistance, job or dating opportunities, joint fellowship, etc.[12]

However, soon thereafter it became clear the growth of the sectarian groups was also slowing, and that in such regions as Europe and Australasia their active membership had already begun to decline. In 2010 Cragun and Lawson found that the growth or decline of membership and participation was a much more complex phenomenon, being impacted by both "supply-side" and "demand-side" factors. The former are factors that are controlled by the group, such as what it teaches and how it presents itself, while the latter factors are related to characteristics and attitudes of the population where the group is attempting to grow.[13]

By comparing the changing membership statistics of Mormons, Adventists, and Witnesses in all countries in which they have been active over time since 1960, and by using the United Nations' Human Development Index, which combines measures of such factors as standard of living, literacy, school enrolment, and life expectancy into a single measure ranging from 0 to 1 for all countries over time, we found a curvilinear relationship between a country's position on the index and growth of the religious groups active there: growth occurs mostly *while countries are modernizing* – that is, while they are between .30 and .80 on the index. There is very little religious growth either below .30, when countries are pre-modern, or above .80, and especially above .90, when they are thoroughly modernized. The latter is where the countries of the Global North viz. Developed World are located; their citizens tend to be both secular and post-modern in their attitudes. Consequently, Bennion and Young found that Mormons grow more rapidly in politically and economically "volatile" countries than in "stable" ones.[14]

Although both Kelley and Iannaccone focused on why such religious groups maintain fervor and commitment, their theory is also useful in understanding the demand-side factors that impact levels of growth by religious constituencies: that is, in understanding who is likely to respond to the religious outreach and who not. A

12   See Iannaccone, "Why Strict Churches are Strong."
13   Ryan T. Cragun and Ronald Lawson, "The Secular Transition: The Worldwide Growth of Mormons, Jehovah's Witnesses, and Seventh-day Adventists." *Sociology of Religion* 71.3 (2010): 349–373.
14   Lowell C. Bennion and Lawrence A. Young, "The Uncertain Dynamics of LDS Expansion, 1950–2020;" *Dialogue: A Journal of Mormon Thought* 29 (1996):8–32.

strict message can offer a salve to population groups feeling alienated as a result of modernization, discrimination, and fear because of war, ill-health, unemployment, family disintegration, or other danger.

The data examined in this paper allow us to go a step further, to compare not just country data, but also the participation of different groups within countries – in this case, indigenous citizens of developed countries in the Global North and new immigrants moving to those countries from homelands in the Developing World.[15] Sectarian groups are likely to attract people with few secular opportunities, those with the least to lose – such as immigrants. On the other hand, people with broad secular opportunities are likely to chafe at the social costs and refuse to join or, if they are already members, push to moderate group rules or choose to exit. Consequently, Bennion and Young find that immigrants to countries in the Global North are more likely to convert than long-standing residents there.[16]

Cragun and Lawson found that this pattern is much more marked among Adventists than Mormons: while Mormon growth is greatest among populations where the Human Development Index is between .50 and .60, Adventist growth is greatest where it is between .30 and .40 – that is, they have high appeal while a population is only just starting to modernize and has very little in material goods, which is often true also of new immigrants to countries in the Global North. I also show that internal tensions are likely to become severe when a religious group endeavors to recruit or to retain diverse constituencies.

# Britain

## Rapid Racial Change, 1952–1997

Adventist growth in Britain had been high early in the 20th century, averaging 8% per annum during the 1910–1920 decade, but it had then declined each decade to 1% per annum during 1940–1950.[17] The president of the British Union in 1950 declared that its "almost static membership" was the Union's "most perplexing problem."[18]

The influx of immigrants from the British colonies in the West Indies to England, and into the urban Adventist congregations, began in 1952, lifting the Adventist growth-rate to 4% per annum during the two decades 1950–1970. West Indians formed a majority among Adventist members in London by the mid-1960s, in the

---

15 I revert here to the older usage because some of the countries from which immigrants are now flowing lie geographically in the Northern Hemisphere.
16 Ibid.
17 Robin Theobald, "The Seventh-day Adventist Movement: A Sociological Study with Particular Reference to Great Britain" (PhD diss., University of London, 1979), 36.
18 Dennis S. Porter, *A Century of Adventism in the British Isles: A Brief History of the British Union Conference of Seventh-day Adventists* (Grantham: Stanborough Press, 1974), 36.

South England Conference by 1968, and the North England Conference by 1975. Black accessions surpassed white accessions in the British Union 2:1 in 1968, rising to 5:1 by 1975, and they have remained high since. The gap in attendance was also dramatic, with black attendance outnumbering white 2:1 in 1975 and a 4:1 disparity among young unbaptized children.[19] By 1997 about 80% of the members of the British Union were of West Indian stock; the membership in Greater London was 92% West Indian, with only 300 of the 8,000 members there being indigenous English. (See Table 2)

**TABLE 2**
**THE CHANGING FACE OF ADVENTISM IN THE BRITISH UNION, 1950-1997**

|  | Membership | Caucasians | West Indians | Others |
|---|---|---|---|---|
| **BRITISH UNION** |  |  |  |  |
| 1950 | 6,666 | c100.0% | c0.0% | c0.0% |
| 1980 | 14,569 | 44.4% | 51.9% | 3.7% |
| 1997 | 18,846 | c16.0% | c80.0% | c4.0% |
| **LONDON** |  |  |  |  |
| 1950 | 1,059 | c100.0% | c0.0% | c0.0% |
| 1980 | 4,088 | 8.9% | 84.8% | 6.1% |
| 1997 | c8,000 | c3.7% | c92.0% | c4.4% |

Sources: Anthony, 1980; Interviews.

The formation of a Ghanaian congregation, with a membership of 80, in London in 1992 was a sign of changes to come: by late in the decade its expanding membership had reached 350.[20] The demographics of the Adventist Church at that time contrasted dramatically with those of the general population, for in London less than 2% of the population was West Indian. The Adventist membership in other major English cities, such as Birmingham, Manchester, and Leeds, was also heavily West Indian. Adventism was seen popularly as a "Black Church," a reputation it has maintained since that time. Meanwhile, the white indigenous membership in the

19   Ibid, 43; Anthony, "Unto the Perfect Day: A Survey of Church Growth among Seventh-day Adventists in the United Kingdom and Eire During the Period 1940–1980."
20   William Ackah, "Diasporas of Faith: Exploring Ethnic and Religious Identity in the Ghanaian Seventh Day (sic) Adventist Community in Britain," Paper presented to the Colloquium on New African Diasporas, School of African and Oriental Studies, University of London, 2000.

Union has declined sharply from a peak of 8,000 to little more than 3,000. This segment was ageing, and was scattered largely among small provincial congregations.

## Diversity Increases, 1997–2018

Legislation in the 1970s largely staunched the flow of West Indian immigrants. Those known as West Indians thereafter increasingly became British-born from the second, and then also the third, generation. However, the flow of immigrants continued, becoming increasingly diverse. In the new century the largest influx came from several countries in Africa – especially Zimbabweans fleeing the excesses of the Mugabe regime, and many others from other former British colonies there – Ghanaians, Zambians, Nigerians, Kenyans, Ugandans, Malawians – who were motivated to flee weak economies, even though many of them were educated professionals who often pursued their careers in small cities and towns in Britain. By 2014 most church leaders saw the number of Adventist Africans in Britain as almost equal with those of West Indian stock; by 2018 the two groups were at least equal, but probably with Africans exceeding the number with roots in the West Indies. There were a total of 20 Ghanaian churches by that time, and several other African groups had multiple churches; the Zimbabweans, probably the largest African group, responded to their hatred of their experience with Apartheid by joining integrated congregations.

By the end of 2017 the membership of the British Union had reached 37,212 – more than double that in 1996. Of the 30,000 whose race was known, 71.4% were black. The fact that 70% of these had been born abroad was evidence of the rapid influx of Africans over the previous 15 years. The members of the Adventist church in Britain had become mostly immigrants or descendants of immigrants – a dramatic change since 1952. By 2018 there were only about 1,000 white British remaining in the Union – secularism and post-modernism had caused the loss of most of the younger generations, so most of those remaining were elderly. Those who attended churches were in mixed congregations.

Even the Scottish, Welsh, and Irish Missions – which had never been large enough to become conferences but had become the most British portions of the union, have now lost that status – they are now only 50% white. Meanwhile, however, a flow of white immigrants, mostly from Eastern Europe (Romanians, Bulgarians, former Yugoslavians, Moldovans, Ukrainians, Poles) but also from South Africa, has been strengthening the white category somewhat. By 2017 the number of white members of the British Union who were born abroad exceeded the UK-born; the largest congregation in Ireland was Romanian, and the presidents of the Irish and Welsh Missions were both Romanians.

The British Union was also experiencing significant Hispanic growth, second only to the African growth; there are now several Portuguese-speaking congregations drawn from Brazil and two Spanish-speaking congregations where the members are mostly Colombians. The most rapidly expanding Asian group is Filipino, although there are several longer-established Indian/Pakistani congregations, especially in the North England Conference.[21]

The ethnic African congregations have been especially successful in recruiting back-slidden members whose origins were in their culture. Their biggest disappointment is the failure of their ambitions to convert the indigenous British. It has become extremely difficult to recruit either British or West Indian pastors – most of those hired are now African and Eastern European graduates of Newbold College. However, the diversity of the British Adventists, and the need for pastors who speak different languages, has forced the hiring of a goodly number of pastors whose education was abroad.

## The Dynamics of Change

The Adventist Church, like the Roman Catholic Church and the Jehovah's Witnesses, is a global church with an "international outlook." Its congregations eagerly welcome visiting missionaries and international visitors and students, who are all appreciated as signs that their world church is fulfilling its mission to evangelize "all nations." Members feel close ties to one another wherever they are because of their shared beliefs. Adventists therefore expected to encounter no major problems in building a multiracial church. However, this did not prove to be the case.

Extensive ethnic change seems almost always to cause tensions and conflict, especially when the changes are rapid. The tensions occurred initially in the existing congregations which immigrants joined, especially if they eventually become a majority of the members. (Where immigrants form new congregations, such as is common when the group speaks a foreign language, this step is omitted.) The second focus of conflict was within the judicatories of the church, especially in the local conferences. Here the Adventist Church is especially prone to conflict because of its structure. It is neither congregational, where there is little at stake in the judicatory, nor highly authoritarian, where members have little room to maneuver, but has democratic forms, with delegates from congregations meeting in conference constituency meetings where the officers and executive committees are chosen. These in turn control the choice and payment of pastors, decisions about opening or closing schools, and the disbursement of funds for evangelism, schools, etc. This structure therefore maximizes the opportunities for groups to compete with one another and the incentives for conflict between entrenched and challenging groups.

The influx of immigrants from the Global South occurred first in England, and it was there that the conflict was most severe, especially in London. Adventism had done well in the West Indies, where it had burgeoned over time. In Jamaica, for

21   Interviews, British Union, North and South England Conferences, 1997, 2014, 2018.

example, there were four times as many Adventists as in Britain by 1964, and a population ratio of 1:40 compared to 1:5,000 in Britain.[22] It was inevitable, then, that Adventists would be among the influx of immigrants from there to England after 1952.

The West Indian immigrants were welcomed when they first attended the inner-city Adventist congregations in England: two studies in the 1960s showed that Adventists provided them with a much warmer welcome than they received from society at large, as they were given opportunities to serve by, for example, performing musically.[23] A survey in the early 1960s showed that while 69% of the immigrants had attended the churches of six mainline denominations in the West Indies, only 4% attended them in England.[24] However, the Adventists, along with Pentecostals and Jehovah's Witnesses, grew rapidly, not only holding most of the West Indians who had been Adventists in the Caribbean, but also attracting many others.[25]

Meanwhile, the indigenous Adventist response passed over time through phases of welcome, puzzlement, and flight.[26] Unlike earlier visitors, whose stay had been temporary, the West Indians remained and their numbers expanded rapidly. Moreover, they soon made their mark because they were uninhibited in a conservative society: they tended to be noisier and more emotional in worship, more legalistic in their mores and judgmental of those who differed from them, more fundamentalist in their beliefs, and more ready to participate in door-to-door outreach activities than the English; they were tardy, wore bright clothing, and their weddings seemed often to follow the birth of a child. Because many of them were eager and committed, as time passed they were given opportunities to teach adult Sabbath School classes, where they presented their different views. As they grew rapidly in number, tensions were exacerbated as the indigenous members felt overwhelmed by the clashing cultures and as immigrants were voted into positions of power within congregations and then introduced changes in the style of worship.

The West Indians, for their part, often felt that they were not accepted as they had expected, as brothers and sisters. The President of the South England Conference during the late-1960s told of being called to many church meetings to deal with

22  Roswith L.H. Gerloff, *A Plea for British Black Theologies: The Black Church Movement in Britain in its Transatlantic Cultural and Theological Interaction*, 2.vols. (Frankfurt am Main: Peter Lang, 1992), 290.

23  Malcolm J.C. Calley, *God's People: West Indian Pentecostal Sects in England* (London: Oxford University Press, 1965) 127; Sheila Patterson, *Dark Strangers: A Study of West Indians in London* (Middlesex: Penguin, 1965); Theobald, "The Seventh-day Adventist Movement," 320–321.

24  Clifford Hill, *West Indian Migrants and the London Churches* (Oxford: Oxford University Press for the Institute of Race Relations, 1963), 22

25  John Rex and Robert Moore, *Race, Community and Conflict* (Oxford: Oxford University Press for the Institute of Race Relations, 1967), 184; Clifford Hill, "From Church to Sect: West Indian Sect Development in Britain," *Journal for the Scientific Study of Religion* (1971): 114–123; Theobald, "The Seventh-day Adventist Movement," 317–320.

26  Porter, *A Century of Adventism in the British Isles*, 42.

congregational tensions, and of finding that neither congregational vote nor administrative fiat could command love.

As the number of immigrants in a congregation expanded, the size of the indigenous English group there tended to contract. Two studies in the late-60s reported a lot of white resentment and flight.[27] Many of the indigenous members fled, sometimes emigrating en masse to Australia, and often moving out to other congregations where, for the time being, they could be with their own, or becoming irregular in their attendance and then ultimately ceasing to attend Adventist services altogether. When the indigenous members became an aging cohort, many died and were not replaced: non-Adventist whites would not attend evangelistic meetings where most of those present were immigrant Adventists and the contacts they had invited, nor did they feel comfortable when invited to the predominantly black churches.

As the number of immigrants in London congregations increased during the 1960s, their white elders formed an organization to provide mutual support. They held regular meetings, whose stated purpose was to retain the leadership of their congregations in order to keep them receptive, at least to some degree, to the conversion of their fellow-countrymen.

For example, in 1989 one English couple told of the transition of one of the London churches, where he had been senior elder for 28 years. When they joined the congregation in 1951 it had 70 members, all indigenous English. Since their congregation was baptizing about 20 converts per year at that time, the indigenous membership grew to a peak of 150. However, only five more indigenous members were baptized between 1966, by which time the congregation was about evenly divided between the two racial groups, and 1989. The first three West Indians, who had arrived in 1953, had been welcomed warmly. However, as immigrant numbers grew rapidly, they gained the power to change the style and atmosphere of worship, and were then resented. Their presence also provoked hostility in the neighborhood of the church, to which they commuted, attracting graffiti saying "Blacks go home!" – an occurrence which embarrassed the indigenous members.

A watershed occurred when a West Indian was appointed as pastor about 1980. What was described as a militant West Indian group was then placed in office: they were much more legalistic in their observance of traditional Adventist mores and they refused to do anything to observe Easter and Christmas, since they had been taught by missionaries in the West Indies that these were not biblical celebrations. The elder resigned his position shortly after the pastor's appointment, and in 1985 he and his wife moved to a more diverse congregation; they also began to travel a considerable distance once per month to meet with "the Amersham Group", an all-white group of Adventists that rented their meeting space from a Quaker congregation, and attended an Anglican Church on Sundays. By 1989 the membership of their former congregation had grown to about 350, only 3 of whom were indigenous English.

27   Rex and Moore, *Race, Community and Conflict*, 184; C.D. Handysides, "West Indian Integration in the SDA Church in Britain," B. Ed. thesis, University of Reading, 1969; Gerloff, *A Plea for British Black Theologies*, 277.

The parallel stories of the change process as West Indians perceived it told, for example, of reaching 85% of the membership in congregations in the 1960s but still being unrepresented among the elders. However, when their consciousness was raised, often by young members who were university graduates or students who gained courage to voice objections, moving from the floor of the church to have reports from nominating committees referred back, they then slowly achieved representation.

Meanwhile, tension between the immigrants and the conferences had also been mounting. The first major incident concerned the New Gallery Evangelistic Center in the West End district of London, which Adventists had bought in 1953 in an attempt to reach out to the higher social classes. Church leaders saw this goal threatened when Adventist West Indians flocked there with friends they hoped thereby to evangelize, fearing that the Center would become identified with immigrants: the sight of a large crowd of West Indians and their children socializing on the street after meetings was at odds with the image that the Center was trying to project. Consequently, in 1959, in spite of the fact that a predominantly West Indian congregation was using the space for worship on Sabbaths, the president of the South England Conference distributed a letter asking West Indians not to attend the evangelistic meetings there, for it had been "established at tremendous cost for evangelizing London's white millions, and particularly the upper social classes."[28] The Conference then moved the unwanted congregation from the Center to another location. These events, plus refusals to rent the Center to Adventist West Indian groups even though it was rented to non-Adventists, deeply offended the immigrants – an offense that was never forgotten.

The tension with the conferences was focused in the late 1960s by some West Indian university graduates and students, most of whom had been born in the West Indies but at least partially educated in England. They were emboldened by their awareness of the American Civil Rights movement, then at its height. The young activists raised the following issues among their peers:

(1) Since the South England Conference had only 2 English-trained West Indian pastors, most congregations with West Indian majorities had white pastors. When they demanded that the Conference import West Indian pastors, they were told this was impossible because of the additional cost of benefit and furlough packages for those with the status of missionaries and the Conference's obligation to hire the graduates of Newbold College in England. However, the college had a reputation of refusing to admit many West Indians. Moreover, even if a cohort of West Indians were now admitted, the activists felt this would take too long to solve the problem.

---

28   South England Conference Committee, Letter "To the Members of [Adventist] Churches in the London Region," Nov. 5, 1959. Reprinted in Gerloff, *A Plea for British Black Theologies*, 759–760.

(2) The Adventist schools were far from West Indian areas, yet West Indian students were facing enormous problems in the public schools both educationally and, from the point of view of their parents, in the socialization they were receiving there, which was loosening the ties of the youth to the church and fostering intergenerational conflict. The West Indian constituency therefore demanded that an Adventist school be established in the Inner London area. However, once again it faced administrative reluctance because of cost.

(3) Since West Indian youth were exiting the church in increasing numbers, the constituency voiced demands for a youth center and youth programs in London to try to stem the hemorrhage.

(4) The West Indians, who were used to a heavy focus on evangelism, felt that this was being neglected in London because of the Conference administration's concern for racial conflict and its fear of adding to it through expanding the proportion of West Indian members. Even the campaigns in the New Gallery Evangelistic Center eventually ceased for a period as the focus of Adventist evangelism was shifted to more remote areas where whites predominated.

(5) These difficulties brought home to the immigrants the disadvantages of not being represented among the church leadership and on the committees. These disadvantages were underlined when London-wide meetings attended mostly by West Indians had no black faces on the platform. However, when they demanded political inclusion they realized that this was impossible to win while most of their pastors were indigenous, for pastors were automatically included among the delegates from their congregations. The church leadership, which had earlier seen the West Indians as temporary visitors who therefore did not need representation at the Conference, now argued that the latter were not capable of handling such administrative posts as Treasurer or even Secretary.

The 1970s were marked by escalating racial tensions, both in society, where Enoch Powell's denunciations of the flow of immigrants ultimately resulted in street violence, and in the Adventist Church. In 1973 the youthful West Indian leaders formed an organization, the London Laymen's Forum (LLF), to pursue their goals. This held meetings in churches on Sabbath afternoons, educating the members concerning the issues and raising their consciousness. The Greater Birmingham Laymen's Association joined the protest in 1974. The LLF published a magazine, *Comment,* analyzing what was at stake, and issued a manifesto. Its leaders spread this far and wide, reaching as far as the General Conference, the world church headquarters in the U.S. They demanded frequent meetings with leaders of the Conference, practicing role-playing in order to press their case most effectively – and were then threatened with church discipline. The president of the British Union dubbed them "self-styled leaders" who had not been appointed by any pastor or even by the immigrant community themselves.[29]

---

29   Gerloff, *A Plea for British Black Theologies,* 302.

In an attempt to respond to the rising pressure and discontent, the president of the British Union traveled to the General Conference in 1974 to seek funds to subsidize the recruitment of pastors from the West Indies. However, he found that rather than gaining the support he sought, he was instead lectured on race relations by Robert Pearson, the President of the General Conference, who had been subjected to the West Indian point of view by prominent West Indian Adventists in the U.S.

The LLF made its discontent public at the constituency meeting of the South England Conference (SEC) in May 1975, demanding greater inclusion in administration because requests for pastors who matched their congregations and for a school were being overlooked. Under their influence, the Plans Committee drafted a resolution recommending proportional representation among pastors, in conference departments, and within the administration and executive committee, and that black pastors be trained or recruited from abroad to serve the predominantly black churches. When there was insufficient time for this resolution to be debated by the full meeting, it was passed on to the Executive Committee, which in turn appointed a subcommittee to address it. The latter rejected the resolution on the grounds that representation should not reflect the makeup of the membership but rather, because of the church's responsibility to evangelize the whole country, the racial distribution of the whole population.

The LLF then increased pressure on church leaders by issuing publicity to the press. In June 1976 the respected *Observer* published an article headlined "Black Adventists Demand a Greater Share of Power." This reported that for the first time a British church faced a situation where the majority of its members were black. Nevertheless, the administrators and pastors of the church in Britain remained predominantly white. "One obvious problem for the Adventist leaders is that they do not want to acquire the public image of being a West Indian organization."[30]

Seeking a possible solution, the British Union initiated a debate about creating a separate West Indian conference overlapping with the territories of the South and North England Conferences, modeled on the racially separate "regional conferences" in the US. Although this had not been its demand, the LLF embraced it as apparently the only route to greater representation. However, the Union was never comfortable with its proposal. Suddenly, in what was seen as a ploy to cut off discussion, the President of the Union, referring to "contention and power-seeking," announced a referendum in October 1976 among all members, an unprecedented means of deciding the issue. Members were allowed only one week to return their ballots. The President's own letter in the *Advent Messenger* was clearly against the proposal, and no counterweight was provided. The proposal was soundly defeated: only 15.5% of the votes, which came from 42% of the members, supported it: it clearly lost within both racial groups.[31] The LLF cried foul, sending an open letter of protest to the

30   Colin Cross, "Black Adventists Demand a Greater Share of Power," *The Observer* (June 27, 1976).
31   Gerloff, *A Plea for British Black Theologies*, 310–314.

Union about the bias in the referendum process and rejecting its result. Its struggle had not been broken.

As an observer member of the British Council of Churches, the representatives of the British Union had frequently been exposed to debates critical of racism in church and society. As the Christian body with proportionately the highest active West Indian membership in Britain, they had tried hard to project an image as a peaceful multiracial church – with some justification, for Adventism had led the way in allowing West Indian participation in congregational leadership. However, its representatives now had reason to fear that fallout from the struggle would harm the image of the Church among other denominations in Britain. When the *Advent Messenger* announced in a January 1977 editorial that "we were happy to report" to a meeting of the Community and Race Relations Unit of the BCC "that of all the British churches, the SDA has been marvelously blessed in nurturing and maintaining a sense of cohesion and brotherhood that transcends race and colour," they were clearly fudging the data.[32] However, when a black layman complained, the editor affirmed his statement, discounting the "tiny though extremely militant minority."[33]

The LLF kept up the pressure on the leadership, calling an assembly of all West Indian Adventists in London in 1977, with Dr Walter Douglas, a well-known West Indian professor at the Adventist Seminary in Michigan, as speaker. An attempt by the Conference to cut attendance there by announcing that Communion would be held on that day in the churches failed, and the meeting had a full house. The LLF also sent a stream of information to the General Conference leadership through educated West Indian Adventists in the U.S. In return, it was kept informed of relevant changes in attitudes and decisions there, and was therefore prepared in advance.

Meanwhile, the LLF resurrected the proposal for a regional conference. Its campaign gathered momentum when, following its urgings, three of the West Indian congregations in London withheld their tithes, banking them instead of passing them to the Conference, pending the settlement of the racial issues. Other members sent their tithes to the West Indies, which in turn caused conflict between two Divisions of the world church when the English demanded that conferences in the West Indies hand over the diverted funds. The conflict over tithes led the LLF to appeal to the General Conference, an action which eventually gave the latter reason to intervene.

Since a constituency meeting of the SEC was scheduled for 1978, the LLF opened negotiations with a white candidate who was planning to challenge the president, and then endorsed him. General Conference President Robert Pearson intervened directly in 1978, taking the British leadership by surprise; the president of the British Union had been under the impression that the purpose of Pearson's visit was to answer his earlier request for funds to import West Indian pastors. However, Pearson in fact imposed a broad solution, for West Indians in the General Conference such as its Secretary, Ralph Thompson, had applied strong pressure. The imposed

---

32  *Advent Messenger* (January 7, 1977).
33  Editorial, *Advent Messenger* (January 19, 1977).

solution, known colloquially as the Pearson Package, rejected the regional conference route. It had two main facets:

(1) Each structural level (the Union and both English conferences) would in future have at least one West Indian officer and one department director, and West Indian representation on all committees; the secretarial staff would also reflect the balance of the constituency. That is, Pearson insisted on proportional representation.

(2) A group of experienced pastors from the West Indies with leadership experience would be brought in, subsidized directly by the General Conference, as had been requested. These would provide the quality personnel needed to occupy the black positions in the leadership.[34]

The English responded to the pressure from above to accept the Package with considerable bitterness, the more so because they were allowed so little time to digest it. The South England Conference's constituency meeting, which followed only two weeks later, was an angry one, as the Package was forced through and its president was forced out, being replaced by the white pastor endorsed by the LLF. Two of the items of the Pearson Package were implemented immediately – an increase of Black committee members at all structural levels and on institutional boards, and the recruiting of seven "top-drawer pastors with leadership potential" from the West Indies.[35]

By mid-1978 both conferences had installed a black secretary and department director. Another black was elected Secretary of the British Union in 1981. That same year, Dr Silburn Reid, the secretary of the SEC, was elevated to its presidency after a difficult, conflicted session in which the report of the nominating committee was referred back to it and the session had to be extended to another day. The SEC had West Indian presidents continuously from 1981 until 2016; in 1996 the position of Secretary also passed to a West Indian. By 1984, the proportion of black ordained and licensed pastors had increased to 37 of 138 (up from six of 132 in 1976), and the majority of pastors in London were black.

Although the proportion of immigrant members in the North England Conference was in fact somewhat higher than in the South England Conference, the former's President remained white to "keep the balance," with a black Secretary, until 1995. However, a black President was then chosen as "the best man available." A West Indian was elected President of the British Union in 1991. He defeated the incumbent white with a nominating committee that was evenly divided racially, and was confirmed narrowly in an unusual secret ballot by all constituency delegates. The executive committees of all three judicatories had black majorities before 1997.

34   E.H. Foster, "More Meaningful Racial Representation in the Seventh-day Adventist Church in the British Isles," *Messenger* 83 (April 21, 1978): 1–2.
35   Gerloff, *A Plea for British Black Theologies,* 330.

The West Indian immigrants in Britain had thus taken several decades after they became the majority group and had gained control of the key decision-making positions in their churches before pressing for leadership positions in the conferences and then the British Union. Similarly, African immigrants lived for over a decade under West Indian decision makers before the first African, Dr Osei, a Ghanaian, was chosen as President of the South England Conference in 2016.

Reid, the first West Indian President of the SEC, started the John Loughborough School in Central London, named for an Adventist pioneer missionary. It initially attracted a lot of favorable attention from the media. However, shortage of funds led it in 1998-99 to apply for funding from both Central and Local Government sources, which opened it to greater scrutiny and less autonomy. The decision led ultimately to a clash of ideals between the Adventist holistic approach and the government's focus on academic attainment. In 2013 the Haringey London Borough Council decided to close the school because of inadequate pupil attainment and falling pupil numbers.[36] Reid also launched "big-tent" evangelism, based on the model used in the West Indies, which led to a boom in conversions of West Indians during the 1980s even though the influx of immigrants had by then been stopped by legislation. He also returned English Adventism to camp meetings, which were well attended by the West Indian membership but not by the indigenous members.

All groups of first-generation immigrants from the Caribbean, Africa, Asia, Latin America, or Eastern Europe, have differed strongly from most indigenous white English concerning behavioral norms and beliefs: it seemed that their influx would have the effect of reversing the trajectory of the Adventist Church in Britain, which had moved a considerable distance from sect towards denomination along the sect-denomination continuum, back towards the sectarian pole. For example, the attitudes of immigrants towards women pastors has made it difficult to find churches willing to accept women theology graduates as their pastors. However, the second, and now third, generations of Adventist West Indians in England have become socialized to British culture. They fought against the legalism and mores of their parents and, like their white counterparts, became much less involved in church outreach programs; to the extent that the British-born from immigrant stock remain active Adventists, they are likely to support the trajectory travelled by the indigenous white English Adventists. However, many of them have moved, like the younger generations of British, to the periphery of the Adventist Church.

The greatest sorrow of the indigenous English has been their inability to reach out successfully to their own countrymen. When it was pointed out that this pattern was congruent with the sharp decline in religious commitment among the English population and that Adventism was not gaining converts even in the areas where there are no immigrants, they replied that the number of indigenous English had earlier been growing slowly but steadily in the cities, but that this is now impossible,

36   Elizabeth Pears, "End of an Era as Black School is set for Closure," *The Voice* (December 26, 2012); "The John Loughborough School," *Wikipedia,* accessed, January 4, 2018, https://en.wikipedia.org/wiki/The_John_Loughborough_School.

for the non-Adventist English avoid evangelistic meetings where the majority in attendance is black. However, given the growing secularization of English society, it seems certain that the Adventist growth-rate would have declined even without an influx of immigrants, as it has in the other countries of Northern Europe.[37] That is, in the words of the director of Church Growth in the South England Conference, "Without immigrants the Adventist Church in England would be reduced significantly; now that immigrants have come in, (our) churches have been given life again."[38]

The Adventist Church in England has become a black Church. The indigenous pastors do not expect to see one of their own as a president again. Indeed, the flow of indigenous theology graduates is drying up as the white membership ages, making growth among the indigenous English even less likely.

## France

Adventism grew slowly among the indigenous French. By the late 1960s there were only about 1,000 members in Metropolitan Paris. However, from that time onwards there was a swelling of the membership there, almost all as a result of the immigration of Adventists and evangelism among their fellows. Most of the immigrants came from the French Antilles – the French-speaking islands of Guadeloupe and Martinique in the Caribbean, whose populations are French citizens who can come and go to France as they wish – with some also from French Guiana. In 1997 over 3,000 of the 3,578 Parisian members came from that region or that stock. There were also about 200 from the former French colonies in Africa (the Malagasy from Madagascar) and Cambodia, and another small group from the former Yugoslavia.

Most of the indigenous French felt they had become strangers in their own congregations and, as their frustration with this situation escalated, they ceased attending church altogether. In the mid-1970s one pastor visited each missing indigenous member, and gathered many of them to form a separate white congregation, Southeast Paris, that was committed to remaining a white bastion. However, when these whites requested letters transferring their memberships from the other churches, the Antilleans were offended, accusing them of racism, even when the rationale given was that such a congregation was necessary in order to evangelize the indigenous French population.

In 1997 this was the one remaining congregation in Metropolitan Paris that was predominantly white. It had been maintained as such because the indigenous French members, in their determination not to allow a repeat of the earlier process, had adhered to an unwritten rule that they would not accept new members who would

---

37    See Cragun and Lawson, "The Secular Transition," for a discussion of secularization theory.

38    Taashi Rowe, "Immigrants Sustaining Adventist Church Membership in Some Regions," *Adventist News Network* (August 5, 2007), accessed, May 24, 2019, https://news.adventist.org/en/all-news/news/go/2007-08-05/immigrants-sustaining-adventist-church-membership-in-some-regions/. Citing Aris Vontzalidis.

raise the immigrant proportion of the membership above ten percent of the total. However, another problem undermined the viability of the congregation, which could not survive as designed without retaining its children: this became impossible given the secularization of their generation. Some other indigenous members continued to be scattered among the predominantly black congregations, but several of these complained to me that they did not feel at home there. Consequently, the number of indigenous French among the Adventists in Metropolitan France continued to plummet, falling to perhaps 200 by 1997 (see Table 3).

**TABLE 3**

**ETHNIC DISTRIBUTION OF THE ADVENTIST MEMBERSHIP IN METROPOLITAN PARIS, 1997**

|  | Membership | Caucasians | Antillians | Others |
|---|---|---|---|---|
|  | 3,578 | c.200 | c.3,000 | c.400 |

Sources: Franco-Belgian Union

Meanwhile, the churches in the centers in the North France Conference outside of Paris also experienced a growing immigrant presence. Consequently, the Caribbean immigrants also formed a clear majority of the membership of the Conference, which stood at 5,484 in 1997. While the South France Conference continued to have an indigenous majority, the immigrant minority there also swelled.

During the next two decades the flow of immigrants to Paris and the other centers in the North France Conference became increasingly diverse, to the point where in 2018 15 non-French language groups were present in the membership, some with several congregations. The largest of the newer groups are Romanians, with 800 members in five congregations. Ghanaians have two churches, one each in Paris and Strasbourg, and Brazilians also have two. Other ethnic groups with a congregation apiece include Filipinos, Russians, Serbo-Croats, Malagasy, Tamil Indians, Hispanics, and a mixed group of Africans worshiping in English. The other 30 churches are French-speaking, with almost all, except for two Haitian and two mixed congregations with a substantial white minority, being Antillean. In recent years the membership of the conference, which had stood at 3,904 in 1970 and 5,415 in 1996, has expanded much more rapidly, reaching 10,349 in early 2018 (see Table 4).

Meanwhile, however, the number of white indigenous French, especially in Paris, has continued to fall. They have lost almost every member of the generation now aged 30 to 50, and almost all of their youth, leaving an aging cohort involved in two mixed congregations situated in Neuilly and Dammarie-lès-Lys on the outskirts of Paris. The paucity of children in this group of Adventists, and the difficulty of attracting other whites given the immigrant majority in the church, the challenge of post-modernism, and the secularity prevalent among the white French, suggest a bleak future for them.

**TABLE 4**

**ETHNIC DISTRIBUTION OF THE ADVENTIST MEMBERSHIP IN NORTH FRANCE CONFERENCE, 2018**

| Membership | Antillians | Caucasians | Eastern Europeans | Others |
|---|---|---|---|---|
| 10,349 | c.5,150 | c.2,700 | c.1,300 | c.1,200 |

Sources: Franco-Belgian Union

In the last five years Europe has received an almost unprecedented flow of refugees from Libya, Iraq, Afghanistan, and Northern Africa, and France has a goodly share of these, who are gathered mostly near the English Channel, frustrated in their hope of settling in Britain. Since most of the refugees are Muslims, they include almost no Adventists. Some Adventist churches, together with ADRA, have become active supplying food and clothing to the refugees, and a few of those helped have attended church services; two of them were baptized in 2017.

The conference has hired a new group of diverse pastors, in order to match the needs and languages of the new immigrants. Some were Eastern European and African graduates of Collonges, the French Adventist college and seminary, but many had been trained in the colleges serving the regions from which the immigrants were drawn.

Seeing the changing racial balance, administrators had divided France into two conferences, North and South, in 1969, in order to maintain a white bastion in the South. However, the black portion of the population of the cities there also began to increase. Nevertheless, in 2018 the membership of the South France Conference, with far fewer immigrants than in the North, remained below 5,000, and was thus less than half of that of the North Conference.

## Dynamics

While the first Antillean Adventists were welcomed to their congregations in Paris by the indigenous French, tensions emerged as their numbers increased, initially in the few churches in the City of Paris and then also in those on the periphery of the city. Although the immigrants were legally French citizens, and thought of themselves as French, the whites saw them as culturally very distinct. While French Adventists tend to focus on "justification by faith" and are far less concerned with behavioral rules, seeing obedience to them as peripheral to salvation, the Antilleans had been evangelized by legalistic American missionaries and therefore lived their religion differently. The latter were also used to more lively worship than were the indigenous French. Many of the indigenous leaders became frustrated as tensions waxed and resigned their positions, preparing the way for the immigrants to assume leadership of their congregations and therefore to change the style of worship. Exiting whites then created new congregations on the periphery, increasing the total number of Adventist churches in metropolitan Paris from six to 15, only to find that immigrants followed them there.

The first, and most dramatic, conflict occurred in the large South Paris church in the late 1960s. Facing an unexpected influx of immigrants, the white members feared being overwhelmed and losing what they had. Once the immigrants formed a clear majority, they organized and demanded an Antillean pastor. When the Conference responded by importing a pastor from Martinique, his arrival split the congregation. Consequently, additional Antillean pastors were added slowly – the total in 1989 was only five. Moreover, most of those hired to serve the Antilleans after the first one were chosen from among those who had pursued their education at Collonges, rather than those who had attended the Adventist college in Haiti or the two English-speaking colleges in the West Indies.

As the black proportion among the membership increased, evangelism among white Parisians became even more difficult. When all Adventists were urged to invite their friends to evangelistic meetings, the blacks proved more committed to outreach and found their friends more eager to attend. When the few white visitors attending found themselves part of an audience that was largely black, they usually did not to return a second time. Moreover, because most of the blacks were younger than the whites, their rate of natural increase has been much greater than that of the indigenous French, even though church officials estimate that they lose about 40% of their youth.

The shortage of Antillean pastors was so severe that a number of churches with black majorities had to accept white pastors. This situation made it difficult for the black pastors to seek higher positions, so that the black presence in the churches was not reflected in the conference leadership and staff. In 1989, by which time there was a clear immigrant majority in the North France Conference, there was only one Antillean departmental leader: nominating committees at constituency meetings, which were still dominated by white pastors, had begun to show concern that the immigrants receive token representation at the Conference. However, there were still no Antillean laypersons on the Conference committee. Black pastors told me then that it was time for a change, and that they expected to see that occur at the constituency meeting later that year. One result of their new determination was considerable tension at the next three constituency meetings: an Antillean was elected as President for two terms at raucous sessions in 1989 and 1993; the tension was maintained in 1997, when, following the retirement of the Antillean president, a white was again elected to the post.

Given the ethnic diversity of the delegates, each constituency meeting of the North France Conference becomes "a battlefield", with each group endeavoring to take power. A second Antillean was elected as president in 2001. The 2013 meeting was especially divided, resulting in the firing of the president, from Mauritius, for breaking the laws governing how churches deal with their finances.

In spite of their numerical dominance at all levels of the administrative structure of the Adventist church, immigrants did not gain leadership positions in the Franco-Belgian Union until 2008, when an Antillean was elected president. However, scandals during his term embarrassed his community. As a result of these scandals, the three constituency meetings that followed surprised when each elected a foreigner as president: a Romanian in North France, an Italian in the South conference, and a Portuguese at the Union.

The immigrants, especially the Romanians and Antilleans, are theologically and behaviorally conservative, unlike the white French. This has given an additional dimension to tensions between the groups. The initial tensions between Romanians and white French concerned the Sabbath behavior of their children; this was followed by disputes over "last-generation theology," which implies that Adventists must be living sinless lives before Christ can return. This highlighted the differing views of grace held by the two groups.

The most fraught issue to be debated at the North France Conference's constituency meeting in 2017 concerned articles written by a theology professor at Collonges in which he had favored accepting the marriage of gay and lesbian couples: these had greatly upset the immigrants, who argued that the conference should cease giving financial support to the college. However, the protest was quelled when Jean-Jack Chafograck, an Antilean with a Th.D. who was elected president of the conference at that session, spoke out in favor of homosexuals being married so long as the relationship was exclusive.[39] To generalize, immigrants have made the North France Conference both theologically and socially conservative, while in contrast the South France Conference is more liberal. However, Chafograck's bold statement in 2017 aligned the North Conference with the position on same-sex marriage adopted earlier by the South Conference.

In the whole of France, about 70% of the Adventist members are immigrants; in the North France Conference this figure jumps to about 80%; and in Metropolitan Paris it is over 90%. There is a brooding sense of desperation among the indigenous French concerning the future of Adventism in France among their own kind, especially in the North.

## The Netherlands

The Netherlands is a small country and the Adventist membership there had matched the country: it was only 2,788 in 1960. However, these numbers have been bolstered by several waves of diverse immigrants over the decades since the 1940s. Some Indonesians had migrated there when their country gained independence in the late 1940s, and these included Adventists; more arrived in the 1950s. Now third-

---

39   Quoting from an interview in Paris, 2018.

generation Dutch, they were described to me as polite and well integrated into the Dutch church. Surinam gained its independence in 1975, but a strong tie persists between the two countries. Many Surinamese came to the Netherlands for education in the 1970s and remained; even more came after a coup in 1980, until the flow stopped when restrictions were imposed because the Surinamers were not Dutch citizens. A Surinamese lay leader reported early tension because their beliefs and norms were more conservative than the Dutch were used to, but my Dutch interviewees always described them positively.

The Antillians from the Caribbean islands of Curaçau and Aruba (the Dutch Antilles) have Dutch citizenship, and therefore the right to live in the Netherlands if they choose. Students came in the 1960s and 70s, and others moved to the Netherlands after a refinery closed in 1969. Large numbers followed them in the 1980s and 1990s, fleeing a weak economy. In spite of their status as citizens, they arrived, unlike the Surinamers, without a felicity with the Dutch language. Although the Dutch had no former colonies in Africa, Ghanaians began to migrate there in the 1990s.

The Dutch Adventists became strongly aware of tensions emerging as a result of the Antillean influx: while they emphasized salvation by faith alone, they found the Antilleans legalistic and with strong views concerning some Adventist doctrines. However, there was also discomfort because they saw them as being indifferent concerning ethics: it was not uncommon for an Antillean to hold strongly to a complex doctrine such as the 2,300 days, but be uncertain who had fathered her children. They also offended the Dutch by frequent requests for rebaptism, apparently regarding multiple baptisms as rendering them better Christians. The Dutch were, moreover, offended by their belief that Dutch Adventists needed to be reconverted, in part because they did not strongly embrace evangelistic outreach. Because the number of Antillean Adventists increased much faster than any other group, both because of a large influx and because of having larger families, the Dutch church leaders regarded the Antilleans with increasing concern.

The initial policy of the Dutch Union was to encourage immigrants to join Dutch churches in order to foster their assimilation, and the Antilleans did this. However, they were uncomfortable there both because of the Dutch language and a neglect of mores they had been taught were important: they were shocked to find that coffee was provided at churches and that Dutch women regularly ornamented themselves with jewelry. They were also extremely critical when the Dutch Union chose to ordain a woman pastor. They put special emphasis on Adventist beliefs in the realm of eschatology, and the expectation that laws would be enacted making Sunday a sacred day and that Adventists who did not observe them would then be persecuted. They regarded the Dutch as liberal, and were seen by them in return as inflexible.

When they requested that Antillean pastors be hired for their congregations, the Dutch union regarded that as opening the way to repeat the trajectory that had resulted in the West Indian immigrants gaining control of most of the Adventist churches in England and then also of the church structure there. There were bitter feelings and white exits when Antillean majorities in large churches in the coastal cities gained control of the church boards and elder positions, and then changed the style of worship. However, in most churches the Dutch continued to control the church board, and did not allow the immigrant minority any power.

In 1995, 15 Ghanaian Adventists who had been discontented in a multi-cultural church in Amsterdam gained permission to found a Twi-speaking congregation. By 1999 it had 75 members, and this number doubled by the beginning of 2001, by which time the attendance was actually close to 250. Adventist Ghanaians have a network when abroad like no other Adventist ethnic group: Matthew Bediako, a Ghanaian who was then Secretary of the General Conference, became mentor of the Amsterdam congregation, for he was President of the Association of Ghanaian Churches Abroad. The strength of this association was demonstrated when the President of the Adventist Ghanaian Union agreed to be the preacher in an evangelistic crusade in Amsterdam in 2000. Such crusades were extremely successful is reconnecting Ghanaians who had backslidden since arriving in the Netherlands because of their discomfort in Dutch-speaking churches or their failure to find employment that did not require them to work on the Sabbath.[40]

The Ghanaians demonstrated the advantages of fostering single-ethnic group congregations to the Union leaders: by becoming cultural centers they could much more readily evangelize members of their ethnic group, reconnect with members who had fallen away, and at the same time they removed the risk that they could become the majority in a formerly indigenous Dutch church, and so take control of it and mold it to suit their culture. The union eventually learned from the Ghanaian example, and stopped insisting that immigrants join existing congregations. Instead, it gave immigrants room to create their own ethnic churches.

By the end of 2000 four new congregations serving a particular ethnic group had been created. However, immigrant members and persons with an immigrant background had grown to the point of being 45% of the Adventist membership in the Netherlands, and the Union leaders were uneasily aware that it would not be long before there was an immigrant majority (see Table 5). The latter were still reluctant to hire ethnic pastors. The first such, a Surinamer hired in 1985, was such a success that in 1993 he was elected as youth director at the Union, thus becoming the first immigrant at church headquarters. However, it was not until 2000 that a second ethnic pastor, a Guyanese who had lived in Surinam, was hired as an intern after raising a new congregation as a volunteer. Meanwhile, a lay Surinamer served on the Union board from 1987–2000. These bellwethers made it clear that, given the percentage of immigrants within the Dutch church, they were very inadequately represented both in the pastorate and in decision-making positions. The union leaders realized the reality of this situation, but they felt they also had to protect Dutch interests and not allow the Dutch Church to follow the trajectory of the British Union

---

40  Koning, "Messengers of Truth: Evangelism by a Ghanaian Seventh-day Adventist church in the Netherlands."

by becoming a black church. The fact that the key advocates of what they regarded an unacceptably conservative theological interpretations and living according to strict rules were often former Antillean pastors who had come to the Netherlands as immigrants made them extra-cautious.

| TABLE 5 |
| --- |

**ETHNIC DISTRIBUTION OF THE ADVENTIST MEMBERSHIP IN THE NETHERLANDS UNION, 2000-2018**

| Year | Membership | Dutch Caucasians | Antillians, Surinamians | Others | All Immigrants |
| --- | --- | --- | --- | --- | --- |
| 2018 | 6,002 | 35% | 45% | 20% | |
| 2014 | 5,736 | 45% | | | 55% |
| 2000 | 4,327 | 55% | | | 45% |
| 1980 | 3,944 | | | | |
| 1960 | 2,788 | | | | |

Sources: Netherlands Union; Adventist Statistics

Realizing that they had to understand what options were available in their situation and to lay plans accordingly, the union leaders chose to hold a seminar to inform and raise the consciousness of the Dutch Adventist Church. Since I had recently published three articles on the impact of an influx of immigrants on the Adventist church in Metropolitan New York, they invited me to be the speaker. I spoke and dialogued with lay representatives, pastors, and the Union administrators and department heads in turn, and interviewed some from each group individually. As requested, I set out to educate them all and to discuss the alternative policies available. It was for them to make choices and steer accordingly afterwards.

In the subsequent years the flow of immigrants slowed because of the enactment of stricter laws, but it also became more diverse, as it had in Britain and France also: the ethnic groups represented among newcomers became predominantly Africans, Eastern Europeans, and Latinos. Although the flow had slowed, the growth in immigrant numbers far exceeded the growth among the Dutch, partly because of the size of immigrant families. Early in 2018, within a union membership that had risen to 6,002, it was estimated that 35% were indigenous white Dutch, 45% were drawn from the Antilles and Surinam, and the remaining 20% were "other" (see Table 5). The immigrants were no longer concentrated mostly in the large coastal cities, but were spread across the Netherlands and its Adventist churches. Recent Antillean immigrants are students desiring to further their education, and thus differ from their predecessors: they feel Dutch, prefer white churches, and integrate more readily.

The union leaders now see secularization, rather than immigrants, as the main reason for the decline of the white membership – the Adventist experience is similar to that of the Dutch mainline denominations, which have declined without any immigrant influx. Indeed, immigrants have been important in bolstering the Adventist membership in the Netherlands: forty years ago the Adventist membership in both Sweden and the Netherlands stood at about 4,000, but now the Dutch have 6,000 but the Swedes, who have had no immigrant influx, have only 2,000. One reason why the growth is slowing is that the children of the immigrants are becoming like the children of the Dutch – they are secularizing and losing interest in the church. This process is especially marked within the Surinamese constituency.

Some of the new immigrant groups have requested pastors who match them ethnically, and some such have been hired. The union leaders are concerned about the Eastern Europeans, whom they regard as often rigid Adventists who promote their version of orthodoxy. Representation in the church administration has broadened significantly in recent years. When I visited the Netherlands in 2014 I discovered that the elected treasurer had resigned and been replaced by an Antillean businessman, who had changed his career in order to help his church. At the constituency meeting in 2016 a Surinamese pastor was chosen as secretary. The immigrants, who had long felt alienated from power in the Dutch Union, are now content: they do not want to push the Dutch out, for they recognize that would likely result in the loss of many indigenous members, but they do want a voice and a share of the power.

There are still deep ethnicity-related fissures over social issues within the Dutch church. At the 2012 business session a large majority of the delegates voted in favor of the ordination of women pastors, and the union soon after ordained the most eligible woman. However, after women's ordination was voted down by the 2015 General Conference Session, mostly because of the votes of delegates from the Global South, immigrant members felt uncomfortable that the Dutch Union continued to oppose a policy endorsed by the General Conference. This was an important reason behind changes of leadership voted in the Union in 2016. Another issue that gained attention at the 2016 session concerned LGBTQ couples: the former Secretary had written an article in the church periodical urging that Adventists listen to them and try to understand them. This was referred to and questioned. There was a strong wish expressed that the periodical be more in tune with the global church: many immigrants, in particular, felt that it had been too progressive. However, this concern did not come from immigrants alone.

Nevertheless, the cultural and religious differences within the constituency are real: the Dutch are traditionally very liberal and not oriented to the World Church; immigrants, in contrast, are conservative and strongly oriented towards being in step with the World Church. Dutch pastors are not so concerned with doctrinal matters, but often care deeply concerning social justice issues. On the other hand, as the immigrants have integrated more into Dutch society, they have become less conservative. For example, after the 2012 Session, the Union contacted five churches seeking to place a woman pastor; four largely white churches in the north refused to take her, but an Antillean congregation, which had earlier been very conservative, accepted her.

In 2002 the Dutch Union decided that it would hire only immigrant pastors who had lived as youth in the Netherlands and been trained in Europe in order to prevent conflicting theologies; it later added a requirement that if potential pastors did not conform with that history, that they at least complete an MA at Newbold College in England. By 2014 only two of the six active immigrant pastors complied with the first stipulation, but the others had completed MAs. One who did not was dismissed. By 2018 there were 8 immigrants among 22 active pastors: 3 Ghanaian, 2 Surinamese, 1 Guyanese, 2 Antilleans. There are still several immigrant congregations with Dutch pastors: they are not complaining about cultural issues, though they would like more emotional than academic preaching.

The Dutch Adventist Church, unlike its counterpart in North France, still has active youth members, but fewer than earlier. The losses are no longer mainly among the white youth, but also among immigrant youth, as both groups are influenced by secularism and postmodernism. The youth leaders recognize that it is possible that they could eventually find themselves in the same situation as the French. In some respects, the attempts to retain the youth divide along ethnic lines. Since it has become almost the norm among all European youth for couples to live together in advance of marriage, the indigenous Dutch pastors have long been willing to recognize such couples as if they were married already, and to encourage them to hold offices in their church; the youth department has also long allowed such couples, and indeed gay and lesbian couples also, to live in rooms reserved for married couples when they attend youth camps rather than reject their coupled status and so risk alienating them totally from the church. On the other hand, such policies offend many immigrant pastors, who would rather risk alienating them – even though they accept members who, while not "living together" parent children.

## An Underlying Pattern

In each of these case studies there was an influx of immigrants, initially mostly from the Caribbean, into an area of Europe where Adventism had been growing slowly. While the first immigrants were welcomed by the indigenous white Adventists, tensions emerged as the flow of immigrants increased and they became active in the churches and successful in evangelism among their peers. This caused some whites to pull back, irritated by the "loud" behavior and legalistic theology of the newcomers. As the latter attained majority status within congregations, there were battles for control there, resulting ultimately in immigrant ascendancy and changes in the style of worship. This greatly increased the flight of whites, some of whom moved to other congregations or founded new ones, only to discover that the pattern was sooner or later repeated there.

Meanwhile, the presence of large numbers of immigrant members and their friends in evangelistic meetings made it very difficult to evangelize whites, and similarly a strong black presence in congregations made it difficult to embed any new white converts there. So conversions of whites declined even further just as many of the white members were becoming discouraged and inactive. That is, the number of white Adventists fell sharply over time against the backdrop of a rapidly growing immigrant membership.

The changing numerical balance within each of the conferences and unions led in turn to tensions there. The initial issue was always the demand from immigrants in churches where they had come to form a majority for pastors who matched them ethnically and culturally – that is, that the conference import them and install them in their churches. When the immigrants realized that the conferences were reluctant to do this, usually using the excuse that they were obliged to hire the graduates of their local colleges to cover their fear that such actions would inevitably change the balance of power within the conference, they became frustrated and, flexing their numbers, began to demand representation at the conference. They realized that if this demand was implemented the result would not only make the conferences more responsive to their expressed needs, but would also result in representatives of their group gaining leadership posts.

The entrenched white leadership usually responded by offering token positions to immigrants. However, rapid growth and then careful organization ultimately allowed the latter to seize the highest positions in the conferences. Once they were entrenched at that level, the immigrants sought representation and the leadership of their respective unions – that is, at the national level or, in the case of France, in the body overseeing the three conferences in France and Belgium. This has been achieved in the British Union but not yet completely in either the Franco-Belgian or the Dutch Union.[41]

In all these cases, the Adventist Church grew much larger during the period of immigrant influx from both the arrival of immigrants who were already Adventists and the successful evangelization of their peers. However, with immigrant majorities and leadership, and a small and declining white membership, Adventism came to be seen, accurately, as primarily an immigrant church in both England and North France; the Dutch have not yet reached that situation. Given the fact that its profiles in these countries had become strikingly different from those of the population of the host societies, this had the effect of further marginalizing the Adventist Church.

Meanwhile, restrictions on immigration and the passage of time are steadily changing the composition of Adventism once again, bringing second- and third-generation immigrants, socialized to their new cultures, to predominance. The Adventist Church has found that it is now having increased difficulty retaining its youth and evangelizing the new generations of immigrants. The problem of retaining immigrant youth is exacerbated by the generation gap between them and their first-generation parents, who have largely retained their immigrant cultures. Moreover, the new generations of non-Adventist immigrants are much less responsive to Adventism because they have developed their own networks, and are not urgently in need of

---

41  Because it is small both numerically and geographically, the Dutch Union is a "union of churches" without constituent conferences.

church-based opportunities to celebrate their cultures since they have become more assimilated to the broader society and have developed avenues for advancement there.

Why has Adventism been transformed so dramatically in each of these cases? Why has its white membership declined so sharply and its immigrant membership grown so rapidly? The analysis demonstrates the utility of the curvilinear relationship formed by the interaction of "demand-side" and "supply-side" factors highlighted by Cragun and Lawson, which also incorporates "strictness" theory as developed by Kelley and Iannaccone, in accounting for these trends.[42]

## Accounting for the Decline of Indigenous White Members

The decline of white members in all cases occurred in contexts where religious participation among whites in general, notably in the established, mainline denominations, had been falling because of secularization. These trends also impacted Adventism in ways that are congruent with secularization and strictness theory, affecting both the enthusiasm of its members and its ability to evangelize others. As the white Adventists had experienced upward mobility, thus gaining greater opportunities within the secular society, they had become less eager to witness personally to their faith, so that the Adventist Church had come to rely more on public evangelistic campaigns for outreach.

At the same time non-Adventists were proving less receptive to evangelistic endeavors. They found Adventism unattractive because of the social costs of its strictness, isolation, and its low esteem, which were linked in part to an often troubled history, such as problems in wartime because of the refusal of its members to serve as regular soldiers. Moreover, the Adventist message of warning concerning an impending apocalypse was less appealing to an increasingly materialistic generation. Meanwhile, the Adventist Church found that its white youth were also increasingly unwilling to embrace the costs of Adventism. That is, the growth-rate through conversions prior to the influx of the immigrants had been barely sufficient to make up for Adventist losses to death and apostasy.

As Adventist growth had slowed, the demographics of its membership became less suitable for internal growth, as its members passed the age of reproduction, thus making decline more likely since there were fewer children to replace the deaths among the aged. That is, the profile of white Adventism had been approaching closer to that of the declining mainline denominations, and had moved away from those sectarian groups, such as the Pentecostals, which were still experiencing growth among whites.

An influx of racially different immigrants was then injected into each of these situations. Nancy Ammerman, reviewing an array of case studies of congregations

---

42   Cragun and Lawson, The Secular Transition: The Worldwide Growth of Mormons, Jehovah's Witnesses and Seventh-day Adventists;" Kelley, *Why Conservative Churches are Growing*, 1971 and 1984; Iannaccone, "Why Strict Churches are Strong."

undergoing community change in the US, remarked that such challenges often kill churches.[43] The latter may, for example, fade away because their memberships and programs no longer match their communities, or they may choose to sell their buildings and move elsewhere. These Adventist churches did not fade away – indeed, they typically grew considerably, for the immigrants mostly spoke the same language as the white members and, being Adventists, assumed that they belonged in the existing congregations; nor could they sell their houses of worship and move their congregations elsewhere, since title to Adventist buildings is vested in the conferences, which would not consider such an option since there were new members operating the churches, filling their pews, and returning tithes. Nevertheless, these Adventist congregations did experience the problems faced by many congregations that become multicultural: tensions caused by clashing cultures and sharply differing social classes.[44]

These Adventist case studies echo the tensions suggested by other studies. Immigrant congregations (and members) are often more conservative than indigenous congregations (and members), as for example the Presbyterian Church USA found with Korean members.[45] Similarly, less educated groups, such as most immigrant groups, tend to be more conservative than their better educated co-religionists. This is true even when they gain opportunities for upward mobility in their new societies: Weber found that the upwardly mobile are ascetic.[46] Their faith may become more important to immigrants in their new societies than it was at home, since it becomes more central to their identity and sense of community, and assists their acculturation.[47] A strict adherence to the beliefs and behavioral rules of their faith allows immigrants to assert their identity: they feel more holy than most white members, whom they see as following compromised versions of faith and practice.

The tensions that developed among Adventists in these case studies as the number of immigrants in their ranks burgeoned had the effect of further eroding the size

---

43   Nancy Tatom Ammerman, *Congregation and Community* (New Brunswick: Rutgers University Press, 1997), 3.

44   Ibid., 198–208.

45   Karen J. Chai, "Competing for the Second Generation: English Language Ministry at a Korean Protestant Church," 295–332, in *Gatherings in Diaspora: Religious Communities and the New Immigration*, eds., R. Stephen Warner and Judith G. Wittner (Philadelphia: Temple University Press, 1998); See also R. Stephen Warner, "The Korean Immigrant Church as a Case and a Model," in *Korean Americans and their Religions: Pilgrims and Missionaries from a Different Shore*, eds., Ho-youn Kwon, Kwant Chun Kim and R. Stephen Warner (Pennsylvania State University Press, 2001).

46   Max Weber, *The Protestant Ethic and the Rise of Capitalism,* trans. Talcott Parsons. (New York: Scribner, 1958, (1904–1905))

47   Will Herberg, *Protestant—Catholic—Jew* (Garden City, NY: Anchor Books, 1960 (1955)); R. Stephen Warner, "Immigration and Religious Communities in the United States," in R in *Gatherings in Diaspora: Religious Communities and the New Immigration*, eds., R. Stephen Warner and Judith G. Wittner (Philadelphia: Temple University Press, 1998), 3–36.

of the previously dominant white groups. Once the flows of black immigrants increased from trickles to floods, creating tensions in urban congregations as newcomers took control, Adventism in all these cases experienced white flight. White members were not only offended by what they saw as unacceptably exuberant worship behavior and legalistic beliefs, but they felt uncomfortable being identified with an immigrant church – an identity that increased the cost of membership further by lowering its status another notch. Moreover, not only did their internal tensions distract Adventists from any outreach they might have otherwise engaged in, but their changing racial demographics made it increasingly difficult to attract potential white converts to Adventism.

The demographics of white Adventism in all these cases became increasingly unfavorable to growth, as the white membership aged and the profile of the denomination shifted, until it gained the reputation of being a black immigrant church. For the indigenous whites, Adventism had become distinctive in yet another way, thus increasing the cost of becoming or remaining a member.

## Accounting for the Rapid Growth of Immigrant Members

Each of these cases occurred against the background of the numerical center of Christianity shifting from the Global North to the Global South, and of this process occurring much more dramatically within Adventism. A second feature of this context has been the strong flow of immigrants from the Global South to parts of the Global North. Where there has been a strong flow of immigrants from parts of the world where Adventists are well represented, such as the Caribbean, it has been inevitable that Adventists would be among them.[48] Since Adventism attracts converts who are looking for opportunities for upward mobility, and often provides the means for this to occur and teaches members to expect it, it may well be that the Adventist representation among immigrants moving from areas where economies are weak to areas where they are strong is greater than a random selection of citizens would provide.

Studies among immigrants to England showed that Adventists were much more successful in retaining the participation of members arriving from abroad than were the established and mainline denominations. This was found to be related to the welcomes they initially received from Adventist congregations, from their sense of the correctness of their beliefs, which they had been taught so well in their homelands, and from the extent to which the immigrants succeeded in creating strong communities in their new congregations. In the opportunities it provided for participation and internal status and in its perspective on the "world," Adventism, like Pentecostalism, offered compensation for the various status and other deprivations

---

48  Similarly, when there is a strong flow from regions where Adventists are poorly represented, as with the recent torrent of refugees fleeing from Syria, Iraq, Afghanistan, and Muslim areas of Sub-Saharan Africa, it is rare to discover Adventists among the immigrants. I was surprised, however, and disappointed, to find few Adventist efforts to provide help to these refugees, in spite of their presence in all three countries studied.

which a racial minority faced in British society – compensations which were not available in the more staid, white-dominated denominations. [49] Such compensators bind underprivileged groups to strict churches.

The number of Adventist immigrants also swelled because of their enthusiasm in reaching out to their backslidden-Adventist peers or non-Adventists. The latter were often open to such outreach, having been shaken loose from their customary ways and ties (including their religious ties) by their migration, and often feeling the need to re-establish communal networks. As immigrants, they had few established opportunities to lose by embracing Adventism and much to gain, such as fellowship in situations where they could celebrate their culture and a new, enclosed status system where there were opportunities for them to rise rapidly. Moreover, because Adventism was much better known in the Caribbean than in Europe, immigrants often had a positive image of it rather than, as among the English, French, and Dutch, being suspicious of it as possibly an unknown cult.

The demographics of the immigrants in turn helped their growth, for they were typically much younger than the indigenous members, eager to bear children, and their families tended to be larger than those of the whites. Consequently, they rapidly took over the children's divisions in their new churches. They therefore also experienced rapid natural increase.

The immigrants, in spite of their numbers, proved to be slow to assert themselves. Initially they were marginalized in society and also the church because of their poverty, relative lack of education, and the prevailing racism – a racism that was expressed in the church as assumptions that immigrants could be neglected because they were temporary visitors who would in due course return home. Those who eventually took the lead in politicizing the immigrants were youthful members who had graduated from universities. Having gained access to opportunities, they now possessed a stake in society and set out to fight for their rights there. Once the immigrants took control of their congregations and then, in turn, also their conferences, the Adventist Church shifted its focus to meeting their needs, providing them with schools and turning its evangelistic thrust towards the newcomers, so that the conversion rate among them increased further.

However, once legislation slowed the influx of immigrants, so that Black Adventism became increasingly a second-generation phenomenon in these societies, and as black Adventists attained higher levels of education and experienced upward mobility, they increasingly mirrored white Adventism in their new societies: they lost more of their youth from the church, became less strict so that they were less eager to be involved in personal outreach, and their demographics became less favorable to

---

49   Rodney Stark and William Sims Bainbridge, *The Future of Religion: Secularization, Revival, and Cult Formation* (Berkeley, University of California Press, 1985); Hill, *West Indian Migrants and the London Churches*, 18–21; Theobald, "The Seventh-day Adventist Movement," 318.

growth. This pattern mirrored that found in other studies.[50] Meanwhile, their non-Adventist peers, having themselves put down roots in their new societies, became less disposed to use foreign churches as their social centers, and were therefore more reluctant to respond to evangelistic outreach, since they now had more to lose by joining a group that still clung to distinctive behavioral norms such as Sabbath observance.

## Conclusion

This paper has tested the usefulness of "secularization theory," in which we incorporated also "strictness theory", in a new role: that of explaining why one religious constituency grows while another declines. It has proved to be effective in this. Adventist distinctiveness and strictness encouraged both close ties and zeal among members who were new immigrants to Europe. It fitted their needs in their new countries, providing them with community, purpose, a status system where they could easily climb, and help with their problems. Consequently, most of those who arrived with Adventist roots clung to them, and others were drawn in by their outreach. They had much to gain from their Adventist connection in their new situation, and as newcomers had little to lose by so separating themselves from the broader society.

In contrast, few whites were drawn to peculiar Adventism, for they had often already been secularized and had much more to lose. Those who had grown up as Adventists had already moderated the rules in order to reduce the costs of membership, making Adventism less distinctive. However, when the immigrants took over they brought a more distinctive brand of Adventism, with higher costs, and also further raised the cost for white Adventists as the denomination gained the reputation of being a "black church." This led to tension, a sense of loss among the whites, and the exit of the majority of them as the impact of the immigrants resulted in a new homogenization of Adventism. Only isolated attempts to create or maintain niche congregations meeting the needs of different kinds of Adventists – different cultures, different educational levels, different music and styles of worship – survived the rapid changes brought about by an overwhelming shift in the makeup of the membership.

These case studies illustrate the continuing relevance of Adventism to many of the people yearning for better opportunities in the Global South – and especially to the new immigrants from such societies seeking a sense of community in the Global North. However, they also starkly illustrate the decline of Adventism in the Global North, a decline that increasingly parallels that of the mainline denominations active there but not the more vibrant sects. Indeed, the failure of Adventism to appeal to second-generation immigrants and its huge losses among the children of its immigrant members underlines the problem that Adventism faces in the Global North.

---

50  Helen Rose Ebaugh and Janet Salzman Chafetz, *Religion and the New Immigrants: Continuities and Adaptations in Immigrant Congregations* (Walnut Creek, CA: Alta Mira, 2000), 431–446.

The problems that indigenous and immigrant Adventists have had worshiping, fellowshipping and working together in the same congregations and conferences in turn illustrate how difficult it is proving to practice Christian love, brotherhood and servant-leadership in a global church. This difficulty is likely to escalate as the relative financial decline of the American church renders it increasingly less able to exercise control through the power of the once almighty dollar.

*Jón Hjörleifur Stefánsson*

# Towards European Seventh-day Adventist Hymnology: Published Hymnals, Native Composers, and Native Adventist Composers

Abstract

Hymnology is currently an underresearched topic in the history of European Seventh-day Adventism. This article is intended as a stepping stone for further research, by striving towards a comprehensive list of Adventist hymnals published in Europe. It also provides figures, albeit incomplete, of the ratio of tunes composed by native composers and native Adventist composers in each country's most recent hymnal. Tentative conclusions are as follows. The ratio of native Adventist tunes is generally low and does not vary greatly, probably because the Church has not encouraged or appreciated musical creativity. The ratio of tunes by native composers varies to quite some extent, apparently in tandem with the strength of the local Protestant musical tradition, perhaps because Adventists feel averse to adopting hymns of Catholic or Orthodox material. The research data behind this article will most heartily be shared with any musician or historian who wants to explore or use it further.

As in all other areas of human life, the vitality of Adventist hymnody can be measured by its growth, development, and renewal. These are the signs of vibrant and rich musical life. Interestingly, it seems that artistic creativity has traveled hand in hand with new religious insights. Whenever Christianity has turned theologically to grow towards the light, sacred music has blossomed. The early Christians not only sang the old Temple hymns but created new ones, some of which are quoted in the New Testament. And the movements that Adventists list in their pedigree – such as the early Reformers, Pietists, Methodists, and Millerites – all showed signs of bursting activity when it came to the publication and creation of music. This means that the vibrancy of a musical tradition may speak of the conditions of the ideological climate in which it thrives.

When European Adventist hymnology is reviewed, from its commencement in the late nineteenth century to the present time, the question arises: How living has this tradition been? How does it vary between the different countries of the continent? To what extent has the Church in each country leaned on the American Adventist hymnals, its native sacred music tradition, and native Adventist composers? These are some of the opening lines of query, but answering them is much harder than it sounds.

To research European Adventist hymnology, first it is necessary to gather and analyze the primary sources, namely all the published hymnals.[1] This is not easily done. Besides the fact the total has barely been studied, other difficulties quickly beset the researcher: The language barriers and the nature of hymnals. Hymnals are published in small amounts, are usually short-lived, and quickly become hard to find. There is probably nowhere on earth where all the published European Adventist hymnals can be consulted in one place. National Adventist church magazines probably contain articles about the preparation and publication of all the hymnals. But hardly any of these magazines are available online to the researcher.[2] For this article I tried my best to collect or learn of the existence of as many of the hymnals as I could, with partial results. Some may say that the results are too incomplete to be published at this time. But given how much time and effort would go into making the picture more complete, I think it is unlikely to appear soon, and that partial results are worthwhile. The incomplete picture hopefully still sheds some informative rays on European Adventist hymnology.

This article gives an overview of European Adventist hymnology by listing the hymnals published in each European country. It states how many tunes in the most recent hymnal of each country were written by native composers and by native Adventists. It is intended as a rough overview of current findings and a stepping stone for future researchers. Due to its preliminary nature, the accuracy of all the details[3] must be taken with a grain of salt, and an enthusiasm for discovering European Adventist music.

Around thirty European countries have produced Adventist hymnals, and around twenty have not published any. The most common reasons for a country not publishing hymnals are reliance on hymnals from other countries where the population speaks the same language, or little to no Adventist presence in the country.[4]

---

1   This article is limited to the general hymnals and excludes the specific ones, such as children's song books, youth hymnals, etc.

2   Scanning them and making them available online would be a tremendous help to European Seventh-day Adventist scholars. Ironically, they must sometimes travel to the United States to find information about the history of the church in Europe.

3   Since this research is in its infancy, I do not go into the myriad methodological details, such as definitions of Europe, nationality, tune authorship, etc. The only importance for present purposes is the alphabetical order used when listing composers and tunes: Scripts and diacritics are ignored so that the items are arranged according to the English alphabet, as far as possible.

4   Albania is preparing its own hymnal. Belarus uses the Russian hymnals. Belgium uses the Dutch hymnals in Flanders (the Dutch-speaking region) and the French hymnals in Wallonia (the French-speaking region). Bosnia and Herzegovina use the Serbian hymnals. Cyprus uses the American and Greek hymnals. Georgia is preparing its own hymnal. Ireland used the English hymnals and now the American ones. Kosovo uses the Serbian hymnals. Luxembourg uses the French hymnals. The microstates Andorra, Liechtenstein, Malta, Monaco, San Marino, and Vatican City have no hymnals. Malta uses the American hymnal,

# European Adventist Hymnals per Country

## Armenia

There has been at least one Armenian hymnal published either in the twentieth or twenty-first century. It is entitled *Spaselov nran* (115 hymns).[5] A text-only edition was published under the same name in 2017 (176 texts).[6] Neither book lists the poets or composers.

## Austria

The Austrian Church used the German hymnals, until it published the first Austrian Adventist hymnal, *Singt unserm Gott* (594 hymns) in 2014.[7] The membership in Austria chose to make their own hymnal due to disagreement over the newest German hymnal, which was regarded as too secular. *Singt unserm Gott* contains 17 tunes by Austrian composers (3%), 6 (1%) of which were composed by Adventists. The composers are Franz Xaver Gruber (1), Bodo Hoppe (1), and Franz Peter Schubert (9).[8] The Adventist composers are Hans Brantner (2), Dietmar Pickhardt (2), and Walter Scharf (2).[9]

## Bulgaria

I have no information on the earliest Bulgarian hymnals. I have received a copy of an accompanist book published during the Soviet Era named *Dukhovni Pesni* (300

---

but I am not sure if there are church members in any of the other microstates. Moldova uses the Romanian and Russian hymnals. Montenegro uses the Serbian hymnals. Portugal uses the Brazilian hymnals. Spain uses the Latin American hymnals. Switzerland uses German hymnals (and now probably the Austrian as well). The small group of believers in Turkey has no Turkish hymnal. No information was found yet on possible Adventist hymnals in Azerbaijan, Georgia, or Ukraine.

5    *Spaselov nran* (N.p.: N.p., n.d).

6    *Spaselov nran* (N.p.: N.p., 2017).

7    *Singt unserm Gott* (Vienna: TOP LIFE Wegweiser-Verlag, 2014).

8    Gruber (1787–1863): #135 "Stille Nacht"; Hoppe (1926–): #511 "Der du neues Leben mir schufst", #42 "Lobet den Herrn, alle Heiden!"; Schubert (1797–1828): #575 "Wohin soll ich mich wenden", #576 "'Ehre, Ehre sei Gott in der Höhe'", #577 "Noch lag die Schöpfung formlos da", #578 "Du gabts, o Herr, mir Sein und Leben", #579 "Heilig, heilig, heilig", #580 "Betrachtend deine Huld und Güte", #581 "Mein Heiland, Herr und Meister", #582 "Herr, du hast mein Flehn vernommen", #583 "Anbetend deine Macht und Größe".

9    Brantner (1946–2017): #267 "Erscheinen meines Gottes Wege", #461 "Sag alles Jesus"; Pickhardt (1970–): #337 "Ob Daniel, David, Mose", #338 "Graue Wälle, Nebelfelder"; Scharf (1927–2008): #222 "Allmächtiger, ewiger Gott", #519 "Wir haben nichts verdienet".

hymns).[10] It seems to be a photo-copy collection of hymns from German and English-speaking hymnals. In the twenty-first century, several youth songbooks have been published: *Khvalete Gospoda* (106 hymns) in 2000[11], *Pesni 2002* (32 hymns) in 2002,[12] *Pesni 2004* (100 hymns) in 2004,[13] and *Ela da peem s radost* (75 hymns) in 2009.[14] *Khvalete* has 4 Bulgarian tunes (4%), *Pesni 2004* has 16 (16%), and *Ela da peem* 23 (31%), and of these 43 tunes all but two were written by Adventists. This is a high ratio, but of course cannot be put into perspective without a hymnal. The non-Adventist composers are Boyan Kushev (1) and M. Marinova (1),[15] and the Adventist ones are: Julia Hinova (1), Ivo Hristov (1), Tanya Ivanova and Veronika Kartalova (11), Donka Mavrodieva (1), Alexandur Milev and Krasimir Lazarov (6), Krasimira Naydenova (1), Nichka Nedeva (3), Plamen Paskalev (7), Ivaylo Petrov (2), Peter Stoilov (4), Kristian Tonchev (1), Kaloyan Voshtanski (1), Borislau Yordanov (1), and Mitko Zhekov (1).[16]

## Croatia and Serbia

In 1917, Albin Močnik published *Pjesmarica* and *Pesmarica*, the first Adventist hymnal in Croatia and Serbia.[17] It was most likely published in both languages. It went through several editions,[18] but it is hard to know how many. There was not

---

10   *Dukhovni pesni* (N.p.: N.p., n.d.).

11   *Khvalete Gospoda* (Sofia: Bulgarian Union of the Seventh-day Adventist Church, 2000).

12   *Pesni 2002* (Sofia: Bulgarian Union of the Seventh-day Adventist Church, 2002).

13   *Pesni 2004* (Sofia: Bulgarian Union of the Seventh-day Adventist Church, 2004).

14   Ела да пеем с радост: библейски седмици [*Ela da peem s radost: Bibleyski sedmitsi*] (Sofia: Bulgarian Union of the Seventh-day Adventist Church, 2009). The authors are listed on the last page [80].

15   Kushev: "Dano da cum tam", HG, 11; Marinova: P #10 "Bozhij Sin".

16   Hinova: GH 16 "Zavinagi c Teb"; Hristov: P #61 "Ochakvane"; Ivanova & Kartalova: E #23 "Dnes i sega", E #28 "Ima iyakoy tuk do teb", E #36 "Molya se", E #38 "Moyat priyatel", E #40 "Nashata zvezda—Isus", E #49 "Praznik e denyat s teb", E #50 "Preklanyam se pred teb", E #65 "Toy nikoga ne spi", E #67 "Utre kbsno shtde", E #9 "Vbdi do men", E #11 "Vseki den"; Mavrodieva: E #7 "Blazheni sme"; Milev & Lazarov: E #35 "Mozhe li nyakoy na tozi svyat", E #47 "Placha za tebe, Erusalim", E #43 "Posht, svetyat zvezdi", E #52 "Priemi me, Gospodi", E #73 "Shte ti se predam", E #64 "Tiho pak potuvash"; Naydenova: P #57 "O, Gospodi"; Nedeva: E #71 "Chuden spasitel imam", E #62 "Tatko nebesen, vuv gryah az zhiveya", E #12 "Vuv hrama tvoy s nadezhda idram"; Paskalev: P #29 "Ela i ti"; GH 82 "Bludniyat cin", P #38 "Imam edna svetla mechta", P #36 "Izpoved", P #60 "Otvori o chi", P #75 "Pozhden den", GH 89 "Vyara, Nadezhda, Liubov"; Petrov: P #2 "Ako mozhesh vse pak da obichash", P #8 "Bozhe moyta dusha"; Stoilov: P #20 "Gospodi sbrtseto mi", P #53 "Iyama da se boish", P #45 "Na Boga az razchitam", P #67 "Poslushay vika mi"; Tonchev: P #84 "Slava na Isusa"; Voshtanski: E #44 "Oda za Postoyniya"; Yordanov: P #74 "Razkriy si ti sbrtseto"; Zhekov: E #24 "Dokosni me".

17   *Pjesmarica* (1917); *Pesmarica* (1917).

18   The only one I found was *Pjesmarica za pobudu i unapređenje kršćanskog života*, 3rd rev. ed. (Novi sad, 1930).

one official and regular hymnal until 1980. The latest edition of the same-titled hymnals I found was the Serbian *Pesmarica* from 1971 (325 texts).[19] In 1980, Dragutin Slankamenac published the first hymnal with notes, *Kršćanske himne* in Croatian and in Serbian (both 490 hymns).[20] It does not contain any Croatian or Serbian tunes.

## Czech Republic and Slovakia

I do not have information about the earliest hymnals from the Czech Republic and Slovakia.[21] There was one hymnal published in Czechoslovakia in 1951 (of which I do not have a copy).[22] In 1968 *Písně sionské* was published (551 hymns).[23] After the division of the two countries, an identical hymnal was published in Czech and Slovak in 2014: *Zpívejme Hospodinu*[24] and *Spievajme Hospodinovi*[25] (400 hymns). The latest hymnals (*Zpívejme / Spievajme*) contain three Czech tunes (<1%). In addition to a Bohemian song (1), the composers are V. Mladý (1) and V. Friml (1).[26]

## Denmark

At least nine Danish Adventist hymnals have been published. The pioneering missionary to Denmark, John G. Matteson, published *Bibelske Psalmer og Lovsange* ('Biblical Psalms and Hymns') in 1868 while he was in the United States.[27] A couple of years later he published an extended version.[28] In 1877, the same year that Matteson arrived in Denmark, he published *Bibelske Psalmer og Lovsange* (71 hymns).[29] In 1881 he published a second edition (353 texts, 110 tunes) which was

19   *Pesmarica: Adventističke crkve za upotrebu pri bogosluženju* (Belgrad: Preporod, 1971).

20   *Kršćanske himne* (N.p.: Yugoslavian Bible Conference, [1980]); *Hrišćanske himne: Nadahnute biblijskim tekstovima* (Belgrade: Preporod, [1980]). The second edition was unchanged. See *Kršćanske himne*, 2nd ed. (Zagreb: Znaci vremena, 1995).

21   There is a website with several more hymnals that I did not have time to incorporate into this article. "Zpěvníky—Noty, Texty, Akordy používající se ve sborech Církev adventistů s.d.," accessed August 5, 2018, www.zpevniky.casd.cz.

22   *Písně sionské* (1968), introduction.

23   *Písně sionské* (1968).

24   *Zpívejme Hospodinu: Sbírka duchovních písní*, 3rd ed. (Prague: The Seventh-day Adventist Church, 2014).

25   *Spievajme Hospodinovi: Zbierka duchovných piesní* (Dotlač, 1995).

26   Bohemian melody: #391 "Hospodin nás viedol sám"; Friml: #386 "Zas vôkol radosť vládne"; Madý: #379 "Pán Boh sa ka ždému do srdca díva"; see Spievajme Hospodinovi, 491.

27   *Bibelske Psalmer og Lovsange*, ed. John G. Matteson (1868).

28   [*Bibelske Psalmer og Lovsange* (?)], ed. John G. Matteson (1870).

29   *Bibelske Salmer og Lovsange til Aandelig Opbyggelse*, ed. John G. Matteson, 1st ed. (Weile: W. Hertz's Bogtrykkeri, 1877); *Salmer og Sanger*, 7.

printed in Battle Creek, Michigan.[30] A third edition appeared in 1891.[31] In 1896, Matteson prepared his last hymnal (840 hymns), which was published some months after his death.[32] Besides writing 122 of the hymns himself and translating "a large number", Matteson composed two of the tunes. The next hymnal was published after Matteson's day, in 1913.[33] In 1924 *Salmer og Lovsange* (834 hymns) were published,[34] and *Salmebog* (508 hymns) was published in 1960.[35]

The most recent hymnal is *Salmebogen* (633 hymns) from 2007.[36] It has 196 Danish tunes (31%), 12 (2%) of which are composed by Adventist composers. The composers are Thorvald Aagaard (2), Georg Bacher (1), Carl Christian Nicolaj Balle (3), Anne Barfoed (3), Christian Barnekow (10), Johannes Beck (1), Andreas Peter Berggreen (17), Valdemar (Walter) Bjerborg (1), Klaus Brinch (3), Christian Bull (1), A. C. Christensen (2), Bernhard Christensen (3), Hans Dammeyer (1), Danish melodies (6), Willy Egmose (5), Arne Elkrog (1), Jens Laursøn Emborg (1), Lasse Toft Eriksen (1), Johanne Fenger (1), Werner Fischer-Nielsen (1), *Forsamlingsmelodi* (1), Kaare Gade (2), Niels Wilhelm Gade (6), Johan Christian Gebauer (1), Joseph Glæser (2), P. Nedergaard Hansen (2), Emil (Wilhelm Emilius Zinn) Hartmann (2), Johan Peter Emelius Hartmann (15), Caspar Christian Hoffmann (2), Hans Holm (4), Bjarne Haahr (2), Ole Jacobsen (1), Knud Jeppesen (4), Hans Anker Jørgensen (1), Erik Kobbelgaard (1), Peter Casper Krossing (1), Erling Kusk (1), Thomas Linnemann Laub (13), Erling Lindgren (2), Eilert Lindorff-Larsen (1), Holger Lissner (2), Jacob Lorentzen (1), Lasse Lunderskov (2), Axel Madsen (2), Niels Kristian Madsen-Stensgaard (1), Jørgen Henrik Malling (1), Finn Mathiassen (2), Jacob Gerhard Meideil (1), Carl Mortensen (1), Otto Mortensen (1), Peter Møller (3), Johan Henrik Nebelong (3), Johannes Konstantin Neergaard (1), Axel Nielsen (1), Carl Nielsen (7), Lars Nielsen (1), Heinrich von (Bendix Conrad Heinrich Andersen von) Nutzhorn (1), Cora Petronella Nyegaard (1), Asger Pedersen (1), Mogens Helmer Petersen (1), Oluf Ring (7), Ulla Ring (1), Henrik Rung (8), Peter Sand (1), Ole Schmidt (4), Johann Abraham Peter Schulz (3), Erik Sommer (7), Lars Sømod (1), Hans Thomisssøn (1), Henning Wellejus (1), Merete Wendler (4), Christoph Ernst

30  *Bibelske Salmer og Lovsange med firstemmige Melodier til aandelig Opbyggelse*, ed. John G. Matteson, 2nd ed. (Battle Creek, MI: Seventh-day Adventist Publishing and Printing Assocation, 1881).

31  *Bibelske Salmer og Lovsange til Opbyggelse*, ed. John G. Matteson, 3rd ed. (Kristiania: Den skandinaviske Forlags- og Trykkeriforening, 1891).

32  *Bibelske Psalmer og Lovsange. En Samling af Religiøse Sange med firstemmige Melodier til Aandelig Opbyggelse*, ed. John G. Matteson (Battle Creek, MI; London; Toronto; Kristiania: Den Internationale Missionsforening, 1896).

33  Preben Jalving told me that a hymnal had been published that year, but he had neither a copy nor more information about it.

34  *En Samling Salmer og Lovsange til Aandelig Opbyggelse* (Kristiania: Skandinavisk Bogforlag, 1924).

35  *Salmebog for syvende dags adventistmenighederne i Danmark* (Dansk Bogforlag, 1960).

36  *Salmebogen. Syvende Dags Adventisten* (Nærum: Dansk Bogforlag, 2007).

Friedrich Weyse (18), August Winding (8), and Hardenack Otto Conrad Zinck (6).[37] The Adventist composers are Kenneth Birch (1), Timon Müller (3), Svend-Erik Pedersen (1), and Carsten Thomsen (7).[38]

## Estonia

The first published Estonian Adventist hymnal I am aware of is two editions of *Siioni laulud*, published in 1913 and 1928.[39] Around the close of the Soviet era, *Vaimulikke laule* was published (1988 and 1994; 506 texts and then 536 texts).[40] The accompaniment book *Kogutud viisid* (1988; 360 tunes)[41] was prepared for the first edition. Neither *Vaimulikke* nor *Kogutud* lists poets or composers.[42]

## The Faroe Islands

The first and so far only Faroese hymnal is *Sálmabók* (376 texts) from 1963.[43] It has three Faroese tunes (1%): one by Jógvan Waagstein (1), and two folk melodies (2).[44]

## Finland

The first Finnish Adventist hymnal was perhaps *Siionin lauluja* (272 texts), published in 1903.[45] Then there were four editions of *Valikoima Siionin lauluja*, published in 1919 (90 texts), 1923 (187 texts), 1928 (302 texts), and 1942 (317

---

37  Due to the number of tunes, they will not be listed, and the reader is referred to the hymnal itself.

38  Birch (1939–): #37 "Gud vil jeg ære"; Müller: #474 "En hjertesag, o Jesus Krist", #475 "Hverdagslivet falder", #558 "Når aftenfreden sænker sig"; S.-.E. Pedersen: #324 "O, tænk hvilken glæde"; Thomsen: #218 "Fremad det går med Jesus", #122 "Gennem rummets tavse nat", #158 "Gud, jeg ser dig komme", #340 "Hvor længe skal hjerterne håbe", #585 "Kolde østenvinde stryger", #186 "Syv bønner har Herren lært os", #267 "Vær blandt os til stede".

39  *Sioni laulud* (Hamburg: Internationali Traktadiselts, 1913); *Siioni laulud*, 2nd ed. (Tallin: SPAdv Eesti Liit, 1928).

40  *Vaimulikke laule*, 1st ed. (1988); *Vaimulikke laule*, 2nd ed. (N.p.: SP Adventistide Eesti Liit, 1994).

41  *Kogutud viisid*. 1988. It was prepared and distributed but never published officially.

42  *Vaimulikke* does cross-reference the texts with other hymnals (see abbreviations above texts, listed on p. 271), but this is often a dead-end, since it often references *Kogutud*, which in turn has no author information.

43  *Sálmabók Føroya sjeynda dags adventista* (Tórshavn, 1963). The hymnal has only the texts, but references all of them to other hymnals. See abbreviations, *Sálmabók*, [469].

44  Folk melodies: #21 "Harra Gud, títt dýra navn og æra", #28 "Var Gud ei við okkum hesa tíð"; Waagstein (1879–1949): #324 "Tíðin rennur sum streymur í á". Though the hymnal does not have notes, which tunes to use from other hymnals is indicated by abbreviations above each text. The abbreviation are listed on p. 469.

45  *Siionin lauluja* (Helsinki: Aikain Vartija, 1903).

texts).[46] The first hymnal with notes was *Adventti-lauluja* (663 hymns), which was published in 1959. [47] In 2001 a multi-denominational hymnal committee – including the Seventh-day Adventist Church – published *Seurakunta laulaa* (351 hymns).[48]

In 2007 the committee published *Församlingen sjunger* (168 hymns) in Swedish, for the Swedish-speaking community in Finland.[49] *Seurakunta* has 129 Finnish tunes (37%!), and 2 of them (<1%) are by Adventists. *Församlingen* has 13 (8%) Finnish tunes. The tunes are by the following composers: Artto Tapani Aittala (1), Wiljam Ensio Aittala (1), Hjalmar Braxén (1), folk melodies (24), Kreeta Haapasalo (1), Pirkko Halonen (1), Pietari (Pekka) Juhani Hannikainen (5), Toivo Ilmari Hannikainen (1), Martti Mikael Hela (1), Alfred Hiilimies (1), Aimo Olavi Huttunen (2), Tuomo Huuhtanen (1), Ruth Jaarla (1), Samuel Jalkanen (2), Konsta Viljami Jylhä (1), Yrjö Karanko (4), Asko Kariluoto (1), Josefiina (Iina) Karttunen (4), Ilta Eveliina Koskimies (1), Ilmari Henrik Reinhold Krohn (1), Ahti Johannes Kuorikoski (1), Toivo Timoteus Kuula (1), Ilkka Taneli Kuusisto (2), Taneli Kuusisto (1), Petri Laaksonen (1), Rudolf Theodor Lagi (3), Lilli Leinberg (1), Johan Primus Leppänen (1), Sofie Lithenius (1), Jaakko Löytty (1), Armas Toivo Valdemar Maasalo (3), Frans Oskar Merikanto (1), Karl Johan Moring (1), Tuomo Nikkola (3), Antti Markus Nissilä (2), Mikko Tapanti Nuutinen (1), Berndt Mikael Nyberg (4), Huugo Henrik Nyberg (1), Mariitta Anneli Palviainen (1), Teuvo Edvard Pärlesten (1), Aino Pekkarinen (1), Elin Aina Sofia von Pfaler (1), Mikko Pietarinen (1), Mika Piiparinen (5), Jouko Piitulainen (1), Kaarina Puljujärvi (1), Heikki William Pöyhtäri (1), Aulis Raitala (1), Tyyne Salokannel (1), Jean Sibelius (1), Emil Siippanen (1), Pekka Simojoki (5), Aatto Soinne (1), Niilo Tuomenoksa (1), Lars Emil Törnwall (1), Uimonen Jorma (1), Eeva Vaija (1), Aarne Armas Vanhakangas (10), Maija-Liisa Kaarina Vättö (2), Väinö Viikilä (1), Väinö Viitasalo (1), Paavo Virtanen (2), and Kaarlo Voipio (1).[50] Adventist composers are Hannu Juhani Huhtala (1) and Vilho Armas Makkonen (1).[51]

---

46   *Valikoima Siionin lauluja*, 1ˢᵗ ed. (Helsinki: Aikain Varija, 1919); *Valikoima Siionin lauluja*, 2ⁿᵈ ed. (Hämeenlinna: Aikain Varija, 1923); *Valikoima Siionin lauluja*, 3ʳᵈ ed. (Hämeenlinna: Aikain Varija, 1928); *Valikoima Siionin lauluja*, 4ᵗʰ ed. (Hämeenlinna: Aikain Varija, 1942). There was also another edition, unchanged from the last one, in 1948: *Valikoima Siionin lauluja* (Hämeenlinna: Kirjatoimi, 1948).
47   *Adventti-lauluja* (Helsinki: Kirjatoimi, 1959).
48   *Seurakunta laulaa* (Jyväskylä: Kirjatoimi, 2001).
49   *Församlingen sjunger* (Vasa: The Swedish Seventh-day Adventist Church in Finland, 2007).
50   Due to the number of tunes, they will not be listed, and the reader is referred to the hymnal itself.
51   Huhtala (1953–): #434 "Kiitos, Herra, että annoit"; Makkonen (1923–1999): #522 "Näen maallisten usvain takaa".

## France

The supposedly first French hymnal, *Hymnes et Louanges* (654 hymns), was published in 1933.[52] The next hymnal, *Donnez-Lui Gloire* (520 hymns) was published in 2007.[53] Joelle Gouel, a French Adventist musician, self-published the hymnal *Les chants du pèlerin* in 2001 (206 hymns).[54] That is the only instance in Europe I am aware of when a church member published an entire hymnal on their own.

## Germany

Germany, Austria, and Switzerland traditionally used a common hymnal. The first hymnal, *Zionslieder*, went through at least two editions in the early twentieth century, with its first publication probably appearing in the late 19th century. In 1908 (the second printing) the hymnal contained 1050 hymns.[55] In 1935 (the tenth printing) a new edition had appeared with 656 hymns.[56] The next hymnals I have information about are *Wir loben Gott* (602 hymns) from 1998,[57] *Leben aus der Quelle* (306 hymns) from 2007[58] and *glauben hoffen singen* (694 hymns) from 2015.[59] In addition, the Seventh Day Adventist Reform Movement published a German edition of its hymnal, *Internationales Gesangbuch* (750 hymns)[60] and their own edition of *Zions-lieder* in 2010 (705 hymns).[61] *Glauben hoffen singen* has ca. 440 German tunes (63%!),[62] and at least 22 (3%) of them are composed by Adventists. The Adventist composers are Harry Buschbeck (1), Erhardt Dan (1), Horst Gehann (5), Oliver Haist (1), Jürgen Hartmann (1), Johannes Kahle (2),

---

52  *Hymnes et Louanges: Recueil de cantiques à l'usage des Églises adventistes de langue française* (1933; Dammarie-les-Lys: Éditions Vie et Santé, 2001).

53  *Donnez-Lui Gloire: Recueil de Cantiques* (Dammarie-les-Lys: Éditions Vie et Santé, 2007).

54  *Les chants du pèlerin* (N.p.: Joelle Gouel, 2001).

55  *Zions-Lieder zum Gebrauch im Hause Gottes und im Heim, Sowie zur allgemeinen Erbauung* (Hamburg: Internationale Traktatgesellschaft, 1908). The hymn number stayed the same until at least the eighth printing.

56  *Zions-Lieder zur Erbauung für Gemeinde und Heim* (Hamburg: Advent-Verlag, 1935).

57  *Wir loben Gott: Geistliche Lieder für Gemeinde und Heim.* Lüneburg: Advent-Verlag, 1998.

58  *Leben aus der Quelle: Lieder der Hoffnung* (Lüneburg: Advent-Verlag, 2007).

59  *Glauben hoffen singen: Liederbuch der Freikirche der Siebenten-Tags Adventisten* (Lüneburg: Advent-Verlag, 2015).

60  *Internationales Gesangbuch*, 2nd ed. (Downey, CA: International Missionary Society, 2005); 4th ed. (Downey, CA: International Missionary Society, 2016).

61  *Zions-Lieder: Zum Gebrauch beim öffentlichen und Haus-Gottesdienst sowie zur allgemeinen Erbauung* (Schwäbisch Gmünd: Wegbereiter Verlag, 2010).

62  Since this is the majority of the tunes, they will not be listed here.

Matthias Kramp (1), Gunther Lüpke (1), Debora Preuß (1), Günter Preuß (5), Hans-Otto Reling (1), and Wilfried Scheel (2).[63]

## Greece

The only Adventist hymnal I have found from Greece is *Psallete eis ton Kyrio* (355 texts) from 1982.[64] The musician index lists only ca. 200 of the tunes, none by a Greek composer.[65]

## Hungary

It seems that the several versions of *Üdv-és Adventi énekek* were the earliest Adventist hymnals published in Hungary, starting in the early twentieth century.[66] The most recent hymnal, *Hitünk énekei* (477 hymns), was published in 2002.[67] It has 25 Hungarian tunes (5%), by the composers Farkas Kálmán (1) and Balázs Székel (2), and published in the cities Kolozsvár (Cluj-Napoca) (21) and Pozsony (Bratislava) (1).[68]

---

63  Buschbeck (1942–): #626 "Die Früchte sind herangereift"; Dan (1963–): # "Der Tag ist nun vergangen"; Gehann (1928–): #638 "Der du die Zeit in Händen hast", #318 "Der Herr bricht ein um Mitternacht", #41 "Gloria Patri", #625 "Kommt, singt ein Lied vom Segen", #145 "Wir warten, Herr, das du dein Wort"; Haist (1971–): #381 "Schritt für Schritt gemeinsam nach vorne"; Hartmann (1961–): "Die ganze Welt ist voll Gesang"; Kahle (1931–): #452 "Dein bin ich, Gott", #157 "Halt im Gedächtnis Jesus Christ"; Kramp (1965–): #393 "Durch Gottes gnade bin ich"; Lüpke (1906–1986): #310 "Bald kommt Jesus Christus wieder"; D. Preuß (1991–): #139 "Mit vollen Herzen stehen wir vor dir"; G. Preuß (1953–): #117 "Ein Segen liegt verborgen", #118 "Herr Jesus, Herr des Sabbattags", #322 "Unterwegs nach Hause", #352 "Wie Gott mich haben möchte", #515 "Wenn Terror diese Welt zerreißt"; Reling (1956–): #105 "Shabbat Shalom"; Scheel (1960–): #514 "In der Mitte der Nacht liegt der Anfang eines neuen Tags", #297 "Komm zu uns, du Kraft des neuen Lebens".

64  *Psallete eis ton Kyrio* (Athens: MANNA, 1982).

65  Ibid., 399–400.

66  *Üdv-és Adventiénekek* (Budapest).

67  *Hitünk énekei: Gyülekezeti énekeskönyv* (Budapest: The Seventh-day Adventist Church, 2002).

68  Kálmán (1838–1906): #179 "Ím, nagy Isten"; Kolozsvár: #365 (1744) "A nap immár felviradván", #3 (1744) "Adj, Úr Isten", #370 (1744) "Adjunk hálát a nagy Úr Istennek", #245 (1744) "Akik bíznak az Úr Istenben", #174 (1744) "Atya Úr Isten", #238 (1555) "Emlékezzél mi történék", #176 (1744) "Felséges Isten", #302 (1744) "Fohászkodom hozzád", #178 (1744) "Hallgass meg minket, Úr Isten", #286 (1744) "Hallgass meg minket, nagy Úr Isten", #373 (1744) "Jézus Krisztus, szentek reménye", #341 (1744) "Jézus Krisztus, szép fényes hajnal", #158 (1744) "Jővel Szentlélek Úr Isten", #263 (1744) "Kegyelmes Isten", #324 (1907) "Megáll az Istennek igéje", #109 (1744) "Menynyei Ige", #166 (1744) "Ne szállj perbe énvelem", #363 (1837) "Örülj, szívem", #322 (1811) "Szűzkölködünk nagy mértékben", #100 (1744) "Ú világosság jelenék", Pozsony: #171 (18th century)

## Iceland

The first and so far only Icelandic hymnal was *Sálmar og lofsöngvar* (471[69] hymns), published in 1995.[70] It contains 24 Icelandic tunes (5%), 11 of which are written by Adventists (3%). Besides five folk melodies (5) the composers are Guðrún Böðvarsdóttir (1), Páll Ísólfsson (1), Tómas Jónsson (1), Sigvaldi Kaldalóns (3), Þorkell Sigurbjörnsson (1), and Sveinbjörn Sveinbjörnsson (1).[71] The Adventist composers are Salómon Heiðar (7), Árni Hólm (2), and Jón Hjörleifur Jónsson (2).[72]

## Italy

The earliest Italian Adventist hymnal that I found is *Cantate all' Eterno*. The editions or printings I am aware of date from 1933 (1st ed.?),[73] 1951 or 1956 (2nd ed.?; 404 hymns),[74] 1985 (3rd ed.),[75] and 1989 (4th ed.).[76] The most recent hymnal is *Canti di lode* (550 hymns), published in 2003.[77] *Canti di lode* has 42 Italian tunes (8%), thereof three composed by Adventists (0.5%). The composers are B.

---

"Elt'evedtem, mint juh"; Székel: #72 "Hálaadásunkban rólad", #309 "Semmit ne bánkódjál".

69  The numbered hymns are 462 + 3 (457b–d) + 6 (additional 1a–6a) = 471.

70  *Sálmar og lofsöngvar* (Reykjavík: Frækornið, 1995).

71  Böðvarsdóttir (1902–1936): #124 "Ég kveiki' á kertum mínum"; folk melodies: #114 "Ég gleðst af því ég Guðsson á", #443 "Gefðu að móðurmálið mitt", #194 "Hún er mér kær", #220 "Í dag er dýrmæt tíð", #330 "Víst ertu, Jesús, kóngur klár"; #5 Ísólfsson (1893–1974): "Lof sé þér, lífsins herra"; Jónsson: #315 "Ó Faðir, gjör mig lítið ljós"; Kaldalóns (1881–1946): #94 "Kirkjan ómar öll", #104 "Nóttin var sú ágæt ein", #444 "Ísland ögrum skorið"; Sigurbjörnsson (1938–2013): #423 "Heyr, himnasmiður"; Sveinbjörnsson (1847–1927): #445 "Ó Guð vors lands".

72  Heiðar (1889–1957): #345 "Ég vil þér fús og feginn hlýða", #420 "Hvöt", #247 "Í ljóssins veldi", #101 "Jólanótt", #310 "Kæri faðir, kenndu mér að biðja", #254 "Ó blessuð stund", #394 "Vér syngjum oft"; Hólm: #346 "Helgaðu Jesú þitt líf", #81 "Tuttugasti og þriðji Davíðssálmur"; #115 Jónsson (1923–): #155 "Guð með oss", #155 "Sjá, eg kem skjótt".

73  *Cantate all' Eterno: Raccolta d'inni e salmi cristiani ad uso delle chiese cristiane avventiste di lingua italiana* (Florence: L'Araldo della Verità, 1933); see The European Library, "Cantate all' Eterno", accessed September 20, 2018, http://www.theeuropeanlibrary.org/tel4/record/resolve?query=%22cantate+all%27eterno%22&provider=P02002&collection=a0086r&identifier=CUB0152872.

74  *Cantate all' Eterno: Raccolta d'inni e salmi cristiani ad uso delle chiese cristiane avventiste di lingua italiana* (Florence: L'Araldo della Verità, [1951 or 1956]).

75  *Cantate all' Eterno: Raccolta d'inni e salmi cristiani ad uso delle chiese cristiane avventiste di lingua italiana*, 3rd ed. (Impruneta [Fl]: AdV, 1985).

76  *Cantate all' Eterno: Raccolta d'inni e salmi cristiani ad uso delle chiese cristiane avventiste di lingua italiana*, 4th ed. (Falciani, Impruneta: AdV, 1989).

77  *Canti di lode: Raccolta di inni cristiani ad uso delle Comunità avventiste del 7° giorno* (Florence: AdV, 2003).

Ancira (1), Del Bene (1), Benemani (1), U. Caporali (2), G. Cento (1), F. Festa (1), folk melodies (3), G. Gasperini (1), G. Gastoldi (1), C. Giampaglia (5), S. Guidetti (1), G. L. Lippolis (8), L. D. de Macchi (1), A. Niccolini (1), Giovanni Pierluigi da Palestrina (1), S. Ragghianti (1), N. G. Rosa (1), V. Sommani (6), E. Taglialatela (1), and F. M. A. Venua (1).[78] Adventist composers are E. Buonfiglio (1) and Ruben Grieco (2).[79]

## Latvia

The only Adventist Latvian hymnal I found is *Jaunās kokļu skaņas* (370 hymns), published in 1992.[80] It lists neither poets nor composers.

## Lithuania

The first Adventist Lithuanian hymnal I have information on is *Kanklių aidai* (133 texts), which was published in 1995.[81] In 2011, *Edeno aidai* (276[82] hymns) was published.[83] It has 14 Lithuanian tunes (5%), 10 of which were written by Adventists (4%). The non-Adventist composer is Laima Sabaliauskaitė (4),[84] and the Adventist ones are Inga Ardževanidze (1), Vigilija Gasevičienė-Černiauskienė

---

78  Ancira: #495 "Figli del gran Re"; Del Bene: #226 "Innalzate il vessil della croce"; Benemani: #303 "Benignamente guardami"; Caporali: #508 "Insieme", #511 "La scelta"; Cento: #516 "E correremo insieme"; Festa: #300 "Gesù, perdonami"; folk melodies: #7 "A te, Signor, s'innalzino", #370 "Pellegrino in questa terra", #181 "Scendi tu nel nostro petto"; Gasperini: #355 "O Creatore, Padre d'amore"; Gastoldi: #122 "Notte stellate, notte beata"; Giampaglia: #286 "È così dolce il nome tuo"; #466 "Erano novantanove"; #451 "O Gesù, la mia luce sei sol tu"; #462 "Ho visto che nel mondo"; #465 "V'è un Edenne"; Guidetti: #277 "Meco dimora, o Dio consolatore"; Lippolis: #228 "Ambasciator di Dio", #442 "Cristo è il pane", #48 "O Cristo, fa' ch'io t'ami ognor di più", #198 "O Gesù, mio buon pastore", #234 "L'ombra della sera", #354 "O Padre, Dio Santo", #331 "Signor che col tuo sangue", #310 "Signor, la voce tua"; de Macchi: #184 "Vieni le grazie a spargere"; Niccolini: #321 "Verso te la voce alziamo"; Palestrina (c. 1525–1594): #337 "Padre, dona pace vera"; Ragghianti: #173 "Lassù su quell monte"; Rosa: #412 "Al Re dei secoli"; Sommani: #450 "Come la cerva anela" #461 "Ecco l'Agnello di Dio", #455 "Quando l'Eterno", #460 "Sii Fedele fino alla morte", #46 "Una lampada al nostro piede", #458 "Vestiti di vesti bianche"; Taglialatela: #211 "Una schiera di credenti"; Venua: #240 "Tu sei del sabato, Gesù, Signor".
79  Buonfiglio: #496 "Forza giovani"; Grieco: #471 "Mille ragioni per credere", #530 "Voglio esserci anch'io".
80  *Jaunās kokļu skaņas: Septītās dienas Adventistu draudzes kopējās dziesmas* (Riga, 1992).
81  *Kanklių aidai: Davsinių giesmių rinkinélis* (1995).
82  238 + 38 (27A, 36A, 38A, 39A, 52A, 61A, 66A, 68A, 70A, 77A, 82A, 84A, 96A, 101A, 105A, 110A, 112A, 115A, 121A, 122A, 129A, 132A, 146A, 148A, 160A, 177A, 185A, 186A, 196A, 200A, 206A, 207A, 208A, 209A, 212A, 219A, 224A, 236A) = 276.
83  *Edeno aidai: Giesmynas* (Amžinoji uola, 2011).
84  Sabaliauskaitė: #70A "Aleliuja!", #207A "Dievas ruošia tau valtelę", #105A "Koks šventas, šventas", #196A "Laimingas, kuris mato kito skausmą".

(1), A. Gončarov (1), Loreta Povilaitienė (1), Remigijus Rabikauskas (2), Žydrūnas Serepinas (1), and Danutė Sinkevičienė (4).[85]

## Macedonia

The oldest Macedonian hymnal I found information about is *Pesnarka*,[86] which is now several decades old (340 hymns). All the hymns were selected from a Serbian hymnal. In 2011 *Gilja e Devleske* (201 hymns), a Romani hymnal, was published.[87] *Gilja* contains 18 tunes (9%) composed by Romani Adventists.[88]

## The Netherlands

The first Dutch hymnal I have information about is *Gezangen Zions*, published in 1936,[89] with a revised edition in 1949.[90] In 1982 *Liedboek voor de Adventkerk* (150 psalms and 271 hymns) was published.[91] It lists neither poets nor composers.

## Norway

The two most recent[92] Norwegian Adventist hymnals are *Salmer og lovsange* (610 hymns), published in 1954, and *Salmer og sanger* (656 hymns), published in

85    Ardževanidze: #201 "Ačiū, Dieve, už šį rytą"; Gasevičienė-Černiauskienė: #219A "Tu palaimink mane viltimi"; Gončarov: #110 "Oišmoky mane, Jėzau, melstis"; Povilaitienė: #154 "Malonės sparnais nusileidai"; Rabikauskas: #200A "Dievas sukūrė", #203 "Tau, tėtuk, tiesiu rankytę"; Serepinas: #185A "Yra pasaulyje viena vieta"; Sinkevičienė: #202 "Dieve, Tau karštai dėkoju", #209 "Dieve, Žemėj šioj plačiojoj", #207 "Lakstom, straksim kaip žvirbliukai", #55 "Tau, Viešpatie garbė".

86    *Pesnarka* (Skopje: Znaci na vremeto, n.d.).

87    *Gilja e devleske* (Skopje: Znaci na vremeto, 2011).

88    This information is from Melita Tomovska, who spoke with a pastor who was involved in preparing the hymnal. The composers for these tunes are not mentioned in the hymnal, which only lists the melographers. The tunes are: #155 "Aven tumen savore", #157 "Devla tut molinaja akana", #186 "Dur me geljum", #151 "Kedisaljem devla sat tre čave", #169 "Ko sveto sijum sine", #189 "Maj šužo maj šužo del", #190 "Miro duho devla", #191 "Me dživdipaste tu aljan", #105 "Mre vasta posavde!", #156 "Nevo berš avilo", #154 "O devel ka avel", #152 "Roden tumare pralen", #95 "Slava tuke isuse!", #187 "Soske te mukhav ti khangiri devla", #98 "Šunen tumen romalen", #188 "Te manga men", #100 "Tri khangiri ten a bistra!", #153 "Udžaraja te ave".

89    *Gezangen Zions: Zangbundel ten gebruike bij de godsdienstoefeningen in het huis Gods en voor den huiselijken kring* ('s-Gravenhage: Internationaal advent-zendingsgenootschap, 1936).

90    *Gezangen Zions: Zangbundel ten gebruike bij de godsdienstoefeningen in het huis Gods en voor den huiselijken kring* (Den Haag: Boekenhuis "Veritas", 1949).

91    *Liedboek voor de Adventkerk: Psalmen en liederen voor de eredienst in kerk en huis uitgegeven in opdracht van het Kerkgenootschap der Zevende-dags Adventisten* (Huis ter Heide: Kerkgenootschap der Z.D.A., [1982]).

2005.[93] *Salmer og sanger* contains 184 Norwegian tunes (28%). The composers are Tore Wilhelm Aas (2), Signe Marie Aaslund (1), Kjell Aasmundrud (2), Wenche Aker (3), Martin Alfsen (1), Trond Andersen (1), Thomas Ball Barratt (2), Martha Bentsen (1), Dag Bjørnestad (1), Oscar Borg (1), Arnold Børud (1), Christian Cappelen (1), Mathias Christensen (1), Alf Fasmer Dahl (1), Sophie Dedekam (1), Gunnstein Draugedalen (4), Alfred Dulin (1), Bjørn Eidsvåg (1), Thor Fjellvang (1), folk melodies (25), Øivind Fragell (1), Thorleif Holm Glad (1), Edvard Hagerup Grieg (1), Johan H. Grimstad (2), Leonard Gunelius Gudmundsen (3), Egil Haugen (3), Else B. Haugen (1), Thore U. Haukner (1), Elevin Heede (1), Alexander Hermansen (1), Trygve Henrik Hoff (1), Bertil Hogganvik (1), Hogne Hogganvik (1), Holm W. Holmsen (1), Jan Honningdal (1), Egil Hovland (10), Laila Posti Høgli (1), Knut Johansson (1), Per Juvang (1), Bjørn Keyn (2), Eyvind Keyn (1), Åsulf Kvammen (1), Trond Kverno (5), Monica de Lange (1), Kenneth Lie (1), Ludvit Mathias Lindeman (15), Nils Lindhjem (1), Knut Løken (1), Alfred Lunde (1), Sigurd Lunde (5), Ingebjørg og Bjørn Olav Lyster (1), Einar Matre (1), Trygve Moe (1), Audun Molde (2), Hans Olav Mørk (1), Olav Nordahl (3), Rikard Nordraak (1), Knut Nystedt (3), Anfinn Øien (1), Kenneth Olsen (1), Mathias Orheim (1), Ragnar Ørstavik (1), Knut Ose (1), Klaus Østby (1), Arve Reigstad (1), Ingar Rekstad (2), Ingfrid Berge Rogstad (1), Birgitte E. Bjørnstad Sæbø (1), Aage Samuelsen (1), Kristin Solli Schøien (3), Christian Sinding (1), Reidar Skaaland (1), Trygve R. Skallerud (1), Ivar Skippervold (3), Arthur Skrede (1), Erik Sommer (1), Lars Søraas, jr. (1), Caroline Walla Sørlie (1), Oskar Stakkeland (1), Per Steenberg (2), Tor Strand (1), Mons Leidvin Takle (1), Tore Thomassen (1), Adolf Thomsen (1), Øivind E. Tønnesen (1), Per Aa. Tveit (4), Sigvald Tveit (10), Sverre Valen (1), Olav Vestre (1), Øystein Wang (2), and Kristian Wendelborg (1).[94]

## Poland

The first Adventist Polish hymnals were *Spiewnik syonski* ([1st ed.], 215 texts), published in 1912,[95] *Śpiewajcie Panu* (50 texts) from 1932,[96] *Pieśni Syońskie* ([2nd ed.], 251 texts, a few with notes) from 1933,[97] which was published in a third

92   The introduction of the 1954 refers to an older hymnal by the same name: "Salmer og lovsanger has been sold out for a long time and there has been a great need for a new church hymnal." *Salmer og lovsange* (Oslo: Norsk bokforlag, 1954), introduction. My translation.
93   *Salmer og sanger—på veien hjem* (Røyse: Norsk bokforlag, 2005).
94   Due to the number of tunes, they will not be listed, and the reader is referred to the hymnal itself.
95   *Spiewnik syonski do ogólnego zbudowania w wierze chrzescijanskiej* (Riga, 1912).
96   *Śpiewajcie Panu* (Warsaw, 1932).
97   *Pieśni Syońskie* (Warsaw, 1933).

edition in 1947 (112 hymns) [98] and a third enlarged edition in 1959 (573 hymns).[99] The next several versions gradually included more and more additional hymns: 13 texts mostly with notes in 1962, 48 hymns in 1967, 96 hymns in 1977 and 1983 (= 670 items).[100] In 1995 *Śpiewajmy panu* was published (700 hymns).[101] It may have some Polish composers.[102]

## Romania

Romania has had a long tradition of hymnals, but I am still in the process of getting a copy of all of them. The most recent one is *Imnuri Creştine* (921 hymns) from 2013.[103] Of all the Adventist hymnals from European countries, this is the most professional one. It contains detailed sourcing about each hymn.[104] *Imnuri Creştine* has 59 Romanian tunes (6%). The composers are Benoni Catană (1), Romulus Chelbegean (2), Leonid Cojocaru (4), Lucian Cristescu (7), Petru Diaconu & Ciprian Jalbă (1), Gabriel Dumitrescu (2), Vasileu Florescu (6), folk melodies (4), Cezar Geantă (10), Costică Grăjdinoiu-Ionescu (1), Paul Jelescu (1), Andrei Lucaci (1), George Natsis (1), Felician Roşca (2), Adrian Stroici (4), Andrei Tajti (1), Ştefan Tajti (1), Gabriel Uţă (7), and Gabriel Vasilescu (3).[105]

---

98  *Pieśni Syońskie*, 3rd ed. (Kraków, 1947). The previous editions counted are the hymnals from 1912 and 1933.

99  *Pieśni Syjońskie*, 3rd rev. ed. (Warsaw, 1959).

100  *Pieśni Syjońskie*, 4th ed. (Warsaw, 1962), 5th ed. (Warsaw, 1967), 6th ed. (Warsaw, 1977), 7th ed. (Warsaw, 1983).

101  *Śpiewajmy panu: Śpiewnik nutowo-tekstowy Kościoła Adwentystów Dnia Siódmego* (Warsaw: Chrześcijański Instytut Wydawniczy "Znaki Czasu", 1995). It was republished unchanged in 2008: *Śpiewajmy panu: Śpiewnik nutowo-tekstowy Kościoła Adwentystów Dnia Siódmego* (Warsaw: Chrześcijański Instytut Wydawniczy "Znaki Czasu", 2008).

102  Some of the composer names sound Polish, such as L. Czernicki, R. Dutkowski, K. Hlawiczka, W. Kadziela, T. Kiewicz, Cz. Kroczek, and K. Lubomirski. In addition to this, ca. 170 of the hymns contain no mention of composer or poet, and some of these 170 hymns may be written by Polish composers.

103  *Imnuri Creştine*, rev. ed. (N.p.: Editura viaţă şi sănătate, 2013).

104  It gives not only the poet, composer, and even arranger, but the original (or earliest known) publication information of both text and tune. It also gives the melody names. This usefulness is regrettably diminished considerably because the index is riddled with errors.

105  Catană (1955–): #434 imnul colportorului; Chelbegean (1957–): #764 "Cele trei solii"; #431 exemplul credinţei; Cojocaru: #754 "Fii credincios!", #767 "Sărbătoarea Sabatului", #762 "Se-aude un cânt", #749 "Vreau să fiu ca Tine"; Cristescu (1949–): #414/893 apă cristalină, #574/575 duh de iubire, #216 dumnezeu veşnic, #380 fapta bună, #434 imnul colportorului, #166 îndreptăţirea, #453 marea trezire; Diaconu (1960–) & Jalbă: #763 "Chemare"; Dumitrescu (1958–): #640 a ta mână, #490 revival; Florescu (1904–1974): #841 "Ce frumos şi dulce", #791 "Din vremi străbune", #875 "Eu sunt copil", #194/905 florescu, #822 "Hai, copile, vin' la Mine!", #337 sfinţirea; folk melodies: #2 aleluia, amin, #111 domnul isus hristos, #110 o, ce veste, #535 voievodeasa lupu; Geantă (1938–): #910 "Aş vrea să duc în lume pacea Ta!", #768 "Cântare de Sabat", #747 "Carte sfântă", #740 "Doamne din ceruri", #585/920 frumos e-al păcii sfânt sălaş, #654 jertfă deplină, #755

## Russia

At least two Russian Adventist hymnals have been published, *Psalmi Siona* (525 hymns) in 1927,[106] and *Gimni Nadezhdy* (385 hymns) in 1997.[107] *Gimni* contains 25 Russian tunes (6%) by the following composers: A. Arkhangelskij (1); O. Bokova (6); D. Bormnjanskij (1); D. C. Bormnjanskij (1); folk melody (1); I. Ganurova (1); V. E. Godunov (1); E. I. Godunova (1); A. Goncharov (2); V. Gumeniuk (1); N. A. Kazakov (1); N. Nikolaev (3); N. N. Pibenko (1); U. Ia. Sokolovskij (1); N. Vasiuk (1); and E. P. Zhimnikov (2).[108]

## Slovenia

In 1974, *Pesmarica* (365 texts), the first official Adventist Slovenian hymnal, was published.[109] It was mostly a translation of the texts from the Croatian and Serbian hymnal *Pjesmarica / Pesmarica*, with some additions.

---

"Legea Ta", #770 "Mama mea", #106/589/918 noapte-adâncă, #532 trei solii; Grăjdinoiu-Ionescu (1900–1994): #454 imnul tineretului advent; Jelescu: #774 "Doamne sfinte Creator"; Lucaci (1987–): #404 vindecare; Natsis: #748 "Fără de Tine"; Roșca (1953–): #675 din amurg, #39 slavă; Stroici (1965–): #427 brațele întinse, $429 iată-mă, trimite-mă, #676 tăticul meu, #528 ziua mielului bland; A. Tajti (1958–): #129 kremel; Ș. Tajti (1957–): #265 dacă...; Uța (1959–): #158 cărarea spre lumină, #185 consacrare, #732 glas de rugă, #608 înserare, #633 lumină și pace, #187 rugă, #853 "Veghetori, sunați din trâmbiți!"; Vasilescu (1936–): #670 în zori edenici, #93 păstorul cel bun, #563 țara minunată.

106 *Psalmy siona: Sbornik dukhovnykh pesnopeniy s notami* (Moscow: H. J. Löbsack—PATMOS, 1927).

107 *Gimny nadezhdy: Sbornik khristianskikh gimnov* (1997).

108 Arkhangelskij: #202: "O, vnemli, Gospodi!"; Bokova: #315 "Bozdajte slavu Gospodu liubvi"; #332 "Byshe solnyshko v nebe podnimaetsia"; #275 "Diudi Zemli, moi sestry i bratia"; #279 "Serdtsa otkrojte Slovu Vsemogushchego"; #360 "Snezhok pushistyj"; #272 "Zvuchit trekhangelskaia vest"; Bormijanskij (1752–1825): #1 "Kol slaven"; Bormijanskij: #36 "Slava, slava Bogy v vyshnikh"; folk melody: #86 "Predvechnyj Dukh, pridi!"; Ganurova: #361 "Vifleem spokojno spit"; Godunov: #380 "Pust na poroge nevedomykh dnej"; Godunova: #350 "Dish pridu k Iisusu"; Goncharov: #182 "Nauchi menia, Bozhe, molitsia"; #193 "Vsem umom Tebia, vsem pomyshlenem"; Gumeniuk: #358 "Nebo Edema"; Kazakov: #323 "Tikhij prazdnichnyj chas"; Nikolaev: #246 "Chem ia bozdam Tebe, Spasitel?"; #215 "Ia khochu, moj Spasitel, liubit"; #339 "Ia ustal—poshli pokoj"; Pibenko: #333 "Zolotye iskry"; Sokolovskij: #355 "Est na nebe strana"; Vasiuk: #351 "Dobrota"; Zhimnikov: #270 "Buriami nosimaia"; #80 "O Dukhe Bechnom i Sviatom".

109 *Pesmarica: Za uporabo pri Božji službi* (Celje: The Seventh-day Adventist Church, 1974). It was later published unchanged: *Pesmarica: Za uporabo pri Božji službi* (Ljubljana: The Seventh-day Adventist Church, 1986).

## Spain

Spain uses the Latin American hymnals. But in 2013 the Church in Spain began publishing *bienvenidosa adorar*, booklets towards a new hymnal (as of now, two issues of 20 and 10 hymns respectively).[110] So far 27 of the tunes (90%) are by Spanish Adventists. The composers are Joel C. Barrios (4), Denis Boidi (2), Martín Borgna (3), Álvaro Calvo Ramón (5), María José Jimeno García (1), Esther Gómez (1), Romina Gómez & Luis Viveros (1), Angelita Gutiérrez & Ana Grané (1), Denny Luz (1), Esther Quiles Peiró (1), Adriana Perera Larrarte (5), Jader Dornelles Santos (1), Luis David Solano Vílchez (1).[111]

## Sweden

The first Swedish hymnal was *Sions sånger* and went through several editions: 1889 (1st ed.),[112] 1927 (3rd ed.; 746 texts),[113] 1948 (3rd rev. ed.; 700 texts),[114] and an undated fourth edition (700 texts).[115] In 1987 the interdenominational Free Church Hymn Committee (Frikyrkliga psalmkommittén), which included the Adventist Church, published *Psalmer och sånger* (784 hymns).[116] A newer revised edition has been published since then.

The 1987 edition has 346 Swedish tunes (44%!). These are by Carl-Bertil Agnestig (3), David Ahlberg (1), Verner Ahlberg (1), Waldemar Åhlén (3), Oscar

---

110 *Bienvenidosa adorar 01* (N.p.: The Seventh-day Adventist Church, 2013); *Bienvenidosa adorar 02* (N.p.: The Seventh-day Adventist Church, 2014).

111 Barrios: #13 "Avancemos", #10 "Bienvenidos a adorer", #15 "Busca la verdad", #4 "Desesaría entrar en tu corazón"; Boidi: #18 "Necesario", #17 "Vivir en Espíritu"; Borgna: #1 "Es el amor de Jesús", #11 "Te devolvemos", #6 "Una expresión de amor"; Calvo Ramón: #30 "Cieling", #8 "En tus manos", #29 "No quiero soñar más", #9 "Que mi hogar sea tu casa", #2 "Reflejo de tu amor"; García: #25 "Tan triste y tan lejos"; Gómez: #20 "Siempre estás aquí"; Gómez & Viveros: #26 "Un corazón triste"; Gutiérrez & Grané: #14 "Juntas las manos"; Luz: #5 "Cómo no cantar"; Peiró: #23 "Venimos a Ti"; Perera Larrarte: #21 "Alza tu mirada", #3 "Por ti", #12 "Quiero ser como Cristo", #16 "Unidos en Espíritu", #19 "Unidos en Jesús"; Santos: #24 "Sábado bendito"; Vílchez: #28 "Mírame".

112 *Sions sånger: En samling af andliga sånger med melodier i notskrift, för religiösa sammankomster och hemmet* (Chicago, IL: n. p., 1889); see Nasjonalbiblioteket, "Sions sånger", accessed September 20, 2018, https://www.nb.no/nbsok/nb/3007ac887d98d40843 99a96de07f1fb6.

113 *Sions sånger: Psalmer och sånger för offentligt och enskilt bruk i kyrka, skola och hem*, 3rd ed. (Stockholm: Skandinaviska förlagsexpeditionen, 1927).

114 *Sions sånger: En rikhaltig samling andliga sånger och psalmer*, 3rd rev. ed. (Stockholm: Skandinaviska förlagsexpeditionen, 1948). The same year a text-only anthology of the third edition was published under the title *Lova hans namn* with 176 lyrics. *Lova hans namn: Ett urval andliga sånger* (Stockholm: Skandinaviska Förlagsexpeditionen, 1949), introduction.

115 *Sions sånger: En rikhaltig samling andliga sånger och psalmer*, 4th ed. (Gävle: Skandinaviska Bokförlaget).

116 *Psalmer och sånger* (Libris Verbum, 1987).

Ahnfelt (7), *Ahnfelts sånger* (5), Johan Alfred Ahlström (1), Lars-Erik Ängeborn
(1), Gustaf Aulén (1), *Barn-Sånger* (1), Bernhard Berglund (1), Ida Björkman (1),
Joël Blomqvist (6), Anders Bond (1), Ingemar Braennstroem (1), Sven-Erik Bäck
(3), Julius Dahlöf (1), Isidor Dannström (1), Gustaf Düben (1), Lars Edlund (1),
Åke Edvinsson (1), Einar Ekberg (1), Elsa Eklund (2), Fredrik August Ekström (1),
Karl Eliasson (1), Gösta Elowsson (1), Gunnar Eriksson (1), Torgny Erséus (12),
folk melodies (24), *Förbunds-Sånger* (1), *Förbundstoner* (1), Roland Forsberg (16),
Nils Frykman (5), Rickard Furustam (1), Anders Gerdmar (1), Gunnar Hahn (1),
Jan-Inge Hall (2), Bertil Hallin (2), Hilding Hallnäs (1), Per Harling (5), Daniel
Helldén (2), *Hemlandstoner* (1), *Hjärtesånger* (2), Gunn-Britt Holgersson (1),
Johan Holmstrand (1), Christer Hultgren (1), Johannes Alfred Hultman (2), Jan
Lennart Höglund (1), Nils Jacobsson (1), Bedrich Janacek (1), Sören Janson (1),
Lennard Jernestrand (2), Sven-Eric Johanson (1), Beatrice F. Johnson (1), Stellan
Jonsson (1), Pelle Karlsson (1), Erland von Koch (2), Åke Kullnes (1), Emmy
Köhler (1), Johan Fredrik Lagergrén (1), Leif Larsson (1), Gustaf Lewenhaupt (1),
J. Olof Lindberg (2), Oskar Lindberg (9), Albert Lindström (1), Curt Lindström
(4), Olof Lindström (1), Tore Littmarck (4), Leif Larsson (1), Gustaf Lewenhaupt
(1), J. Olof Lindberg (2), Oskar Lindberg (8), Albert Lindström (1), Curt
Lindström (4), Olof Lindström (1), Tore Littmarck (4), *Lofsånger och Andeliga
Wisor* (2), Johann Christian Lotscher (1), Lars Åke Lundberg (9), Leif Lundberg
(1), Peter Lundén (1), Kjell Lönnå (2), *Melodier till Sions Nya Sånger* (3), Ingmar
Milveden (1), Moberg (3), Svante Myrén (1), Anton Nilsson (1), Hjalmar Nilsson
(1), Preben Nodermann (1), Otto Nordlund (1), Gustaf Nordqvist (1), Hans
Nyberg (1), Jacob Nyvall (2), Johan Melcher Öjerholm (1), Alex Olovson (1),
Birger Olsson (1), Daniel Olson (2), Ingemar Olsson (1), Otto Olsson (2), August
Östlund (1), Christer Palm (1), Gunnar Petersén (1), Emil Peterson (1), Lewi
Pethrus (1), Eva Pettersson (1), *Pilgrims-Sånger* (3), published in Sweden (17), Bo
Ramviken (1), Börge Ring (1), Karl-Olof Robertson (7), David Rondin (1),
Waldemar Rudin (1), Amanda Sandborg-Waesterberg (2), Göran Sandén (1), Uno
Sandén (2), *Sanningsvittnet* (1), Wilhelm Sarwe (1), *Segertoner* (1), *Sions Nya
Sånger* (2), *Sionstoner* (1), Anders Gustav Sjöblom (1), Karl Gustaf Sjölin. – Due
to the number of tunes, they will not be listed here; the reader is referred to the
hymnal itself.

## The United Kingdom

The United Kingdom used to have its own hymnal. *Hymns for Use in Divine
Worship* was published in 1906 (1413 texts).[117] The first edition of *The Advent
Hymnal* was published in 1915[118] and the second edition in 1928 (725 hymns).[119]

---

117  *Hymns for Use in Divine Worship* (London: International Tract Society, 1906).
118  *The Advent Hymnal: A Collection of Standard Hymns and Gospel Songs Suitable for All
      Kinds of Religious Services,* 1st ed. (Watford: International Tract Society, 1915).

*The New Advent Hymnal* was published in 1952.[120] Sometime after this the American hymnal took over. Since I did not procure a copy of the *New Advent Hymnal*, the *Advent Hymnal* of 1928 will be analyzed instead. It has 321 English, five Irish, eight Scottish, and 15 Welsh tunes, or 349 tunes (44%)[121] from the four nations of the British Isles.[122] At least 30 of those tunes (4%) are by English Adventist composers: Albert Kingsley Armstrong (2), Douglas Albert Raoul Aufranc (3), Edwin Barnes (2), and Joseph Harker, Jr. (23).[123]

## Working Analysis

Since I have still not managed to collect all the European Adventist hymnals, any analysis can only be rudimentary. First, it is striking how difficult it is to research this topic. The nature of hymns makes them hard to find, as has been mentioned in the introduction. But even when they are found, the research difficulty is aggravated when their production is less than satisfactory. When they lack internal information their analysis is very time consuming or even impossible.[124] These difficulties underscore the importance of researching the topic further.

They also illustrate the second point, and that is how the bureaucratic disconnect in the Church has affected its hymnals and musical life. Europe is a continent, and yet the musical efforts of the Church in each country seem to be islands interconnected with but few boats or bridges. It is true that most of the countries borrow from the other countries' hymnals to some extent. Yet this is sometimes to a little and a selected extent. The overall picture emerges that the countries are unaware of the entirety of the hymnals and do not benefit from the

119  *The Advent Hymnal: A Collection of Standard Hymns and Gospel Songs Suitable for All Kinds of Religious Services*, 2nd ed. (Watford: The Stanborough Press, 1928).

120  *The New Advent Hymnal: A Collection of Hymns and Gospel Melodies for Public and Family Worship and Private Devotion* (Alma Park: Stanborough Press, 1952).

121  As in older hymnals, the same tune is often used more than once. This of course offsets the true ratio. Another factor that would have to be considered for the true ratio is that there were at least 55 tunes whose nationality I could not verify, but that had either an English tune name, composer, or were from a hymnal published in England.

122  Since this is nearly half the hymnal, the tunes will not be listed.

123  Armstrong (1884–1965): #91 CHOSEN HILL, #430 TRENTHAM; AUFRANC (1892–1980): #478 CHERWELL, #273 HIGH SALVINGTON, #197 PEVENSEY; BARNES (1864–1930): #428 MORTON, #605 WHEN THE KING SHALL CLAIM HIS OWN; HARKER, JR. (1880–1970): #451 ADDYCOMBE, #211 CHATSWOOD, #362 CHILLINGHAM, #593 CRAGSIDE, #609 "THE DAY IS FAST APPROACHING", #533 DENESIDE, #150/233 DYKES, #194 HOLY REST, #303 INVOCATION, #120 JULIAN, #510 LOVE'S MELODY, #196 MEMORIUM, #725 "OUR GOD SHALL COME", #138 PARACLETE, #276/486 PATMOS, #290 REAPERS, #272 SANTEE, #579 SIMONSIDE, #429 ST. DAVID'S, #275 STANBOROUGH PARK, #702 "TO SEE HIS FACE", #555 "WE FOLLOW IN HIS STEPS", #293 WINSCOMBE.

124  When a hymnal does not list poets or composers, one must both know the native language and how to read or play music to identify the texts and tunes.

labor of their colleagues. For instance, in some countries the hymnals lack information about the poets and composers, which makes the hymnals less professional and useful, even when the information is readily available in the hymnals of another country.

But even with an incomplete picture, some elements can still be detected about native tunes. In respect to the number of tunes by native composers, the countries can be divided into three groups. First are the countries that have a high number of native tunes (30% or more): Germany, Denmark, Finland, Norway, Sweden, and the United Kingdom. These countries all have a long Protestant history, and the Church has drawn on the native Protestant musical tradition. The second group of countries have some native tunes (8% down to barely a percentage): Austria, the Faroe Islands, Hungary, Iceland, Italy, Lithuania, Romania, and Russia. And then there are countries that have apparently no native tunes, such as the Czech Republic and Slovakia. While I cannot say what distinguishes the second and third group, it seems clear that overall the Church feels more comfortable adopting Protestant music than Catholic or Orthodox music. There are probably many reasons for this, such as tradition and theology. Adventism grew out of American Protestantism and was therefore familiar with the Protestant hymnal tradition, and it is always easier to adopt the known rather than the unknown. The Adventist Church is also Protestant and in general regards the Catholic and Orthodox Churches as apostate, and is probably hesitant in identifying too much with their music tradition.

When it comes to the number of native Adventist tunes, there is no discernible geographical factor. The highest number is found in the booklets published in Bulgaria and Spain, and then in the hymnals of Lithuania and the United Kingdom. The highest number is probably found wherever creativity is welcomed or not seen as a threat to the hymnal tradition. For instance, the Bulgarian and Spanish booklets are not replacing a hymnal. Adventist musicians compose sacred music all over Europe, but usually their music is self-published on CDs or some online media. It rarely finds its way into the hymnal or – in countries where the hymnal has fallen prey to the projector – to the wall. Is it of too poor quality? Is it too little known? These are questions that would be interesting to explore.

The theological spectrum of the Church also seems to be a factor. Where "liberal" choices have been made, such as working with other denominations in the preparation of a hymnal, or in including more "contemporary" music, the ratio of native tunes has also been high. This is the case in Denmark, Finland, Germany, Norway, and Sweden. The spectrum seems to be irrelevant to the number of native Adventist tunes. Apparently – and regretfully – musical creativity does not seem to be important in either "conservative" or "liberal" Adventist praxis of music. On both sides it is assumed that the Church will borrow and not be itself a fountain of music.

There is however a way to see a brighter picture here and that is when all the pieces are put together into one mosaic of European Adventism. While any given hymnal might be limited, if you line up all the European Adventist hymnals together, a much richer sound is heard. While this crosses over the historical boundaries of the article into the praxis of the present and future, I would like to propose increased co-operation between all the musical departments in Europe, increased use of the sacred native musical tradition (and not only the Protestant ones), and increased facilitating and usage of Adventist musical compositions. When future European Adventist hymnals are being prepared, if all the other countries' sacred musical traditions were consulted – as well as all the native musical talent within the Church – each country would be enriched by the native and Adventist music from all the other countries. For all the Adventist talk about "iron and clay," or the impossibility of European co-operation, I think it would be wonderful if Adventists would break the mold and show what pan-European co-operation can do, in this instance in the area of music. It is at least a sweet sounding possibility.

***

## Acknowledgements

Since European Adventist hymnology has barely been studied, help from others was essential to gather information. I would like to thank the following people for their assistance: Ela Ardelean, church member from Romania; Hanne Berntsen, Norwegian publishing house; Kennet Engblom, pastor in Finland; Laura Fantasia, church member from Italy; Preben Jalving, director of HASDA, Denmark; Birgitta Kip, church member from Sweden; Neven Klačmer, director of the Historical Archives of the Adriatic Union; Jaanus-Janari Kogerman, treasurer of the Estonian Conference; Joel Niininen, retired director of the Finnish publishing house; Heinrich Patryarcha, pastor in Poland; Ivaylo Petrov, church member from Bulgaria; Alvaro Calvo Ramón, music director of the Spanish Union; Melita Tomovska, Macedonian publishing house; Deividas Vanagas, treasurer of the Lithuanian Conference.

# PART II

# EUROPEAN ADVENTISM
# FACING VIOLENCE

*Daniel-Adrian Neagu*

# In the Name of Right Faith against Real Faith: The Persecution of Seventh-day Adventists in Romania during the Interwar Period

Abstract

The period between the two world wars meant impressive growth and development for the Seventh-day Adventist Church in Romania. From very few members at the beginning of the 20th century, they grew to 12,000 members in 1930 and to 25,000 in 1948. This impressive and unexpected evolution led to a wave of persecution from the Orthodox Church through the local authorities, despite laws that seemed favourable to Seventh-day Adventists. Churches were vandalized, members were arrested and beaten, colporteurs' books were confiscated without reason, and soldiers lost their decorations. The persecution was so cruel that some lost their lives after the beatings they had received. Secret military orders demanded that the Adventists must be stopped, despite the laws that guaranteed their rights and freedoms. This aspect of Romanian Adventism in the period is, therefore, typical of the early reality of Adventists in Europe in several respects.

According to official statistics, in 1900 the Seventh-day Adventist Church in Europe had 7,042 members, over 2,000 of whom lived in Germany.[1] Ten years later, in 1910, the official statistics mentioned over 21,262 members and confirmed an Adventist presence – at least through missionaries – in most European countries: the Netherlands, Belgium, Austria, Switzerland, Sweden, Norway, Finland, Iceland, Denmark, Russia (where there was even a mission in Siberia), Spain, Portugal, Italy, France, the Balkan region (comprising Romania and Bulgaria), Serbia, Greece, Hungary, Turkey, England, Ireland, and Scotland. This was an impressive boom judging by the hesitation which the Adventist leaders first approached the idea of a European mission. After another ten years, in 1920, the official statistical report spoke about approximately 48,460 members, and besides the previously mentioned countries, the report also contains the names of three other countries: Czechoslovakia, Poland, and Lithuania. Counting another fifteen years, in 1935, there were already three Adventist divisions in Europe and a total number of 109,238 members, 92,824 of whom lived on the European continent and 19,709 in the Soviet Union. At the same time, Adventist believers in Europe were involved in the conversion of inhabitants of Africa and areas of India by sending funds and missionaries to those territories.

However, this growth was not uniform, as Adventism was not well received everywhere. Moreover, the European countries had their own Christian traditions, a

---

1    See *Annual Statistical Reports* for 1900, 1910, 1920, 1935.

situation quite different from the one in the United States, reflected in the way the various European groups of believers chose to apply in their lives the details of the Adventist lifestyle.

Each country has its own history with regard to how Seventh-day Adventism arrived in its territory and the way in which it developed. There are, however, several constants common to all countries: one among them is the important role of literature evangelists and of publications; another is opposition from local people. This opposition sometimes went to the point of persecution, and some of the believers had to pay with their lives for the fact of waiting for Jesus Christ and of keeping the seventh-day Sabbath. Even if this opposition was not as aggressive in Western Europe as it was in Eastern and Southern Europe, it confirmed what the apostle Paul said, that "everyone who wants to live a godly life in Christ Jesus will be persecuted" (2 Timothy 3:12, NIV).

## Persecution of Adventists in Europe in the Early Period

From the sources available several statements regarding opposition and persecution of Adventist believers in Europe should be mentioned. The *Home Missionary* issue of August 1897 contains a long report about missionary activity in the then Central European Conference.[2] Besides data about the number of members and activities of missionaries and literature evangelists, it says,

> Small as our work is, yet its effect is best seen by the various articles and pamphlets being published against us. We have had plenty of free advertisement from the pulpit and the religious press.[3]

However, besides the opposition coming from the pulpit and the religious press, one case is presented that is much more dramatic:

> One case where one of our brethren refused to send his children to school on the Sabbath, has gone as far as Berlin, but has been decided against him. The man has spent weeks already in prison and sustained great financial loss. Others, again, obtained permission in other parts, and in one case even in a high school. Sunday laws are becoming very strict, and in numerous cases heavy fines were imposed.[4]

In the *Advent Review and Sabbath Herald* issue of November 3, 1904, another interesting case is presented, this time from Switzerland.

> Dr. DeForest stated that in 1896 when the Institut Sanitaire began sanitarium work in the quarters formerly occupied by our Basel publishing house, there was a great deal of prejudice against our people because of the Sunday persecutions we had been passing through in that city; but one of the very police men who helped to arrest Elder Holser at

---

2    "Central European Mission Field," *The Home Missionary*, 9.7 (August 1897): 161-164.
3    Ibid., 163.
4    Ibid., 164.

that time, has recently been under treatment in the Institut Sanitaire, and is now recommending our principles to comrades.[5]

In Germany, the matter was no different. A. Olsen tells of the beginnings of Adventist preaching in Saxony,

> Evangelistic work in Saxony was begun under G[erhard] Perk, who, being a foreigner, was sent out of the country in 1902. K. Sinz, a native of the country, continued the work, but for a time under great difficulties. At every meeting there were two or three detectives present to make note of all that was said or done.[6]

Another major difficulty for the Adventist believers in Germany was Sabbath keeping for those conscripted to military service. As Schwartz reports,

> one young man explained to a court martial that he could cite a hundred Bible texts for observance of the Sabbath on Saturday. If shown one text calling for Sunday observance, he would agree to work. A confrontation with the military chaplain ended in the young Adventist's favor, and the court simply decided to dismiss him from the army. Others were not as fortunate; they spent months and years in prison, until finally army medical examiners began to find all manner of excuses for rejecting Seventh-day Adventist recruits.[7]

Similarly, the Adventists in Spain had their own story.

> Consider Spain and Italy. For centuries they have been bastions of Roman Catholicism. Their religious liberty record was bad—especially Spain's. It has often been difficult for Adventists even to get married there. Church services had to be held in buildings with no identification, and behind closed doors and windows.[8]

The beginning of the World War I brought new difficulties even for the Adventist youths who found understanding from the military authorities so as to be drafted as non-combatants. Such a group of young men from England, who were sent to a military prison in France for the crime of not working on the Sabbath, had to faithfully suffer the consequences of their decision.

> Here they were ordered to do prison work on the Sabbath, and on their refusal, were put in irons, and sentenced to various kinds of exhausting punishment. They were also put

---

5    Guy Dail, "The General European Conference," *The Advent Review and Sabbath Herald* 81.44 (November 3, 1904): 14.

6    M. Ellsworth Olson, *The Origin and Progress of Seventh-Day Adventists*, (Washington, D.C: Review and Herald Publishing Association, 1926, second edition), 409.

7    Richard W. Schwartz, *Light Bearers to the Remnant* (Mountain View, CA: Pacific Press Publishing Association, 1979), 220.

8    Bert B. Beach, *Record* (June 19, 1993): 4

in solitary confinement, and then told individually that the rest had given in. All, however, stood firm.[9]

Evidently, similar difficulties were also present during World War II.[10] An article in the *Australasian Record* in 1947 summarized the situation after the war.

> More than 9,000 Adventists of many nationalities have been forcibly transplanted or have fled before political and religious persecution in Europe. Thousands have fled on foot for hundreds of miles, pulling small waggons filled with things they were able to save from their homes. Others were crowded into cattle cars. All left behind them a bitter trail of woe.[11]

These are only a few portrayals of the persecution and opposition which Seventh-day Adventist believers in Europe met. In some countries – e.g. Russia or Turkey – the cases were much more frequent and much more violent.

## Religious Persecution in Romania

Seventh-day Adventists in Romania were confronted with persecution and opposition from their very beginning. We do not know too many details about the 1870–1881 period, i.e. the period between the arrival of Czechowski in Piteşti and the moment in which Toma Aslan, the leader of the group of believers in this city, established contact with the European Adventist mission. However, after this year, there is more and more frequent evidence about the difficulties and persecution they faced.

In 1913, A. C. Bourdeau published, in a periodical with statistical data[12] of the European Division, several memories in relation to his visit in Romania after 1884. The portrayal of the small group of Adventists in Piteşti is impressive. Thus, we find that,

9    Francis McLellan Wilcox, *Seventh Day Adventists in Time of War* (Takoma Park, Washington, D.C.: Review and Herald Publishing Association, 1936), 262

10   Schwartz says that "in all of the occupied countries many hardships were suffered by Adventists, both as individuals and as a church. Food and many basic necessities were in short supply and therefore rationed. Dutch Adventists found that frequently the meager food supplies that did become available appeared on the Sabbath. This put their principles to the test. Other areas suffered when their leaders were removed for forced labour or to concentration camps." Schwartz, 438

11   D.G. Rose, "Without Our Help Many Will Die," *Australasian Record*, 51.40 (October 6, 1947): 1. The article continues, "Many more than the nine thousand started out, but exhaustion, cold, and starvation greatly reduced their numbers. Day and night, without food and without rest, they fled. Pitiful and shocking were the scenes. A large part of the babies starved to death. People of every age succumbed. Husbands had to bury their own wives, and wives their own husbands. The experiences defy description, yet the fate awaiting them in their exile was little better. They were thrust under the cold, forbidding ruins of the destroyed cities of Germany, or into large, overcrowded, wooden, barracks, a family to a room."

12   *European Division Conference of SDA, Quarterly Report* 2.2, (Second quarter, 1913): 34–36.

compared to the salon of the Aslans, which could accommodate 40-50 persons (probably the same salon in which Czechowski had preached), Toma had asked his father's permission to use a family storehouse that could accommodate "hundreds or even thousands of persons." After asking and receiving the permission from the authorities to gather there, the series of lectures began in a Sunday evening, with an attendance of "thousands of persons." The windows were wide open, and the listeners everywhere.

The event aroused such an interest that the entire city came to listen to the preacher who had arrived from America. One evening, an Orthodox priest asked permission to speak, in an attempt to attenuate the impact of the American missionary's preaching, and at the end of the lecture Bourdeau had to be escorted by the police in order to prevent possible incidents. The authorities tried to send him out of the country, but as a result of negotiations, it was agreed that the meetings could continue only in Aslan family's salon.

After 1888, there is no information about the Pitești group in Adventist periodicals, the reason being related to the subject of this study: due to persecution, the church members in this city scattered throughout the country or chose to emigrate. One of them, Toma Aslan's brother Mitică, who was chosen an elder of the church in Bucharest after 1900, would tell, "The creditors began persecuting us. They called us Jew-Christians. The traders all hated us. We were persecuted and stricken by fate. We lost everything. However, God did not leave us."[13]

Nevertheless, this was only the beginning. The following sections present an analysis of the phenomenon of persecution of Romanian Adventist believers that takes into account the evolution of the legislative framework, testimonies from military archives, and internal documents of the Adventist Church in this period.

## The Legislative Framework in the 1920s

Until the beginning of the 1920s, the Adventists' religious freedom was indirectly guaranteed by the 1866 Constitution, which said (title II, art. 5) "The Romanians enjoy freedom of conscience, freedom of education, freedom of the press and freedom of gathering."[14] Pertaining also to the question of individual liberties, article 21 of the Constitution said, "Freedom of conscience is absolute. Freedom of all denominations is guaranteed as their celebration does not interfere with public order or the good morals."[15]

However, the emergence of fast-spreading new protestant denominations among Romanian citizens drew the attention of the Romanian ecclesiastical and political authorities. Publications of the Orthodox hierarchs and heated debates in the parliament seemed to make it necessary to regulate the functioning of the new religious

13  Mitică Aslan in V. D. Cojea, *Vechi cărări advente* (Cernica: CARD, 1998), 31.
14  *Constituția României*, published in *Monitorul Oficial*, 142 (June 1, 1886): accessed April 21, 2013, http://www.cdep.ro/pls/legis/legis_pck.htp_act_text?idt=37755.
15  Ibid.

denominations, i.e. especially, the Baptists and the Seventh-day Adventists, but also the Bible Students (later called Jehovah's Witnesses), and other Christian groups that appeared after the beginning of the 20th century.

The law was necessary indeed as in some areas the authorities felt free to resort to all kinds of abuses against those who abandoned their ancestral faith – imprisonment, beating, denial of legitimate rights, writing down in papers of identity the designation "Adventist heretic" instead of one's nationality, etc.

On January 24, 1921, the Ministry of Internal Affairs issued the circular Order no. 2180, published in the *Official Bulletin* on February 6, 1921, which stated that gatherings of officially unrecognized denominations had to be held according to the regulations specific to the public gatherings, and that "their own cult is allowed only in their own houses of prayer."[16] This was easier said than done since most of the public gatherings of the unrecognized denominations took place in the parishioners' own houses, the few believers in each locality not having enough funds or understanding from the local authorities to open a specific place of worship.

On April 1, 1921, the Ministry of Religious Affairs issued another circular Order (no. 15831), in which it was stated explicitly, "We do not recognize any kind of sectarian organization" – targeting again especially the Adventists and the Baptists. About these two denominations it is stated towards the end of the order that the gatherings of the Adventist and Baptist cults "are admitted only according to the provisions of the law ... As a result, sectarians will not be able to publicly manifest any kind of act specific to their cult without knowledge and permission from the rightful authorities."[17] Worship could be held locally only in houses of worship and only with the consent of the Ministry of Religious Affairs and "under no circumstance in private houses."[18] The preachers could be only Romanian citizens and they could only serve one local church.

These difficult conditions for the small groups of believers were a constant source of abuses from the police, but also a challenge for the believers to build houses of prayers with their own means. The last point of this circular order provided that tithe and all other offerings of the members be used exclusively in the benefit of the local community and that at the end of each year local communities hand over to the prefect's office up-to-date financial statements as well as the following year's budget, with the provision that the prefect's office send them further to the government. This regulation was interpreted by both Baptists and Adventists as an interference with their internal affairs, which they accepted could be examined by financial authorities, but held that the state cannot establish the purpose of freely offered funds. This order

---

16    See "Ordinul Circular 2180/January 24, 1921," *Buletinul Oficial* 1 (February 6,1921) cited in Dumitru Popa, *Pagini din istoria bisericii adventiste de ziua a șaptea din România 1921-1936* (București: Editura Viață și Sănătate, 2008), 40.

17    Order 15831/April 1, 1921, cited in Popa, *Pagini din istoria bisericii adventiste de ziua a șaptea din România 1921-1936*, 40–41.

18    Ibid.

drew numerous protests both from the Baptist Union[19] and from the Union of Adventist Churches, governing bodies that were thus abolished, the only recognized entities being the local congregations.

The official recognition of the Adventist Church (as a religious association at the beginning) came through Decision no. 32950/June 1921. The Seventh-day Adventists were recognized afterwards in several repeated ministerial decisions, such as: Decision no. 12794/1924, Decision no. 75734/January 29, 1925, or Decision no. 24536/May 29, 1926, which is in fact an application of the Law of the cults. We could also mention Decision no. 114119/August 21, 1933, as well as other decisions and resolutions of the Ministry of Religious Affairs, which specify each time that "the exercise of the Adventist and Baptist cult is free."[20] This freedom was, however, recognized in a different way by the authorities, many of them making reference to certain secret orders that explicitly provided a basis for the persecution of Seventh-day Adventists.

## Adventists Facing Secret Orders

The recent declassification of the documents from the Military Archive, Religious Service section, brought to light new elements regarding the purpose and role of military priests. One of the major objectives of their activity was to fight against what they perceived as the "sectarian offensive." Their declarations, sometimes quite bellicose towards Adventists or Baptists, must be understood, however, in the Romanian interwar context, in which for many people nationalism was the appropriate expression of their love for their country, and Orthodoxy was deemed the highest form of *românism* (that is, the national sentiment of the Romanians, the Romanian spirit).

All the documents bear the 'strictly secret' mark and, according to military laws and regulations, can be studied only after they have been declassified. Being secret correspondence, it was unknown to the Adventist or Baptist leaders whose denominations were targeted; therefore, we do not have their answer to some of the allegations against them.

Another aspect is that not all the declarations of the military confessors or their superiors were official positions of the Romanian Army, nor can we find in the legislative system a reflection of their opinions. However, the postponing of a decision regarding the legal recognition of the cults allowed by the law and the outlawing of the Adventists by General Ion Antonescu in 1942 can be attributed to this nationalist current in the Romanian society.

---

19  The Union of the Baptist Churches in Romani had been established in 1919, and for 1921 statistics speak of 633 churches and 21,193 members. In 1931, these numbers are double: 1,521 Baptist churches with 47,025 members on the Romanian territory (cf. *Baptist Handbook*, 1937, and the data offered by C. Adorian at the World Congress of the Baptists in 1923).

20  See Order 32950/1921; Order 12794/1924; Order 75734/1925; Order 114 119/ 1933 etc. in Popa, 45–46.

The first declarations we want to mention describe what in the author's view are the problems that the country had to face as a result of the new sects being tolerated by the authorities, but especially show the hidden aspects of the existence of those sects. For the reader of the rich anti-sectarian literature of the time, these statements only repeat the texts disseminated in the press or in various publications in order to stop the missionary impetus of the new religious denominations. Therefore, we believe they must not be separated from the context of that time.

Thus, we find the idea that "through their religious ideology ... sectarianism causes a real revolution in every separate conscience, stealing it forever from the family, from the society, from the state."[21] In another document, issued by the Inspectorate of the Military Clergy to the Superior Council for the Defence of the Country, the demand is made that some measures proposed by the Inspectorate be accepted and that the representatives of the clergy be invited when the sectarian matter will be discussed.

About Adventists in Romania, it was claimed that they were dangerous

> because they are international, mostly enemies of the state, and thus separated from the body of the people and possessed by interests foreign to our nation and state, [and because] through their propaganda they endanger the existence of our people and the foundation of our national state."[22]

This document was a response to a solicitation from the Supreme Council for the Defence of the Country, following an analysis of a special study commission. The Adventists and the Baptists appear on the list of the sects that need to be fought, although they functioned in a legal framework. The solicitation was sent to the Bishop of the Army in order to be given an answer. The answer listed the dangers posed by the new Christian cults, "*We have shown the great danger that all sects pose to the people and to the country in general, and especially to the army*" (emphasis in the original).[23]

In this same document we read that these religious groups are dangerous because

> they are not properly religious movements, of good faith, but they are political currents, of bad faith, fuelled with money and foreign propagators, with the hidden goal of demoralize us and ruin the grand edifice we... accomplished."[24]

To complete the dark picture, the religious cults were marked as Communist and anarchic movements who fought to break the Romanians from the faith that made them distinct, for "by disintegrating the church, the Romanian people itself will disintegrate and, with it, our national state."[25]

---

21   Historical Military Archives (HMA), Religious Service fund (RS), file 101/1927, f. 8.
22   HMA, RS fund, file idem, refer to footnote 17.
23   Ibid., Folio 22.
24   Ibid.
25   Ibid.

The authors of the document notice with "indescribable pain" that "even an officer registered as a sectarian." Therefore, the demand was made that the sectarians be isolated or grouped in order not to make propaganda and not to be promoted. In the same document, the Minister of Religious Affairs, which recognized the preachers of the religious denominations, was also sanctioned, as well as certain army leaders who ignored previous documents on the same subject or who mentioned that the army cannot discriminate. In the last paragraph the demand was made: that "the Minister of Public Instruction ... [should] not tolerate students without knowledge of the state religion, as this measure is not unfair to any sectarian since they receive in the system of their sect only adult people."[26]

This situation is similar to another one that developed in Focşani, where in the unit's report for the year 1926 there appear 27 "sectarian" soldiers. The Army Bishop sent a secret letters to the religious confessor in which he asked that in agreement with the Commander of the Regiment "the sectarians be so divided in subunits that they not form compact masses."[27] The answer is unexpected: the 27 soldiers were of the Roman Catholic religion, and their presence on the Adventists' list was a simple mistake.[28]

Sometimes, in order to find out precisely if the soldiers supported certain Christian sects or not, letters were sent to the priests in the parishes to which they belonged, or the parishes themselves announced their arrival. In the Buzău garrison, captain-priest Matei Popescu offers a detailed report[29] of his way of working with the soldiers against the sectarian danger, mentioning among his methods of persuasion the "hours long" discussions on the Holy Scriptures, but also the fact that, when they are discovered, "these traitors to their people are taken to the Commander." If these methods failed to change their religious convictions, "they [were] delivered to the Prosecutor's Office."[30]

Although none of the 2,500 recruits declared himself to be a sectarian, priest Matei Popescu was determined to ask each priest from the villages where soldiers went on their Easter vacation to confirm whether they were suspected of relationships with religious sects or not. Likewise, all the priests in the Buzău Bishopric were obliged to "report all the sectarian soldiers in the commune, in order to follow them."[31]

In spite of close surveillance and a rather inimical attitude, the fact that the "sectarians" did not cause harm to the military itself was also noted. In a memorandum

---

26   Ibid., Folio 23.
27   Ibid., Folio 68.
28   Even though the Inspectorate received confirmation from the unit that the 27 alleged Adventists were in fact Catholics, they asked again the priest to recheck the situation, although the result is the same as that from the final report of the unit.
29   Ibid., Folio 63.
30   Ibid., Folio 63.
31   Ibid., Folio 63.

of the Inspectorate of the Military Clergy to the 1st Army Division, written in response to an account received in 1931, it is stated, "the fact is encouraging that the few sectarians present in the units have had no activity harmful to the institution, that they behave well during their service, that they work conscientiously, they are honest and they always strive to obey the orders they are given."[32] In the report of the Second Army Division for the January–June 1931 period, it is stated that "as for the fulfilment of their duties, the sectarians are no different from the rest of their companions-in-arms."[33] Despite such favourable reports, surveillance and control measures did not cease. Thus, in the memorandum to the 1st Army Division mentioned above, it is stated that in order to discover all the sect's members, it was indicated that "the informing officers and unit commanders search in detail all incoming and outgoing correspondence."[34]

As to Major[35] Păunescu's activities after he became an Adventist, a note dated May 13, 1927, signed by the Inspectorate of the Military Clergy and addressed to the Minister of War, personnel service, says, "If possible, take all the necessary measures against Reserve Major Păunescu, so that he as a soldier stops making Adventist propaganda, which, despite all explanations, is against the people and the country."[36]

The idea that Adventists are against the people is not unusual for the historical context back then, and would constantly reappear in the correspondence, despite the example of World War I, in which Adventist soldiers typically fought with determination wherever they were sent. For instance, a note dated April 1, 1931, written by the Protopope of Caliacra, says, "Adventists are known to be against the oath, the bearing of weapons, the church, and the hierarchy."[37]

There is much evidence that, while the Adventist soldiers were fighting on the front and were being decorated during both World War I and World War II, their wives and children were being persecuted back home. There is, for instance, a case of a family for whose child the priest organized a public procession during which he christened the child in a baptistery filled with cold water, during winter, while his father was away on the front. Shortly after, the child died. Some of the soldiers, especially during World War II, were decorated for distinguished service, only to have their decorations withdrawn because they would not carry out small duties in the barracks on the Sabbath day.[38]

---

32  HMA, RS fund (Military Clergy Direction), file 4/1931, f. 1.

33  Ibid., Folio 18.

34  Ibid., Folio 2.

35  Petre Paunescu (1882–1972) was a major of Romanian Army who became an Adventist in 1919, then studied at Friedensau and from 1922 was pastor in Romania before becoming the president of the Adventist Bible School in Stupini, Brasov.

36  HMA, RS fund, file 101/1927, Folio 127.

37  HMA, RS (Military Clergy Direction) fund, File 4, 1931, Folio 21.

38  See Viorel Achim, *Politica regimului Antonescu față de cultele neoprotestante: Documente* (Polirom: N.P., 2013), 491–492.

## The Memorandum about Persecutions

In 1924, the administration of the Adventist Church in Romania addressed the Minister of Religious Affairs with a memorandum regarding cases of religious persecution suffered by Adventist believers in Romania in the previous few years.[39] The document is 72 pages long and in its first part tells the story of 25 cases of persecution, while its second part contains declarations of the witnesses and forensic certificates trying to prove the validity of these cases.

Even though the entire document cannot be reproduced here, a short presentation of several cases will help illustrate the varieties of the religious persecution in this period. In the county of Bacău, 13 Adventist members were arrested while in the house of prayer and were forced to walk 70 kilometres; finally, they were locked up in prison by the police. In the same county of Bacău, but in a different locality, the house of prayer, which was ready to be inaugurated, was burned down completely. In the same place, the funeral of a child was put off for nine days because the local authorities did not allow it due to the fact that the parents of the child were Adventists. In the same county, three adults and a 10-year-old child were beaten an entire night in a police station in order to persuade them to abandon their faith.

In another locality, a hamlet named Dorobanţ, in the same region of Moldova, on January 12, 1924, the priest and the mayor, together with over 200 local citizens, forced their entry into the house of prayer of the Adventist Church on the Sabbath while the Adventist believers were praying. They confiscated the Bibles and the hymnbooks, took them to the police and two of the believers were severely beaten. In Nicşeni an Adventist member was taken by force to the Orthodox Church on the day of the Epiphany, was forced to touch the icons as if kissing them, and then a cross was put on his back as a mockery and he was forced to wear it on the streets.

In order to prevent a religious wedding celebration in Botoşani, the local authorities mobilized a military brigade in front of the church; the soldiers formed a battle position and forbade the Adventist members to come near the house of prayer, even if this was not forbidden by the law. In another village, Andrieşeni, the same document says the priest told the people that came to confess to go and beat the Adventist members and drive them away from their locality. Heeding his advice, several Orthodox Christians went and beat savagely Adventist Ruxanda Creţu until they rendered her unconscious.

In Radauţi County, a young Adventist couple who wanted to have their civil wedding ceremony had to wait for two years because the authorities refused to release their civil status documents. In a locality in the county of Brăila, a visiting member of the Adventist Church was arrested, severely beaten and chased away on the ground that he wanted to abandon the faith of his ancestors. In several localities in southern

---

39   The document can be found in the Archives of Romania Union, and also at The National Central History Archives of Romania, Minister of Cults and Public Instruction (MCPI) fund, 131/1922, Folio 66.

Romania, the above-mentioned document speaks about many cases in which gendarmes burst into the house of prayer and violently beat the people who had gathered there, then arrested them and threatened them even saying that they would be killed for their faith. A priest decided to stop the development of the Adventist Church in his locality, the village of Poieneşti-Mănăstirea, Vaslui County at any cost and forced two of his parishioners to leave their wives because they had become Adventists.

These are only a few cases. Even if the persecutions and their repercussions varied across the country, the Adventist believers in the interwar period suffered the most for their faith. The most famous is the case of the preacher Gheorghe Oresciuc, who was assassinated in Bucovina, on January 22, 1932[40] He was not going to be the only one. More brethren would suffer the same fate shortly after and later in communism period.[41]

All this tide of persecution culminated in 1942 with the closing of the houses of prayer and the cancelling of every religious freedom for the Adventists.[42] However, the hand of God was over them, and he did not allow the Adventists in Romania to be deported in Siberia, although General Ion Antonescu, who was in charge of the Romanian state at the time, had issued a deportation order.[43]

## Conclusion

All these details underline the fact that the persecution of the Seventh-day Adventists in Europe in general and in Romania in particular was a complex phenomenon that must be carefully analysed and understood with its multiple phenomena. Religious intolerance of the masses was many times accompanied by the involvement of the local and religious authorities, and also by a rather ambiguous legislative framework.

The examples of these believers are an opportunity for the researcher to understand elements newly found in the sources, and an opportunity for those who nowadays have the same faith to know the cost with which this good news was brought to us. Even if their names are never forgotten in the heavenly books, we have the duty not to ignore them in the books of this earth either, especially since the spirit of intolerance is still present even today.

---

40   The case was presented in a national newspaper *Dimineaţa*, in 25th January 1932
41   Well-known names are Vasile Azanfirei, Gheorghe Pascalu in the inter-war period, and Cling Constantin, Dumitru Roman in comunism
42   The law no. 927, December 1942 – Popa, *Pagini din istoria bisericii adventiste de ziua a şaptea din România 1936-1955,* (Bucureşti: Editura Viaţă şi Sănătate, 2015), 120
43   For more datails see Achim, *Politica regimului Antonescu faţă de cultele neoprotestante. Documente,* 491–492.

*Yevgeniy Zaytsev*

# The Seventh-day Adventist Church in the USSR during World War II

Abstract

The article covers the history of the Seventh-day Adventist Church in the Soviet Union during World War II (1939–1945). It analyses the social, political and religious situation in the country in this period, which helps understand the incredibly hard conditions that the denomination faced during the war. It is a clear example of how extremely difficult Adventist existence could be in some parts of Europe. Lack of historical data, related to the absence of a centralized church organization and official periodicals, does not allow us to explore the topic widely enough; however, extant information is sufficient to estimate the level of pressure put on the church by external circumstances and to see instances of divine guidance in this history.

The Second World War (1939–1945)[1] is probably the least studied period in the history of the Seventh-day Adventist Church in the USSR, for several reasons. First of all, state policy aimed at eradicating religion from life in Soviet society. By the beginning of the war, due to the Soviet state's policy against the church, practically all Protestant associations – including the SDA Church – had ceased their legal and factual existence. There were almost no legal Protestant congregations left. Their revival and official registration would take place only at the end of the war. Furthermore, although in 1939–1940 the territories of the Baltic States, Western Belorussia, Western Ukraine, and Moldavia, where there were a lot of Protestant congregations including Adventist ones, had been added to the USSR, they had not been integrated into the life of Soviet society yet, and therefore information about them is scattered and contradictory in nature. Finally, the Council for Religious Affairs, whose records serve as the main official source of information about the history of Russian Protestantism in this period, was not established until 1944.

This study attempts to trace the history of the Seventh-day Adventist Church in the Soviet Union during the Second World War (1939–1945). It will analyse the socio-political and religious situation in the country during this period, which will help understand the incredibly difficult conditions in which the denomination found itself during the war. The shortage of historical data resulting from the lack of a centralized church organization and official periodicals makes it impossible to present the topic widely enough. However, the information provided will be sufficient to

---

1   The title *The Great Patriotic War* will also be used in this article. This is the title of the war used in the USSR history textbooks.

assess the degree of pressure from external circumstances on the church during this time period and see God's guidance in the history of the church.

## The Socio-political and Religious Situation in the USSR on the Threshold of the War

During the 1930s the Soviet state was taking a tougher stance against religious organizations as compared to previous years. The central purpose of policy on religion was to reduce, as much as possible, the place that religion and the church had in Soviet society. Religious groups were fought against as "anti-socialist and counter-revolutionary" phenomena and organizations, and therefore typical means of struggle against them included the imposition of administrative and criminal measures, extrajudicial acts, and repression. In broad terms, such a policy was a manifestation of the general political course chosen by Stalin and his associates. In general, this course can be described as the construction of "barracks socialism" with a minimum of personal rights and freedoms for citizens of the USSR.[2]

In 1938, the Permanent Commission on Cults, which had been established to resolve issues related to the activities of religious organizations, was dismissed. This meant the elimination of the very possibility of contact between the government and religious organizations, which became a natural consequence of the party and Soviet institutions' policy aimed at building a "non-religion society." Efforts by a small number of public figures who were members of the Commission, including its chairman Petr A. Krasikov, who sought to rectify the incorrect course of the state's church policy, were in vain.[3] At the all-Union level, only one departmental structure was left, which dealt with the problems of religion and the church – the People's Commissariat of Internal Affairs of the USSR (NKVD). Within its structure, in the Secret Political Directorate, there operated a special department "for combating church and sectarian counter-revolution."[4]

By 1937 the Soviet Union, according to the plans of the Union of Militant Atheists, established as far back as 1925, was to turn into a country of mass atheism. The Central Council of the Union of Militant Atheists was active in implementing both its own plans and state tasks, as it understood them. Its chairman Yemelyan Yaroslavsky, the main anti-religious leader of the time, was urging for active, offensive

2    For more detailed information about this period in the state-church relations in the USSR see I. A. Kurlyandskiy, *Stalin, Vlast, Religiya (Religioznyy i Tserkovnyy Factory vo Vnutrenney Politike Sovetskogo Gosudarstva v 1922–1953)* (Moscow: Kuchkovo Pole, 2011).

3    For more detailed information about the activities of the Commission on Cults see O.B. Prikazchikova, "Deyatelnost Postoyannoy Tsentralnoy Komissii po Voprosam Kultov (1929–1938)," *Vestnik PSTGU II: Istoriya Russkoy Pravoslavnoy Tserkvi* 31 (2009): 41–76.

4    M. I. Odintsov, *Vlast I Religiya v Gody Voiny* (Gosudarstvo I Religioznye Organizatsii v SSSR v Gody Velikoy Otechestvennoy Voiny 1941–1945) (Moscow: Rossiyskoye Obyedineniye Issledovateley Religii, 2005), 12.

actions at the "anti-religious front." By 1940, the Union had 96,000 groups and more than 3 million members. The circulation of anti-religious publications in the period between 1928 and 1940 reached 140 million copies.[5] Taking into account the Soviet government's policy to destroy religion completely, we can understand why the opinion on the necessity of the total elimination of religious cult legislation became widespread among members of the Communist Party and Soviet activists by the end of the 1930s.[6]

Churches and prayer houses were closed all over the country. Orthodox church buildings were used as production workshops, warehouses, and clubs, whereas monasteries were used as prisons and colonies. The campaign to close the churches was conducted primarily in the countryside. The Union of Militant Atheists mobilized the Communist Party and trade union organizations, cultural centres, and production committees for this purpose. The collection of signatures for closing a church was encouraged, while collection of signatures against its closure was considered counter-revolutionary and punished accordingly.

To combat Protestant organizations, the Communist Party and Soviet agencies often emphasized their foreign origin and membership in international church organizations. They considered the leaders of Protestant communities enemies, spies, and agents of the West.[7] The main Protestant churches, therefore, ceased to exist. As early as 1929 the Union of Baptists was dissolved, the building of the Union was confiscated, the work of training ministers was stopped, and all printed media were discontinued. The Union of Evangelical Christians ceased to exist after the arrest of its leader Y. I. Zhidkova. The Mennonite brotherhood shared the sad fate of the Baptists and Evangelical Christians. The leaders were arrested, the prayer houses closed, and the believers' assemblies stopped.

The Seventh-day Adventist Church was not an exception to the rule. Like all other religious organizations, it experienced ideological and physical pressure from the state. Initially, the SDA Church was boycotted by all publishing houses, printing houses and post offices, which meant the cessation of the publication of any spiritual literature. Then the churches and prayer houses started being closed, and mass arrests of active members of the denomination began. It was particularly hard for the SDA church members during this difficult period due to a rather strange initiative by the Soviet government. In 1929 they introduced a six-day week with five workdays and one day off.[8] It was virtually impossible for SDA church members to find a job that

---

5    A. I. Abdusamedov, R. M. Aleynik, B. A. Aliyeva et al., "Soyuz Voinstruyushchikh Bezhbozhnikov SSSR," in *Ateisticheskiy Slovar*, ed. M. P. Novikova (Moscow: Politizdat, 1985, 2nd revised ed.), 240–241.

6    M. I. Odintsov, "Khozhdeniye po Mukam," *Nauka i Religiya* 7 (1990): 56, 57.

7    M. I. Odintsov, Kochetova A.S. *Konfessionalnaya Politika v Sovetskom Soyuze v Gody Velikoy Otechestvennoy Voiny 1941–1945* (Moscow, 2014), 24.

8    The seven-day week was returned on June 26, 1940, under the Decree of the Presidium of the Supreme Soviet of the USSR "On Shifting to 8-Hour Working Day, Seven-Day Week, and on Prohibiting Unauthorized Leave of Workers and Officers from Factories and Institutions."

would allow them to freely observe the commandment of God – "Remember the Sabbath day to keep it holy." Faithful members of churches had, at best, to change their jobs several times a year, and at worst to remain unemployed at all and be included into the category of "parasites." Many believers were declared "disenfranchised." This meant that they were deprived of the opportunity to get medical aid or receive bread cards, did not have the right to vote, and could not get a job at a factory or at a government agency.

At the plenum of the SDA All-Union Council, held in 1931, due to the liquidation of local church conferences and in order to preserve at least some kind of leadership over congregations, the SDA Church established the Integrated Union with a council of five people and introduced the institution of commissioners of the SDA Integrated Union. However, by the end of the 1930s, all members of the council and all the Integrated Union's commissioners had been arrested and convicted. The data collected with great difficulty shows that during this period about 150 ordained ministers and elders and more than three thousand members of the church were repressed.[9] T. N. Nikolskaya notes that if until the mid-1930 religious ministers and activists were usually sentenced to exile or various terms of imprisonment, in the late 1930s they were typically given the death penalty.[10]

The Soviet authorities did not leave family members of the repressed ministers, including children, at peace. They were considered sons or daughters of a "public enemy." Mothers were intimidated and threatened that their children would be taken away if they continued to educate them in their religious faith. The church ministers who were not imprisoned could be arrested for only one single visit to the family of a repressed person and for rendering it some kind of assistance. For this reason, many members of the Church were deprived of church communication, including the opportunity to participate in the Lord's Supper for a long time.[11]

The responsibility for managing the Church in this difficult period rested with G. A. Grigoryev. The last original working document, dated April 1934, written in uneven handwriting and signed by Heinrich J. Löbsack after his arrest, read:

To regional and district commissioners of the SDA All-Union Council in the USSR. Hereby I entrust Grigorey Andreyevich Grigoriev, a former authorized representative for

---

9    For more information about the SDA church members repressed in 1930s see N. A. Zhukalyuk, *Vsponinayte Nastavnikov Vashih (Istoriya Adventistov Sedmogo Dnya v Litsah)* (Kyiv: Self Published, 1999); Dmitry O. Yunak, *Istoriya Tserkvi Khristian ASD v Rossii*, 2 vols. (Zaokskyy: Istochnick zhizni, 2002). The Saint-Petersburg Martyrology contains information about ten Seventh-day Adventists repressed in that period. See *Sankt-Peterburgskiy Martirolog.* (Saint-Petersburg, 2002), 404–405.

10   T. K. Nikolskaia, *Russki protestantizm i gosudarstvennaia vlast v 1905–1991 godah* (St. Petersburg: Publisher House of the Europe University of St. Petersburg, 2009), 102.

11   From the memoirs of a daughter of a repressed Adventist pastor Anton F. Grinenko, who died in GULAG in 1943. See N. A. Zhukalyuk, *Vspominayte Nastavnikov Vashih*, 133–134.

the West Siberian Region, current member of the Central Council, to conduct the activities and management of the Seventh-day Adventists All-Union Council temporarily until re-election. (The date is unreadable) April 1934.[12]

From this moment until the end of the Second World War, G. A. Grigoriev would remain the only representative of the SDA All-Union (Integrated) Council.

Thus, during the years of Stalinist repression, the Seventh-day Adventist Church, like the associations of Russian Baptists and Pentecostals, which according to the authorities were "class alien organizations to workers," which should be combatted decisively, was virtually annihilated. The main Bolshevik expert on issues of "sectarianism," F. M. Putintsev, reported in 1935 "to the top" that in the Far Eastern district alone the number of Protestant congregations decreased by more than 3.5 times: in 1929 there had been 311 Protestant congregations in the territory of the Far Eastern district, and in 1932 there were only 86 of them.[13]

## Conventional Policy of the Soviet Union during the War

For the Soviet Union the war started on June 22, 1941. The war, named in the USSR history textbooks "Great Patriotic War," become a most serious test for all the people living in the territory of this vast country. Many cities were destroyed and villages were burnt down. Overall, the casualties in the USSR reached 26.6 million people. The Patriotic War required the mobilization of not only organizational, financial, and material resources, but also moral, spiritual, and patriotic ones.

Ten days after the beginning of the war, the head of the Soviet government and the Communist Party, I. V. Stalin, addressed the nation over the radio. This was one of the few speeches addressed not to "Communists, Komsomol members and non-Party people," but to the heart of every Soviet person. Thus it began with the words: "Comrades! Citizens! Brothers and sisters! The soldiers of our army and navy! To you I address, my friends! ... A serious danger looms over our Motherland."[14] The appeal to Soviet citizens as brothers and sisters, more common in the church environment, emphasized the fact that religion, despite a long-term campaign to impose an atheistic worldview, was still an integral part of the life of many Soviet people. This appeal indicated that now, in the face of a national threat, the Soviet authorities would have to revise their attitude towards religion. In short, it would require a change in the confessional policy of the state.[15]

12  From the SDA Church Archive, *Reports of AUCSDA Board meetings*, 1920–1934, Leningrad, 235.

13  F. M. Putintsev, *Politicheskaya Rol i Taktika Sekt* (Moscow: Gosudarstvennoe Antireligioznoe Izdatel'stvo, 1935), 405.

14  *Pravda*, June 3, 1941, 1–2.

15  For further information about this see: M. I. Odintsov, A. S. Kochetova, *Konfessionalnaya politika v Sovietskom Soyuze v Gody Velikoy Otechestvennoy Voiny 1941–1945* (Moscow, 2014). The authors describe in detail practical changes in the position and activities of the Soviet authorities which made a large contribution to the "religious renaissance" in the Soviet

From the time of the all-Union census of 1937 it had not been a secret for the party-Soviet leadership that a significant part of the Soviet Union's population considered themselves believers. In the first months of the Great Patriotic War, the inadequacy and perniciousness of the state policy towards religion and the church formed in the 1930s became obvious. The illusions about the successful and universal "overcoming" of religion and the victory of the atheistic movement had dissipated, giving way to the truth – there were millions of believers in the country who were unfairly restricted in their ability to satisfy their religious needs freely and openly.[16]

Many researchers note that the patriotism of Soviet people in the first days of the war was to no small extent fuelled by the Orthodox Church.[17] Following the appeal of the head of the Russian Orthodox Church, Metropolitan Sergius (Stragorodsky) of Moscow and Kolomna, who spoke on the very first day of the beginning of the Great Patriotic War, other religious groups such as the Renewal Orthodox Church, the Georgian Orthodox Church, the Armenian Apostolic Church as well as the leaders of Muslim, Jewish, and Buddhist organizations, expressed their patriotic position. The sense of patriotism turned out to be stronger than past and bitter grievances. Addressing believers with patriotic messages, they called upon them to fulfil their religious and civil duty properly and to render all possible material assistance to the needs of the front and the home front.[18]

At the beginning of the war, the authorities intended to build constructive relations with Protestant organizations as well. As T. N. Nikolskaya noted,

> patriotism, readiness to defend one's country, did not always mean readiness to fight with arms in hand. Believers prayed for their homeland, conscientiously worked in industry, agriculture, hospitals, servicing the Soviet Army, collected money to help orphans, wounded, war-affected areas, etc., were ready to serve in medical and other detachments that do not require carrying weapons, used international relations to support the USSR.[19]

Union during the war and promoted widespread patriotic activities of believers and religious organizations both within the inner regions of the USSR and in the temporarily occupied Soviet territory. They also study the foreign policy factor, which positively affected the religious policy of the Soviet state.

16   M. I. Odintsov, "Sovietskoye Gosudarstvo i Religioznye Organizatsii v SSSR v Gody Velikoy Otechestvennoy Voiny 1941–1945," *Svoboda Sovesti v Rossii: Istoricheskiy i Sovremennyy Aspekty*, Issue 12, Collection of articles (Saint-Petersburg: The Russian Scholars of Religion Union, 2016), 8.

17   M. I. Odintsov, "Patrioticheskoye Sluzheniye Russkoy Pravoslavnoy Tserkvi v Gody Velikoy Otechestvennoy Voyny," *Svoboda Sovesti v Rossii: Istoricheskiy i Sovremennyy Aspekty*, Issue 2, Collection of Articles (Moscow: The Russian Scholars of Religion Union, 2005), 363–381.

18   For further details see M. I. Odintsov, A. S. Kochetova, *Konfessionalnaya Politika v Sovietskom Soyuze v Gody Velikoy Otechestvennoy Voyny 1941–1945*.

19   T. N. Nikolskaya, *Russkiye Protestanty v Gody Velikoy Otechestvennoy Voiny 1941–1945*, 48.

Thus, the Baptists, for instance had the opportunity to address their fellow believers abroad. In February 1942, they reported on their activities to the President of the Baptist World Alliance (BWA), D. G. Rashbrook, voicing their desire to unite with the Evangelical Christians into a single alliance,[20] and expressed their hope to establish permanent ties with foreign co-religionists. The established Provisional Council of Evangelical Christians and Baptists took a patriotic position during the war. In particular, in an appeal letter to the believers, its leaders wrote:

> In our days, Europe shudders under the wheels of the military machine of Hitler's Germany. Hitlerism inscribed on its banner: "The conquest of the world! The enslavement of mankind! The re-establishment of a new cult of Nazism on earth!" The danger for the work of the Gospel is great ... Germany wants to match the name of the bloody Fuhrer against the name of Christ dear to all the Christians. May God save humanity from this! Three great powers: our native Russia, England, and the USA have united ... their weapons to repel the formidable forces ... of aggression ... and to save Europe from the danger of enslavement looming over it. Let every brother and every sister fulfil their duty to God and to the Motherland in the hard days that we are experiencing. We, the believers, will be the best warriors on the front and the best workers in the home front! Our beloved Motherland should remain free.[21]

Members of local congregations of Evangelical Christians and Baptists organized garment tailoring and repair services, collection of clothes and other items for the families of the deceased and for the soldiers, helped in caring for the wounded and the sick in hospitals, and cared for orphans in orphanages. They used the money collected in the congregations to build the "Merciful Samaritan" sanitary plane, which was used to take seriously wounded soldiers to the rear.[22]

Silent recognition of the patriotism of believers and religious organizations was felt in the position of the government authorities, which during the first two years of the war actually adopted an approach of non-interference in the country's church life. As a result, general church fundraising and extracurricular activities were conducted; there were no obstacles to mass worship and ceremonies; churches' publishing activities expanded; religious centres were recognized *de facto* and allowed to establish links with foreign religious organizations; churches and prayer houses were opening; and some religious leaders were released from prison.

During the war all public anti-religious propaganda was stopped and the Union of Militant Atheists was terminated. Instead, the official press published articles about the patriotic activities of the Orthodox Church. Paradoxical as it may sound, the war in some sense was salutary for religion in the Soviet Union, contributing to a warming of relations between the state and the church.

---

20  It is important to draw attention to this situation, witnessing the existence of objective tendency of related churches to unity, independent from the state.
21  *Istoriya Yevangelskikh Khristian-Baptstov v SSSR* (Moscow: Izdatelstvo VSEHB, 1989), 229.
22  Ibid.

Then the Soviet government took steps to settle the relationship, primarily the one with the Russian Orthodox Church. A special body – the Council for the Affairs of the Russian Orthodox Church, headed by G. G. Karpov – was set up under the Council of People's Commissars to connect the government with the Orthodox Church.[23] The Council started to function in September 1943. The task of the Council included the organization of relations between the state and the Church. At the local level this task was fulfilled by the Council's commissioners, who acted as a liaison between local authorities and the church.

## Confessional Policy of Germany in the Occupied Soviet Territory

In order to better understand the situation in which religious organizations – including Protestants in the occupied territory – found themselves, it is important to pay attention to the religious policies of the Germans.[24] The German strategy of destroying the USSR in the course of the "blitzkrieg" was largely founded on the hope that the dissatisfaction of Soviet people with the political regime, including its national and religious policy, would become a kind of ally of the Third Reich in the struggle against Bolshevism. Hence the significant attention the Germans paid to religion in the territory they occupied. In an effort to take control over the activities of religious organizations, the occupation authorities set up departments for administering church affairs under city councils. Their activities included the selection of church personnel, administering churches, scheduling church services, etc.

The documents of various German departments recorded the significant religious revival in the Soviet territories occupied during the first months of the war. The main department of imperial security, for example, noted that, "among the part of the population of the former Soviet Union freed from the Bolshevik yoke, there is a strong desire to return to the authority of the church or churches, which is especially true to the older generation, while the younger generation looks at it indifferently."

---

23  About the foundation and activities of the Council see M. I. Odintsov, T. A. Chumachenko, *Sovet po Delam Russkoy Pravoslavnoy Tserkvi pri SNK SSSR (SM SSSR) i Moskovskaya Patriarchia: Epocha Vzaimodeystviya i Protivostoyaniya. 1943–1965* (Saint-Petersburg: [n.p.], 2013).

24  M. V. Shkarovsky, *Politika Tretyego Reiha po Otnosheniyu k Russkoy Pravoslavnoy Tserkvi v Svete Arhivnyh Materialov 1935–1945 Godov* (collection of documents) (Moscow, 2003). A large massive of documents on the policy of German authorities towards religious cults in the occupied territory was published in the book: *Russkaya Pravoslavnaya Tserkov v Gody Voiny 1941–1945*: Collection of documents (Moscow, Krutitskiy courtyard publishing house, 2009), 519–649. See also: M. I. Katin, "Tretiy Reih: Ideologi Natsizma o Formirovanii 'Novoy Religii', ob Otnoshenii k Pravoslvnoy Ruskoy Emigratsii I o 'Novom Religioznom Poryadke' na Okkupirovannoy Sovetskoy Territorii," *Svoboda Sovesti v Rossii: Istoricheskiy I Sovremennyy Aspekty*, Issue 10, Collection of articles (Saint-Petersburg: Russian Scholars of Religion Union, 2014), 62–80.

In that regard, it was suggested that a "new class of preachers," trained and capable of "interpreting religion to the people" free of national history, traditions, and culture, should be admitted to the occupied territories.[25]

Considering the role of Orthodoxy, special attention was paid to the activities related to the Russian Orthodox Church in the occupied territories. At the same time, it should be mentioned that in their strategic plans the leadership of the Third Reich aimed at destruction of the Russian Orthodox Church as a historical and national-cultural phenomenon of the Russian and other Orthodox peoples of the USSR. It was supposed to be replaced by the same "new" religion and a state church, which the ideologists of Nazism were planning to set up.[26]

In general, the German authorities sought to make maximum use of religious issues in the occupation zone for their ideological purposes. The press, flooded with materials about "terror," unleashed by the Bolsheviks against religion and believers, simultaneously emphasized that the new government would bring religious freedom. The invaders persistently "recommended" the priests, in sermons and during church ceremonies, to express loyalty to Hitler and the Third Reich as well as to hold special prayer services for the victory of the German army and the "salvation of the Motherland" from the Bolsheviks. The distribution of all sorts of religious and edifying literature was also encouraged.[27]

The Ministry of Occupied Eastern Territories, created for the civil administration of the territories of the USSR seized during the war, sought to use Protestants for its own purposes as well. Thus, in Belarus, permission was obtained to set up a Pentecostal centre headed by the "bishop" I. K. Panko. The occupation authorities gave the All-Ukrainian Union of Evangelical Christians permission to resume their activities under the direction of G. I. Ponurko.[28] By the end of 1943 the union included almost 350 congregations with over 11 thousand members. It should be mentioned that the occupation authorities insisted on uniting (as they had in Germany) Pentecostals with Evangelical Christians and Baptists of Ukraine,[29] who could also function freely. However, not all leaders and believers took this step. At the same time, all those leaders who opposed the association were subjected to Gestapo arrests

25    Rossiisky Gosudarstvenny Arhiv Socialnoy I Politicheskoy Istorii (RGASPI) (Russian State Archive of Social Political History), Fond 17, Description 125, Case 92, List 23–25.

26    About the main features of the "new religion" see: M. I. Katin, "Tretiy Reih: Ideologi Natsizma o Formirovanii 'Novoy Religii', ob Otnoshenii k Pravoslavnoy Russkoy Emigratsii I o 'Novom Mirovom Poryadke' na Okkupirovannoy Sovietskoy Territorii".

27    M. I. Odintsov, and A. S. Kochetova, *Konfessionalnaya politika v Sovietskom Soyuze v Gody Velikoy Otechestvennoy Voiny 1941–1945*, 99.

28    The chairman of the Union, G. I. Ponurko, was recognized by the German authorities as the "bishop of the Episcopal church of Christians of Evangelical faith." This title was more common for the German authorities. A significant factor for approving this candidacy was that Ponurko had spent nine years in prison, suffering for his faith.

29    According to some information, this union ("united Christ's Church") was to include the Seventh-day Adventists. See D. V. Vedeneyev, *Ateisty v mundirah. Sovetskiye Spetssluzhby I Religioznaya Sfera Ukrainy* (Moscow: Self Published, 2016), 122.

and imprisonment. Besides, in Western Ukraine, the resurgent Pentecostalism was subjected to violence by Ukrainian nationalists (Banderites). A number of church ministers were killed by the Nationalist Security Service.

In general Protestant organizations (Lutherans, Evangelical Christians, Baptists, Pentecostals, Adventists) had the opportunity to function in the occupied territory. According to data collected later by Soviet state security agencies, during the years of occupation up to 4,200 Protestant congregations resumed their legal activities in the Ukraine alone. For example, whereas in 1940 there were 426 prayer houses of Evangelical Christians and Baptists in the Ukrainian SSR, in 1942 there were 2778 of them, and they had about one hundred thousand believers.[30]

## The Creation of the Council for Religious Affairs under the CPC of the USSR

On May 19, 1944, the Council of People's Commissars adopted a resolution to set up another state body, the Council for Religious Affairs, which administered "relations" with all other religious organizations, except for the Orthodox ones. On June 6, 1944, I. V. Polyansky was approved as the organization's chairperson. The rights and responsibilities, as well as the area of competence and organizational structure of the new Council, were similar to the ones of the Council for the Russian Orthodox Church.

The Council's responsibilities included considering the questions raised by leaders of religious cults, drafting legislative acts and resolutions related to the issues of these religious cults, monitoring the correct and timely implementation throughout the territory of the USSR of laws and decrees by the USSR Government related to religious cults, the general recording of churches and prayer buildings, and the compilation of statistical reports on data submitted to the Council by local Soviet bodies.[31]

The Council supported religious organizations' and believers' petitions related to their spiritual activities, registration of religious congregations, opening religious buildings, and publication of religious literature. In late February 1945, the Soviet government, on the recommendation of the Council for Religious Affairs, decided to defer mobilization of the clergy of a number of churches, including the Seventh-day Adventist Church.[32]

30  See Ibid., 122.
31  E. N. Duplenskaya, "Soviet po Delam Religioznyh Kultov pri SM SSSR: Istoriya Sozdaniya, Osnovnye Napravleniya Deyatelnosti," *Svoboda Sovesti v Rossii: Istoricheskiy I Sovremennyy Aspekty* (Moscow, 2004).
32  Gosudarstvenny Arhiv Rossiiskoy Federatsii (GARF) (State Archive of Russian Federation), Fond 6991, Description 3, Case 12, List 99–100.

The Council had its own representatives in the Councils of People's Commissars of union and autonomous republics and in regional and district executive committees. In early 1945, a manual entitled "Instruction on the Activities of Commissioners" was developed and approved, in which the main directions of their activities were determined and specified.

The very first reports received by the representatives of the Council for Religious Affairs already showed how difficult it was for local authorities to accept the idea of the need to ensure citizens' right to freedom of conscience and the rights of religious groups. There were widespread refusals to consider any requests from believers regarding setting up prayer houses, administrative sanctions regarding applicants for registration, and red tape in the application process. The representatives reported that local authorities "dodged" believers' requests to return to them the religious buildings that had been previously reserved for state and public needs. In addition, local authorities did not allow believers to hold meetings, did not let the clergy into settlements, did not allow the repair of religious buildings, arbitrarily closed existing prayer buildings, confiscated property of religious societies, unduly arrested clergymen, insulted believers, and broke up prayer buildings.[33]

I. V. Polyansky, in his work, tried to take into account the political views of religious leaders, their patriotic attitude during the occupation of the Soviet territory, and their loyalty to the reestablished Soviet power. At the same time, the Council for Religious Affairs was extremely harsh towards those religious associations that the state referred to as "anti-state, anti-Soviet and fanatical sects." These included the Adventist Reform Movement, Dukhobors, Malevans, Methodists, Molokans, the new Israel, Pentecostals, Satanists, Jehovah's Witnesses, Skoptsy, Khlysty, and some others. The Council (as the state in general) perceived them not so much as religious, but as political organizations, and therefore did not consider it possible even to raise the question of their legalization and subsequent registration. All of them were under the constant control of state security agencies.

One of the religious movements to which the Council for Religious Affairs paid considerable attention was the evangelical movement. This was primarily due to the gradual liberation of the territories of Belarus and Ukraine, previously occupied by fascists, accomplished by the Soviet troops in 1944. Before re-establishing Soviet power, the task was to formulate a policy towards numerous evangelical organizations that operated here: Evangelical Christians, Baptists, Pentecostals and Adventists. This process turned out to be very, very difficult. Official authorities had a more or less favorable position towards Russian Orthodoxy, and all other churches, denominations, associations, and cults had to prove their right to exist. Negative attitudes towards them had already risen in connection with the fact that during the years of occupation the evangelical congregations in general managed to restore organizational ties, opened prayer houses, and even resumed the activities of previously closed centres.

33   See for instance, ibid.

In the autumn of 1943, leaders of the Provisional Council of Evangelical Christians and Baptists were permitted to return from evacuation to Moscow and begin restoring church structures and establishing permanent ties with fellow believers abroad. In October 1944, a conference was held in Moscow, which would later be called the 37th All-Union Congress of Evangelical Christian Baptists. Following the discussion of the main issue of merging the organizations, they adopted a resolution. It read: "Burying all disagreements of the past, from two unions – the union of Evangelical Christians and the Baptist Union – to create one union – the Union of Evangelical Christians and Baptists with the All-Union Council of Evangelical Christians and Baptists as the governing body, residing in the city of Moscow."[34] The materials of the congress were made public in the first issue of the journal ACECB, "Bratsky Vestnik," the publication of which was sanctioned by the authorities. In 1945 during the so-called "August meeting," Pentecostals were included in the Union of Evangelical Christians-Baptists.

## The SDA Church during the War

The war became a serious shock for the entire Soviet society, including Seventh-day Adventists. For the latter, the war was particularly difficult given the fact that for historical reasons among the Seventh-day Adventists there were many ethnic Germans. During the war they were arrested as "unreliable" and taken to the forced labor in camps or mobilized into the labor army. The Adventists, refusing to take up arms, were also mobilized civilian facilities, in mines, in logging, and sometimes in extremely difficult conditions. They had to work in the construction of military installations and church veteran Arnold Rebein recalls that the situation of the Adventists drafted into the labor army hardly differed from the conditions in a detention camp.[35] Despite these difficulties, Adventists generally considered being drafted into the labor army as a real opportunity to serve the Motherland without taking up arms.[36]

At the same time, members of Adventist congregations, along with the entire Soviet people, did everything in their power to support the war effort: they served in the Red Army, did their duty in medical units, worked as translators, drivers, signalmen, military musicians, etc. SDA church pastor D. O. Yunak recalls that

---

34  *Istoriya Yevangelskih Hristian-Baptistov v SSSR*, 232.

35  A. Rebein, *Po Milosti Tvoyey…* (Zaokskyy: Istochnik Zhizni, 1997), 129.

36  D. A. Fokin, "Kak Zhili I Trudilis Veruyushchiye v Voinu: Povsednevnaya Kultura Protestantov v Period Velikoy Otechestvennoy Voyny," *Svoboda Sovesti v Rossii: Istoricheskiy I Sovremennyy Aspekty*, Issue 12, Collection of articles (Saint-Petersburg: Russian Scholars of Religion Union, 2016), 69.

among the Adventists there were those who served in combat units, some were taken as sappers, some as communication officers, someone was sent to the most dangerous sections of the front – a lot depended on the commanders who either understood the feelings of believers, or vice versa – they mocked, they tried to break their religious views.[37]

The only representative of the All-Union (Integrated) Council of the SDA Church remaining at large by the beginning of the war, G. A. Grigoryev, along with the leaders of other religious associations living in Moscow, in October, 1941 was evacuated to the city of Ulyanovsk, where he stayed until August, 1942.[38] According to Grigoriev's memoirs, reported by Pastor V. I. Sorokin, on the eve of his departure, I. V. Stalin summoned him, remembering that many years ago he told him about the prophecies of the Bible. Summoning him, Stalin asked: what did he think, according to the Bible, would the Germans take Moscow? Brother Grigoriev replied to this: "They will not. The world empire, according to the book of the prophet Daniel, will no longer be, Europe will not be united under the rule of Hitler. God will punish Hitler through Russians."[39]

## The SDA Church and Pacifism

For many believers, including Adventists, the war sharply aggravated the problem of military duty and weapon bearing. This was especially true for convicted pacifists. The Criminal Code of the RSFSR, even in peacetime, dictates various degrees of punishment for evasion of military service due to religious reasons: from application of the rules of the Red Army's disciplinary Charter (correctional labour or 1 to 5 years of imprisonment) to the death penalty.[40] And this despite the fact that the Law on Military Obligations of August 13, 1930 provided for the possibility for traditional pacifist sects to do civil service instead of military, or (in wartime) to serve in the auxiliary parts of the Red Army. In practice, this law was not observed and for evasion of military duties due to religious convictions, pacifists generally bore criminal responsibility. M. Y. Krapivin notes the fact that during the period between 1935

37  Ibid.
38  The information found in some publications, for instance D. O. Yunak, *Istoriya Tserkvi Hristian Adventistov Sed'mogo Dnya v Rossii, 1886–1981*, vol. 1 (Zaoksky: Istochnik Zhizni, 2002), 328) that G. A. Grigoryev in Autumn 1941 was sent out of Moscow and taken to Ulyanovsk, where he lived near Patriarch Aleksiy (Simanskiy), is not completely accurate. In Autumn 1941, Grigoryev along with leaders of other religious centres were evacuated to Ulyanovsk. The head of the Russian Orthodox Church of that time, metropolitan Sergiy (Starogorodskiy), elected as the patriarch only in September 1943, lived there at the same time as well. Metropolitan Aleksiy (Simanskiy) spent the wartime in blockaded Leningrad and visited Ulyanovsk for a few days only in 1943. He was elected as the patriarch only in January 1945.
39  This and other such "memoirs" have no documented evidence, and therefore can be considered only mythologization of the past.
40  See articles 68, 69, 594, 595 193–13. The Criminal Code of RSFSR. (Moscow: [n.p.], 1938), 36–37, 43–44, 98.

and 1941 there were no recorded cases of religious pacifists exercising their right to alternative service.[41]

The law on universal military service, adopted on September 1, 1939, did not provide refusal to serve in the Red Army for any reason at all, including religious beliefs. Therefore, pacifistic believers who were drafted against their will to the armed forces and who refused to take up arms, were punished by military courts.[42] Thus, the Chairman of the Council for Religious Affairs, I. V. Polyansky, in his "Report on the Religious Situation in the USSR" to the Central Committee of the Central Committee of the All-Union Communist party of the Bolsheviks, mentions the fact that an Adventist third-year student of the Dnepropetrovsk Medical Institute, being called to the Red Army, refused to take up arms. Six students of the Medical Institute came to the military registration and enlistment office to apply for his release from military service. Commenting on this situation, Polyansky noted that

> the leader of this community, just like many members, is looking at the military service negatively, allowing each believer to resolve this issue "in line with his conscience." However, those members of the community who agree to take up arms and serve in the Red Army, are excluded from the community.[43]

It should be noted that at the end of the war, Protestants, along with the current ministers of other religions and confessions, were exempted from conscription into the army according to the decision of the commission for exemptions and draft postponement adopted on February 26, 1945. But this option was extended only to elders of Evangelical Christians, Baptists, and Seventh-day Adventists elders and preachers.[44]

The Seventh-day Adventist Church has never adopted the tenet of completely abandoning any form of military service, as manifested in the extreme version of the pacifist position. Adventists were ready to fulfil their civic duty as long as the orders of the authorities and the military command were not in conflict with their conscience and God's law.[45] The following examples narrate the life of some leaders and

---

41  M. Y. Krapivin and A. G. Dalgatov, "Sektantskij Antimilitarizm I Problemy Stroitel'stva Rossijskih Vooruzhennyh Sil (1918 – 1939)," *Vlast', Obshhestvo I Reformy V Rossii (XVI – nachalo XX* (Saint-Petersburg: [n.p.], 2004), 441.

42  Thus, an Adventist minister I. M. Cherkasov was convicted for refusing to take up the arms twice – during the Soviet-Finn war and the Great Patriotic War. See Yunak, *Istoriya Tserkvi Hristian Adventistov Sed'mogo Dnya v Rosssii,* vol. 1, 277.

43  GARF. F.R. – 6992. op. 3. d. 10. l. 69.

44  A letter from the chairman I.V. Polyanskiy to the chairman of the Novgorod regional union of March 8, 1945. State archive of Novgorod Region (GANO). Fond 4110, Description 4, Case 23, List 1.

45  D. Heinz mentions three main reasons why Adventists adopted the principle of refusing to take part in military actions bearing weapons: 1. Conviction that taking part in military activities contradicts the Christian faith, especially the "Thou shalt not kill" commandment. 2. Eschatological tendency to nonconformity and distance from all worldly matters. 3. Unwillingness to profane Sabbath – the day of weekly rest in line with a commandment – by doing

church members who faced the Law on General Military Duty during the War. It should be noted that many leaders and members of the church managed to avoid this law only because they had already been repressed earlier and served their sentence in the Gulag for their faith, and their imprisonment lasted during the wartime.[46]

In January 1944 the senior pastor in the Zhitomir region (Ukraine), Vitaliy G. Slyusarenko, and local ministers Kalenik, Kalinchuk, Lavrenchuk, and Ivan and Veniamin Tarakhtelyuk were drafted into the army. For refusing to take the military oath, they were all arrested and thrown into the prison of Berdichev. A few days later, exhausted and hungry, the half-dressed people were taken to the frost and put against a long wall. The verdict was read: execution. Several shots rang out simultaneously, but none of the men fell – the marksmen shot over their heads. In this way the prison authorities tried to frighten the believers and get them to take up arms, and then send them to the front. These brethren were ready to face death under a hail of bullets and splinters in order to save the wounded or engage in other work, but they refused to kill. The brave prisoners were taken back to the cell. The next day they did shoot Ivan Tarakhtelyuk to death, hoping to shake the faith of his comrades, but the rest of the men remained unshakable. Consequently, the authorities announced a new sentence – ten years in prison. They were sent to Zhitomir prison, and then to Syktyvkar (Komi ASSR) for heavy and dangerous work related to logging. Adventist prisoners had to live among criminals, thieves, and murderers; they had to starve and freeze. The guards treated the believers with the utmost contempt, considering them traitors to their homeland.[47]

There were cases when Adventists refused to take up arms and they were offered the opportunity to fulfill their duty to the motherland through service without weapons. This happened to a young preacher, a graduate of the Bible Institute in Brasov (Romania), Alexander F. Parasei. During the war, he was in a Romanian concentration camp in Botosani. In 1944, the prisoners of the concentration camp were liberated by the Red Army, and Alexander found himself in the military unit of the Third Byelorussian Front, where he served as the head of the uniforms warehouse. He reached Berlin with his detachment and met Victory Day on May 9, 1945, in Lower Silesia, from where he was demobilized and returned home.

Unusual was the fate of another Adventist minister, Ignat S. Bondar, who on the first day of the war, on June 22, 1941, was summoned to the military enlistment office and sent to the Lukyanovka barracks. In the military unit, located in Brovarsky forests, Bondar served as an instructor for chemical protection. After the 600,000-

---

the service. See Daniel Heinz, "Adventisty Sed'mogo Dnya I Otkaz ot Uchastiya v Voyennyh Deystviyah v Rossiyskoy Imperii," *Dolgiy Put' Rossiyskogo Patsifizma: Ideal Mezhdunarodnogo I Vnurennego Mira v Religiozno-Filosofskoy I Obshchestvenno-Politicheskoy Mysli Rossii*, ed. by T. A. Pavlov (Moscow: [n.p.], 1997), 173.

46  Thus, the deputy chairman of the All-Union Council, I. A. Lvov, repressed in 1934, spent over 20 years in the camps and as an exile, and was released only in 1955, 10 years after the end of the war. See N. A. Zhukalyuk, *Vspominayte Nastavnikov Vashih*, 273.

47  Ibid., 272–273.

strong grouping of Soviet troops was surrounded, most of the soldiers were taken
prisoner. Bondar miraculously managed to escape captivity, and he returned home,
to Kiev. Before the war all the ministers of the Adventist church in Kiev were repressed, the congregation was closed, and the prayer house was confiscated. Now,
under the conditions of German occupation, Bondar was actively engaged in rebuild-
ing the destroyed community of believers and began to conduct worship services with
a small group in a basement-like damp room. Soon the authorities gave the community a house of the Karaite Kenesa (Karaite synagogue) and in the difficult time of
war, in just one and a half years, the Kiev church baptized 185 new members.

Even more surprising was the fate of Dmitry K. Kolbach, a graduate of the Warsaw Theological Seminary, which he left in 1939. Before the invasion of German
troops in the USSR, Kolbach, a talented musician, organized in his hometown of
Pozharka, Volhynia (Ukraine), a large brass band consisting of 30 musicians. With
the outbreak of the war, all the members of the orchestra, young people of military
age, received draft notices that required them to come to the military commissariat
and subsequently get sent to the front. The young minister decided to propose to the
military commissar to take the entire Adventist orchestra along with their instruments into a musical division so that they could all complete their military service in
this manner. The proposal was accepted, and by the end of the war, having fulfilled
its civic duty, the whole orchestra returned to its home community.

A truly difficult life was that of Adventist preacher Vitaliy I. Prolinsky, who was
baptized in 1943. The village of Uladovka, where he lived, was completely burned
down by the Nazis on January 9, 1944. Over 400 people were burnt or shot to death
that day – including Vitaliy's father. Vitaliy, along with other young members of the
church, was captured by the Germans and sent to a concentration camp. For refusing
to work on Saturday, he and his friends were sentenced to death by shooting. Yet just
at the moment when the escorts had already received permission from the camp com-
mandant to shoot the "sabbatarians," the American air force arrived, and during the
air raid the young Adventists managed to escape and hide in the nearest forest. After
the liberation of Ukraine from Germany, Vitaliy was drafted into the active army,
where he served in the construction battalion until the end of the war.

## The SDA Church and Collaboration

It was mentioned earlier that the German authorities in the occupied territory tried
to use religion in order to persuade the population to join their side. Thanks to the
promotion of the new authorities, the life of many Protestant congregations intensified noticeably. In the occupied territories they even held church congresses and established Protestant alliances.[48] Many prayer houses, closed under the Soviet

48   T. N. Nikolskaya, "Russkiye Protestanty v Gody Velikoy Otechestvennoy Voiny, 1941–
     1945," *Svoboda Sovesti v Rossii: Istoricheskiy I Sovremennyy Aspekty*, Issue 12, Collection
     of articles (Saint-Petersburg: Russian Scholars of Religion Union, 2016), 45.

authorities, were opened, and religious centres in many regions were restored. Vitaly Nikitchenko, chairman of the republic's KGB (in 1954–1970), in his report to the Central Committee of the Ukraine's Communist party, stressed that during the occupation there was a revival in sectarian movements, "the doctrine of which is based on the anti-Soviet platform" such as the Pentecostal Zionists, the Reformed Adventists, the Jehovah's Witnesses, the Il'inians, the True Orthodox Church, the Podgornovtsy, the Joannites, the Innokentyans, the Khlysty, the Murashkovtsi, and others.[49]

This revival of Protestant activities in the occupied territories would later turn against them. After the liberation of these territories by the Red Army, many religious ministers and activists were convicted of complicity with the occupation regime. The accusation of collaboration would become one of the main arguments against Russian Protestantism in the post-war years.[50]

The question of the collaboration of Russian Protestants remains open to this day. Although such accusations of believers regarding cooperation with the occupiers were often used in anti-religious propaganda, in specific cases it is difficult to verify whether a particular employee or member of a Protestant community actively cooperated with the invaders and whether he was a believing Protestant at that moment.

It is known that the occupation authorities and representatives of the special services actively supported and "infiltrated" the Adventist community, especially the members of Adventist Reform Movement. As Soviet counterintelligence established later, in the occupied territory, individual reformers cooperated with the new administration and they were used for special propaganda, intelligence, and counterintelligence work. Activists of the Kiev Adventist community – Yakov and Vladimir Reiner – voluntarily cooperated with the German authorities and campaigned for loyalty to the invaders. The son of F. Gladkov, a Seventh-day Adventist minister responsible for the Kharkov and Dnipropetrovsk region, and pastor of one of the congregations in Donbass, served the Germans distributing anti-Soviet leaflets.[51]

One can imagine the conflicting feelings experienced by believers in the occupied territories during the wartime when they were forced to determine their attitude towards the new government. Living in the Soviet Union, many of them had experienced oppression on religious grounds, had survived persecution for their faith, and had lost their loved ones. The constant violation of rights and freedoms, a brutal insult to religious feelings had certainly caused a negative attitude towards the Soviet authorities in believers. Even more complex was the attitude towards the Soviet authorities of the people living in the territories recently annexed to the USSR, where national and political problems were added to religious ones. It is not a secret that some of them believed German propaganda, which promised freedom of religion, and went on to cooperate with the new authorities on matters of religious activity.

49  Departmental State Archive of the Ukrainian Security Service (OGA SBU). Fond 1, Description 21, Case 2, List 16.
50  Nikolskaya, *Russkiye Protestanty v Gody Velikoy Otechestvennoy Voiny,*121.
51  OGA SBU, F. 9, D. 89, L. 105–108. Cited from D. V. Vedeneyev, *Ateisty v Mundirah. Sovietskiye Spetssluzhby I Religioznaya Sfera Ukrainy* (Moscow: [n.p.], 2016), 123.

After the end of the war, many collaborators would experience all the horrors of the GULAG once again, being condemned by the Soviet authorities for assisting the occupation forces. Thus, G. Ponurko who was actively involved in the reconstruction of the Union of Evangelical Christians in the occupied territory of Ukraine, was arrested in April, 1945, charged with collaboration, and sentenced to prison until 1954.[52] The head of the Adventist Reform Movement, V. A. Shelkov, was sentenced to death in 1945 for his ties with the German invaders. Two months later, the death sentence was replaced by ten years of imprisonment.[53] On September 17, 1955, a decree was issued by the Presidium of the Supreme Soviet of the USSR entitled "On the amnesty of Soviet citizens who collaborated with the occupiers during the Great Patriotic War of 1941–1945."

## Restoration of the SDA Church Organization

Returning to Moscow in August 1942, G. A. Grigoriev, engaged in the pastoral care of the Moscow community of believers, was making efforts to restore the activities of Adventist congregations in the liberated Soviet territories. As soon as some territory was liberated from the occupation and as postal services were re-established, Grigoriev sent encouraging letters, assuring the believers of the relentless prayerful support from the church leadership. He constantly stressed the need to restore at least some organization in order to make it easier to solve the problems of the church ravaged by repressions and the war.[54]

The authorities did not impede the revival of the All-Union Council of Seventh-day Adventists (AUCSDA). At Grigoriev's request, F. V. Melnik and A. G. Galladzhev were allowed to move to Moscow and take part in the work of the All-Union Council of Seventh-day Adventists. I. V. Polyansky assisted A. G. Galladzhev in moving to Moscow. In a letter to the representative for the Kazakh SSR, N. Sabitov, he wrote:

> In Moscow there is the "All-Union Council of Seventh-day Adventists" – the centre of a widespread and significant religious organization. Currently this centre is represented for various reasons only by its chairman, G. Grigoriev. Grigoriev applied to the Council for Religious Affairs for permission for a number of senior officials of the organization to move to Moscow in order to staff its centre and improve its efficiency. Alexey Georgiyevich Galladzhev, currently residing in the South-Kazakhstan region, is chosen as one of these workers ... I ask you to take urgent measures to ensure that Galladzhev

---

52  V. Franchuk, *Prosila Rossiya Dozhdya u Gospoda*, vol. 2 (Kyiv: [n.p.], 2002), 364.

53  F. Fedorenko, *Sekty, Ih Vera I Dela* (Moscow: Publishing House of Political Literature, 1965), 194. Although in some Soviet sources Shelkov is mentioned as "an active aider of Fascists," specific charges mention only his studying at German language courses and organizing in the region of the Caucasus Mineral Waters about 10 groups of Adventist-Reformers. See L. E. Voronin, *Adventism I Reformism* (Stavropol: [n.p.], 1983), 58–59.

54  Dmitry O. Yunak, *Istoriya Tserkvi Hristian ASD v Rossii*, vol. 1 (Zaokskyy: Istochnik Zhizni, 2002), 318.

gets the pass and other documents necessary to travel to Moscow together with his daughter Rosanna Alekseevna Galladzheva (13–15 years old), without any hindrance. Report to the Council via telegram when executed.[55]

By the autumn of 1945, the first post-war composition of the Administrative Council of the SDA Church was formed. Under the All-Union Centre they set up an institution of republican commissioners, who started to visit congregations and served as a link between them and the centre. They sent letters to SDA congregations in the Ukraine, Latvia, Estonia, Belarus and elsewhere, reading:

> At its recent meeting on November 21 this year (1945), the All-Union Seventh-day Adventist Council assigned the work functions for the sake of productivity and planned work as follows: G. A. Grigoryev – chairman of the All-Union Council of Seventh-day Adventists; A. G. Galladzhev is his deputy and secretary; F. V. Melnik is a cashier (treasurer). In the forthcoming Week of Prayer, we all have the privilege of offering our prayers to God so that He will continue to help us successfully build, restore or renew the ways for the Eternal Gospel (Isaiah 58:12) so that the ship of our faith keeps travelling under the power of the Holy Spirit unhindered.[56]

In addition, the new management of the All-Union Council of Seventh-day Adventists requested the timely sending of statistical and financial reports to the centre, as well as organizing "collection of donations for the needs caused by the destruction during the war and for the widows and orphans of the families of front-line soldiers." They recommended putting the collected money in local state-owned banks, as did the believers of other confessions.

All these efforts produced positive results: in 1946 there were in the USSR 300 congregations with 13,300 members and about 75 ministers. The largest number of them operated in Ukraine, Moldova, and the Baltic States. In the RSFSR only a few congregations were registered – in Moscow, Gorky, Rostov-on-Don, Taganrog, and Stavropol. In Central Asia not a single church was registered.

Correspondence with the leaders of the World Organization of the SDA Church resumed. Grigoryev sent letters to the General Conference president, Charles Watson, not knowing that his presidential term had expired in 1936. This fact indicates the degree of isolation of the Seventh-day Adventist Church in the Soviet Union. It should be noted that immediately after the allies opened the second front, the stream of postal mail literally rushed in to Moscow. Edgar Chernyavsky in his brochure on P. A. Matzanov wrote:

> Our brothers abroad knew nothing about the situation of the Church in the Union. All ties were broken, but since the United States entered into an alliance with the USSR in the fight against fascism, brothers started sending letters to the old, known address of the mailbox in Moscow to learn something about the fate of the Church. The mailbox was constantly filled with letters, but there was not a single Adventist who could deal with

---

55 See GARF, Fond 6991, Description 3, Case18, List 1.
56 Cited from Yunak, *Istoriya Tserkvi Hristian ASD v Rossii*, 318–319.

this correspondence. When Grigoriev returned to Moscow, all this correspondence was handed over to him.[57]

At the same time, unresolved problems in the relationship with the state persisted. Permission to hold a congress with the subsequent election of leaders was not given. Many Adventist congregations were refused registration; thus they actually worked illegally, sometimes seeking formal recognition for years.[58] P. S. Kulyzhsky recalled:

> Unregistered congregations were then in a very difficult situation. Leaders of registered congregations could not attend them, as the authorities did not give them permission to do so. Unregistered congregations did not have the right to apply for their religious centre. And so, it turned out that the whole Adventist community was divided in two groups: the sons and stepchildren. This was the situation of unregistered churches in the Russian Federation, Kazakhstan, Uzbekistan, Tajikistan, and Kyrgyzstan.[59]

Many state leaders did their best to restore their pre-war policies, aimed at the complete eradication of religion from the life of the Soviet society. The chairman of the Council for Religious Affairs at the Council of Ministers of the USSR, I. V. Polyansky, in his Memorandum to the Central Committee of the AUCP (B) (All-Union Communist Party of Bolshevics) of August 31, 1945, expressed extreme concern over the widespread activation of the operations of religious organizations. He writes that,

> The growth of religious activity of believers ... is observed everywhere and in all religious groups. In some republics, districts, and regions this growth is slower, and in others it is faster, sectarians (Evangelicals, Baptists, Seventh-day Adventists, Pentecostals, etc.) are active in one place, and in the other – Muslims, Old Believers, Jews, Catholics, etc. The activity of believers is expressed in the application to the Authorized Council for the registration of religious congregations, the increase in religious rites (baptism, wedding), the involvement of children and youth in the religious activities of a cult, etc.[60]

The chairman of the Council was particularly concerned about young students turning to God. Giving numerous examples of this trend, he, in particular, mentioned

---

57   See E. Chernyavskiy, *P. A. Matsanov, Fenomen Rukovoditelya Adventistkogo Dvizheniya v Sovietskom Soyuze* (Riga: Self-published, 1997; typewritten). The first, currently known, official message from the General Conference president V.G. Branson was sent to P. Matsanov in December 1953. In line with the rules of that time, the letter was initially delivered to the Council for Religious Cults. In it, representatives of the Adventist society in the USSR were invited to take part in a General Conference session in San-Francisco (USA, May–June 1954), and if it was not possible, to report the activities of Adventists in the Soviet Union. See GARF, Fond 6991, Description 4, Case 10, List 28, 29, 32, 33.
58   For instance, the SDA community in Leningrad in 1946 was never registered despite the petitions from A. G. Galladzhev, P. A. Silman and others. In 1955, A. I. Kholodkov, visiting the community from Moscow, managed to buy a house, but they were denied registration for the reason that it was a redevelopment area.
59   V. V. Teppone, *Iz Istorii Tsekvi ASD v Rossii* (Moscow: [n.p.], 1990), 124.
60   GARF, Fond 6991, Description 3, Case 10, List 61–73.

that for the previous two to three years a group of the "Seventh-day Adventist sect," consisting of 12 people, had emerged and taken shape among the students of the Dnepropetrovsk Medical Institute.[61]

To resume publication of periodicals of the SDA church, P. A. Matzanov, who had a solid experience in publishing, was invited to move from Riga to Moscow in 1947. Starting from 1929 and up to 1940, every three months he had published a magazine entitled *Review of World Affairs* in Russian. The magazine was published in several thousand copies and was distributed mainly among the Russian population in Latvia, Lithuania, and Estonia.

By 1947 the AUCSDA included the following members: G. A. Grigoriev as the chairman; A. G. Gallaghev as secretary-treasurer; P. A. Matzanov as deputy chairman and editor; F. V. Melnyk as a member of the AUCSDA; an elder of the Moscow SDA Church; B. D. Yakovenko as member of the AUCSDA, and an authorized representative of the Council for the Ukraine. The AUCSDA office was located at building no. 22, 1st Meshchanskaya street (now Prospekt Mira), next to the Greek Embassy. Grigoriev and Matzanov with their families lived in the same house.

Members of the AUCSDA, using their authority, were actively visiting congregations and getting acquainted with the situation on the ground. Elders and pastors were ordained wherever they were needed. Beside the Ukraine, representatives of the AUCSDA were appointed in Moldova, Latvia, and Estonia. All the leading members of the SDA Church met in Moscow annually to resolve current issues.

A year later, in 1948, permission was received from the Council for Religious Affairs to expand the Council first to 11, and then to 17 people, including the Audit Commission. The expanded Council was called the "Plenum." Such a name was given to this supreme organ of Adventist administration in the USSR, not in accordance with the *Church Manual*, but based on the model of the Soviet state system of administrative-party management existing in the country that listed a chairman, the presidium, the plenum, and the congress. At the end of 1948, the "Plenum" of the AUCSDA already had 13 members. Its members constantly travelled around the country, facilitating the registration of old and new congregations through local authorities, and recreating the vertical organization of church administration.

One cannot say that all members of the church were satisfied with the established all-union organization. Some did not want to recognize the church leadership, shaped, as they thought, by the will of one person. There were doubts about the legitimacy of the leadership approved by the Council for Religious Affairs. It is true that the post-war church organization was not formed according to the church charter, and the top five church leaders were not elected by delegates sent to the congress from all congregations and conferences. But it should be remembered that there was simply no possibility of holding a congress in line with the canons of the international Seventh-day Adventist Church. The very fact of contacts between church leaders and the state, which was also changing its religious policy and made concessions to many

61   Ibid.

religious organizations and believers, cannot be imputed to anyone. These religious leaders, due to the historical circumstances in which they found themselves when they were called to build up the church, are worthy of recognition, for they sincerely and bravely fulfilled their duty to God, the Motherland and other believers.

## Conclusion

Summing up this research, one should emphasize once again how extremely difficult Adventist existence could be in some parts of Europe and how complex is the problem posed by the scarcity of information on the history of the Seventh-day Adventist Church in the Soviet Union during the period under study. The Church faced the war almost without a head. Church leaders, most pastors, and elders were oppressed. Some organizational activities of the church had not been carried out since 1931, and all of the church's printed publications had been closed.

At the same time, the analysis of the socio-political situation in the country and the nature of state-church relations – painstakingly collected information about the state of religious organizations including the Protestant ones – allows us to conclude that the Seventh-day Adventist Church remained viable, and despite the circumstances related to the war, continued to live its inner life, hidden from the external viewers. Believers gathered together, held worship services, and prayed for their loved ones who had gone to war or were in prison. Inter-congregational ties had practically ceased. Information about the establishment of any centralized church organization in the temporarily occupied territory was not found. It was not possible to find documents reflecting the position of the church leadership in relation to the war. Therefore, in those difficult circumstances each member of the church acted in accordance with his or her own conscience, trying to be faithful to God and to their civic duty. God led his Church through the crucible, and by the end of the war, thanks to a change in state-church relations, it was possible to set up a centralized church-governing body, to establish contacts with all congregations, and to begin the process of the slow and gradual restoration of the church's life.

*Michal Balcar*

## Clash or Embrace? Seventh-day Adventists and the Totalitarian Regimes in Czechoslovakia (1939–1989)

Abstract

The subject matter of this paper is to describe, compare, and analyse the relationship between Seventh-day Adventism and totalitarian governments in former Czechoslovakia, specifically under Nazi rule from 1939 to 1945 in *Protectorate of Bohemia and Moravia* and under Communism between 1948 to 1989. It will focus on identifying points of conflict, as well as of cooperation between church and state. Particular emphasis will be put on a comparison of the two regimes and the search for a reason why they were perceived differently within the church.

The history of the 20th century in Central Europe presents the researcher with a unique opportunity to compare two totalitarian regimes – Nazism and Communism. The subject of this paper is to compare the attitude of Seventh-day Adventists in former Czechoslovakia towards these two political ideologies. The conclusion might, hopefully, not only be useful for Adventists in the Czech and Slovak Republics, but in the whole of Europe, since the history of the region is similar in many ways.

### Seventh-day Adventism in Czechoslovakia under Nazi Rule (1939–1945)

The title of this section might seem a bit misleading, since Czechoslovakia as an independent state did not exist between 1939–1945.[1] The dismantling of the country began a year before with the Munich Agreement.[2] The aftermath – loss of border regions, the so-called *Sudetenland* – had a huge impact on the life of the Seventh-day Adventist church as well. A significant number of Adventists of German ethnicity (even though citizens of Czechoslovakia) suddenly became citizens of Nazi Germany and the North Bohemian Conference became part of the East German Union.

---

1   For more details on general history of Czechoslovakia during the World War II, see, for example, Maria Dowling, *Czechoslovakia, Brief Histories* (London: Arnold, 2002), 58–79.

2   For more detailed description, see David Faber, *Munich, 1938: Appeasement and World War II* (New York: Simon & Schuster, 2010).

On March 14, 1939, an independent Slovakian State was declared by a clerico-fascist government. A day later, the German army occupied remaining parts of former Czechoslovakia and established a *Protectorate of Bohemia and Moravia*. This came as a shock to most of the Czech speaking Adventists.[3] Karel Poledník, later the president of Central Bohemian Mission field, recalls: "Early morning March 15th, my wife turned the radio on, just to hear that German army is approaching Brno from Vienna. She started crying and wanted to escape, only to realize that the whole republic is occupied."[4]

The Seventh-day Adventist Church had not been recognized by the state authorities as a church and its legal status had been that of an *association* since the Austrian-Hungarian Empire. It operated under the name of Czechoslovakian Union of the Seventh-day Adventists. During the time of the Protectorate, it only slightly changed the title to Czecho-Moravian Union.

Immediately after the establishment of the Protectorate, the church found itself in conflict with new ruling power. The denomination was forced to close down the publishing house in Brno. The reason for the closure is unclear: according to some accounts, it might have had something to do with a book titled *Svítání* ("Dawn") by Richard Rühling, who was "interpreting prophecies in a way opposite to the policies of Reich."[5] Jiří Piškula, the author of the only comprehensive history of Adventism in Czechoslovakia, believes that the reason lay in several anti-Nazi articles published in the Seventh-day Adventist magazines.[6] It is likely that authorities acted on information given by a former Seventh-day Adventist and book colporteur, Otmar Swatek.[7]

Later in March 1939, a local church in Vojkovice (Moravia) was also closed. According to an eyewitness account, it was due to a complaint to the authorities from an extended family of a new Adventist convert.[8] All local churches were forced to use bilingual signs, and all the employees had to prove "Aryan" origin.

The association (Czecho-Moravian Union of Seventh-day Adventists) voluntarily dismantled itself on August 30, 1942 according to the board minutes.

3   Such an attitude was completely in line with general population of Czechoslovakia. See for example Peter Demetz, *Prague in Danger: The Years of German Occupation, 1939–45. Memories and History, Terror and Resistance, Theatre and Jazz, Film and Poetry, Politics and War* (New York: Farrar, Straus and Giroux, n.d.); chapter: "Third Reich Suddenly."

4   Emanuel Duda, *Tak Nás Bůh Vedl: Adventní Hnutí v Čechách a Na Moravě* (Self-Published, n.d.), 23.

5   Michal Balcar, "Seventh-day Adventists in the Protectorate of Bohemia and Moravia, 1939–1945" (Sázava Theological Seminary, 2002), 11.

6   For instance an article by C. B. Haynes, "Dark Clouds of Hatred," published in Slovakian, "Straž nad Tatrami" in 1938 (no. 6, p. 65), or a front page article by J. Marcolla, "Our Firm Leader," inevitably alluding to Adolf Hitler (for Marcolla, the leader obviously was Jesus Christ). Cf. Jiří Piškula, *Dějiny Církve Adventistů Sedmého Dne v Čechách, Na Moravě a ve Slezsku* (Praha: Advent-Orion, 2009), 78.

7   More on Swatek in chapter "Seventh-day Adventists in Protectorate and Jewish Issue."

8   Interview with Ludvík Svrček, March 14, 2000.

Only after the war was it explained that this was due to pressure from the authorities. However, this forced move was not aimed at Adventists in particular, as many similar associations were shut down in an attempt to suppress any civil activities. The church was made to establish a liquidation committee, whose job was to shut down all church activities and sell off any remaining properties. Members of the committee kept stalling the work, even by resorting to bizarre means. For example, they used an excuse that they could not proceed because the chairman, Josef Doubravský, had broken his leg while riding a sleigh. Such behaviour is part of a Czech cultural tradition called "švejkování," which describes avoiding responsibility by pretending to be a fool.[9] However, the legal termination had very slight effect on the life of the church, so some accounts express uncertainty as to whether the church was officially closed down or not.

## Clash or Embrace – Persecution, Resistance, and/or Cooperation in the Protectorate

Most of the clashes with the regime were over the Sabbath issue. Since 1942 all of the adult men from the Protectorate had been obliged to perform forced labour in (mainly) German factories. There were even several martyrs among the Seventh-day Adventists in the Protectorate. The two most prominent were Jan Biehaj and Miloš Hlávka. Both were arrested for refusal to work on Sabbath.

It is worth mentioning that the church was far from united in this attitude. In the very church where Biehaj had come from, Lazy (in Silesia), a church elder named Pavel Guznar claimed that there was no need to always observe Sabbath since "this is no end-time, no time of persecution."[10] After Biehaj was arrested, he later died in the Auschwitz-Birkenau concentration camp. Hlávka's story is very similar. There were probably others who were persecuted, as attested by Josef Doubravský (then the president of the Union), who wrote in a letter in 1947 that "many an Adventist died in a concentration camp because of the Sabbath".[11]

There are not many cases of known Adventist resistance against the Nazi authorities. These include mainly sheltering wanted people, which was obviously very dangerous. However, these cases seem to have been occasioned by circumstances more than being a result of active resistance.

Similarly, there are no known cases of active collaboration with Nazi authorities.[12] Sometimes, the leadership of the church, as well as ordinary church members, expressed a positive attitude towards the regime. Examples of this support

---

9 Jaroslav Hašek's literary masterpiece describing a fictional soldier, Josef Švejk, is a part of the Czech cultural canon. Some even claim that it describes typical behavior of Czech people during times of hardship. Jaroslav Hašek, *The Good Soldier Svejk: And His Fortunes in the World War* (London: Penguin Classics, 2005).

10 Balcar, "Seventh-day Adventists in the Protectorate of Bohemia and Moravia," 35.

11 Piškula, *Dějiny Církve Adventistů Sedmého Dne v Čechách*, 81.

12 By "collaboration" I mean an active cooperation and support of Nazi regime.

were an obituary of Reinhard Heydrich, a deputy Reich protector and high-ranking Nazi officer, in the *Bible Quarterly* together with an announcement of military successes of German armies, as well as an appeal to support the German Red Cross. Some church members expressed positive attitudes towards the new policies. For instance, a certain Brother Gomola wrote to Josef Doubravský in 1943, "Praise the Lord and Hitler, too, for doing so much for worrying dads. Much more than all of the democratic do-nothings together".[13]

## Seventh-day Adventists in the Protectorate and the Jews

It is very natural to ask about the relationship of Adventists towards Jews, since it was one of the main issues of the time. The evidence is, however, inconclusive. We have preserved pictures of entrances to local churches displaying bilingual signs reading: "Betsaal/Modlitebna – Juden Verboten/Židům zakázáno" (Prayer House – Jews No Entry).

An account written by F. A. Ludwig, who ran the official Adventist publishing house until 1939,[14] and whose wife was Jewish, claims that in 1941 the leadership of the denomination from Prague ordered the expulsion of all Jewish and half-Jewish ("*Mischling*") members of the church. In Brno alone, where Ludwig had come from, this meant expelling nine members. However, this claim cannot be corroborated from any other source. Similarly, Ludwig maintains that a member of the church of Jewish origin, Frieda Redlich, was expelled before being transported to the concentration camp. On the other hand, Ludwig later found himself in dispute with the denomination, so his account shows some bitterness and should be taken into consideration cautiously.[15] On the other side, we can find testimonies about Jews saved by Adventists. Even Josef Doubravský, the Union president himself, was said to have adopted a Jewish girl in order to save her, according to his daughter.[16]

## Seventh-day Adventists in Sudetenland

The initial reaction of the Sudeten German Seventh-day Adventists was quite different from that of the Czechs mentioned above. In *Adventbote* from April 1939, there was an article expressing the views of German Seventh-day Adventists, reading: "Bohemia and Moravia with some islands of German population, and also Prague, city so important for German history, now belong to the Reich. By establishing the

---

13  Balcar, "Seventh-day Adventists in the Protectorate of Bohemia and Moravia," 33.
14  First under his own name – Ludwig & Co, later as a manager of Advent Publishing House.
15  Piškula, *Dějiny Církve Adventistů Sedmého Dne v Čechách*, 81. All information comes from the private archive of Daniel Heinz, Friedensau.
16  Balcar, "Seventh-day Adventists in the Protectorate of Bohemia and Moravia," 18.

Protectorate, bulwarks of enemy powers deep within our Lebensraum have been destroyed."[17]

In contrast to that, the former North-Bohemian Conference (now Sudeten Conference) faced the threat of being officially closed down. Similarly to the situation in the Protectorate, this was probably not directed against the Adventists, but against all civil activities in Sudetenland.[18]

## Provisional Conclusion

Generally, the Czech Adventists did not see the Nazis favourably, but mainly because they were "German." Thus, we can conclude that the Seventh-day Adventists in the Protectorate neither fully clashed nor embraced the regime. They simply tried to survive it, mostly by trying to avoid conflicts.

# Seventh-day Adventists in Czechoslovakia and the Communist Regime

After brief three years of re-established democracy in Czechoslovakia, a new threat for the church emerged with the communist coup d'état in February 1948. However, it was not perceived as a threat from the beginning. In 1948 Josef Doubravský, president of the Union, wrote to the Belgian Union, that religious freedom was fully maintained.[19] It is plausible that many Adventists looked quite favourably upon the communist government. Most of the members were from the lowest social class and the communist focus on improving working conditions for the factory and agricultural workers might have been seen as appealing. In fact, one of the leading Czech historians of the communist period, Professor Karel Kaplan, claims that "many"[20] members of the church were also actually members of the Communist party.

The denomination even managed to fulfil its long-term dream – full government recognition of the church. The application was submitted to the Ministry of Education on April 18, 1948 (only 3 months after the coup), and it was approved on July 15, 1950, with a few conditions. Josef Doubravský, the Union president, had to pledge allegiance to the new communist republic, promising not to do anything

17 Some of the words are intentionally kept in German, just to demonstrate that the church leadership fully adopted the political vocabulary of the time. "Lebensraum in Osten" was a term/programme justifying Nazi military expansion to the countries to the east of Germany. Piškula, *Dějiny Církve Adventistů Sedmého Dne v Čechách*, 74.

18 For more see Johannes Hartlapp, *Siebenten-Tags-Adventisten im Nationalsozialismus* (Göttingen: V&R Unipress, 2008), 438.

19 Piškula, *Dějiny Církve Adventistů Sedmého Dne v Čechách*, 93.

20 Karel Kaplan, *Stát a Církev v Československu v Letech 1948–1953* (Brno: Doplněk, 1993), 73. Such a claim is at the moment very difficult to corroborate, since the complete lists of the members of the KSČ (communist party) have not been published yet.

against the republic and its regime. The authorities also reserved the right to approve all the members of the Union board. This clearly demonstrates a certain amount of naiveté on the side of the church leadership, which was inclined to underestimate the intentions of the regime.

## Prohibition of the Church (1952–1956)

Between 1950 and 1952 there were some warning signs as to the goals of the government. It forced the denomination to significantly lower the number of pastors and increased the pressure regarding Sabbath work.

On October 1, 1952, members of the interim leadership of the church were invited to the Ministry of Education, and to their total shock were given a document regarding the complete prohibition of all the activities of the church in Czechoslovakia. The reason cited was that the church headquarters worked "actively against the constitution and values of the republic."[21] All the pastors were assigned new jobs in factories, all of the theology students were dismissed. All buildings were confiscated by the state. The authorities did not encounter any major resistance.

However, the church kept on living. Members met in private houses, and the pastors conducted services in spite of their new work assignments. After several unsuccessful attempts, the church was granted permission to legally restart its activities in Czechoslovakia on September 18, 1956, on the condition that the "religious life of the denomination will not be in conflict with the constitution of the republic."[22]

The crisis was over; however, the consequences were of major proportions. The firm stance of some and the will for compromise of others caused huge internal tensions within the denomination, which lasted up until the mid-1960s. The slow liberation of the regime in 1960s was welcomed by the Adventists. The church even tried to receive rehabilitation regarding the unlawful prohibition in 1952 and restitution of confiscated property. Unfortunately, the courts were not able to reach any verdict before 1970, and the political situation completely changed with the Soviet occupation of the country in 1968.

The 1970s and 1980s were decades of very good official cooperation between the church and the authorities. The leading figure of church/state cooperation was the president of the church, Oldřich Sládek, laureate of several state awards.

---

21   One of the members, Antonín Pražan, recalls crying for the first time after 30 years at that moment. 117.
22   National Archives, 49d Adventists, 996/1969.

## Clash or Embrace – Persecution, Resistance, and/or Cooperation During Communism (1948–1989)

There seemed to be a big miscalculation on the side of authorities as far as Seventh-day Adventism was concerned. As mentioned above, church members were positively inclined towards the regime, in spite of its declared atheism. This completely changed during the time of prohibition (1952–1956). During this period, several pastors were arrested and later accused of "gathering against the republic" and were given prison sentences from five to seven years.[23]

It is noteworthy that it was the unsuccessful experience with the resistance of the Seventh-day Adventist Church that made the authorities choose a softer approach with other groups, for example towards the Baptist Church:

> After the end of the trial with the Baptist pastors, the SUC[24] had to reconsider its approach towards the church and its members. Complete prohibition of the church, dismissal of its pastors, and confiscation of its property is not recommended after the very unfortunate experience with the Adventist church, which went underground and grows even stronger.[25]

A huge conflict developed over obligatory Saturday school education. The usual reaction of the authorities was a financial fine. However, there are also several known cases when the children were institutionalized after their parents refused to send them to school on Saturdays.[26] The leadership of the denomination was trying to reach a compromise between the demands of the regime and principles of the church; however, this compromise was criticized by those members who took a firm stance and refused to oblige under pressure. The result was distrust between some churches and Union administrators, as well as a lowering of tithe income in the 1950s.[27]

Many SDA members were imprisoned during the 1950s. Most of them were soldiers refusing to serve on Saturdays. Later on, the authorities provided an option to avoid two years of compulsory military service. Many a young Adventist chose to work for ten years as a coal miner instead of serving in the army.

Naturally, the church was the object of interest for the secret police (StB).[28] Jiří Piškula, the author of the only serious historical work on Seventh-day Adventism in Czechoslovakia, even claims that since 1956, it was a commonplace practice for all

---

23  These sentences were quite low, since the state prosecutor was considering accusing the pastors of treason, which could have attracted even the death penalty. Piškula, *Dějiny Církve Adventistů Sedmého Dne v Čechách*, 122.

24  Státní úřad pro věci církevní – State Office for Church Matters.

25  National Archives, SUC, box 4. inv. no. 54.

26  National Archives, Ministry of Education, box 50.

27  Piškula, *Dějiny Církve Adventistů Sedmého Dne v Čechách*, 125.

28  StB stands for Státní bezpečnost (State Security).

of the members of church leadership to be collaborators[29] of secret police.[30] Such a claim is actually difficult to corroborate, since most of the files were shredded in the aftermath of the Velvet Revolution in 1989. However, the insight that cooperation was quite close is supported for example by a secret police report expressing hope that through Czech Adventists, StB might be able to infiltrate the General Conference in the USA.[31] What makes it even more plausible is the fact that the denominational leadership lived in constant fear of a new prohibition of the church, and thus was inclined to make all kinds of compromises. However, as Piškula points out:

> one must be very careful in evaluating cooperation of individuals with the secret police. Some of the agents and collaborators were in contact with the secret police in order to secure some position in the church. On the other hand, others were under pressure and even found strength to refuse cooperation after a few meetings. Some agents provided misleading information, while others only reported on foreign trips without any valuable information. Many people refused to cooperate straight away.[32]

## Clash or Embrace? Seventh-day Adventists and Totalitarian Regimes in Czechoslovakia

This final section suggests some possible answers to the rhetorical question posed as the title of this paper. Was the relationship between the Seventh-day Adventists and the totalitarian regimes on Czechoslovakia a clash or an embrace?

### Not an Embrace, Since Adventists Were Not to Be Involved in Politics

In both contexts – Nazism and Communism – Seventh-day Adventists were not active as far as their relationship with the regimes is concerned. The Nazi authorities persecuted only those who were actively opposing their interests, and the Adventists were not among them. The *modus vivendi* of the church could be described as follows: "Let's keep our heads down and wait until it's over." As one of the administrators of the Church reflected upon his interrogation by the Gestapo: "As the Seventh-day Adventists, we should never be involved in political affairs."[33]

Ideologically, this attitude evidently comes from a very strong Seventh-day Adventist emphasis on the separation of church and state. That is why it is somewhat curious that leaders of the church in Czechoslovakia strived to obtain state

---

29   This was the lowest possible rank, with agents' being those who cooperated willingly, usually for financial or other gain.
30   Piškula, *Dějiny Církve Adventistů Sedmého Dne v Čechách,* 180.
31   Ibid., 181.
32   Ibid.
33   Balcar, "Seventh-day Adventists in the Protectorate of Bohemia and Moravia," 45.

recognition in the early 1950s, in spite of the fact that it meant more control from the authorities.

As far as the Communists are concerned, the situation was different. They wrongly evaluated the Seventh-day Adventist church as a threat and decided to completely prohibit all of its activities. The result was twofold. (1) For the authorities this move seemed unsuccessful, and they gave up after realizing that the church had gone underground. (2) However, in the long term, it was successful, since the denominational leadership had lived in constant fear of a new prohibition and was inclined to compromise with the regime. Thus, we can conclude that officially the church adopted a position of an embrace, because it felt that the other option (possibly resulting in a new prohibition) was going to be much worse.

## Not a Clash, Since Nazis and Communists Were not the "Real" Enemies

The only real clash with the authorities of both regimes was over the Sabbath issue. It was either about obligatory Saturday school education, or about refusal to work on Sabbath in connection with military service. The church was only marginally involved with the Jews during the Nazi occupation,[34] and it completely ignored the clash over human rights issues (Charter 77) in the 70s and 80s, even though the issue of religious freedom is one of the cornerstones of Adventist identity. The reason for this might lie in the denomination's rigid eschatology. This is nicely summarized by the quote mentioned above, "This is no end-time": therefore there was, in some leaders' opinion, no need to be overly strict. The same principle could be applied to the regimes themselves. "This is no eschatological enemy," so there was no need to stand against it.

The silence of the denomination was not only outward, but also in its thinking. Theology, and eschatology in particular, strongly shapes one's understanding of reality. In retrospect, we can see the 20th century as a period of two of the most "evil"[35] ideologies that this world has seen so far, even though such a characterization might be inappropriate in historical research. Yet Seventh-day Adventists are still waiting for the real oppression to begin, because it must be over the Sabbath, and it must be by the Roman Catholic Church. It is a historical irony that the end of the Sabbath oppression was brought about with the introduction of two-day weekend, which the majority of the Czech population welcomed as an opportunity to spend more time at their weekend houses, without realizing that this is a matter of cosmic conflict.

---

34  In spite of being theologically closest to Judaism among all Christian denominations, there have never been any close ties to the Jewish community. For more on this topic see Jacques Doukhan, *The Mystery of Israel* (Silver Spring: Review and Herald, 2004).

35  It is still a matter of heated debate, but it is estimated that the communist regimes killed about 100,000,000 victims and Nazis about 25,000,000. See Stephane Courtois, *The Black Book of Communism: Crimes, Terror, Repression* (Cambridge, Massachusetts: Harvard University Press, 1999).

*Gheorghe Modoran*

# The Romanian Adventist Church under the Communist Regime

Abstract

While the purpose of Communism was to eradicate religion and to impose atheism, each country developed its own model concerning the relation between state and church. In 1944, the Romanian Adventist Church emerged from an orthodox military dictatorship during which it had been prohibited and declared illegal. It entered the phase of another regime: communist dictatorship. During a consolidation period of four to five years, the church enjoyed freedom. Once the regime was consolidated, harsh measures, which aimed at the gradual destruction of the church, were taken, targeting churches, pastors and missionary work. It was, however, surprising that all the restrictive and repressive measures against the church were taken by the authorities indirectly, through the church leaders. All Union Presidents from the time of Communism were imposed by the regime and the majority of the church leaders were agents of the *Securitate* (the State Security Department). Cooperation with the *Securitate* was the most difficult challenge that the church faced during the Communist era. In spite of unimaginable control of pastors and leaders by the authorities, God cared for the church. The denomination did not disappear as the regime envisioned, but grew.

The arrival of Communism in Romania was possible through the presence of the Soviet army. The Communist party had only 1000 members in 1944.[1] The Seventh-day Adventist Church emerged from an orthodox military dictatorship (1940–1944) during which it had been prohibited and declared illegal. It then entered the phase of another regime: Communist dictatorship. Communism may be considered one of the most dangerous forms of dictatorship because while it spread fear and terror, it presented itself as a democratic regime with noble objectives. During the first period of the Communist regime, the Soviet model of Communism was exported to all countries that were satellites to Moscow. This also covered religion and the relationship between state and church.[2]

The purpose of Communism was to eradicate religion and to impose atheism. Over time, each Communist country developed its own model of relations between state and church: a more liberal one in Poland, Hungary, Yugoslavia, where Bibles

---

1 Constantin Hlihor, "Armata Roşie în România şi Evoluţia Regimului Politic," *Arhivele Totalitarismului* 2 (1995): 54.
2 Ioan Chiper, "Modelul Stalinist de Sovietizare a României," *Arhivele Totalitarismului* 2 (1995):10, 23.

could be found in libraries, religious programs were broadcast on radio and TV, religious literature was published; and a rather strict model in Russia, Bulgaria, and Romania.

The most difficult situation for Adventists was experienced in Russia and Bulgaria. Here two parallel Adventist church organizations existed: one official, recognised by the state, which had accepted restrictions imposed by the regime, and the other one unofficial, an underground, persecuted church, which had rejected the interference of the state in church issues. Many of the pastors and believers were arrested, tortured, or imprisoned. Children from these families were taken away by the state and put in foster homes. The story of the Soviet Gulag is well known.

## Years of Freedom and the Ensuing Prohibition

During the first four to five years of consolidation of the regime, all churches enjoyed freedom. Given the lack of popular support, Vasile Luca and Gheorghe Gheorghiu-Dej, leaders well known for their Stalinist views, pleaded for caution and moderation, strongly arguing that "It would be a crime to transform the church into an enemy."[3] Adventist churches were reopened, pastors reemployed, the theological institute and the publishing house resumed activity, canvassing was reorganised, public evangelistic meetings were held,[4] and new churches were established and built. Church leaders could participate in international meetings of the Division and General Conference and world church leaders could keep official contact with church leaders from Romania.

Once the regime was consolidated around 1949–1950, harsh measures, which aimed at the gradual destruction of the church, were taken. The freedoms which had been granted were now taken back. By 1949 the theological institute and the publishing house had been confiscated.[5]

Numerous other prohibitions followed: the closing of churches; the dismissal of pastors; the prohibition of baptisms, the prohibition of religious activities outside of church buildings (except small funerals) and on other days except the Sabbath; the suppression of the Sabbath School in groups with teachers, of the Children's Sabbath School, and of the baptismal class; the suppression of choirs and orchestras; the prohibition of youth meetings; the prohibition for church members to visit other churches, and for pastors to preach in other churches than those mentioned in their

3   Cristian Vasile, "Romanian Communists and the Church," *Arhivele Totalitarismului* 1–2 (2002):131.
4   Archive of the National Council for the Study of the Securitate Archives (ACNSAS), Informative Fund, file 6883. f. 64. The note of the Regional Police Inspectorate for Bucharest, April 8, 1947.
5   ACNSAS, Documentary Fund, file 6899, vol. 4, f. 186. Archive of the State Secretariat for Church Affairs (ASSC), file 93/1952, vol. 2, f. 4, 5. Note from the Polygraphic Centre no. 3 to the Adventist Church, March 20, 1952; Note from the Union of Conferences to the Polygraphic Centre no. 3, March 28,1952.

accreditation; prohibition of canvassing and missionary work; the prohibition to circulate Bibles and any religious literature; the prohibition to buy or build churches; and the prohibition of contacts with the world church leadership.

Even though the objective of the authorities was very clear – to eliminate all influence of religion – the restrictive and repressive measures against the church were taken indirectly. The communist ideology proclaimed the superiority of the "communist democracy" over the capitalist democracies and "imperialism". Communism was presenting itself as a regime which respected human rights and freedoms. In view of preserving this image, the policy was to impose all the measures taken against the church indirectly through church leaders. The motto of that time was, "let us destroy the church through the hierarchy."[6] Thus the authorities could reply to members or pastors protesting against the measures that it was their own leaders who took the measures, not them. The authorities strictly required church leaders to refrain from justifying these measures as coming from the regime and forced them to take full ownership and responsibility.

## Merging of Churches

Authorities considered that the discrepancy in organizational terms was quite wide between "Neo-Protestant"[7] and historic churches (Orthodox, Catholic, Protestant churches). While a parish of historic churches included on average around 1000 believers, Neo-Protestant churches were allowed to be organized with a minimum of 20 registered members and many were functioning with even fewer individuals. A table comparing the situation of different churches with similar membership from 1960 may illustrate this situation:[8]

| Churches | Membership | Number of churches | Number of clerics |
|---|---|---|---|
| *Unitarian* | 73 973 | 128 | 112 |
| *Baptist* | 78 298 | 867 | 475 |
| *Evangelical Synodal Presbyterial* | 32 429 | 37 | 35 |
| *Adventist* | 32 535 | 549 | 437 |

Needless to say, Neo-Protestant churches were relatively fewer in these comparisons given the fact that they did not baptise children who were therefore not counted

6    Adrian Nicolae Petcu, "Slujitorii Altarului în Anii democrației Populare", *ProMemoria* 3 (2004):318.
7    At the time (and starting from the early 20th century), this was the Romanian term commonly used for Baptists, Adventists, and Pentecostals. These Free Churches did not adopt the term, and today most of them call themselves "Evangelicals."
8    ASSC, file 103/1960, vol. 13, f. 49.

in the membership. Moreover, none of the Neo-Protestant churches received financing from the state, as opposed to the historic churches, in order to justify the requirements of the authorities related to a minimum number of members per church. These comparisons by the government were just a pretext to justify restrictive and repressive measures the authorities were envisaging.

The real objective of the authorities was to reduce the number of Neo-Protestant churches by merging existing ones and imposing on members the duty to move to a larger church. This process took place over several phases. The first phase took place in 1951, when out of a total of 3,943 Neo-Protestant churches, only 2,013 were allowed to continue. The table below indicates these reductions.[9]

| Church | Number of churches in 1951 | Membership | Number of churches closed | Remaining number of churches | Percentage of churches closed |
|---|---|---|---|---|---|
| Baptist | 1 327 | 52 942 | 513 | 814 | 39% |
| Adventist | 1 380 | 27 518 | 793 | 587 | 67% |
| Brethren Assemblies[10] | 454 | 10 970 | 289 | 165 | 64% |
| Pentecostal | 782 | 21 444 | 335 | 447 | 43% |
| Total | 3 943 | 112 874 | 1 930 | 2 013 | 49% |

Due to these measures, almost half of the Neo-Protestant churches were closed. The most affected were the Adventists; the least affected the Baptists. This is explained by the fact that Adventist had a large number of churches with fewer than 20 registered members.

Starting with 1959, a second phase of church merging took place. The Department for Church Affairs communicated to territorial inspectors the criteria for merging: the number of members, the distance from other churches, and the number of churches in the same town or village. Based on these criteria the authorities operated new mergers and issued new authorizations. In this phase, not only small churches (with fewer than 20 members) were closed, but also big churches with hundreds of members where two or more congregations existed in the same place.

## Baptisms

Since it was considered the main means of church growth, the authorities took drastic measures to limit the number of baptisms. They made baptism authorizations conditional upon presentation of a certificate proving that individuals have left the denomination they belonged to. New converts mostly came from the majority Orthodox Church, and Orthodox priests usually refused to issue such a certificate.

9    Ibid., file 103/1951, vol. 3, f. 1, 2.
10   In Romanian, Biserica Creştină după Evanghelie

Moreover, if a priest agreed to issue these certificates, he was reprimanded by the authorities.

Later on, baptisms of believers coming from other churches were entirely prohibited. Admitted to baptism, but only with long delays, were the children of Adventist families who reached the age of legal responsibility (18 years). There were attempts to nullify some baptisms when it was discovered that young people baptized from Adventist families had been born before their parents became Adventists and had been baptized as babies into the Orthodox Church.

Outdoor baptisms were completely prohibited in order not to create an occasion for proselytizing. Baptism was permitted only in church baptisteries with the participation of the family and the closest relatives.[11] Baptism of "intellectuals" (i.e. anyone with university degrees) was prohibited.

The performing of an unauthorised baptism was considered a legal crime punished by law: the offense of illegal conversion.[12] Active pastors that were discovered to have conducted illegal baptisms were fired. Therefore, many baptisms took place in hiding by night. The author of this article was baptised by a retired pastor in a bathtub in the presence of only three persons. Because of the risks it entailed for pastors, ordained elders performed this function for a while.[13]

## Regulations of Religious Activities

After 1944, during the first years of religious liberty, Neo-Protestant churches started to hold religious activities during the week as well as on the regular day of worship. For the Adventists these were mainly Sundays for evangelistic purposes and Wednesdays for prayer. Starting in 1954, these services, as well as other activities that were taking place in the churches in Romania, became strictly regulated by the Ministry of Church Affairs. Following the pattern of indirect action, the authorities were asking church leaders to present these measures not as an obligation imposed by the state, but as a measure stemming from within the organisation.[14]

If initially the Romanian Union sent written complaints and raised objections to the decision of the authorities to close down meetings during the week, after the intervention of the Ministry of Church Affairs, the leaders changed course and brought arguments in favour of the regulation. To justify the discontinuation of Sunday meetings, leaders even used Biblical arguments,[15] including the fourth commandment, which foresaw the day of worship as only the Sabbath. The Union

11   ACNSAS, Informative Fund, file 2672, vol. 5, f. 214.
12   Article 309, Criminal Code 1968.
13   ASSC, file 93/1960, vol. 13/2, f. 205. Roşca Dumitru, an Adventist pastor, performed an illegal baptism in 1960.
14   Iosif Ţon, *Confruntări* (Oradea: Cartea Creştină, 2000), 61.
15   ASSC, file 96/1955, vol. 4c, f. 29.

President, Dumitru Florea, was arguing: "Unfortunately, we have not strictly re-spected the fourth commandment of the Decalogue and we have become lazy and we have feasted also when we were supposed to work."[16]

The President of the Muntenia Conference was commended in the report of the regional inspector to the Ministry of Church Affairs because he had "documented well why the internal directive of the Union was needed." The argument of the Pres-ident was the following: "Until ten years ago we were persecuted and we were forced to celebrate even on Sundays, because if our believers were seen by the authorities working on Sundays, they were persecuted. But now, when the democratic regime has given us the freedom we did not have, it is appropriate to follow the teachings of the Bible which say that we should work six days and celebrate the seventh day – instead, because of circumstances in the past, we did not respect this and we cele-brated Sundays as well, violating the word of the Bible."[17] Thus the regime at times even succeeded in influencing the theological argument inside the church.

## Measures against Sabbath School and Baptismal Classes

Another restrictive measure initiated by the Department of Church Affairs and the *Securitate*[18] was the suppression of adult Bible teaching through Sabbath School groups. They considered Sabbath School to be the religious service which exerted the greatest influence on believers. The functioning of the Sabbath School through a group of seven to ten people studying a Bible topic led by a teacher was considered by the authorities as a powerful training tool, motivating believers to do evangelism and fostering resistance to the measures initiated by the Department of Church Af-fairs. The role of Sabbath School teachers was seen as impressing on believers "exces-sive mysticism" and exerting constant influence on their conscience.[19] Despite opposition from churches, during one year (1960), Sabbath School groups were sup-pressed in all Adventist churches under the pressure exerted by the Department of Church Affairs on Union leaders.[20]

The study in groups was replaced by a public presentation from the pulpit of the study lesson. While the initial intention of the authorities had been to entirely sup-press the Sabbath School in two phases – suppression first of the groups, followed by its entire elimination in the second phase – the strong opposition of churches to the

16  Ibid., file 93/1954, vol. 3, f. 24.
17  Ibid.
18  The Department of State Security (common name: Security or *Securitate* in Romanian) was the intelligence service in Romania during the communist period. It was under the Ministry of Internal Affairs most of the time. As an instrument of the Romanian Communist Party, whose directives it brought to fulfilment, the *Securitate* played a leading role in maintaining a climate of terror, becoming guilty of countless crimes and human rights violations, while func-tioning as a political and ideological police.
19  ASSC, file 93/1960, vol. 13/2, inv. 99, f. 234.
20  Ibid.

first phase led them to abandon the second. The authorities also realised that with only one person presenting from the pulpit, the Sabbath School became easier to control.

As a parallel, the authorities also imposed the suppression of children's and youth Sabbath School classes. The argument used was that they were not members of the church.[21] Following the measures taken, the official teaching of the children and youth ceased for about 20 to 25 years in all Neo-Protestant churches. Together with education received in the family, some churches continued a secret training programme for children and youth during the whole period when this prohibition was in force, i.e. until the 1980s.[22] More than ten years after the suppression of the Sabbath School groups, the second type of adult Bible teaching – the baptismal class – was also suppressed.[23]

## Preaching and Distribution of Bibles

Only authorised persons – pastors and elders – were allowed to preach. Other members of the church board were allowed to preach only later. Sermons concerning the end of the world and the second coming of Christ were prohibited, being considered alarmist and in contradiction with the bright and luminous future the communist

21  Ibid., Research Directorate Fund, file 93/1960, vol. 8, f. 22: "Through the Department of Church Affairs, it should be discussed with the central leadership of churches to determine them to eliminate the instruction of children and youth in churches as these are not members of the church."

22  Ibid., file 93/1960, vol. 8, inv. 95, f. 90. An inspector of the Department for Church Affairs was reporting about a new method used by the Adventist Church to instruct children: during adult Sabbath School, teachers were inviting children to the front rows and asking them special questions. Ibid., f. 1–2. During the inspection of the Department of Church Affairs in one of the congregations in Bucharest called Grant Church, the inspectors found a group of 15 children at the balcony of the church participating in instruction under the leadership of a teacher. Only following intervention from the Union and commitment by the local church not to continue this practice was the authorisation for running the congregation retrieved. However, the authorities continued to suspend the authorisation of the pastor, Marin Enache. See also ACNSAS, Informative Fund, file 5114, f. 26. In November 1965, the source Fabian A. was informing that "in the Popa Tatu church in Bucharest, the Adventist pastor Zăbavă Ion allows the organisation of a children's Sabbath School in the basement (cloak room). Children from other churches in Bucharest were coming here together with their parents, as pastors in those churches did not have the courage to organise activities for the children."

23  In June 1972, a note from the Department of Church Affairs to the inspector in Prahova County announced the suppression of the baptismal class; see ASSC, file 1/1972, f. 95. This was valid for the entire country. The Note no. 15058/June 28,1972 mentioned: "We inform you that recently the leadership of the Adventist Church has decided to suppress the baptismal class in all churches. It is your duty to ensure the enforcement of this measure so that it is not replaced by other activities."

ideology was depicting.[24] Missionary sermons were prohibited because they encouraged proselytising. The sermons had to include social aspects such as the agricultural targets fixed by the authorities, the "fight for peace" and the benefits of the regime. Purely biblical sermons were considered inadequate, distracting the people from the realities of life.[25]

The Bible was the book which was most sought after and cherished by Neo-Protestants. Bibles were very rare and expensive, as their circulation and commercialisation was prohibited. Those who entered Romania from abroad were asked questions about three things: if they were carrying Bibles, guns or drugs. All three were considered dangerous, but the Bibles were listed first. To help churches under communist regimes to have access to Bibles, on the other side of the Iron Curtain, commercial companies were established with the objective of transporting them under cover in trucks, together with other merchandise. Others made double walls for cars or vans to hide Bibles and to smuggle them into the communist world. Many Bibles were introduced into Romania from Germany by barges on the Danube.[26] Another method, particularly used to transport Bibles within Romania, was to hide them in beehives together with a few frames with wax and bees. Many Romanians and foreigners took great risks and some were imprisoned because of the distribution of Bibles. Their trials and sentences triggered a wave of international protests.[27]

## Sabbath Keeping

The Sabbath was the greatest challenge that the Seventh-day Adventist Church had to face, which distinguished it from the other Neo-Protestant churches. Adventist believers had great difficulties concerning the observance of the Sabbath at work, in school and in the army. During the communist time, Saturday was an official working day. Countless Adventists, especially educated persons, lost their employment because they refused to work on Sabbath. The first category that was targeted – teachers – was chosen because of the influence they exerted on the young generation in the most direct way. For this reason all Adventist teachers were dismissed from their jobs.[28] The author of the article was a history teacher at the time of becoming an Adventist and only managed to keep the position for one year before being fired.

---

24  Ibid., file 93/1953, vol. 13B, f. 1. Report: "Hostile Manifestations in the SDA Church," [Manifestări ostile în Biserica Adventistă de Ziua a Şaptea.], January 27, 1953.
25  Idem, dosar 93/1957, vol. 13/2, f. 68.
26  ACNSAS, Informative Fund, file 261352, vol. 1, f. 163.
27  ACNSAS, Informative fund, file 130545, file 8. Declaration of Pastor Gheorghe Piţurlea, February 26, 1975.
28  ACNSAS, Reţea fund, file 303405, vol. 2, f. 55. See also: ACNSAS, Informative fund, file 126, f. 19–26. Memoir of pastor John Stoiu, December 15, 1981.

Saturday was also a regular school day. Parents of children who did not attend school on Sabbath faced great difficulties. They were threatened with loss of employment or had to pay fines. Adventist children who kept the Sabbath were humiliated, despised, mocked, made to repeat school years, prevented from graduating or expelled.[29] Under pressure from the authorities, church leaders and many pastors pressurized parents, asking them to obey the authorities. The situation was even harder for those who refused to send their children to school on Sabbath, as many others had followed the church recommendations and were in their turn exerting pressure.

Pastors who did not manage to convince parents to send their children to school on Sabbath were often moved to other churches or, if their own children did not attend school on Sabbath, they could be sanctioned with the withdrawal of their credentials. Moreover, local congregations were threatened with the cancelling of their authorization.[30] During the whole communist period, some parents, children and even some pastors chose to resist, despite pressures from the church leadership and measures from the authorities meant to force them to change course.[31] While some of the Union leaders were visiting churches to plead in favour of school attendance on Sabbath, other pastors and even some leaders supported those who resisted, which resulted in losing their credentials.[32]

29   ACNSAS, Informative Fund, file 131545, f. 36.
30   ASSC, Research Directorate Fund, file 109/1963, vol. 2, inv. 29, f. 225. In the Războieni church, where the majority of Adventist children were not attending school on Sabbath, the authorities asked for the intervention of the church leadership under the threat of withdrawing congregational authorisation.
31   ACNSAS, Network Fund, file 628, f. 147. The Securitate was mentioning that in Moldova "fanatism" was so intense that almost all pastors were not sending their children to school on Sabbath. The leaders of the Bacau Conference preferred rather to have their authorisation withdrawn than to be considered as "sold to the state."
32   Ibid., Informative Fund, file 73569, f. 4. Pastor Ion Vulvară was called before the board of the Sibiu Conference in the presence of the inspector for Church Affairs, and was ordered to send his children to school on Sabbath. The inspector's conclusion was: "He is very stubborn, he refuses." Although threatened with the withdrawal of his credentials as pastor, Ion Vulvară declared that he could not change his position, even if he would need to pay with his own life. See also ibid., file 131545, f. 36. Pastor Gheorghe Pițurlea submitted a written request to the Ministry of Education and to the Education Section in Bacau to approve the re-examination of his son, who needed to repeat the school year due to absences on Saturdays. The Education Section approved the re-examination, but the school fixed the exam once again on Saturday and his son needed to repeat the year once more (ibid., Documentary Fund, file 141, vol. 1, f. 44). Gheorghe Procsch was accused of "instigating the parents of children from Laslea to not allow them to attend school on Saturday". Ibid., file 141, vol. 2, f. 224. It was also mentioned that pastor Gabriel Vasilescu was not sending his children at school on Saturday and that, as counsellor of the Bucharest Conference, he was refusing to solve similar problems in other churches, justifying himself as follows: "I am not sending my children, how can I go and tell others to send theirs?" See ASSC, Research Directorate Fund, file 96/1952, vol. 2, inv. 108, f. 3. The President of Bacău Conference, Gheorghe Graur "was not sending children to school on Saturday, asking for interventions at the state authorities to have this right acknowledged."

Impressive sometimes was the solidarity of other children with the persecuted Adventist pupils. In one case, the school principal tried to coerce an Adventist pupil to stay in school on Friday evening after sunset. He made sure that the pupil was inside and ordered the school door to be locked. Realizing what was happening, the Adventist pupil started to cry, as he had never before been at school at the beginning of Sabbath. Seeing his anguish, his colleagues helped him to escape by tying their clothes into a rope so he could climb down from the window.[33] Sometimes children were not understood in their determination to observe the Sabbath even by their own parents: two brothers, high school students, decided not to go school any more on Sabbath, and, at their pastor's recommendation, their parents sent them away from home.[34]

However, the most challenging situation was for Adventists drafted into the Army. Given their reluctance to participate in military instruction, young Adventists were usually sent to detachments employed for construction work. Many of those who refused to work on Sabbath were sentenced to two to five years of prison. Some of them went to prison two or three times. After release from prison, they were sent back to a military unit, and they were asked: "Did you rehabilitate yourself? Do you now work on Saturday?" If the answer was negative they would be tried and sentenced again.[35]

It is regrettable that these youths did not have the support of the church. The leaders of the church and pastors encouraged and even exerted pressure on them to obey military orders. During the trial of such a young man, two church leaders came to inform the president of the military tribunal that the young Adventist man was not following the church position and presented him as a fanatic, an extremist with "reformist" ideas. During his imprisonment he was chained, beaten, starved because he refused to work on Saturday in spite of the irony of the situation.[36]

## Cooperation with the State Security Department (*Securitate*)

During the Communist era, in order to have total control over the church the *Securitate* needed informants from the ranks of the leaders, the pastors and lay members. Among those who consented to cooperate with the *Securitate*, there were several motivations:

(1) To be promoted to various offices or functions. It was a well-established fact that one could not be appointed to church leadership positions without the support of the authorities.

(2) To obtain certain privileges: travel outside the Iron Curtain, appointment in the more materially prosperous districts, protection in the case of committing certain

33   Napoleon Stoica, *Bastonul Mareșalului* (Cernica, CARD, 2005), 149–151.
34   Paul Boeru, "Ministry under Fire", Unpublished Manuscript, n.d., 129.
35   ACNSAS, Documentary Fund, file 6899, vol. 1, f. 70.
36   Ibid., Informative Fund, file 226,434, f. 52.

illegal acts, obtaining an ID card in a city that was closed to new inhabitants (e.g. the capital Bucharest or other large "exclusive" cities), help in getting the children enrolled in college etc.

(3) As a result of blackmail: based on their past, or their parents' past (former right-wing sympathizers, former members of parties that had been outlawed), moral slippage, contact with relatives in Western countries. Other reasons for blackmail were the so-called offences against the law: baptisms without authorisation, proselytizing, maintaining relationships with western foreign nationals etc. In absence of reasons for blackmail, these could also be staged by the *Securitate* (e.g. domestic electricity theft, theft at work, relationships with political prisoners).

(4) Following threats, pressures, beatings and torture. In some cases persons were taken to desolate places, threatened with shooting and that no one would ever find out what happened to them. Others were taken to underground facilities of the *Securitate*, were threatened that they would never get out until they signed their consent to cooperate. Others were pressured with a gun on the table, others with a gun to their head. If the person would not consent, the action would be repeated until the person gave in. Some gave in, but others resisted. Some of those who initially gave in under pressure and agreed to cooperate retracted after a while, telling the authorities that they could do whatever they wanted with them, but would not cooperate as they could not oppose their conscience anymore.[37]

A few cases related to this latter category exemplify the challenges Adventists faced and the methods used by the *Securitate*:

(1) Pastor Bazil Păcuraru was hijacked from the street, taken by force into a car, and driven around between two officers for hours without knowing any destination or location. He was threatened and forced to agree to cooperate.[38]

(2) An elder of a church, Ion Iordache,[39] was threatened in all manners possible, with invented reasons for blackmail – all to no effect. Then the *Securitate* used the threat which was the most difficult to resist to: "You don't want to cooperate? You will come yourself to beg to become our informant. What will you say when a car runs over one of your children when he returns from school?" The elder understood that the only way to protect his family was to leave the country illegally. He went to the border to scout the terrain and to find someone to help him. He returned home without saying a word to his family and started preparations. The following week the radio news service announced the death of two *Securitate* officers in a car accident. They were exactly the two officers that had investigated him and threatened his child with a car accident. The elder did not leave the country, nor was he called again to the *Securitate*.[40]

---

37   ACNSAS, Network Fund, file 189148, vol. 1, f. 12, 13.

38   Interview with pastor Lazăr Forray.

39   ACNSAS, Documentary Fund, file 141, vol. 14, f. 47–48. Note of Securitate State Department to Securitate of Dâmbovița country, October 17, 1987.

40   Interview with elder Ion Iordache.

While the collaborators loyal to the authorities enjoyed leading offices, trips to the Western world, and many other privileges, others who refused had to suffer terribly or even paid with their lives for their attitudes. One pastor, Dumitru Roman, started the construction of a church. He was called by the *Securitate* and was asked to cease the building process. Because he did not obey, one evening he was taken to the *Securitate* and nobody knew where he was for three days. Upon his return, all his body was covered in bleeding wounds: he had been beaten countless times these three days. Every time he was beaten until he lost consciousness, and then they put him in a bathtub with cold water. After regaining consciousness they continued to beat him. Despite all this, the pastor refused to become an agent of *Securitate*.

A while after his full recovery, the leadership of the church decided to transfer him to another district where five churches needed to be built. After opening a new building site, the authorities tried to stop him again. They threatened him, harassed him, but he did not stop. Then the *Securitate* decided to kill him: he was poisoned. After some months spent in hospital, where his family was not allowed to visit him, he died at the age of only 38.[41]

Another pastor, Vilhelm Moldovan, one of the most capable pastors in Romania during communist times, untiringly organized series after series of evangelistic meetings in different places. Moreover, at his home, he organized study hours for students – both Adventists and non-Adventists. Among the participants was also the daughter of an important *Securitate* officer in town. The officer threatened him numerous times that if he did not stop he would end badly. One evening, when he returned from an evangelistic meeting, a large unmarked truck, without any lights, was parked on the road. The pastor saw it too late, crashed his car into the back of the truck and died instantly. The threat had been fulfilled.[42]

Many other opponents of the regime who refused collaboration with the *Securitate* were sent to psychiatric hospitals and were treated according to the commands of *Securitate* with drugs that made them lose their minds.[43] Thus the *Securitate* came almost to complete control of the church. Nothing was possible without the approval of the regime:

(1) Admission to the Seminary was organized only once every four years and only four students were allowed for each graduation. There were, therefore, more professors than students.

(2) Employment, transfer or ordination of pastors was also controlled.

(3) Every meeting of the leading church boards (Union and Conferences) was also controlled – a representative from the Department of Church Affairs was always present.

---

41 Gheorghe Modoran, *Biserica prin pustiul roșu* (Pantelimon: Viață și Sănătate, 2013), 531–534.

42 Interview with retired pastor Adalbert Orban.

43 Studii CNSAS, *Totalitarism și rezistență, teroare și represiune în România Comunistă*, coord. Gheorghe Onișoru (București: CNSAS, 2001), 187–190.

(4) The salaries of the pastors and the church budget were also controlled and strictly capped at levels that barely allowed subsistence.

(5) Even the purchase of firewood or employing cleaning staff for the church buildings was a matter of state approval, as these persons were to be good informants.[44]

Thus, one of the first measures taken after the regime was consolidated was to impose new leadership on the church composed of pastors fully subjected to the regime and willing to accept and defend the restrictions imposed by the authorities.[45] Once promoted, the new leaders were permanently blackmailed with the loss of their function and their replacement with others willing to cooperate, in case they refused to implement the imposed measure. Therefore, one of the Union presidents during the communist period installed by the regime, Pavel Crişan, was reasoning: "Instead of having someone else brought in and willing to impose the restrictions requested by the authorities, it would be better that I apply them and stay in office."[46]

All Union presidents from the time of communism were imposed by the regime and were agents of the *Securitate*. Formally, during the 56 years of communism, the church held elections six times. Only one president (Ştefan Năilescu) came to this function through elections. The authorities had to threaten the delegates with the cancellation of the elections if they did not agree to vote for him. For all the following presidents (Pavel Crişan, Ion Tachici and Dumitru Popa), elections were only organized one or two years after these had been installed through appointment, i.e. once the authorities were sure that their choice would obtain the votes of the delegates. The leaders were usually voted for unanimously, as it was known that they had been selected and were imposed by the regime. Therefore, there was no use for delegates to expose themselves unnecessarily to risks arising from voting against the candidates.

On one particular occasion when the delegates tried to oppose the election of the person appointed by the authorities as President of one of the Conferences, the process was prolonged long after midnight, when the delegates were tired and voted as they were asked to, just to be able to return home as many had to go to work early the following morning.[47] In this manner the elections in the church became a formality. While the leaders appointed by the authorities were calling the believers to fast and pray for God's Spirit to lead the elections, they already had in their pockets the list prepared by the authorities with the names that had to be voted.

In spite of this unimaginable control by ignoble pastors and leaders, God cared for his church. The church did not disappear, as the regime envisioned, but grew. During communism, the Seventh-day Adventist Church in Romania overtook nu-

---

44  ACNSAS, Informativ fund, file 1798, vol. 2, f. 92. See also Romanian Adventist Union Archive, Correspondence with "Minister of Cult" for approval to buy fire wood.

45  Modoran, *Biserica prin pustiul roşu*, 598.

46  ACNSAS, Informative Fund, file 137608, vol. 3, f. 48. Informative note, "P. Georgescu," May 10, 1958.

47  Archive of Adventist Union, Minutes of the General Elective Assembly of North. Transilvania Conference, Cluj, March 20, 1955.

merically the denomination in Germany with its then three Unions, reaching towards the end of the communist period 70,000 members. Despite all restrictive and
repressive measures taken by the regime, the Adventist church thus increased by over
40,000 members during the 56 years of the communist period.

*Daniel Heinz*

# Faithful unto Death:
# The Legacy of Adventist Martyrs in Europe[1]

## Abstract

This article, one of the first covering this particular topic, examines the influence and witness of some outstanding European Adventist martyrs who lost their lives as a result of political and/or religious persecution. The chapter explores three different periods in European history (Ottoman Empire, Soviet Communism and German Fascism) when it was particularly difficult for Adventist church members to live according to their religious convictions and be faithful to God's commandments. The courageous witness of these martyrs is a true model of Christian discipleship.

Christian martyrs are believers in Christ who lost their lives prematurely, in situations of witness, as a result of human hostility and violence. Since the day Stephen was stoned for the cause of Christ, Christian martyrs have sealed their faith with blood for nearly two thousand years. They remained true to God even when it cost them dearly. In their life and death, Christ's words were fulfilled: "If anyone would come after me, let him deny himself and take up his cross and follow me. For whoever would save his life will lose it, but whoever loses his life for my sake will find it" (Matt 26:24–25, ESV).

The twentieth century entered the annals of history as *the* century of martyrs. In that century, more Christians were killed for their faith than in any previous century. In Turkey, Christian Armenians and Assyrians endured terrible persecution. Between 1894 and 1923, around 1.5 million people of these ethnic groups perished in a national genocide which has been called "a holocaust before the Holocaust" (Elie Wiesel). The war against Christianity, waged by modern dictators of both communist and fascist persuasions, resulted in indescribable sufferings. It led to a death toll that has not been calculated to this day.

The period of persecution under the Soviet regime stretched, roughly speaking, from 1917 to 1965, with the years of terror during Stalin's rule (1929–1941) being the darkest ones. The Russian author Aleksandr Solzhenitsyn estimates that in the years 1937 to 1939 alone, around 1.7 million were shot by Soviet militia. Stalin's number of victims has been roughly estimated at fifteen million. Even though the majority of these victims perished on "political" grounds, the Christians who died tragically or deliberately due to their religious convictions number several million.

---

1    Translated from German by Jón Hjörleifur Stefánsson.

The Stalinist "purges" are indeed without precedent in world history.[2] Even though National Socialism's reign of terror was much shorter than the Stalinist one, the systematic and perfected annihilation of Jews and Jewish Christians during that time reached atrocious proportions. And even the more recent past – if we, for instance, consider only the persecution of Christians during the Chinese Cultural Revolution – is soaked with the blood of millions of martyrs.

It is true that Christians today can speak freely about their faith in Western societies. Yet human rights experts have demonstrated that even today Christianity remains the most persecuted religion worldwide.[3] It is estimated that in recent years around 100,000 Christians were killed annually at a global level.[4] In many Islamic states in the Near East, Asia, and Africa, violence against Christians is particularly strong. The life of the Christian Church is dependent on the faith-expressions of these courageous witnesses. The early church father Tertullian (2nd/3rd century) stated: "*Semen est sanguis Christianorum*" – "The blood of Christians is the seed of the Church."[5] A church that does not know or forgets its martyrs, cuts itself off from its own history and loses its value and purpose.

Seventh-day Adventists also count many martyrs among their ranks, especially in Europe. They were killed as "Christian heretics" in the Ottoman Empire, died under torture in the dungeons of the Soviet secret police or in Siberian labor camps, completely isolated from the outside world. Some were killed by Nazi henchmen due to non-violence, conscientious objection to military service or refusal to work on Sabbath. Some lost their lives as missionaries in Africa, Asia, and Latin America. Their persecutors were not only militant non-believers or hostile atheists, but also fanatics from non-Christian religions. Some Adventists even fell victim to ecclesiastic or Christian violence, especially in Orthodox countries such as Tsarist Russia, Romania, Serbia, and Bulgaria. Besides this, the story of many Adventist martyrs is still unknown.[6]

---

2    With regard to the persecutions of Christians in the Soviet Union I refer to the groundbreaking study of my late friend and colleague Hans-Christian Diedrich, which appeared shortly before his untimely death in 2008: "*Wohin sollen wir gehen…" Der Weg der Christen durch die sowjetische Religionsverfolgung* (Erlangen: Martin-Luther Verlag, 2007). With great appreciation and thankfulness, I look back at our fruitful cooperation in establishing various lists of Christian martyrs for the Soviet period, which were partially published in his book.

3    Thomas Schirrmacher, *Christenverfolgung heute. Die vergessenen Märtyrer* (Holzgerlingen: Hänssler, 2008), 6–65.

4    See Christof Sauer, "Kann man Märtyrer zählen und wenn ja, wie? Gegensätzliche Ansätze," in *Jahrbuch Verfolgung und Diskriminierung von Christen 2018*, eds. Thomas Schirrmacher, Max Klingberg, and Martin Warnecke (Bonn: Verlag für Kultur und Wissenschaft, 2018), 39.

5    *Apologeticum* 50,14.

6    The present article is based on various studies done by the author over a period of many years. I just refer to two pieces which contain most of the information presented in this article: "Gemeinde unter dem Kreuz: Das Vermächtnis adventistischer Märtyrer," *Adventecho*, October

## Adventist Martyrs: Uncomfortable Witnesses?

What do we know about Adventist martyrs in Europe? What place do they occupy in the life and thought of the Adventist Church? Surprisingly, no monograph has been written in the field of Adventist martyrology so far. The topic is obviously not yet part of the spiritual or theological mindset of the Church even though Adventists have developed a biblical end-time scenario that includes the persecution of faithful believers by anti-Christian powers. While the heritage of the martyrs as "models of faith" (not as "saints" or "mediators" as in Roman-Catholic tradition!) is alive in the historical consciousness of other Protestant denominations (e.g. the Mennonites),[7] the Adventist Church takes hardly any official notice of its own martyrs. It almost seems as if the Adventist community has forgotten them.

The reasons for this apparent "martyr forgetfulness" are probably multifaceted: ignorance about their particular history due to insufficient sources of information, a certain degree of apathy towards the topic in general due to the pluralistic influence of modern times, or even a more fundamental and conscious rejection of the past, which, as some may feel, does not fit into an "enlightened" context of a modern and progressive church seeing itself as future-oriented rather than fixated on "dark times." Thus the more attractive aspects of the Gospel are usually presented whereas the difficult and challenging ones passed over in silence. However, Paul did not keep silent when he wrote these words in prison: "All who desire to live a godly life in Christ Jesus will be persecuted" (2 Tim 3:12, ESV). Do Christians, including Adventists, not die for their faith today? They do! The readiness to suffer in the sense of "self-denial" and "carrying the cross" is still required of all those who wish to follow Jesus wholeheartedly, honestly and consistently.

Uncompromising martyrs who lived out their faith to the last consequence always have been a challenge to the church. In fact, they reflect the true crisis that exists within the church, a church that prefers to ensure its survival in some given situation by entering into complicity or compromise with the ruling power, thus going directly against the divine commandment and human conscience.[8] The painful contrast between aspiration and reality in the life of a church is manifested by the powerful and clear witness of its martyrs. And thus the memory of martyrs may indeed raise uncomfortable questions: If their nonconformist choices were right, did all the other true believers go astray? Are there ultimately only two positions to be taken, for or against? Or how should the biblical commandment – "We must obey God rather

2006, 25–28; "Christusbekenner unter Halbmond, Sowjetstern und Hakenkreuz: Adventistische Märtyrerschicksale im 20. Jahrhundert," *Adventecho*, November 2006, 23–26.

7    Cf. Jochen-Christoph Kaiser, "Die Wiederentdeckung der Märtyrer im 20. Jahrhundert," in *Gewalt gegen Christen,* eds. Georg Plasger and Heinz-Günther Stobbe (Leipzig: Evangelische Verlagsanstalt, 2014), 265–280.

8    See Daniel Heinz, "Dem Gebot und Gewissen verpflichtet: Freikirchliche Märtyrer," in "*Ihr Ende schaut an…*": *Evangelische Märtyrer des 20. Jahrhunderts,* eds. Harald Schultze and Andreas Kurschat (Leipzig: Evangelische Verlagsanstalt, 2. ed., 2008), 85–89.

than men" (Acts 5:29) – be understood in practice? How important are biblical doctrines to me in times of trouble and temptation? Do I have a solid, Bible-based personal conviction, a living and independent trust in God, or are all my religious convictions more or less shaped by the socio-cultural environment in which I live? Do I shy away from inevitable conflicts to live comfortably or at least to survive under pressure, or do I have the courage to resist and suffer even at the risk of my life? Do I ultimately tend to forget the witness and legacy of Christian martyrs to avoid inner struggle?

Despite the diversity of their sufferings, Adventist martyrs have one thing in common: They are uncomfortable for us because they represent a radical challenge to our Christian life, reminding us of the apocalyptic warning to Laodicea: "So, because you are lukewarm, and neither hot nor cold, I will spit you out of my mouth" (Rev 3:16). At the same time, they encourage us to follow the Master by carrying the cross willingly and patiently, for – to put it in the words of Heinrich J. Löbsack – it is "a burden that is light in view of the signs of the approaching Advent," a burden that "uplifts us in the light of eternity."[9] Löbsack, who was murdered in a labor camp, and who had furthered the Adventist missionary cause in Russia and the Soviet Union with untold sacrifices, concludes: "I know no disappointment, for I 'have tasted the powers of the world to come' (Heb 6:5)".[10] This strong eschatological assurance – "to stand finally with all the perfected saints on Mount Zion!" – gave Adventist martyrs the strength to remain faithful to God despite despair, doubts, fears, and sufferings, as they faced the greatest, final trial of their life.

## Persecution, Hardship, and Death

This article can mention only a few examples of Adventist martyrs from various epochs. Their stories exemplify the stories of many others who suffered a similar fate. Some remain forgotten, are unknown, or lost to memory until today. This ambiguous situation is characteristic of many Adventist martyrs, who suffered and died in anonymity and loneliness, completely cut off from the outside world in prisons, in concentration or labor camps. The perpetrators methodically covered the traces of the victims as if they never had existed. I was continually reminded of this fact during the weary research into files of the Soviet secret police, which were intentionally scattered all over the country to make any investigations as difficult as possible. In many cases, documents were redacted to hide the truth behind them. For nearly thirty years the author has endeavored to collect biographical information about Adventist martyrs in Russian and Ukrainian archives with rather limited success. The "operative documents" (spy and police reports), for example, are still closed to the public to this

9   See Daniel Heinz, "Heinrich J. Löbsack: Pioneer, President and Poet of the Adventist Church in Russia, 1870 – 1938," *Journal of the American Historical Society of Germans From Russia (AHSGR)* 21.1 (1998):11–16.
10  Ibid., 13.

day. Once all relatives of a repressed or executed person have passed away, archives and police refuse categorically to cooperate with investigators or historians, and no files are released.

When the Turkish authorities realized the purpose of my investigations in Istanbul in 1995, they became furious and blocked access to all archives. Until the present day, the Turkish government officially denies the Armenian genocide. Historians often face closed doors. What remains is the certainty that those who were persecuted and killed are not forgotten by God. Their names neither "drown" in the water nor "burn up" in the flames (Isa 43:1–2). The fragmentary historical records that do exist – whether transcripts of court proceedings or a personal farewell note – may demonstrate, sometimes in a deeply moving way, the strong faith of the victims. This faith was not free from doubt or fear, but it held on to the end. Often this work of uncovering history will simply remain a tentative but intricate search for traces, with few historical results, a challenge for every researcher, but, spiritually, most rewarding.

First, we will look at Adventist victims of Greek and Armenian background in the Ottoman Empire who lost their lives in the course of the Young Turks revolution. They were not only political victims, for they died as confessing and practicing Christians in a hostile and intolerant Islamic environment. Although the Ottoman Empire was, historically, geographically, and culturally, never part of Europe – even though it had subjugated in the course of history large territories of southeastern Europe – the little flock of Greek and Armenian Seventh-day Adventists within its borders always considered itself to be more European than Oriental in its cultural outlook and orientation. Next we will consider the group of martyrs during the time of German National Socialism and Soviet Stalinism – both totalitarian regimes which were profoundly atheist and hostile to Christianity. As for European Adventist martyrs who died as missionaries in non-European mission fields – mostly due to sickness and exhaustion, but also through violence – their story, unfortunately, lies beyond the limited scope of this presentation. Nevertheless, we should not forget any single Adventist martyr in our historical work. They are heroes of faith, even if they did not consider themselves as such. If we forget their names, even unintentionally, we allow them – metaphorically – to suffer "death" a second time – in our memory, and their witness for us is forever lost.

## *"God Has Satisfied My Spiritual Hunger": Diran Tcherakian*

The annihilation of the Armenian Adventist congregations is one of the saddest chapters in Adventist mission history.[11] This dark chapter remains more or less unknown to the present day. In 1914, there were around 350 Adventist church members, most of them ethnic Armenians, scattered all over Turkey. Of those, more than 250 lost

11    See Daniel Heinz, "Adventisten im Osmanischen Reich – Ein Fallbeispiel für islamische In-
      toleranz," in 'For You Have Strengthened Me'. Biblical and Theological Studies in Honor of
      Gerhard Pfandl in Celebration of His Sixty-Fifth Birthday (St. Peter/Hart: Seminar Bogenho-
      fen, 2007), 453–478.

their lives in the years to come, among them around 50 children or youth. Very few seem to have converted to Islam to save their lives. One of the first martyrs was the untiring Dzadour G. Baharian, who has become known as the Adventist "father" and "apostle" of the Armenians. Kurdish soldiers murdered him in 1914 close to Sivas, while he was on a missionary journey. Baharian was ordered to renounce Christ and accept Islam on the spot. When he resisted and folded his hands for prayer, he was shot in cold blood. The murderers then sold his clothes and belongings in the market place. Other Adventists preachers followed Baharian into death in the following months and years, some with their families: E. Ayvazian, B. Touzdjian, M. Ashikian, H. Apovian, H. Shadarevian, O. Pirenian, and finally Diran Tcherakian. Those who were not killed immediately perished during the so-called "death marches," which were organized by the Turkish army. The prisoners, sometimes whole families with their children, were led through rough mountain and desert areas for hundreds of miles without regular food and water – until they perished in the blazing heat.

Diran Tcherakian was a famous Armenian poet and college teacher who decided in 1921 to travel through Anatolia as an itinerant preacher to comfort the threatened, frightened and isolated Adventist church members on his way. He was among those who later perished in one of these numerous death marches. We are relatively well informed about the martyrdom of Tcherakian, since he was already famous during his lifetime, so that the entire Armenian people mourned his death. Tcherakian also managed to leave behind written notes during the march, which found their way back to the Adventist members in Constantinople, where the mission office was located. In addition, there were also some eyewitnesses who reported his death in oral and written form later on. Even the *Armenian Soviet Encyclopedia,* published in Yerevan from 1974 to 1986, honored Tcherakian with an entry that acknowledged his literary accomplishments for the Armenian nation.[12]

Tcherakian, the restless and searching poet, had become a fervent Adventist believer in 1915 and, according to his own testimony, saw in the return of Christ the fulfillment of his deep spiritual longing. After the death of Baharian, the forty-year-old took over the pastoral care of the small Armenian flock that had survived the genocide. This Tcherakian did until 1921, when he himself was arrested in Konya and convicted, since he refused to renounce his faith in court. He had preached about his favorite topic, the soon-coming "kingdom of God". The Turkish authorities, however, accused him of "rebellion." Two sturdy brothers from the local Adventist group were convicted with him, and shot dead within a few days after the trial. Tcherakian's ordeal began on April 14, 1921. For several months he was forced to walk in chains, beaten and tortured by mounted militiamen, traversing the barren mountainous area of Anatolia. Gradually all his belongings were taken from him. With a small Bible in his hands he preached to his fellow prisoners while walking.

---

12   The State Museum of Yerevan dedicates one exhibition room to the life and work of Diran Tcherakian as an outstanding Armenian writer and philosopher. However, no information is given on his later life as an Adventist lay pastor and missionary.

After having travelled around one thousand kilometers, the convict colony reached the Kurdish city of Diyarbakir on the banks of the river Tigris in June. They now faced the deadly Syrian desert beyond the river. Along the way, women and children from Armenian villages, taking pity on the prisoners, had given them food or washed them and their clothes. Any prisoner who could not walk further was now left behind to die. Tcherakian was struck by fever and, finally, his feet could not carry him any longer. His fellow-prisoners, who had listened to his short sermons on the march, being themselves in deepest misery and totally exhausted, did not want to leave the preacher behind and decided to carry him on their backs until strength forsook them too. Yet, they did not give up and convinced some officers, in exchange for Tcherakian's coat, to lift him unto a horse and tie him to the saddle. A few hours later Tcherakian passed away. In one of his final words, he exhorted his companions to keep together and not to allow their faith and love to cease.[13]

## "All the Kingdoms of This World Shall Pass Away": Karl G. Harreß

Since Adventists distanced themselves from state and politics on the one hand, and kept to the divine commandment and their conscience on the other, they often found themselves in conflict with the authorities. They did not openly show political opposition, but valued loyalty to God above loyalty to the government according to the principle "We must obey God rather than men" (Acts 5:29). However, this stance was not an iron rule but left to the individual church member's understanding and interpretation. At times, it caused those members who took the rule very seriously not only sufferings, but also loneliness and isolation, as they could not rely on the spiritual support of their own local congregation or denominational leadership. Frequently church leaders or even close fellow believers accused them of religious hubris, ostentation, or fanaticism. Thus, they eventually became "strangers" in the ranks of their own congregation, which saw political or social adjustments as a means of survival and, therefore, distanced itself from members who would not bend or compromise.

We are reminded of the Adventist minister Karl G. Harreß.[14] He grew up in the province of Thuringia and was working as a pastor in Oldenburg at the time of his arrest. His wife, Frieda, described him as "a level-headed man, who already in 1939

13    Some vital information on Tcherakian I owe to the late Professor Nourhan Ouzounian, an Armenian Adventist scholar and linguist. He invited me to his home in Montreal in 2001 where we attempted to reconstruct the biography of Tcherakian on the basis of the primary sources in his collection.

14    See my article in Schultze and Kurschat, 307–308. Cf. also Johannes Hartlapp, "Karl Georg Harreß – Ein adventistischer Märtyrer," *Dialog* (Theologische Hochschule Friedensau) (July–September 2014): 8. For the difficult situation of the Adventist Church during the Nazi regime, I refer to Johannes Hartlapp's monumental study, *Siebenten-Tags-Adventisten im Nationalsozialismus* (Göttingen: V & R unipress, 2008).

perceived the catastrophe that was about to befall the German nation." In December 1941, he held public lectures on the occasion of the annual week of prayer. Unnoticed by Harreß, three undercover *Gestapo* agents were sitting in the audience pretending interest in the message he presented. At the end of one lecture, they suddenly arrested him. After intense police interrogation, Harreß honestly admitted his opposition to the Nazi regime, which he based on the message of the prophet Daniel that no earthly kingdom will last (Daniel 2).

He was taken into "custody" and finally judged by the People's Court (*Volksgerichtshof*). In February 1942, the 55-year old pastor was transferred to the Sachsenhausen-Oranienburg concentration camp, where he was left to the whims of the guards. Already severely weakened, he was put to the task of cleaning sidewalks with a toothbrush. Many times he collapsed unconscious. Soon thereafter, he was transferred to the concentration camp of Groß-Rosen in Lower Silesia, which claimed many victims due to the grueling forced labor in the granite quarry. Harreß managed to send some short letters to his wife from the camp. One letter reveals that he refused to use the greeting "*Heil Hitler*". The courageous preacher died on July 6, 1942, as a result of the severe conditions. It is uncertain whether the official cause of death – poor blood circulation – corresponded to reality. Harreß was one of the few German Adventist martyrs in the "Third Reich". We may also think of Adventist conscientious objectors, some of whom are known to us by name: Fritz Bergner, Hans Brüning, Otto König, Franz Partes, Herbert Schwalbe, Franz Dlugosch, Willi Kollmann, not to forget Erich Mertinat, a young dentist from Treuburg, East Prussia, who refused to kill but was permitted to serve as a medic. Bergner, born 1903 in Berlin, who was a simple locksmith, saw his conscription to the *Wehrmacht* as "the most difficult trial" in his life ("I was in constant conflict with my religious convictions").[15] At first he complied with the orders, but could not go against his conscience for long. In 1942, in the battle turmoil on the Eastern front, he affirmed: "I would rather be shot than raise a weapon against the enemy." Bergner was deemed "unworthy to bear arms" and handed over to the *Gestapo*. A few months later he died in the Dachau concentration camp. We do not know the real cause of his death.

When Hans Brüning of Rostock was enlisted in 1943, he attempted to flee to Switzerland. Before he could cross the border he was arrested and convicted for desertion. Soon after, Brüning was executed in the city of Posen by the *Gestapo*. Franz Partes from Vienna and Otto König from Eastern Prussia were already advanced in age when they were drafted into the *Volkssturm* in the very last phase of the war. The latter stated: "I can only serve one *Führer* and I do not want to be unfaithful to Him at the end of my life."[16] Both were convicted and died under unknown circumstances. Even though he was physically disabled – visually impaired – Herbert Schwalbe from Dresden was conscripted to the armed forces, and died as a conscientious objector and deserter. Franz Dlugosch, an Adventist merchant and staunch

---

15   On Fritz Bergner and Hans Brüning, see Heinz, in: Schultze and Kurschat, 232–233; 244.
16   Heinz, "Gemeinde unter dem Kreuz," 27.

pacifist from Lossen in Silesia, suffered a similar fate when he was shot in 1940 in Łódź/Litzmannstadt for rejecting to bear arms. In 1937, he had already been imprisoned for "fleeing the flag". Willi Kollmann, born 1914 in Neustrelitz, had been a colporteur and a student at the Adventist Seminary in Neandertal. After having finished a specialized training with the German *Luftwaffe*, Kollmann worked as a cargo pilot, mainly in the Ukraine. He brought food and medical supplies to frontline soldiers on his plane, a *Heinkel* He 111. Kollmann even received a military medal of honor ("honor roll clasp" or "*Frontflug-Spange*") for his courageous service. In March 1944, however, he was ordered to change planes and work as a bomber pilot. Being a staunch Christian, Kollmann refused repeatedly. He was then ordered before a military tribunal but was suddenly shot on April 27, 1944, at Jaroslaw in Eastern Poland, before the court was able to decide on a final verdict.[17]

When the German army had to withdraw in Bobruisk (Mogilev) at the White Russian frontline in June 1944, Mertinat was left behind with a large group of heavily wounded German soldiers. As a devout Christian he had volunteered to take care of them since they were unfit for transport. When the Soviet army took over, these wounded soldiers were most probably executed together with Mertinat. Nothing was heard of them and Mertinat's fate has been a mystery ever since.[18]

Some Adventists lost their lives because they had protected Jews by helping them to hide or flee the country. For example, Zoltán Kubinyi, an Adventist military officer of a Jewish work battalion from Hungary, freed around 140 Jewish prisoners, while he himself was taken prisoner and later found death in a Siberian labor camp.[19]

Finally, we should not forget the brave conscientious objectors among the German "Reform Adventists," of whom seven died just between 1941 and 1943 in the prison of Brandenburg-Görden.[20] Of all churches and denominations – with the exception of the Jehovah's Witnesses – Adventists and Reform Adventists account for the highest number of conscientious objectors (around eighteen, though the number of unreported cases is higher!), a historical fact that was previously unnoticed in research literature.[21]

---

17  See Daniel Heinz, "Adventist Opposition to War in Europe: Cases of Nonconformity and Conscientious Objection," in *Adventists and Military Service: Biblical, Historical, and Ethical Perspectives*, eds. Frank Hasel, Barna Magyarosi, and Stefan Höschele (Madrid: Sateliz 2019), 147.

18  Interview with Walter Mertinat (brother of Erich), Freiburg/Br., 8. 11. 2002.

19  See Daniel Heinz, ed., *Freikirchen und Juden im "Dritten Reich". Instrumentalisierte Heilsgeschichte, antisemitische Vorurteile und verdrängte Schuld* (Göttingen: V & R unipress, 2011), 298, 302, 304.

20  The author refers to the short biographical entries that he dedicated to them in the encyclopedia edited by Schultze and Kurschat (2008, see footnote 7). Cf. also Ines Müller ed., *Du sammelst meine Tränen. Glaubenszeugen im Nationalsozialismus* (Naumburg/Saale: Edelstein Verlag, 2014).

21  See Heinz, "Dem Gebot und Gewissen verpflichtet: Freikirchliche Märtyrer," 94.

## "I Have Tasted the Powers of the World to Come": Heinrich J. Löbsack

Adventists were hit particularly hard in the Soviet Union. During the time of the persecutions under Stalin (1924–1941) entire congregations were wiped out. Around 70% of all preachers and church leaders were killed. 3000 to 4000 church members, more than one fourth of the entire Soviet Adventist membership, died due to persecution, hunger, and detention in labor camps. It is impossible to calculate the precise number of Adventist martyrs in the Soviet Union. A few relatively well-documented cases are now known after many years of research and investigation.[22]

The White Russian preacher Alexander M. Gryc (Gritz) represents one of these cases. Gryc testified of his faith openly in his East-Siberian captivity in 1944 until he was tied to a tree in the extreme cold and water was poured over him until he froze stiff. The Russian-German leaders Jacob K. Reimer and Jakob W. Kraus, who had studied in Friedensau before World War I, were shot in labor camps in the late 1930s for refusing to work on Sabbath and for conducting baptisms in secret. A particularly agonizing fate was that of the president of the entire church work in the Soviet Union, Heinrich J. Löbsack.[23] On the night before March 21, 1934, a black car stopped outside his home in Durowa Street 22, Moscow. Undercover secret service agents stepped out and knocked loudly at the door of apartment 19 of the wooden house, built in traditional Russian fashion. The Volga-German Adventist preacher from the village of Frank had spent years of sacrificial work as colporteur, pastor and superintendent in the largest country on earth. He had now grown old but was still undeterred in his service for the church. He quietly opened the door. "Genrich Ivanovitsch Lebsak!" one of the men shouted, "You are under arrest!" Before Löbsack was put into handcuffs, he called out to his fellow workers in the mission house: "Brethren, keep on working and do not become discouraged, because the work of God is like a river and cannot be stopped." These were the last words of the doomed preacher to his congregation. They represent a legacy to this day.

No other person accomplished as much for the Adventist cause in Russia as he did. From 1890 onwards, Löbsack had been an itinerant preacher and a church leader on the frontlines. In 1927, if we just look at one year of his life, he traveled 46,000 km by train, ship, car, and on horseback to visit Adventist congregations scattered all over the country. Adversity, persecution, and imprisonment run like a red thread through his life. He often found himself "chased like a hunted deer." His missionary spirit came from a deep eschatological assurance, which he expressed in 1906 in one of his many poems in the following words: *"Du machtest mich zum Himmelsbürger,*

---

22  The author conducted more than fifteen field trips between 1994 and 2015 to states and cities of the former Soviet Union searching for biographical information on Adventist martyrs among local congregations and in various public archives. Most of the material he found is not yet ready for publication, but still gives an idea of the vast extent of state suppression and annihilation during the Communist years.

23  On Löbsack, see my article in Schultze and Kurschat, 602–603.

*Befreit von Angst; Drum will ich, Herr, für Dich auch sterben, Wenn Du's ver-langst.*[24] At that time Löbsack, of course, did not know that he would have to suffer precisely this fate one day.

The highlights of his career as a church leader were the recognition of the Adventist Church through a declaration of tolerance issued by Tsar Nicholas II. in 1906, the reorganization of the Church as a "Federation of Unions" (*All-Räte-Bundesunion*) at the beginning of the new era of the Soviet Union, the doubling of membership from 1920 to 1927 under his presidency (from 1920 on), and the founding of a publishing house. At the same time, Löbsack realized that the Soviet state was increasingly tightening its iron grip on the Church through new restrictions and repressions. At two Adventist conferences held in Moscow in 1924 and 1928, he attempted to find a compromise with the state and the party, especially with regard to the question of military service.

In 1924, he issued a formal declaration stating that each member "had to solve the question of military service according to its own conscience." In 1928, however, under severe pressure from the authorities, Löbsack proclaimed that henceforth members must fully accept "military service in all its forms." Church members who failed to adhere to this guideline were to be considered as "false teachers" and dismissed. Consequently, various dissident Adventist underground movements arose in the country, which refused to accept the church's compromise with the state. After 1929 (and the then new laws restricting religion), the situation in Moscow became gradually unbearable for Löbsack. Secret police officials now summoned him almost daily for negotiations and interrogations that lasted for hours, with Löbsack always barely escaping arrest. Once again, he tried to appease his suppressors. This time, in June 1933, he published a circular in which he encouraged Adventist Kolchos farmers to work on the Sabbath during harvest time, a highly controversial move by the faithful church leader. Löbsack did not want the smoldering wick of the suppressed Church to go out entirely, and, therefore, for one last time tried desperately to accommodate, hoping to finally win the favor of the authorities.

Yet his efforts were doomed from the start. Later in prison he confessed to his wife in tears how much he regretted these compromises. It had become clear to him: "The tyrants want one thing only: The complete annihilation of the Church and our death." After his arrest Löbsack was interrogated every night for three weeks in the infamous Lubyanka and Butyrka prisons in Moscow until he caved in. The court records give only a vague description of the harassment and punishments he suffered in the torture chambers of the NKVD.[25] The goal was to break the body and mind

---

24    Translation: "You made me a citizen of Heaven / And freed me from all fear / And, therefore, Lord, I would also die for You / If you would so require."

25    The secret police agency, Stalin's instrument of terror, was named NKVD which stands for People's Commissariat of Internal Affairs. From 1954 until 1991, it was called KGB (translated in English as "Committee for State Security"). After the collapse of the Soviet Union the secret intelligence service took a new name: FSB – Federal Security Service.

of the prisoner. After Löbsack collapsed, he was taken to the prison hospital to recover so that the trial could continue. It is obvious from the court records that the author was able to study between 1994 and 1995 at the FSB[26] archives in Moscow that both the charges against and the confessions by Löbsack were falsified. Every defendant was brought to the point where he or she admitted their "mistakes" and after a Kafkaesque process ritually pledged to "improve." Löbsack's "confession" of counterrevolutionary activities as defined in Article 58 of the Russian Soviet Penal Code (RSFSR) was brought about through torture, as seen from the later rehabilitation record.

When visited by his wife, he uttered only one wish: "I want to die." Löbsack was sentenced to three years of solitary confinement in a labor camp close to Yaroslavl, northeast of Moscow. Almost nothing is known about his detention conditions. Some of the individual cells in the camp were very small and cold, with a low ceiling and could be submerged in water. At the end of his sentence, Löbsack was offered freedom if he recanted his faith. He refused. It is possible that he died in the camp in 1938. An eyewitness claims to have seen a guard beating Löbsack to death with the butt of his rifle. It was later reported that he was executed by a firing squad during the Great Purge. Until today the exact place, time, and circumstances of his death remain unknown. The family received no official death notification and his grave has not been located.

## "Consider the Outcome of Their Way of Life, and Follow Their Faith" (Heb 13:7)

The power of Adventist martyrs lies in the fact that they illustrate in a dramatic way what it means to glorify God and be true to his commandments in a world ruled by dark forces. In spite of obstacles and doubts, they remained faithful unto death. The light in their sufferings was the hope in Jesus, the soon-returning King. They saw themselves as subjects of his reign, which is everlasting. And for that, it was worth it both to live and to die.

Dark forces – does the present look much different? No, because true Christianity was never "cheap". The well-known Protestant evangelist, youth pastor, and author, Theo Lehmann, writes, admittedly in a somewhat provocative way: "Never before, when we look at the world as a whole, have there been so many Christian martyrs. In this respect, our lives in Germany and in Western Europe are like an island of blessing. . . . Yes, friends, we still dance in our Christian house parties, while the body of Christ bleeds from a thousand wounds in other countries. We still market the Christian faith under the cheap slogan 'Christianity is cool.' But what will we do, when one day Christianity is not 'cool' anymore, but a dangerous liability? Who will be sustained by these superficialities when not sitting in church but in prison? When

26   See ibid.

there is no more happy dancing but terrible torture?"[27] May the witness of the martyrs always remind us that it was first and foremost Jesus who went to the cross for us. It is from Him alone that the believer receives strength to be a true disciple. Those who live "under the cross" and are persecuted for His sake, He embraces in His infinite love and mercy, and declares that theirs is the kingdom of heaven (Matt 5:10). They are the true examples of faith and discipleship.

27    Theo Lehmann, "Das Land ist still," *Idea Spektrum* (May 26, 2004): 3.

# Part III

# European Adventists, the Public, and the Christian Other

*Reinder Bruinsma*

# The European Union and the Adventist Church

Abstract

This paper examines the views of Seventh-day Adventists with regard to the nature and possible future of the European Union. Some of the elements of the biblical prophecy of Daniel 2 have traditionally been interpreted as foretelling the failure of any political attempts to unite a major part of Europe. While Adventists have not turned away from this interpretation, current Adventism does not place much emphasis on it, apart from more critical comments from representatives at the conservative edges of the church. The developments around a likely rupture between the United Kingdom and Europe has attracted relatively little attention. On the other hand, there is appreciation for some practical advantages that the EU has brought.

Seventh-day Adventists have always had an uneasy relationship with attempts at forging greater political unity in the world and in Europe in particular. A significant element in their traditional views on end-time events is the expectation that before Christ's coming the world will be ruled by a world-wide religio-political power, with key roles for the papacy and for the United States of America. At the same time Adventists have maintained that all attempts at creating a united Europe will ultimately fail.

## Daniel 2

A few chapters in the apocalyptic portions of the Bible, i.e. the Book of Daniel and the Book of Revelation, form the basis for these views about the future. Since this paper deals with Europe and the European Union – the current attempt to establish a major degree of economic and political unity in Europe – the second chapter of the Book of Daniel is our main focus.

Daniel 2 tells the story of a dream by King Nebuchadnezzar, who ruled over the Neo-Babylonian empire from ca. 605 to ca. 562 BC. When the king awakes he has forgotten his dream, and he expects his spiritual advisers to tell him what he saw in his dream and also its significance. When his entourage of "wise men" is unable to do this, the young Judean prince Daniel, who had been exiled to Babylon, is the one who is able to do what the "wise men" failed to do. Daniel reminds the king of the statue of different metals that he saw in his dream, and subsequently explains the meaning of the dream. The head of gold, he says, symbolizes the rule of Babylon, while the body parts made of silver, brass and iron are symbols of the empires that were to follow. In the end a big stone – the Kingdom of God – would strike at the feet, composed of a mixture of iron and clay, and usher in a totally new era.

Different views developed regarding the identity of those empires, but early in the Christian age both Jews and Christians agreed on a four-kingdom schema: (1) Babylon; (2) some combination of Media and Persia; (3) Greece and Macedonia, including the empire of Alexander the Great and the kingdoms of the Diadochi; and (4) Rome.[1] When the Roman empire collapsed, Christian exegetes did not relinquish this schema but reinterpreted it in order to include the major powers of their own days.[2] In post-Reformation Protestantism the Babylon, Medo-Persia, Greece, Rome schema became the standard interpretation.[3]

As the centuries went by, gradually more attention was given to the feet of the statue and to the ten toes.[4] Ephraim Huit, in the first systematic commentary to appear in the American colonies, suggested a worldwide application. He identified the ten toes as Britain, France, Germany, Spain, Italy, Africa, Asia, Greece, Syria and Egypt.[5] Other commentators from that time rather saw the ten toes as powers that arose on the territory of the Roman Empire. This became the dominant view of Seventh-day Adventists. Uriah Smith (1832–1903), the most prestigious interpreter of apocalyptic prophecy in early Adventism, listed the ten nations which were symbolized by the ten toes as: "Huns, Ostrogoths, Visigoths, Franks, Vandals, Suevi, Burgundians, Heruli, Anglo-Saxons and Lombards."[6] Smith acknowledged that he had simply adopted the view of Machiavelli (1469–1529; an Italian diplomat, politician, historian, philosopher, humanist, and writer of the Renaissance period), which had been endorsed by several authorities that Smith had consulted.[7]

Surprisingly enough, Adventists could get very agitated about this topic of the ten toes and, and especially about the identity of each of the ten powers that were symbolized by the toes. When in 1888 the General Conference met in Minneapolis and began its discussion of the important issue of righteousness by faith, the atmosphere had already been thoroughly poisoned by acrimonious debates about a slight

---

1   Carol E. Newson, *Daniel: A Commentary*, Old Testament Library (Louisville, KY: Westminster John Know Press, 2014), 85; James A. Montgomery, *A Critical and Exegetical Commentary on the Book of Daniel* (Edinburgh: T&T Clark, 1964 ed.).

2   Newson, 88.

3   Leroy E. Froom, *The Prophetic Faith of our Fathers*, vol. II (Washington, DC: Review and Herald Publishing Association, 1948), 784, 785.

4   Exegetes of the prophetic books of Daniel and of John the Revelator usually point to the parallel between the ten toes of the statue and the ten horns of the beast that is portrayed in Daniel 7, and the ten horns of the beast of Revelation 13 and 17.

5   Froom, vol. 3, 63.

6   Uriah Smith, *Thoughts Critical and Practical on the Book of Daniel* (Battle Creek, MI: Review and Herald, 1873), 62.

7   Smith, 62; George R. Knight, *From 1888 to Apostasy: The Case of A. T. Jones* (Hagerstown. MD: Review and Herald Publishing Association, 1987), 35.

revision of the list of the nations that were symbolized by the ten toes.[8] Uriah Smith saw this revision as "a tearing up of old truth."[9]

Not all Adventist interpreters insisted that the number ten was to be taken in a literal sense. George McCready Price (1870–1963), who is best known for his role in the creationist debate, also wrote a commentary on Daniel. Commenting on the ten toes in Daniel 2, he argued that "ten" is used "as an indefinite but comparatively large number, rather than as an exact number."[10] Several other Adventist exegetes agree with him on that point.

The mixture of clay and iron was, and is, often explained as denoting weakness and fragility. Some see this mixture as referring to the many marriages between members of the royal families in a significant number of the European countries. The British Queen Victoria (reigned 1837–1901) has often been called "the grand-mother of Europe". Others point out that the mixture of clay and iron may well refer to an alliance between religion and politics.[11] Much emphasis was laid on the fact that, in spite of intermarriages, military exploits and international treaties, no lasting unity was ever achieved – in fulfilment of the words in Daniel that state that the brittle clay and the hard iron "will not remain united" (2:43, NIV).

Roy Allan Anderson, in his book *Unfolding Daniel's Prophecies*, like many commentators before him (and after him), points to the futile attempts of Charle-magne, Charles V, Louis XIV, Napoleon, Kaiser Wilhelm and Adolph Hitler to unite most of Europe. He also refers to the 4,568 treaties and international agree-ments that "have been signed, sealed – and broken – and to the League of Nations which functioned between 1920 and 1939, but did not prevent World War II."[12]

More recent Adventist commentators, though adhering to the continuous-his-torical method of interpretation, are rather more circumspect in dealing with the ten toes and their ultimate fate.[13] William H. Shea stresses that since the collapse of the Roman Empire the nations of Europe have not "cleaved" to one another. He

8    A.T. Jones wanted to replace the Huns by the Alemanni. See Knight, *From 1888 to Apostasy*, 35.
9    George R. Knight, *A User-Friendly Guide to the 1888 Message* (Hagerstown, MD: Review and Herald Publishing Association, 1998), 53.
10   George McCready Price, *The Greatest of the Prophets* (Mountain View, CA: Pacific Press Publishing Association, 1955), 80.
11   Desmond Ford, *Daniel* (Nashville, TN: Southern Publishing Association, 1978), 98, 99.
12   Roy Allan Anderson, *Unfolding Daniel's Prophecies* (Mountain View, CA: Pacific Press Publishing Association, 1975), 51. See also F.D. Nichols, ed., *Seventh-day Adventist Bible Commentary*, vol. 4 (Washington DC: Review and Herald Publishing Association, 1955), 775, 776.
13   See, Reinder Bruinsma, "Is the Adventist Hermeneutical Approach to Daniel and Revelation Changing?" Paper presented at the European Theology Teachers' Convention, April 2013. This paper concludes that the most qualified Adventist scholars who have in recent years writ-ten on the interpretation of apocalyptic prophecy are considerably less explicit in the interpre-tation of certain symbols than the more popular authors who are found at the fringes of the church.

asks: Will the European Common Market and the political affiliation of European countries break with this trend? Shea allows for the fact that they may agree upon certain political principles and enter into trade agreements, but the European countries will retain their own national identity.[14] Zdravko Stefanovic has written the most recent Adventist commentary on the Book of Daniel. His remarks on the ten toes are remarkably brief. He feels that the union of the two incompatible elements (iron and clay) can only result in tension. Behind this tension is the bipolar character of the kingdom. It is both strong and brittle at the same time. It will never become as strong as iron as Rome was in the past.[15] Interestingly enough, Stefanovic makes no reference to the European Union, even though he himself is a European by birth and was writing his commentary at a time when the EU was already a powerful institution.

## The European Union

Today, the European Union serves 510 million people in twenty-eight member states. Great Britain is currently negotiating its exit from the EU, but several other states (e.g. in the Balkans and Turkey) are anxious to join the organization. The basis of the European Union was laid when, in 1957, six countries (Germany, France, Italy, the Netherlands, Belgium and Luxembourg) formed the European Economic Community. The Maastricht Treaty (1992) created the much more comprehensive European Union. A major expansion took place in May 2004 when ten new member states were added. The Union deals with common economic, social and security policies of its member states. Much in Europe has changed because of the free movement of goods and persons within the EU, and of the Schengen-arrangement, which allows for unrestricted travel in a large part of Europe. Another major achievement is the successive adoption of a single currency by nineteen countries.

From the start the European Union has met with enthusiasm but also with firm resistance among Europe's population. Some would like to see further European integration, while others feel Brussels already controls far too much. In a number of countries populist, anti-EU parties do what they can to strengthen anti-EU sentiments. But there have also been religious objections. Many Bible believing Christians feel that, on the basis of Daniel 2, the EU must be considered a failed project from the start, but others argue that the EU-project is, in actual fact, inspired and promoted by the Roman Catholic Church. A little *Googling* on the internet will lead to numerous websites that express widespread unease among large groups of (mostly evangelical) conservative Christians about the alleged Catholic roots of the

14  William H. Shea, *Daniel 1–7* in *The Abundant Bible Amplifier* (Boise, ID: Pacific Press Publishing Association, 1996), 144, 145.
15  Zdravko Stefanovic, *Daniel, Wisdom to the Wise: Commentary on the Book of Daniel* (Nampa, ID: Pacific Press Publishing Association, 2007), 107, 108.

EU. The flag that the Council of Europe shares with the European Union, for instance, is alleged to have a strong association with the Virgin Mary. The flag has twelve stars on a blue field; these stars are said to have been inspired by the halo of twelve stars around the head of Mary on many Catholic paintings and illustrations. Moreover, it is frequently stressed that the flag was officially adopted by the Council of Europe on December 8, 1955 – the day that also happened to be the annual Day of Mary's Immaculate Conception![16] This connection with Roman Catholicism has been strongly denied by officials of the EU, but it continues to be cited by many conservative Christians, including key representatives of a number of Adventist "independent ministries". And this aspect is also not fully absent from mainline Adventist thinking. For example, in a short video that was prepared by the *Adventist Review / Adventist World*, Dr David Trim, the director of the Office of Archives and Statistics of the world church, commented on recent developments in the European Union. He emphasized that maintaining or further building the unity in Europe remains challenging, since there are so many factors that compete with the ideology of a united Europe. In this context he refers to a book written by the Italian politician Romano Prodi – a former Italian prime minister and president of the European Union between 1999 and 2004 – in which it is stated that the only thing that can hold the countries with all their own national interests together is loyalty to the [Catholic] church.[17]

Although there is a surprising lack of written and digital sources, it seems that, in general, so far the Adventist Church has displayed a mostly positive attitude towards the European Union. When the EU expanded in 2004 with ten additional countries (the Turkish part of Cyprus and nine countries that once were under Soviet influence or domination in Central and Eastern Europe), the presidents in the two European regions ("divisions") of the Adventist Church commented that the inclusion of these countries into the EU would also strengthen international ties within the church.[18] "The practical implications of integrating ten more countries into the EU could benefit church operations and communication as well," they said. It was also noted that the widespread use of the euro would make it easier to move funds across borders with less hassle, and that easier movement of people across the EU might lead to migration of church members from one country to another. The increased income of those migrants, who would move from economically challenged to more prosperous countries, could result in increased tithe income.[19]

---

16  See for instance, "The 'Virgin Mary' Flag of the European Community," accessed July 15, 2018, www.propheticrevelation.net/misc/euroflag.htm. There are many sites on the internet that make similar claims.

17  "BREXIT and Prophecy," July 15, 2018, https://www.adventistworld.org/brexit-and-prophecy/

18  Mark Kellner and Ray Dabrowski/ANN/ANR, "Church leaders watchful as EU expands," *Record* (June 19, 2004): 6.

19  Ibid.

Two departments of the church are most directly affected by developments in the EU. The department for Public Affairs and Religious Liberty of the Inter-European Division (headquartered in Bern) decided that Dr Liviu Olteanu, its director, ought to be located in Brussels (Belgium), where much of the action was now expected to be. Besides being the observer and representative of the religious liberty arm of the church (the International Association for the Defense of Religious Liberty) in Geneva, New York and Vienna, Olteanu is also a representative of that organization to the Council of Europe in Strasbourg, to the European Parliament in Brussels and in Strasbourg, and to the O.S.C.E. (Organization for Security and Co-operation in Europe).

The Adventist Development and Relief Agency (ADRA) has recently also strengthened its presence in Brussels. Its aim is to, more than in the past, be active in the field of advocacy, with a view to fighting inequality, social injustices and human rights infractions in developing countries. The EU is an important player in this area and being close to its offices and to key people is seen as a huge advantage. The European Union also has very substantial funding for development and relief projects in many countries all over the world. The Brussels office of ADRA coordinates efforts by European ADRA-donor offices (most notably in Germany, Denmark, the United Kingdom and Rumania) to apply for this European funding. In 2017 the total amount of approved ADRA-EU projects was 38.4 million euro. (It should be noted that many of these projects are implemented over a two or three-year period.) The amount of EU funding for ADRA projects in 2018 is estimated to be about 13.6 million euro.[20]

## Brexit and Future Developments

At the time of the writing of this paper the negotiations between the United Kingdom and the European Union are still taking place. At this moment the outcome – whether it will be a "soft" or a "hard" Brexit – remains uncertain. For some prophecy-watchers, Brexit fulfils the Daniel 2 prophecy, and they predict that Brexit is just the beginning of a further unraveling of the EU.

The *Adventist Review* commented on the Brexit referendum in a very restrained manner. An article, written by the communication director of the Trans-European Division of the Adventist Church, cited some of the leaders of the Trans-European Division, who acknowledged the decision made by the British people, but at the same time called for continued co-operation and for unity and love across man-made borders. They also indicated that a Brexit might have some negative financial

---

20  Information received by letter from Mr. João Martins, the executive director of the ADRA-EU office in Brussels, March 6, 2018.

and operational effects for the division, which in due time would need to be stud-ied.[21]

This is the only item about this topic of any substance that I could find in the mainline Adventist news media. But reactions are much less restrained in media that are operated by "independent" Adventist "ministries", to the right of center. Take, for instance an article in *Our Firm Foundation*, in which the author argues that Brexit is a welcome departure from the global agenda of those who want to unite the entire world under one religion.[22] The problem with the EU, we are told, is that it is run by Jesuits. The Jesuits are the ultimate culprits, who are doing what they can to implement the global agenda and the ultimate victory of the papacy.[23] A website that, according to its name, claims to represent "the Adventist under-standing of prophecy", states that prophecy does not forecast a total dissolution of the EU, but a very real weakening. In the end, prophecy tells us, the United States of America will be the only remaining super power in the world. "When we see the Brexit vote thus tearing Great Britain from the EU, we can rest assured that the days of the [God's] kingdom are nearer than we first believed."[24] Similar sentiments were voiced by Clifford Owusu-Gyamfi, an Adventist pastor in Geneva.[25] Another fringe-Adventist website, however, takes a slightly differently approach and asks whether a "yes" vote during the British referendum would have compromised the Adventist prophetic understanding. The author, Filipe Reis, replies: "No, not at all!" And the reason is simple: "While iron and clay do not unite, it is also true that they are together, side by side." He concludes that the nations of Europe will not unite, but as iron and clay are together, the nations of Europe "will be united in many organizations and purposes."[26] It is interesting to note that – as far as I have been able to ascertain – prominent speakers at the right fringe of the church, as e.g. Doug Batchelor and Walther Veith, have (so far?) been reticent in commenting at any length about a connection between Daniel 2 and Brexit.

21  Victor Hulbert, "Trans-European Division Responds to Brexit Vote," *Adventist Review, Ad-ventist Review Online*, accessed June 25, 2016, https://www.adventistreview.org/church-news/story4131-trans-european-division-responds-to-brexit-vote.

22  Bruce Telfer, "Brexit and the Global Agenda," *Our Firm Foundation* (August 2016): 20, 21.

23  Ibid.

24  Garrick Augustus, "Brexit in Bible Prophecy," accessed July 15, 2018, https://sdapro phecies.com/2016/07/02/brexit-in-bible-prophecy.

25  Clifford Owusu-Gyamfi, "Brexit and the Apocalyptic Consciousness of the Adventist," ac-cessed July 15, 2018, http://www.cliffordowusugyamfi.com/brexit-and-the-apo calyptic-consciousness-of-the-adventists.

26  Filipe Reis, "The UK Brexit and Daniel 2," accessed July 15, 2018, http://www.fulcrum7. com/blog/2016/6/24/the-uk-brexit-and-daniel-2. This critical website also strongly promotes the doctrine of male headship.

## An Interesting Question

One very interesting question is whether the Seventh-day Adventist church members in Europe are in any way influenced in their political sympathies and voting strategies by their religious views. Do the traditional convictions, based on Daniel 2, that a united Europe has no future, make the average Adventist more of a Euroskeptic than he would otherwise be? To my knowledge there are virtually no data about the political affiliations of European Adventists, let alone data about changes in voting patterns among Adventists. The only data I am aware of have been furnished to me by Pastor Jurrien den Hollander in the Netherlands. Pastor den Hollander is a trained researcher, who has initiated some major surveys of Adventist church members in the Netherlands Union. A survey in 2010 included questions about an individual's political affiliation and how the interviewee voted in the last Dutch general election. Out of over fifteen hundred respondents only forty-seven (about three percent) indicated that they had voted for the PVV (*Partij voor de Vrijheid*), which is a Dutch populist party that is more anti-EU than any of the other parties). This is (to my relief) significantly below the national average of about 15 percent. This might, at the very least, indicate, that (around 2010) Dutch Adventists were less inclined to cast an anti-EU vote than the Dutch populace in general. In other words: according to this survey, there was no indication that the prophetic convictions of Dutch Adventists made them more inclined to vote for a party that has a *Nexit* as one of its main political aims.[27]

## Conclusion

It may come somewhat as a surprise that the Adventist Church and its media have remained largely silent about developments in the last few decades with regard to the European Union project, and, more recently, with regard to Brexit. Earlier on Adventists had much more to say about the prophecy of the ten toes of iron and clay – made of substances that will never "cleave together", and about its fulfilment in a continued fragmentation of Europe, in spite of past efforts to bring most of Europe again under one rule. Have Adventists perhaps learned from earlier mistakes, when predictions failed to materialize, and has mainline Adventism perhaps become less inclined to jump upon events and trends in the world of politics and religion, and to tie these to a prophetic interpretation, with the risk of having to modify or change its views as time goes on? Unfortunately, it seems that speakers and organizations on the conservative fringe of the church display much less reticence and continue to make rash statements about the Roman Church, Sunday

---

27 Netherlands Union Conference, *Survey of Membership Involvement, 2010.* Researchers: Prof. dr. ing. H.A. Rijken, A.M. Staal, M. Nagtegaal, J. den Hollander.

laws, ecumenical conspiracies, etc. Yet, the EU and the Brexit have not (yet?) excited these voices at the fringe to the extent that one might have expected.

It would, I think, be of particular interest to have more information about the political leanings of Seventh-day Adventists in Europe, and to discover how these political preferences are informed by their religious views, in particular with regard to prophetic fulfilments. Hopefully this will be the topic of some future study.

*Michael Pearson*

# Geography of the Heart:
# Spiritual Belonging and Familiar Landscapes

### Abstract

Our spiritual identity develops significantly in response to any geographical place which has shaped us, particularly any that we call "home". Natural and built landscapes profoundly affect and reflect cultural development, and so influence our personal spiritual growth. It follows then that certain dangers may face members of the Seventh-day Adventist Church which prides itself on being a "global family". The principal among them is a sense of rootlessness. The dangers may be increased for Adventists in Europe by the fact that the principal events in the Adventist narrative have taken place, and continue to take place, elsewhere. And so tensions arise between our natural habitat and our spiritual belonging.

## An Unfamiliar Theme

Adventist scholars, like most of their Protestant peers, have focused on matters of time (and eternity), rather than of place. We have spilt much ink on the seventh day and the prophetic time-line. We often speak of salvation history but rarely of salvation geography. This paper seeks to offer some remedy by exploring the influences of church and nation – or rather country – in the formation of personal spiritual identity. The word "country" is more appropriate here because our concern is with our rootedness in our own particular landscape, our natural habitat, rather than with political or ethical issues, like military service or church-state relations, which may share borders with the topic. The paper seeks to focus on landscapes rather than on cultures. Yet geographical and cultural influences may prove impossibly difficult to separate.

This paper is simply intended to start a conversation by sketching out the territory. It includes some autobiographical reference. I do not claim to be exposing universal truths here, yet I would be surprised if my experience were unique. And if there is some substance to the claims made here it has implications for Adventist mission, nurture and retention in Europe. Though the literature on this theme is not extensive, a number of writers have ventured along various paths through the territory.

## The Land

The Bible uses equivalents for the word "home" nearly 250 times. Walter Brueggemann in *The Land* tells how God promised His people a safe space. He says, "the yearning to belong somewhere, to have a home, to be in a safe place, is a deep and moving pursuit". He believes, "our humanness is always about historical placement in the earth". He adds that our wholeness, our joy, our personal ease as well as our social coherence all derive from "physical dirt freighted with social meanings derived from historical experience. . . . There are no meanings apart from roots". Place "has historical meanings; . . . important words have been spoken which establish identity; . . . vows have been exchanged."[1]

Brueggemann concludes that the central human problem which the Bible confronts is homelessness, rootlessness – ever since God asked Adam: "Where are you?" The Bible frequently exhorts us to "Remember! Remember!" Central biblical characters find their way back to Sinai, to Bethel, to the Jordan river, to Jerusalem and other special places. It reminds us of our need for rootedness, belonging, location, placement in community – in short, our own story. Without such rootedness, without a place to call home, an intolerable burden is placed on the individual's private experience of God. Without such rootedness most cannot cope and give up. Vance Packard's *A Nation of Strangers* (1972), and Peter Berger's *The Homeless Mind* (1973), reveal early worries about an emerging modern western rootlessness nearly half a century ago.

## The Altar

Barbara Brown Taylor picks up the theme of Jacob at Bethel highlighted in Brueggemann's book. "Surely the Lord is in this place and I did not know it! How awesome is this place! And he was afraid and said: "This is none other than the house of God, and this is the gate of heaven."[2] God meets us at a time and in a place which become special to us, so special that we erect an altar, at least in our minds. Time moves inexorably on and, in the modern world, we may well choose to do the same.

Taylor identifies a potential problem here. It is a certain existential restlessness. It is a restlessness which may hamper Christian mission in general, and, no doubt, Adventist mission. Taylor says: "They will travel halfway around the world . . . to take part in a mission trip to Belize. The last place most people look is under their feet".[3] She cites a well-known saying of the fourth-century Desert Fathers: "Go to your cell and your cell will teach you everything." We sometimes find it difficult to be still where we are, to face our masked selves, to bear witness there to what we have learned of God.

Christian mission may sometimes involve a running away. It seems, says Taylor, that there is some sort of deep-seated human wish to escape one's place because we suspect that somehow our spiritual lives, our pursuit of mission will be easier, livelier,

1    Walter Brueggemann, *The Land* (London: SPCK, 19780), 2–5.
2    Gen 28: 6-7, NRSV.
3    Barbara Brown Taylor, *An Altar in the World* (London: Canterbury Press, 2009), iv.

more authentic, away from our place. For our everyday place forces some uncomfortable realities upon us. It demands that we make personal connections and commitments. It may also often involve a dull, daily grind. As a highly mobile Adventist community, we do well to give this some serious thought.

## The Parish

Andrew Rumsey, in his *Parish: An Anglican theology of place* (2017), notes that the nineteenth-century radical, William Cobbett, confessed that he was committed to the Church of England partly "because it bears the name of my country."[4] Rumsey goes on to argue that our own spirituality develops significantly in response to the geographical place where we find ourselves. In much of Europe, spirituality has for centuries been focused in the parish – a few square kilometres. We easily ignore this even though the local place, the altar, holy ground, the land, play such a large part in the biblical narrative.

This paper suggests that there is such a thing as a "geography of the heart", that God accesses us partly through local topography, and that the Adventist Church is unwise if it ignores this. If there is a gulf between our current physical experience of the world in Europe and the contours of our faith, our spiritual lives may be negatively affected. And just as important, to other Europeans our faith may seem unattractive, even unintelligible. Attachment to place is important in mission.

## The "Enchanted Place"

It is David Brown's book, *God and Enchantment of Place,* which perhaps comes closest to my subject here. He says that "enchantment of place" means that place has a special potential for "engendering a sense of divine presence". God may often be "mediated through nature and culture."[5] Mountains may elicit very different responses to God from plains, forests from the sea. He cites Brueggemann's view that all places are "storied". Particular places are invested with value and significance for different reasons. They may be national landmarks, significant locations in religious history or family life, or the setting for personal epiphanies and so on.

We have a deep attachment to place. Places become part of our identity, part of our own human story. These significant places may be natural or man-made. A significant encounter with God can take place anywhere. This "enchanted" place need not be a church. Our favourite walking place, a wild valley or even a car park can become holy ground. God's grace is not uniquely dispensed through Christian community. Furthermore, encounter with God need not be mediated by words – difficult for children of the Reformation to accept perhaps. When that encounter does happen, that

---

4   Andrew Rumsey, *Parish: An Anglican Theology of Place* (London: SCM Press, 2017), 6.
5   David Brown, *God and Enchantment of Place* (Oxford: Oxford University Press, 2004), 23–24.

place becomes significantly, divinely, "storied". Brown laments the fact that the church has withdrawn from theological engagement with that wider world beyond words which may reveal the presence of God.

Brown uses the example of landscape painting, a particularly European genre, to press his central case. In the $18^{th}$ century, painters began using a physical, empty rectangle to frame their open-air painting. And from that we get our word "picturesque" – what fits well within the frame to make a picture. We all seek to do the same with our experience of God. We experience God for the most part in context, in a familiar frame of meaning, of which the physical landscape, natural or built, is part. Context is crucial. All the particularities of the Incarnation tell us that place is central to the Christian story. Place is also crucial in our contemporary experience of God and in our witness to that experience. Our context is European. It is vital to our witness that God has encountered and continues to encounter us on our own patch of European soil. We all have our own special places, none more important than another. What happens if the narrative attaching to our physical environment does not cohere with that of our spiritual experience?

## Sacred Spaces

Philip Sheldrake in *Spaces for the Sacred* (2001) and *Spirituality and Theology* (1998) summons various witnesses to press the case. Heidegger's concept of *dasein* is vital – to be a person is to be there, to be there in a particular place. Sheldrake says place is interpreted space, citing Brueggemann again: "Place is space, has historical meanings where some things have happened which are now remembered and which provide continuity and identity across generations."[6] Sheldrake adds that place is often significant in our early spiritual development. He says landscapes "carry us beyond ourselves and beyond the immediate. They are our first intimations of the sacred."[7] "Place has also the capacity to reveal and evoke the sacred or the deepest meaning of existence; . . . the timeless and the deep can be found and in this is both grace and revelation." [8] "Without a sense of place there is no centring of the human spirit." [9] There is a visceral dimension to our experience of God.

Without this grounding which place provides we may be in some spiritual danger. "'Place is space that has the capacity to be remembered and to evoke our attention and care. We need this if life is to be conducted well. We need to think about where we are and what is unique and special about our surroundings so that we can better understand ourselves and how we relate to others,'" [10] citing Lyndon and Moore. "The skyscrapers, airports, freeways and other stereotypical components of

---

6   Brueggemann, *The Land*, 5.
7   Sheldrake, *Spirituality and Theology*, 168.
8   Ibid., 169.
9   Ibid., 190.
10  Ibid., 194. Quoted from *Chambers from a Memory Palace* (Cambridge, Mass.: MIT Press, 1994), xxii.

modern landscapes – are they not the sacred symbols of a civilization that has deified reach and derided home?"[11] citing Buttimer. In an increasingly placeless culture we have become "standardized, removable, replaceable, easily transported from one location to another,"[12] citing Berleant. Our bodies are forever "on the road". More worrying still, so too are our minds, our spirits.

Sheldrake issues a serious warning: "If we are placeless people without roots we are not only insecure but also in danger of abusing the world and the people around us in a vain attempt to create artificial identity we do not naturally experience." [13] A forced search for identity in an unfamiliar place makes us insecure and more likely to abuse others. It is a timely warning to the Adventist Church struggling to find its identity, not least in Europe. In the end restlessness, rootlessness may well produce a violence within from which the stranger may well suffer.

Sinai, Shiloh, Horeb's burning bush and so many other places in Scripture all confirm that the Infinite God is made known only by "acts of self-placement."[14]

## The Patria

Keith Clements in his *A Patriotism for Today* (1984) speaks about patriotism, devotion to country. Interestingly, he focuses his analysis through the lens of the life and death of Dietrich Bonhoeffer, so fiercely German and deeply Christian that he was forced into the agonizing choice over the Nazi tyranny. The Third Reich had many ambitions but one was the reconfiguration of borders, and the transformation both of the man-made and the natural landscape. Bonhoeffer was clear about his identity. He said: "Now I stand before you not only as a Christian, but also as a German . . . who confesses gratefully that he received from his people all that he has and is."[15] "We cannot escape our national identity any more than we can slough off our skin; . . . we are in and of the country – we *are* our country."[16]

Clements then asks us the very uncomfortable question which Bonhoeffer confronted: "We feel a deep need to belong . . . but what happens if the suspicion arises of dishonourable action by the group to which we belong?"[17] What happens if the place which has nurtured us seems suddenly strange? What happens if the people with whom we have long shared our place behave dishonourably? "My country right or wrong" is the rallying cry of the patriot and it raises a question faced by some

11  Ibid., 190. Quoted from Annie Buttimer, "Home, Reach and the Sense of Place," in *The Human Experience of Place and Space*, eds., Annie Buttimer and David Seamon (London: Croom Helm, 1980), 174.

12  Ibid., 191. Quoted from Arnold Belearnt, *The Aesthetics of the Environment* (Philadelphia: Temple, 1992), 86–87.

13  Ibid., 168.

14  Ibid., 175.

15  Kenneth W. Clements, *A Patriotism for Today* (Bristol: Bristol Baptist College, 1984), 85.

16  Ibid., 94.

17  Ibid., 93.

Adventists in Europe over the years. It may concern the Church at the local or the highest level. The question of "dishonourable action" has surfaced again over issues of unity and compliance, and seriously troubles many members, of various persuasions, in the Adventist Church. It requires a deeply thoughtful response.

## Disconnect

So what are the implications of all this?

When I was a child the small Adventist church I attended generously paid for my subscription to the weekly publications *Our Little Friend* and *Primary Treasure.* They were shipped from the USA and printed on glossy paper. They were clearly American artefacts. I scarcely read a single word. The cars pictured were far too big for British roads. There were no Dutch barns or verandas in my London suburb, neither racoons nor rattlesnakes in my country. Baseball diamonds were a strange foreign invention. Here were the seeds of a disconnect growing in my mind.

Later I also noticed that the mission stories normally were about South America or Africa, rarely Europe. There were no references to the "Great Dark Day" or the "falling of the stars", important elements in Adventist prophetic understanding, in European sources. They might as well have been events on a different planet.

Something of this disconnect has persisted into my adult years as an Adventist believer in Europe. While I am glad enough that people are being brought to Jesus in Latin America, I am more preoccupied with the fact that the gospel as understood by Adventists has negligible appeal to inhabitants of my town, my country or any other in Europe.

When the reach of the Church is global, it is likely that my Church will be less inclined to relate to what is happening in my country. The passing of seasons in my small place, the particularities of topography which do so much to shape our lives, will be largely ignored. This effect is exaggerated by the fact that the primary historical and geographical references in the Adventist narrative remain American with little awareness of other narratives. The success stories which get retold are from Africa, South America and the Far East. I understand about the world church and its needs. *But why would people in my place recognize the importance of my church when my church does not recognize the importance of my place?* All of this threatens to force a wedge between my spiritual identity, my sense of belonging, and my attachment to my country.

Landscape does inevitably influence the development of cultural practices. When the sense of particular significant human activity taking place in particular significant spaces breaks down, then spiritual danger lurks. Place is undoubtedly part of the narrative.

## Belonging

Central to all of this is the importance of a sense of belonging and belonging is a very complex phenomenon. We may, for example, begin to sense that we no longer belong in a physical place which nevertheless remains on the surface familiar. It has to be acknowledged that eventually any clear distinction between country as landscape and country as culture begins to break down.

We are faced with two central questions: Who are we? Who do we want to become? The matter of belonging underlies current conflicts within Adventism like women's ordination, sexual identity issues, hermeneutics, unity, compliance. What kind of community do I wish to belong to? Who does the Church belong to? Members of voluntary communities need to have a sense that they belong. There must be things which bind them together as people. When people do not sense the bond, do not identify, they drift, they leave. So, some indigenous European church members may have left feeling that local church culture lacks any congruence with life in the space they occupy. Maybe native Europeans do not care to join because they see our church as belonging to incomers, people nurtured in another landscape. The church may be seen as a kind of island somehow anchored off the mainland. There must be common points of reference, some of which will be inevitably and inextricably tied to physical space.

This feeling of not quite belonging cannot be ignored. I wonder whether the fact that I am Adventist means that I do not quite belong as an Englishman? Does the fact that I cherish many things about my country mean that I cannot quite belong as an Adventist? Does my Englishness, my European-ness, somehow fight with my Adventist-ness?

Kathleen Norris talks of "the place where I have wrestled my story out of the circumstances of landscape and inheritance." [18] Somehow, I need to craft these various elements of my life – including the landscape, natural and fabricated – into a coherent whole, to make meaning.

## Globalism and Rootlessness

Theresa May generated some hostile responses when she said in 2016 that "if you believe you are a citizen of the world then you are a citizen of nowhere." [19] But there is a sense in which she is right. In all forms of globalism much local colour is eventually lost. Shopping centres look increasingly the same the world over. There is a "dumbing down" process. Everything is melded into some common, tasteless soup.

So the danger is that we may produce a kind of "globish Adventism". As with "globish" versions of the English language, active vocabulary is reduced from the

18  Cited in Philip Sheldrake, *Spirituality and Theology* (London: Darton, Longman, Todd, 1998), 168. See also Philip Sheldrake, *Spaces for the Sacred* (London: SCM Press, 2001).
19  "Theresa May's Conference Speech in Full," accessed May 20, 2018, www.telegraph.co.uk/news/2016/10/05/theresa-mays-conference-speech-in-full/.

500,000 words in the language to a couple of thousand functional words. All possibility of nuance, elegance, restraint and mystery is lost. That is a disaster in the spiritual life where we struggle to "see in a mirror, dimly".[20] The Christian faith is then all too easily turned into a mere product, a superficial message, a shallow experience – an implant or an import.

## Beyond Place – A Tension

A number of these writers, however, are quick to identify a serious tension. "A God of freedom could never be comfortably contained in one place".[21] While we must attend to the land, our place, we must transcend it too. Otherwise we become a local sect, as the early church sometimes was. It is important to heed the warning, to recognize the very real dangers of settlement. Stagnation and an unwillingness to change, a sense of entitlement, a sense of superiority, an inclination to defensiveness, all threaten. Spiritually speaking, it is healthy to feel something of an alien. Being displaced is a central part of the Bible story. Nostalgia may set in, dangerous because it misrepresents not only the past but thereby also the present and the future.

However, if anything, Adventists seek to *transcend* at the expense of *attending* – we may settle for a global "one-size-fits-all" spirituality. Then we are deracinated. Lost. There is the danger of a disembodied spirituality at variance with the "scandalous" particularity of the incarnation. We must understand and interpret our spiritual experience in the light of our living in Germany, Italy, Serbia, and all that this implies, not in outposts of a multi-national corporate church.

Rumsey says: "We cannot know God by leaping beyond the limits of our place on earth, but only by encountering God and his saving work within space and time, within our actual physical existence."[22] The NT writers addressed their writings to particular groups of believers in particular places, well aware of the natural and cultural particularities of the life of the city or region to which they wrote.

The Gospel needs to be understood, lived and communicated by us with the particularities of space and time which we share with all Europeans if it is to be accessible and meaningful to them. Rumsey says: "many clergy today, [are] engrossed with global dynamics well beyond their influence."[23] It is true of many who find the larger church political issues more engrossing than the business of everyday living as a Christian in our street, among our mountains, by the sea, in our suburb, in our city – in our place.

20   1 Cor 13:12, NRSV.
21   Sheldrake, *Spirituality and Theology*, 175.
22   Rumsey, *Parish*, 18–19.
23   Ibid., 164.

## Importance of Place and Its Significance for the Church in Europe

This is not simply an account of the geography of a particular heart which has wrestled its particular meaning in one particular place. It is more than that. If we are to counter the problems of rootlessness, loss of Adventist identity, the consequent haemorrhaging of members, we must confront the causes. So, there follow some concluding thoughts on causes and remedies.

Firstly, in Adventism there was a coincidence in time of the formation of a nation (the USA) and the foundation of the Church. The two identities may have become somewhat conflated. Europeans may feel somewhat dispossessed by the fact that the formative events in Adventist history took place several thousand miles away – in Portland in Maine, Battle Creek in Michigan, Elmshaven in California – and continue to do so – San Antonio in Texas, Silver Spring in Maryland, or Glacier View in Colorado. Our American connection may be both boon and bane. *So we need to explore further and cherish our European Adventist narratives. We need to re-assess our dependence on our host church in the USA and avoid an unhealthy co-dependency.*

Secondly, New World settlers fled both religious intolerance and complacency in the Old World. Might modern church leaders also see Europe as hopelessly secular and the church as irredeemably liberal? Pope Francis, a South American of course, in a speech to the European Parliament on 25 November 2014, controversially described Europe as, morally and spiritually speaking, a "barren grandmother".[24] It was an unhelpful remark. And it would be unfortunate if senior Adventist leaders shared this sentiment. *A pastor struggling to make Jesus known in secular Frankfurt or Amsterdam needs all the encouragement and understanding she can get from her leaders in the world church. Her place is not their place.*

Thirdly, in our case, who exactly is my European, Croatian, Danish, Belgian neighbour? How can the gospel as understood by Adventists make compelling sense to them? In all our enthusiasm to reach people from "every nation and tribe and language and people"[25] we may lose sight of our geographical neighbour. We lift our gaze into the distance and overlook what is at our feet. It demands that *we ask again: Who exactly is my neighbour?* How does the everyday experience of sharing space affect our common life?

Fourthly, place is also neighbourhood. Many Adventists have to, or choose to, travel some considerable distance from home to their church, and then only once a week. This will often mean that the church easily becomes a commuter church not a community church; the emphasis is on movement not place. A commuter church

---

24 "Pope Francis Calls Europe an 'Elderly and Haggard' Grandmother," *Financial Times*, (November 25, 2014): accessed May 4, 2018, https://www.ft.com/content/ec0503e0-749d-11e4-b30b-00144feabdc0.
25 Rev 14:6, NRSV.

has no opportunity to embed itself in the life of the community. Place therefore becomes unimportant in its thinking. The existence of an infinity of virtual communities poses a further threat. *A core of members living close to the church building is thus vital to its flourishing. Local churches need to set about the lengthy and difficult task of embedding themselves in the local community and earning its trust.*

Fifthly, pastors also often have little opportunity to form real attachment to place. It is difficult to see that the important relationships which underlie the kingdom of God can be formed amidst frequent exchanges of personnel. This highlights a deep structural problem. The more committed we are to a place, the more invested it becomes with personal meaning generated by routines, practices, shared values, by mutual love and respect, by walking, talking, eating, shopping, playing together. It may then, for us, become "deep place". *A pastor's commitment to place is central.*

Sixthly, multitudes of people living in Europe are rootless. There is a deep need to belong. Swiss Christian psychologist Paul Tournier says "Deprivation of love and deprivation of place overlap". [26] *There is opportunity for the local church to become a place of genuine welcome and resource – of belonging. We must learn hospitality as holiness.*

Finally, unless the Seventh-day Adventist Church has a sense of its place, its rootedness in Europe, it can have no enduring place in the hearts of Europeans. *In short, the Adventist Church in Europe will have no rich history to tell unless it respects the geography of the heart, unless it pays greater attention to hearts nurtured by the natural and cultural landscapes of Europe.*

---

26   Rumsey, *Parish*, 75. See also Paul Tournier, *A Place for You* (London: SCM Press, 1968), 27.

*Marianne Thieme*

# Being a Politician and an Adventist in Europe[1]

My name is Marianne Thieme and I am the co-founder of the Party for the Animals and leader of the parliamentary group in the Dutch House of Representatives. This evening I will talk about our animal rights party, why we founded it and what we hope to achieve. Dr Stefan Höschele asked me to tell you a little bit more about why I am interested in animal rights, the environment and nature, and why I started a political party for these issues instead of collecting signatures for, let's say, a ban on seal hunting, donating money for this good cause or being active in an animal rights NGO. I will also tell you something about why I became an Adventist eleven years ago.

I studied law at the Erasmus University in Rotterdam. Even before my studies, I took a great interest in the plight of animals in our society. To my great disappointment, my law course devoted precious little attention to the issue of animal rights. I've been raised in a Roman Catholic family. As long as I remember, I had a great love and admiration for nature and animals and I wanted to protect them. I became a vegetarian when I was a student. My parents always pointed at the beautiful but vulnerable animals and nature, and they taught me to treat them with respect. My mother used to sit with her cat on her lap, saying "you know, Marianne, people can invent big computers and build cars, but this innocent little creature here is so perfect and capable of doing things people can't do. People could never create such a lovely and loving creature. They can just watch it, take care of it, but most of all they shall have to respect it and give it its freedom." Such an approach worked for me, and if you respect other creatures, you will want to protect them. That's why I became an animal advocate.

I grew up at the Veluwe near Arnheim. I was always amazed at the many concrete stables and sheds where animals like chickens and pigs had to live, crammed together. Stables without daylight, without enough space, where other creatures are living as if they are no more than things, means of production. It became clear to me that it was often the Orthodox Christians who owned factory farming companies. And that they assumed that man ruled the universe, more in particular, ruled the animals, that they could control the lives of animals to suit themselves.

I was shocked to learn that the Catholic Church blessed bull fights. When I also found out that the church blessed the weapons of people who shoot animals for fun ... in special "St. Hubertus Masses" ... I decided to turn my back on the church.

---

1   The oral presentation style has been preserved in this published version.

I kept on believing but I could not handle the way in which many Christians treated the earth and animals.

Fifteen years ago, I learned about Seventh-day Adventists and their thoughts about vegetarianism. Together with my belief and my animal advocacy, the Adventist Church appealed to me and since February 2006 I am an Adventist. I found that the Adventist Church paid more than average attention to our living environment, which is why there are a great many vegetarians and vegans among its church members. But when I had just become a member, I was frequently told that living a vegetarian life was kind of old-fashioned. I was quite surprised because it is actually quite popular and trendy to be a vegetarian these days.

I experienced first-hand that we live in a time when many people strongly distrust people with Christian beliefs. In 2007, one of our political supporters, a celebrated writer and animal protectionist, Maarten 't Hart, became furious when he found out that I was a Christian and, in particular, a Seventh-day Adventist. He wrote articles and was interviewed on national television, discrediting me both as a person and as a politician. He accused me of having a hidden political agenda to turn everybody to these dumb and sectarian people who believe in fairy tales. Opponents of religion believe that Christians are people with a hidden agenda. And unfortunately, those thoughts often become stronger because of the way politicians of Christian parties propagate or justify their lack of sustainability and solidarity while holding the Bible in their hands. Or want to have state regulation to keep the Sunday rest. This is a shame because it stigmatises people and beliefs. I also think that people believe that Christian politics plays a harmful role. And that is one of the reasons why I convincingly chose to set up a secular political party.

I believe that church and State should be strictly separated. All our voters and members have different backgrounds: they are atheists, humanists, Buddhists, Christians, Muslims, agnostics, young, old, liberals, socialists, conservatives, but they all share a common goal: to create a society where compassion, sustainability, personal freedom and responsibility are the leading principles in everything we do. Not the short-term interests of people who are leading, not the assumed rights of the strongest, but the interests of the weakest should be first taken into account. And until now, animals are always at the bottom of people's list.

In the circles of animal protectors, it is often assumed that the protection of animals is at odds with being a member of a Christian church. Because attention is focused on man in most churches and the interests of man prevail over all other life on earth. However, I can see that the focus of attention on man is reflected in almost all churches and ideologies. Yet I have also seen that most religions and beliefs are fundamentally focused on treating life, also that of animals, respectfully. The name giver of the Christian belief said: "Inasmuch as ye have done it unto one of the least of these my brethren, ye have done it unto me." I think we should also include animals in this.

It is important to conclude that people are often only busy with themselves. That they consider themselves as the top of civilisation. And with that, as a yardstick for all things. They find it more fascinating to talk about the origin of life and the possibility of life on other planets, than about how valuable life on *this* earth is and how they can protect it. While only a little imagination is needed to dissociate the right to protect life from a vision on the origin of life. Anyone who believes that life was created by a higher power should be able to realise that humans bear responsibility and that they are in debt to that higher power for the way they treat other creatures.

Prince Pierre Troubetzkoy said: "Why should man expect his prayer for mercy to be heard by What is above him when he shows no mercy to what is under him?" Anyone who believes that life is a product of time and coincidence should be aware that the mere coincidental circumstance that the one form of life is one or several evolutionary steps behind the other, should not be a reason to treat other evolutionary relatives with so much contempt. It would be highly questionable to subdue "relatives" who are genetically closely related to man, and to treat them disrespectfully. I believe that it is essential that we focus more on the way we treat other living creatures.

What is the value of having discussions about the origin of lives if we neglect to protect those lives? On the other hand, it is more than clear that religious and ethical inspiration does encourage people to spare other living beings, to spare animals, to treat them with respect and to take their interests seriously.

When we founded the world's first political party for the animals in 2002, many people could not believe their ears, and some became really angry. How can someone found a Party for the Animals while children are dying of hunger in Africa? While there are many wars and many refugees. While there is unemployment and we're running out of commodities. In short, while there are many human problems that need to be solved instantly. But instead you are worried about animals? Is the Party for the Animals not the height of decadence? Some kind of betrayal? That makes animals more important than people?

I told everyone who asked me that question at the time that the problems of animals and those of people cannot be dissociated. People and animals live together on a small planet that is not kept in balance because of the way people treat animals. We, humans, are the only kind that destroys its own living environment. We have caused global warming that leads to floods and hunger. The Dutch writer Jan Wolkers once said: "If there were no people on the earth, I would be able to believe in God".

Jozef Keulartz, a Dutch environmental philosopher, describes the meaning of other forms of life on earth for people wonderfully. He says, "The enormous diversity of species and ecosystems is a form of wealth. If a species becomes extinct, a way of living and a perspective on the world disappears, which will never come back." Human life on this planet would be much poorer and a lot more lonely if people were only surrounded by their own species and the items they have created themselves. Other species enrich our existence, for example because they have a completely personal perspective on the world, they confront people with a critical view, hold up a mirror to them, inspire them, fascinate them, or make them scared. They give meaning to the world. Our world.

Ellen G. White writes in her book *Education*:

> How beautiful the psalmist's description of God's care for the creatures of the woods – "The high hills are a refuge for the wild goats; And the rocks for the conies." Psalm 104:18. He sends the springs to run among the hills, where the birds have their habitation, and "sing among the branches." Psalm 104:12. All the creatures of the woods and hills are a part of His great household. He opens His hand, and satisfies "the desire of every living thing." Psalm 145:16.[2]

Man is part of nature. But we often fail to treat the freedom of other living creatures with respect. And are disrespectful towards the earth. That is why nature reserves are disappearing rapidly, and animals are becoming extinct. And the future of large groups of people and animals is threatened.

It is of course unacceptable that people use nature to such intensive extent that it dramatically changes the living conditions on earth. That the living environment of people themselves and of other forms of life becomes worse, smaller or even disappears. That people start to drift as a result and flee the hunger and drought. Our children and grandchildren will be confronted with the effects of this even more than we are.

For that reason, it is very important that we behave in such a way that it has the least impact on others and the earth. That we will not consume and produce more than the earth can handle. But we use too much energy, we waste too many commodities like timber and food. We now live, as calculated by the World Wildlife Fund, as though we have four earths at our disposal.

Money seems more important than living. The fact that we only have an eye for economic interests without having an eye for our living environment is criminal. Animals cannot talk. But a good Christian knows the life of animals according to the Bible. Religious people used to say: "If a farmer is converted, the animals will notice first."

Did you know that livestock farming worldwide produces more greenhouse gases than all cars, trucks, aircraft, vessels and trains together? This is because the cows in the meat and dairy industry produce a great deal of methane gas by belching and farting. Yes, this is not a tasty story. Methane gas is twenty-five times more potent than $CO_2$ from, for example, coal-fired power plants and cars. And we have quite a number of cows, pigs and chickens in the world.

70 billion agricultural animals are bred and slaughtered worldwide every year, mainly for the rich West. 600 million of those animals live – and die – in this tiny damp country of ours. While I am telling you this story, 1,100 animals are slaughtered in the Netherlands every minute. After this lecture of 50 minutes, 6 million animals have been slaughtered in the world.

---

[2]    Ellen G. White, *Education* (Mountain View, CA: Pacific Press, 1903), 118.

Ellen White wrote in 1905:

> Animals are often transported long distances and subjected to great suffering in reaching a market. Taken from the green pastures, and traveling for weary miles over the hot, dusty roads, or crowded into filthy cars, feverish and exhausted, often for many hours deprived of food and water, the poor creatures are driven to their death, that human beings may feast on the carcasses.[3]

How true this is when you look at today's practices!

The Dutch Government already said in 2004 that meat, milk and eggs are the most polluting products of everything that we eat. Last year, Germany's Federal Environment Agency called for higher taxes on animal products, stating that meat and dairy farming is more damaging to the environment than producing cereals, fruits or vegetables. And let's not forget the huge deforestation which is mainly caused because countries like Brazil use billions of acres of land to grow cattle food intended for the factory farming industry in the West.

The climate is changing incredibly fast. We should now more than ever prevent the emission of greenhouse gases and deforestation. If all Dutch people did not eat meat one day a week, it would reduce the emission of greenhouse gases as much as taking 1.1 million cars of the road for a year long. A meat eater in a Toyota Prius emits more greenhouse gas than a vegetarian in a Hummer SUV.

We all know that science has established a link between eating too much fat and serious illnesses, such as cardiovascular disease, various types of cancer, obesity and diabetes. I challenge you to name one illness that is linked to a vegetarian diet. There are currently more than 600 million vegetarians worldwide, so plenty of opportunities to display any potential diet problems. But the reverse is the case. In February 2013, I was at the Loma Linda University to give a lecture at the International Congress on Vegetarian Nutrition. Scientists from reputable universities all reported without exception that vegetarians are healthier, and on average live longer than meat eaters.

Ellen White wrote in the *Ministry of Healing* in 1905, mind you:

> Flesh was never the best food; but its use is now doubly objectionable, since disease in animals is so rapidly increasing. Those who use flesh foods little know what they are eating. Often if they could see the animals when living and know the quality of the meat they eat, they would turn from it with loathing. People are continually eating flesh that is filled with tuberculous and cancerous germs. Tuberculosis, cancer, and other fatal diseases are thus communicated.[4]

And: "Think of the cruelty to animals that meat eating involves, and its effect on those who inflict and those who behold it. How it destroys the tenderness with which

---

3    Ellen G. White, *Ministry of Healing* (Mountain View, CA: Pacific Press, 1905), 314.
4    Ibid., 313.

we should regard these creatures of God!"[5] Ladies and gentlemen, I became a vegetarian when I was 23, and a vegan when I was 42. I got to know the Adventist Church eight years later and was so happy to see so many vegetarians and vegans, well more than in any other church, because of the works of Ellen G. White.

But to my surprise, a lot of Adventists told me this message of White was, with all due respect they added, a little bit old-fashioned. Old-fashioned? I was so surprised. All the things she said about a healthier life with no animal products, her compassion towards animals, her advice not to smoke cigarettes, the fact that Adventists were the first religious group of people who had health programmes to stop smoking, vegetarian products ... that was all "so 20th century"?

I was astonished. Right now, at this moment, it is a very relevant and up-to-date message. It is unbelievable that Adventists are not visible in the discussion about the impact of meat on climate change, obesity, animal welfare and the food crisis. Now is the time I should say! More than ever! Now is the time to stand up and show that you are involved and you have practical solutions to make this world a better place. To let people know what stewardship really means.

The Adventist Church was one of the first to produce meat substitutes, if I recall it correctly. The massive meat consumption is completely out of step with reality. The facts surrounding the animals themselves, nature, the environment, public health, biodiversity, the climate, world food distribution and the prevention of worldwide crises involving animal diseases, speak for themselves.   It is no surprise that the Netherlands was the first country in the world to have a political Party for the Animals. But what about the existing political parties? Haven't they paid enough attention to animal rights issues, nature and the environment so far? Well, animal welfare and rights is "a side dish" for the few traditional political parties who, according to their parties' manifestos, are willing to defend it. But it is a key anti-issue for those politicians who believe that animal rights are high-priced nonsense. In 2002, the farmers' representatives of the governmental parties were keen to reverse all animal welfare measures from the last 20 years as swiftly as possible.

The so-called animal friendly parties, like the Greens, just let it happen without *any* protest. Although our law states that animals are sentient beings with an inherent value, animals have become objects once again, intended only to serve the appetite and the economic purposes of people and commerce. This is why the plan to set up a Party for the Animals was hatched in late 2002, after the fall of the government. The idea was, a party that would initially serve to remind the parliamentary parties about their good intentions. We started with just four people, and no budget.

After the Party for the Animals was founded, we received a huge number of enthusiastic phone calls. I recall a lady who was very moved, telling me how wonderful she thought it was that at the age of ninety she was to see an actual party for animals. She herself had been active in the women's emancipation movement in the 60s and could still vividly remember how she and her fellow activists gave a toast

5    Ibid., 315.

to women's rights and vegetarianism. They felt a bond with all groups, be it man or animal, that were, and still are, oppressed.

Ladies and gentlemen, I am sure you can imagine that the majority of the people mocked us for starting a party for animals. They made fun of us, they could not believe their ears when they heard of our existence. What's next: a party for bicycles or a party for plants? Didn't we know we were the laughing stock of the country and we were never going to make it into parliament? I think it has something to do with the fear or belief that a party for the animals automatically betrays humans or threatens the social and economic order. The very same fears that for example the abolitionists encountered during their fight against slavery.

But there were also people, feminists, famous authors, intellectuals and opinion leaders, who saw us as the next emancipation movement. After the liberation of slaves, women, giving rights to children, the next logical step was to consider the interests of animals seriously. To look beyond the interests of our own species.

And, ladies and gentlemen, all these emotions of anger, hope, disbelief, sarcasm are very useful, I can assure you. It takes emotions to start a debate, to move people, to achieve social change. All other social movements were first ignored, then ridiculed, even criminalized. But in the end they won!

It immediately became evident that our strategy worked when we participated in the elections of January 2003. We got a lot of free publicity and overnight, other parties adopted animal welfare as an issue in their election programs and communications. Many other parties jumped on the bandwagon. They started to do more for animals as a result of our role as a "pacer or pacesetter in the marathon." They realized that animal rights were becoming an increasingly important issue for the electorate.

Some political analysts said that they were convinced that we were not just a flash in the pan, or a publicity stunt that had got out of hand. They called our party a new political movement, the only exponent of the 'new politics'. At that time, and still now, people in our country were *and are* really fed up with politics, and do not trust any politician. The Party for the Animals has attracted not only people who care about animals and the environment but also people who have wanted to protest against the political establishment. Of course, we had to write a manifesto that, besides the animal issues, also had to reflect viewpoints regarding health care, pensions, education, foreign affairs etc.

We decided to be brief on those issues in our first manifesto. Ninety percent of the pages were about animals and green issues Because, let's face it, more than 90% of the election programs of other parties were addressing human issues, short term human interests. *Real* one issue parties I would say.

It was quite extraordinary and surprising to see that when we went through these other issues, we jointly arrived at the same viewpoints in no time at all. In the years that followed we developed four main principles as a framework to develop viewpoints: compassion, sustainability, personal freedom and personal responsibility.

Ladies and gentlemen. During the TV broadcast of the election results in 2003, to everyone's surprise the Party for the Animals nearly got a seat! Within two months of campaigning, with no budget! Four years later, on November 22, 2006, for the first time ever in the world, voters elected members of a Party for the Animals to a national parliament. With two, and nearly three, seats, we achieved a victory. Our breakthrough gave a real drive to push even harder for our cause.

Our tools vary, from participating in debates with Secretaries of Government Departments, to asking parliamentary questions, to proposing measures through petitions the parliament votes on. Like a ban on *enriched* cage systems for laying hens. Make no mistake: An enriched cage is nothing more than a decorated battery cage. Battery cages are banned in the EU. We managed to get a larger budget for alternatives to animal experiments. And the government also provided a 6 million Euro budget to stimulate the innovation on meat alternatives.

Besides the use of the traditional political instruments, we use more activist-like methods. Political analysts and historians see this as a form of "expressive politics" instead of the more traditional "instrumental politics" which is more focused on compromises, to act within the political conventions and try to better the status quo instead of questioning the current social and economic system.

In 2007, when we were just elected, one of the female Ministers thought it appropriate at the installation of the new cabinet to pose for the cabinet photo wearing fox fur around her neck. I decided to wear my "own" fox during the first debate in the Lower House after the elections. All the newspapers wrote about it, partly because making a statement like that in the rather formal Lower House is simply not done. The public loved it. And the minister sent me a letter saying that she liked my alternative. I have never seen her with fur around her neck after that.

In 2008 we asked our former Prime Minister Balkenende about an official dinner where our former Queen Beatrix served *foie gras* to her guests. *Foie gras* is liver from force-fed ducks and geese. No politician had ever asked a parliamentary question about such issues before. The prime minister apologized and said this would be a one-off mistake, and it would never happen again!

We push other, bigger political parties to start being more animal friendly: Fur farms for example. In 2006, our two socialist parties started an initiative to ban fur farms in our country and this initiative got the majority of the votes three years ago. My impression is that this is an immediate, in some way opportunistic, reaction to our existence as a party.

Many environmental and animal organizations have to work hard to get their five minutes in the spotlight of politics. It is really special that we have managed to get our foot in the door. At the moment we have 74 seats: 18 seats in regional parliaments, 15 seats in parliaments for water management, 33 seats in 18 city councils, 5 seats in the National parliament, 2 seats in the Senate and 1 in the European parliament.

Since March this year we are rising even further in the polls! We could get 8 seats if there were to be National elections today. 14 to 18% of all Dutch voters consider voting for our party. Last month we more than doubled our seats in 15 city councils. In parliament, a lot of animal unfriendly politicians are frustrated about the fact that our party manages to dominate any debate on livestock farming. One of our biggest opponents, the Christian Democratic Party, stated on National television that, to their irritation, since the Party for the Animals has been in parliament, they have had to talk about animals every day!

Since 2006, during the debates on the agricultural budget, 80% of the speaking time of all parties in parliament is now taken up by animal issues. And the Minister of Agriculture stated that this had happened for the first time in history. More and more insiders acknowledge that they initially saw us as a passing phase, but that they now see us as a new and permanent factor to be reckoned with.

The difference between being an animal rights party instead of a lobby group is that other politicians see an animal rights party as a competitor and a threat to their seats, losing them votes, and a lobby group as just something you can ignore. That's a huge factor of successful campaigning.

I would like to take a brief look ahead. The way in which we have set up the economy has brought some of us enormous wealth, but is now threatening to bring about great damage and destruction to our planet, people and animals. People have come to realise that business as usual is no longer possible. There are companies and governments who think so, but it is not a coincidence that everywhere in the world there is a growing resistance coming from public society and individuals. That means that all these concurrent crises really can be a turning point.

Our way of life not only harms animals and nature but also threatens our health and that of future generations. Despite the financial crisis, during which many people had a *tendency* to think in terms of short-term personal interests, our parties for the animals in the world are growing and we achieved the best election results in our history this year [2018].

Ladies and gentlemen, I would like to conclude. I am convinced that in order to change our way of life, to make it sustainable and led by principles of compassion, we have to shift our focus from being man-centred to being planet-centred. We are on the threshold of a new era. Our interactions with other living creatures must change, just as the way in which we interact with each other will also have to. This new era will not come to pass without a struggle. The established order, which has a *vested* interest in exploiting animals, will use all its powers to resist. Yet, just as the tobacco industry's seemingly untouchable position of power crumbled away as a result of changing social attitudes, so will progressive social insights into animal rights also ensure that animals are no longer the pariahs of this planet. I am proud to be part of a movement that is the exponent of this new era. The time is ripe.

Ladies and gentlemen, throughout the world more and more Parties for the Animals are being set up. There are 18 Parties for the animals at the moment. The Portuguese party has seats in city councils and one in the national parliament. The German party won a seat in the European parliament. The British Animal Welfare Party has a seat in the city council of Alsager in England, and the Australian Animal Justice Party has a seat in the senate of New South Wales. Although it is quite a paradigm shift we want to achieve, although it is ambitious and hard work with lots of counter force, we are on our way.

It reminds me of a great quote of Margaret Mead in the 1940s: "Never doubt that a small group of thoughtful, committed citizens can change the world; indeed, it is the only thing that ever has." She is so right: think about other social movements that changed the world; it all started with just a few people.

The Party for the Animals has never played a compromise game since it entered the Dutch Parliament. It was and is a principle-driven political movement, stressing the uniqueness of its political message and its unwillingness to find common ground with its mainstream political adversaries.

This is also what attracted me to the Seventh-day Adventist Church. In contrast to other Christian churches, it has always remained true to its reformationist heritage and message. Where others have lost their soul in the ecumenical movement, the Seventh-day Adventist church should remain the salt of the earth.

Ladies and gentlemen, Martin Luther is said to have stated, "If I knew that tomorrow was the end of the world, I would plant an apple tree today!" He is a tremendous example for people who believe that this world will not last but do not want to be fatalistic. We can make this world a better place, and that's also our assignment. It always seems impossible until it is done!

*Tiziano Rimoldi*

# Italian Seventh-day Adventists, Military Service and Conscientious Objection (1946–1986)

Abstract

For a decade after World War II, Italian Seventh-day Adventists followed an approach to military service that combined bearing arms with requesting permission to rest on Sabbath. Thanks to the dynamic advocacy of some ministers, the Italian Seventh-day Adventist Church was able to secure Sabbath keeping privileges in the military. Then, in line with a growing movement in favor of conscientious objection, outside and inside the Church, the Italian Union approached the Italian government, asking the right to perform alternative civil service for Adventist draftees. This right was granted in an agreement signed in 1986 and turned into a law in 1988. This achievement was pioneering and still remains an inspiration for other denominations and for fellow Adventists in other European countries.

The crisis contributing to the Reform Movement schism in Germany induced the executive committee of the European Division, assembled in Gland, Switzerland, on January 2, 1923, to approve the following statement:

We assert the justice of rendering tribute, custom, and honor to earthly governments, as enjoined in the New Testament. We revere the law of God contained in the Decalogue as explained in the teachings of Christ and exemplified in His life. For that reason we observe the seventh-day Sabbath (Saturday) as sacred time; we refrain from secular labor upon that day, but engage gladly in works of necessity and mercy for the relief of suffering and the uplift of humanity; in peace and in war we decline to participate in acts of violence and bloodshed. We grant to each of our church members absolute liberty to serve their country, at all times and in all places, in accord with the dictates of their personal conscientious conviction.[1]

While the declaration clearly, but not explicitly, opted in favor of a non-armed service, because of Sabbath keeping and the refusal to participate in acts of violence and bloodshed, it left freedom of conscience to church members. In releasing the statement, the president of the General Conference was aware that "[e]ven now, in some parts, where delicate situations still exist, our brethren need special wisdom and judgment in handling such declarations."[2]

---

1  See W.A. Spicer, "Our European Brethren and Noncombatancy," *Review and Herald* 101.10 (March 6, 1924): 4, 5.
2  Ibid., 4.

Italy, because of Fascist militarism, was one of these "parts" where the decision to "decline to participate in acts of violence and bloodshed" could not be taken without suffering serious consequences.[3] Italian Adventists followed the setting outlined by Ludwig Conradi, who "insisted only on Sabbath keeping by Adventist military personnel during peacetime."[4] In fact, Italian Adventists, in a declaration of 1932, upheld Sabbath keeping in the military, recommending "[t]hat the young people drafted should toil to remain faithful to the observance of the 4th commandment."[5] This was the line followed by the Italian Adventist Church for decades.

After the Second World War, in the Italian Republic, established in 1946, despite the repealing of fascism and militarism, still "[t]he defense of the country [was] a sacred duty for every citizen" and "[m]ilitary service [was] obligatory within the limits and in the manner set by law" (Italian Constitution, article 52).

In this setting, young Italian Adventists

> reluctantly accepted to perform military service. They were forced by law to learn to use weapons, but they were convinced that there would never be an opportunity for them to use them to kill, and in any case, they would never kill. The carrying out of an armed military service was not fully in harmony with the religious faith of the young Adventists, even though the commandment "not to kill," in fact, was not violated.[6]

## Sabbath Keeping in the Military

As we have seen, Sabbath keeping was the main concern for Adventist draftees, obtained by means of individual agreements with their officers. The Religious Liberty Department (RLD) of the Italian Union intervened in difficult cases, like that of soldier Carmelo Di Maggio,[7] who, in 1956, refused to participate in military instruction on Sabbath. His case was solved by Dr Gianfranco Rossi, the Director of the

3    Jehovah's Witnesses, and their journal, *The Watch Tower*, were precisely targeted because of their open hostility against dictatorial regimes, militarism, and war. After the issuing of the Ministry of Interior's circular letter of August 22, 1939, no. 441/0277713, about 150 Jehovah's Witnesses (almost all the registered members!) were arrested and condemned and 26 of them sent to the Special Tribunal for the defense of the State for a more severe punishment: they were sentenced to two to eleven years of prison. See P. Piccioli, *Il prezzo della diversità. Una minoranza a confronto con la storia religiosa in Italia negli scorsi cento anni* (Napoli: Jovene, 2010), 67–104, 343–355.

4    Douglas Morgan, "Between Pacifism and Patriotism," *Adventist Review*, accessed March 18, 2018, http://archives.adventistreview.org/2003-1535/story5.html.

5    "Verbale delle sedute amministrative della Seconda Assemblea dell'Unione Italiana tenuta a Firenze, dal 2 al 5 giugno 1932, nei locali di via Trieste, 17," *Il Messaggero Avventista* 7.6 (July 1932): 6.

6    Gianfranco Rossi, *Lotte e vittorie degli avventisti italiani per la libertà religiosa* (Firenze: Edizioni ADV, 2007), 89.

7    The son of Carmelo Di Maggio recounted his father's story in Ismaele Di Maggio, "In Cpr* per il sabato," *Il Messaggero Avventista* 81.4 (April 2007): 25–27.

RLD, by means of a personal visit to the officer in charge. In this, and other similar cases, his argument was based on article 19 of the Italian Constitution, which affirms religious liberty for everyone,[8] and on the authorization for Adventist students to keep the Sabbath he had obtained from the Ministry of Education a few months before.[9]

In 1958, encouraged by these successes, the eleventh constituency session of the Italian Union approved the following deliberation, in line with the one approved in 1932:

> We recommend: … 3. To young people who are subject to military service, to be loyal to the Lord by letting the superiors know the principles of the professed faith and asking them to be able to observe the Lord's day freely.[10]

In 1959, due to the case of private Cateno La Versa, who was put in jail for his Sabbath observance, Dr Rossi got in touch personally with the Minister of Defense, Honorable Giulio Andreotti, and various parliamentarians, asking for a general authorization for Adventists draftees to keep the Sabbath. Before the final decision in the trial of La Versa was taken, three circular letters (Army, Navy, and Air Force) were issued in December 1959,[11] allowing Adventist servicemen to enjoy the Sabbath rest, except in case of an imperative need of service. When the final hearing of the trial took place, even the military prosecutor asked that the charge be dismissed. Cateno La Versa was acquitted.[12]

In 1962, the twelfth constituency session of the Italian Union approved a declaration recommending "*to young people*, called to serve the homeland, to remain faithful to the Lord, making known to their superiors our principles of "nonviolence" and asking them to be free to keep the Sabbath.[13] While the Sabbath remained the focus, it was the first time in which the Italian Adventist Church connected it with

---

8    "Anyone is entitled to freely profess their religious beliefs in any form, individually or with others, and to promote them and celebrate rites in public or in private, provided they are not offensive to public morality."

9    Rossi, *Lotte...*, 59, 60.

10   "I lavori dell'assemblea," *Il Messaggero Avventista* 33.10 (October 1958): 12.

11   See the documents in Rossi, *Lotte...*, 411, 412.

12   See Rossi, *Lotte...*, 79–82; Gianfranco Rossi, "Il fratello La Versa è stato assolto," *Il Messaggero Avventista* 35.2 (March–April 1960): 5, 6.

13   *Deliberazione n. 9. Dipartimento Libertà religiosa*,"I lavori dell'assemblea," *Il Messaggero Avventista* 37.10 (October 1962): 12.

nonviolence. This was a sign that a certain sensibility toward nonviolence and conscientious objection, little by little, was emerging in the Italian Adventist Church, in
line with the developments in civil society[14] and in other denominations.[15]

In 1966, the thirteenth constituency session of the Italian Union approved the
following deliberation:

> Considering the importance of helping our young people to clearly understand the posi-
> tion they have to take in the face of the problem of military service, so that they avoid
> enlisting in fighting corps, we recommend:
> (1) To the MM.VV. [Missionary Volunteers] Department to organize educational
> courses on this topic;
> (2) To Church leaders to encourage young people, in order to be more easily enrolled in
> medical corps, to follow, where possible, medical education courses.[16]

What had simply been evoked in the declaration of 1962 now was clearer. Because
of the position young Adventists were expected to take, they should be encouraged
to avoid armed military service and, by means of specific training, enroll in medical
corps, in line with the strategy adopted in the USA with the Military Cadet Corps.[17]

## "Thou Shalt Not Kill"

After the permission for observing Sabbath rest in the military was achieved,[18] Dr
Rossi started working on the noncombatancy side of the military service issue. The
*casus belli* came up with the case of the Adventist conscript Graziano Pocecco. In
1969, while serving in the Navy, Pocecco asked to be transferred to medical service,
because of his desire not to bear arms. Since the Ministry of Defense was late in
answering, Pocecco asked for help from the Union. Dr Rossi sent a letter to the
Minister of Defense in September 1969. He used as his main topic the commandment "Thou shalt not kill" of the Decalogue, mentioning the historic position of

---

14   See Giorgio Rochat, ed., *L'antimilitarismo oggi* (Torino: Claudiana, 1973); Roberto Diodato,
     *Pacifismo* (Milano: Editrice Bibliografica, 1995).
15   On May 26–30, 1966, the Evangelical Churches in Italy celebrated their congress in Rome,
     with the participation of a delegation from the Italian Union. The congress approved a reso-
     lution proposing to the government a bill on conscientious objection. See Antonio Caracciolo,
     "Uniti per l'Evangelo," *Il Messaggero Avventista* 40.7 (July 1965): 2, 3.
16   "I lavori dell'assemblea," *Il Messaggero Avventista* 41.10 (October 1966): 12.
17   See "Noncombatancy," *Seventh-day Adventist Encyclopedia*, M-Z, Commentary Reference
     Series 11 (Hagerstown, MD: Review and Herald, 1995), 185.
18   See Gianfranco Rossi, "Un documento significativo," *Il Messaggero Avventista* 35.5 (Septem-
     ber–October 1960): 10, 11.

noncombatancy the Seventh-day Adventist Church took in 1863, and making specific references to the situation of Adventist draftees in the USA and in Belgium.[19] The answer of the Ministry of Defense was positive and Pocecco was assigned to a non-armed service. Because of this favorable experience, the fourteenth constituency meeting of the Italian Union of 1970 approved this resolution:

> Resolution no. 7 – Unarmed military service.
> Given that the Sixth commandment, illustrated by the teachings and examples of Jesus and the Apostles, does not permit a Christian to kill his fellow men under any circumstance, even if declared enemies of the Homeland;
> Considering, that the official position of our Church is to serve in unarmed military service;
> Considering, that the Ministry of Defense has practically recognized that our young people, for their religious convictions, can be assigned to such a service;
> We vote to recommend to our preachers to persuade young people so that, when they are called to serve the Homeland, they ask to be assigned to a non-armed service, preferably to the medical corps, using for this purpose the forms already prepared by the Religious Liberty Department.[20]

This resolution was accompanied by another one, encouraging young people to enlist in the Adventist Volunteer Service Corp, considering the possibility to substitute military service with it.[21] For the first time, the Italian Adventist Church explicitly said that the official position of the Church was to serve in unarmed military service, which in the previous declarations had only been implicit. This position was derived directly from the Ten Commandments and the example of Jesus and the Apostles.

## Noncombatancy in a New Setting

In 1972, the Italian Parliament approved Law no. 772, "Rules for the recognition of conscientious objection." With this law, any conscript who declared himself in any situation opposed to the personal use of weapons for essential reasons of conscience, could now satisfy his obligation to military service in an alternative way, either non-armed military service[22] or civil service. Only religious, philosophical, or

---

19  On August 31, 1945, the Belgian Ministry of Defense, answering a request from the Chief Chaplain of the Belgian Army, issued a circular letter granting to Seventh-day Adventist draftees to be assigned to the Medical Service of the Army, providing they can prove they are Adventists. During their service, they would also be entitled to enjoy Sabbath as the day of rest, but could be asked to perform compensatory work on Sunday. See document in Rossi, *Lotte...*, 417.

20  *Delibera n. 7. Servizio militare non armato*, "I lavori dell'Assemblea," *Il Messaggero Avventista* 45.10 (October 1970): 7.

21  *Delibera n. 8. Corpo di Servizio Volontario Avventista*, "I lavori dell'Assemblea," *Il Messaggero Avventista* 45.10 (October 1970): 7.

22  In reality, non-armed military service was never implemented. See Rodolfo Venditti, *L'obiezione di coscienza al servizio militare* (Milano: Giuffré, 1994, 2nd edition), 90, 129, 130.

moral convictions were accepted. A commission evaluated the motives[23]: if its advice was favorable, the Ministry of Defense approved the request with a decree.

Considering the new context created by Law no. 772, the fifteenth constituency meeting of the Italian Union of 1973 approved the following deliberation:

> Deliberation N. Unarmed Civil Service.
> Considering:
> (1) The importance of fidelity to the principles of the Bible and of the Spirit of Prophecy;
> (2) The possibilities offered by Italian laws:
> We recommend to all the young Adventists called to military service to orientate themselves towards the civil or unarmed service and we invite them to ask for information from the responsible leaders.[24]

In November 1974, Dr Rossi explained in the denominational magazine that on the basis of the examples of Jesus, the Apostles, and of the Christian Church of the first centuries, "a Christian cannot kill and cannot bear arms in a fought war."[25] He then explained the official position of the Church,[26] encouraging Adventist draftees to apply for the substitutive civil service and ask explicitly to serve in an Adventist institution. Moreover, in February 1975, Dr Rossi asked the Ministry of Defense to recognize the Italian Adventist institutions as centers where conscientious objectors could fulfill their alternative civil service, according to Law no. 772 of 1972.[27] While

---

23  The commission was formed by a magistrate of the Court of Cassazione (president), a general or an admiral, a university professor in ethics, a lawyer from the legal service of the State, and a psychology expert. See article 4, Law no. 772 of 1972.

24  "Delibera N, Servizio Civile non armato," *Il Messaggero Avventista* 48.10 (October 1973): 119. About Ellen G. White and military service, see George R. Knight, "Military Service," in *Ellen G. White Encyclopedia*, eds., Denis Fortin, Jerry Moon (Hagerstown, MD: Review and Herald, 2013, 2nd edition,), 981, 982.

25  Gianfranco Rossi, "Obiezione di coscienza," *Il Messaggero Avventista* 49.11 (November 1974): 128.

26  The official position of the Church on military service and noncombatancy was presented many times in *Il Messaggero Avventista*: "Non combattenti. Posizione di 'non combattenti': quella di chi è contrario al servizio militare armato," *Il Messaggero Avventista* 53.1 (January 1978): 13, 14 [it is a translation of the entry "Noncombatancy" in the *Seventh-day Adventist Encyclopedia*]; John Graz, "1860: avventisti, schiavismo e guerra civile americana," *Il Messaggero Avventista* 53.4 (April 1978): 62–64; "Gli ordini degli ufficiali e la verità, sono compatibili?" *Il Messaggero Avventista* 55.6 (June 1980): 93; Antonio Caracciolo, "No alla guerra e alle armi," *Il Messaggero Avventista* 60.9–10 (September-October 1985): 156, 157. In the Graz article, it is specified that "there are religious movements that claim that a true Christian has to be a conscientious objector. It is not enough for them to be non-combatants, that is, to be enrolled in the army and not to take up arms, to work in medical corps or as a chaplain, because they say they cooperate in the war. This is an interesting position and must be respected anyway."

27  Specifically, in the middle and high school of IACB, and in the largest Italian Adventist churches with a community center for elderly and needy people, no-smoking plans, temperance activities, etc. See document in Rossi, *Lotte...*, 424–426.

waiting for the answer, the Italian Union Executive Committee created a commission on Civil Service, with Dr Rossi (at that time secretary of the Italian Union) as chairman, Hugo Visani (at that time Director of the Youth Department), and Eliseo Cupertino (at that time Director of the Lay Activities Department). On December 10, 1975, Dr Rossi signed the agreement with the Ministry of Defense for the recognition of a certain number of Adventist civil service centers.[28]

In March 1976, an article by Dr Rossi confirmed the possibility of serving in Adventist institutions and reported that already around ten Adventist draftees applied for civil service and that three had already been assigned to civil service in the church of Turin and in the Istituto avventista di cultura biblica (IACB) [Italian Adventist College].[29] The Adventist Church was the first among the Italian Evangelical Churches[30] to sign this kind of agreement with the Ministry of Defense.[31]

In April 1976, the Ministry of Defense issued a general declaration confirming that young Adventists opposed to the use of arms for essential reasons of conscience could serve in non-armed military or civil service, according to Law no. 772 of 1972.[32] With this declaration, examination of the Adventist draftees' motives would become a *pro forma* matter. The Executive Committee decided in 1979 to entrust the managing of the Adventist Civil Service to the Youth Department.[33] From 1976 to 1979, there were more than forty conscientious objectors serving in Adventist institutions.[34]

In December 1982, the Executive Committee took the action to ask Adventist conscientious objectors for a sort of "civil disobedience":

Alternative Civilian Service – Voluntary Service
Considering that according to the law in force a conscientious objector is exempted from service if the call from the Ministry of Defense arrives after 18 months [from the application],

---

28  See document in Ibid., 427–434. An excerpt of the agreement was published in "Estratto della Convenzione fra il ministero della Difesa e la Chiesa Avventista italiana," *Il Messaggero Avventista* 51.3 (March 1976): 30.

29  Gianfranco Rossi, "Servizio Sostitutivo Civile,", *Il Messaggero Avventista* 51.3 (March 1976): 28, 29.

30  Gianfranco Rossi, *Dipartimento Libertà religiosa,* "I lavori dell'assemblea," *Il Messaggero Avventista* 51.5 (May 1976): 64. In Italy, the term "Chiese evangeliche" [Evangelical Churches] includes almost all the historical Protestant denominations (Waldensians-Methodists, Lutherans, Baptists, Brethren, etc.), Seventh-day Adventists, and some Pentecostal Churches.

31  Rossi, *Lotte...*, 95.

32  See document in ibid., 435.

33  Executive Committee of the Italian Conference, September 18, 19, 1979, Action no. 20 *Servizio Civile – gestione,* in "Le decisioni del Comitato della Federazione," *Il Messaggero Avventista* 54.11 (November 1979): 164.

34  Gianfranco Rossi, *Rapporto del Dipartimento della Libertà religiosa. Servizio Civile,* "I lavori dell'assemblea," *Il Messaggero Avventista* 54.12 (December 1979): 181.

Voted to ask young people who have applied to serve in the alternative civilian service to voluntarily start working in the Work from the sixth month from the submission of the application, and for the duration of the remaining 12 months of service [...].[35]

In a later action, the Italian Union transformed the aforementioned "request" into *a sine qua non* condition for those desiring to spend their alternative civilian service in an Adventist institution.[36]

## A Shift in the Italian Adventist Culture

From the mid-70s, the decisions taken by the Italian Union to promote the alternative civil service were supported and pushed forward by an internal movement, particularly evident within the younger generation. A consistent and vocal group of young people now shared what single Adventist draftees previously upheld. At the same time, the Italian Union contributed to create this shift in the Italian Adventist culture allowing Union officers, department directors, pastors, and young people, to express their voices freely in favor of conscientious objection in the pages of *Il Messaggero Avventista*, the official magazine of the Italian Union. For example, during December 6–8, 1975, a group of young Adventists from Northern Italy, considering that substitutive civil service was the "best instrument to express our obedience to God, our love towards men and the respect of state authority," approved a resolution asking for "our competent institutions and our communities to help and defend the young people that would act accordingly" and asking young people and pastors of other Adventist local churches to comply.[37]

At the sixteenth Italian Union constituency session of April 1976, the first three young men performing their alternative civil service in an Adventist institution gave their testimony in favor of civil service.[38] By the end of November 1976, sixteen young Adventists were working in the civil service in an Adventist institution.[39] The Italian Union organized a convention for them at IACB, March 7-8, 1977.[40] In the

35   Executive Committee of the Italian Union, Plenary Session, December 6–8, 1982, Action no. 140, *Servizio sostitutivo civile. Ferma volontaria.* See also "Dal mondo avventista," *Il Messaggero Avventista* 58.3 (March 1983): 46.
36   Executive Committee of the Italian Union, May 26, 1983, action no. 323, *Ferma obbligatoria obiettori.* See "Dall'Unione," *Il Messaggero Avventista* 58.11 (November 1983): 156.
37   Giovanni Leonardi, "Giovani avventisti e servizio sostitutivo civile,", *Il Messaggero Avventista* 51.3 (march 1976): 31.
38   Gianfranco Rossi, *Dipartimento Libertà religiosa*, "I lavori dell'assemblea," *Il Messaggero Avventista* 51.5 (May 1976): 64.
39   *Servizio Sostitutivo Civile*, "Dal mondo avventista," *Il Messaggero Avventista* 52.1 (January 1977): 12.
40   The cover of the May 1977 issue of *Il Messaggero Avventista* was dedicated to the First National Convention of Conscientious Objectors in the Substitutive Civil Service serving in Communities or Institutions of the Italian Conference of Seventh-day Adventist Churches. At the convention were present Rolando Rizzo, Mario Maggiolini (president of the Italian Union), Gianfranco Rossi, Clark Smith (at that time Associate Director of the Youth Department of the General

summer of 1978, the group of conscientious objectors serving in the Adventist School in Naples sent a report to *Il Messaggero Avventista*, lamenting the fact that there were young Adventists serving in the military, while the brethren drafted in Czechoslovakia preferred to spend ten years in prison.[41]

The Associazione Diplomati Universitari Avventisti (AUDA)[42] [Association of High School Graduates and University Students] played an important role in promoting nonviolence and conscientious objection among young Adventists. The theme of its second convention, held during March 23–27, 1978, was the end of the world. The hundred participants of the convention formed a silent parade, with banners and signs,[43] in the streets of Rimini, ending in the main theatre of the city, where some conscientious objectors gave their testimonies.[44] In presenting one of the speakers of the convention, Carlo Cassola,[45] an influential Italian prize-winning novelist

Conference and member of the National Service Organization committee), Nino Bulzis (director of the Youth Department of the Euro-Africa Division). A final document and a report were published by E. Mangano, and B. Marchese, "Servizio Sostitutivo Civile," *Il Messaggero Avventista* 52.5 (May 1977): 68.

41   G. Albanese, D. Benini, G. Mosca, C. Urso, "Napoli. L'opera degli obiettori nella scuola di Chiesa. Dal mondo avventista," *Il Messaggero Avventista* 52.7–8 (July–August 1977): 123. Later, one of these young conscientious objectors wrote a short, but intense, account of his experience, in Daniele Benini, "Perchè è importante essere obiettori di coscienza," *Il Messaggero Avventista* 54.1 (January 1979): 12. D. Benini guided a team of volunteers and conscientious objectors of the Opera Sociale Avventista during the emergency caused by the Irpinia (Southern Italy) earthquake of November 23, 1980. See "Laici avventisti in soccorso," *Il Messaggero Avventista* 56.1 (January 1981): 4–6.

42   AUDA was organized on April 7, 1977. While it was an autonomous organization, its creation was approved by the Executive Committee of the Italian Conference, on recommendation of the Education and Missionary Volunteers Department. The purpose was to create a place where educated Adventist young people could freely discuss current themes and problems and find new ways to cooperate with the Church. See *AUDA – Associazione Universitari e Diplomati Avventisti*, "Dal mondo avventista," *Il Messaggero Avventista* 52.1 (January 1977): 12. Pastor Rolando Rizzo and Dr. Rossi, the promoters of the AUDA, were elected counselors of the association. See *Raduno AUDA – Abetone 7–11 aprile 1977*, "Dal mondo avventista," *Il Messaggero Avventista* 52.1 (January 1977): 13; M. Di Silvestre, "AUDA. 1° Convegno Nazionale," *Il Messaggero Avventista* 52.6 (June 1977): 88, 89. From the beginning, AUDA received the support not only of the Italian Union, but also of the Euro-Africa Division, and invited high profile speakers, e.g. Jean Zurcher (at that time Secretary of the Euro-Africa Division), Raul Posse (president of the Adventist Seminary in Sagunto, Spain, and member of UNESCO).

43   The slogans were: "We are for the brotherhood with all the peoples," "Wake up! Realize. The end of the world is near," "We are for global and total disarmament," "We want a world of love, cooperation, and peace," "We are for the overcoming of militarism." See pictures in *Il Messaggero Avventista* 53.5 (May 1978): 72–74.

44   Giuseppe De Meo, "Studenti che attendono il ritorno di Cristo," *Il Messaggero Avventista* 53. 5 (May 1978): 72–75.

45   Gianfranco Rossi, "Carlo Cassola e la fine del mondo," *Il Messaggero Avventista* 53. 5 (May 1978): 71, 72. The other speaker of the convention was professor Bryan W. Ball, Newbold College. Carlo Cassola (1917–1987) in his last years engaged in an antimilitarist campaign.

and essayist, favoring unilateral disarmament, Dr. Rossi explaining the reason for his invitation, said,

> We also agree on another point with Carlo Cassola and that is on the proposal to over-come militarism, that is, on the proposal of unilateral disarmament, as a premise for the whole. Our consent to this proposal is only a logical consequence of our position as be-lievers and Christians [...]. Furthermore, as Christians, that is, as followers of Jesus Christ, we cannot be but non-violent. And, therefore, we Seventh-day Adventist Christians, wanting to follow Jesus' teaching and example, cannot but be opposed to violence, con-trary to the use of weapons, opposed to killing anyone, also because there is a command-ment of God that says precisely, "Thou shalt not kill."[46]

In the period of June 28 – July 12, 1980, a survey was launched among Italian Adventists focusing on two topics: military service and conscientious objection, and the inspiration of Ellen G. White.[47] In the same issue of *Il Messaggero Avventista* announcing the survey, an article from the editors appeared, quoting extensively the *Testimonies* and clearly affirming the "incompatibility between military orders and truth [as] justified by the Decalogue, precisely from the IV[th] and the VI[th] commandment," saying also that "it is not easy to reconcile this position [to consider licit taking up arms to defend your own country from an enemy attack] with the Gospel... We think that this work of sensitization must continue until we understand fully that as Christians we must always cooperate for the life of our fellow human beings and never, in any case, for their death."[48]

The questions and the answers from the survey about our topic were: Is it Christian to take up arms to defend the homeland in case of an enemy attack? (Answers were: Yes 6%, No 77%, Don't know 13%; blank 4%); Is it Christian to accept military service and practice shooting? (Answers: Yes 4%, No 85%, Don't know 6%; blank 5%); Is it a duty for the Christian to be a conscientious objector? (Yes 80%, No 8%, Don't know 6%; blank 6%); Is it a duty for the Christian to be noncombatant? (Yes 77%, No 13%, Don't know 6%; blank 4%).[49] There were 1,254 responses to the survey, among a membership of 4,750, which represents 26.4% – a significant response rate.

> In 1977, he started the Lega per il Disarmo [League for Disarmament] and a long tour of public speeches. He then started a committee promoting the organization of a convention of intellectuals on the end of the world, held in Florence in 1982.

46  Giuseppe De Meo, "Studenti che attendono il ritorno di Cristo," *Il Messaggero Avventista* 53.5 (May 1978): 73.

47  "Sondaggio di opinione, rispondono gli avventisti italiani del 7° giorno," *Il Messaggero Avventista* 55. 6 (June 1980): 83.

48  "Gli ordini degli ufficiali e la verità, sono compatibili? Possiamo ricevere il sigillo di Dio, os-servando il sabato e impugnando le armi?," *Il Messaggero Avventista* 55. 6 (June 1980): 93.

49  "Risultati del sondaggio di opinione sugli avventisti italiani del 7° giorno," *Il Messaggero Avventista* 55.10 (October 1980): cover.

## Proposals to Change the *Church Manual*

In 1981, the Executive Committee invited Ulrich Frikart[50] to be one of the speakers at the sixth annual convention of AUDA and lecture on the theme "War, Violence and Conscientious Objection."[51] Frikart's presentations received the main attention[52] and fueled the decision of AUDA to approve this concluding resolution:

The Concluding Resolution
We, members of the A.U.D.A. gathered in Velletri from 8 to 12 April 1982, expressing our gratitude to God for the blessings, grace and fraternal communion we enjoyed at this meeting of study and reflection, we submit and recommend to the whole church, at the next assembly of the Italian Union and the governing bodies of the church (executive committees of the Italian Union, the Euro-Africa Division and the General Conference) our firm and precise concluding resolution expressed in two proposals arising from the two topics discussed and debated: "War, Violence and Conscientious Objection", and "Which Church?."

a. Adventism and Military Service
*Considering* that we live in the time of the balance of terror in which the insane arms race imposes on the Church to clearly witness, more than the grass-roots movements do, the right of man to life, as expressed by the VI[th] commandment,
*considering* that the same VI[th] commandment, understood in the light of the Sermon on the Mount, imposes on the Christian the prohibition to kill even in case of defensive war, *considering* that armed military service is a logical preparation for war, and that the young Adventist who performs this service does not give a testimony consistent with his faith, *considering* that the position of the Seventh-day Adventist Christian Church lends itself to misinterpretations, as is clear from serious incidents that occurred during the last two World Wars, such as to cause splits in our Movement,
*considering* that the Adventist Church gives considerable dignity to the local communities, of which Conferences, Unions, and the General Conference perform representative functions, and considering that from an opinion poll carried out two years ago by "Il Messaggero Avventista" to which 26% of the members of the then Italian Conference

50   At that time a Credentialed Missionary, Director of the Education Department of the Swiss Union Conference and of the French Swiss Conference, and principal of the Renens Secondary School.
51   The other theme of the convention was "Quale Chiesa?" ["Which Church?"], presented by Rolando Rizzo. See Emanuele Santini, "Guerra, violenza e obiezione di coscienza," *Il Messaggero Avventista* 57.6 (June 1982): 88.
52   In his speeches, he affirmed that violence is an ineliminable component of man. Christians are a people that do not orient their violence against other men, but through love, transform violence into non-violence, which is not a passive attitude. Non-violence implies to turn the other cheek and recognize the uniqueness of each human person. In regard to the relation between the Adventist Church and the State he suggested that there should be a constant dialectic, not disinterest. He considered it a pity that the Adventist Church, at least in Switzerland, was not a member of any organization trying to establish an alternative civil service. See Santini, "Guerra, violenza e obiezione di coscienza," 89–91, 93. A part of Frikart's presentation on Romans 13:1 and Matthew 22:17, is reported in "Dobbiamo sottometterci allo Stato?," *Il Messaggero Avventista* 57.6 (June 1982): 91.

answered (over 1,200), it turns out that a very high percentage (80%) considers it *incumbent* for a Christian to be a conscientious objector,

*considering* that the problem of the consumption of alcoholic beverages and toxic substances is considered rightly important by our Church to the point of making it a test of discipleship, and that paradoxically the transgression of the 6th [sic] commandment is instead left to the discretion of consciences,

*considering* that in countries where the possibility of alternative civilian service exists, it happens that various young Seventh-day Adventists quietly opt for armed military service, *we propose* that in case of a call to arms, if the alternative civilian service is not possible for various reasons, the choice to serve exclusively in *non-armed medical service corps* becomes a test of discipleship.

Additional Considerations.

We appreciate the consistency with which Seventh-day Adventists remain faithful to the commandment of the Sabbath by undergoing severe restrictions to their liberty in some countries to the point of imprisonment, but we believe that the VI[th] commandment should be observed with the same dignity and firmness, transgressed by armed military service.

We do not believe that armed military service can be justified by stating that the young man will shoot in the air. Even if he did so, by embracing the rifle, he would silently declare that he is ready to kill, and there would be a lack of loyalty, inconsistency and false testimony, the latter a sin indicated in the spirit of the IX[th] commandment.[53]

It was a time in which the Seventh-day Adventist Church in general was sensitive to the themes of peace and nonviolence in its own peculiar perspective. An example of this sensitivity can be seen in the document voted in the meeting of the Euro-Africa Division (EUD), held in Oertlimatt (Switzerland), on May 29, 1984. The delegates released a *Declaration of Peace*,[54] with a specific paragraph on nonviolence:

This peace it is not the result of human ability. On the contrary, it is the gift of God, the fruit of His justice, obtained through obedience to His commandments (Isaiah 32:17), in particular to that that requires respect for another's life: "Thou shalt not kill". In fact, this justice condemns violence in all its forms and requires us to love even our enemies. "If it is possible, as much as depends on you, live peaceably with all men."[55]

In the document, there is also a clear warning against open participation in grassroots movements for peace: while Adventists should be more and more involved in favor of peace, with different actions, they should avoid "participating in whatsoever

53  "La risoluzione finale," *Il Messaggero Avventista* 57.6 (June 1982): 90.
54  In order to get the original text, I have consulted the secretariat of the Inter-European Division and the European Archives for Seventh-day Adventist History, Friedensau, but was not able to find it. A special thanks to Dr Daniel Heinz, the director of the European Archives, for showing me that in that period there were various studies and declarations on war and peace circulating in European Adventist circles.
55  "Dichiarazione di pace," *Il Messaggero Avventista* 59.8–9 (August–September 1984): 116.

public demonstration – even a march for peace – in contrast with our spiritual mission in the world."[56]

The EUD document on peace encouraged the Executive Committee to take the action to adopt the AUDA resolution of 1982 and to transmit it through the appropriate denominational channels, asking for the inclusion as a test of discipleship in the *Church Manual* the fact that in case of a call to arms, if the alternative civilian service is not possible for various reasons, the only possible choice would be to serve in non-armed medical service corps.

In adopting the AUDA resolution, the Executive Committee added a long statement:

> We unanimously consider ourselves to be in solidarity with the considerations made and with the awareness of the insufficiency of our current regulations regarding the problem of violence, arms, war, and armed service.
>
> Unanimously we formally ask that the Committee of the Division carefully considers this document and, following the planned channels, brings to the General Conference a proposal that improves our current position.
>
> We kindly ask you to reflect on the following points:
>
> (1) The ambiguity of our proclaiming ourselves "non-combatants".
>
> In all the official documents, we declare that historically we have always proclaimed ourselves "non-combatants." Not all of this is correct. It would be better to say that we have simply recommended this position to our young people. In other words, we are observers of the Sabbath, we are teetotalers ... but we are not noncombatants.
>
> When this position is not evidence of discipleship, it becomes too subjective a subject, an object of dialectics, not a truth to be affirmed.
>
> (2) The damage this position has caused to the church.
>
> This ambiguous position has caused considerable damages to the church, we mention a few:
>
> - The splits in Germany for the active participation of many German brothers in the First World War.
> - The even more massive presence of many German brothers in the army during the last world war.
> - Vietnam has seen numerous Adventist soldiers at work.
> - The Maldives Wars saw Adventist military fighters on both sides.
> - In the USA and in other countries, many young people even voluntarily enter a military career.
> - In Italy, despite the certainty of the substitute civil service, there are young people who choose the armed service.
>
> We believe it is appropriate to correct this position decisively.
>
> (3) The reasons invoked for the maintenance of this ambiguous position.
>
> The reasons normally invoked to maintain the current position are:
>
> (a) The need to obey the state.

56  Ibid. Dr. Rossi, in the letters' column of *Il Messaggero Avventista*, considered that the march for peace that took place in Rimini (see above) was not "in contrast with our spiritual mission in the world" and therefore perfectly compatible with it. See Gianfranco Rossi, *Coscienza e ubbidienza*, "A colloquio con i lettori," *Il Messaggero Avventista* 60.2 (February 1985): 18.

(b) The problem not explicitly solved in the T.N. [sic] self-defense in extreme cases (aggression to family members, to own country ...)

(d) [sic] Career soldiers accepting the truth.

We consider all these reasons to be serious, perhaps sufficient to not reach extreme, utopian, and unrealistic positions, or, as citizens of free countries (that live in a normal situation), to place unbearable burdens on those who live in extreme situations both collective and personal.

However, in conscience, we believe that this cannot justify the current position of the Church.

We believe that it is possible to arrive at a statement of principle that safeguards the church from contradiction.

The principle of rejection of violence must be clearly established as a means of resolving any problem of human relations. This principle must be affirmed with absolute clarity even if, at the level of church discipline as for any other possible infringement of the norm, the situations must be examined in their simplicity.

(4) If it is necessary to be cautious in extreme cases, there are no reasons to tolerate the voluntary enlistment, the renunciation of the civil substitutive service, or the service in the medical corps.

(5) Proposal

Based on the above considerations, we formally ask the Plenary Committee of the Division to propose to the General Conference that:

(A) The confession of faith is reviewed and it contains the enunciation of the Adventist understanding of the truth about violence, about the army.

(B) That it becomes evidence of discipleship not to voluntarily undertake under any circumstances a military career. To choose, if forced, however, always the alternative civil service where it exists or enrollment in unarmed or medical corps.

We look forward to a careful examination of our problem and awaiting your motivated reply, even to correct us, we send fraternal greetings.

The Union Committee of Italian Adventist Churches.[57]

According to a chronicle of *L'opinione*, the monthly journal of the Italian Adventist youth,[58] the Executive Committee of the EUD constituted a commission to examine the proposal of AUDA, backed by the Italian Union.

57   Executive Committee of the Italian Union, February 21, 1985, Action No. 957, *Posizione Movimento Avventista* 'Sulla Violenza'. See "Obiezione di coscienza: cambierà il manuale?," *L'opinione* 1.0 (April 1985): 3. The delay in taking this action (the document was from 1982, while the action was taken in 1985) was explained by pastor Rolando Rizzo in Rolando Rizzo, *Una precisazione*, "A colloquio con i lettori," *Il Messaggero Avventista* 60.7 (July 1985): 98. Rizzo was the man in charge of presenting the AUDA document to the Executive Committee, being a member of both. A certain delay was due to his busy agenda, then he decided to study further the current position on the topic. After that, he sent the document to "America" [General Conference], which sent it back, asking for review by the Division. Then the Executive Committee took its time to discuss the text.

58   The first name of the journal was *L'opinione. Mensile di informazione avventista* 1.0 [sic] (April 1985), then *L'opinione della gioventù Avventista* from 1.0 bis [sic] (May 1985), then *L'opinione. Mensile della gioventù avventista* 4.6 (June 1988). I will refer in this paper simply to *L'opinione*.

Finally, the EUD voted to promote the insertion of the topic of military service in the *Church Manual*,[59] but the text they approved was not the document sent by the Italian Union, but the text of a "lost" declaration approved by the General Conference assembly in 1954,[60] with the elision of the words "in time of war":[61]

*Relationship to Government in Time of War*
Whereas, the Autumn Council in Cleveland, Ohio, in 1951, and again in Washington, in 1952, recommended that a statement on "The Relation of Seventh-day Adventists to War" be prepared which could be incorporated into our General Conference statement of beliefs; wherefore,
*We recommend* that the following be adopted and inserted in the beliefs as found in the *Church Manual:*

The Relationships of Seventh-day Adventists to Civil Governments and War
There are two divinely established institutions, the church and civil governments; genuine Christianity manifests itself in good citizenship and loyalty to civil governments; the breaking out of war among men in no way alters the Christian's supreme allegiance and responsibility to God or modifies his obligation to practice his beliefs and put God first in all things.
This partnership with Jesus Christ, who came into this world not to destroy men's lives but to save them, causes Seventh-day Adventists *in time of war* [italics provided] to take a noncombatant position, following their Divine Master in not taking human life but rendering all possible service to save it. In their accepting of the obligation of citizenship, as well as its benefits, their loyalty to government requires them to serve the state in any noncombatant capacity, civil or military, in war or peace, in uniform or out of it, which will contribute to saving life, asking only that they may serve in those capacities which do not violate their conscientious convictions.[62]

59  Forty-Seventh Meeting of the Euro-Africa Division, Montreaux, Switzerland, November 12, 1986, 8:00 hrs., Action no. 563 *Military Service/Church Manual-Request of Italian Union:* "VOTED, that the following be adopted and inserted in the fundamental beliefs as found in the Church Manual: 'Our partnership with Jesus Christ, who came into this world not to destroy men's lives but to save them, causes Seventh-day Adventists to take a noncombatant position, following their Divine Master in not taking human life but rendering all possible service to save it...'".

60  In fact, this statement was never inserted in the *Church Manual*. In 1959, the General Conference Committee, aware of the fact that "[t]he material appearing in the *Church Manual* must be voted at the time of General Conference session," nevertheless, sensing that "certain part of it should undergo revision," decided to "withhold from the *Church Manual* for the present this statement [...], and that further consideration be given to it at a future quadrennial session." See General Conference Committee, Forty-Fifth Meeting, January 22, 1959, 10:00 a.m., 209.

61  "Rettifica della divisione sulla obiezione di coscienza. Ecco il nuovo documento proposto a Washington", *L'opinione* 3.2 (February 1987): 1.

62  Proceedings of the General Conference, Forty-seventh Session, May 24–June 5, 1954, Seventh Meeting, May 27, 1954, 3:00 p.m., in *Review and Herald* 131.26 (May 31, 1954): 139. In fact, this statement was never inserted in the *Church Manual*. In 1959, the General Conference Committee, aware of the fact that "[t]he material appearing in the *Church Manual*

The proposal never made its way to the plenary session of the General Conference,[63] despite the successive requests of the Italian Union, and the Seventh-day Adventist Church maintained its position on military service, contained in the statement of 1972.[64]

## Conscientious Objection in the Agreement between the Adventist Church and the Italian State

The Italian Constitution of 1948, in its article 8.3, established that the relations with the denominations other than the Roman Catholics "are regulated by law, based on agreements with their respective representatives." For decades, this paragraph was not implemented. In the seventies, the Federation of the Evangelical Churches in Italy (FCEI) and other denominations that were in good relations with it (Seventh-day Adventists, Assemblies of God, etc.), asked the government to open discussion for the establishment of an agreement, according to Article 8.3 of the Constitution. In 1977, the Italian Union received the communication that the government was ready to open the negotiation.[65]

The Italian Union constituency session of June 1982 voted to start negotiation with the government; in the list of sixteen topics to be included in the agreement, four were directly connected with military service and civil service: "4. Spiritual assistance to Adventists who serve in unarmed military service. ... 7. Postponement of service for theology students. 8. Ministers exemption from military service. 9. Civil service."[66]

---

must be voted at the time of General Conference session," nevertheless, sensing that "certain part of it should undergo revision," decided to "withhold from the *Church Manual* for the present this statement […], and that further consideration be given to it at a future quadrennial session." See General Conference Committee, Forty-Fifth Meeting, January 22, 1959, 10:00 a.m., 209.

63  The president of the EUD, Edwin Ludescher, in his letter of February 28, 1991, explained the process that the recommendation of the EUD passed through. On April 25, 1989, the *Church Manual* Committee discussed the request, considering that, before it could be introduced in the *Church Manual*, the officers of the EUD should consider all its implications. On September 28, 1989, the officers of the General Conference and of the EUD discussed the issue. As they were not convinced about the issue, they decided to recommend to the Annual Council of the General Conference in 1989 not to take any action. See "La posizione avventista sul servizio militare," *Il Messaggero Avventista* 73.10 (November 1998): 14, 15.

64  One Hundred Forty-ninth Meeting, General Conference Committee, Autumn Council, October 17, 1972 8:00 a.m., 1171. This resolution was published in its Italian translation in Roberto Vacca, "Martiri, obiettori e soldati," *L'opinione* 12.6 (June 1996): III.

65  For different reasons, the discussion started only in 1986. See Rossi, *Lotte...*, 201–269.

66  "I lavori dell'assemblea," *Il Messaggero Avventista* 57.8–9 (August–September 1982): 132, 133.

In a dossier of Adventist texts, provided by Pastor Ignazio Barbuscia for the commission, there was a section containing some documents about alternative civil service and military service. The first document was a statement produced by the Italian Union explaining the position of the Adventist Church on military service:

> In accordance with the teaching of the Holy Scripture, the Christian Adventist Church believes that "the Authorities of the State are from God" and that due respect and obedience should be given to them in everything, except in what contrasts with the supreme divine law. As is known, one of the commandments of the Decalogue prescribes "Thou Shalt Not Kill" and the Adventist Church believes that this commandment, understood in the light of the teaching and example of Jesus and the Apostles, involves the opposition to the use of weapons even for the purpose of defense, but does not exclude the possibility of serving the country in *unarmed military service.*
> It professes this position of faith since its first organization (U.S.A., 1863, attachment no. 2) supporting it in all the countries of the world in which it operates.[67]

Then follows the *Statement of Principles* approved by the General Conference on August 2, 1864.[68] It is noteworthy to see that the rationale for noncombatancy in the 1864 statement lies in the teaching of the Bible, as "contrary to the spirit and practice of war," and in the requirements of the fourth commandment, while the Italian Union statement affirms that it is in the sixth commandment. The third document of the section was a newspaper article about Alberto Long, a Seventh-day Adventist, among the first Italian conscientious objectors, in World War I.[69]

When the commission for the drafting of the agreement between the Italian Union and the Italian Republic divided in sub-commissions to examine the draft proposed by Adventist representatives, the articles about non-armed military and civil service and Sabbath observance were dealt with by the same sub-commission, composed of Dr Rossi and Professor Carlo Cardia. Some regulations concerning peculiar themes dear to Adventists,[70] including noncombatancy,[71] were difficult to obtain in

---

67  It was the document already sent to the Ministry of Defense in 1969: "La posizione della Chiesa Cristiana Avventista sul servizio militare notificata al Ministero della Difesa in data 16/9/1969," *Speciale Documentazione per le Intese*, Dipartimento per gli Affari Pubblici e la Libertà Religiosa, Unione italiana delle Chiese Cristiane Avventiste del 7° Giorno, 20.

68  In Francis M. Wilcox, *Seventh-day Adventists in Time of War* (Washington D.C.: Review and Herald, 1936), 58.

69  On Alberto Long, see Tiziano Rimoldi, "The Italian Adventists during World War I – The Story of Alberto Long," *The Impact of World War I on Adventism*, Friedensau: Institute of Adventist Studies, forthcoming 2019.

70  The other themes were Sabbath keeping and the status of colporteurs. See Gianfranco Rossi's interview in "L'intesa segna un momento storico per il nostro paese e per l'opera avventista mondiale," *Il Messaggero Avventista* 62.2 (February 1987): 20–23.

71  Ignazio Barbuscia, "L'Intesa è diventata legge!," *Il Messaggero Avventista* 64.1 (January 1989): 6–8.

the drafting commission. Special prayers were offered for that and the draft was approved under "miraculous" circumstances.[72]

The agreement was signed on December 29, 1986, and approved by the Italian Parliament as Law November 22, 1988, no. 516: "Norms for the regulation of the relations between the State and the Italian Union of Seventh-day Adventist Christian Churches." Article 6 of Law no. 516 of 1988 deals with non-armed military and civil service:

> 1. The Italian Republic, acknowledging that the Adventist Christian Church is for reasons of faith contrary to the use of weapons, guarantees that Adventists subject to the obligation of military service are assigned, upon their request and in compliance with provisions for conscientious objection, to the civil substitutive service.
> 2. In the event of a recall to arms, Adventists who have served in the military are assigned, at their request, to the civil substitutive service, to the non-armed military service or to the medical services, in relation to the service needs.
> 3. Religious ministers of the Adventist Christian Church have the right, at their request, to be exempted from military service or to be assigned to the civil substitutive service. This possibility is granted to ministers of worship with care of souls even in case of general mobilization. In this case, the ministers of worship without care of souls are assigned to the civil substitutive service or to the medical services.

Article 7 of Law no. 516 of 1988 deals with the religious assistance of Adventists serving in the military:

> 1. The soldiers belonging to the Adventist Christian Churches have the right to take part, in the fixed days and hours, in the Adventist religious and ecclesiastical activities that take place in the places where they are for reasons of their military service.
> 2. If there are no Adventist Christian Churches in the place where they serve, the soldiers belonging to the Adventist Christian Churches can still obtain, in compliance with particular service requirements, permission to attend the nearest church within the provincial area, upon declaration of the competent ecclesiastical bodies.
> 3. In the event of the death of soldiers in service belonging to the Adventist Christian Churches, the competent military command shall adopt, in agreement with the deceased's relatives, the necessary measures to ensure that the funeral is performed by an Adventist minister.

Article 14 of Law no. 516 of 1988 deals with the IACB and in its third paragraph specifically prescribes that "[t]he students of the aforementioned Istituto can enjoy the same postponements of military service granted to students of schools of the same length." Article 17 of Law no. 516 recognizes the right for Seventh-day Adventists to

---

72  In the last meeting of the drafting commission, most of the government members were late; the only two punctual members discussed the problematic issues with the Adventist representatives and easily reached an agreement; when all the late members arrived, the already agreed upon text was promptly approved. See Gianfranco Rossi interview in "L'intesa segna un momento storico per il nostro paese e per l'opera avventista mondiale," *Il Messaggero Avventista* 62.2 (February 1987): 23.

observe the Sabbath rest from sunset Friday to sunset Saturday. Among the different categories of Adventist workers, professionals, and business operators entitled to the "the right to enjoy, at their request, the Sabbath rest as the weekly rest" only those "assigned to the alternative civil service" were included, while Adventist soldiers were not explicitly mentioned.

According to Dr Rossi, the agreement sent an important message, in line with the teaching and deeds of Christ, the apostles and the martyrs of the Church of the first centuries, to a world full of violence, contrasts, struggles and wars:

> [h]umanity must be helped to reach maturity, to understand that we must learn to coexist peacefully with others, with those who are different by race, religion, language, national-ity, etc. Problems can be solved through dialogue, discussion, exchange of views and not by violence and war. The law of the jungle is not a human law, it is not a civil law. If humanity came to be mature and civil, there would be no need for armies. This is the message of peaceful coexistence, which the Adventists, with their position as non-com-batants, can launch to their Italian compatriots.[73]

## Conclusions

Despite the fact that in 1986 the Italian Union secured for Adventist draftees the right to conscientious objection, it continued the promotion of conscientious objec-tion, particularly by means of its two official journals, *Il Messaggero Avventista* and *L'opinione*, which constantly published news, letters, original and translated articles, official documents and declarations, book reviews, interviews, and conscientious ob-jector reports on the topic.

The regulation of conscientious objection contained in the agreement of 1986 was contested by some politicians, scholars, and journalists, which considered it an unfair privilege.[74] Italian Adventists were forerunners of a change of perspective. In fact, Italy, in line with other European countries[75] and international human rights bodies,[76] in 1998 recognized conscientious objection to military service as a personal right for all,[77] and practically abolished obligatory military (or civil) service from Jan-uary 1, 2005, onward.[78]

---

73  Rossi, *Lotte...*, 320, 321.
74  See, for example, Antonio Guarino, *Obiezione di coscienza e valori istituzionali* (Napoli: Jovene, 1992), 118–146.
75  See European Consortium for Church-State Research, *Conscientious Objection in the EC Countries*, Proceedings of the Meeting Brussels-Leuven, December 7–8, 1990 (Milano: Giuffré, 1992).
76  See European Court of Human Rights, Grand Chamber, Case of Bayatyan v. Armenia (Ap-plication no. 23459/03), July 7, 2011, 10–17, http://hudoc.echr.coe.int%2Fapp%2Fconver-sion%2Fpdf%2F%3Flibrary%3DECHR%26id%3D001-105611%26filename%3D001-105611.pdf&usg=AOvVaw2_kJkTm8siemgssgtWiry0 (accessed April 6, 2018).
77  Law no. 230 of 1998.
78  Law no. 226 of 2004.

Moreover, Article 6 of Law no. 516 of 1988 continues to be an inspiration for other denominations. In fact, a similar norm was included in three agreements signed by the Italian Republic in 2012, with the Apostolic Church in Italy, the Buddhists, and the Hindus:

Article 4. Military service

1. The Republic, acknowledging that the UBI [Italian Buddhist Union] is for spiritual reasons contrary to the use of weapons, guarantees that, in the event of restoration of compulsory military service, the members of the organizations represented by it, subject to the obligation of military service, are assigned, at their request and in compliance with the provisions on conscientious objection, to the civil service.

2. In case of recall in service the members of the bodies represented by the UBI, who have served in the military, are assigned, at their request, to the civil service or medical services, in relation to service needs.

*Bernard Sauvagnat*

# Adventist Involvement with European Bible Societies

Abstract

Since the 1980s, several Adventists have worked for *French Bible Society* to collaborate in new translations or revisions of the Bible: *La Nouvelle Bible Segond (NBS), édition d'étude*, published in 2000, *La Bible expliquée*, published in 2004, *Ze Bible*, published in 2011, and a complete revision of the *Bible en Français courant* (BFC), to be published in 2020. Others have been involved with Bible Societies in Belgium, the Netherlands, Switzerland, Portugal, and other countries. This paper presents a first account of the French story and adds some notes and observations on the Adventist participation the other four countries mentioned.

During the last 40 years, Adventist Bible scholars and administrators have been called to participate in Bible translation, revision, edition, or education projects of several national Bible Societies in Western Europe. This paper will trace instances of collaboration with Bible Societies in France, Belgium, the Netherlands, Portugal and Switzerland. There has certainly been other Adventist involvement with Bible Societies in Europe[1] and in other world regions; this paper is, therefore, merely a partial attempt at describing and evaluating the larger story, while other regional cooperations could be the subject of other research initiatives.

## Adventist Involvement in the French Bible Society

### *Administration*

The French Bible Society is organized in two different entities: the Alliance Biblique Française (ABF), which is a non-profit association preparing various projects to make the Bible available and understandable to the French-speaking public and is financed by gifts; and the Société Biblique Française (SBF), which is a commercial society selling the products prepared by the ABF, and financed by its commercial activities.

---

1  On March 31, 2018, I heard a colleague from Romania saying that some Adventists worked with Orthodox scholars on Bible translation in Romania. After the presentation of this paper in Friedensau on April 24, 2018, a colleague from Iceland mentioned that there was also Adventist involvement with the Iceland Bible Society. For an account from Norway, see Tor Tjeransen, "Adventists and Cooperation with Other Denominations in the Bible Societies," in *Faith in Search of Depth and Relevancy: Festschrift in Honour of Dr. Bertil Wiklander*, ed. Reinder Bruinsma (N.p.: Trans-European Division of Seventh-day Adventists, 2014), 497–506.

Both entities are members of the United Bible Societies (UBS or, in French: Alliance Biblique Universelle, ABU). Before 2012, when the ABU was completely reorganized, the ABF/SBF was the leader of a taskforce called Francosec to coordinate the projects of the French-speaking Bible Societies including those of Belgium, Switzerland, Québec, and several African and Asian countries. This explains why the good relations between the Seventh-day Adventist Church and the ABF/SBF had a positive influence on the other French-speaking Bible societies. The Seventh-day Adventist Church has had a representative on the board of the ABF/SBF since the 1980s. Their commitment was always well received, and the denomination has been a regular and welcome partner of the ABF/SBF.

Pastor Emile Sauvagnat (Publication Director of the Franco-Belgian Union (FBU) already had friendly relations with Jean Barral, General Secretary of the ABF, when Pastor Marc Boegner was chairman of the ABF/SBF board in the 1950s.[2] Dr Maurice Verfaillie (General Secretary, FBU 1988–1995) was invited by Pastor Jacques Stewart, then President of the Fédération Protestante de France (FPF), to become a member of the board of the ABF/SBF.[3] Jean-Pierre Boyer, as General Secretary of the ABF/SNF, was happy to welcome an Adventist representative on that board. When Verfaillie was called to serve as Public Affairs and Religious Liberty Director of the then Euro-Africa Division of SDA in 1995, I was proposed by the FBU to take his place on the board of the ABF/SBF. I stayed on that board from 1995 to 2012 and became vice-president of the ABF (2010–2012). At that time I served as Sabbath-School and Personal Ministries Director at the FBU. Dr Jean-Jack Chafograck (Northern France Conference President) succeeded on the board from 2012 to 2018 and became President of the ABF (2015–2018). Since May 17, 2018, Pastor Matthieu Fury, the Education Director of the North France Conference, is the Adventist representative on the board of the ABF.

## The Nouvelle Bible Segond – édition d'étude

In 1988, Maurice Zehnacker, FBU President, asked Dr Jean-Claude Verrecchia, at that time director of the SDA Institute of Bible Correspondence School (IEBC), to offer his collaboration to the ABF for adding introductions to the last revision of the Louis Segond Bible, called "à la colombe,"[4] published in 1978. At that time this Bible was the most used French version among evangelicals. Verrecchia[5] was selected to become one of the four members of the editorial committee, together with Jean-Claude Dubs (Reformed), Mario Echter (Pentecostal) and Henri Blocher (Evangelical). Thus he became the first Adventist member of an academic ABF

2    Personal memories of B. Sauvagnat, son of E. Sauvagnat (died in 1985).
3    M. Verfaillie in a telephone conversation with B. Sauvagnat, March 12, 2018.
4    This revision of the Louis Segond Bible 1910 was published in 1978 by the SBF with a dove as logo. This is why it is usually called "à la colombe" in France (colombe in French means dove).
5    Jean-Claude Verrecchia, e-mail to author, February 27, 2018.

committee. While working on this project, the team noticed that the translation needed a thorough revision. It was decided, therefore, to prepare what is called now *La Nouvelle Bible Segond edition d'étude* – a study Bible version.

The work for this version took nearly fourteen years. Verrecchia wrote the introductions to the books of Daniel, Revelation, Hebrews, Colossians, and Philippians, as well as many entries in the glossary. Knowing the French-speaking Adventist scholars, Verrecchia suggested that the committee ask for their contribution. Dr Richard Lehmann, then president of Salève Adventist University, read and corrected the translation and notes of Paul's epistle to the Colossians.[6] Dr Roland Meyer, then lecturer of Systematic Theology at the Faculté Adventiste de Théologie (FAT) in Collonges-sous-Salève, worked on the text and notes of the two epistles to the Corinthians.[7] Dr Bernard Sauvagnat, then pastor of the Campus church in Collonges, wrote the introductions to the gospel according to Luke and to the Acts of the Apostles, and revised the translation and notes of Acts. For the translation we were required both to follow the 27th edition of Nestle-Aland and to stay faithful to the classic translation style adopted by Louis Segond at the end of the 19th century.

When the translators' and revisers' work was finished, Françoise Thaeder, a retired copy editor at the Adventist French publishing house, was asked to read the texts for correction. Finally, Corinne Egasse, then secretary of the FAT, having worked before for the Adventist publishing house in France, spent almost 500 hours in proof-reading from June 2000 to January 2002, when the text was already in the printing process. She worked closely with Didier Fougeras, who was the editorial secretary of the ABF, and corrected most of the text,[8] except the books of Ruth, Job, and Psalms which were given to other proof-readers, among whom was an Adventist retiree, Hélène Pfenniger,[9] who had worked both for the FBU offices and for the Adventist French publishing house. All the Adventist contributors of this large project evidently worked to the satisfaction of the FBU leadership; this project thus facilitated future joint projects with the ABF.[10]

## La Bible expliquée; Ze Bible; Bible Exposition

The *Bible expliquée* project aimed at adding to the margins of the Bible en Français courant (BFC, a dynamic translation of the Bible comparable to the New English Bible) short explanatory comments to help readers unfamiliar with the Bible to understand it better. Each comment was to be written by two persons of different Christian confessions – a Bible scholar and a non-scholar. Verrecchia was asked by

6   Richard Lehmann, e-mail to author, September 26, 2017.
7   Roland Meyer, unpublished text sent attached to in e-mail to author, February 27, 2018.
8   C. Egasse, e-mail to author, February 27, 2018.
9   C. Egasse, e-mail to author, March 8, 2018.
10  Verrecchia, e-mail to author, March 6, 2018.

Christian Bonnet (ERF), then General Secretary of the ABF, to work with Bettina Cottin (ERF), a female minister, to comment on the epistle to the Hebrews.[11]

*Ze Bible*, a Bible for young people, was one of the largest projects of the ABF so far. Eleven Christian organizations working for young people became partners. Among them was the Youth Department of the SDA Church in France. The project included a printed Bible using the text of the Bible en Français courant (BFC), with many helps and tools, but also a special website and pages on social networks (YouTube and Facebook), aiming at the development of a community of young readers of the Bible. A series of videos was produced to nurture these webpages and songs were composed to stimulate interest in the Bible and its life-changing message.

Seven years (2004–2011) of teamwork were necessary to complete the project. The two successive Adventist youth leaders of the FBU, Paul-Louis Ferrandez (2004–2008) and Pascal Rodet (2008–2011), were members of the managing and editorial committees. The responsibility of those two committees was to lead the project and validate the different texts written to help Bible readers. Pascal Rodet is still on the managing committee because the digital part of the project is continuing.[12]

Two other Adventist youth leaders, Philippe Anquetil (South France Coference, SFC) and Gabriel Samperio (SFC), as well as three Adventist scholars, Dr Richard Lehmann (FAT), Pierre Franco (SFC, and representing the Adventist Church in the Bible committee of the FPF), and Dr Jean-Claude Verrecchia (FAT) were among the writers of comments, notes, portraits and other tools for young readers. Anquetil and Samperio wrote the comments on 2 Samuel.[13] Franco wrote the comments on Galatians together with a Roman Catholic.[14] Lehmann wrote the comments on the Pastoral Epistles; Verrecchia[15] wrote several articles of the Tools. One of them, the Canon, was very sensitive because the committee had decided to include the deuterocanonical books, a resolution that upset the Evangelicals. Beyond the scholarly work and the contributions toward applicability, the Adventist input is evident in a note about present Sabbath observance, which mentions not only the Jews but also the SDA Church.

Beyond these Bible versions for contemporary readers, the ABF had promoted the Bible for several decades through a classic itinerant exposition made of several boards. When it needed renewal, it was decided to create a new interactive and dynamic exposition: *La Bible, patrimoine de l'humanité* (The Bible, Heritage of Humanity). Once more Verrecchia was called to participate in this project. He wrote several boards – amongst others, one on Bible manuscripts, another on materials on which the Bible has been or is available, and one on the Bible translations.

---

11   Verrecchia, e-mail to author, February 27, 2018.
12   P. Rodet, e-mail to author, March 6, 2018.
13   Ph. Anquetil, e-mail to author, March 6, 3018.
14   P. Franco, e-mail to author, March 6, 2018.
15   Verrecchia, e-mail to author, February 27, 2018.

## The Bible in French Sign Language (LSF)

In December 2007, the ABF editorial committee decided to publish a book of the Bible for the French-speaking deaf and hearing impaired. One of the secretaries employed in the office of the South France Conference of SDA, Valérie Lefebvre, was already committed to serving this group of people; therefore, she was invited to participate in this project. In turn, she invited a young Adventist woman, Marjorie Chanzy, who was learning sign language, to work for this project as a volunteer.[16] The gospel of Luke was chosen and divided into nine sections of two or three chapters each. Each section was translated by one of the nine teams in four countries (France, Switzerland, Belgium and Congo Brazzaville). Fifteen Bible scholars worked with these teams to check the accuracy of the translations compared to the Greek text of the gospel. A special vocabulary of 90 words or phrases was created. Several meetings of the French and Swiss teams took place on the SDA Campus of Collonges. The video recording took place during the winter 2009–2010, and three DVDs were published in May 2010.[17]

## Revision of the Bible en Français courant (BFC)

First published in 1982, this dynamic translation of the Bible is among the most appreciated products of the ABF. It was revised in 1997. When the first edition appeared, I was editor of the *Signes des temps* magazine; after reading it, I wrote to the ABF asking for a revision of Daniel 8:14 on behalf of the SDA Church – because it said "1150 days and 1150 nights." The 1997 edition took account of our request, and the text now says, "2300 nights and mornings."

In 2016, the editorial committee of the ABF decided it was time to do a complete revision of this translation. Dr Valérie Duval-Poujol, a Baptist scholar, who teaches the Septuagint at the Catholic University of Paris, was asked to lead in this revision project. She called for the collaboration of several Adventist scholars: Richard Lehmann[18] for Philemon, Roland Meyer[19] for 1 Corinthians, Bernard Sauvagnat for 1, 2 and 3 John, and Jean-Claude Verrecchia[20] for 1 and 2 Timothy and Colossians. Each reviser works on the text, the notes and the introduction of the books; they follow the 28th edition of Nestle-Aland and a detailed guide, which reflects the philosophy of this particular translation. This work is still in process.

---

16   V. Lefebvre, e-mail to author, March 13, 2018.
17   ABF, *Dossier de presse* LFS (pdf format), Paris, April 2010.
18   Lehmann, e-mail to author, September 26, 2017.
19   Meyer, e-mail to author, February 27, 2018.
20   Verrecchia, e-mail to author, February 27, 2018.

## Belgium and the Netherlands

In these two countries there are three Bible Societies: two in Belgium, one French-speaking (French Belgium Bible Society, FrBBS) and one Flamish-speaking (Flamish Belgium Bible Society, FlBBS), and one in the Netherlands (NLBS), that is Dutch-speaking, a language very close to Flamish, also spoken in Surinam. In 2003 Dr Rudy van Moere,[21] an SDA minister and then Professor of Old Testament at the Protestant Theological Faculty of Brussels University, who speaks the three languages, became a member of the board of the FlBBS, and was elected vice-president, a function he filled until 2006. In 2004 he was invited to be a guest member of the board of the NLBS, because he was one of the supervisors of the Nieuwe Bijbelvertaling, a high quality inter-confessional Bible. From 2006 to 2011, he was a member of the FrBBS. From 2004 to 2016, he served as NLBS board member and as advisor of the FlBBS board. In 2016 he wrote commentaries for the Bijbel in Gewone Taal, a Bible in fundamental Dutch using idiomatic expressions typically Dutch and not Flamish.

The French-speaking Belgian Bible society closely cooperates with its French counterpart and promotes and sells its Bible editions. But it also has its own publishing projects, which are promoted in other French-speaking countries as well. It produced, for instance, the Luc Magazine and the Marc Magazine, which present the gospels according to Luke and to Mark as modern magazines. In 2004 two SDA ministers were members of the Constituency of the FrBBS: Rudy Van Moere and Jacques Rase. In 2008 Jacques Rase was elected board member and vice-president. Another SDA pastor, Michel Mayeur, who had been editor of the Adventist magazine *Signes des temps*, also served as copy editor for publications of the FrBBS in several instances. Several other Adventist representatives continue serving the FlBBS, NLBS, and FrBBS.[22]

## The Swiss Bible Society

Eleven local or cantonal Bible Societies, one of them created in 1804, formed the Alliance Biblique Suisse in 1947. This Alliance became the Swiss Bible Society (SBS) in 1955. The SDA Swiss Union was accepted as member of the SBS in 1994 with a right to vote in its constituency meetings. By the end of 2002, a letter was sent by the SBS looking for new board members because there were only three members left while its policy required seven. The Swiss Union proposed Reto Mayer as candidate, and the constituency voted his name in 2003. He became the first SDA member of this board. In 2005, he was elected vice-president; then, in 2013, when the former

---

21  R. Van Moere, e-mail to author, March 19, 2018.

22  R. Van Moere is still a member of the board of the FlBBS and NLBS and member of the consultative committee of the FlBBS. Jacques Rase, as vice-president, is now working on the strategic plan of the FrBBS for 2020. Tom de Bruin, a Dutch SDA minister is also a member of the Constituency of the NLBS. Johan Delameillieure, a Belgian SDA minister is a member of the consultative committee of the FlBBS. See J. Rase, e-mail to author, March 1, 2018.

president resigned, he was appointed president. The SDA Church is eager to support SBS projects, and the other partners – mainly Protestant denominations – developed a positive view of Adventists.

The German-speaking churches (GSC) of Switzerland wished to have a Bible exposition adapted from the French one: La Bible, patrimoine de l'humanité. The SDA church provided crucial financial support to this project. The exposition was presented for the first time at the assembly of the GSC in Zurich in 2017. As most of the members of the SBS are from the mainline Protestant churches, Reto Mayer notes, "One of my aims was, as far as possible, to present the Bible as God's Word rather than just a product, a book to sell. This challenge has been met through meditations introduced in each board and constituency meeting."[23]

## The Portuguese Bible Society

Dr Teofilo Ferreira, an Adventist pastor from Portugal, former missionary to Israel, professor of Old Testament at the Adventist Faculty at Collonges until 1994, and associate director of the Ellen White Estate in Silver Spring, was one of the Old Testament translators of the Biblia para Todos (The Bible for everyone), an inter-denominational edition. The translation was done directly from Hebrew and Greek and not from other languages as sometimes happens. Ferreira was invited in 1975 by the Portuguese Bible Society (PBS) to join the small translation team. They knew his expertise on Biblical Hebrew and this relationship continued during all the years he worked in Jerusalem, France and the USA.

This translation was to be a team effort. The team was composed of three Protestant and three Catholic translators. Ferreira translated seven books of the Old Testament and revised the translation of seven other books from 1973 to 1993.[24] When the entire Old Testament text had been finished and was to be reviewed, he was invited with another translator to read it completely for corrections.

His collaboration with the PBS continued in other projects from 1999 to 2009, mainly as a reviser. Moreover, he remained a member of the translation team even in the years before. Recently, Ferreira participated in a special Bible Project sponsored by the PBS, which focused on putting the Book of Psalms to music for young people; the British Bible Society participated as well.[25]

## Conclusion

These instances of cooperation demonstrate the interest of European Adventists in the Bible. Adventist contributions were possible because of the high quality of training of ministers and scholars in Biblical languages. Moreover, the general

---

23   R. Mayer, unpublished text attached in e-mail to author, March 1, 2018.
24   T. Ferreira, e-mail to author, March 13, 2018.
25   Ferreira, e-mail to author, March 6, 2018.

atmosphere of brotherhood in Christian universities and churches in Europe facilitated the inclusion of Adventist scholars among the scientific teams of the Bible Societies.

*Stefan Höschele*

# The Adventist Encounter with Free and State Churches on the Old Continent

Abstract

When Adventists appeared on the European religious scene, they encountered situations that differed markedly from the American "free religious market" setup. Hence their encounter with both state and free churches was largely characterized by friction and, to some degree, a lack of interest in understanding each other. At the same time, this story of conflict provided a crucial learning opportunity to the denomination as a whole, which led to a differentiated picture by the late 20th century. This paper presents four case studies and evaluates types and developments in the Adventist relationship with other Christian churches in Europe.

This paper results from a crossover of a nine-year research project (ended in 2016) on global Adventist interchurch relations[1] and a first attempt to sort out patterns of how this relational story enfolded on the Old Continent. The latter element certainly needs to be developed much further. At the moment, there are only a few academic inquiries into any aspect of how Adventists interacted with other churches in Europe;[2] and the few that exist focus on a portrayal of institutional history, concentrating on the denominational stance vis-à-vis ecumenism at large (e.g. in France and Germany).[3] The following is, therefore, an incomplete mosaic; yet even the little that is available provides us with important insights.

## Conflicts with State Churches, Competition with Free Churches

From the distance of almost one and a half centuries, the 1870s and 1880s not only appear as another era altogether, but it is also easy to overlook that it was much less globalized. In fact, when the first Seventh-day Adventist communities developed in

---

1    Stefan Höschele, "Interchurch Relations in Seventh-day Adventist History: A Study in Ecumenics," habilitation thesis, Charles University, Prague, 2016. For an annotated collection of key texts, see Stefan Höschele, *Interchurch and Interfaith Relations: Seventh-day Adventist Statements and Documents*, Adventistica 10 (Frankfurt a. M.: Lang, 2010).

2    The most significant to date is probably Christopher Peake, "Seventh-Day Adventists in Britain in Relation to Their Host Community in the Early 20th Century," in David Trim and Daniel Heinz, eds., *Parochialism, Pluralism, and Contextualization: Challenges to Adventist Mission in Europe (19th–21st Centuries)*, Adventistica 9 (Frankfurt a. M.: Lang, 2010), 93–116.

3    For details, see the case studies below.

Europe in the last quarter of the century, North America and Europe were quite different worlds, especially with regard to religion. The vibrant, experience-oriented Christianity of the USA with its revivalist heritage differed markedly from the traditional leaning in much of European Christendom. Of course Europe had exported all of its confessional brands to America; however, in the New World, these brands transformed into denominations, this curious new mode of being Christian that a secular state produced in connection with a free religious market.

Seventh-day Adventists were not only children of the American way of religious life in many ways, including a happily competitive approach to other Christian movements. Once they decided to propel their mission beyond the boundaries of the continent of origin, they also faced such a variety of religious setups that the encounter with these was a learning experience in itself. Such encounters were characterized – at least for the first generations – mainly by strain, misgivings, oppression and persecution,[4] and often misunderstanding.[5] Nevertheless, it was such situations of conflict that would, ultimately, help the denomination to grow in terms of the competency to differentiate, to develop with regard to ecclesiology, and to appreciate the heritage of the Reformation as well as the Christian Church in general – and, ultimately, even some aspects ecumenism, which was otherwise viewed in a rather sceptical manner.[6]

For the representatives of this young and dynamic American denomination, which aimed at proclaiming the last message to the world, the necessary shift in their *modus operandi* was not easy. In the 19th century, such a thing as religious liberty was merely a theory and largely unknown in much of Europe. Unlike the USA, each territory had a state church or, at least, such a powerful majority religion that movements that did not find their place within these existing religious structures *had* to be considered intruders. In this regard, Europe was much like South America at the time, only that the bewildering diversity of state Christianities – Roman Catholic, various types of Orthodox, Lutheran, and Reformed – made a systematic and consistent mission approach to the continent as a whole much more difficult.

Adventist historiography usually depicts the denomination's past as a story of advance, growth, and the overcoming of obstacles. The European story modulates this picture: the denomination did not play its role as naturally in much of its European history for the reason that the religious landscape looked so different from the

---

4   For the Austrian example, see Daniel Heinz, "Kein Platz zwischen Thron und Altar: Freikirchliche Mission im Alten Österreich (bis 1918) am Beispiel der Adventisten [No Space between Throne and Altar: Free Church Mission in Old Austria (until 1918) – the Adventist Examples]," manuscript, 2018, due to be published in *Freikirchenforschung*. To Guy Dail, Austria "seemed quite a European Tibet" (ibid., 4 / *Review and Herald*, February 11, 1909, 13).

5   The exception to this rule was the Seventh Day Baptist support of early Adventist missionary activities in Great Britain; see Harry H. Leonard, "John N. Andrews and England's Seventh Day Baptists: 'We Are Brethren'," *Adventist Heritage* 9 (1984): 50–56.

6   Bert B. Beach's book *Ecumenism: Boon or Bane?* (Washington, D.C.: Review and Herald, 1974), the first and so far only book-length treatment of the theme, came about largely as a result of his experiences in Europe.

open market in the USA. In many parts of Asia and America at large, many aspects of Adventist operations in the USA could be imitated, even with regard to intra-Christian encounters; in Europe, Adventists were thrust into a situation that was non-typical for the peculiar SDA ways.

Time and space do not allow a discussion of identity issues and terminology – such as the question of where and when Adventists perceived and presented themselves as a "movement" or a "church," and what the ascription of being "a sect" did to them (as was the case in many European contexts and until quite recently). The latter actually calls for a study of its own.[7] Yet the very fact that Adventists could not neatly perpetuate their identity as it had been formed in America – a denomination that called itself church but prefers a "movement" self-understanding – in most areas of the Old Continent implies that there was a considerable amount of perplexity to deal with.

Whatever the denomination's self-conceptualization was, the majority churches throughout Europe considered groups such as the Adventist "sectarians" a danger to peace, to the social fabric, and – of course – to their unquestioned status of power. Thus any new, small or imported movement had to develop a self-conceptualization that dealt with the common lack of positive esteem by the religious establishment. In some countries, Adventists came to be considered one of the free churches, like Baptists, Methodists, and groups like the Mennonites, which had existed since earlier periods. Yet these free churches hardly cooperated among each other in those early years and mostly viewed Adventists as further competitors. And this they were, for many Adventist communities in Europe actually arose among those who belonged to free churches already.

## Four Brief Case Studies

At this point, it is helpful to turn to a few specific countries to note the variety of paths and the issues arising in peculiar contexts.[8] On each of these countries – and indeed on each other European country – a full paper, and in some instances even a major study, could be written with regard to the relationship with other churches and Christians.[9] The purpose of these short case studies is to highlight both the diversity and some common themes in the European Adventist encounter with the ecclesial Other.

---

7   A somewhat odd precursor study is the first doctoral dissertation by a German Adventist theologian: Johannes Schwital, *Großkirche und Sekte: Eine Studie zum Selbstverständnis der Sekte* [Majority Church and Sect: A Study on the Self-understanding of the Sect] (Hamburg: Saatkorn, 1962), originally a Dr. phil. dissertation, University of Frankfurt, 1961.

8   The countries for these case studies have been arranged in alphabetical order.

9   As is the case with other topics, writing a complete overview is hardly possible at the moment. In several cases, there are no comprehensive histories of Adventism in a particular country; and where such histories exist, historians often need to be polyglot in order to be able to use

## Estonia: From Conflict to Ecumenism in a Post-Christian, Neo-Pagan Context

Adventists in Estonia number about 1,500 today, down from over 2,200 in the mid-20th century. Beginnings[10] were somewhat conflict-ridden, as mostly in the story of Adventism: the denomination came in response to a call by a woman from St Petersburg in 1897, who wanted her Baptist relatives in Tallinn to know the Adventist faith. Recruiting members from other free churches was common at the time but evidently caused frictions, as did the general missionary work among the Orthodox. Adventist preaching at the time was apparently forbidden in Russia (to which Estonia belonged), which changed only in 1904, at least for the Estonian part.

Little is known about interchurch encounters locally and nationally in the phase of independence (1920 to 1940), but the Soviet period brought the dissolution of the denominational organization as well as other severe hardships – as in most other socialist states – and an unprecedented closeness to other Christians. Church buildings were shared with other Christian denominations,[11] and frictions were apparently stronger inside Adventism than with other churches. A major conflict concerned the relationship to Charismatic phenomena;[12] which implies that severe challenges from the Christian Other can also arise in one's own ranks.

Soon after independence, the Estonian Seventh-day Adventist Church became a guest member in the Estonian Council of Churches, building on the "mutual respect and understanding between Christian Churches" that had developed in the Communist era.[13] Today, Adventists are full members in this Council[14] – in a context of a society where 54% declare themselves non-religious and 16% do not state to which religion they belong (if any; 2011 figures). In fact, Estonians are the nation in Europe where neo-paganism has the strongest influence. It seems comprehensible, therefore,

them. In several instances, fine monographs on Adventism in a country contain little or nothing on the encounter with other Christians and churches (e.g. the comprehensive work by Ernesto Ferreira, *Arautos de Boas Novas: Centenário da igreja Adventista do Sétima Dia em Portugal, 1904*–2004 [Lisbon: UPASD, 2008]). Thus one has to rely largely on clippings from those secondary sources that happen to include sections or memories relevant to the topic (see, e.g., the 2-page section "La intolerancia durante una dura y larga posguerra [Intolerance during a hard and long post-war period]," in *Compartiendo la Esperanza: Cien años de adventismo del séptimo día en España* [Madrid: Editorial Safeliz, 2003], 152–153.

10    Voldemar Viirsalu, "Estonia," in Hugh I. Dunton, Daniel Heinz, Dennis Porter and Ronald Strasdowsky, *Heirs of the Reformation: The Story of Seventh-Day Adventists in Europe* (Grantham: Stanborough, 1997), 78–84, here 78–79.

11    Ibid., 80.

12    Ibid., 83–84. Viirsalu reports that several pastors developed an interest in charismatic phenomena in the 1970s.

13    Ibid., 84.

14    For a history of Estonian ecumenism, see Riho Altnurme, ed., *History of Estonian Ecumenism* (Tartu: University of Tartu Press; Tallinn: Estonian Council of Churches, 2009).

that today Estonian Adventists stress their positive relationship with other Christians and view the non-Christian majority as the major missionary challenge.

## France: Making Friends among the Protestants

France has never been an easy territory for Adventists. The religious situation that they encountered there was characterized by a heritage that included state persecution of Huguenot Protestants, anti-religious sentiments as evidenced in the French Revolution, and a population that was overwhelmingly Roman Catholic, at least in name. This mix resulted in a broad-based opposition to the type of religion that Adventists brought and, consequently, in very slow growth.

Most success of the earliest Adventists apparently took place among Protestants and, more specifically, Baptists.[15] This was common at the time; Methodists and Darbyites (Plymouth Brethren) also mainly targeted Protestants – evidently because Roman Catholics were much slower to respond. However, Adventists may have gone farther than the others in this situation of "direct competition."[16] Later paths of opening[17] towards other Christians and churches include activities by physician Jean Nussbaum, the well-known Adventist lobbyist for religious liberty, and his disciple Bert Beach, child to American missionary parents and equally well-known religious liberty advocate and prime interchurch networker, with a close connection with France.[18]

It is in the 1990s that the SDA Church made steps towards becoming members of the Protestant Federation (Fédération Protestante). Debates and some opposition continued through the 1990s, but in 2006 and after considerable discussion among representatives of the other Protestants,[19] Adventists became full members. No doubt

---

15  Sébastien Fath, "Les relations entre les adventistes et les autres protestants," in Fabrice Desplan and Regis Dericquebourg, eds., *Ces protestants que l'on dit adventistes* (Paris: L'Harmattan, 2008), 19–27, here 25–26.

16  Ibid., 26. Fath goes on by referring to a specific example from 1897 in Nice; see ibid.

17  Cf. the title of the paper by Richard Lehmann, "L'Église adventiste en France: Chemins d'ouverture," in Desplan and Dericquebourg, eds., *Ces protestants que l'on dit adventistes*, 101–119.

18  He obtained his doctorate from the Sorbonne and through his knowledge of French remained close to Adventists in the country throughout the decades.

19  For more details, see Lehmann, "L'Église adventiste en France: Chemins d'ouverture," and Jean-Paul Willaime, "L'intégration des adventistes du septième jour à la Fédération Protestante de France," in Desplan and Dericquebourg, eds., *Ces protestants que l'on dit adventistes*, 89–99.

such a membership was conceivable because this was a *Protestant* council[20] in an unambiguous minority context.[21]

## Germany: Becoming a Free Church

In Germany, the earliest Adventists found a situation that was more diverse than in many other European countries. Roman Catholic, Lutheran and some Reformed territorial churches dominated the religious scene. The Radical Reformation had added flavour to this mix since the 16th century, and Baptists, Methodists and a number of indigenous free-church type movements made the existence of religious diversity more plausible than in nations where essentially everyone had shared the same confession for centuries.

Ludwig Richard Conradi and at least some of his followers intended to build positive relationships with representatives of other Christian traditions mainly in the context of Protestant foreign mission initiatives.[22] In spite of the common reservations at the time, at least some mission leaders viewed Adventists in a positive light; the well-known Julius Richter even counted them among the "free churches"[23] – a rare assessment at the time. Although Adventists were advised – after an application to be accepted into the German Mission Council – to withdraw their request, this step shows that at least from an Adventist perspective, cooperative and constructive encounters with other missionary-minded Protestants were deemed reasonable.[24]

20   According to oral information by Bernard Sauvagnat, this membership in the Protestant Federation at times prompted unforeseen opportunities of mission and ministry – as in Morocco, where an Adventist pastor was called through the Federation to serve Adventist and other students in the country in 2014.

21   This situation is similar to the developments in Spain in some respects; cf. Ley 24/1992 de 10 de noviembre [Law 24/1992 of November 10], November 12, 1992, no. 272 [on FEREDE (Federation of Evangelical Religious Entities of Spain)], *Boletín Oficial del Estado*, online: http://www.boe.es/boe/dias/1992/11/12/pdfs/A38209-38211.pdf, accessed February 1, 2016. This law actually provides for freedom from work and from exams on Saturdays for Adventist employees and students.

22   Cf. Johannes Hartlapp, *Siebenten-Tags-Adventisten im Nationalsozialismus unter Berücksichtigung der geschichtlichen und theologischen Entwicklung in Deutschland von 1875 bis 1950*, Kirche – Konfession – Religion 53 (Göttingen: Vandenhoeck & Ruprecht, 2008), 577–580; on the general relationship with other churches in the same period, see 66–78.

23   Julius Richter, "Zweihundert Jahre deutscher Missionsgeschichte," in Julius Richter, ed., *Das Große Buch der deutschen Weltmission* (Gotha: Klotz, 1935), 14–15.

24   For more details, see Stefan Höschele, "Gaststatus als Modell von Ökumenizität? Siebenten-Tags-Adventisten und die Arbeitsgemeinschaft christlicher Kirchen in Deutschland – Hintergründe, Entwicklungen und Einsichten [Guest Status as a Model of Ecumenicity? Seventh-Day Adventists and the Council of Christian Churches in Germany – Background, Developments, and Insights]," *Freikirchenforschung* 18 (2009): 194–195.

During the GDR period, when the number of Protestant church members steadily decreased, Christians finally found themselves to be a minority.[25] Seventh-day Adventist leaders first established informal but positive interdenominational contacts[26] and then applied for a guest status in the then AGCK (Association of Christian Churches) in 1974. This organization was the GDR version of a national council of churches, and although there was no guest category, the "observer" status that was granted made Adventists virtually members of the association, just like Roman Catholics, who were also observers. The subsequent cooperation was conspicuously free of conflict.[27]

In Western Germany, such positive contacts did not exist, and it was only in 1993 that the denominational leaders decided to apply for a guest status in the reunified German Association of Christian Churches (ACK). This status was granted in the same year.[28] In the ACK context, observer status implied potential non-agreement with its trinitarian basis, which is why the "guest" category seemed by far preferable. In the same year, Adventist leaders were surprised by vigorous protests of a vocal minority of members who claimed that this new status compromised Adventist beliefs.[29] This led to several years of attempts at explaining this step to the members and a "test phase" until 1997,[30] i.e. until the status could be confirmed by constituency meetings.

25  This and the following paragraphs are borrowed almost verbatim from Höschele, "Interchurch Relations in Seventh-Day Adventist History," 324–325.
26  Manfred Böttcher, *Dialog und Zeugnis: Interkonfessionelle Kontakte und Konflikte einer Freikirche in der DDR* (Frankfurt a.M.: Lang, 2001), 19–72, mentions participation in the Association of Churches and Religious Communities in Berlin and in weeks of prayers of the Evangelical Alliance, the solidarity among construction soldiers (i.e. conscientious objectors) belonging to different denominations, Adventist employees in Protestant hospitals and similar institutions, and cooperation in the field of church music. Cf. also Dieter Leutert, "Die Adventgemeinde in der DDR und ihr Verständnis zur Ökumenischen Bewegung," in Träder, ed., *Ökumene: Verpflichtung oder Versuchung?* (1983), 57–70.
27  Böttcher, *Dialog und Zeugnis*, 86–87, 109–110.
28  For details of this event and the ensuing debate, see Stefan Höschele, "Gaststatus als Modell von Ökumenizität?," 195–201.
29  A comprehensive analysis of the debates in those years is presented by Thomas Spiegler, "Darstellung und Analyse der Diskussionen um die Gastmitgliedschaft der Gemeinschaft der STA in der Arbeitsgemeinschaft Christlicher Kirchen in Deutschland," Diplom thesis, Theologische Hochschule Friedensau, 1999.
30  For a discussion of interchurch relationships and the ACK by the denominational leadership in Germany, see Gemeinschaft der Siebenten-Tags-Adventisten in Deutschland, *Unser Verhältnis zu anderen Kirchen, Freikirchen und Gemeinschaften*, Adventgemeinde heute 1 (Hannover: Gemeinschaft der Siebenten-Tags-Adventisten in Deutschland, 1993); Gemeinschaft der Siebenten-Tags-Adventisten in Deutschland, *Vierundfünfzig Fragen und Antworten zum Verhältnis der Gemeinschaft der Siebenten-Tags-Adventisten zu anderen Kirchen und zur Arbeitsgemeinschaft Christlicher Kirchen in Deutschland (ACK)*, Adventgemeinde heute 3 (Hannover: Gemeinschaft der Siebenten-Tags-Adventisten in Deutschland, [1997]).

Apart from many local encounters, ranging between hostile and amiable, the most remarkable instance of encountering a particular confessional group was the series of conversations with representatives of the Lutheran Church in Germany (VELKD, which comprises only a part of the Protestant Church in Germany, EKD), between 1985 and 1987.[31] It did not have the nature of an interchurch dialogue but was mainly intended as a kind of examination of Adventists by the Lutheran side. A follow-up series of meetings that began in 2017 on the basis of a Lutheran recognition of Adventists as one of the Free Churches indicates that an encounter between Adventists and other Protestants at eye level is actually possible.

## Hungary: Uneasy but Close Free Church Relationships in a Socialist Society

With regard to Hungary,[32] the one episode that is most well-known in the Adventist collective memory is particularly significant for its effects on the denominational discourse on interchurch relations. Adventists in most countries worldwide shunned involvement in the major ecumenical organizations, i.e. national councils of churches, throughout the 20th century. If participation was an option for the respective church leaders, consultant or observer status was their choice in most cases.[33] Until the end of the 20th century, full membership occurred only in two very small countries – the Bahamas and Belize.[34] In the Hungarian case, however, active involvement in an entity that was generally regarded as ecumenical caused considerable tension. While the situation was rather complex and arose within a context of state pressure, infiltration by the secret service and isolation from the global denomination, the 1975 schism in Hungary was directly linked to the authorities' attempts to control Christians by uniting free churches in a common council.

The Hungarian Council of Free Churches had been initiated by Christian leaders themselves but soon came under the influence of the government office of church

---

31   From these conversations arose a statement entitled "How Do Adventists View Their Relationship to Other Churches?," which was approved by the Biblical Research Committee of the Euro-Africa Division. For the text and comments, see Stefan Höschele, *Interchurch and Interfaith Relations: Seventh-Day Adventist Statements and Documents*, Adventistica 10 (Frankfurt a. M.: Lang, 2010), 77–81.

32   Most of the text in this section is taken from Höschele, "Interchurch Relations in Seventh-Day Adventist History," 323–324.

33   In 1985, Adventists were "Fraternal Associates" of the National Council in Kenya (a lower status than "Associate Members"); in Rwanda and the Solomon Islands, they were an "Associate Member"; in England the status was status that of a "consultant-observer"; cf. the respective pages in *Directory: Christian Councils* (Geneva: World Council of Churches, 1985).

34   Ibid. Full membership in the Swedish Mission Council was different from membership in organizations that mainly represented an ecumenical agenda.

affairs. A few Adventists were strongly involved in the leadership of this organization,[35] and in 1975 some denominational leaders and about 10% of a total membership of 6,000 left their church, mainly with reference to "ecumenical involvement." Attempts at reconciliation failed due to hardened positions and power issues on both sides until in 1984 the schismatic "Egervari group"[36] formed an organization of their own.[37] This church, the Christian Advent Community (KERAK), grew to a membership of over 1,600 in the post-1989 era.[38]

After the peaceful revolution, attempts at reunion failed,[39] and by the year 2000, communication ceased. In 2011, new conversations began, and in 2015, the leaders of both churches signed a "Joint Declaration on Settling the Past and Building a Common Future," a kind of "healing of memories" agreement.[40] Although a full reunion (e.g. by forming a new conference under the Hungarian Union leadership) seemed impractical for leaders of the regional Trans-European Division, a partial reunion was achieved in that almost all KERAK leaders became pastors of the Seventh-day Adventist Church. About half of the KERAK members joined the denomination individually until mid-2016 – the others preferred to uphold their own organization.[41] In spite of the partial reconciliation, the general relationship to other free churches in Hungary remained distant, and the "Hungarian schism," as it has become known, remained a sign to many Adventist leaders that aiming at closer relations with other denominations is potentially divisive for the SDA Church itself.

---

35 Cf. the overly positive report by an Adventist who was involved in the leadership of this Council of Free Churches, Sándor Palotay, "Les Églises libres," in Jozsef Lukacs, ed., *Ensemble pour une bonne cause: L'État socialiste et les Églises en Hongrie. Études, déclarations, documents* (Budapest: Corvina, 1978), 179–189.

36 It was named after Oszkar Egervari, a former conference president, who became the group's leader.

37 For different perspectives on what happened in those years, see Edwin Ludescher, G. Ralph Thompson, and Neal C. Wilson, "The Hungarian Situation," *Ministry* 58.4 (1985): 11, 21; and Sidney Reiners, "Betrayal in Budapest," *Adventist Currents*, September 1986: 10–15.

38 On the history of Hungarian Adventists after World War II, see the dissertation by Zoltán Rajki, *A H. N. Adventista Egyház története 1945 és 1989 között Magyarországon* [The History of the Seventh-day Adventist Church in Hungary between 1945 and 1989], Societas et Ecclesia 6 (Budapest: Advent, 2003); on the schism, see Zoltán Rajki, *Az Egervári-mozgalom: A Keresztény Advent Közösség kialakulása és vallásszabadsági küzdelmei a Kádár-korszak második felében (1975–1990)* [The Egervári Movement: The Formation and Religious Liberty Struggles of the Christian Advent Community in the Second Half of the Kádár Era (1975–1990)] (Budapest: Gondolat Kiadó, 2012).

39 A significant attempt, with meetings, a joint declaration signed, and committees to work out details, was already made in October 1989; see "Hungarian Church – Report," GC Minutes, October 9, 1989, GC Archives.

40 "Adventist Church in Hungary Reconciles with Breakaway Group after 40 Years," *Adventist News Network*, May 1, 2015.

41 Information provided by Csaba Simon, SDA pastor in Békés, and László Szabó, Hungarian lecturer of mission studies, Theologische Hochschule Friedensau, Germany.

## Types of Relationships and Developments

The four case studies have shown that interchurch relationships strongly depend on contextual factors such as (1) the relative strength of Christianity in a country, (2) the degree to which one church has power in a given region, (3) the presence of movements that resemble Adventism ("free churches"), and (4) political factors. The variety of relational options – ranging from positive to negative, from close to distant, and from strong to weak exertion of power by majority churches – is so large that an adequate discussion cannot be presented here. However, it is certainly safe to state that Europe, with its multi-faceted cultural, religious and political contexts, confronted Adventism with an abundance of challenges in terms of relating to the Christian Other – not only in the beginning, when most such encounters were negative and some were characterized by the use of power on the side of the existing religious groups.

On a global level, Adventist interchurch relationships and concomitant concepts of Christian unity (see appendix[42]) slowly developed from a purely spiritual approach [7][43] to a relatively complex whole comprising six types of a total of eight approaches that are common in the Christian world. By the end of the 20th century, some degree of "ecumenism of life" [8] was the norm rather than the exception for many Adventist communities. The denomination participated in the Global Christian Forum and other forum-type processes and events [6], it had experimented with theological dialogues [5 / partly 2]; and Adventists were active in a number of ministry organizations such as the Bible Societies[44] together with certain Evangelicals and in some cases even a rather broad spectrum of churches [4]. In some cases they no longer even rejected ecumenical organizations (which they had done in the late 19th and early 20th centuries, mainly for apprehensions regarding possible Sunday legislation and because any type of unity that did not build on the Sabbath was viewed with utmost suspicion).

This general trend took place both in North America and in Europe, and in some respects more in Europe than in the Adventist land of origin – especially with regard to experiments in conciliar ecumenism. Yet altogether it is not easy to compare what happened on the two continents, for in many cases, developments took place on an

---

42  The appendix summarizes the eight major models of interchurch relations and ecumenism, derived from a comprehensive theory elaborated in Höschele, "Interchurch Relations in Seventh-day Adventist History: A Study in Ecumenics," 15–83.

43  Numbers in brackets indicate the type of interchurch relationships viz. unity concepts connected with them as found in appendix.

44  See Tor Tjeransen, "Adventists and Cooperation with Other Denominations in the Bible Societies," in Reinder Bruinsma, ed., *Faith in Search of Depth and Relevancy: Festschrift in Honour of Dr. Bertil Wiklander* (N.p.: Trans-European Division of Seventh-day Adventists, 2014), 497–506.

altogether local level.[45] In general, it appears that the direction was the same: a diversification of interchurch activities and modes, with full mutual recognition [2] being excluded as a goal and organic union [1] never being an option.

The unwillingness to engage in activities aiming at the latter two types of ecumenical activity (which are the ones most commonly cited as goals in the Ecumenical Movement) also explains why Adventists hardly engaged in bilateral relationships with any specific church anywhere going beyond friendly theological discussion for better mutual understanding. The Protestant state churches or former state churches mainly aim at forming a network of denominations that mutually recognize each other, e.g. in the European Leuenberg community (Community of Protestant Churches in Europe / CPCE). Adventists, by way of contrast, did not view such a type of "church growth" as theologically mandated. Nor did they expect any organization to join theirs (except for other sabbatarians), as Roman Catholics did for a long time, thus aiming at organic union. In this regard, European Adventists did not differ from Adventists elsewhere in any way.

The overall development is, therefore, one from a rather proselytizing and "sectarian" mission mirroring oppression and persecution by the established churches, soon giving way to a cautious general distance to churches as organizations. Non-membership in major ecumenical organizations as a rule changed into observer and guest status in several instances. There were very few direct relationships with particular churches, but a growing appreciation of the Christian Other,[46] which generally went beyond what is common in North America.[47] As in the USA, this largely applied to Protestants and, particularly, to free churches.[48]

---

45   The SDA Periodical Index has hundreds of references tagged "interdenominational cooperation"; most of them are from North America – because the SDAPI mainly reflects magazines from that area. Much of what is reported there concerns sharing pulpits in special cases, making friends with people from other denominations, giving a home to other churches on Sundays, women's meetings, meeting dignitaries of other denominations, and the like. Similar events could have been reported from Europe.

46   See e.g. Bryan W. Ball, *The English Connection: The Puritan Roots of Seventh-Day Adventist Belief* (Cambridge: Clarke, 1981); and Hans Heinz, "Nikolaus Ludwig Graf Zinzendorf: Wertschätzung und Auseinandersetzung aus adventistischer Sicht [Nikolaus Ludwig Count Zinzendorf: Appreciation and Debate from an Adventist Perspective]," *Freikirchenforschung* 3 (1993): 65–75.

47   The exception is the overwhelming North American Adventist appreciation of Mennonites; see Cepha Ang'ira, "A Consistent Esteem: Seventh-Day Adventists' Attitudes towards the Mennonites," research paper, Theologische Hochschule Friedensau, 2010.

48   For the Adventist discourse on Catholicism, see Reinder Bruinsma, *Seventh-Day Adventist Attitudes toward Roman Catholicism, 1844–1965* (Berrien Springs: Andrews University Press, 1994), and "Roman Catholicism," in Ray Dabrowski, ed., *Statements, Guidelines and Other Documents*, 3rd ed. (Washington, D.C.: Communication Department, General Conference of Seventh-day Adventists, 2005), 90–91.

# Appendix: Unity Concepts & Types of Interchurch Relations

| Types | Typical activities | Examples | Nature of unity |
|---|---|---|---|
| **A. Juridical** | | | |
| (1) organic union | unification negotiations | United churches, reversed schisms | institutional, formal |
| (2) mutual recognition | consensus dialogue | Leuenberg Church Fellowship, Porvoo Communion | |
| **B. Cooperative** | | | |
| (3) cooperative-federal | council resolutions | WCC, NCCs, other conciliar types of ecumenism | diaconical-missional |
| (4) alliance model | service strategizing | Bible Societies, interdenominational mission societies | |
| **C. Communicative** | | | |
| (5) "ecumenism of profiles" | debate | denominational alliances (on various levels) | interactive, processual |
| (6) forum | conversation | Global Christian Forum, Christian World Communions | |
| **D. Experiential** | | | |
| (7) "spiritual unity" | prayer, worship | Pietism, mystics, 19th century Disciples of Christ | natural, given, spontaneous |
| (8) "ecumenism of life" | everyday activities | interchurch families | |

# PART IV

# CONCLUSION & BIBLIOGRAPHY

*Rolf J. Pöhler*

# Bringing the Treasures into the City of God: The Contribution of European Adventism to the Global Church

"The city does not need the sun or moon to shine on it. God's glory is its light, and the Lamb is its lamp. The nations will walk by the light of the city. The kings of the world will bring their glory into it. . . . The glory and honor of the nations will be brought into it." (Rev 21:23–26 NIRV)

## Abstract

Adventists in Europe comprise less than 2% of the total membership of the Seventh-day Adventist Church and may seem to be of little significance to the denomination as a whole. In spite it its diversion and lack of cohesion, European Adventism shares certain commonalities – the result of adaptation and acculturation. These may not make it appear an ideal church. Still, the essay argues, Adventism in Europe may contribute significantly to the growth and wellbeing of the global church. Among its "treasures" are its cultural sensitivity, Protestant identity, conscientious adaptability and critical loyalty. The future will show how these features will join up with the missionary zeal, social cohesion and spiritual commitment which Adventist immigrants bring to Europe.

The last grand vision of the Apocalypse of John – and of the Bible itself, for that matter – presents to the marveling spectator a magnificent symbolic description of the bride of Christ in her perfected state (Rev 21:9–22:5). Couched in the imagery of a cubic-shaped city (analogous to the most holy place in the Jewish tabernacle) made of pure gold and precious stones (indicating her priceless value), the New Jerusalem – alias the church of Christ – is honored by the very presence of God, who lives among his people (Rev 21:3). It is "the glory of God" that enlightens the city, making all other sources of light, even the sun, superfluous (Rev 21:11.23; cf. 22:5).

Besides these two references to the Shekinah, the term "glory" (Greek: *doxa*) appears two more times in this context. According to vv. 24–26, the nations and their kings will bring their "glory" into the city of God. The imagery is taken from Isaiah 60, where the future grandeur of Jerusalem after the exile follows the coming of the glory of Yahweh, which causes the nations of the earth and their kings to come to Jerusalem to worship God. On their pilgrimage to the city they bring with them their "glory," that is, their wealth and treasures (Isa 60:5.9.11.13; cf. 66:12) to be used as sacrifices and to adorn the temple.

This apocalyptic vision refers to the bride of Christ in the eternal kingdom to be established on the new earth (Rev 21:1-2); still, it may also contain a valuable lesson for the church in its present, earthly state. Even today, the church may be compared to a city (Matt 5:14; Heb 12:22), a temple (1 Cor 3:16–17; Eph 2:19–22; 1 Pet 2:4–8), God's people/Israel (1 Pet 2:9; Gal 6:16) and the bride of Christ (2 Cor 11:2; Eph 5:22–32; Rev 19:7). While the reference to "nations" and "kings" in John's vision is due to its rootedness in Isaiah's down-to-earth expectation of a future national restitution of Israel and should, therefore, not be taken literally, it has a more immediate bearing on a church whose members come from "every nation, tribe, language, and people" (Rev 14:7 NIV).[1]

Today, the Seventh-day Adventist Church likes to characterize itself as a "world church" and proudly displays its multicultural makeup. One of the most impressive events at a so-called "General Conference" is the pageant of the nations, when representatives of about 200 countries dressed in their national costumes walk across the stage in front of delegates and visitors from all over the globe. The vast diversity and multiethnic composition is one of the greatest assets of the Adventist church, but also one of its biggest challenges. How can this huge resource of cultures and experiences, traditions and insights, talents and commitments be utilized for the benefit of the whole church in an incredibly multifarious world?

Compared to the fast-growing membership of more than 22 million people, Adventists in Europe make up only a fraction of the total membership of the church (< 2%). They may become even more marginal in the future with the center of gravity moving steadily toward the global South. Can and will European Adventists contribute something significant and lasting to the world church currently and in years to come? Will they be remembered for dirndls and lederhosen, Swiss chocolate and Eurodollars or for other treasures they bring into the city of God? In what way can European Adventism – if there is such a thing at all – enrich the global Adventist community? And is such an input desired at all by the leadership of the church and by fellow believers in other world regions, or are European Adventists regarded as too insignificant and idiosyncratic to be considered a blessing to the global church?

## Is There Room for a Regional Adventism? Missiological Considerations

The first time I seriously asked myself this question was when, in 2012, I was invited to Australia to give some presentations in Sydney and at Avondale College. Until then, my life and work had exclusively centered on Europe and North America. To visit the region "Down Under" provided a new experience and challenge to me. Could I, as a European, contribute something to my colleagues and fellow believers on the other side of the globe? Was I to assume that my own cultural imprint, faith experience and theological stance would be applicable and relevant in a quite

---

1    What has been said so far can be applied to the church of Christ in general – at all times and in all places. In view of the precise theme of this symposium, I will limit myself in this essay to the Seventh-day Adventist Church.

different setting of a distant continent? With such thoughts in mind, I prepared a presentation for the Avondale Staff Colloquium on the question, "Is there a place for a 'regional theology' in Adventism?" As I recall it, it got the liveliest response from the audience during my stay in Australia.

Based on my doctoral research on doctrinal developments in Adventism, there can be no question that Adventist theology underwent significant changes in the course of time, both with regard to basic teachings (like the Trinity) and distinctive doctrines (like the sanctuary). These developments were partly homogeneous (deepening existing views), partly heterogeneous (correcting previous beliefs) in nature. Among the factors contributing to these adjustments were prophetic disconfirmation (like the disappointment of 1844 and the outcome of WWI), new cultural experiences (e.g., in mission fields) and church growth and internationalization. In other words, changing contexts breed new convictions.[2]

What holds true for a longitudinal (chronological) study of development is no less applicable to a cross-sectional (contemporaneous) analysis. As new insights and customs do not necessarily replace old (historic) views and habits but may exist side by side with them, so also in varying cultural, religious and social settings different positions and traditions may arise and carry the day. Inevitably, this brings forth a certain diversity of views and customs in the church. These, too, may be either homogeneous (harmonious) or heterogeneous (contrasting) in character. Inasmuch as culture and religion, society and church constantly interact, faith is always, to some degree, contextual and acculturated in a specific time and place. (Still, it should not be bound to it but transcend it.) Thus, different and even diverse manifestations of Seventh-day Adventism are possible, if not to be expected.

According to Hanz Gutierrez,[3] "there is today no one universal Adventism, culturally neutral and valid everywhere. There are rather various Adventisms, complementary, coexisting, but also irreducibly in tension with each other. European Adventism legitimately represents one of them."[4] While the claim of multiple Adventisms may be seen as an exaggeration, it cannot be questioned that the globalization of the Adventist church entails an increasing amount of local and regional peculiarities. The concerned and sustained effort by the denomination's top leadership to foster church unity by imposing uniformity of beliefs and policies on a worldwide scale is telling evidence of the very existence of such diversities.

2    For details, see Rolf J. Pöhler, *Continuity and Change in Adventist Teaching: A Case Study in Doctrinal Development,* Friedensauer Schriftenreihe, Series A: Theologie, vol. 3 (Frankfurt: Peter Lang, 2000).

3    Hanz Gutierrez is a Peruvian theologian, philosopher and physician. Currently he is Chair of the Systematic Theology Department at the Italian Adventist Theological School of Villa Aurora and director of the CECSUR (Cultural Center for Human and Religious Sciences) in Florence, Italy.

4    Hanz Gutierrez, "The De-Europeanization of European Adventism – European Holzwege II" (10 July 2014): accessed July 10, 2018, https://spectrummagazine.org/article/c olumn/2014/07/10/de-europeanization-european-adventism-%25E2%2580%2593-european-holzwege-ii.

Seen from a missiological perspective, the divine commission to bring the gospel to everyone and to plant churches everywhere implies the dynamic, cross-cultural interaction between the bearers and the recipients of the message. While the eternal gospel is universally relevant and applicable, its proclamation must be adjusted to the understanding and needs of the people it is supposed to reach. In other words, the global outreach of the church requires the conscious adaptation and responsible acculturation to the respective local contexts.[5] After all, it does make a substantial difference whether the Adventist message enters a Hindu, Buddhist, Islamic or Traditionalist culture in the 10/40 window or an Eastern Orthodox or a secular/postmodern society in Europe. Keeping the world church together requires genuine appreciation of the variety of manifestations and indigenizations of the Adventist faith and ethos.

## Adventism in Europe or European Adventism? Empirical Observations

Looking at the Seventh-day Adventist Church in Europe, the question needs to be asked at the outset, is there such a thing as a "European Adventism" at all, showing some kind of cohesion and solidarity? There are several reasons why this expression may seem rather inappropriate and actually misleading.

To begin with, of the 47 countries of the European subcontinent (population: 750 million), only 28 belong to the European Union (500 million inhabitants). Even this conglomerate of geographic regions and climate zones, political systems and economic divides, cultures and languages can hardly be called a "unit." True, the European Union has overcome the bellicose nationalism that had characterized Europe in the past (leading to two world wars that started in Europe) and has created the so-called "Eurozone," an economic and monetary union comprising 19 countries (population: 337 million). However, recent developments give reason to expect that the centrifugal forces of nationalism will trump the willingness to sacrifice privileges for the sake of the common good. Thus, to speak of a "European Union" may one day turn out to be an anachronistic misnomer. Is the project "Europe" failing and falling apart?

In addition, from an Adventist prophetic perspective, the European Union may be interpreted as a venture that is doomed to fail from the outset. Traditionally, Adventists have understood Daniel 2:41–44 to refer to Europe (the heir of the Roman Empire) as "a divided kingdom," made up of a mixture of strong and brittle nations "that will not remain united" (NIV). When, in 1957, the European Economic Community was formed, Adventist evangelists prophesied its downfall in no uncertain terms. While these confident predictions have not come true (yet) and are rarely expressed today, they may linger on subconsciously in the Adventist mind,

---

5   On this, see Chigemezi Nnadozie Wogu's paper in this volume ("Scripture, Traditions, and Contexts: European Adventist Approaches to Contextualization").

preventing any serious attempt by European Adventists to create a kind of "Adventist European Union" (or Division, for that matter) on their own. Conversely, a united European Adventism might become a showcase model for the biblical and Adventist vision of a church comprised of people from "every nation, tribe, language, and people."

But even if the forming of a united Adventist church in Europe would gain ground among church members and become the aspiration of the leadership of the European Divisions and Unions, there would be formidable challenges in the way of such an endeavor. The very diversity of history, languages and cultures may prove to be an unsurmountable obstacle.[6] Europe is irreducibly and irreversibly heterogeneous and the Adventist church has a share in this condition. To indicate the compartmentalized state of Adventism in Europe: There are ca. 375,000 church members in the three European Divisions, comprising more than 100 Unions, Conferences and Local Fields.[7] In comparison, the Southern Union Conference in the North American Division alone has a membership of 290,000 in only eight Conferences.

There are few signs indicating that a "European Adventism" is actually emerging. There is fairly little cooperation between the three Divisions. In spite of long-held notions regarding the desirability of an Adventist university in Europe, the main graduate schools (Collonges, Friedensau, Newbold) are acting quite independently.[8] Union Conferences try to run their own theological seminaries offering Master's programs. Cultural and theological reservations add to a situation that places heavy financial burdens on the denomination. Apart from some notable exceptions, the trend seems to be dispersal rather than integration.[9]

Thus, it appears that European Adventists – even in the higher echelons of the church – lack a true *Wir-Gefühl* (feeling of togetherness), a shared vision and a common goal. Their allegiance to the worldwide Adventist church may actually be more pronounced than is their sense of belonging together and of facing common challenges peculiar to the European continent. On the whole, Adventists in Europe do not display a notable European Adventist identity. While they identify each with

6    The European Union has 24 official languages, with English, French and German being considered procedural languages. The Sabbath Worship Service of the Belgian-Luxembourg Conference (2,500 members) in Brussels, where I preached some years ago, was opened in ten languages.

7    See "2017 Annual Statistical Report: 153rd Report of the General Conference of Seventh-day Adventists for 2015 and 2016," (Maryland: Office of Archives, Statistics and Research, 2018, revised): accessed, May 45, 2018, http://documents.adventistarchives.org/St atistics/ASR/ASR2017.pdf.

8    There is no sustained cooperation between them. Together, the three schools have (only) about 550 students (ibid.).

9    At the last European Theology Teachers Convention (ETTC) in 2017, a European Adventist Society of Theology and Religious Studies (EASTRS) was launched. The scholarly journal *Spes Christiana*, published by Friedensau University, is projected to be co-edited by faculty members from several major institutions.

their own countries and cultures, their linkage with Adventism in other European countries and cultures can hardly be felt.

At the same time, however, it must be recognized that Adventism in Europe shares commonalities that are binding the different church entities and regions together as companions in fate. In spite of its cultural and religious diversity, internal tensions, contradictions and antagonisms, "Europe" denotes a world region distinguished by its common history, cultural imprint, economic systems, political institutions and juridical traditions. More than any other continent (except Australia), Europe is characterized also by secularism and postmodernism. While 75% of the population still formally belongs to a Christian church, in some regions only a small minority are practicing Christians (especially in Czechia and the former GDR). Surveys generally indicate that this trend will continue and become even more pronounced.

This situation creates a formidable challenge for Adventists in Europe. To live in a predominantly secular and postmodern society shapes the thinking and doing of Christians – including Adventists – unavoidably and in a sustained manner. The peculiarities of European Adventism are to a considerable extent due to this fact. Just as Adventists living in a Buddhist, Hindu, Islamic or Jewish culture need to accommodate to their environment, so European Adventists are also adjusting to their cultural setting. Consequently, missionary concepts and evangelistic methods, too, must be adapted to an audience that views organized religion quite critically and no longer shares many of the traditional Christian beliefs and values.[10] New converts and a new generation of Adventists are echoing the society in which they live.

Seen from the outside, European Adventists may, therefore, appear somewhat worldly and lacking in missionary zeal. Besides, there seems to be a want of theological orthodoxy, denominational identity and church loyalty. As a result, European Adventists are generally not regarded as role models by the worldwide Adventist community. However, to view the Adventist church in Europe from the vantage point of a more religious, traditional or submissive society may easily lead to false conclusions and premature judgments. In order to understand the situation and challenges of European Adventists and appreciate their manifestation of the Adventist faith, it is important to take an internal perspective. This may even help prepare the global Adventist church for the challenges of the future – if not today. Thus, the reality faced by European Adventism now may be a herald of what tomorrow will be happening in other parts of the world, too. European Adventists may therefore have a pioneering role in the church.

10   The situation in Eastern and Southeastern Europe is somewhat different because of the influence of the Orthodox Church and also for other historical and cultural reasons.

# How Can European Adventism Enrich the World Church? Theological Reflections

The remainder of this essay will be devoted to the question, Can Euro-Adventism effectively enrich the world church and, if so, in what ways can it contribute to the life and progress of the denomination? In the past, Europe has supported the Adventist mission in a significant way, particularly through money and manpower. Tithe and mission offerings flowing from the more affluent countries in Europe have raised the budget of the General Conference and enabled it to support mission endeavors in new fields.[11] And in the latter part of the twentieth century, a number of theologians coming from and/or being educated in Europe have helped in the buildup of Andrews University and its Theological Seminary, the flagship educational institution of the church. They have all left their distinguished marks on the worldwide church.[12]

The rapid increase in church membership in the Two-Thirds World, economic advances of the church in other regions outside of North America, and the rising number of educational institutions worldwide have left Europe as being of lesser importance for global Adventism. Money and manpower from the Old World no longer contribute to the church as formerly. Will European Adventism, at last, sink into insignificance? Not necessarily. There may be other, less visible but no less valuable gifts which Europe can share with the rest of the Adventist world. The intellectual, religious, political, cultural and social history and context of Europe have left a permanent imprint on Christianity in general and on Adventism in particular and have conveyed important lessons that should not be forgotten. It is these treasures that European Adventism can contribute to the world church.[13]

## Cultural Sensitivity

Arguably, no one has had a more formative influence on European Adventism than Ludwig R. Conradi, the German-born pioneer missionary and longtime leader of the Adventist mission work in Europe.[14] For almost half a century, he shaped the face and theology of Adventism, not only in Germany but also in central and eastern

---

11   For example, the Week of Prayer offerings in the German-speaking countries are consistently a multiple of what is donated elsewhere in relation to tithes and other financial contributions.

12   For example, Niels-Erik A. Andreasen, Raoul Dederen, Gerhard F. Hasel, Hans K. LaRondelle, and Peter M. van Bemmelen. Mention should also be made of archeologist Siegfried H. Horn and of former General Conference President Jan Paulsen.

13   The following deliberations reflect this author's personal biography and social upbringing in (the Western part of) Germany.

14   This statement hints at the rivalry that existed between the strong-willed leader and the influential prophet, Ellen White.

Europe.[15] His name stands for the distinct kind of Adventism that spread to much
of Europe and even beyond.[16] Conradi's far-sighted and successful mission strategy
was characterized by a sensible accommodation to the respective political, cultural
and religious context. The strong prejudice and opposition of the established
(national or people's) churches to any new religious movements prompted him to
keep distinctive and potentially divisive teachings in the background. Only after the
confidence of the people had been won were new and unknown truths to be
preached. The primary concern was to find *Anknüpfungspunkte* (points of contact)
that would create interest in new truths.[17]

To this effect, presentations of Bible truth were supported by references to Church
Fathers, Protestant theologians and Catholic authors. "In this way, the orthodoxy of
the Adventist faith was to be substantiated by taking into account contemporary
Protestant trends and church historical research."[18] Instead of going on the offensive
and engaging in polemical debates, the eternal gospel was presented in a prophetic
framework, showing concurrences with other believing Christians and compatibility
with various Protestant traditions. A more recent example of such a bridge-building
approach can be found in a little book by Otto Gmehling, President of the Central
European Division from 1964 to 1970. In about 60 pages he quotes non-Adventist
authors – mostly 20th century theologians – 30 times. This indicates not only his
erudition but also his objective to locate Adventism in European theological thought
and to spell it out as a theologically reflected expression of Christianity.[19]

15  "Vom ersten Tag seines Wirkens als adventistischer Missionar prägte Conradi fast für ein
    halbes Jahrhundert die deutschen und darüber hinaus die mittel- und osteuropäischen
    Adventgemeinden in Lehre und Erscheinungsbild maßgeblich." ["From the first day of his
    ministry as an Adventist missionary, Conradi shaped the German – and beyond that, the
    Central and Eastern European – Adventist churches in teaching and appearance.] Johannes
    Hartlapp, *Siebenten-Tags-Adventisten im Nationalsozialismus* (Göttingen: V&R unipress,
    2008), 35.

16  Adventist missionary work in Europe had officially started with John N. Andrews, who, in
    1874, had moved to Basel and worked from there primarily as writer and editor until his death
    in 1883. To what degree he had promoted a European kind of Adventism, is a matter of
    debate. For an enlightening discussion of his mission strategy as well as its success and failure,
    see Gilbert M. Valentine, "J. N. Andrews and the 'Success' of the European Mission," in this
    volume.

17  On Conradi's missionary approach, see Daniel Heinz, *Ludwig Richard Conradi: Missionar,
    Evangelist und Organisator der Siebenten-Tags-Adventisten in Europa* (Frankfurt: Lang,
    1998); idem, "The Development of Seventh-day Adventist Missionary Dynamic in Europe:
    Assessing the Contributions of Michael B. Czechowski, John N. Andrews, and Ludwig R.
    Conradi," in *Parochialism, Pluralism and Contextualization: Challenges to Adventist Mission
    in Europe 19th – 21st Centuries,* eds. David J. B. Trim and Daniel Heinz (Frankfurt: Lang,
    2010), 51–62; and Erich W. Baumgartner, "Charisma and Contextualization: Leadership
    Lessons from the Emerging Adventist Church in Central Europe, 1864–1914," ibid., 63–82.

18  Hartlapp, 72.

19  Otto Gmehling, *Christus der Herr im Glauben und Leben der Siebenten-Tags-Adventisten*
    (Hamburg: Advent-Verlag, 1965).

Conradi's strategic missionary vision entailed not only methods adapted to changing circumstances, but also a different way of arguing in presenting the Advent(ist) message. He wanted to overcome the stigma of Sabbathkeepers as an American "sect" by presenting them as an indigenous Protestant movement rooted in European culture. To this end, he conducted extensive historical research showing that the historicist interpretation of Daniel and the Revelation was known in Europe long before and independent of William Miller. The same also holds true for the historical proof that the Sabbath had been observed by Christian groups in the Old World. Conradi saw in Sabbath-keeping Adventism the continuation and completion of the European revival movements that had their origin in the sixteenth-century Reformation. Thus, the Reformers, Anabaptists, Puritans, Pietists, Moravians and other groups were actually European precursors of the end-time Adventist movement.

More than in other European regions, Conradi's contextualizing approach to mission has sharpened the profile of German Adventism as a church committed to the principles and ethos of the Protestant Reformation. Thus, Adventists in Germany prefer to see themselves, not as a national branch of an American movement, but as an indigenous free church molded by the European context and culture.

## Protestant Identity

It is this Protestant heritage that gives European Adventism its special flavor. While the key players of the sixteenth-century Reformation were living in central Europe, the impact of the events they set in motion could be felt all over Europe and even beyond. The Reformation and the Counter-Reformation changed not only the Christian church but even the course of history. Martin Luther's courageous stance against a corrupt church and his uncompromising testimony before the Emperor resonated in the hearts and minds of Advent believers who themselves faced opposition and harassment by political and religious powers. Through her book *The Great Controversy,* Ellen White embedded the story of the Reformation deeply in the Adventist mind. It goes without saying that the Adventist church in countries that had witnessed these events and/or were most affected by them see these events as part of their own history.

Theologically speaking, the so-called *particula exclusiva (sola gratia, sola fide, solus Christus, sola scriptura)* provide the Adventist message with a sound biblical foundation and a crucial hermeneutical criterion. However, the consistent application of these Protestant principles is more an aspiration than a reality. For example, the 1888 General Conference is often said to have been the turning point from a works-and-law-oriented theology to a faith and grace emphasis. However, the 1888 revival was no clear-cut affirmation of Reformation theology as can be seen by the ensuing perfectionism of its proponents. The ambient noise of the Methodist and Holiness movements produced a somewhat different understanding of and emphasis on salvation than is the case in a Lutheran and Reformed setting in Europe.

The same can be said about the Christocentric principle. In a leaflet printed in 1905 for a conference of the *Deutsche Vereinigung*, a statement entitled "Glaubensgrundsätze der Siebenten-Tags-Adventisten" was enclosed, which is arranged in a strictly Christ-centered manner. In 14 sentences, all points of faith are explicitly related to Jesus Christ – in total 36 times. (I am not aware of any comparable Adventist statement of faith.) Sixty years later, Otto Gmehling, in his aforementioned book, argued that all distinctive Adventist teachings arise from Christ as their center and constitute no sectarian peculiarities.[20] If Adventists want to be truly Christ-centered, then belief in Jesus Christ will not be one doctrine among others but rather the hermeneutical foundation and true center of all teachings, including the distinctive Adventist beliefs. Because of its historical Reformation background, European Adventism is particularly conscious of the need to apply this principle fully in all preaching, teaching, and writing.[21]

Speaking of hermeneutics, Adventist theology has, from the very beginning, acknowledged the sola scriptura principle as foundational to all Christian faith and practice. At the same time, the great esteem Adventists have for their founding mother and gifted prophet has led to conflicting views and practices regarding the proper application of the Protestant Scripture principle. In the new 1980 statement of Fundamental Beliefs, Ellen White's writings were called an authoritative "source of truth" (#17). This phrase was opposed by some Adventists who were aware of its use in Catholicism for church tradition in distinction to the Bible. There were church members and at least one pastor who left the church in protest against this decision. In reaction to it, in the German Church Manual the phrase was translated by "voice of truth" ("eine bevollmächtigte Stimme der Wahrheit"), a rendering that lies in the semantic range of the word "source" but avoids the misleading association with the Catholic two-source theory.[22]

Another illustration for the European Reformation-induced sensitivity of European Adventism is the alternative baptismal vow found in the Church Manual. It consists of only three questions, the second of which reads as follows: "Do you accept the teachings of the Bible as expressed in the Statement of Fundamental Beliefs of the Seventh-day Adventist Church, and do you pledge by God's grace to live in harmony with these teachings?" The expression "these teachings" can be related both

---

20   *Christus der Herr im Glauben und Leben der Siebenten-Tags-Adventisten*, 3.

21   For a discussion of this principle, see Rolf J. Pöhler, "Die Rechtfertigung durch den Glauben als hermeneutisches Prinzip: Christozentrische Schriftauslegung und adventistische Theologie," *Spes Christiana* 11 (2000), 46–60.

22   In 2015, the expression was replaced by the phrase "Her writings speak with prophetic authority" (#18). – "Für Conradi, der ein Leben lang die Vision vor Augen hatte, am Abschluss der von Luther begonnenen Reformation mitzuarbeiten ... musste das fundamentalistische Verhältnis zu Ellen G. White eine Missachtung der Bibel darstellen" ["To Conradi, who for a lifetime envisioned to contribute to the completion of the Reformation begun by Luther ... the fundamentalist relationship to Ellen G. White must have constituted a disregard of the Bible"]. Hartlapp, 241.

to "the teachings of the Bible" or to "the Statement of [Adventist] Fundamental Beliefs," a most unfortunate vagueness that is unacceptable from a true Reformation perspective. Consequently, the German Church Manual has removed the ambiguity by changing the ending of the sentence into *"the teachings of the Word of God."*

Unquestionably, the need for renewal applies to every church – the Adventist denomination not excluded. Every genuine revival and reformation is based on this insight. *Ecclesia Adventistica semper reformanda.* This applies to spiritual matters as much as to theological issues. If the Adventist church wants to remain truly a Protestant church, it should heed the timely counsel of its prophet: "How shall we search the Scriptures? Shall we drive our stakes of doctrine one after another, and then try to make all Scripture meet our established opinions, or shall we take our ideas and views to the Scriptures, and measure our theories on every side by the Scriptures of truth?" (Review & Herald, July 26, 1892). Euro-Adventists with a Reformation imprint are seismographs who sense tremors before others notice them.[23]

## Conscientious Adaptability

To be a Protestant Christian in the spirit of the sixteenth-century Reformers implies the willingness to answer for one's convictions and to take a stand for what is right according to one's conscience – if necessary, even alone against the rest. This is the attitude Adventists have taken up from the beginning, often at a high price. Faced by unsympathetic societies, intolerant churches and repressive states, their commitment to truth as they had come to understand it led to deprivation, suffering, persecution, and even death. During much of the twentieth century, European Adventists experienced tremendous challenges, particularly under the National Socialist and Communist regimes, which were inimical to religion and put severe pressure on those who wanted to live their faith according to their own convictions. Those who stood up for their beliefs were often put in prisons and labor camps, harassed, tortured and killed. The untold story of these faithful witnesses will one day become known.

Under such dire circumstances, believers learned to be circumspect in living out and sharing their faith and to adapt to capricious conditions. Some were more courageous than others. Those carrying responsibility had to weigh the consequences of their actions for their families and churches. In the free West everyone will emerge unscathed if he plasters billboards labeling the pope the antichrist or calls Donald Trump an Egomaniac and a notorious liar. However, making strident attacks in a safe environment that protects freedom of speech and belief is altogether different from risking one's life and liberty under a repressive regime or in view of a hostile church. European Adventists have learned to behave in a more circumspect manner,

---

23   The 2015 ETTC Convention was devoted to the *Ecclesia semper reformanda* principle. See *Ecclesia Reformata, Semper Reformanda,* Proceedings of the European Theology Teachers' Convention, Newbold College of Higher Education, 25–28 March 2015, ed. Jean-Claude Verrecchia (Bracknell, Berks.: Newbold Academic Press, 2016).

to show their loyalty to the state without denying their commitment to God. Their experiences in conscientiously adapting to circumstances are valuable in view of an uncertain future.

Today, Europe is marked by widespread secularism and pronounced individualism. In a postmodern society everyone can believe and live according to his own liking. The resulting freedom and the right of self-determination are a blessing to the church, which no longer faces persecution and oppression. However, there is a downside to this new cultural megatrend. On the one hand, an aggressive secularism can become a new threat to the church, demanding submission to secular values in conflict with biblical views. On the other hand, postmodern relativism with its resulting loss of certainties makes it harder for the church in bringing people to a point where they make firm decisions for Christ and the church. To convey biblical and Adventist beliefs in a pluralist environment is a formidable challenge.[24]

To survive and thrive in the secular and postmodern societies of contemporary Europe, Adventists also need the virtue of conscientious adaptability. With it, European Adventism will not succumb to a secular mentality, which robs faith of its spiritual substance. Nor does it adopt an attitude of total opposition, which denounces the postmodern mindset as intrinsically hostile to the gospel. As under authoritarian regimes, Adventists need to take a stand for what they believe in (even against an uncomprehending majority) and at the same time accommodate to new cultural contexts (without betraying their loyalty to Christ). As in the past, it requires courage and commitment as well as prudence and circumspection. As different as these contexts seem to be, they have at least two things in common: The church may seem to be unable to cope with the challenges it faces, but God still has his faithful witnesses. Life-style evangelism remains the most effective form of winning disciples for Christ.

## Critical Loyalty

Conradi's missionary strategy was linked to his strong drive for independence. From 1901 until 1907, he was the leader of a "European General Conference," an indication of the rivalry existing between him and the "General Conference" located in the United States. The tensions concerned not only matters of church organization but also of theology. In Conradi's mind, European Adventism was to be a kind of counter project to the American Advent movement. Though these ideas did not meet with approval by leaders and members alike, until today there remains a certain suspicion that European – or, more precisely, German – Adventism is on an independent course trying to distance itself from the world church. Two world wars, which placed America and Germany in direct conflict with each other, and the

24  See Rolf J. Pöhler, "Religious Pluralism: A Challenge to the Contemporary Church," in *Cast the Net on the Right Side ...: Seventh-day Adventists Face the Isms,* eds. R. Lehmann, J. Mahon, B. Schantz (Newbold College, Bracknell, Berkshire: European Institute of World Mission, 1993), 81–89.

downsizing of the "Central European Division" to comprise only Germany after World War II have kept this notion alive. The socialist GDR and the Berlin Wall intensified the relative isolation of Germany.

Apart from Conradi's regrettable defection and the political fallout of two world wars, there is also a feeling that in some parts of Europe, not least in Germany, there exists a certain nonconformist, critical mentality, particularly among the more educated members of the church. From an American viewpoint, Europeans may seem, in part, pretty intellectual, if not arrogant. Critical questions regarding certain church teachings (e.g., on creation, the sanctuary, and Ellen White) and policy decisions (like on women's ordination) reinforce the notion that European Adventism is, to some degree, insubordinate.

From a European perspective, this seeming spirit of independence is an expression of the intellectual mindset that characterized Europe since the rise of rationalism, the Renaissance, the Reformation and the Enlightenment. In addition, the history of Europe has amply demonstrated the consequences of following authorities uncritically. The ability to ask probing questions and the willingness to critique and to disagree is part and parcel of the European mentality. Unsurprisingly, Adventists are participating in it. According to Daniel Heinz, in German Adventism there exists "a general critical mood, which should not at all be judged negatively, for it can contribute in a fruitful way to the clarification and deepening of the Adventist deposit of faith."[25] This statement can be applied to other parts of Europe as well.

A fitting illustration for this is the extensive adaptation of the Sabbath School Quarterly for the German and Swiss churches. Since 1990, a group of pastors have been reviewing and actually rewriting the Quarterly in order to make it more palatable to those church members who are dissatisfied with the American Standard Edition. The two criteria for the reworking of the material are Biblical faithfulness and cultural contextuality. A majority of church members prepare for Sabbath School with the help of the German edition, while others use the (translated) Standard Edition. Coupled with this alternative, in Germany, Sabbath School attendance is considerably higher than in other parts of the (Western) world. In spite of this success story, there is strong opposition coming from a small but vocal segment of the church, reinforced by some top leaders of the church who consider the *one* Quarterly indispensable for keeping the worldwide church doctrinally united. For years, there was considerable pressure to stop the project.

This example illustrates the challenge faced by Adventism in Europe. On the one hand, it is a loyal part of the worldwide Adventist church and will remain so in the future. On the other hand, it is called by God to bring the Advent(ist) message to the peoples of Europe in a way they can understand and accept. This requires a conscious attempt to reach the people where they are (and not where others may be).

25  "… eine allgemeine geistig kritische Gestimmtheit, die dem deutschen Adventismus eignet und durchaus nicht negativ beurteilt werden sollte, da sie in fruchtbarer Weise zur Klärung und Vertiefung des adventistischen Glaubensgutes beitragen kann." Heinz, *Ludwig Richard Conradi*, 111.

Encouraging open and unbiased Bible study is not an option, but a necessity. A faithful servant will give others food at the proper time and in a proper manner (Matt 24:45).

Critical loyalty calls for loyal criticism. The Seventh-day Adventist Church needs people who are loyal to it, but not uncritical, and who criticize it, when needed, out of loyalty. European Adventists are in a good position to do so. Given the needed mental astuteness, the experience of walking upright in the face of opposition, and a first-hand knowledge of the needs of people around them, Adventists across Europe constitute a widely varied community that, while being united with the global Adventist church, is rooted in the contemporary culture, inspired by a Protestant ethos, and committed to God's truth.

## Conclusion

The above-named treasures are not the exclusive possession of European Adventism or even of global Adventism, for that matter. They are also found in other places and churches. Still, they are somewhat typical for European Adventism. Inasmuch as experience shapes theology – one is reminded here of Martin Luther's dictum *sola experientia facit theologum* – the experience of Adventists on the European continent has formed their DNA. It is therefore pertinent to develop a church profile that is genuinely European.[26] As such, it can and will be a benefit to Adventists in other regions of the world. This does not imply any claim of superiority or specialness. To the contrary, small as it is in numbers compared to the more than 22 million Adventists worldwide, European Adventism may give a humble testimony to the miraculous guidance and remarkable blessing it has received throughout the decades. The rich diversity of manifestations and experiences within European Adventism is in itself a reason to be grateful.

What of the future? For quite some time now, European Adventism has been undergoing lasting changes due to the influx of Adventist immigrants. This will most likely continue. As a result, the term "European Adventism" will develop new and different meanings. Will this lead to a diffusion of European traits with those coming from other cultures of the world and will it finally make European Adventism indistinguishable from the rest of the Adventist world? While I hope that European Adventism will not lose its special profile, watering down its identity, I also believe that there must be no withdrawal into an introspective and isolated mentality. Not only are immigrants here to stay, they can also enrich the Old Continent by their own gifts. We must learn to recognize and appreciate the splendor they bring: young

---

26  Cf. Rolf J. Pöhler, "Die theologische Entwicklung und Eigenheit des deutschen Adventismus," in *Adventhoffnung für Deutschland: Die Mission der Siebenten-Tags-Adventisten von Conradi bis heute,* eds. Daniel Heinz and Werner E. Lange (Lüneburg: Saatkorn-Verlag, Abt. Advent-Verlag, 2014), 249–262.

believers, a missionary spirit, social cohesion, commitment and enthusiasm, and much more.

In addition, European Adventism must not foster a Eurocentrism in place of a global perspective. We live in *one* world and Christ has *one* church on earth. As Hanz Gutierrez has pointed out, European Adventists must learn to dialogue at three levels: with European society, with global Adventism, and within European Adventism itself. "These various Adventisms present in Europe need to learn to interact, dialogue and confront each other with respect – critically, but also with generosity." While the "De-Europeanization of European Adventism" through demographic (ethnic) changes may be securing its survival, it is also jeopardizing its uniqueness by blending with a globalized form of Adventism.[27] Only the future will tell which direction European Adventism will be taking.

27  See the following articles by Hanz Gutierrez, "The Eurosceptic Adventist Soul – European Holzwege I," June 12, 2014, https://spectrummagazine.org/article/ column/2014/06/12/ eurosceptic-adventist-soul-%E2%80%93-european-holzwege-i; "The De-Europeanization of European Adventism – European Holzwege II" July 10 2014, https://spectrummagazine. org/article/column/2014/07/10/de-europeanization-european-adventism-%E2%80%93-european-holzwege-ii; "For a European Dialogical and Experimental Adventism – European Holzwege III," August 14, 2014, https://spectrummagazine.org/article/column/2014/08/ 14/european-dialogical-and-experimental-adventism-%E2%80%93-european-holzwege-iii; "From a Voracious to a Wise Depressive Narcissism – On European Adventism – I," April 9, 2015, https://spectrum magazine.org/article/2015/04/09/voracious-wise-depressive-narcissism-european-adventism-i; "Euthanasia and Christian identity: The Dutch Way. On European Adventism II," May 14, 2015, https://spectrummagazine.org/article/2015/05/14/ euthanasia-and-christian-identity-dutch-way-european-adventism-ii; "Adventist Vegetarian ism, The Czech Way – On European Adventism III," June 11, 2015, https://spectrummag azine. org/article/2015/06/11/adventist-vegetarianism-czech-way-%E2%80%93-european-adventism-iii.

*Jón Hjörleifur Stefánsson and Eudritch Jean*

## Seventh-day Adventism in Europe: A Working Bibliography

This is one of the first academic bibliographies on Seventh-day Adventism in Europe, if not the first one. Since this academic field is young and the sources scattered, the bibliography is of modest proportions and a work in progress. We apologize for any important works that we overlooked – and would appreciate it if such information would be conveyed to us. Despite its incompleteness, this bibliography is a start, and hopefully a helpful one to those who want to study further.

The bibliography begins with works that cover the European continent or a region of it, works on important Seventh-day Adventist (SDA) pioneers in Europe, and then covers the largest offshoot group in Europe (the Reform Adventist Movement). The main part of the bibliography is dedicated to the various European countries alphabetically. The English alphabetical order is followed. This means that diacritics are ignored, and all letters are treated like their closest English counterparts. When punctuation marks are part of the title, the punctuation marks follow the rules of the language in which the work was written.

Please note that each section is divided into two parts. Published books, pamphlets, and articles appear first, and unpublished theses, dissertations, and manuscripts follow after the space of one line. No titles were located for the history of the SDA Church in the following European countries: Cyprus, the Faroe Islands, Kosovo, the microstates (Andorra, Liechtenstein, Malta, Monaco, San Marino, and the Vatican), Montenegro, North Macedonia, and Slovenia.

When recording theses and diploma works that were written at SDA colleges in Europe, the colleges are referred to by their English names. For those who know them by their native names, both are listed here for clarification:

| | |
|---|---|
| Adriatic Union College | Adventističko teološko visoko učilište |
| Adventist University of France–Collonges | Campus Adventiste du Saleve |
| Belgrade Theological Seminary | Beogradski Teološki Fakultet |
| Friedensau Adventist University | Theologische Hochschule Friedensau |
| Hungarian Adventist Theological College | Adventista Teologiai Foiskola |
| Italian Adventist University "Villa Aurora" | Istituto Avventista di Cultura Biblica Villa Aurora |
| Polish Senior College of Theology and Humanities | Wyzsza Szkola Teologiczno-Humanistyczna |

| | |
|---|---|
| Sazava Theological Seminary | Teologický seminář CASD |
| Romanian Adventist Theological Institute | Institutul Teologic Adventist |
| Zaoksky Adventist University | Zaokskaya Dukhovnaya Akademiya |

Some of the theses and dissertations are available online. To save space the URLs will not be given for each item. Instead, note how the databases can be accessed: those available at Andrews University can be found by searching at Digital Commons, https://digitalcommons.andrews.edu. Those from the Italian Adventist University are listed on their website, http://www.villaaurora.it, under Corsi › Facoltà die Teologia › Elenco laureate, and marked with a floppy disk symbol.

The compilers gleaned as many titles as they could from existing bibliographies and sources. [1] We also relied largely on the help of personal contacts and sister institutions. We want especially to thank Adrian Neagu (Romania), Andris Pešelis (Latvia), Aneta Berkan (Poland), Daniel Heinz (Austria/Germany), Iosif Diaconu (Romania), Yurii Zakhvataiev (Russia), Ivaylo Vasilev Petrov (Bulgaria), Klaudia Głowacka (Poland), Tiziano Rimoldi (Italy), Yvonne Johansson Öster (Sweden), the staff at the Center for Adventist Research (USA) and the Finnish SDA Archives for their assistance and contributions. Given the nature of the project, we have undoubtedly overlooked some mistakes and errors, and for these we ourselves accept full responsibility. Thankfully, Friedensau Adventist University will make an online version of this bibliography available on their website, and that version will continue to be corrected and updated.

In addition to this bibliography, we recommend the *Seventh-day Adventist Encyclopedia*, Gary Land's *Historical Dictionary of Seventh-day Adventists*, and the forthcoming *Encyclopedia of Seventh-day Adventists*. These works contain articles on both European countries and individuals, which were too numerous (and often too short) to be added to the present work.

***

---

1    Gilbert Abella and Vera May Schwarz, "Dissertations, Theses, and Major Research Papers Related to the Seventh-day Adventist Church: A Bibliography," TMs, Loma Linda University, 1988; Gary Land, "Bibliography," Historical Dictionary of the Seventh-day Adventists, Historical Dictionaries of Religions, Philosophies, and Movements 56 (Lanham, MD: Scarecrow Press, 2005), 381–469; Jón Hjörleifur Stefánsson and Terry Dwain Robertson, "Seventh-day Adventist Dissertations and Theses in Religion," Faculty Publications 3, Digital Commons, Andrews University, 2015.

# The Continent or Specific Regions

## Published

*52. Generalkonferenz der Siebenten-Tags-Adventisten. Wien, Österreich 10–19 Juli 1975.* Vienna: Austrian Union of SDAs, 1975. 62 pp.

"1874–1974: Centenaire de l'Eglise Adventiste en Europe." *Revue Adventiste,* October 1974. A special issue. 24 pp.

Andross, Matilda Erickson. *Sunshine and Shadow in Southern Europe.* Washington, DC: Review and Herald, 1939. 192 pp.

Baumgartner, Erich W. "Charisma and Contextualization: Leadership Lessons from the Emerging Adventist Church in Central Europe, 1864–1914." In *Parochialism, Pluralism, and Contextualization,* edited by Trim and Heinz, 63–81.

Baumgartner, Erich W., ed. *Re-Visioning Adventist Mission in Europe.* Berrien Springs, MI: Andrews University Press, 1998. xiv, 280 pp.

*Bericht über den ersten Kongreß der Europäischen Adventjugend in Chemnitz vom 17. bis zum 22. Juli 1928.* Hamburg: Advent-Verlag, 1928. 103 pp.

*Biographisch-Bibliographisches Kirchenlexikon.* Nordhausen: Verlag Traugott Bautz, 1975–. Contains many entries by Daniel Heinz on SDAs, mostly from Germany and Russia.

Christian, Lewis Harrison. *Pioneers and Builders of the Adventist Cause in Europe.* Mountain View, CA: Pacific Press, 1937. 164 pp.

Christian, Lewis Harrison. *Sons of the North and Their Share in the Advent Movement.* Mountain View, CA: Pacific Press, 1942. 250 pp.

"Conférence Générale Utrecht 1995." *Revue Adventiste,* September 1995. 16 pp. Special issue on the 56th session of the General Conference, held in Utrecht, Netherlands.

Dumitrescu, Cristian. *"Historical Sketches of the Foreign Missions of the Seventh-day Adventists."* In *The Ellen G. White Encyclopedia,* edited by Fortin and Moon, 870.

Dunton, Hugh, Daniel Heinz, Dennis Porter, and Ronald Strasdowski, eds. *Heirs of the Reformation: The Story of Seventh-day Adventists in Europe.* Grantham: Stanborough Press, 1997. 274 pp.

Fortin, Denis, and Jerry Moon, eds. *The Ellen G. White Encyclopedia.* Hagerstown, MD: Review and Herald, 2013. 1465 pp. Articles cited separately.

Gerber, Robert. *Le mouvement adventiste: Origines et développement.* Dammarie-les-Lys: Les Signes de Temps, 1950. 271 pp.

Heinz, Daniel. "Adventist Opposition to War in Europe: Cases of Nonconformity and Conscientious Objection." In *Adventists and Military Service: Biblical, Historical, and Ethical Perspectives,* edited by Frank Hasel, Barna Magyarosi, and Stefan Höschele, 135–49. Madrid: Safeliz, 2019.

Heinz, Daniel. "Christian, Lewis Harrison." In *The Ellen G. White Encyclopedia*, edited by Fortin and Moon, 342.

Heinz, Daniel. "Das Historische Archiv der Siebenten-Tags-Adventisten in Europa." In *Geschichte—Gesellschaft—Gerechtigkeit: Festschrift für Baldur Pfeiffer zum 70. Geburtstag*, edited by Johannes Hartlapp and Stefan Höschele, 41–50. Berlin: Frank und Timme, 2007.

Heinz, Daniel. "The Development of Seventh-day Adventist Missionary Dynamic in Europe: Assessing the Contributions of Michael B. Czechowski, John N. Andrews, and Ludwig R. Conradi." *Spes Christiana* 11 (2000): 128–39. Also in *Parochialism, Pluralism, and Contextualization*, edited by Trim and Heinz, 51–61.

Heinz, Daniel. "Freikirchliche Märtyrer im 20. Jahrhundert: Definitionen Problemfelder und Perspektiven der Forschung." *Evangelische Arbeitsgemeinschaft für Kirchliche Zeitgeschichte—Mitteilungen* 22 (2004): 65–80.

Heinz, Daniel. "The Law of God, Individual Conscience, and Antimilitarism: Seventh-day Adventist Commitment to Nonviolence." In *Szabadegyházak, vallási kisebbségek és a diktatúrák Európában a 20. században,* edited by Daniel Heinz, Rajki Zoltán, and Simon Ervin, 57–71. Budapest: Gondolat Kiadó, 2013.

Heinz, Daniel. "Origin and Growth of the Seventh-day Adventists in North America and Europe and Their Outreach in Africa." In *The Development of the Seventh-day Adventist Church in Eastern Africa—Past, Present, and Future*, edited by K. B. Elineema, 31–39. Dar-es-Salaam: Dar-es-Salaam University Press, 1995.

Heinz, Daniel. "World War I." In *The Ellen G. White Encyclopedia*, edited by Fortin and Moon, 1289–1290.

*Historical Sketches of the Foreign Missions of the Seventh-day Adventists*. Basel: Imprimerie Polyglotte, 1886. vii, 294 pp.

Home Missionary and Missionary Volunteer Worker Council. *Report of Home Missionary and Missionary Volunteer Workers' Council Held in Posen, Poland, July 10–16, 1935*. Edgware, Middlesex: Northern European Division, 1935. 100 pp.

Kobialka, Martin H. *Mehr als Brot: Wesen und Werk der Adventmission*. Frankfurt am Main: Akademische Studien Frankfurt am Main, 1975. 199 pp. Europeans played an important role in many early missions of the worldwide SDA Church.

Koziróg, Bernard. *Geneza, dzieje i teologia adwentyzmu w latach 1831–1939: Wydanie drugie uzupełnione*. Podkowa Leśna: Signa temporis, 2008. 302 pp.

Pfeiffer, Baldur Edmund. *The European Seventh-day Adventist Mission in the Middle East 1879–1939*. European University Studies, Series XXII 161. Frankfurt am Main: Peter Lang, 1981. 123 pp. Republished as *Die Adventmission im Nahen Osten*. Archiv für internationale Adventgeschichte 7. Frankfurt am Main: Peter Lang, 1996. vii, 123 pp.

Pfeiffer, Baldur Edmund, ed. *Seventh-day Adventist Contributions to East Africa,*

*1903–1983.* Frankfurt am Main: Verlag Peter Lang, 1985. 121 pp.

Polok, Władysław. *Geneza i wczesny rozwój adwentyzmu europejskiego.* ("Genesis and Early Development of European Adventism.") Podkowa Leśna: Signa Temporis, 2008. 223 pp.

Schumacher, Sigrun, and Gerhard Padderatz, eds. *ASI: Geschichte und Geschichten.* Mundelsheim: Basista Media, 2012. 219 pp. History of Adventist Laymen's Services and Industries in the USA and Europe.

Spalding, Arthur W. *Origin and History of Seventh-day Adventists.* 4 vols. Washington: Review and Herald, 1962. 2:191–212, 225–38; 3:333–58; 4:221–302.

Spicer, William Ambrose. *Our Story of Missions for Colleges and Academies.* Mountain View, CA: Pacific Press, 1921. 86–204.

Spicer, William Ambrose. *Providences of the Great War.* Washington, DC: Review and Herald, 1923. 236 pp.

Szigeti, Jenő. "Duna Unió 1912–1919." ("The Danube Union 1912–19.") In *A magyarországi Adventista Egyház Történetéből,* 1972.

Trim, David J. B., and Daniel Heinz, eds. *Parochialism, Pluralism, and Contextualization: Challenges to Adventist Mission in Europe (19th–21st Centuries).* Adventistica 9. Frankfurt am Main: Peter Lang, 2010. 208 pp.

Ulrich, Bernhard. *Die Entwicklung und Organisation des europäischen Adventwerkes von 1874–1938: Einführender Hintergrund zum Verständnis L. R. Conradis.* Darmstadt: Published by the Author, 1978. 81 pp.

## Unpublished

Bajic, Milan. "Planting Adventist Communities of Faith among Muslims in Unentered Areas of the Balkans." DMin dissertation, Andrews University, 2005. viii, 142 pp.

Cupertino, Giuseppe. "Ecclésiologie et mission: Étude sur la genèse de la mission adventiste (1844–1901)." MA thesis, Adventist University of France–Collonges, 1984.

Días, Joaquim. "Seventh-day Adventist Education in Southern Europe, Italy, Spain and Portugal." Term paper, Andrews University, 1977. 28 pp.

Dinţă, Andrei-Mihai. "Răspândirea mesajului Adventist în Europa." ("The Spread of the Advent Message in Europe.") BA thesis, RATI, 2017.

Eißner, Thomas. "Rezeption von Ellen G. White im deutschsprachigen Raum 1845–1915." Diplom thesis, Friedensau Adventist University, 2008.

Stele, Galina I. "An Analysis of Growth in the Euro-Asia Division (1985–1995) Leading to a Strategy for Developing Home Churches." DMin dissertation, Andrews University, 1996. x, 283 pp.

Tompkins, Paul. "Bringing Home Our Adventist Prodigals: A Strategic Plan to Reclaim Youth in the Trans-European Division." PhD Dissertation, Andrews University, 2009. viii, 154 pp. 21–71.

Van Rijn, Hendricus Gerardus. "Seventh-day Adventist Publishing Work: The Necessity of Decolonizing: The History and Purpose of an American-Centered Enterprise." TMs, VU Amsterdam, 1978. 129 pp.

Vaucher, Alfred-Félix. "Origins of the Seventh-day Adventist Church in Europe." 1974. Unpublished paper. 27, 8, [6] pp.

# Historical Personalities

## John Nevins Andrews in Europe

### Published

Campbell, Michael W. "Andrews, John Nevins and Angeline (Stevens)." In *The Ellen G. White Encyclopedia*, edited by Fortin and Moon, 294–95.

Campbell, Michael W. "Andrews, Mary Francis." In *The Ellen G. White Encyclopedia*, edited by Fortin and Moon, 295–96.

Heinz, Daniel. "Andrews, John Nevins (1829–1883)." In *Biographisch-Bibliographisches Kirchenlexikon*.

Leonard, Harry, ed. *J. N. Andrews: The Man and the Mission*. Berrien Springs, MI: Andrews University Press, 1985. xi, 355 pp. Biography, results of a symposium which took place at the French Adventist Seminary in Collonges, France, from August 30 to September 1, 1983, on the centenary of Andrews' death.

Leonard, Harry H. "The Adventist Rubicon: John N. Andrews and the Mission to Europe." In *Parochialism, Pluralism, and Contextualization*, edited by Trim and Heinz, 31–50.

Leonard, Harry H. "John N. Andrews and England's Seventh Day Baptists: 'We Are Brethren.'" *Adventist Heritage* 9, no. 1 (1984): 50–56.

Sanon, Sully. "Interpersonal Supports: A Prophet-Scholar Model." *Ministry* (April 2018): 17–20.

### Unpublished

Posavec, Darko. "Život i rad Johna Nevinsa Andrewsa." ("The Life and Work of J. N. Andrews.") BA thesis, Adriatic Union College, 2008.

Van Bignoot, Johan A. "J. N. Andrews, Seventh-day Adventist Missionary-Editor in French Speaking Europe." MA project report, Andrews University, 1980. 96 pp.

Van Bignoot, Johan A. "A Study of J. N. Andrews' Mission-Philosophy in Les Signes des Temps (1876-1883)." Term paper, Andrews University, 1979. 66 pp.

Vanuxem, Nicole. "John Nevins Andrews: pionnier de l'Eglise adventiste du septième jour en Europe. Une étude du personnage et de sa théologie à travers ses articles parus dans «Les signes des temps» de juillet 1876 à octobre 1883." MA thesis, Adventist University of France–Collonges, 1986.

# Ludwig Richard Conradi

## Published

Hartlapp, Johannes. "Eine vergessene Liebe: Ludwig Richard Conradi und die Adventgemeinde." *Spes Christiana* 17 (2006): 69–83.

Heinz, Daniel. "Conradi, Louis (Ludwig) Richard." In *The Ellen G. White Encyclopedia*, edited by Fortin and Moon, 346–48.

Heinz, Daniel. "Conradi, Ludwig Richard (1856–1939)." In *The Modern Encyclopedia of Religions in Russia and the Soviet Union*. Gulf Breeze, FL: Academic International Press, 1988–.

Heinz, Daniel. "L. R. Conradis missionarischer Durchbruch: Ein Modell für die Zukunft?" In *Die Adventisten und Hamburg*, edited by Pfeiffer, Träder, and Knight, 146–161.

Heinz, Daniel. *Ljudvig Richard Konradi: Missioner, evangelist i organizator Tserkvi Adventistov Sed'mogo dnya v Evrope i v Rossii*. Enlarged edition. Nikolaev: MedNa, 2006.

Heinz, Daniel. *Ludvig Richard Konradi: Misioner, evangelizator i organizator na adventistite ot sedmija den v Evropa*. Sofia: Nov Život, 2014. Enlarged edition.

Heinz, Daniel. Ludwig R. Conradis evangelistisches 'Erfolgrezept' und das Wachstum der Adventisten in Deutschland." In *Adventhoffnung für Deutschland*, edited by Heinz and Lange, 31–42.

Heinz, Daniel. *Ludwig Richard Conradi, Missionar, Evangelist und Organisator der Siebenten-Tags-Adventisten in Europa*. 3rd Edition. Archiv für internationale Adventgeschichte 2. Frankfurt am Main: Peter Lang, 1998. 138 pp.

Heinz, Daniel. "Ludwig Richard Conradi: Patriarch of European Adventism." *Adventist Heritage* 12, no. 1 (1987): 17–24.

Padderatz, Gerhard. *Conradi und Hamburg: Die Anfänge der deutschen Adventgemeinde (1889 bis 1914) unter besonderer Berücksichtigung der organisatorischen, finanziellen und sozialen Aspekte*. Kiel: Published by the Author, 1978. [Dr. phil. dissertation, Kiel University.] vi, 298 pp.

## Unpublished

Gerhardt, Johann Helmut. "L. R. Conradi, the Development of a Tragedy." Term paper, Andrews University, 1977. 27, [4] pp.

Grob, Fredy. "Conradi and the Consequences of His Apostasy." Term paper, Andrews University, 1974. iii, 25 pp.

Kaiser, Denis. "Ludwig Richard Conradi (1856–1939): Seventh-day Adventist Missionary in Europe." Term paper, Andrews University, 2010. 73 pp.

Langhof, Rüdiger. "Die Missionsstrategie Ludwig Richard Conradis: Zu den Möglichkeiten heutiger Mission." Diplom thesis, Friedensau Adventist University, 1997. 61 pp.

Schmidl, Christina. "Adventism in Germany under Carl Ludwig Richard
Conradi." Term paper, Newbold College, 1989. 20, [1] pp.
Van Rijn, Hendricus Gerardus. "A Biography of Louis Richard Conradi."
Term paper, Andrews University, 1970. 42 pp.

## Michael Belina Czechowski

### Published

Dąbrowski, Rajmund Ładysław. "Czechowski, Michael Belina." In *The Ellen G.
White Encyclopedia*, edited by Fortin and Moon, 356–57.
Dąbrowski, Rajmund Ładysław. *M. B. Czechowski First Adventist Missionary to
Europe: American Sources.* Published by the Author, 1972. 97 pp.
Dąbrowski, Rajmund Ładysław. "M. B. Czechowski: Pioneer to Europe."
*Adventist Heritage* 4, no. 1 (1977): 13–23.
Dąbrowski, Rajmund Ładysław, and Bert B. Beach, eds. *Michael Belina
Czechowski, 1818–1876: Results of the Historical Symposium about His Life
and Work Held in Warsaw, Poland, May 17-23, 1976, Commemorating the
Hundredth Anniversary of His Death.* Warsaw: Znaki Czasu, 1979. 551 pp. The
text is both in English and in Polish.
Frei, Jacques. *Recueil de documents concernant Michael Belina Czechowski.* Zürich:
Published by the Author, 1971. 154 pp.
Heinz, Daniel. "Czechowski, Michael Belina (1818–1876)." In *Biographisch-
Bibliographisches Kirchenlexikon.*
Korsak, Andrzej Michał. *Pucybut Boży: opowieść o Michale Belinie- Czechowskim.*
("God's Shoes: The Story of Michael Belina-Czechowski.") Warsaw:
Chrześcijański Instytut Wydawniczy "Znaki Czasu," 1997. 500 pp.
Koziróg, Bernard. *Ksiądz Michał Belina-Czechowski.* Warsaw: Znaki Czasu,
1992. 169 pp.
Nowlan, Connie Wells. *The Man Who Wouldn't Listen.* Trailblazers. Mountain
View, CA: Pacific Press, 1982. 96 pp.
Polok, Władysław. "Prekursorska działalność Michała Beliny-Czechowskiego."
("The Precursor Activity of Michał Belina-Czechowski." *Signa Temporis*,
no. 12 (2007): 185–203.
Popa, Dumitru. *Biografii ale pionierilor Bisericii advente din România: Mihail
Belina Czechowski, 1816–1876.* ("Biographies of Romanian Adventist Church
Pioneers: Mihail Belina Czechowski, 1816–1876.") Bucharest: GraFix Print,
1995. 151 pp.

### Unpublished

Bujak, Adam R. "Biography of M. B. Czechowski." Term paper, Andrews
University, 1975. iii, 25 pp.

Chmielewski, Józef. "Życie i działalność Michała Beliny-Czechowskiego." ("The Life and Work of Michael Belina-Czechowski.") BA thesis, Polish Senior College of Theology and Humanities, 2010.

Dąbrowski, Rajmund Ładysław. "M. B. Czechowski, First Adventist Missionary to Europe (American Sources)." Term paper, Andrews University, 1972. 102 pp.

Krall, Jack. "M. B. Czechowski, Independent Missionary to Europe." Term paper, Andrews University, 1975. 25 pp.

Schori, Markus. "Michael Belina Czechowski et l'origine du mouvement adventiste en Suisse." Thesis, Adventist University of France–Collonges, 1979.

Schulze, Alexander Christian. "Michael Belina Czechowski: Pionier der Siebenten-Tags-Adventisten in Europa." Diplom thesis, Friedensau Adventist University, 2001. 169 pp.

Vaucher, Alfred Félix. "Michael Belina Czechowski: A Self-Sent SDA Missionary to Europe, 1818–1876." TMs, 1980. 77 pp.

Zoltán, Rajki. *Egy Amerikai Lelkész Magyarországi Missziója.* ("The Mission of an American Pastor in Hungary.") Budapest: Lucidus, 2004. 183 pp.

## *Ellen G. White in Europe*

### Published

Barham, Nigel G. "England." In *The Ellen G. White Encyclopedia*, edited by Fortin and Moon, 805–806.

*Centennial Symposium: Ellen G. White and Europe, 1885/1887–1987.* Bracknell: Ellen G. White Research Centre, Europe, 1987. [ix], 477 pp.

Delafield, Dwight Arthur. *Ellen G. White in Europe: Prepared from Ellen G. White Papers and European Historical Sources.* Washington, DC: Review and Herald, 1975. 320 pp.

Delafield, Dwight Arthur. "The Productive Years in Europe, 1885–1887: A Picture of Ellen White, the Many-Sided Prophet." Silver Spring, MD: Ellen G. White Estate, 1987.

Dumitrescu, Cristian. "Italy." In *The Ellen G. White Encyclopedia*, edited by Fortin and Moon, 907–908.

*Ellen G. White and Europe: Symposium Papers 1987.* Bracknell: Ellen G. White Research Centre, Europe, 1987.

Fortin, Denis. "Norway." In *The Ellen G. White Encyclopedia*, edited by Fortin and Moon, 1005.

Graybill, Ron and Gerte Graybill. "Ellen White in Copenhagen." *Adventist Heritage* 1, no. 2 (1974): 36–42.

Heinz, Daniel. "Europe." In *The Ellen G. White Encyclopedia*, edited by Fortin and Moon, 810–813.

Heinz, Daniel. "Germany." In *The Ellen G. White Encyclopedia*, edited by Fortin and Moon, 841.

Rolland, Jean-Luc. "France." In *The Ellen G. White Encyclopedia*, edited by Fortin and Moon, 826–827.

Schantz, Hans Jørgen. "Denmark." In *The Ellen G. White Encyclopedia*, edited by Fortin and Moon, 763.

Schantz, Hans Jørgen. Ellen G. White i Danmark: En beskrivelse af Ellen Gould Whites tre besøg i Danmark, 1885–1887, og deres betydning. Odense: Dansk Bogforlag, 1987. 85 pp.

Zürcher, Jean Rudolf, and Robert W. Olson. *Ellen G. White in der Schweiz: 1885–1887*. Krattigen: Advent-Verlag, ca. 1985. 50 pp. Also published in French as *Ellen G. White en Suisse 1885–1887*. Zürich: Union Suisse des Eglises Adventistes, n.d. 64 pp.

## Unpublished

Riches, Rex. "The Beginnings of Expansion in the British Mission of the Seventh-day Adventist Church 1887–1902 in the Light of History and the Personal Opinions of Ellen G. White." Term paper, Andrews University, 1974. ii, 44 pp.

Riches, Rex. "The Failure of the British Mission of Seventh-day Adventists, 1878–1887 in the Light of History and the Personal Opinions of Stephen N. Haskell and Ellen G. White." MA project report, Andrews University, 1973. 40 pp.

# The Seventh Day Adventist Reform Movement

## *Published*

Balbach, A. *The History of the Seventh Day Adventist Reform Movement*. Roanoke, VI: Seventh Day Adventist Reform Movement, 1999. x, 664.

Christian, Lewis Harrison. *The Aftermath of Fanaticism; or, A Counterfeit Reformation*. Washington, DC: General Conference of Seventh-day Adventists, 1957? 76 pp.

Dill, Viktor Y. *Reformisty: Ucheniye i istoriya*. ("The Reform Adventists: Their Teachings and History.") Zaokskiy: Istochnik zhizni, 2009.

Engelhardt, Adam. "Mişcarea de reformă: Origine, istorie şi situaţie actuală." ("The Reform Movement: Origin, History, and Current Situation.") BA thesis, RATI, 1997.

*Erweckung und Reformation unter dem Adventvolk*. Hannover: Missionsverlag für Glaubens- und Gewissensfreiheit, 1997. 156, xi pp.

Fleschutz, Hans. *Und folget ihrem glauben nach!: Gedenkbuch für die Blutzeugen der Siebenten-Tags-Adventisten Reformationsbewegung: Zeugnisse der Treue und Standhaftigkeit aus Deutschland dunklen Tagen*. Heilbronn: Internationale

Missionsgesellschaft der Siebenten-Tags-Adventisten    Reformationsbewegung, n.d. 59 pp.

Hartlapp, Johannes. "Die Siebenten-Tags-Adventisten im Ersten Weltkrieg und die Entstehung der 'Reformationsbewegung'." In *Adventhoffnung für Deutschland*, edited by Heinz and Lange, 43–66.

Heinz, Daniel. "Brugger, Anton." Heinz, Daniel. In *'Ihr Ende schaut an...'*, edited by Harald Schultze, Andreas Kurschat, and Claudia Bendick.

Heinz, Daniel. "Der Widerstand der Reformationadventisten im 'Dritten Reich.'" *Jahrbuch des Dokumentationsarchivs des österreichischen Widerstandes* (2002): 88–98.

Heinz, Daniel. "Hanselmann, Johann Georg." Heinz, Daniel. In *'Ihr Ende schaut an...'*, edited by Harald Schultze, Andreas Kurschat, and Claudia Bendick.

Heinz, Daniel. "Metzner, Gottlieb Karl." Heinz, Daniel. In *'Ihr Ende schaut an...'*, edited by Harald Schultze, Andreas Kurschat, and Claudia Bendick.

Heinz, Daniel. "Münch, Alfred." Heinz, Daniel. In *'Ihr Ende schaut an...'*, edited by Harald Schultze, Andreas Kurschat, and Claudia Bendick.

Heinz, Daniel. "Pacha, Viktor." Heinz, Daniel. In *'Ihr Ende schaut an...'*, edited by Harald Schultze, Andreas Kurschat, and Claudia Bendick.

Heinz, Daniel. "Pietz, Günter E." Heinz, Daniel. In *'Ihr Ende schaut an...'*, edited by Harald Schultze, Andreas Kurschat, and Claudia Bendick.

Heinz, Daniel. "Przyrembel, Gustav." Heinz, Daniel. In *'Ihr Ende schaut an...'*, edited by Harald Schultze, Andreas Kurschat, and Claudia Bendick.

Heinz, Daniel. "Ranacher, Julius." Heinz, Daniel. In *'Ihr Ende schaut an...'*, edited by Harald Schultze, Andreas Kurschat, and Claudia Bendick.

Heinz, Daniel. "Zrenner, Leander Josef." Heinz, Daniel. In *'Ihr Ende schaut an...'*, edited by Harald Schultze, Andreas Kurschat, and Claudia Bendick.

Kramer, Helmut H. *The Seventh-day Adventist Reform (German Reform)*. Hagerstown, MD: Biblical Research Institute, 1988. vi, 89 pp.

Ruttmann, Hermann. *Die adventistische Reformationsbewegung, 1914–2001: Die internationale Missionsgesellschaft der Siebenten-Tags-Adventisten Reformationsbewegung in Deutschland*. Köln: Teiresias, 2002. 348 pp.

*SDA Reform Movement: Origin and Early Experiences*. Sacramento, CA: Seventh Day Adventist Reform Movement, 195-. 39 pp.

Tobler, Gustav. *Gott gibt sein Volk nicht auf: Reformation oder "Reformationsbewegung"?* Zürich: Advent-Verlag, 158 pp.

## Unpublished

Felea, Enoh. "Statornicia organizaţiei bisericii AZŞ în mijlocul atacurilor reformiste." ("Stability of the SDA Church Organization amidst the Reformist Attacks.") BA thesis, RATI, 1999.

Mandemaker, Gerard W. "Geschichte und Lehre der 1914 in Deutschland entstandenen 'Reformationsbewegung' der Siebenten-Tags-Adventisten." Term paper, Andrews University, 1972. iv, [67] pp.

Prună, Laurenţiu. "Istoria confesiunii adventiştilor reformişti." ("History of Reform Movement.") BA thesis, RATI, 2006.

Teubert, Holger. "Die sogenannte Reformationsbewegung." Diplom thesis, Seminar Marienhöhe, n.d. 62 pp.

Teubert, Holger. "Lehrentwicklung bei den Reformadventisten." Diplom thesis, Friedensau Adventist University, 1996. 79 pp.

Zaitsev, Evgeniy V. "The Origin of the Reform Movement in the Seventh-day Adventist Church in Russia." Term paper, Andrews University, 1996. 53 pp.

# Countries

## Albania

### Published

Dabrowsky, Ray. "Albania's Dawn: The Only Country that Officially Declared Itself Atheist Opens Its Doors to Adventism." *Spectrum* 22, no. 1 (March 1992): 24–29.

Hamilton, Bill, and Bhasker Solinka. *Albania, Who Cares?* Grantham: Autumn House, 1992. 156 pp, [16] pp of plates.

### Unpublished

Rice, Leigh Russell. "Leadership Development in Albania: Equipping Young Pastors for Apostolic Leadership." DMin dissertation, Andrews University, 2005. x, 163 pp. 75–77.

## Armenia

### Published

*Egitkhanoff, Marie Abelian, and Ken Wilson. Terror by Night and Day: An Armenian Girl's Story.* Mountain View, CA: Pacific Press, 1980. 144 pp.

Heinz, Daniel. "While Justice Lingers." *Adventist Review*, December 2015, 26–30. On the Armenian Genocide.

Sarkisyan, Ashot S. N*euzheli eto bylo?: Ocherki iz istorii Tserkvi Adventistov Sed'mogo dnya v Armenii.* ("Did It Really Happen?: History of the SDA Church in Armenia.") Dnepropetrovsk: Lira, 2003. 160 pp.

Tavoukdjian, Serpouhi. *Exiled: Story of an Armenian Girl.* Washington, DC: Review and Herald, 1933. 126 pp.

## Unpublished

Krieger, Viktor. "Die Siebenten-Tags-Adventisten in Armenien 1890–1991: Organisation und Wachstum einer Minderheitskirche." MA thesis, Friedensau Adventist University, 2011. 77 pp.

## *Austria*

## Published

Heinz, Daniel. "Church, Sect, and Government Control: Seventh-day Adventists in the Habsburg Monarchy." *East European Quarterly* 23, no. 1 (1989): 109–115.

Heinz, Daniel. *Church, State, and Religious Dissent: A History of Seventh-day Adventists in Austria, 1890–1975.* Archives of International Adventist History 5. Frankfurt am Main: Peter Lang, 1993. 206 pp. (Unpublished version: Heinz, Daniel. "Church, Sect, and Government Control, a History of Seventh-day Adventists in Austria, 1890–1975." PhD dissertation, Andrews University, 1991. 266 pp.)

Heinz, Daniel. "Kein Platz zwischen Thron und Altar—Freikirchliche Mission in Altösterreich (bis 1918) am Beispiel der Adventisten." *Freikirchen-Forschung* 27 (2018): 39–54.

Heinz, Daniel. "Lešovsky, Wilhelm Heinrich (1901–1976)." In *Biographisch-Bibliographisches Kirchenlexikon.*

Heinz, Daniel. "Repression, Toleranz, und Legalität: Siebenten-Tags Adventisten in Österreich: Geschichte, Organisation, und Wachstum einer Minderheitskirche." *Österreichisches Archiv für Recht und Religion* 48, no. 2 (2001): 323–344.

Heinz, Hans. "'Ich denke an die Taten des Herrn' (Ps 77,12): Ein autobiographischer Blick zurück." *Spes Christiana* 21 (2010), 13–23.

## *Azerbaijan*

## Published

Yunak, Dmitry O. *Vspomnite prezhde byvsheye. Istoriya Tserkvi ASD v Azerbaydzhane.* ("Remember the Past: History of the SDA Church in Azerbaijan.") Tula, 2004.

## Belarus

### Published

Myshepud, S. A. *Iz istorii sekty Adventistov Sed'mogo dnya na territorii Belorussii.* ("The History of the SDA Denominaton in Belarus.") Minsk, 1989.

Ostrovskiy, Moisei Iosifovich. "Perevod domov, nakhodyashchikhsya v zhilom fonde, v status kul'tovyh zdaniy, zdanii Tserkvi Adventistov Sed'mogo dnya v Belorusii." DMin dissertation, Zaoksky Adventist University, 2011.

Yunak, Dmitriy O. *Dlya roda posleduyushchego: Istoriya Tserkvi ASD v Belorussii.* Minsk, 2005.

## Belgium

### Published

Van Rijn, Hendricus G. *100 JAAR Adventkerk in Belgie.* 1996. 16 pp.

Vandenvelde, Georges. *Special centenaire: 100 ans d'Adventisme en Belgique et au Grand-Duche du Luxembourg.* Bruxelles: Federation belgo-luxembourgeoise des Eglises Adventistes du 7eme jour, 1996. 15 pp.

## Bosnia and Herzegovina

### Published

*An Idea of Bosnia.* Grantham: Autumn House in association with Feed the Children, 1996. 281 pp.

## Bulgaria

### Published

Grozev, Atanas. *Moyat zhivot na focus.* ("My Life in Focus.") Sofia: EL WAY, 2018. Autobiography of a church leader during the Communist Era.

Kumanov, Kiril. *Sŭborŭ t. 25-27 oktomvri 1968 g.* Sofia: Sŭyuz na TSASD, 2018. 143 pp.

Nakova, Petia. *Propovednikat i cherniyat kon: Biografichen roman.* ("The Preacher and the Black Horse.") Sofia: Iztok zapad, 2012. Biography on church leader Emil Dimitrov.

Patterson, Rae. *Front Line Bulgaria.* Hagerstown, MD: Review and Herald, 1998. 80 pp.

Shemkov, Kiril. *Vyara zad bodliva tel: Radost v stradaniya.* ("Faith behind Barbed

Wire: Joy amidst Suffering.") Sofia: Nov zhivot, 2016. Autobiography.
Tomas, Alfred. *Nachalo i razvitie na Adventnoto delo v Bulgariya.* ("Origin and Development of the Adventist Work in Bulgaria.") 1st ed. Sofia: Adventna misiya, 1938. 44 pp. 2nd ed. Sofia: Nov zhivot, 2017. 96 pp.
Yorgov, Mikhael. *Po stramninata na zhivota.* Vol. 1. Sofia: N.p., 2001. Autobiography. There are two other volumes.

## Unpublished

Krumov, Vladimir. "An Analysis of Demographic Developments of the Bulgarian SDA Church: Recommendations for Mission Strategizing." MTS thesis, Friedensau Adventist University, 2016. vi, 139 pp.

## *Croatia*

See also Yugoslavia.

## Published

Golubič, Mirko. *10-godišnjica srednje vjerske škole i 50-godišnjica teološke škole adventističke crkve u SFRJ.* Čakovec: Adriatic Union College, 1980. 43 pp.

## Unpublished

Đidara, Ivan. "Povijest Adventističke crkve u Hrvatskoj s posebnim osvrtom na Dalmaciju." ("History of the Adventist Church in Croatia, with a Particular Focus on Dalmatia.") PhD dissertation, University of Split, 2016. 292 pp.
Đidara, Ivan. "Povijest Kršćanske adventističke crkve—mjesne crkve u Osijeku—od njezinih početaka 1907. do raspada SFR Jugoslavije 1992, uz kratki osvrt do 2007." ("The History of the SDA Church—the Local Congregation in Osijek—from the Beginning in 1907 until the Breakup of Yugoslavia in 1992.") MA thesis, Evangelical Theological Seminary (Osijek, Croatia), 2007. 271 pp.
Đidara, Miroslav. "Developing a Deeper Understanding of God: A Strategy for Revitalizing the Seventh-day Adventist Church in Croatia." DMin dissertation, Andrews University, 2005. x, 198 pp.
Klačmer, Neven. "Pojava i razvoj upravnih struktura i institucija Kršćanske adventističke crkve u Hrvatskoj 1902–2004." ("The Origin and Development of the Administrative Structure and Institutions of Seventh-day Adventist Church in Croatia, 1902–2004.") BA thesis, Adriatic Union College, 2004. 102 pp.
Medić, Branka. "Propovijedaše evandjelje svim gradovima." ("Preaching the Gospel in All the Towns.") BA thesis, Adriatic Union College, 1986. 81 pp.

Mihaljcic, Jovan. "The Teaching Ministry of the Church and How It Is Practiced through the Week-Day Religious Instruction in the Seventh-day Adventist Church in the Socialist Republic of Croatia." DMin dissertation, Andrews University, 1987. viii, 300 pp.

## Czech Republic

### Published

Passer, Radim. *3½ Years or the American Dream in the Czech Republic.* S.p.: Maranatha, 2006. 250 pp. Autobiography.
Piškula, Jiří. *Dějiny Církve adventistů sedmého dne v Čechách, na Moravě a ve Slezsku.* ("History of the SDA Church in Bohemia, Moravia, and Silesia.") Prague: Advent-Orion, 2009. 202 pp.

### Unpublished

Činčala, Petr. "A Theoretical Proposal for Reaching Irreligious Czech People through a Mission Revitalization Movement." PhD dissertation, Andrews University, 2002. xi, 287 pp.
Doleček, Radek. "Koncepce adventistických škol v ČR." ("The Concept of Adventist Schools in the Czech Republic.") BA thesis, Sazava Theological Seminary, 2001.

## Czechoslovakia

### Published

Laufersweiler, Erich Theodor. *Im Schatten seiner Hand: Erlebnisse eines jungen Christen in der Armee der CSSR.* QuoVadis: Heidelberg, 2012. 213 pp.

### Unpublished

Balcar, Michal. "Adventisté sedmého dne na území Protekrorátu Čechy a Morava v letech 1939–1945." ("Seventh-day Adventists in the Protectorate of Bohemia and Moravia, 1939–1945.") BA thesis, Sazava Theological Seminary, 2001.
Duda, Emanuel. Vývoj a pokrok adventního díla v československu. BA thesis, 1972. 54 pp.
Piškula, Jiří. "Das Verbot der Siebenten-Tags-Adventistenkirche—Ein Beispiel für Verfolgung der Freikirchen in der Tschechoslowakei." *Communio Viatorium* 49, no. 3 (2007): 361–69.
Svoboda, Oldrich. "Histoire de l'éducation théologique de l'Église adventiste du

septième jour en Tchécoslovaquie." MA thesis, Adventist University of France–Collonges, 2004.

## Denmark

### Published

Carter, Erik C. "Matteson, John Gottlieb." In *The Ellen G. White Encyclopedia*, edited by Fortin and Moon, 462.

Carlsen, Leif. *Men få er udvalgte*. Systime, 1989. 189 pp.

Chilson, Adriel D. *Gospel Viking*. Washington, DC: Review and Herald, 1981. 128 pp. Biography of John Matteson.

Edwards, Josephine Cunnington. *Son of the Vikings*. Nashville, TN: Southern Publishing Association, 1972. 126 pp.

Hartmann, Walder, and others. *Vejlefjord: Et springbræt til fremtiden*. Viborg, 2015. 168 pp.

Jensen, Kamma. *Himmerlandsgården: En del af dit liv*. TopTryk Grafisk, 2017. 104 pp. 40 year anniversary, 1977–2017.

Lodahl, Anders Bank, and Jørn Hansen. *Skodsborg Badesanatorium, persilleslottet som blev Nordens største kursted*. University of Southern Denmark
Studies in History and Social Science 565. Odense: Syddansk Universitetsforlag, 2018.

"Ottosen, Carl Jacob." In *The Ellen G. White Encyclopedia*, edited by Fortin and Moon, 485.

Pedersen, Kaj. *Syvende Dags Adventistkirken i Danmark*. Nærum: Dansk Bogforlag, 2007. 172 pp.

"Rasmussen, Anna M." In *The Ellen G. White Encyclopedia*, edited by Fortin and Moon, 496.

Raft, Carl. *Bondedrengen, der blev verdensprædikant: Historien om min morfar J. C. Raft*. Herning: Poul Kristensen, 1997.

Schantz, Børge and Hans Jørgen Schantz, eds. *Var det umagen værd?: Danske syvende dags adventister i fremmedmissionen*. Nærum: Dansk Bogforlag, 1999. 304 pp.

Schantz, Hans Jørgen. *I troens bakspejl*. Odense: Dansk Bogforlag, 1998. 100 pp.

"Skodsborg Sanitarium." In *The Ellen G. White Encyclopedia*, edited by Fortin and Moon, 1168.

Strayer, Brian E. "Johnson, Lewis." In *The Ellen G. White Encyclopedia*, edited by Fortin and Moon, 428–429.

## Unpublished

Andersson, Ellen Lya. "A Study of Seventh-day Adventist Education in
Denmark." PhD dissertation, Loma Linda University, 1985. x, 233 pp.
Bayer, Birthe. "The Beginning of Adventism and the First Danish College,
1890–1898." Term paper, Andrews University, 1979. ii, 37 pp.
Lodahl, Anders Bank. "Skodsborg Badesanatorium, på kanten af det offentlige
sundhedsvæsen og den ortodokse medicin i 1898-1992." PhD dissertation,
University of Southern Denmark, 2017.

## *Estonia*

### Published

Viirsalu, Raely. *Kuldne maa ja koduta rahvas.* N.p.: N.p., 2001. 131 pp.
Viirsalu, V. *Loojangu eel: Kristuse taastuleku kuulutajad.* N.p.: Published by the
Author, 2001. 136 pp.

## *Finland*

### Published

Aittala, Wiljam. *Aapiskujalta Tähkäpolulle: Wiljam Aittala muistelee.* ("From
Aapiskuja to Tähkäpolku: Memoirs of Wiljam Aittala.") Tampere:
Kirjatoimi, 1994. 204 pp. Autobiography.
*Että totuus saisi siivet: Kirjatoimi 1897–1972. Kirjatoimen kustannustoiminnan
historiaa ja kustannustuotteiden luettelo.* Tampere: Kirjatoimi, 1972. 87 pp.
History of the literature work and the publishing house.
Halminen, Hjalmar. *Jumalan lähettiläänä: Kirjaevankelista kertoo kokemuksistaan.*
("God's Messenger: The Experiences of a Literature Evangelist.") Tampere:
Kirjatoimi, 1967. 127 pp. Autobiography.
Helminen, Auvo. *Aihetta itkeä ja nauraa.* ("Laughter and Tears.") Ylöjärvi:
Published by the Author, 2004. 113 pp. Autobiography of a pastor.
Helminen, Auvo, ed. *Suunnan muutos: Elämää muuttavia uskonvalintoja
sukupolvien ketjussa.* ("Changing Course: Life Changing Decisions of Faith
from Generation to Generation.") Tampere: Kirjatoimi, 2007. 190 pp.
Adventist church members relate how they found the Adventist Church.
Ketola, T. N. *Hengellisiä liikkeitä: Historiallinen tutkielma Suomen
adventtiliikkeestä.* ("Spiritual Movements: A Historical Thesis on the Adventist
Movement in Finland.") Turku: Published by the Author, 1952. 247 pp;
Helsinki: Akateeminen Kirjakauppa, 1952. xi, 246 pp.
Kuusisto, Arniika. *Growing up in Affiliation with a Religious Community: A Case*

*Study of Seventh-day Adventist Youth in Finland.* Research on Religious and Spiritual Education 3. Münster: Waxman, 2011. 174 pp.

Lillas, Bengt. *Aseeton taistelija.* ("Unarmed Soldier.") Helsinki: Published by the Author, 1963. 157 pp. Memoirs of a pastor during the Finnish-Russian War (1939–1940).

Luukkanen, Elsa, and Olavi Rouhe. *Laulu armosta: Elsa Luukkanen muistelee.* ("Songs of Grace: Memoirs of Elsa Luukkanen.") Tampere: Kirjatoimi, 1980. 213 pp. Biography on Elsa Luukkanen. Published in English as *Elsa, Sweet Singer of Finland.* Translated by Leo L. Raunio. A Destiny Book. Mountain View, CA: Pacific Press, 1980. 144 pp.

Luukko, Heikki, ed. *Kemistin elämäntarina: Henning Karström.* ("The Life of a Chemist: Henning Karström".) Porvoo: Media7 Julkaisut, Porvoo, 2014. 242 pp. Autobiography by Karström, edited by Luukko.

Rintala, A. Y. *... kunnes päivä valkenee: Mietteitä ja muistelmia.* ("Until the Day Dawns: Thoughts and Memories.") Tampere: Kirjatoimi, 1963. 187 pp. Autobiography of a pastor and church leader.

Rintala, Aarne. *Työtä ja kaskuja: Plastiikkakirurgi muistelee.* ("Work and Jokes: Memoirs of a Plastic Surgeon.") Sulkava: Published by the Author, 2004. 168 pp. Autobiography.

Rouhe, Olavi. *Mies Hengen virrassa: Arvo W. Arasolan elämä ja sanoma.* (A Man Led by the Holy Spirit: Life and Message of Arvo W. Arasola.") Tampere: Kirjatoimi, 1995. 126 pp. Biography on Arvo W. Arasola.

Rouhe, Olavi, ed. *Nykvaika* no. 49, 1994. Special issue of the magazine, entitled "Adventtiseurakunta Suomessa 100 v." ("Adventist Church in Finland 100 Years.") Tampere: Kirjatoimi, 1994. 68 pp.

Saarinen, Anneli. *Särkynein siivin matkalla vapauteen.* ("On the Way to Freedom with Broken Wings.") Tampere: Kirjatoimi, 1995. 71 pp. Memoirs of a Literature Evangelist who became seriously ill.

Tarvainen, Toivo. *Vankeudesta vapauteen.* ("From Imprisonment to Freedom.") Helsinki: Kirjatoimi, 1949. 48 pp. Autobiography of a prisoner who became a SDA in prison.

*Toivonlinna 1932–1982: Toivonlinnan koulun 50-vuotisjuhlakirja.* ("Toivonlinna 1932–1982: 50th Anniversary of the Toivonlinna School.") Tampere: Kirjatoimi, 1982. 112 pp.

Tuchtenhagen, Ralph. "Die Religionsfreiheit in Finnland." *Gewissen und Freiheit* 40 (1993): 8–20.

Viirla, Antero. *Elämä on palvelua ja antamista: Lääkärin ja hammaslääkärin omaelämäkerta.* ("Life is Serving and Giving: An Autobiography of a Doctor and a Dentist.") Tampere: Published by the Author, 2012. 94 pp.

## Unpublished

Helminen, Aimo. "Developing a Strategy for Growth in the Seventh-day Adventist Church in Finland Using the Natural Church Development Approach Based on a Case Study in the Turku Seventh-day Adventist Church." DMin dissertation, Andrews University, 2006. x, 157 pp.

Helppi, Rauno Tapio. "The Beginning of the Seventh-day Adventist Church in Finland." Term paper, Andrews University, 1973. 24 pp.

Kuhalampi, Harri. "A Qualitative Study of the Factors Contributing to the High Incidence of Women in Ministry and Leadership in the Seventh-day Adventist Church in Finland." MA thesis, Newbold College, 2001. 110 pp.

Lempinen, Kai. "Church Growth in Finland: A Thematic Analysis of Two Growing Churches." MA thesis, Newbold College (University of Wales), 2017. 102 pp.

## *France*

### Published

"Avec vous pour témoigner." *Revue Adventiste*, June 1997. 16 pp. Special issue on the 75th year anniversary of the French publishing house, Editions Vie et Santé.

"Cinquantenaire de la Maison d'Edition Les Signes des Temps 1922–1972." *Revue Adventiste*, June 1972. 36 pp. Special issue.

Delaporte, Ernest Pierre. *I Was a Catholic Priest*. Mountain View, CA: Pacific Press, 1973. 127 pp.

Desplan, Fabrice, and Regis Dericquebourg, eds. *Ces protestants que l'on dit adventistes* [Those Protestant Called Adventists]. Paris: L'Harmattan, 2008.

Kempf, Jean, and Sigrid Kempf. *Il te montrera la voie que tu dois choisir*. Dammarie-les-Lys: Vie et santé, 2011. 251 pp. Autobiography.

Poublan, Gérard. *Histoire de Louis Carayon: Fondateur des eglises adventistes du Tarn*. N.p.: n.p., 199-.

Poublan, Gérard. *Naissance et développement de l'église adventiste à Toulouse*. N.p.: N.p., 1997? 161 pp.

### Unpublished

Bican, Jean-Rémy. "Histoire et développement de l'Église adventiste d'Annemasse." MA thesis, Adventist University of France–Collonges, 1985.

Bouvier, Daniel E. "Attitudes of French Seventh-day Adventists toward Seventh-day Adventist Schooling and Education." EdD dissertation, Loma Linda University, 1984. xxi, 273 pp.

Coffin, Ronald. "Approche sociologique d'un groupe minorieux religieux:

L'église adventiste en France." PhD dissertation, Université des Sciences Humaines de Strasbourg, 1981.

Hutin, Claude. "Les origines du mouvement adventiste en France (jusqu'en 1920)." 3 vols. Thesis, Adventist University of France–Collonges, 1966. 140, 93, 33 pp.

Joachim, Roland L. "Influences on the Enrollment in the French Adventist Seminary from 1904 to 1941." Term paper, Andrews University, 1982. ii, 30 pp.

Kis, Miroslav Mirko. "Beginnings of Seventh-day Adventism in France, 1884-1901." Term paper, Andrews University, 1975. ii, 43 pp.

Martin, Jean-Michel. "Les origines et l'implantation du mouvement adventiste du septième jour en France: 1876–1925." PhD dissertation, Institut Protestant de Théologie, Paris, 1980. 386 pp.

Monet, Gabriel. "L'Église de l'espérance: Genèse et développement de 2001 à 2005: Regards sur la création d'une église contemporaine à Paris." MA thesis, Adventist University of France–Collonges, 2005.

Nagler, Raphaël. "Etude de l'impact d'une radio locale adventiste: Radio Semnoz." MA thesis, Adventist University of France–Collonges, 2003.

Nobre, Rickson. "L'immigration vers un pays plus développé a-t-elle affecté la vie religieuse des immigrants adventistes lusophones installés en Suisse et en France?" MA thesis, Adventist University of France–Collonges, 2006.

Roesch, Gabrielle I. "Vegetarian Practices among Seventh-day Adventists in France." MA thesis, Andrews University, 1986. 2, iv, 72 pp.

Vertallier, Bruno R. "A Design for Spiritual Formation during the Academic Life of the Adventist Seminary Students at Collonges-sous-Salève, France." DMin dissertation, Andrews University, 1993. vi, 180 pp.

Vertallier, Bruno R. "Campagne d'évangélisation de Marseille 1988: Bilan analytique et critique." MA thesis, Adventist University of France–Collonges, 1990.

## Georgia

### Unpublished

Namoradze, Sergo. "Church Growth Theory and the Development of the Seventh-day Adventist Church Mission in Georgia: A Case Study." PhD dissertation, Adventist International Institute of Adventist Studies, 2018.

# Germany

## Published

N.B.: Because of the large number of brochures, these are found in a separate section immediately following this part.

Allweiss, Werner. *Die Adventgemeinde und der Nationalsozialismus: Texte und Dokumente.* Konstanz: N.p., 1986. 83 pp. Extended version of a lecture delivered on October 19, 1985 in Freudenstadt, Germany.

Barsukov, A., ed. *Die Siebenten-Tags-Adventisten.* Vol. 1 of *Freie Kirchen in Gelsenkirchen.* Gelsenkirchen: N.p., 2018. 105 pp.

Birsgal, Johanna. *August Birsgal: Ein Leben für den Glauben.* Heiligenrode: Published by the Author, n.d. 228 pp. Biography of her father, August Birsgal.

Blaich, Roland. "Religion under National Socialism: The Case of the German Adventist Church." *Central European History* 26, no. 3 (1993): 225–280.

Blaich, Roland. "Selling Nazi Germany Abroad: The Case of Hulda Jost." *Journal of Church and State* 35 (1993): 807–30.

Böttcher, Manfred. *Dialog und Zeugnis: Interkonfessionelle Kontakte und Konflikte einer Freikirche in der DDR.* Friedensauer Schriftenreihe, Reihe B, Gesellschaftswissenschaften 4. Frankfurt am Main: Peter Lang, 2001. 143 pp.

Böttcher, Manfred. *Die Adventgemeinde in der DDR: Eine Gratwanderung von 1949 bis 1990.* Lüneburg: Advent-Verlag, 2007. 220 pp.

Böttcher, Manfred. "Die Entwicklung der Gemeinschaft in der Deutschen Demokratischen Republik." In *Adventhoffnung für Deutschland,* edited by Heinz and Lange, 173–190.

Böttcher, Manfred. *Gratwanderungen einer Freikirche im totalitären Regime: Die Gemeinschaft der Siebenten-Tags-Adventisten in der DDR von 1945 bis 1990.* Friedensauer Schriftenreihe, Reihe B, Gesellschaftswissenschaften 9. Frankfurt am Main: Peter Lang, 2006. 219 pp.

Böttcher, Manfred. *Wagnis des Glaubens: Dialog und Zeugnis der Advent gemeinden in der DDR.* Hamburg: Norddeutscher Verband, Siebenten-Tags-Adventisten, 2001. 186 pp.

Bromba, Walter. *F-STA 100: Zur Geschichte der Frankfurter Adventgemeinden.* Frankfurt am Main: Bromba, 1992. 162 pp.

Campbell, Michael W. "Ings, Jennis L. (Hussman) and William." In *The Ellen G. White Encyclopedia,* edited by Fortin and Moon, 421–22.

Day, Dan. *Burning Hope: The Story of Hans Mayr.* Boise, ID: Pacific Press, 1987. 80 pp.

*Ein Zeugnis des Glaubens: 75 Jahre Friedensau.* Berlin: Union-Verlag, 1974. 131 pp.

Elineema, K. B. "German Adventist Contributions to Eastern Africa." In *Die Adventisten und Hamburg,* edited by Pfeiffer, Träder, and Knight, 110–131.

Fischdick, Eberhard. *Helfende Hände: Die Geschichte des Advent-Wohlfahrts werkes in Deutschland.* Darmstadt: Advent-Wohlfahrtswerk, 1988. 160 pp.

Fischer, Roland E. *Bildung im Gottesdienst: Die Bibelschule der Adventgemeinde.* Frankfurt am Main: Peter Lang, 2008. 272 pp.

"Frey, Henri." In *The Ellen G. White Encyclopedia,* edited by Fortin and Moon, 382.

Hartlapp, Johannes. "Der Umgang mit der NS-Vergangenheit in den deutschen Adventgemeinden." *Freikirchenforschung* 15 (2005–2006): 324–352.

Hartlapp, Johannes. "Die Blütezeit der Adventmission in Deutschland 1889–1933." In *Die Adventisten und Hamburg,* edited by Pfeiffer, Träder, and Knight, 70–87.

Hartlapp, Johannes. "Die Entwicklung der Gemeinschaft der Siebenten-Tags-Adventisten in der Weimarer Republik." In *Adventhoffnung für Deutschland,* edited by Heinz and Lange, 67–88.

Hartlapp, Johannes. "Die Gemeinschaft der Siebenten-Tags-Adventisten während der Zeit des Nationalsozialismus." In *Adventhoffnung für Deutschland,* edited by Heinz and Lange, 89–112.

Hartlapp, Johannes. "Eine vergessene Liebe: Ludwig Richard Conradi und die Adventgemeinde." *Spes Christiana* 17 (2006): 69–84.

Hartlapp, Johannes. "Kirchenpolitik im 'Dritten Reich': Der Umgang des Sicherheitsdienstes der SS mit den kleinen Religionsgemeinschaften." *Spes Christiana* 14 (2003): 141–154.

Hartlapp, Johannes. *Siebenten-Tags-Adventisten im Nationalsozialismus unter Berücksichtigung der geschichtlichen und theologischen Entwicklung in Deutschland von 1875 bis 1950.* Kirche—Konfession—Religion 53. Göttingen: V&R unipress, 2008. 684 pp.

Hartlapp, Johannes. "Siebenten-Tags-Adventisten und die Herausforderung der Weimarer Republik." In *Glaube und Zukunftsgestaltung: Festschrift zum hundertjährigen Bestehen der Theologischen Hoschschule Friedensau: Aufsätze zu Theologie, Sozialwissenschaften und Musik,* edited by B. Oestreich, H. Rolly, and W. Kabus, 211–230. Frankfurt am Main: Peter Lang, 1999.

Hartlapp, Johannes. "Stellungnahmen zum Nationalsozialismus und der NSDAP in Zeitschriften deutscher STA vor der faschistischen Machtübernahme 1933." *Spes Christiana* 9–10 (1998–1999): 48–63.

Hartlapp, Wolfgang. *Wanderer, kommst du nach Friedensau: Erlebnisse, Erfahrungen, Erinnerungen.* Spröda: Akanthus, 2009. 175 pp.

Heinrich, Guido, and Gunter Schandera. *Magdeburger Biographisches Lexikon—19. und 20. Jahrhundert: Biographisches Lexikon für die Landeshauptstadt Magdeburg und die Landkreise Börderkreis, Jerichower Land, Ohrekreis und Schönebeck.* Magdeburg: Scriptum Verlag, 2002. Contains several entries on German SDAs by Daniel Heinz.

Heinz, Daniel, ed. *Adventisten machen Schule: 50 Jahre Seminar Schloß Bogenhofen, 1949–1999.* Vienna: Wegweiser Verlag, 1999. 119 pp.

Heinz, Daniel. "Bergner, Fritz." In *'Ihr Ende schaut an...'*, edited by Harald
    Schultze, Andreas Kurschat, and Claudia Bendick.
Heinz, Daniel. "Brüning, Hans." In *'Ihr Ende schaut an...'*, edited by Harald
    Schultze, Andreas Kurschat, and Claudia Bendick.
Heinz, Daniel. "'Da warst auch du wie einer von ihnen': Freikirchen und Juden
    im 'Dritten Reich': Traurige Bilanz und spätes Bekenntnis." *Kirchliche
    Zeitgeschichte / Contemporary Church History* 30, no. 1 (2017): 175–189.
Heinz, Daniel. "Dem Gebot und Gewissen verpflichtet: Freikirchliche
    Märtyrer." In *'Ihr Ende schaut an...'*, edited by Harald Schultze, Andreas
    Kurschat, and Claudia Bendick, 85–98.
Heinz, Daniel. "'Die Baptisten sind unser Vorbild!'" In *"Die Bibel hat die Schuld
    daran...": Festschrift zum 175. Jubiläum der Oncken-Gemeinde in Hamburg
    2009*, edited by Dietmar Lütz. 177–190. Hamburg: WDL-Verlag, 2009.
Heinz, Daniel. "Eberhardt, Walter Heinrich [1902–1980]." In *Magdeburger
    Biographisches Lexikon*, edited by Guido and Schandera.
Heinz, Daniel. "Erbe und Auftrag: Aus der Vergangenheit lernen und
    hoffnungsvoll in die Zukunft blicken." In *Adventhoffnung für Deutschland*,
    edited by Heinz and Lange, 263–270.
Heinz, Daniel. "Exklusivität und Kontextualisierung: Geschichte und
    Selbstverständnis der Siebenten-Tags-Adventisten in Deutschland."
    *Freikirchen-Forschung* 10 (2000): 31–50.
Heinz, Daniel. "Friedensau und Ostafrika: Ein Beitrag zur Missionsgeschichte."
    *Zeitschrift für Heimatforschung / Sachsen-Anhalt* 9 (2000): 58–64.
Heinz, Daniel. "Großer Glaube, kleine Schritte: Zur Geschichte der
    protestantischen Freikirchen in Dessau mit besonderer Berücksichtigung der
    Adventgemeinde (1908–2008)." *Dessauer Kalender.* (2009): 116–125.
Heinz, Daniel. "Harreß, Karl Georg." In *'Ihr Ende schaut an...'*, edited by Harald
    Schultze, Andreas Kurschat, and Claudia Bendick.
Heinz, Daniel. "Herkunft, Identität und frühe Prägung der Siebenten-Tags-
    Adventisten in Deutschland." In *Adventhoffnung für Deutschland*, edited by
    Heinz and Lange, 11–30.
Heinz, Daniel. "Horn, Sigfried Herbert Nathan [1908–1993]." In *Magdeburger
    Biographisches Lexikon*, edited by Guido and Schandera.
Heinz, Daniel. "Kotz, Ernst [1887–1944]." In *Biographisch-Bibliographisches
    Kirchenlexikon*.
Heinz, Daniel. "Kotz, Ernst [1887–1944]." In *Magdeburger Biographisches
    Lexikon*, edited by Guido and Schandera.
Heinz, Daniel. "Kriegsverdienstverweigerer und religiöser Pazifist: Der Fall
    Anton Brugger und die Haltung der Siebenten-Tags-Adventisten im Dritten
    Reich." *Jahrbuch des Dokumentationsarchives des österreichischen
    Widerstandes* (1996): 41–56.
Heinz, Daniel. "Lindermann, Johann Heinrich [1806–1892]." In *Biographisch-
    Bibliographisches Kirchenlexikon*.

Heinz, Daniel. "Löbsack, Georg Samuel [1893–1936]." In *Magdeburger Biographisches Lexikon*, edited by Guido and Schandera.

Heinz, Daniel. "Meyer, Erich [1879–1958]." In *Magdeburger Biographisches Lexikon*, edited by Guido and Schandera.

Heinz, Daniel. "Michael, Curt Wilhelm [1884–1945]." In *Magdeburger Biographisches Lexikon*, edited by Guido and Schandera.

Heinz, Daniel. "Michael, Wilhelm C." In *'Ihr Ende schaut an…'*, edited by Harald Schultze, Andreas Kurschat, and Claudia Bendick.

Heinz, Daniel. "Missionarische Offenheit in der Welt, ideologische Anpassung in Deutschland: Siebenten-Tags-Adventisten und Juden in der Zeit des Nationalsozialismus." In *Freikirchen und Juden im "Dritten Reich": Instrumentalisierte Heilsgeschichte, antisemitische Vorurteile und verdrängte Schuld*, edited by Daniel Heinz, 281–308. Göttingen: V & R Unipress, 2011.

Heinz, Daniel. "Mueller, Wilhelm [1888–1971]." In *Biographisch-Bibliographisches Kirchenlexikon*.

Heinz, Daniel. "The Pietist Roots of Early German Adventism." In *Parochialism, Pluralism, and Contextualization*, edited by Trim and Heinz, 83–91.

Heinz, Daniel. "Reider, Rudolf [1887–1973]." In *Biographisch-Bibliographisches Kirchenlexikon*.

Heinz, Daniel. "Seventh-day Adventists and the Persecution of Jews under the Nazi Regime." In *Thinking in the Shadow of Hell: The Impact of the Holocaust on Theology and Jewish-Christian Relations*, edited by Jacques B. Doukhan, 193–208. Berrien Springs, MI: Andrews University Press, 2002.

Heinz, Daniel. "Simon, Bruno Ernst [1887–1944]." In *Magdeburger Biographisches Lexikon*, edited by Guido and Schandera.

Heinz, Daniel. "Von der Klappermühle zur Kirchlichen Hochschule—100 Jahre Friedensau, 1899–1999." *Zeitschrift für Heimatforschung / Sachsen-Anhalt* 8 (1999): 56–61.

Heinz, Daniel. "Wiederkunftshoffnung und Weltmission: Streiflichter aus der Geschichte der Siebenten-Tags-Adventisten in Berlin." In *"Mit uns hat der Glaube nicht angefangen": Wie die Freikirchen in Berlin begonnen haben*, edited by Ökumenisch-Missionarisches Institut des Ökumenischen Rates Berlin-Brandenburg, 175–188. Berlin: WDL-Verlag, 2001.

Heinz, Daniel, and Werner E. Lange, eds. *Adventhoffnung für Deutschland: Die Mission der Siebenten-Tags-Adventisten von Conradi bis heute*. Lüneburg: Advent-Verlag, 2014. 303 pp.

Heinz, Hans. "Die theologische Prägung der Siebenten-Tags-Adventisten in Deutschland mit besonderer Berücksichtigung ihrer nordamerikanischen Wurzeln." In *Die Adventisten und Hamburg*, edited by Pfeiffer, Träder, and Knight, 32–45.

Horn, Sigfried. *Promise Deferred*. Washington, DC: Review and Herald, 1987. 95 pp. Autobiography.

Höschele, Stefan. "Die deutsche adventistische Weltmission bis zum Zweiten Weltkrieg." In *Adventhoffnung für Deutschland*, edited by Heinz and Lange, 113–26.

Ising, Walter K. *Unter den Arabern im Morgenlande*. Hamburg: Advent-Verlag, 1924. 335 pp. A shortened version published in English as *Among the Arabs in Bible Lands*. Mountain View, CA: Pacific Press, 1924. 213 pp.

Johnsen, Carsten. *The Part of the Story You Were Never Told about the Four Seers of Hamburg: A Tragic Event in Recent S.D.A. History*. Redlands, CA: The Untold Story Publishers, Center of Christian Realism, n.d. 63 pp.

Knight, George. "From Shut Door to Worldwide Mission: The Dynamic Context of Early German Adventism." In *Die Adventisten und Hamburg*, edited by Pfeiffer, Träder, and Knight, 46–69.

Kongress der europäischen Adventjugend. *Bericht über den ersten Kongress der europäischen Adventjugend in Chemnitz vom 17. bis zum 22. Juli 1928*. Hamburg: Advent-Verlag, 1928. 103 pp.

Leutert, Dieter. "SED-Regime und Adventgemeinde." In *Glauben heute*, edited by Elí Diez, 49–62. Lüneburg: Advent-Verlag, 1998.

Link, Fritz-Gerhard. *Aus Gottes Hand: Die Anfänge der Adventgemeinden im deutschen Südwesten von 1887 bis 1914 sowie Blickpunkte bis 2015*. Baden-Württemberg: Freikirche der Siebenten-Tags-Adventisten, 2015. 184 pp.

Machel, Edgar. *Vergangenheit und Zukunft: Eine Gemeindewachsstumsstudie des Westdeutschen Verbandes der Siebenten-Tags-Adventisten von 1945–1990*. Frankfurt am Main: Peter Lang, 2002. 164 pp.

Mueller, Harald. "Die rechtliche Stellung der Siebenten-Tags-Adventisten in Deutschland." In *Adventhoffnung für Deutschland*, edited by Heinz and Lange, 127–36.

Mundy, Susi Hasel, and Maylan Schurch. *A Thousand Shall Fall: The Electrifying Story of a Soldier and His Family Who Dared to Practice Their Faith in Hitler's Germany*. Hagerstown, MD: Review and Herald, 2001. 172 pp.

Naumann, Ingrid. *Umarme das Unmögliche: Biografie*. Wien: Top Life Wegweiser-Verlag, 2014. 205 pp.

Paul, Eva. *Weder Tod noch Leben: Eine siebenbürgische Lebensgeschichte*. Lüneburg: Advent-Verlag, 2017. 331 pp.

Pfeiffer, Baldur Edmund. "Die deutsche Adventmission im Nahen Osten und Afrika: Interkulturelle Auseinandersetzungen." In *Die Adventisten und Hamburg*, edited by Pfeiffer, Träder, and Knight, 132–45.

Pfeiffer, Baldur Edmund, ed. *Die Siebenten-Tags-Adventisten in Deutschland: Bilddokumentation*. Hamburg: Advent-Verlag, 1989. 63 pp.

Pfeiffer, Baldur Edmund, Lothar E. Träder, and George R. Knight, eds. *Die Adventisten und Hamburg: Von der Ortsgemeinde zur internationalen Bewegung*. Archiv für internationale Adventgeschichte 4. Frankfurt am Main: Peter Lang, 1992. vii, 161 pp.

Pöhler, Rolf J. "Die theologische Entwicklung und Eigenheit des deutschen Adventismus." In *Adventhoffnung für Deutschland*, edited by Heinz and Lange, 249–262.

Reiche, Lothar, ed. *Als Adventist in der DDR: Erfahrungen*. Lüneburg: Advent-Verlag, 2001. 267 pp.

Rochat, Joyce. *Survivor*. Berrien Springs, MI: Andrews University Press, 1986. xii, 332 pp. Biography of Siegfried Horn.

Rühling, Richard. *Quer durch Persien*. Hamburg: Advent-Verlag, 1934. 93 pp.

Scholz, Johannes. "Die Siebenten-Tags-Adventisten und die Wehrfrage in der SBZ und in der DDR 1945–1990." *Freikirchenforschung* 13 (2003): 130–173.

Schulze, Harald, Andreas Kurschat, and Claudia Bendick, eds. *'Ihr Ende schaut an...': Evangelische Märtyrer des 20. Jahrhunderts*. 2nd ed. Leipzig: Evangelische Verlagsanstalt, 2006. Contains many entries on German and Russian SDAs and Reform SDAs by Daniel Heinz.

Simon, Irmgard. *Die Gemeinschaft der Siebenten-Tags-Adventisten in volkskundlicher Sicht*. Münster: Aschendorff, 1965. 228 pp.

Stotropp, Ilka Annette. *Die Gesundheitsphilosophie der Siebenten-Tags Adventisten am Beispiel ihres Gesundheitswerkes in Deutschland*. Studien zur Geschichte des Krankenhauswesens 43. Herzogenrath: Murken-Altrogge, 2003. 175 pp.

Teubert, Holger. "Die Beziehungen der Siebenten-Tags-Adventisten zu anderen Kirchen und christlichen Organisationen." In *Adventhoffnung für Deutschland*, edited by Heinz and Lange, 237–248.

van Treeck, Klaus-J. "Unsere Freikirche in Deutschland: Die organisatorische Entwicklung von der Pionierphase bis zur Gegenwart." In *Glauben heute*, edited by Eli Diez, 43–57. Lüneburg, 2011.

Wietrichowski, Heinz. *Vom Alleinsein in der Welt: Tagebücher, Kalenderblätter, Jahresrückblicke 1945–2013*. Berlin: Pro Business, 2013. 528 pp. Autobiography.

Wilhelm, Lothar. "Die Haltung der Gemeinschaft der Siebenten-Tags-Adventisten zur Militärfrage (Wiederbewaffnung, Waffen- und Zivildienst, Militärseelsorgevertrag) in der BRD 1945–1990." *Freikirchenforschung* 13 (2003): 174–179.

## Brochures

*25 Jahre Altenheim Uelzen 1969–1994*. N.p.: N.p., 1994. 32 pp.

*50 Jahre Seminar Marienhöhe 1924–1974*. N.p.: N.p., 1974. 138 pp.

*70 Jahre Adventgemeinde Bad Aibling*. N.p.: N.p., 1989? 90 pp.

*75 Jahre Adventgemeinde in Hanau*. N.p.: N.p., n.d. 16 pp.

*75 Jahre Adventgemeinde in Kaiserslautern*. Kaiserslautern: Siebenten-Tags-Adventisten-Gemeinde, 1975. [24] pp.

*75 Jahre Adventgemeinde Kirchheim/Teck: 1908–1983.* N.p.: N.p., 1983. 27 pp.

*75 Jahre Adventgemeinde Köln: Jubiläumsfeier am 4. März 1978.* Köln: Gemeinschaft der Siebenten-Tags-Adventisten, 1978. 16 pp.

*75 Jahre Adventgemeinde Luzern 1912–1987: Eine kleine Chronik...* N.p.: N.p., 1987. [121] pp.

*75 Jahre Adventgemeinde Treysa 1922–1997.* Treysa: Adventgemeinde Treysa, 1997. [16] pp.

*75 Jahre Advent-gemeinde Universitätsstadt Tübingen.* Stuttgart: Baden-Württembergische Vereinigung, n.d. 32 pp.

*75 Jahre freie Wohlfartsarbeit.* N.p.: N.p., n.d. [30] pp.

*75 Jahre Friedensau: Ein Zeugnis des Glaubens.* N.p.: Gemeinschaft der Siebenten-Tags-Adventisten, 1974. 131, [5] pp.

*75 Jahre Krankenhaus Waldfriede.* Berlin: Krankenhaus Waldfriede, n.d. [56] pp.

*90 Jahre Adventgemeinde Augsburg.* Augsburg: Adventgemeinde Augsburg, 1995. 24 pp.

*90 Jahre Adventgemeinde Stadtroda.* Stadtroda: Adventgemeinde Stadtroda, 2004. [7] pp.

*90 Jahre Krankenhaus Waldfriede)(1920–2010).* Berlin: Krankenhaus Waldfriede, 2010. 56 pp.

*100 Jahre Adventgemeinde Augsburg: Unterwegs in die Zukunft | 1905–2005.* Augsburg: Gemeinde der Siebenten-Tags-Adventisten, 2005. 29 pp.

*100 Jahre Adventgemeinde Bielefeld.* N.p.: N.p., 1999. 34 pp.

*100 Jahre Adventgemeinde Bochum.* Bochum: Bochum Gemeinde der Siebenten-Tags-Adventisten, 2003. 54 pp.

*100 Jahre Adventgemeinden in München: 1897–1997.* München: Gemeinschaft der Siebenten-Tags-Adventisten, 1997. 35 pp.

*100 Jahre Adventgemeinde Lüdenscheid.* N.p.: N.p., n.d. 11 pp.

*100 Jahre Adventgemeinde Mannheim.* N.p.: N.p., n.d. 26 pp.

*100 Jahre Adventgemeinde Stuttgart 1895–1995.* Stuttgart: Adventgemeinde Stuttgart, 1995. 82 pp.

*100 Jahre Adventgemeinde Tegel 1913–2013.* Tegel: Adventgemeinde Tegel, 2013. [14] pp.

*100 Jahre Adventgemeinde Tübingen 1908–2008.* N.p.: N.p., 2008. [12] pp.

*100 Jahre Adventgemeinde Würzburg 1910–2010: Chronik.* Würzburg: Adventgemeinde Würzburg, 2010. 28 pp.

*100 Jahre Gemeinde Magdeburg 1895–1995.* Magdeburg: Adventgemeinde Magdeburg, 1995. 38 pp.

*100 Jahre Gemeinschaft der Siebenten-Tags-Adventisten in Solingen.* Hamburg: Grindeldruck, 1976. 24 pp.

*100 Jahre Siebenten-Tags-Adventisten Bonn 1905–2005.* N.p.: N.p., 2005. 35, [1] pp.

*100 Jahre Siebenten-Tags-Adventisten in Dortmund.* Dortmund: Adventgemeinde Dortmund, 2003. 24 pp.

*100 Jahre Siebenten-Tags-Adventisten in Köln.* N.p.: N.p., n.d. 36 pp.

*110 Jahre Adventgemeinde Chemnitz 1899–2009.* CD. 2009.

*1895–1970: Hamburger Verlagshaus der Siebenten-Tags Adventisten.* N.p.: N.p., 1970. [48] pp.

*1897–1997 Adventgemeinde Essen: Zwischen gestern und morgen.* Essen: Adventgemeinde Essen, 1997. 22 pp.

*1914–1989 Adventgemeinde Calw.* N.p.: N.p., 1989. [12] pp.

*1921–1971 Haus Neandertal der Siebenten-Tags-Adventisten.* Hannover: Grundstücks- und Heimverwaltung, Westdeutscher Verband, 1971. [56] pp.

*Adventbotschaft im Herzen des Schwabenlandes.* Stuttgart: Baden-Württembergische Vereinigung, 1979. 48 pp.

*Advent-Gemeinde 75 Jahre Schlangen.* N.p.: N.p., 1985. 20 pp.

*Advent-gemeinde Görlitz: Festschrift zum 100jährigen Bestehen 1904–2004.* N.p.: N.p., 2004. 44 pp.

*Advent-gemeinde Hameln: 75 Jahre: 1912–1987.* N.p.: N.p., 1987. 15 pp.

*Adventgemeinde Reutlingen 1909–1984.* Stuttgart: Baden-Württembergische Vereinigung, 1984. 32 pp.

*Advent-Mission im Rheinland: Hundert Jahre nach dem Besuch E. G. Whites im Rheinland.* Darmstadt: Gemeinschaft der Sieben-Tags-Adventisten in Deutschland, 1987. 24 pp.

*Advent-Wohlfahrtswerk Altenheim Uelzen e. V.* N.p.: N.p., n.d. 16 pp.

Arnold, Rudolf. *Krankenhaus Waldfriede: 1920–1975.* Hamburg: Grindeldruck, 1975. Gedenkschrift anläßlich der Einweihung des Krankenhaus-Neubaues am 7. Mai 1975 und des 55jährigen Bestehens am 15. April 1975. Unpaginated.

Binanzer, Walter. *100 Jahre Adventbotschaft im Herzen des Schwabenlandes.* Stuttgart: Siebenten-Tags-Adventisten, 1995. 82 pp.

Binanzer, Wilhelm. *München unter der Adventbotschaft.* München: Gemeinschaft d. Siebenten-Tags-Adventisten, Südbayerische Vereinigung, 1966. 36 pp.

Breu, F. *Mein Leben mit Gott: Aufzeichnungen und Erfahrungen aus der Feder des Jubilars Ferdinand Breu anläßlich seines 90. Geburtstages am 30. Januar 1996.* N.p.: N.p., 1996? 82 pp.

*Chronik zum 85jährigen Jubiläum der Adventgemeinde Göttingen.* N.p.: N.p., n.d. 19 pp.

*Chronik zur Einweihung der Kapelle der Advent-Gemeinde Romanshorn.* N.p.: N.p., n.d. [20] pp.

*Einladung zum 80jährigen Jubiläum 1908–1988: Adventgemeinde Ludwigsburg.* N.p.: N.p., 1988. [16] pp.

*Festschrift 100 Jahre Adventgemeinde Nürnberg 1900–2000.* Nürnberg: Adventgemeinde Nürnberg, 2000. 81 pp.

*Festschrift Marienhöhe: 1999 75 Jahre.* Darmstadt.: Marienhöhe, 1999. 52 pp.

*Geschichte der Gemeinde Steyr.* N.p.: Adventgemeinde Steyr, 1996. 46 pp.

Gnüchwitz, Bodo. *Die Wachtelburg zu Werder a/H: Historie und Gegenwart.* Werder/Havel: Förderverein Freundeskreis Wachtelburg e. V., n.d. 141 pp.

Gössler, Rudolf. *70 Jahre Adventgemeinde Bad Aibling* [Chronik der Adventgemeinde Bad Aibling]. Bad Aibling, 1989. 90 pp.

*Hamburger Verlagshaus der Siebenten-Tags-Adventisten: 1895–1970.* Hamburg: Saatkorn-Verlag, 1970. [48] pp.

Hartkop, Johann Heinrich Frederich. *Die Internationale Traktatgesellschaft in Hamburg.* Hamburg, 1912. 24 pp. Gedenkschrift über die Entstehung und Entwicklung der Internationalen Traktatgesellschaft in Hamburg.

Kopp, Marianne. *1907–1997: 90 Jahre Adventgemeinde Heidenheim.* N.p.: N.p., 1997. 44 pp.

*Krankenhaus Waldfriede 1920–1975: Gedenkschrift anläßlich der Einweihung des Krankenhaus-Neubaues am 7. Mai 1975 und des 55jährigen Bestehens am 15. April 1975.* Berlin-Zehlendorf: Krankenhaus Waldfriede, 1975. [30] pp.

*Neandertal 1921–1996: …im Blick zurück liegt der Weg nach vorne.* Neandertal: Adventgemeinde Mettmann-Neandertal, 1996. [30] pp.

Pfeiffer, Baldur Edmund, ed. *Advent-Mission im Rheinland: Hundert Jahre nach dem Besuch E. G. Whites im Rheinland.* Frankfurt am Main: Peter Lang, 1981. 24 pp.

*Siebenten-Tags-Adventisten: Chronik: Vom Beginn in Deutschland bis zur Gegenwart, 1875–2004.* Hamburg: Gemeinschaft der Siebenten-Tags-Adventisten in Deutschland, 2004. 98 pp.

Scharfschwerdt, Edwin. *75 Jahre Krankenhaus Waldfriede.* Berlin: Werbeagentur Kapella & Hubmeier, 1995.

Schneider, Robert. *Gemeindechronik zum 100-jährigen Jubiläum der Adventgemeinde Annaberg: 1910–2010.* Annaberg-Buchholz: Adventgemeinde Annaberg, 2010. 75 pp.

*Schritte in ein neues Leben: Bilder und Texte zum 125-jährigen Jubiläum der ersten adventistischen Taufe im Rheinland: Die Adventgemeinde Solingen und ihre Anfänge.* Solingen: Adventgemeinde Solingen, n.d. [14] pp.

Schröer, Olaf. *100 Jahre Adventgemeinde Heilbronn: 1902–2002.* N.p.: N.p., 2002.

*Siebenten-Tags-Adventisten in Dresden-Löbtau: 1909–2009.* N.p.: N.p., 2009. 32 pp.

*…so fing es an!: 80 Jahre Adventgemeinde Göppingen.* N.p.: N .p., 1986. [21] pp.

## Unpublished

Bonilla, Benjamin. "Latino Adventism in Germany. A Case Study of Spanish-speaking Seventh-day Adventists in Adventist Congregations across Germany." MTS thesis, Friedensau Adventist University, 2017.

Daniel, Gudrun. "Die Zumutung christlicher Ethik im Dritten Reich unter besonderer Berücksichtigung der Haltung der Siebenten-Tags-Adventisten und der Zeugen Jehovas zum Nationalsozialismus." Diplom thesis, Friedensau Adventist University, 2003. 113 pp.

Decker, Edward Thomas. "Weiss Juden: The Story of the Seventh-day

Adventist Church in the Third Reich." MA thesis, University of Denver, 1968.
    192 pp.
Gäbel, Stephan. "Adventgemeinde und Charismatische Bewegung in
    Deutschland." MA thesis, Friedensau Adventist University, 2011. 187, 101 pp.
Gattman, Heinz-Ewald. "Die missionarischen Konzepte der Siebenten-Tags-
    Adventisten in Deutschland unter besonderer Berücksichtigung der Jahre
    1992–2005. ThD dissertation, University of South Africa, 2008.
Gattman, Heinz-Ewald. "Mission als gelebter Auftrag Jesu Christi:
    Untersuchung für den Bereich des ehemaligen WDV für die Jahre 1992–1996
    unter besonderer Berücksichtigung ausgewählter Vereinigungen und
    ausgewählter Missionsmethoden." Diplom thesis, Friedensau Adventist
    University, 1998. 157 pp.
Gomer, Andreas. "Gemeinde auf dem Weg: Russlanddeutsche STA in
    Deutschland im Spannungsfeld von Religion, Migration und Integration." BA
    thesis, Friedensau Adventist University, 2017. 103 pp.
Gunjevic, Sasa. "Untersuchung missionarischer Projekte der Jahre 2006–2009
    der Freikirche der Siebenten-Tags-Adventisten in Deutschland auf ein
    prozesshaftes Missionsverständnis." MA thesis, Friedensau Adventist
    University, 2009. 69 pp.
Hall, Bruce Wayne. "Render Unto Caesar: State, Identity and Minority
    Churches in the German Democratic Republic, 1945–1989." PhD dissertation,
    State University of New York at Buffalo, 2003. ix, 299 pp.
Hartlapp, Johannes. "Military Service: A Comparative Study between the New
    Testament Teaching and the Attitude of German Adventists." MA thesis,
    Andrews University, 1993. v, 170 pp.
Kanev, Emil. "Erfolgreiche Evangelisation in den osteuropäischen Ländern
    unter den Bedingungen der politischen Wende." Diplom thesis, Friedensau
    Adventist University, 1997. 136 pp.
Machel, Edgar. "Eine Gemeindewachstumsstudie des Westdeutschen
    Verbandes der Siebenten-Tags-Adventisten von 1945–1990." DMin
    dissertation, Fuller Theological Seminary, 1994. 23, vi, 274 pp.
Mager, Johannes E. "The Transfer of Ministers in the Seventh-day Adventist
    Church of the German Democratic Republic and Its Effects on the Minister's
    Service and Family life." DMin dissertation, Andrews University, 1982. 5, ix,
    244, 8 pp.
Mickan, Andreas G. "Gemeindeneugründung in Ostdeutschland:
    Hintergründe, Gründe und Zusammenhänge." Diplom thesis, Friedensau
    Adventist University, 1999. 122 pp.
Müller, Ekkehardt. "Towards a Model of Congregational Evangelistic
    Campaigns in the Seventh-day Adventist Churches in West Germany." DMin
    dissertation, Andrews University, 1987. 3, viii, 254 pp.
Neumann, Matti. "Deutsche adventistische Missionare in der Zeit zwischen den

beiden Weltkriegen: Biographisch-bibliographische Fallbeispiele." MA thesis, Friedensau Adventist University, 2019. 120 pp.

Patt, Jacob M. "The History of the Advent Movement in Germany." PhD dissertation, Stanford University, 1958. x, 446 pp.

Rau, Rudolf. "Gemeinde und Zukunft? Die Rolle des Hauskreises im Gemeindeaufbau der Adventgemeinde in Deutschland." Diplom thesis, Friedensau Adventist University, 2003. 64 pp.

Rebant, Vitali. "Buchevangelisation in Deutschland in der Zeit von 1945–1961 unter Berücksichtigung des Wachstums der Gemeinde in dieser Zeit." BA thesis, Friedensau Adventist University, 2015. 39 pp.

Scheel, Matthias. "Schuldverarbeitung und Schuldbekenntnisse der Freikirchen nach dem Dritten Reich." MA thesis, Friedensau Adventist University, 2007. 124 pp.

Seiler, Alexej. "Gemeindegründung in Deutschland seit 1989: Eine Untersuchung in der Gemeinschaft der STA." MA thesis, Friedensau Adventist University, 2007. 83 pp.

Sinda, Baraka. "Background, Establishment, and Prospects of the Ghanaian Seventh-day Adventist Churches in Germany: A Case Study of Immigrant Adventism." MTS thesis, Friedensau Adventist University, 2014. 80 pp.

Spiegler, Thomas. "Darstellung und Analyse der Diskussionen um die Gastmitgliedschaft der Gemeinschaft der STA in der Arbeitsgemeinschaft Christlicher Kirchen in Deutschland." Diplom thesis, Friedensau Adventist University, 1999. 69 pp.

Tiessen, Andreas. "Seelsorgerliche Aspekte bei der Integration Russlanddeutscher Aussiedler in den deutschen Adventgemeinden." Diplom thesis, Friedensau Adventist University, 2002. 70 pp.

Wojtyto, Marek. "Historia niemieckich zborów Kościoła Adwentystów Dnia Siódmego na terenie diecezji pomorskiej i wschodniopruskiej ("History of the German SDA Congregations in the Conference of Pomerania and East Prussia.") MA thesis, Christian Theological Academy, 2008. 85 pp.

Wolter, Berndt Dietrich. "Planting Diverse Ethnic Seventh-day Adventist Churches in Berlin, Germany." DMin dissertation, Andrews University, 2009. xi, 178 pp.

## Greece

### Published

Latsha, Mabel. *Determined!* Mountain View, CA: Pacific Press, 1983. 128 pp. Biography on Harry Aristo Mataxas.

# Hungary

## Published

*A H. N. Adventista egyház: elismertetésének 20. évfordulója, 1957–1977.*
Budapest: H. N. Adventista egyház, 1977. 61 pp.

Erdélyi, László. *Egy ember az embertelenségben.* Budapest, 2005. 84 pp.
Biography on László Michnay, who helped more than fifty Jews escape the
Holocaust.

Erdélyi, László. *"Ő nekem választott edényem" 100 éve született Id. Szigeti Jenő
1906–1977.* Budapest: Advent Kiadó, n.d. 90 pp.

Kish, Alex. "Did the First Hungarian Baptist Become the First Hungarian
Adventist?: Johann Rottmayer and the Practice of Free Church Missions in
Nineteenth Century Central Europe." *Journal of European Baptist Studies* 7,
no. 1 (Sep 2006): 23–43.

Rajki, Zoltán. "A Békés megyei adventista megtérési történetek elemző
vizsgálata 1945 és 1956. közötti években." *Theologiai szemle* 2 (2000):
108–111.

Rajki, Zoltán. "A. H. N. Adventista Egyház története Magyarországon 1945–
1958 Között." ("The History of the Adventist Church between 1945 and 1958
in Hungary.") *Magyar Egyháztörténeti Vázlatok / Essays in Church History in
Hungary* 1–2 (1999): 109–152.

Rajki, Zoltán. *A. H. N. Adventista Egyház története 1945 és 1989 között
Magyarországon: doktori disszertáció.* ("History of Seventh-day Adventists in
Hungary, 1945–1989: A Doctoral Dissertation.") Budapest: Advent Kiadó,
2003. 208 pp.

Rajki, Zoltán. "A Hetednapi Adventista Egyház missziója Magyarországon a
rendszerváltozás után a statisztika tükrében." *Theologiai szemle* 1 (2009):
43–53. Also published under the same title in *ATF szemle / Adventista szemle*
(2009/1): 31–54.

Rajki, Zoltán. "A Hetednapi Adventista Egyház regionális jellemzői a 21.
század elején Magyarországon." In *Ami rejtve van s ami látható: Tanulmányok
Gereben Ferenc 65. születésnapjára,* edited by Melinda Czászár and Gergely
Rosta, 377–93. Budapest: Loisir Kiadó, 2008.

Rajki, Zoltán. "A Hetednapi Adventista Egyház tagsága családi megoszlása a
2006. évi felmérés szerint." *ATF szemle / Adventista szemle* (2008/2): 43–73.

Rajki, Zoltán. "A Hetednapi Adventista Egyház tagságának társadalmi
összetétele Magyarországon a 2006. év elején." *ATF szemle / Adventista szemle*
(2007/2): 34–71.

Rajki, Zoltán. "Adventisták felekezetközi kapcsolata a Duna medencében a
dualizmus utolsó évtizedeiben." In *Utánad, Olvasó!: A 70 éves Kamarás István
tiszteletére,* edited by János Géczi and Péter Makai, 103–110. Veszprém:
Pannon Egyetem, 2011.

Rajki, Zoltán. "Az adventista misszió társadalmi bázisának alakulása Magyarországon 1945 és 1989 között." *Egyháztörténeti szemle* 2 (2008): 67–85.

Rajki, Zoltán. "Az adventisták családi állapot szerinti megoszlása a 21. század elején a 2001. évi népszámlálás adatai alapján." *ATF szemle / Adventista szemle* (2008/1): 32–71.

Rajki, Zoltán. *Az Egervári-mozgalom.: A Keresztény Advent Közösség kialakulása és vallásszabadsági küzdelmei a Kádár-korszak második felében (1975–1990).* Budapest: Gondolat Kiadó, 2012. 161 pp.

Rajki, Zoltán. "Egy államilag manipulált kisegyházi választás: Az 1958. évi unióválasztás története a Hetednapi Adventisták Felekezete életében." In *"Taníts minket úgy számlálni napjainkat. . .": Tanulmányok a 70 éves Kósa László tiszteletére,* edited by Iván Berényi, Eleonóra Géra, and Gábor Richly, 367–375. Budapest: ELTE Eötvös Kiadó, 2012.

Rajki, Zoltán. *Egy Amerikai lelkész Magyarországi missziója: John Friederick Huenergardt élete és korának adventizmusa.* Budapest, 2004. 183 pp. The mission work of J. F. Huenergardt in Hungary.

Rajki, Zoltán. "Egy sikeres misszió története: A Hetednapi Adventista Egyház kialakulása és fejlődése a Kárpát-medencében az Osztrák-Magyar Monarchia idejében." *ATF szemle / Adventista szemle* (2006/1): 29–50.

Rajki, Zoltán. "H. N. Adventista Egyház a statisztika tükrében Békés megyében 1945–1956." *ATF szemle / Adventista szemle* (1999/3–4): 231–240.

Rajki, Zoltán. "H. N. Adventista Egyház irattárának forrásai. Magyar egyháztörténeti vázlatok." (1999/3–4): 231–240.

Rajki, Zoltán. "Legitimációs válság a H. N. Adventista Egyházban a hatvanas évek közepén." *Valóság: Társadalomtudományi közlöny* 5 (2001): 84–96.

Rajki, Zoltán. "Szabadegyházak egyháziasítása az 1960-as években Magyarországon." In *Szabadegyházak, vallási kisebbségek és a diktatúrák Európában a 20. században,* edited by Daniel Heinz, Zoltán Rajki, and Ervin Simon, 105–118. Budapest: Gondolát Kiadó, 2013.

Rajki, Zoltán, and Jenő Szigeti. *Szabadegyházak története Magyarországon 1989–IG.* Budapest: Gondolat Kiadó, 2012. 406 pp. History of the Evangelical Churches in Hungary.

Szigeti, Jenő. *"És emlékezzél meg az útról...": Tanulmányok a magyarországi szabadegyházak történetéből.* (" 'And Remember the Way...': Studies from the History of the Hungarian Free Churches.") Budapest: Szabadegyházak tanácsa, 1981. 292 pp. History of the Evangelical Churches in Hungary.

Szigeti, Jenő. *Fejezetek A H.N. Adventista Egyház Magyarországi Történetéből.* ("Chapters from the History of the Seventh-day Adventist Church in Hungary.") Engedelyszam: Adventista Egyház, 1985. 212 pp.

Szigeti, Jenő. *Isten tanítani küldött.* Budapest: Aranyforrás Kiadó, 2017. 267 pp. Autobiography.

## Unpublished

Árvai, Gergely. "Egy adventista prédikátor élete." ("The Life of an SDA Preacher.") BA thesis, Hungarian Adventist Theological College, 2004. 47 pp. Biography on pastor Árvai Henrik.

Czinege, Sándor. "A Budapesti Advent Kórus története 1941-től 2011-ig." ("The History of the Budapest Advent Choir from 1941 to 2011.") BA thesis, Hungarian Adventist Theological College, 2015.

Drechsler, Sharolta. "'The Open Door' in Hungary, and the Past and Present History behind It." Term paper, Andrews University, 1977. [21] pp.

Fehér, János. "A magyarországi szabadegyházak közjogi helyzetének alakulása a felszabadulástól napjainkig." ("The Development of the Official Status of the Hungarian Free Churches, from Liberation to the Present.") BA thesis, Hungarian Adventist Theological College, 1975. 57, 2 pp.

Hegyi, Árpád. "Nagy-Sármás H. N. Adventista gyülekezeti körzetének misszió története." ("The History of the Adventist Church's Mission in Nagy-Sármás and Its Surroundings.") BA thesis, Hungarian Adventist Theological College, 1993. 42 pp.

Juhász, Károly. "A Hetednapi Adventista Egyház könyvkiadásának története Magyarországon." ("History of SDA Publishing in Hungary.") BA thesis, Hungarian Adventist Theological College, 2009. 48 pp.

Kassai, Csaba Péter. "Az első budapesti adventista gyülekezet története." ("History of the First SDA Church in Budapest.") BA thesis, Hungarian Adventist Theological College, 2000. 72 pp.

Kormos, Erik. "A hajduböszörményi adventista gyülekezet kialakulása: Fejlődéstörténete napjainkig." ("The Establishment of the SDA Church in Hajduböszörményi: Its Development to the Present Day.") BA thesis, Hungarian Adventist Theological College, 1998. 43 pp.

Kovács, Tibor. "A H. N. Adventista Egyház missziójának bemutatása 1939–1949 között." ("Mission of the SDA Church from 1939 to 1949.") BA thesis, Hungarian Adventist Theological College, 2004. 37, 2 pp.

Kovács, Vilmos Ervin. "Az Adventista Egyház missziói fejlődése Magyarországon 1985 és 1995 között." ("Development of the Adventist Mission in Hungary, 1985–95.") BA thesis, Hungarian Adventist Theological College, 2004. 66, 4 pp.

Simon, Csaba. "A Hetednapi Adventista Egyház pécsi gyülekezetének története az alapítástól az 1975-ös szakadásig." ("The History of the SDA Church in Pécs from Its Foundation to the 1975 Break.") BA thesis, Hungarian Adventist Theological College, 2006. 100 pp.

Simon, Istvan. "Scindarea bisericii adventiste din Ungaria în 1975." ("The Split of the Adventist Church in Hungary in 1975.") BA thesis, RATI, 1999.

Szabó, László. "Mission Theology in Face of Reality: A Missiological Study of the Seventh-day Adventist Church in Hungary in the Context of the Fall of Communism." PhD dissertation, University of Wales, 2015.

Székely, Edmond. "A lelkipásztori szerepek változása a Magyar Unióban a XXI. Század fordulóján." ("Changes in Pastoral Roles in the Hungarian Union in the 21st century. At the Turn of the Century.") BA thesis, Hungarian Adventist Theological College, 2012.

Szilvási, András. "Increasing Pastoral Job Satisfaction and Efficiency in the Seventh-day Adventist Church in Hungary." DMin dissertation, Andrews University, 2005. 78–127.

Zloyomi, Renata Edit. "Erdelyi Adventistak magyarorszagon." ("Hungarian Adventists in Transylvania.") BA thesis, RATI, 2004.

## Iceland

### Published

Guðmundsson, Júlíus. *Minningapættir úr starfi Aðventsafnaðarins á Íslandi.* Reykjavík: Frækornið, 1994. 81 pp.

Heiðar, Helgi. *Views through My Lenses: Helgi's Saga: Eye Surgeon Shares His Eventful Journey from Iceland to America.* Centralia, WA: Published by the Author, 2013. 221 pp.

### Unpublished

Guðmundsson, Jørgen Eric. "A Strategy for Revitalization and Growth of the Seventh-day Adventist Church in Iceland." DMin dissertation, Andrews University, 2006. xii, 323 pp.

Kristjánsson, Guðni Geir. "Personal Aspects of Olaf J. Olsen's Missionary Life." MA thesis, Andrews University, 1977. [23] pp.

Snorrason, Björgvin Martin Hjelvik. "Pastor David Oestlund and the Beginnings of the Seventh-day Adventist Church in Iceland." Research paper, Andrews University, 1975. 70 pp.

Þórðarson, Steinþór Breiðfjörð. "A Study of Factors Related to the Numerical Growth of the Seventh-day Adventist Church in Iceland from 1950 to 1980." DMin dissertation, Andrews University, 1985. 4, xii, 253 pp.

Þórðarson, Steinþór Breiðfjörð. "The Seventh-day Adventist Church in Iceland since 1928." Research paper, Andrews University, 1973. iii, 61 pp.

# Ireland

## Published

Campbell, Percy Tilson and Ida May (Bauer)." In *The Ellen G. White Encyclopedia*, edited by Fortin and Moon, 460–461.

Farrell, Monica. *From Rome to Christ: The Story of a Spiritual Pilgrimage*. 5th ed. Glebe, Australia: Protestant Publications, 1947. 32 pp.

## Unpublished

Blackburn, Phillip. "The Life and Work of William Hutchinson, the First Serious Seventh-day Adventist Missionary to Ireland." Term paper, Andrews University, 1974. [7] pp.

# Italy

## Published

*1898–1998: Cento anni di Avventismo a Roma*. Rome: Department of Public Affairs and Religious Liberty, Italian Union of the Seventh-day Adventist Church, 1998. 64 pp.

Albisetti, Alessandro. "I matrimoni degli acattolici: Avventisti e Assemblee di Dio in Italia (ADI)." *Quaderni di diritto e politica ecclesiastica* 1 (1988): 83–92.

Barbuscia, Ignazio. *Organizzazione della Chiesa cristiana avventista italiana: Cenni storici, delibere, statistiche, progetti*. Rome: Published by the Author, 1984. 59 pp.

Bognandi, Dora. "Luisa Chiellini: Siamo donne non pupattole." In *Scelte di fede e di libertà. Profili di evangelici nell'Italia unita*, edited by Dora Bognandi, and Mario Cignoni, 140–142. Torino: Claudiana, 2011.

Bognandi, Dora, and Davide Romano, eds. 1*50 anni (1864–2014) della presenza avventista in Italia – la storia, la missione, le sfide e la testimonianza*. Firenze: Edizioni AdV, 2014. 175 pp.

Coppola, Raffaele. "Le intese con l'Unione avventista e le Assemblee di Dio in Italia con particolare riguardo ai contenuti normativi." In *Normativa ed organizzazione delle minoranze confessionali in Italia*, edited by Valerio Parlato, and Giovanni Battista Varnier, 39–50. Torino: Giappichelli, 1992.

De Meo, Giovanni. "Alfred-Felix Vaucher (1887–1993): Un secolo d'avventismo." *Adventus* 2 (1994): 5–117.

De Meo, Giuseppe. *"Grane di sale": Un secolo di storia della Chiesa christiana avventista del 7° giorno in Italia (1864–1964)*. Torino: Editrice Claudiana, 1980. 256, [2] pp.

Evangelisti, Franco. *Breve atoria della Chiesa avventista nel mondo, in Italia, a Cesena: 12 Aprile 1935–28 Settembre 2002*. N.p.: Published by the Author, 2002. 117 pp.

Favergiotti, Anna. "Le Intese con le Chiese Avventiste e Pentecostali (artt. 34-38 l. 22 novembre 1988, n. 516)." *Le Nuove leggi civili commentate* 13, no. 2 (1990): 466–469.

*Gli avventisti a Trieste: 1923–2003*. N.p.: Chiesa cristiana avventista di Trieste, 2003. 120 pp.

Heinz, Daniel. "Vaucher, Alfred-Félix (1887–1993)." In *Biographisch-Bibliographisches Kirchenlexikon*.

Long, Enrico. "Alberto Long: Obiettore di coscienza." In *Scelte di fede e di libertà. Profili di evangelici nell'Italia unita*. Edited by Dora Bognandi and Mario Cignoni. Torino: Claudiana, 2011, pp. 172–174.

Long, Gianni. "Le intese con l'Unione avventista e con le Assemblee di Dio in Italia." *Quaderni di diritto e politica ecclesiastica* 4 (1987):119–136.

Margiotta Broglio, Francesco. "Libertà religiosa e sistema di rapporti tra Stato e Confessioni religiose: Le "Intese" del 1986 con le Assemblee pentecostali e con le Chiese avventiste." *Rivista di studi politici internazionali* 4 (1987): 548–549.

Musselli, Luciano. "Le Intese con le Chiese Avventizie e Pentecostali." *Le Nuove leggi civili commentate* 13, no. 2 (1990): 440–446.

Musselli, Luciano. "Le Intese con le Chiese Avventiste e Pentecostali (artt. 1–33 l. 22 novembre 1988, n. 516)." *Le Nuove leggi civili commentate* 13, no. 2 (1990): 447–466.

Rimoldi, Tiziano. "Gian Luigi Lippolis: Predicatore avventista antifascista." In *Scelte di fede e di libertà. Profili di evangelici nell'Italia unita*, edited by Dora Bognandi and Mario Cignoni, 157–160. Torino: Claudiana, 2011.

Rimoldi, Tiziano. "I ministri di culto nella Chiesa avventista del 7° giorno e nella Chiesa evangelica valdese." *Daimon* 3 (2003): 171–193.

Rimoldi, Tiziano. "Il dialogo ecumenico dal punto di vista avventista." In *Cristianesimo Cristianesimi: Fra conflitti e ricerca di pace*, edited by M. Salani, 117–140. Pisa: Edizioni Plus–Pisa University Press, 2011.

Rimoldi, Tiziano. "Il finanziamento delle confessioni religiose in Italia: La Chiesa cristiana avventista del settimo giorno." *Il Diritto ecclesiastico* 3–4 (2006): 490–507.

Rimoldi, Tiziano. "Il riconoscimento dei titoli di studio rilasciati dall'Istituto avventista di cultura biblica." *Coscienza e Libertà* 43 (2009): 124–137.

Rimoldi, Tiziano. "Il riposo sabatico avventista." *Il Diritto ecclesiastico* 1 (2000): 101–114.

Rimoldi, Tiziano. "The Italian Adventists during World War I: The Story of Alberto Long." Proceedings of the Symposium "The Impact of World War I on Seventh-day Adventism." Institute of Adventist Studies, Friedensau Adventist University, May 12–15, 2014. Forthcoming.

Rimoldi, Tiziano. "La Chiesa avventista del settimo giorno e lo stato fascista."
   *Annali di Storia moderna e contemporanea* 6 (2000): 605–623.
Rimoldi, Tiziano. "L'intesa con la Chiesa avventista." *Coscienza e Libertà* 31
   (1998): 16–27.
Rimoldi, Tiziano. "L'intesa con la Chiesa avventista del 7° giorno." Unpublished
   manuscript, 2004.
Rimoldi, Tiziano. "Matrimoni misti e rito religioso: Ordinamenti confessionali a
   confronto: Cattolico, valdese, avventista." *Adventus* 16 (2006): 61–84.
Rimoldi, Tiziano. "Relazioni Chiesa-Stato: La Chiesa avventista del settimo
   giorno: Alcune vicende." *Il Diritto ecclesiastico* 3 (1998): 682–690.
Rimoldi, Tiziano. "Un commento degli avventisti." *Quaderni del Circolo Rosselli*
   96 (2007): 69–73.
Rossi, Gianfranco. *Lotte e vittorie degli avventisti italiani per la libertà religiosa.*
   Firenze: Edizioni AdV, 2007. 560 pp.
Spini, Giorgio. "Gli avventisti in Italia." *Bollettino della Società di studi valdesi* 150
   (1981): 59–73.
Tallini, Damiano. "Il percorso compagnon e i suoi presupposti pedagogici.
   Analisi teorica di un'esperienza educativa." BA thesis, Istituto avventista di
   cultura biblica "Villa Aurora," 2016.
Valsiglio, Cristian. "Il riposo sabbatico e il licenziamento discriminatorio." *Il
   Diritto ecclesiastico* 1 (2000): 114–120.

## Unpublished

Barbuscia, Ignazio. "L'Aisa e lo scoutismo: Un modello educativo cristiano." BA
   thesis, Italian Adventist University, 2007. 89 pp.
Breci, Gionatan. "Etiopia: storia di una missione avventista: Dalla nascita
   dell'interesse missionario avventista fino all'invio di missionari italiani." MA
   thesis, Italian Adventist University, 2012. 132 pp.
Calà, Stefano. "Fatti dell'era fascista nelle pagine dei periodici avventisti italiani."
   BA thesis, Italian Adventist University, 2010. 144 pp.
Fantoni, Vittorio. "Les vicissitudes vécues par l'Église adventiste italienne dans
   son refus d'adhérer à la Fédération évangélique: Histoire et problèmes." MA
   thesis, Adventist University of France–Collonges, 2005.
Gravante, Elisa. "La Fondazione Adventum (1994-2004): Una risposta al
   fenomeno usura in Italia." BA thesis, Italian Adventist University, 2012. 105 pp.
Loide, Migliore. "Da Battle Creek a Niscemi, un viaggio lungo cento anni: Storia
   della Chiesa cristiana avventista di Niscemi." BA thesis, Italian Adventist
   University, 2007.
Long, Alberto. "Alberte Michele Long from Torre Pellice, Italy." 1977. 39 pp.
   Autobiography.
Pontvik, Dag-Kristian, "La Radio Voce della Speranza Firenze: Storia di
   un'emittente avventista." BA thesis, Italian Adventist University, 2005. 71 pp.

Rizzo, Rolando. "Ellen G. White e la Chiesa avventista italiana." MA thesis, Adventist University of France–Collonges, 2003.

Stănescu, Vasile-Emil. "Le origini di Reach Italia e le sue relazioni con la Chiesa avventista del 7° giorno." BA thesis, Italian Adventist University, 2015.

Zagara, Daniele. "Attitude des parents adventistes d'Italie vis-à-vis des moyens utilisés pour la transmission des valeurs religieuses à leurs enfants." MA thesis, Adventist University of France–Collonges, 1988.

## Latvia

### Published

Bendža, Ieviņa. "Blaubergi: Ženija un Valentīns." *Kopējā Ceļā*, 1996/3, 4–6.

Čerņevskis, Edgars. *Adventes kustība Latvijā.* ("The Advent Movement in Latvia.") Riga: Patmos, 1998. 54 pp.

Čerņevskis, Edgars. "Mūsu celmlauži: Alberts Ozols." *Adventes Vēstis*, August 1997, 9.

Čerņevskis, Edgars. "Mūsu celmlauži: Aleksandrs Eglītis." *Adventes Vēstis*, September 1997, 7–8.

Čerņevskis, Edgars. "Mūsu celmlauži: Andrejs Sproģis." *Adventes Vēstis*, April 1997, 7–8.

Čerņevskis, Edgars. "Mūsu celmlauži: Čolderu Dzimta." *Adventes Vēstis*, April 1999, 4–5.

Čerņevskis, Edgars. "Mūsu celmlauži: Elmārs Krievs." *Adventes Vēstis*, May 1998, 4.

Čerņevskis, Edgars. "Mūsu celmlauži: Hermanis Linde." *Adventes Vēstis*, February 1998, 4–5.

Čerņevskis, Edgars. "Mūsu celmlauži: Jānis Dreimanis." *Adventes Vēstis*, July 1997, 7–8.

Čerņevskis, Edgars. "Mūsu celmlauži: Jānis Driķis." *Adventes Vēstis*, November 1997, 7–8.

Čerņevskis, Edgars. "Mūsu celmlauži: Jānis Sproģis." *Adventes Vēstis*, March 1997, 7–8.

Čerņevskis, Edgars. "Mūsu celmlauži: Jēkabs Šneiders." *Adventes Vēstis*, May 1997, 7–8.

Čerņevskis, Edgars. "Mūsu celmlauži: Kārlis Roze." *Adventes Vēstis*, June 1997, 4–5.

Čerņevskis, Edgars. "Mūsu celmlauži: Kārlis Sutta." *Adventes Vēstis*, January 1998, 4–5.

Čerņevskis, Edgars. "Mūsu celmlauži: Pāvels Macānovs." *Adventes Vēstis*, March 1999, 4–5.

Čerņevskis, Edgars. "Mūsu celmlauži: Pēteris Purmalis." *Adventes Vēstis*, December 1997, 4.

Driķis, Juris. "Draudzes dzīvības avots." *Adventes Vēstis*, September 2016, 6–7.
Pešelis, Andris. "Adventistu periodika." *Adventes Vēstis*, September 2016, 14–19. Written at the 110-year anniversary.
Pešelis, Andris. "Adventistu periodika Latvijā." *Adventes Vēstis*, January 2010, 14–15.
Pešelis, Andris. *Septītās dienas adventistu Latvijas draudžu vēsture.* ("History of the SDA Church in Latvia.") Riga: Patmos, 2013. 368 pp.
Raģe, Valija. "Adventistu misijas seminārs Sužos." *Adventes Vēstis*, November 2018, 14–15.
Rasmusens, Steens. *"Draudzes vēstures kurss" ar papildinājumiem par Latviju no J. Šneidera.* ("Church History Course with Additonal Material on Latvia from J. Šneider.") Riga: Latvijas Rakstu Apgādība, 1924. 54 pp.
Šaripovi Leonards, and Aina Šaripovi. "Velta un Edgars Čerņevski." *Kopējā Ceļā*, 1996/2, 3–4.

## Unpublished

Galeniece, Anna. "A Historically and Culturally Contextualized Proposal for Health Evangelism in Latvia." DMin dissertation, Andrews University, 2002. ix, 166 pp.
Kreslins, Andis. "The Challenge of Communicating Christ's Post-Ascension Ministry in a Culturally Sensitive Way to a Postmodern Latvian Society in [the] 21st century." MA thesis, Newbold College, 2004. 73 pp.

## *Lithuania*

### Published

Oželis, Danielius. *Viešpaties vynuogynas: Trumpa Septintosios dienos adventistų bažnyčios istorija Lietuvoje.* ("The Lord's Vineyard: A Short History of the SDA Church in Lithuania.") Kaunas: Spindulio spaustuvė, 2012. 168 pp.

## *Luxembourg*

### Published

Cools, Marc D. *Conduit par Dieu: Un missionaire raconte.* Published by the Author, 2018. 128 pp.

# Moldova

## Published

Andrusyak, V. I. *Nepobyezhdennaya Tserkov' v Bozh'ikh rukakh: Iz istorii tserkvi ASD v Moldove.* ("Undefeated Church in God's Hands: History of the SDA Church in Moldova.") Zaokskiy: Istochnik zhizni, 2011. 287 pp.

Yunak, Dmitriy O. *I pomni ves' put': Istoriya Tserkvi ASD v Moldavii.* ("History of the SDA Church in Moldova.") Kishinev, 2000. 311 pp.

Osadchuk, P. V. *Dlya Slova Bozhiya net uz: Evangel'skoye sluzheniye v usloviyah totalitarizma.* ("The Word of God Cannot Be Fettered: The Gospel during Totalitarian Rule.") Publishing Department of the SDA Church in Moldova, 2005.

## Unpublished

Leahu, Stefan. "Origin and Progress of the Seventh-day Adventist Church in Moldova: A Historical Survey." MA thesis, Friedensau Adventist University, 2016. 159 pp.

Sîrbu, Alexandru. "Istoria şi dezvoltarea bisericii adventiste de ziua a şaptea din unitatea teritorială autonomă găgăuză." ("History and Development of the Seventh-day Adventist Church in the Autonomous Gagauzian Territory.") BA thesis, RATI, 2000.

Tarlev, Ilie. "Scurt istoric al primei comunităţi adventiste de ziua a şaptea din raionul Criuleni." ("Brief History of the Seventh-day Adventist Community of Criuleni District.") BA thesis, RATI, 1999.

Zamostean, Gheorghe. "Istoria dezvoltării Bisericii Adventiste de Ziua a Şaptea din Moldova în timpul comunismului." ("History of the Development of the Seventh-day Adventist Church of Moldova during Communism.") BA thesis, RATI, 2000.

Zgherea, Ianoş. "Fenomenul religios adventist în Hânceşti, Lăpuşna." ("The Adventist Religious Phenomenon in Hancesti, Lapusna.") BA thesis, RATI, 2000.

# Netherlands

## Published

Ford, Herbert. *Flee the Captor.* 1st ed. Nashville, TN: Southern Publishing, 1966. 373 pp. 373 pp. Biography on Jean Henri Weidner.

Heinz, Daniel. "Weidner, Jean Henri (1912–1994)." In *Biographisch-Bibliographisches Kirchenlexikon.*

Koreman, Megan. *The Escape Line: How the Ordinary Heroes of Dutch-Paris*

*Resisted the Nazi Occupation of Western Europe.* Oxford: Oxford University Press, 2018. xiv, 410 pp.

Noorbergen, Rene. *Shadow of Terror: A Compelling Memoir Surging with Hope and Courage.* Washington, DC: Review and Herald, 1990. 141 pp.

Tilstra, Albertine Klingbeil. *A Dutchman Bound for Paradise.* Washington, DC: Review and Herald, 1980. 126 pp. Biography of missionary Klaas Tilstra.

Van Rijn, Hendricus Gerardus. "100 Jaar Adventkerk in Nederland." *Advent Exposé,* 1987, no. 1, special issue. 105 pp.

## Unpublished

De Raad, Robert K. "Contributions Made by Conradi to the Work in Holland." Term paper, Newbold College, 1981. 17 pp. Center for Adventist Research, James White Library.

Koning, Daniëlle Tabitha. "Importing God: The Mission of the Ghanaian Adventist Church and Other Immigrant Churches in the Netherlands." PhD dissertation, Vrije Universiteit Amsterdam, 2011. 231 pp.

Koning, Gerrit Hendrik. "Louis Richard Conradi's Work and Influence: vis a vis, The Development of the Seventh-day Adventist Church in the Netherlands." Term paper, Andrews University, 1975. 34 pp.

Stijnman, Andre H. M. "The Holland Language Publications in the History of the 19th Century S. D. A. Movement in North America." Term paper, Andrews University, 1973. 38 pp.

Tilstra, Albert Cornelius. "The History of the Seventh-day Adventist Church in the Netherlands." Term paper, Andrews University, 1970? 29 pp.

Versteegh, H. Dietrich. "Holland in Focus in the Years 1874–1893." Term paper, Andrews University, 1975. 37 pp.

## *Norway*

## Published

Abrahamsen, Karl. *Norsk Bokforlag 100 ar.* Oslo: s.p., 1979. 101 pp.

Helgesen, Kjell. *Da adventismen kom til Norge.* Røyse: Norsk Bokforlag AS, 2015. 260 pp.

Johannessen, Terje. *De skandinaviske adventismens begynnelse og vekst.* 3 vols. Skjern: Øko-Tryk, 2017. 480, 480, 377 pp.

La Bianca, M. Olav, and Valerie J. Breedlove. *Where God Has Led.* S.p.: Published by the Authors, 2011. 318 pp. Biography of M. Olav La Bianca.

Matteson, John G. *Mattesons Liv.* College View, NE: International Publishing Assocation, 1908.

Paulsen, Kari. *Against All Odds: A True Story.* Nampa, ID: Pacific Press, 2015. 151 pp. Autobiography.

Torkelsen, Edwin. *Ellen G. White og Norge 1885/1887–1987.* Røyse: Signum Forlag, 1988. 243 pp.

## Unpublished

Aune, Kjell. "A Contextual Analysis of the Seventh-day Adventist Church in Norway, with Suggestions for Renewal and Growth." DMin dissertation, Andrews University, 2005. x, 270 pp.

Lisle, Per. "The Seventh-day Adventist Church in Norway: A Bibliography." 2000. 129 pp. Center for Adventist Research, James White Library.

Snorrason, Björgvin Martin Hjelvik. "The Origin, Development, and History of the Norwegian Seventh-day Adventist Church from the 1840s to 1889." PhD dissertation, Andrews University, 2010.

Thompson, Steven Wayne. "Story of the Norwegian Mission School: The First Decade, 1921–1931." Term paper, Andrews University, 1971. 15, [2] pp.

## *Poland*

### Published

*80 lat Wyższej szkoły teologiczno-humanistycznej im. Michała Beliny-Czechowskiego w. Podkowie Leśnej.* Polish Senior College of Theology and Humanities, 2006. [15] pp.

Folaron, Stefan and Robert Janik. *Społeczno-wychowawcza doktryna i działalność Kościoła Adwentystów Dnia Siódmego w Polsce i RFN w latach 1949–1995.* ("Socio-Educational Doctrine and Activity of the SDA Church in Poland and the FRG [Federal Republic of Germany], 1949–1995.") Częstochowa: Wydawnictwo Wyższej Szkoły Pedagogicznej w Częstochowie, 1997. 163 pp.

Koziróg, Bernard. "Diecezja Południowa Kościoła Adwentystów Dnia Siódmego w latach 1928–1939 w relacjach czasopisma 'Sługa Zboru.'" ("History of the Southern Conference of the SDA Church, 1928–1939, as Reported in the Magazine Sługa Zboru.") *Signa Temporis,* no. 1 (1991): 75–96.

Koziróg, Bernard. *Dzieje Diecezji Wschodniej Kościoła Adwentystów Dnia Siódmego w Polsce.* ("History of the Eastern Polish Conference.") Warsaw: N.p., 1988. 44 pp.

Koziróg, Bernard. "Dzieje Diecezji Zachodniej Kościoła Adwentystów Dnia Siódmego w Polsce w latach 1928–1939 w relacjach czasopisma 'Sługa Zboru.'" ("History of the Western Conference of the SDA Church in Poland as Reported in Sługa Zboru, 1928–1939") *Signa Temporis,* no. 1 (1991): 127–141.

Koziróg, Bernard. "Narodziny polskiego adwentyzmu. Wykład wygłoszony podczas inauguracji roku akademickiego w Wyższej Szkole Teologiczno-Humanistycznej w Podkowie Leśnej." ("The Birth of Polish Adventism: Lecture Presented at the Inauguration of the Academic Year at the Polish Senior College of Theology and Humanities in Podkowa Leśna.") *Signa Temporis*, no. 20 (2013): 85–91.

Koziróg, Bernard. *Z dziejów polskiego adwentyzmu...: Zjednoczenie Południowe i Zjednoczenie Zachodnie w latach 1918–1988.* ("From the History of Polish Adventism: The Southern and Western Conferences, 1918–1988.") Podkowa Leśna: Signa Temporis, 2013. 184 pp.

Łozowski, Stanisław Zbigniew, ed. *"Aż dotąd pomagał nam Pan'": Adwentyści w Lublinie w latach 1914–2004.* ("'Hitherto the Lord Has Helped Us': Adventists in Lublin, 1914–2004.") Warsaw: Znaki Czasu, 2004. 96 pp.

Łyko, Zachariasz. *Adwentyzm.* Warsaw: Znaki Czasu, 1970. 320 pp.

Łyko, Zachariasz. *Kościół Adwentystów dnia siódmego.* Warsaw: Znaki Czasu, 1988. 238 pp.

Łyko, Zachariasz. *Kościół Adwentystów dnia siódmego: historia, nauka, ustrój, posłannictwo.* Warsaw: Chrześcijański Instytut Wydawniczy "Znaki Czasu," 2000. 524 pp. History of Seventh-day Adventists in Poland and explanation of Adventist beliefs.

Łyko, Zachariasz. "Od 'Kursów kaznodziejskich' w Warszawie do 'Wyższej Szkoły Teologiczno-Humanistycznej' w Podkowie Leśnej." ("From Preaching Courses in Warsaw to the Polish Senior College of Theology and Humanities in Podkowa Leśna.") *Signa Temporis*, no. 7 (2004): 119–136.

Łyko, Zachariasz. "Osiemdziesięciolecie 'Znaków Czasu.'" ("Eighty Years of *Signs of the Times*.") *Signa Temporis*, no. 1 (1990): 97–108.

Łyko, Zachariasz. *Sytuacja prawna Kościoła Adwentystycznego w Polsce międzywojennej 1918–1939.* ("The Legal Situation of the Adventist Church in Poland in the Interwar Period, 1918–1939.") Warsaw: Znaki Czasu, 1979. 380 pp.

Łyko, Zachariasz. *Zarys dziejów Kościoła Adwentystycznego w Polsce: Kompendium.* ("Outline of the History of the Adventist Church in Poland: A Compendium.") Podkowa Leśna: Polish Senior College of Theology and Humanities, 1990. 62 pp.

Makowska, Marzanna. "Adwentystyczne Seminarium Duchowne w latach 1926–1945." ("The Adventist Seminary, 1926–1945.") *Signa Temporis*, no. 9 (2005): 87–99.

Makowska, Marzanna. *Dzieje i znaczenie eklezjalno-edukacyjne adwentystsycznej szkoły teologicznej (1926–2006).* Podkowa Leśna: Signa Temporis, 2008. 118 pp. History of the Polish Adventist college.

Mazurek, Wanda, and Sandra Piecha-Olech. *Adwentyści w Katowicach 1910–2015: Kronika Zboru Kościoła Adwentystów Dnia Siódmego w Katowicach.* ("Adventists in Katowice 1910–2015: Chronicle of the SDA Church in

Katowice.") Katowice: Kościół Adwentystów Dnia Siódmego Zbór w Katowicach, 2015. 82 pp.

Walter, Marek. *Dzieje zborów Kościoła Adwentystów Dnia Siódmego na Kresach Wschodnich w latach 1888–1945.* Warsaw: Znacki Czasu, 2015. 618 pp.

Walter, Marek. *Dzieje zborów Kościoła Adwentystów Dnia Siódmego na Śląsku w latach 1898–1945.* ("History of the Seventh-day Adventists in Silesia, 1898–1945.") Warsaw: Znaki Czasu, 2012. 297 pp.

Walter, Marek. *Dzieje zborów Kościoła Adwentystów Dnia Siódmego, na Ziemi Lubuskiej, Kujawskiej i Łódzkiej w latach 1893–1945.* Warsaw: Znaki Czasu, 2019. 759 pp.

Żukaluk, Mikołaj. "Wspólne korzenie adwentyzmu w Polsce i zachodniej Ukrainie." ("The Common Roots of Adventism in Poland and Western Ukraine.") *Signa Temporis,* no. 15 (2009): 71–75.

## Unpublished

Adamczyk, Andrews. "The Rise and Development Seventh-day Adventists in Poland." Term paper, Andrews University, 1971. 18 pp.

Czajka, Czesław. "Dzieje Diecezji Wschodniej Kościoła Adwentystów Dnia Siódmego w latach 1988–1991." ("Activity of the Polish Western Conference of the Seventh-day Adventist Church 1988–1991.") BA thesis, Polish Senior College of Theology and Humanities, 2001.

Dąbrowski, Rajmund Ładysław. "Catholic and Adventist Encounter with the Marxist State in Poland." Term paper, Andrews University, 1972. 53 pp.

Firak, Krystyna. "Powstanie, rozwój, doktryna I działalnośc Kościoła Adwentystów Dnia Siódmego w Polsce." ("Establishment, Development, Doctrine and Activity of the SDA Church in Poland."). MA thesis, Higher Pedagogical School, 1993. 190 pp.

Harasim, Mirosław. "Reformacja i adwentyzm na Pogórzu Karpackim." ("Reformation and Adventism in the Carpathian Foothills."). BA thesis, Polish Senior College of Theology and Humanities, 2005. 53 pp.

Janik, Robert. "Społeczno-wychowawcze znaczenie doktryny i działalności Kościoła Adwentystów Dnia Siódmego w Polsce." ("Socio-Educational Significance of the Doctrine and Activity of the SDA Church in Poland.") MA thesis, Higher Pedagogical School, 1988. 247 pp.

Koziróg, Bernard. "Kościół Adwentystów Dnia Siódmego w Polsce: Diecezja Wschodnia." ("Seventh-day Adventist Church in Poland: Eastern Conference.") MA thesis, Christian Theological Academy, 1988, 81 pp.

Krysta, Jan. "Geneza i rozwój adwentyzmu w Polsce ze szczególnym uwzględnieniem Śląska Cieszyńskiego." ("The Origin and Development of Adventism in Poland with a Special Emphasis on Silesia of Cieszyn.") BA thesis, Polish Senior College of Theology and Humanities, 2007.

Maikowski, Mariusz. "Działalność ewangelizacyjna i duszpasterska KADS w

Zakładzie Karnym w Siedlcach w latach 1988–1993." (Evangelism and Pastoral Work of the SDA Church in the Prison in Siedlce between 1988–1993.") BA thesis, Polish Senior College of Theology and Humanities, 2002.

Morozowski, Krzysztof. "Rozwój i działalność kolportażu w Polsce w latach 1992–2005." ("Development and Activity of the Colporteur Ministry in Poland, 1992–2005.") BA thesis, Polish Senior College of Theology and Humanities, 2006.

Pakosz-Stekla, Wioletta. "Historia zboru Kościoła Adwentystów Dnia Siódmego w Jaworzu." ("History of the SDA Congregation in Jaworze.") BA thesis, Polish Senior College of Theology and Humanities, 2010. 58 pp.

Sobkowiak, Mariusz. "Historia adwentyzmu na ziemi rzeszowskiej." ("The History of Adventism in Rzeszów.") BA thesis, Polish Senior College of Theology and Humanities, 2003.

Trzpil, Grzegorz. "Czynniki hamujące wzrost Kościoła Adwentystów Dnia Siódmego w Polsce." ("Factors that Inhibit Growth of the Seventh-day Adventist Church in Poland.") BA thesis, Polish Senior College of Theology and Humanities, 2009.

## Portugal

### Published

Ferreira, Ernesto. *Arautos de Boas Novas: Centenário da Igreja Adventista do Sétimo Dia em Portugal (1904–2004)*. Lisbon: União Portuguesa dos Adventistas do Sétimo Dia, 2008. 790 pp. The first work on the history of the Adventist Church in Portugal.

### Unpublished

Gouveia, Daniel F. M. "A Cross-Centered Evangelistic Preaching Strategy for the Seventh-day Adventist Church in Canelas, Portugal." DMin dissertation, Andrews University, 2016. ix, 173 pp.

Rentfro, Charles Allen. "History of Adventist Pioneers in Portugal." 1979. TMs. 20 pp.

## Romania

### Published

*Aste și memorii referitoare la situația comunității Evanghelice Adventiste din România*. Bucharest, 1923.

Berecz, Sophie, and Arpad Soo. *In His Hands*. Nampa, ID: Pacific Press, 2002.

159 pp. Biography of Arpad Soo.

Budd, Greg. *One Miracle after Another: The Pavel Goia Story.* Hagerstown, MD: Review and Herald, 2010. 160 pp.

Cojea, Vasile Dragu. *Adventiştii de ziua a 7-a în timpul regimului comunist.* N.p.: N.p., 2004. 63 pp. The Adventist Church during the Communist period.

Cojea, Vasile Dragu. *Adventiştii de ziua a şaptea în ilegalitate (1942–1944) şi legalitate.* ("Seventh-day Adventists in Illegal (1942–1944) and Legal Times.") Bucharest: Viaţă şi Sănătate, 2007. 191 pp.

Cojea, Vasile Dragu. *Asuprirea adventiştilor de ziua a şaptea în ciuda l egalităţii şi în afara ei 1930–1943.* ("Oppression of SDAs despite Their Legal Status, 1930–1943.") 2000? 192 pp.

Cojea, Vasile Dragu. *Biserica Adventistă sub comunism.* ("The Adventist Church during Communism.") Cernica: CARD, 2003. 122 pp. See *The Seventh-day Adventists of Romania during the Communist Regime.*

Cojea, Vasile Dragu. *Cărări vechi şi noi: documente de istorie Adventistă.* ("Old and New Paths: Documents of Adventist History.") Bucharest: CARD, 1999. 528 pp. Short biographies of the first Adventist pastors of the Romanian Adventist Church.

Cojea, Vasile Dragu. *Lumini şi umbre.* ("Light and Shadows.") Bucharest: CARD, 2001. 487 pp. Short biographies of important Adventist pastors and missionaries who worked in Romania.

Cojea, Vasile Dragu. *The Seventh-day Adventists of Romania during the Communist Regime.* Translated by Lucia Pavlov. Bucharest: Viaţă şi Sănătate, 2008. 117 pp.

Cojea, Vasile Dragu. *Stefan Demetrescu: Ofiţer, pastor, avocat, 1882–1973.* ("Stefan Demetrescu: Officer, Pastor, Lawyer, 1882–1973.") Bucharest: Viaţă şi sănătate, 2007. 72 pp. Biography on Stefan Demetrescu.

Cojea, Vasile Dragu. *Vechi cărări advente.* ("Old Adventist Paths.") Bucharest: CARD, 1998. 464 pp. Manuscripts, stories, and diverse documents about the beginnings of the Adventist work in Romania.

Cojea, Vasile Dragu. *Vechi înscrisuri advente.* ("Old Adventist Writings.") Bucharest: Viaţă şi Sănătate, 2003. 519 pp. Compilation of short sermons, letters, and manuscripts by the Adventist pastors Petre P. Paulini and Stefan Demetrescu.

Fitzai, Corneliu-Ghiocel. *Mişcarea Adventistă de Ziua a Şaptea din România* ("Seventh-day Adventist Movement in Romania.") Translated from French by Laura Maftei. Selimbar: Clever Books, 2009. 660 pp. See Fitzai's dissertation in the unpublished section.

Gehann, Günther. *Întreita Solie în Austro-Ungaria şi România 1869–1938.* ("The Three Angel Mesage In Austro-Hungaria and Romania.") Cernica: Graphé, 2008. 260 pp.

Gehann, Günther. *Predigt das Evangelium: Die Geschichte der Adventbewegung in Siebenbürgen und Rumänien von der Gründung der Gemeinschaft bis zum Zweiten Weltkrieg*. Kludenbach: Gehann Musikverlag Kludenbach, 2001. 328 pp.

*Institutul Bibilic Brasov-Stupini 1949–1999 Ani de robie*. ("Brasov-Stupini Bible Institute, 1949–1999. Years of Bondage.") Bucharest: CARD, 1999. 52 pp.

Iosif, Váradi. *Persecuţia comunistă în istoria adventă din Romănia*. ("Communist Persecution in Romanian Adventist History.") Dej: DSG Press, 2002. 464 pp.

Modoran, Gheorghe. *Biserica prin pustiul roşu: Rezistenţă şi compromis în adventismul din România în perioada comunistă (1944–1965)*. 2 vols. ("The Church in the Red Desert: Resistance and Compromise in Romanian Adventism during the Communist Era.") Vol. 1: Pantelimon: EVS, 2013. Vol. 2: Bucharest: Alege Viata, 2018. 639, 640 pp.

Modoran, Gheorghe. "Evoluţia oraganizatorică a Bisericii Adventiste de Ziua a Şaptea din România în perioada interbelică." ("The Organizational Evolution of the SDA Church in Romania during the Interwar Period.") *TheoRhēma* 5, no. 1 (2010): 101–124.

Modoran, Gheorghe. "Începuturile Bisericii Adventiste pe plan Mondial şi în România." ("The Beginning of the SDA Movement Worldwide and in Romania."). *TheoRhēma* 3, no. 1 (2008): 174–217.

Modoran, Gheorghe. "'Tovább kell vinnetek' (TKV): Grupare a rezistenţie anti-comunitsă în Romănia." ("'Tovább kell vinnetek' (TKV): An Anticommunist Resistance Faction in Romania.") *TheoRhēma* 12, no. 1 (2017): 91–120.

Neagu, Daniel-Adrian. "Istoria Bisericii Adventiste din România, de la începutul secolului XX, refelctată în rapoartele statistice ale Conferinţei Generale." ("The History of the SDA Church in Romania, Starting with the Beginning of the Twentieth Century, as Reflected in the Statistic Reports of the General Conference.") *TheoRhēma* 5, no. 1 (2010): 124–142.

Neagu, Daniel-Adrian. "Istoria Bisericii Adventiste din România reflectată în primele ediţii ale colecţiei *Imnuri Creştine*." ("The History of the SDA Church in Romania Reflected in the First Editions of *Adventist Hymns* collection.") *TheoRhēma* 9, no. 1 (2014): 97–116.

Pasos, Sperantza. *Hope in Present Danger: A True Story*. N.p.: Always Hope, 2011. 228 pp. Autobiography.

Petrescu, Valeriu. *Presa adventistă din România 1884–2002*. ("The Adventist Press in Romania 1884–2002.") Bucharest: Viaţă şi Sănătate, 2002. 128 pp.

Pey, Gil. *Lacrimi târzii*. Bucharest: Viaţă şi Sănătate, 2008. 341 pp.

Popa, Dumitru. *Biografii ale pionierilor Bisericii advente din România: Toma Aslan şi Istoria Bisericii Advente din România până la 1900*. Bucharest, 1997. 134 pp.

Popa, Dumitru. *Die Gemeinschaft der Siebenten-Tags-Adventisten in der sozialistischen Republik Rumänien*. Bucharest: I. P. Buletinul Oficial, 1983. 96 pp.

Popa, Dumitru. *Eben-Ezer: "Credincioşi adevărului în dragoste!": Comunitatea*

*Bucureşti-Labirint 1923–2003.* ("Eben-Ezer: Faithful to the Truth, in Love: Bucureşti-Labirint Congregation, 1923–2003.") Bucharest: Viaţă şi Sănătate, 2003. 155 pp.

Popa, Dumitru. *Pagini din istoria: Bisericii Adventiste de Ziua a Şaptea din România.* 3 vols. ("Pages from the History of the Romanian SDA Church.") Bucharest: Viaţă şi Sănătate, 2008–2015. 768, 631, 592 pp.

Popa, Dumitru. *The Seventh-day Adventist Church in the Socialist Republic of Romania.* Bucharest: Curierul Adventist, 1983. 61 pp. Also published in French as *L'église des adventistes du septieme jour de la Republique Socialiste de Roumanie.* Bucharest: Curierul Adventist, 1983. 95 pp.

Rosca, Năstăsescu-Beniamin. *Adventismul în România: Scurtă istorie pentru cei tineri.* ("Adventism in Romania: A Short History for Young People.") Bucharest: CARD, 2003. 58 pp.

Rotaru, Ioan-Gheorghe, Dan Iulian Opriş, and Beniamin Roşca-Năstăsescu. *O istorie a Adventismului de Ziua a Saptea din Romania.* Bucharest: Viaţă şi Sănătate, 2009. 341 pp.

Tarita, Doru, and Karaq Kerbs. *A Way of Escape: An Unforgettable Story of Fear, Courage, and a Run for Freedom.* Hagerstown, MD: Review and Herald, 2007. 131, [8] pp. Biography on Doru Tarita.

## Unpublished

Alboş, Aurel. "Seminarul teologic adventist în perioada comunistă." ("The Adventist Theological Seminary during the Communist Period.") BA thesis, RATI, 2007.

Aldea, Traian. "Impactul adventismului în teologia ortodoxă românească." ("The Impact of Adventism in Romanian Orthodox Theology.") BA thesis, RATI, 1996.

Andrei, Adrian. "Persecuţiile împotriva confesiunilor neoprotestante baptistă şi adventistă de ziua a şaptea în perioada interbelică." ("The Persecution against the Adventist and Baptist Neo-Protestant Denominations in the Interwar Period.") BA thesis, RATI, 2006.

Arcaş, Emanuel. "Creşterea Bisericii Adventiste de ziua a Şaptea din România în perioada postcomunistă." ("The Development of the Romanian SDA Church in the Post-Communist Period.") BA thesis, RATI, 2011.

Bârsan, Gabriel. "Istoria Bisericii Adventiste din judeţul Argeş." ("History of the Adventist Church in Arges County.") BA thesis, RATI, 1997.

Berejnec, Adrian Mihai. "Monografia istorică a Bisericii Creştine de Ziua a Şaptea din zona Caransebeşului." ("History of the Seventh-day Adventist Christian Church in the Caransebes Area.") BA thesis, RATI, 1999.

Calinciuc, Gheorghe. "Dezvoltarea mişcării advente în zona Rădăuţi." ("The Development of the Adventist Movement in the Rădăuţi Area.") BA thesis, RATI, 1998.

Calotă, Ionel. "Eseu de istorie adventă în zona Vălenii de Munte." ("Essay on Adventist History in the Vălenii de Munte Area.") BA thesis, RATI, 1997/1998.

Ciobanu, Dănel. "Fenomenul adventist religios în Peretu, Teleorman." ("The Religious Phenomenon of Adventism in Peretu, Teleorman.") BA thesis, RATI, 1998.

Ciurea, Beniamin. "Eseu de istorie adventă în Teleorman." ("Essay on Adventist History in Teleorman.") BA thesis, RATI, 1997.

Costescu, Costel Vili. "Speranta TV–Romania: a Unique Denominational Television Channel in Europe." MA thesis, Newbold College, 2012. vii, [9], 98 pp.

Crăciun, Ciprian. "Dezvoltarea Bisericii Adventiste în districtul Calafat." ("Development of the Adventist Church in Calafat District.") BA thesis, RATI, 1997.

Cristescu, Lucian David. "Istoria Institutului Teologic Adventist din România." ("The History of the Adventist Theological Institute in Romania.") BA thesis, RATI, 2005.

Dafina, Corneliu. "Istoricul Bisericii Adventiste de Ziua a Şaptea din judeţul Gorj." ("History of the Seventh-day Adventist Church in Gorj County.") BA thesis, RATI, 1997.

Dragoş, Gabriel. "Monografia istorică a Bisericii Creştine Adventiste de Ziua a Şaptea Bărăşti-Haţegui judeţul Hunedoara." ("The Historical Monograph of the Seventh-day Adventist Christian Church in Bărăşti-Haţegului Hunedoara County.") BA thesis, RATI, 1997.

Fitzai, Corneliu-Ghiocel. "Origines et actualité du mouvement adventiste du septième jour en Roumanie." 2 vols. PhD dissertation, Université Paris-Sorbonne, 2007. 480, 256 pp.

Gabriel-Ion, Ichim I. "Istoria bisericii adventiste în judeţul Vaslui." ("History of the Adventist Church in Vaslui County.") BA thesis, RATI, 2015.

Goran, Mihai Octavian. "Lucrarea de colportaj în România." ("Literature Evangelism in Romania.") BA thesis, RATI, 2014.

Graur, Cristina Oprica. "Dezvoltarea Bisericii adventiste în perioada interbelică." ("Development of the Adventist Church in the Interwar Period.") BA thesis, RATI, 2007.

Ilyes Janos, Bela. "Monografia comunităţiilor adventiste din câmpia Sărmaşului." ("Monograph on the Adventist Congregations on Sarmasu Plain.") BA thesis, RATI, 1997.

Krisán, Olivér. "A mezőfelei hetednapi adventista közösség kialakulása." BA thesis, Hungarian Adventist Theological College, 2004. On Hungarian Adventists in Romania.

Mărgărit, Benu. "Istoria Bisericii Adventiste din judeţui Ialomiţa." ("History of the Adventist Church in Ialomita County."). BA thesis, RATI, 1997.

Mihai, Marian. "Istoria bisericii adventiste din judeţul Buzău." ("History of the

Adventist Church in Buzau County.") BA thesis, RATI, 2000.

Modoran, Gheorghe. "Istoria confesiunilor neo-protestante din România perioadei contemporane." PhD dissertation, Alexandru Ioan Cuza University, 2008. 300 pp.

Mohorea, Ticu. "Studiu asupra Bisericii Creştine Adventiste de Ziua a Şaptea din judeţul Vrancea." ("Study on the Seventh-day Adventist Christian Church in Vrancea County.") BA thesis, RATI, 1998.

Nagy, Karoly. "Istoria adventă în Tg. Mureş şi împrejurimi." ("History of the Adventist Church in Tg. Mures and Vicinity.") BA thesis, RATI, 1997.

Neagu, Daniel-Adrian. "Istoria Bisericii Adventiste de Ziua a Şaptea din România şi impactul ei asupra societăţii româneşti 1870–1932." ("History of the Seventh-day Adventist Church in Romania and Its Impact on Romanian Society 1870–1932.") PhD dissertation, University of Bucharest, 2013. 306 pp.

Orban, Ioan. "Istoria adventă privind Clujul şi împrejurimile." ("History of the Adventist Church in Cluj and Vicinity.") BA thesis, RATI, 1997.

Pârcălab, Ioan. "Eseu de istorie adventă privind partea de jos a judeţului Mureş, cuprinzând oraşele Târnăveni şi Luduş." ("History of the Adventist Church in the Lower Part of Mures County, Comprising the Towns of Târnăveni and Luduş.") BA thesis, RATI, 1997.

Petrof, Sorin. "Adventismul în societatea contemporană românească." ("Adventism in Contemporary Romanian Society.") BA thesis, RATI, 1997.

Poenariu, Ioan Gelu. "Biserica Adventistă de Ziua a Şaptea în Perioada Antonesciană." ("The SDA Church during the Antonescu Period.") BA thesis, RATI, 2007.

Pop, Iacob. "Istoria adventă pe Valea Gurghiului." (History of the Adventist Church in the Gurghiu Valley.") BA thesis, RATI, 1997.

Roman, Liviu. "Istoricul adventismului în judeţul Bihor fenomen religios unic." ("History of Adventism in Bihor County: A Unique Religious Phenomenon.") BA thesis, RATI, 1998.

Rotaru, Ioan Gheorhe. "Monografia adventă a judeţului Sălaj." ("History of the Adventist Church in Sălaj County.") BA thesis, RATI, 1997.

Sălcianu, Constantin. "Reflectarea istoriei Bisericii Adventiste din România în presa oficială a Bisericii." ("The History of the Romanian Adventist Church as Reflected in the Official Publications of the Church.") BA thesis, RATI, 2009.

Simion, Violeta. "Influenţa participării la comunitatea religioasă a romilor din cartierul Simileasca, oraşul Buzău." ("Influence of Roma Participation in the Religious Community in the Simileasca Neighborhood, Buzau.") BA thesis, RATI, 2003.

Sîrbu, Alexandru. "Istoria şi dezvoltarea Bisericii Adventiste de Ziua a Şaptea din unitatea teritorială autonomă găgăuză." ("The History and Development of the SDA Church in the Autonomous Gagauzian Territory.") BA thesis, RATI, 2000.

Soponariu, Ionel. "Monografia istorică a Bisericii Adventiste de Ziua a Şaptea din zona Lugojului." ("History of the SDA Church in the Lugoj Area.") BA thesis, RATI, 1997.

Stan, Beniamin. "Istoricul Bisericii Adventiste din judeţul Tulcea." ("History of the Adventist Church in Tulcea County.") BA thesis, RATI, 1999.

Szasz, Tiberiu. "Monografia Bisericii Adventiste din Sic." ("The Sic Adventist Church.") BA thesis, RATI, 1998.

Tarlev, Ilie. "Scurt istoric al primei comunităţi adventiste de ziua a şaptea din raionul Criuleni." ("A Brief History of the First Seventh-day Adventist Church in the Criuleni District.") BA thesis, RATI, 1999.

Tolan, Ioan. "Monografia istorică a Bisericii Creştine Adventiste de Ziua a Şaptea Macea, judeţul Arad." ("History of the Seventh-day Adventist Christian Church in Macea, Arad County.") BA thesis, RATI, 1997.

Ungureanu, Emanuel-Dumitru. "Viaţa Bisericii Adventiste de Ziua a Şaptea din România în comunism (1945–1989)." ("The life of the Romanian Seventh-day Adventist Church in the Communist Era, 1945–1989.") PhD dissertation, Babeş-Bolyai University, 2016. 1120 pp.

Valeriu, Petrescu. "Contribuţia presei adventiste române la dezvoltarea Bisericii Adventiste din România." ("The Contribution of the Romanian Adventist Press to the Development of the Adventist Church in Romania.") BA thesis, RATI, 1997.

Zamfir, Nicuşor. "Istoria Bisericii Adventiste din Alexandria şi împrejurimi." ("History of the Adventist Church in Alexandria and Vicinity.") BA thesis, RATI, 1997.

Zeiler, Beniamin. "Monografia istorică a Bisericii Creştine Adventiste de Ziua a Şaptea Socodor, judeţul Arad." ("History of the Socodor SDA Church, Arad County.") BA thesis, RATI, 1997.

Zgherea, Valentin. "Biserica A.Z.Ş. din U.R.S.S. şi mişcările disidente." ("The SDA Church in the Soviet Union and the Dissident Movements.") BA thesis, RATI, 2000.

## Russia

### Published

*100 let Tserkvi khristian Adventistov Sed'mogo dnya v Moskve.* ("100 Years of the Church of SDAs in Moscow.") Moscow, 2005.

Abadir, Raya. *Out of Russia and Back: A Life of Surprises.* CreateSpace Independent Publishing Platform, 2016. 426 pp. Autobiography.

Andrusyak Vsevolod, Lev Bondarchuk, Aleksey Yevgrafov, Aleksey Oparin, Pavel Liberanskiy, and Dmitriy Yunak. *Vozveshchaya Slovo: Ocherki ob istorii adventistskogo knigoizdaniya.* ("Heralding the Word: Essays on the History of Adventist Publishing.") Zaokskiy: Istochnik zhizni, 2017. 352 pp.

Antonova, Olga Abramovna. *Pod maskoy svyatosti.* ("Under the Mask of Holiness.") Omsk: Knizhnoye izdatel'stvo, 1962. 44 pp.

Balalayeva, N. M. *Adventizm Sed'mogo dnya v Priamur'ye v period imperializma.* ("Seventh-day Adventism in the Amur Region during the Period of Imperialism.") Khabarovsk: Uchenyye zapiski Khabarovskogo Gosudarstvennogo Pedagogicheskogo Instituta, 1969.

Beitzakhar, Michael Simonivitch. *Light through the Shadows: The True Life Story of Michael Simonivitch Beitzakhar.* Translated and edited by Daniel V. Kubrock. Washington, DC: Review and Herald, 1953. 184 pp.

Bolotnikov, Alexander, and Gina Wahlen. *True Believer.* Hagerstown, MD: Review and Herald, 1997. 176 pp. Biography of Alexander Bolotnikov.

Booth, Bradley. *Dare to Stand Alone.* Hagerstown, MD: Autumn House, 2008. 128 pp. Biography of Ivan Gumenuk.

Booth, Bradley. *The Seventh-day Ox and Other Miracle Stories from Russia.* Hagerstown, MD: Review and Herald, 2011. 192 pp.

Buz, D., and I. Buz. *Nash put' ne usypan tsvetami.* ("Our Path Is Not Strewn with Flowers.") Kyiv: Dzherelo zhittya, 2003. 144 pp.

Chernevskis, E. P. A. *Matsanov: Fenomen rukovoditelya Adventistskogo Dvizheniya v Sovetskom Soyuze s 1960 po 1981 gg.* Riga: Patmos, 1997.

Dreyling, I. M. *Vospominaniya i opyty.* ("Memories and Experiences.") Zaokskiy: Istochnik zhizni, 2003. Autobiography.

Euro-Asian Division. *Osnovy social'nogo ucheniya: Tserkvi khristian Adventistov Sed'mogo dnya v Rossii.* ("Basics of Social Studies of the Christian Church of Seventh-day Adventists in Russia.") Moscow: Istochnik zhizni, 2009. 284 pp.

Finley, Mark. *The Cross and the Kremlin.* Fallbrook, CA: Hart Research Center, 1992. xi, 95 pp.

Finley, Mark. *Moscow Miracles.* Fallbrook, CA: Hart Research Center, 1993. 112 pp.

Gomer, D. *Perezhivshiye epokhu.* Kaliningrad: Yantarnyy skaz, 2007.

Gonchar, P. *Vmeste s Rossiyey: K 120-letiyu Tserkvi khristian ASD.* ("Together with Russia: 120 Year Anniversary of SDAs in Russia.") Moscow: Russkiy pechatnyy dom, 2006.

Heinz, Daniel. "Adventisty Sed'mogo dnya i otkaz ot učastija v voennych dejstvijach: Istoričeskaja perspektiva." (SDAs and the Conscientious Objection in Russia: Historical Perspective.") In *Nenasilie kak mirovozzrenije i obraz žizni: Istoričeskij rakurs,* edited by T. Pavlova, O. Šalimov, and D. Sdvižkov, 116–27. Moscow: Institut Vseobščej Istorii RAN, 2000.

Heinz, Daniel. "Adventisty Sed'mogo dnya i otkaz ot uchastiya v voyennych deystviyach v Rossiyskoy Imperii." ("SDAs and Conscientious Objection in Russia.") In *Dolgiy put' rossiyskogo pacifizma: Ideal mezhdunarodnogo i vnutrennego mira v religiozno-filosofskoy i obshchestvenno-politicheskoy mysli Rossii,* edited by Tatjana A. Pavlova, 172–176. Moscow: Institut Vseobshchey Istorii RAN, 1997.

Heinz, Daniel. "Arnhold, Gustav A." In *Ihr Ende schaut an...*', edited by Harald Schultze, Andreas Kurschat, and Claudia Bendick.

Heinz, Daniel. "Chistoe gosudarstvo' i antimilitarizm: V. A. Shelkov i ,Vernye i Svobodnyye Adventisty Sed'mogo Dnya' v Sovetskom Soyuze." In *Postizhenie ideala: Iz istorii mirotvorchestva i intelligencii: Sbornik pamyati*, edited by Daniel Heinz and Denis A. Sdvizhkov, 26–36. Moscow: Institut Rossiyskoy Akademii Nauk, 2005.

Heinz, Daniel. *Dushi pod zhertvennikom.* ("The Souls under the Altar.") Khar'kov: Fakt, 2010. 375 pp. This book is about Adventist pastors who were killed in the Soviet Union during the regime of Stalin.

Heinz, Daniel. "Galladscheva-Löbsack, Amalie." In *Ihr Ende schaut an...*', edited by Harald Schultze, Andreas Kurschat, and Claudia Bendick.

Heinz, Daniel. "Heinrich J. Löbsack: Pioneer, President, and Poet of the Adventist Church in Russia, 1870–1938." *Journal of the American Historical Society of Germans from Russia* 2 (1998), 11–16.

Heinz, Daniel. "Kraus, Jakob W." In *Ihr Ende schaut an...*', edited by Harald Schultze, Andreas Kurschat, and Claudia Bendick.

Heinz, Daniel. "Löbsack, Heinrich Johannes." In *Ihr Ende schaut an...*', edited by Harald Schultze, Andreas Kurschat, and Claudia Bendick.

Heinz, Daniel. "Löbsack, Heinrich Konrad." In *Ihr Ende schaut an...*', edited by Harald Schultze, Andreas Kurschat, and Claudia Bendick.

Heinz, Daniel. "Neufeld, Paul K." In *Ihr Ende schaut an...*', edited by Harald Schultze, Andreas Kurschat, and Claudia Bendick.

Heinz, Daniel. "Origin and Growth of the Adventists in Russia. A Historical Survey." *Journal of the American Historical Society of Germans from Russia* 10, no. 4 (1987): 39–43.

Heinz, Daniel. "Pilch (Pilkh), Paul." In *Ihr Ende schaut an...*', edited by Harald Schultze, Andreas Kurschat, and Claudia Bendick.

Heinz, Daniel. "Remfert, Karl F." In *Ihr Ende schaut an...*', edited by Harald Schultze, Andreas Kurschat, and Claudia Bendick.

Heinz, Daniel. "Shelkov, Vladimir Andreyevich (1895–1980)." In *Biographisch-Bibliographisches Kirchenlexikon.*

Heinz, Daniel. "Woitkiewicz, Ludwig," In *Ihr Ende schaut an...*', edited by Harald Schultze, Andreas Kurschat, and Claudia Bendick.

Heinz, Daniel, and O. Beznosova. "Adventisty Sed'mogo dnya." ("Adventists, Seventh-day.") In *Nemcy Rossii: Enciklopediya / Die Deutschen Russlands: Enzyklopädie.* Moscow: ERN/ERD, 1999–.

Heinz, Daniel, Aleksey Oparin, Dmitriy Yunak, and Andris Peshelis. *Fotochronika Tserkvi Adventistov Sed'mogo dnya v Tsarskoy Rossii—SSSR—SNG, 1882–2012.* ("Illustrated History of the Seventh-day Adventist Church in Imperial Russia, the Soviet Union, and the CIS Countries, 1882–2012.") Kharkov, 2012. 128 pp.

Jacques, John G, and Adelaide D. Wellman. *Escape from Siberian Exile.*

Mountain View, CA: Pacific Press, 1921. 288 pp.

Jesske, Waldemar Samuel. *Banished.* Nashville, TN: Southern Publications, 1967. 135 pp. Biography.

Kulakov, Mikhail. *God's Soviet Miracles: How Adventists Built the First Protestant Seminary in Russian History.* Boise, ID: Pacific Press, 1993. 128 pp. History of Zaoksky College.

Kulakov, Michail, and Maylan Schurch. *Though the Heavens Fall: Not Gulags, Not the KGB, Not Even Stalin Himself...* Hagerstown, MD: Autumn House, 2008. 191 pp. Autobiography of Michail Kulakov.

Löbsack, H. J. *Velikoye Adventistskoye dvizheniye i Adventisty Sed'mogo dnya v Rossii.* Kiev: Patmos, 1918; Rostov-on-Don: Al'tair, 2006.

Lohne, Alf. *Adventisten in Russland.* Hamburg: Saatkorn-Verlag, 1985. 176 pp. Published in English as *Adventists in Russia.* Edited by Raymond H. Woolsley. Washington, DC: Review and Herald, 1987. 159 pp.

Matsanova, Anna, and Pavel Matsanov. *Po ternistomu puti.* ("On the Thorny Path.") Moscow: Tserkov' khristian Adventistov Sed'mogo dnya, 1995. 288, [24] pp.

Murray, Katharine. "Soviet Seventh-day Adventists." *Religion in Communist Lands* 5, no. 2 (Summer 1977): 88–93.

Oparin, A. A. *Kogda plachut sosny.* ("When Pines Weep.") Kharkiv: Fakt, 2007. 120 pp.

Otis, Rose Marie Niesen. *Soviet Sonrise.* Washington, DC: Review and Herald, 1990. 158 pp.

Paeske, Hellmuth. *Wendepunkt Rußland: Umwandelnde Erlebnisse.* Hamburg: Saatkorn-Verlag, 1989. 63 pp.

Ponomarov, Alexander. *Desperate Escape: A True Story of Faith through Relentless Persecution.* Translated by Jacob Volkov and Alex Swiridoff. Hagerstown, MD: Review and Herald, 1999. 223 pp.

Reiners, Sidney. *Russia: The Anguish of Adventism.* 3rd ed. Grand Rapids, MI: Christians in Crisis, 1985. 53 pp.

Sapiets, Marite. "One Hundred Years of Adventism." *Religion in Communist Lands* 12, no. 3 (Winter 1984): 256–273.

Sapiets, Marite. *True Witness: The Story of Seventh Day Adventists in the Soviet Union.* Edited by Anne Thompson. Keston College Book no. 32. Oxford: Keston College, 1990. 299 pp.

Sapiets, Marite. "V. A. Shelkov and the True and Free Seventh-day Adventists of the USSR." *Religion in Communist Lands* 8, no. 3 (Fall 2008): 201–217.

Scoggins, Jeff and Rebecca. *Hope for the Thirsting: How 300 Young Church Planters Are Changing Lives in the Former Soviet Union.* Berne: Office of Global Mission, General Conference of Seventh-day Adventists, 2003. 96 pp.

Suvorova, Olga. *My tolko stoim na beregu...* ("We Only Stand on the Shore.") Moscow: EKSMO, 2012. 299 pp. Journalist Suvorova's interviews with Mikhail P. Kulakov.

Teppone, V. *Iz istorii Tserkvi Adventistov Sed'mogo dnya v Rossii.* ("Pages from the History of the SDA Church in Russia.") Kaliningrad: Yantarnyy skaz, 1993. 324 pp.

Yunak, Dmitriy O. *Istoriya Tserkvi Adventistov Sed'mogo dnya v Rossii.* ("History of the SDA Church in Russia.") 2 vols. Zaokskiy: Zapadno-Rossiyskiy Soiuz Tserkvi khristian ASD, 2002. 448, 453 pp.

Yunak, Dmitriy O. *Put' nadezhdy: Yubiley 70-letiya Trokhangel'skoy vesti v Nikolayevke.* Tserkov' ASD, 2009. On the 70 Year Anniversary of the SDA Church in Nikolaeyvka.

Yunak, Dmitriy O. *Tserkov' ASD v Rossii: dokumenty iz gosudarstvennykh, partiynykh i tserkovnykh arkhivov.* ("The SDA Church in Russia: Archival Documents.") Tula, 2004.

Yunak, Dmitriy O., and L. V. Yunak. *O letakh minuvshikh.* ("About the Years Which Have Passed Away.") Tula, 2009.

*Zaokskaya Dukhovnaya Akademiya: Vchera i segodnya.* Zaokskii: Zaoksky Adventist University, 2008. 45 pp. History of Zaoksky Theological Seminary.

Zaitsev, Evgeniy V. "1917 god v istorii Tserkvi Adventistov sed'mogo dnya v Rossii." *Svoboda Sovesti v Rossii: Istoricheskiy i sovremenniy aspekty (Sbornik Statey),* no. 13 (2017): 55–80.

Zaitsev, Evgeniy V. "Istoria soblyudayushchikh subbotu na Rusi." *Obraz i Podobie,* no. 2 (1993): 44–50.

Zaitsev, Evgeniy V. "Adventistiy Sed'mogo dnya v Rossii: Tserkov' traditsionnaya ili netraditsionnaya?" *Svoboda Sovesti v Rossii: Istoricheskiy i sovremenniy aspekty (Sbornik Statey),* no. 3 (2006): 225–242.

Zaitsev, Evgeniy V. *Istoriya Tserkvi Adventistov Sed'mogo dnya v Rossii.* ("History of the Seventh-day Adventist Church in Russia.") Zaokskiy: Istochnik zhizni, 2008. 543 pp.

Zaitsev, Evgeniy V. "Stavropol—kolybel rossiyskogo adventizma." *Adventistskiy vestnik* 87, no. 4 (2015): 23–25.

Zaitsev, Evgenii V. "Tserkov' Adventistov sed'mogo dnya v period massovykh repressiy 30kh godov." *Pastyr' dobry,* no. 7 (2004): 24–39.

Zaitsev, Evgeniy V. "Tserkov' Adventistov Sed'mogo dnya v pervye gody sovetskoy vlasti." *Pastyr' dobryy,* no. 6 (2003): 36–45.

Zaitsev, Evgeniy V, and G. I. Stele. "Tserkov' Adventistov sed'mogo dnya v Rossii v gody Pervoy mirovoy voyny 1914–1918 gg." *Svoboda Sovesti v Rossii: Istoricheskii i sovremennii aspekty (Sbornik Statey),* no. 12 (2016): 100–122.

Zakhvataiev, Yurii. "Po ternistomu puti." Documentary in 19 parts. YouTube video. Posted by "Telekanal Nadezhda," September 12, 2016 to September 28, 2019 (one to be posted still). https://www.youtube.com/watch?v=eVr mZVX_n48&list=PLChh24LqEiIEov598x3D3P2WVWgaNwsSH&index=18.

Zhigankova, Elena. *Resources on the Seventh-day Adventist Church in Tsarist Russia, Former Soviet Union and Contemporary Russian Federation: An Attempt at Classification.* N.p.: Published by the Author, 2012. 20 pp.

Zozulina, Avgustina. *Zhizn' Tiny*. Zaoksky: Istochnik zhizni, 2012. 544 pp. Biography.

Unpublished

Balich, Natal'ya Leonidovna. "Identifikatsiya veruyushchikh v religioznykh obshchinakh: sociologicheskiy analiz (na primere Adventistov Sed'mogo dnya)." ("Identification of Believers in Religious Communities: A Sociological Analysis, Using the Example of Seventh-day Adventists.") PhD dissertation, Minsk, 2010.

Bondarchuk, Lev Ivanovich. "Izdanye i rasprostranenye adventistskoy literatury v Rossii." ("Publication and Distribution of Adventist Literature in Russia.") DMin dissertation, Zaoksky Adventist University, 2011.

Dubov, Alex. "Early History of the Seventh-day Adventist Church in Russia." Term paper, Andrews University, 2010. 22 pp.

Harbeson, Leonard Stanley. "A Brief History of the Seventh-day Adventist Church in Russia." Term paper, Andrews University, 1972. 19 pp.

Jacobson, Melvin V. "A History of the Work of Seventh-day Adventists in Russia." Term paper, Seventh-day Adventist Theological Seminary, 1944. 70, [1] pp.

Lentin, V. "Sekta Adventistov Sed'mogo dnya v SSSR: Issledovaniye dinamiki, social'no-demograficheskogo sostava i sovremennoy ideologii." ("The SDA Sect in the USSR: Investigation of Dynamics, Socio-Demographic Composition, and Modern Ideology.") PhD dissertation, Moscow, 1966.

Lim, Jae-Myeong. Missiological Approach to Russian Koreans in Sakhalin: A Korean Seventh-day Adventist Perspective. MA thesis, Adventist International Institute of Advanced Studies, 1996.

Matsela, Dmytro. "Die religiösen Unterdrückungsmechanismen im frühen Sowjetstaat dargestellt am Beispiel der Siebenten-Tags-Adventisten, 1922–1930." MA thesis, Friedensau Adventist University, 2012. 132 pp.

Morar, Mikhail K. "A Strategy for Public Evangelism in Russia." DMin dissertation, Andrews University, 1998. viii, 242 pp.

Murga, Vasiliy Viktorovich. "Sozdanie novykh tserkvei s pomoshch'yu grupp literaturnykh evangelistov v Zapadno-Rossiyskom Soyuze." ("Establishing New Churches with the Help of Literary Evangelism Groups in the West Russian Union.") DMin dissertation, Zaoksky Adventist University, 2011.

Oliynyk, Lyudmyla. "Storia della Chiesa, storia di miracoli. Nascita e crescita della Chiesa Avventista nell'Impero Russo." BA thesis, Italian Adventist University, 2017. 71 pp.

Patrushev, A. I. "Novyye religioznyye dvizheniya na Urale v kontse XX–nachale XXI vv. (na primere Tserkvi mormonov i Tserkvi Adventistov Sed'mogo dnya)." ("New Religious Movements in the Urals in the Late Twentieth to the Early Twenty-First Century: The Mormons and The SDA Church.") MA thesis, Ural Federal University, 2014. 106 pp.

Seiler, Evgenij. "Anfänge und Fortschritt der Adventgemeinde in Russland mit besonderer Berücksichtigung der Gemeindeentwicklung auf der Krim 1886–1928." MA thesis, Friedensau Adventist University, 2009. 86 pp.

Stele, Galina I. "An Analysis of Growth in the Euro-Asian Division (1985–1995) Leading to a Strategy for Developing Home Churches." DMin Dissertation, Andrews University, 1996. x, 283 pp. 10–103.

Tree, Garett B. "The Russian Mission: Seventh-day Adventism, Bolshevism, and the Imminent Apocalypse, 1881–1946." MA thesis, University of Montana, 2017. 126 pp.

Volkov, John Alexis. "History of the Seventh-day Adventist Church in Russia (1881-1921)." Term paper, Andrews University, 1973. 16 pp.

Ward, Mary Jane. "Protestant Churches under Soviet Rule, 1917–1945: A Study of Soviet Relation with the Lutherans, Mennonites, Seventh-day Adventists, and Pentecostals." PhD dissertation, George Washington University, 1980.

Zgherea, Valentin. "Biserica A.Z.Ş. din U.R.S.S. şi mişcările disidente." BA thesis, RATI, 2000.

## Serbia

See also Yugoslavia.

### Published

Ivanović, Slavica Stojanović. *Sinajska ruža*. Niška Banja: Published by the Author, 2000. 82 pp. Autobiography.

Lorencin-Slavujević, Anica. *Savremeni junaci vere*. Nova Pazova: Preporod, 2013. 147 pp.

### Unpublished

Đurčik, Igor. "Istorijski razvoj prvih grupa Adventista na teritoriji današnje Vojvodine." ("Historical Development of the First Adventist Groups in the Territory of Today's Vojvodina.") BA thesis, Belgrade Theological Semimary 2000.

Lukić, Branko. "Misiološko-strateški plan za ponovno osnivanje crkve sa primenom na grad Užice." ("Mission Strategy for the Re-establishment of the Church with Application to the City of Uzice.") BA thesis, Belgrade Theological Semimary 2002.

# Slovakia

## Published

Štefanec, Augustín. *Pamätajme, ako nás Pán viedol.* ("Remember How the Lord Led Us.") Sázava: Advent-Orion, 1995. 50 pp.

## Unpublished

Kučera, Jozef. "Vznik cirkevného spoločenstva CASD v Trenčíne a jeho prezentácia v regióne." ("The Origin of the SDA Church in Trenčin and Its Presentation in the Region.") MA thesis, Matej Bel University, 2014. 48 pp.

# Soviet Union

See Russia

# Spain

## Published

*Compartiendo la Esperanza: Cien años de adventismo del septimo día en España.* Madrid: Safeliz, 2003. 269 pp.

## Unpublished

Garcia, Luis Francisco. "The Missionary History in Spain." Term paper, Andrews University, 1979. 18 pp.

Gutierrez, Jose Lopez. "Historia de la Iglesia Adventista del Septimo Dia de España (1903–1978)." PhD dissertation, Universitat de Valencia, 1991.

Melgosa, Julian. "A Brief History and Present Situation of the Seventh-day Adventist Education in Spain." Term paper, Andrews University, 1981. v, 56 pp.

# Sweden

## Published

Blomdahl, Rune. *Adventistsamfundet 100 år.* Gävle: Skandinaviska bokförlaget, 1980. 60 pp.

Blomdahl, Rune. *Nyhyttan: Från bergsmansgård till kurort.* Skandinaviska bokförlaget, 1961. 72 pp. Nyhyttan was the first SDA missionary school in Sweden (1898–1932), and later became a health center (1932–1998).

Delding, Vera: *Kära mor och far.* Nyhyttan: Published by the Author, 2016. Letters from Swaziland, 1980–1983. The Deldings operated both a stationary and a mobile dental clinic during these years.

Gidlund, Carl. *En skolas historia: Ekebyholm 1950.* Ekebyholm: Ekebyholms Missionsskola och Carl Gidlund, 1950. 31 pp.

Karlsson, Britta. *Ett liv i Herrens tjänst.* Rimbo: Skandinaviska bokförlaget, 2008. 122 pp. Autobiography of a Bible worker and a pastor's wife.

Karström, Henning. *En kemists levnadshistoria.* Rimbo: Skandinaviska bokförlaget, 2011. 228 pp. Autobiography. Professor, later principal at Toivonlinna and Ekebyholm.

Lindén, Ingemar. *Biblicism, Apokalyptik, Utopi: Adventismens historiska utveckling i USA samt dess svenska utveckling till o. 1939.* Acta Universitatis Upsaliensis Studia Historico-Ecclesiastica Upsaliensia 19. Uppsala: Uppsala University, 1971. 494 pp.

Norlin, Birgitta. *Stockholms församling 125 år.* Stockholm: The Seventh-day Adventist Church of Stockholm, 2009. 48 pp.

Öster, Yvonne Johansson. *De gick till fots.* Rimbo: SDA Media, 2005. 16 pp. Anniversary magazine celebrating 125 years of Adventism in Sweden.

Öster, Yvonne Johansson. *Hur blev det med fru Bergström?* Rimbo: Skandinaviska Bokförlaget, 2013. 192 pp. Biography of Hanna Bergström, wife of Ruben Bergström. They were pioneer missionaries to Cameroon.

Öster, Yvonne Johansson. *Till jordens yttersta gräns: Svenska adventistmissionärers liv och verksamhet.* Stockholm: Skandinaviska bokforlaget, 2018. 415 pp.

Sjölander, Pearl. *Utmaningen.* Gävle: Skandinaviska bokförlaget, 1990. 166 pp. Biography on Margot Spånghagen, during her first years in West-Africa.

*Svenska Sjundedags Adventisternas historia.* Chicago: Sjundedags Adventisternas svenska avdeling, 1928. 370 pp.

Svenson, Ragnar. *Stockholms Adventist församling 90 år jubileumsskrift.* Gävle, Skandinaviska Bokförlaget, 1974. 32 pp.

Westphal, Barbara Osborne. *Ana Stahl of the Andes and Amazon.* Mountain View, CA: Pacific Press. 127 pp. Biography of Ana Christina Stahl, missionary to South America.

Wiklander, Gösta. *Adventkyrkan i Göteborg 100 år!* Göteborg: The Seventh-day Adventist Church of Göteborg, 1996. 61 pp.

Wiklander, Gösta. *De kallade honom Baba Duniyary, Landsfader.* Stockholm, 2006. 219 pp. Biography of Ruben Bergström (1899–1981), missionary to Cameroon.

Wiklander, Gösta. *Från stabbläggare till förkunnare.* Rimbo: Skandinaviska bokförlaget, 2012. 223 pp. Biography of his father Alfred Anderson, who was a pastor, evangelist, Bible teacher, and conference president.

Wiklander, Gösta. *I vår Herres tjänst: Missionsarbetare inom Adventistsamfundet i*

*Sverige 1880–1997.* Göteborg: Adventistsamfundets Svenska Union, 2001. 169 pp.

Wiklander, Gösta. *Julius Persson: Svensk predikant och den första svenske missionären till ett land utanför Europa.* Rimbo: SDA Media, 2007. 36 pp.

## Unpublished

Svensson, Ragnar. "Gävle sjundedagsadventistförsamling 85 år: 1888–1973." Unpublished manuscript. 1972. 14 pp.

Svensson, Ragnar. "Minnesskrift: Adventrörelsen i Dalarna 1885–1910." Unpublished manuscript. Unpublished manuscript, 197[?]. 109 pp.

Svenson, Ragnar. "Minnesskrift Örebro Adventistförsaamling: Pionjärer och församlingsbyggare i Närke." Unpublished manuscript.

Svensson, Ragnar. "Minnesteckningar: Sjundedags Adventistsamfundet i Finland 1892–1972." Unpublished manuscript. 1972. 36 pp. About the Swedish Adventists in Finland, who belonged to the Swedish Union after the division of the East Nordic Union in 1955. In 1981, the Finnish-Swedish Conference was transferred to the Finnish Union.

## *Switzerland*

## Published

*1883–1963: 80 Jahre Advent-Gemeinde Basel: Chronik zum Andenken an das Wirken der Pioniere des Adventwerkes in Basel.* Basel: N.p., 1964. 155 pp.

*1902–2002: Festschrift 100 Jahre Freikirche der Siebenten-Tags-Adventisten in Winterthur.* Winterthur: Freikirche der Sibenten-Tags-Adventisten in Winterthur, 2002. 30 pp.

Buser-Wyss, A., et al. *Chronik zum Andenken an das Wirken der Pioniere des Adventwerkes in Basel.* Basel: E und C. Spittler, 1964. 155 pp.

Domanyi, Thomas, ed. *Du hast uns—Herr—gerufen, 1887–1987: 100 Jahre Adventgemeinde Zürich.* Zürich: Carta Druck, 1987. 191 pp.

Heinz, Daniel. "Erzberger (or Erzenberger or Erztberger), James 'Jakob.'" In *The Ellen G. White Encyclopedia*, edited by Fortin and Moon, 370–71.

Heinz, Daniel. "Oster, Frank Friedrich (1881–1960)." In *Biographisch-Bibliographisches Kirchenlexikon.*

Lecourt, Nancy J. "Clinique 'La Lignière': The First Seventy Years of Seventh-day Adventist Medical Work in Switzerland, 1896-1966." *Adventist Heritage* 9, no. 2 (1984): 3–11.

Lenoir, Thierry, ed. *Reflets: Un siècle au service de la santé.* Dammarie-lès-Lys: Vie et Santé, 2004. 122 pp. The centenary of the sanitarium La Lignière.

Poublan, Gérard. *Souvenirs d'une missionnaire centenaire: Louise-Herminie Roth,*

*100 ans.* Clapiers: Published by the Author, 1992. Unpaginated. Biography of Mrs Louise-Herminie Roth who served as missionary in Switzerland.

"Roth, Mary Amberg." In *The Ellen G. White Encyclopedia,* edited by Fortin and Moon, 502.

Thomann, Elisabeth, and Donaldo Thomann. *Aus besonderem Holz geschnitzt [Papito Thomann].* Spillern: Wegweiser-Verlag, 2008. 168 pp. Biography of Eduardo Thomann, a Swiss who immigrated to Chile with his family. He converted to Seventh-day Adventism and became a pioneer.

Übersax-Nork, Otto. *Von guten Mächten wunderbar geborgen: Glaubenserfahrungen eines Auslandschweizers im Dritten Reich in den Jahren 1940–1944.* Zürich: Advent-Verlag, 2004. 63 pp. Autobiography.

"Vaucher, Jules-Alfred." In *The Ellen G. White Encyclopedia,* edited by Fortin and Moon, 532–33.

"Vuilleumier, Albert Frederic." In *The Ellen G. White Encyclopedia,* edited by Fortin and Moon, 533.

Waber, Karl. *Streiflichter aus der Geschichte der Siebenten-Tags-Adventisten in der Schweiz: Von den Anfängen 1865 bis 1901.* Zürich: Advent-Verlag, 1995. 255 pp.

Waber, Karl. *Streiflichter aus der Geschichte der Siebenten-Tags-Adventisten in der Schweiz: Schweizer Vereinigung 1901–1929.* Zürich: Advent-Verlag, 1995. 219 pp.

## Unpublished

Roth, Larry A. "Obscure Details concerning the History of the Seventh-day Adventist Work in Switzerland." Term paper, Andrews University, 1966. iv, 39 pp.

# Turkey

## Published

Heinz, Daniel. "Adventisten im Osmanischen Reich—ein Fallbeispiel für islamische Intoleranz." In *"For You Have Strengthened Me": Biblical and Theological Studies in Honor of Gerhard Pfandl in Celebration of His Sixty-fifth Birthday,* edited by Martin Pröbstle, 453–78. St. Peter am Hart, Austria: Seminar Schloss Bogenhofen, 2007.

Olson, Mildred Thompson. *Diamondola.* Washington, DC: Review and Herald, 1966. 192 pp. Biography of Diamondola Keanides Ashdod.

## Unpublished

Bairaktar, Viatcheslav. "Zwischen Verfolgung und Duldung: Zur Situation

einer christlichen Minderheitskirche in der Türkei am Beispiel der Siebenten-
Tags-Adventisten in der Zeit von 1889–1915." Diplom thesis, Friedensau
Adventist University, 2001. 132 pp.

Olson, Mildred Thompson. "Theodore Anthony, the Shoemaker Missionary of
Turkey. Zadour Baharian, the 19th century Paul of Asia Minor." Unpublished
manuscript. 199-. 8 pp. Center for Adventist Research, James White Library.

## Ukraine

### Published

Bailey, Ellen. *Katya's Gold: What Will Her Dreams Cost Her?* Washington, DC:
Review and Herald, 2008. 123 pp. Biography of Katya Anatolyevna.

Berecz, Sophie, and Theodor Pawluk. *Hunted by the KGB: The Theodor Pawluk
Story.* Nampa, ID: Pacific Press, 2008. 217, [6] pp.

Hann, William Henry. *The Grizzly Bear of Russia.* N.p.: Published by the
Author, 1992. iv, 124 pp. Autobiography.

Heinz, Daniel. "Manchen, Michael." In *'Ihr Ende schaut an…'*, edited by Harald
Schultze, Andreas Kurschat, and Claudia Bendick.

Kuromiya, Hiroaki. *Conscience on Trial: The Fate of Fourteen Pacificsts in Stalin's
Ukraine, 1952–1953.* Toronto: University of Toronto Press, 2012. x, 212 pp.

Oparin, A. A. *Pobedivshiye vremya.* Kharkiv: Fakt, 2009.

Oparin, A. A. *Psalmy, napisannyye krov'yu.* ("Psalms, Written in Blood.")
Kharkiv: Fakt, 2007.

Oparin, A. A. *Yubileynyy god: Ocherki istorii adventizma v Khar'kove.* ("Jubilee:
Essays on Adventist History in Kharkiv.") Kharkiv: Fakt, 2006.

Oparin, A. A., and V. I. Begas. *Belyy kamen': Ocherki istorii Adventizma na
Yekaterinoslavshchine.* ("White Stones: History of the SDA Church in
Ekaterinoslav Region.") Kharkiv: Fakt, 2009. 136 pp.

Oparin, A. A., and Dmitriy O. Yunak. *Zholtaya reka.* Kharkiv: Fakt, 2008.

Parasei, A. F., and N. A. Zhukalyuk. *Bednaia, brosaemaia bureyu: Istoricheskie
ocherki k 110-letnemu yubileyu Tserkvi ASD v Ukraine.* Kiev: Dzherelo
zhittya, 1997. 340 pp. History of the SDA Church in Ukraine.

Sitarchuk, Roman A. *Adventisty s'omogo dnya v ukrains'kich zemlyach u skladi
Rosiys'koy Imperii.* ("SDAs in Ukraine in the Russian Empire.") Poltava:
Skaytek, 2008. 323 pp.

Zhukalyuk, Nikolay A., and V. Lyubashchenko. *Tserkov' khristian Adventistov
Sed'mogo Dnya v Ukraine.* ("The SDA Church in Ukraine.") 2003.

Zhukalyuk, Nikolay. A. *Vspominaite nastavnikov vashikh.* Kiev: Dzherelo zhittya,
1999. 672 pp.

## Unpublished

Koval', Bogdan Vladimirovich. "Deyatel'nost' Tserkvi khristian-Adventistov Sed'mogo dnya po utverzhdeniyu printsipov svobody sovesti v svete realiy sovremennogo ukranskogo obshchestva (1991–2008 gg.)." ("The Activities of the Seventh-day Adventist Christian Church to Affirm the Freedom of Conscience in the Light of the Realities of Modern Ukrainian Society, 1991–2008."). BA thesis, Zaoksky Adventist University, 2009.

## *The United Kingdom*

### Published

Barham, Nigel G. "Opening of the British Mission." *Adventist Heritage* 9, no. 2 (1984): 12–18.

Barham, Nigel G. "Walter E. Read and the British Union Conference." *Adventist Heritage* 5, no. 1 (1978): 16–23.

Buckley, Robert M. "Dr Robert M Buckley." The SDA Church in the UK and Ireland. http://adventist.org.uk/adventist-history/documents/dr-robertm-buckley. Autobiography.

"Camp Hill History." The SDA Church in the UK and Ireland. http://adventist.org.uk/adventist-history/documents/camphilll-history.

Cupit, Wilf, and Stephen Ham. "The History of the Chesterfield Company of Seventh-day Adventists 1910–1983." Updated June 25, 2001. The SDA Church in the UK and Ireland. http://www.adventistchurches.org.uk/history/chstrfld/chstrfld.htm

Elias, K. A. "Blessings of a Lifetime." The SDA Church in the UK and Ireland. http://adventist.org.uk/adventist-history/documents/lifetime-of-blessings. Autobiography.

Gerloff, Roswith L.H. *A Plea for British Black Theologies: The Black Church Movement in Britain in its Transatlantic Cultural and Theological Interaction.* 2 vols. (Frankfurt am Main: Peter Lang, 1992).

"Gilbert, Frederick Carnes." In *The Ellen G. White Encyclopedia*, edited by Fortin and Moon, 387.

Grieve, Mary. "History of the Aberdeen Seventh-day Adventist Church." The SDA Church in the UK and Ireland. November 1999. Updated June 25, 2001. http://adventist.org.uk/adventist-history/documents/aberdeen-church-history.

Hagstotz, Gideon D. *The Seventh-day Adventists in the British Isles, 1878–1933.* Lincoln, NE: Union College Press, 1936. 231 pp.

Hill, Joyce. "A History of the Church School in Plymouth, Devon." 1971. The SDA Church in the UK and Ireland. http://adventist.org.uk/adventist-history/documents/church-school-history.

Marriner, Noah. "Noah Marriner: God Always Answers." 1998. The SDA

Church in the UK and Ireland. http://adventist.org.uk/adventist-history/documents/norah-marriner. Autobiography.

Marshall, D. N., ed. *100 Years of Mission 1906–2006*. Grantham: Stanborough Press, 2006. *Messenger* 111, no. 17. Special issue. 31 pp. Available online at Center for Adventist Research.

Marshall, D. N., ed. *A Century of Adventism in the British Isles*. Grantham: Stanborough Press, 2000. 31 pp. Special issue of *Messenger* celebrating 100 years of Adventism in the British Isles. Available online at adventist.org.uk.

Marshall, D. N., ed. *The Story of Seventh-day Adventists in the British Isles 1902–1992*. Grantham: The Stanborough Press, 1992. 48 pp. Available online at adventist.org.uk.

Meredith, William Henry. Edited by Brian P. Phillips. *Pages from a Minister's Diary: President 1926–32, British Union Conference*. Pontypridd: B. P. Phillips, 1991. 55 pp.

Myles, Nora. "Personal Recollections: A Resumé of My Early Recollections of the Dundee Church and a Few Outstanding Personalities Who Influenced My Life throughout the Years." Personal Recollections. May 1999. Updated June 25, 2001. The SDA Church in the UK and Ireland. http://adventist.org.uk/adventist-history/documents/personal-recollections.

Peake, Christopher. "Seventh-day Adventists in Britain in Relation to Their Host Community in the Early 20th Century." In *Parochialism, Pluralism, and Contextualization*, edited by Trim and Heinz, 93–115.

Porter, Dennis S. *A Century of Adventism in the British Isles: A Brief History of the British Union Conference of Seventh-day Adventists* (Grantham: Stanborough Press, 1974).

Riches, Rex. *Establishing the British Mission of the Seventh-day Adventist Church 1863–1887*. Greensboro, NC: Published by RoseMarie Riches, 1996. v, 338 pp.

"Scotland Church History: The Seventh-day Adventist Church in Scotland: 90th Anniversary (1992)." 1992. Updated June 25, 2001. The SDA Church in the UK and Ireland. http://adventist.org.uk/adventist-history/documents/scotland-church-history.

"Stanborough Park Church History." Updated November 21, 2007. The SDA Church in the UK and Ireland. http://adventist.org.uk/adventist-history/documents/stanborough-park-church-history.

Surridge, Mrs R. N. "Life of Ernest Bernard Phillips, 1892–1977." The SDA Church in the UK and Ireland. http://adventist.org.uk/adventist-history/documents/life-of-ernest-bernard-phillips. Biography on Ernest Bernard Phillips.

Vine, R. D., ed. *A Century of Adventism in the British Isles: A Brief History of the British Union Conference of Seventh-Day Adventists*. Grantham: Stanborough Press, 1974. 48 pp.

Walton, J. C., ed. "Dundee Church Historical Sketch." August 1977, rev.

September 1999. Updated June 25, 2001. The SDA Church in the UK and
Ireland. http://adventist.org.uk/adventist-history/documents/dundee-church-
historical-sketch.

## Unpublished

Barham, Nigel G. "The Progress of the Seventh-day Adventist Church in
Great Britain, 1878–1974." PhD dissertation, University of Michigan, 1976.
428 pp.

Beardsell, Derek Crowther. "A Study of an Administrative Decision that
Influenced the Structure of the British Adventist College." Term paper,
Andrews University, 1982. v, 22 pp.

Beardsell, Derek Crowther. "A Study of Selected Administrative issues in the
History and Development of Newbold College." PhD dissertation, Andrews
University, 1983. 3, xxx, 499 pp.

Boothby, Janelle. "Newbold College." Term paper, Andrews University, 1981.
28 pp.

Davis, Anthea Natalie. "West Indian Immigrants and Administrative Politics in
the Seventh-day Adventist Church in Britain circ. [sic.] 1950–1980." MA thesis,
University of London, 2003. 70 pp.

Greenlaw, Ken Michael. "Items from the History of the Northern England
Conference." Term paper, Andrews University, 1973. Unpaginated.

Griffiths, Herbert. "The Impact of African Caribbean Settlers on the Seventh-
day Adventist Church in Britain 1952–2001." PhD dissertation, University of
Leeds, 2003. [xiv], 320 pp.

Hagstotz, Gideon D. "The Seventh-day Adventists in the British Isles, 1878–
1933." PhD dissertation, University of Missouri, 1935. 231 pp.

Lawrence, Errol A. "Church-Growth Strategies for Increasing the White
Membership of the Seventh-day Adventist Church in the South England
Conference." DMin dissertation, Andrews University, 2006. viii, 298 pp.

McHarty, A. "Loughborough and the Founding of the English Mission." Term
paper, Andrews University, 1974. 23 pp.

Oddie, John Burton. "A Preliminary Investigation into the Beginnings of the
Health Work in the British Isles." Term paper, Andrews University, 1975. iii,
34 pp.

Peck, Adrian. "Church Growth in Britain: A Thematic Analysis of Two
Growing British Churches." MA thesis, Newbold College, 2014. 143 pp.

Phillips, Brian Pugh. "A Century of Adventism in Wales 1885–1985: A History
of Seventh-day Adventism in Wales and the Border Counties." PhD
dissertation, University of Glamorgan, 1992. 412 pp.

Philpott, Joseph. "Church Growth in the North England Conference of the
Seventh-day Adventist Church: A Quantitative Analysis into Who Are Joining
This Church." MA thesis, Newbold College, 2018. 95 pp.

Riches, Rex. "Establishing the British Mission of the Seventh-day Adventist Church 1863–1887." PhD dissertation, Fairfax University, 1995. viii, 692 pp.

Theobald, Robin. "The Seventh-day Adventist Movement: A Sociological Study with Particular Reference to Great Britain." PhD dissertation, University of London, 1979.

## Yugoslavia

See also Bosnia and Herzegovina, Croatia, and Serbia.

### Published

Šušljić, Milan. *Bićete mi Svedoci: Prilozi za istoriju Hrišćanske adventističke crkve na području jugoistočne Evrope.* Belgrad, 2004. 454 pp.

Vitorovich, Ann. *Any Way Out: Twin Brothers, Two paths, No Chance.* Hagerstown, MD: Review and Herald, 2010. 202 pp. Biography.

### Unpublished

Dedic, Branislav. "Historique du mouvement adventiste en Yougoslavie (1904–1940)." Diplom thesis, Adventist University of France–Collonges, 1972.

Fritz, Anton. "A History of the Seventh-day Adventist Work in Northern Yugoslavia." Term paper, Andrews University, 1970. 13, [1] pp.

Milosavljevic, Radivoje Rade. "Master Planning for Church Growth in Serbia." DMin dissertation, Andrews University, 2001. xv, 278 pp. 64–69.

Mladjen, Dragan. "The Problem of Apostasy among the Second Generation Adherents of Yugoslav Seventh-day Adventist Churches: A Project Report." MA thesis, Andrews University, 1984. 126 pp. Available online at research.avondale.edu.au.

Obradovic, Dragomir. "Seventh-day Adventist Educational Work in Yugoslavia." Term paper, Andrews University, 1981. 23, [6] pp.

Schubert, Branimir. "Développement de l'œuvre d'éducation adventiste en Yougoslavie de 1926 à 1976, et sa contribution à la propagation de l'evangile." MA thesis, Adventist University of France–Collonges, 1987.

# Contributors

**Bernard Sauvagnat,** Dr ès Sciences religieuses
Retired professor of New Testament, Faculté adventiste de théologie,
Collonges-sous-Salève, France
sauvagnat.bernard@orange.fr

**Chigemezi-Nnadozie Wogu,** MTS
Research Associate, Institute of Adventist Studies, Friedensau Adventist University, Germany;
PhD student, Vrije Universitiet, Amsterdam
chigemezi.wogu@thh-friedensau.de

**Daniel Heinz,** PhD
Director of the European Archives of Seventh-day Adventist History, Friedensau, Germany
daniel.heinz@thh-friedensau.de

**Denis Fortin,** PhD
Professor of Historical Theology, Seventh-Adventist Theological Seminary,
Andrews University, Michigan, USA
fortind@andrews.edu

**Eudritch Jean,** MTS
Assistant Chaplain, Friedensau Adventist University, Germany
eudritch.jean@thh-friedensau.de

**Gheorghe Modoran,** PhD
Retired university lecturer, Romania
gmodoran@gmail.com

**Gilbert M. Valentine,** PhD
Retired Professor of Leadership and Administration, School of Education,
La Sierra University, California, USA
gvalenti@lasierra.edu

**Jón Hjörleifur Stefánsson,** MA
PhD candidate, Vrije Universiteit Amsterdam
j.hjorleifur.stefansson@gmail.com

**Marianne Thieme**
Founder, Party for the Animals, PvdD, Dutch Politician and Animal Rights Activist

**Michael Pearson,** PhD
Retired ethicist living in the UK
mpearson@newbold.ac.uk

**Michal Balcar,** MA
PhD cand., Charles University, Prague; Pastor in Prague
michal.balcar@casd.cz

**Neagu Daniel-Adrian,** PhD
Editor-in-Chief, Romanian Adventist Publishing House
adrianneagu@viatasisanatate.ro

**Petr Činčala,** PhD
Assistant Professor of World Mission, Director of the Institute of Church Ministry, Seventh-Adventist Theological Seminary, Andrews University, Michigan, USA
cincala@andrews.edu

**Reinder Bruinsma,** PhD
Retired church administrator, scholar and author
reinder@bruinsmas.com

**Ronald L. Lawson,** PhD
Professor Emeritus, Queens College, CUNY, New York
sondleywriter@gmail.com

**Rolf J. Pöhler,** ThD
Professor of Systematic Theology, Friedensau Adventist University, Germany
rolf.poehler@thh-friedensau.de

**Sergo Namoradze,** PhD
Lecturer of Applied Theology, Theological Seminary,
Ukrainian Adventist Centre of Higher Education, Ukraine
snamoradze@gmail.com

**Stefan Höschele,** PhD
Professor of Systematic Theology and Adventist Studies,
Friedensau Adventist University, Germany
stefan.hoeschele@thh-friedensau.de

**Tiziano Rimoldi,** PhD
Lecturer of Church History, Law and Religion, Italian Adventist University, Florence, Italy
t.rimoldi@avventisti.it

**Yvonne Johansson Öster,** MA, MA
Retired mission historian in Sweden
yvonne.joster4@gmail.com

9 783935 480536

# DRIVEN

### A MEMOIR BY: CRAIG R. BAXLEY

Visit Craig R. Baxley at www.CraigBaxley.com
Or write author@CraigBaxley.com

Formatting, Editing, and Cover Design by Michele Pollock Dalton
of Barr26 Creative Services | www.Barr26CreativeServices.com

Printed in the United States of America

Paperback ISBN: 979-8-9851952-2-4
Hardcover ISBN: 979-8-9851952-3-1
eBook ISBN: 979-8-9851952-1-7

First Edition Printed March 2021
Second Edition Printed November 2021

# The True Story of a Stuntman

### A Stunt Coordinator, Second Unit, and Director in the Motion Picture Industry

# WHAT READERS SAY

## About "Driven"

**Baximum Overdrive! Essential reading for Golden Age Action fans!!**

Director Craig R. Baxley is best known to action fans for his 'Holy Trinity' of kickass classics (Action Jackson, Dark Angel aka I Come In Peace, and Stone Cold) and to horror hounds as Stephen King's go-to guy for Made for TV creepshows (Storm of the Century, Rose Red, and Kingdom Hospital).

His latest project is "Driven," a memoir of his life and career from stunt performer to feature film director – and what a ride it is. While we've been living vicariously through the movies he made, this guy has just LIVED.

 -ADAM HOWE

**If you like movies you must read this book!!**

I LOVED THIS BOOK!! Such an insight to the world of Hollywood! You don't realize what goes on behind the scenes until you read this book!! EXCELLENT READ!!!

 -VANESSA MALLORY

# TABLE OF CONTENTS

# FOREWARD

## by Ken W. Hanley

There's something incredibly bittersweet about the fact that, in 2020, the Academy of Motion Picture Arts and Sciences presented the Academy Award for Best Supporting Actor to a performer inhabiting the role of a stuntman. This is not to say that the actor in question did not deserve the accolade; in fact, his performance was perhaps the most memorable in one of 2019's most discussed films. However, the win happened to shine a light on one of Hollywood's most tenuous relationships - as the Academy otherwise refuses to celebrate the under-appreciated, yet absolutely necessary, stunt performer.

Let's not kid ourselves: Hollywood was built on the bruises, blood, burns, and broken bones of the men and women who have brought countless spectacular moments to our screens over the years.

Before films had sound and color, they had stuntmen, falling from horses, from trains, diving from rooftops onto moving trains, and occasionally risking near certain death for a cheap laugh.

Yet, there has always been a renegade nature to the stunt game. It is often considered to be an accessory of the action and comedy genres and culturally opposed to the glamorous and dazzling productions that put Hollywood on the map.

Stunt performers, as a result, have often had to fight tooth and nail for every ounce of respect that they can find in the film business. It's odd to think that those who take the most risk on a film production, whether it be behind the wheel of a spinning vehicle or falling out of a helicopter engulfed in flames, are stereotyped as the least valuable player by producers and financiers.

But while some stuntmen and stuntwomen are able to parlay

their expertise into second unit work, dramatic acting, and even the coveted director's chair, there are far fewer magazine cover stories and celebratory docuseries dedicated to those taking the bumps of our beloved movie stars.

Of the myriad stories, scandals, and myths that could have served as his inspiration, one could wonder why Quentin Tarantino decided to focus Once Upon a Time, his love letter to 1960s Hollywood, around an actor and his stuntmen. Tarantino has never been quiet about his appreciation for stunt performers and their craft, previously having put his stunt crew front and center in such films as *Kill Bill* and *Death Proof.*

But one might assume Tarantino decided to pivot his focus from the likes of Charlie Manson and the rise of the Spaghetti Western to highlight instead the fictional equivalent of such notable stuntmen-actor partnerships like Clint Eastwood and Buddy Van Horn, Burt Reynolds and Hal Needham, and Warren Beatty and Craig R. Baxley.

For Craig Redding Baxley, stuntwork is in the blood, having followed in the footsteps of his father, Paul - a legendary stunt coordinator in his own right. However, I'm not here to tell his story. I'm sure you'd rather hear it from the man himself. I would rather set the table by sharing with you how I best know Mr. Baxley: an expert architect of hard-hitting, grit-filled cinema.

Hyperbolic? Maybe so. But wrong? Not a chance in hell. Without discounting his stellar stunt work for action stalwarts like Walter Hill and Don Siegel, or his fantastic Stephen King television adaptations, Baxley's triptych of action cult classics, composed of *Stone Cold, Dark Angel,* and *Action Jackson,* still turn heads and drop jaws to this day.

Sporting a blue-collar charm in every frame of his directorial work, Baxley created three timeless testaments to the type of old-school action film that rarely has the big screen in this day and age. He's a goddamn artist within his craft, utilizing the camera as a brush while motorcycle chases, ball-busting dialogue, and big-ass explosions are his colors of choice. But while many action epics have sunk into obscurity over the years, Baxley's films tend to grow in reverence as more cinema fans appreciate his no-bullshit approach to providing escapist entertainment at the highest level possible.

To be honest, my first exposure to Craig R. Baxley was *Rose Red,* a mini-series event that was somewhat of a perfect storm, airing around the time that my appreciation for horror and Stephen King began to deepen. I also remember vividly being scared through much of it, while being introduced to a number of talented character actors whose work I would relish for years to come, including Melanie Lynskey, Julian Sands, Jimmi Simpson, and Matt Ross. Yet while *Rose Red* blew me away in my formative years (and holds up superbly to this day), this was still a time before the likes of streaming and IMDB, so I truly had no idea what I was missing in his previous work.

Nevertheless, Baxley's work could not be denied. Discovering *Action Jackson* late into my teenage years, I couldn't quite believe what I was watching, having been overwhelmed by the unabashed one-liners, mind-melting plot twists, and the practical action set pieces that often prompted my fist flying victoriously through the air. Soon enough, I was passing around the DVD like it was a designer drug and began my search for the rest of Baxley's feature film credits.

With the merging DVD-by-mail service called "Netflix" at my behest, I soon tracked down *Sniper 2*, a rather exceptional direct-to-video entry in the Sniper franchise, followed by *Dark Angel*, also known as *I Come in Peace*. While *Dark Angel* had the same brawn, bullets, and blow-ups as *Action Jackson*, I began to greatly appreciate Baxley's work as a storyteller as well - revealing the film's big twist in a shockingly measured and clever way. Add the fantastic chemistry of Dolph Lundgren and Brian Benben and some truly amazing special effects, and suddenly, I realized I was dealing with a whole different beast.

Sadly, it would be a number of years before I caught *Stone Cold*, but I did so in possibly the best circumstances: on 35mm in a theater filled with action junkies at my local Alamo Drafthouse. Although I knew I was in for a treat from the jump, I could not have anticipated how hard this movie would kick me in the balls. It had everything I could have wanted from an action film: a fishing boat explosion in the first five minutes, a crazy bare-knuckle gladiator fight on a beach, redneck bikers going to war with both the mafia and the government, and even a Komodo dragon. As soon as credits rolled on the most bonkers third act in film history, I knew that I would be singing the praises of Baxley for as long as I remained a connoisseur of the best and boldest action cinema.

To that end, I am proud to remain one of Baxley's most vocal advocates. I was shocked and honored when he reached out to me following my FANGORIA article regarding his film, and that sentiment goes double for the opportunity to pen this little introduction for his most personal and introspective work to date. I'm excited to dig into the true stories behind Craig R. Baxley, and I hope you are as well. If they're anything like the badass fictional adventures he has previously unleashed on the world, we're in for a hell of a ride.

# PREFACE

## The Beginning

*Never fret for an only son; the idea of failure will never occur to him.*
GEORGE BERNARD SHAW

The late sixties, seventies, eighties, and early nineties were known as the golden era of stunt work in the motion picture business. The action prior seems to have become dated and artificial in the eyes of a new generation wanting more modern reality.

The seventies became a creative high point in the industry. It gave rise to some of the most memorable subject matter - questioning the truth of the times that enlightened and entertained, the likes of which we may never see again. It was a watershed of movies like *The Godfather, Bonnie and Clyde, Taxi Driver, The Wild Bunch, Butch Cassidy and the Sundance Kid,* and *It's a Mad Mad Mad Mad World.* During that golden era of stunts, the talent was unparalleled, and the innovations in rigging were groundbreaking.

The goal during those years was to create a safe environment while doing some of the most outrageous stunts ever done. Not thrill show stunts. These stuntmen, like magicians, were innovators with incredible knowledge of rigging. And they had the ingenuity and physical talent to back it up, creating the illusion of something so much more.

The amount of work available was amazing. So was the money. Back in the early days, a stuntman had to be an all-around performer if they expected to be successful. A top stuntman had to be adept at car work, motorcycle work, horse work, high work, fire work, water work, and various types of fights. And, in most cases, an all-around athlete.

In the seventies, if a stuntman was in town and he was good, he could work three or four jobs in one day at one studio. But you never heard the names of those top stuntmen; they were usually under the radar. The ones you did hear about were usually self-promoting, mostly full of shit. A lot of them had nicknames they had given themselves, like "Danger." Periodically, they would even appear on talk shows or make specials about themselves.

Stuntmen became the highest paid members of the Screen Actors Guild during those years - the top ten percent. That was before CGI, wire work, and shifter cars. Before the era of the "specialist."

In 1971, from the stuntmen chosen on the James Bond film *Diamonds are Forever*, four were picked to be the three motorcyclists: Bud Ekins, a legendary racer who did the motorcycle lay-down in Steve McQueen's *Bullitt*; Everett Creach, the motorcycle stunt double on the Evel Knievel film; J. R. Randall, primarily known for his horse work; and myself, a twenty-year-old surfer and motocross racer. It was my first S.A.G. job in the motion picture industry.

Early on, it was clear J.R. was having trouble and was not going to cut it, so Bud, Everett, and I went on to do all the motorcycle work on the film. I was hired for two weeks; two weeks turned into three and a half months.

*Diamonds are Forever* was filmed in Las Vegas, Palm Springs, and Oceanside, California. During filming, I befriended the British Director of Photography, Ted "Teddy" Moore. He was one of the finest DP's I ever had the pleasure of working with. He'd done a couple of other Bond films prior to that: *Thunderbolt, Goldfinger, Doctor No, From Russia with Love, The Man with the Golden Gun*, and *Live and Let Die*.

One day, Teddy and I were sitting together at a piano on the set. Ted was quietly playing as he told me the story about the first time he worked with my father. It was in 1954 on *The Black Knight* in London, England. My father doubled Alan Ladd (the Black Knight) and did a sword fight with Peter Cushing.

At the end of the fight, Peter Cushing's character was killed and was to fall one hundred feet from the castle battlement. The company had hired a stuntman by the name of Paddy Ryan. Paddy had done the legendary seventy-five-foot fall on *Ivanhoe* in 1951. The cast and crew were setting up and preparing for the stunt as hundreds of spectators were gathering. Teddy and his crew were at the bottom of the battlement running four cameras. Paddy was to fall a hundred feet into a catcher made of cardboard boxes, eight feet high.

When action was called, it was dead silent. Nothing. No Paddy.

Ted told me, "After a couple of seconds, your father leaned out and motioned for us to cut the camera. They needed five minutes, then he disappeared. Five minutes later, he leaned out again and waved, we rolled our four cameras again, and the director called action."

Ted paused for a moment. "Out shot Cushing's stunt double, falling one hundred feet. The fall was perfect; he landed dead center in the catcher. The crew cheered and swarmed him, pulling him out of the boxes." Ted looked me in the eye. "I just stood there looking at your father, Paul Baxley, and smiled."

\* \* \* \* \*

Was it serendipitous that my father was the stunt coordinator on *Diamonds Are Forever*, considering my wife Valerie's grandfather, Dick Borland (probably one of the greatest Key Grips that ever lived), was on the same film?

I think so. Valerie's father, Ken Borland, was also working on the film as the Dolly grip.

It was a great location; we all had such a great time working on the film together. It was Dick's last film; he retired after *Diamonds Are Forever.*

I can't forget to mention another man in Valerie's family who made such a lasting impact on me: Geoff Stevens, an Englishman - Valerie's uncle. He was a stunt skater in the Ice Capades. He actually held the world record for a time, jumping over twelve barrels.

\* \* \* \* \*

The end of *Diamonds Are Forever* was epic: six chopper gunships descending on an oil rig five miles out at sea while firing rockets and mounted machine guns. Every stuntman on the rig was watching the mock-up rockets streak down. Fireballs, explosions, stuntmen hitting spot tramps, squib hits, and fire everywhere. As a twenty-year-old kid, it didn't matter that I got some minor bruises and burns. I just thought my life couldn't get any better than this. Little did I know.

I am a proud third-generation filmmaker. My father's father, Paul Sr., ran the paint and miniature department at Warner Brother Studios in the late forties and fifties. He was also an amazing artist. The more I was around him growing up, the more I realized there was a bit more to the man. He cheated at cards and golf, and who knows what else. That and he always called me 'Skip,' which was my cousin's name.

My father, along with Richard Talmadge and David Sharpe, were probably the best all-around athletes and stuntmen the business has ever known. Richard was a member of a famous Russian acrobatic family that performed for the Barnum and Bailey Circus. In his teens, Davey was the National A.A.U. (Amateur Athletic Union) Tumbling Champion two years in a row.

My father's pole vaulting record at Eagle Rock High School was a Los Angeles city record that stood for over sixteen years. He was also an All-City quarterback in high school and became an All-American quarterback in college.

My grandfather introduced Richard to my father after World War II; Richard brought him into the business shortly after that.

\* \* \* \* \*

I remember going to work with my father in 1958; I had just turned eight. It was on a film called *Some Like it Hot*. I was very excited; I was watching him and the crew set up for a stunt. My father and another stuntman, Carey Loftin, were discussing the stunt with the director, Billy Wilder. When action was called, my father came roaring around the corner in a black 1929 Ford model A; suddenly, a Ford Ambulance shot into fame and center punched the model A, flipping it over on its roof as planned. I thought it was one of the coolest things I'd ever seen.

As the company moved on and started to set up for the next scene, my father introduced me to a lady in a white dress who was watching the stunt; her name was Marilyn Monroe.

Paul Baxley diving onto Davey Sharp

SWEET AND SOUR . . . Runaway truck provides exciting scene in "The Ugly American." But not all are as "sweet" to film as this one. A sour scene from the Marlon Brando film is described in the adjoining columns.

**Los Angeles Times article,** *The Ugly American*

My father doubled some of the biggest stars in Hollywood, among them James Dean, Alan Ladd, Paul Newman, and Marlon Brando, with whom he did over a dozen films, including *The Godfather*, on which he was the stunt coordinator and second unit director. More about that later.

The first time I met Marlon in 1961, it was on the set of *One Eye Jacks* in Monterey, California. My father co-directed the film, doubled Marlon, and was the stunt coordinator and second unit director. He did the same for *Mutiny on the Bounty* in 1962.

The next year I graduated from junior high school. I was seated like everyone else, waiting in the dark auditorium. I looked over at my mother and noticed she was quietly crying. Unbeknownst to me, my mother heard earlier on the news that a stuntman was almost killed on the set of *The Ugly American* - that he was almost crushed by a massive truck that had careened off a cliff onto him below.

They were about to announce the guest speaker. Suddenly, the doors behind us opened, light spilled in, and a man on crutches walked down the aisle and sat down next to me. It was my dad - he'd just come from the hospital after the accident on set.

The guest speaker came out; it was my idol, Rafer Johnson, the 1960 Olympic Gold Medalist in the Decathlon. As I sat there between my mother and my father, we were all mesmerized by his words.

\* \* \* \* \*

I continued to hang out with my father and Marlon on the sets of *Morituri* in 1965 and *Appaloosa* in 1966. The last time I saw Marlon, my father had invited me to have lunch with them. It was at a restaurant on Ventura Blvd. in Studio City, Albion's, now called Mistral.

As I sat there, I thought back on the first time I met Marlon. Then he had a 32-inch waist. Now he was on two chairs that had been pushed together for him to sit on. Marlon was such a handsome man. A beautiful man. He always said to me, "My boy, how are you?" To this day, I don't understand what happened to him.

\* \* \* \* \*

In 1966, I went to work with my father in Saugus, California. He was stunt coordinator, doubling Paul Newman on *Harper*. I was getting an education on how the motion picture business worked - about respect.

My father was one of the most successful stunt coordinators and second unit directors through the fifties, sixties, seventies, eighties, and later on, my shows in the nineties and into the early part of the new millennium.

To say my father was a womanizer would be quite an understatement. He liked women; he had lots of them. His affair with Sophia Loren in 1957 while in Spain filming *The Pride and the Passion*, and *Boy on the Dolphin* in Greece was the beginning of the end of my parent's marriage. Those two trips, plus the period of a year and a half that my father spent on *Mutiny on the Bounty* in Tahiti, was the end of their marriage.

I was more affected by my parent's divorce than my older sister. I wanted to be like my father, and at the same time, nothing like him. I wanted to be in the motion picture business. But not as a stuntman, as a production designer.

Growing up, my mother always encouraged me to explore my creativity. She knew I loved to illustrate, draw, and paint. She always said, "You can recognize a good artist by how their work makes others feel."

When I was nineteen, I signed up for the art director apprentice program at Universal Studios. I took a couple of classes at a junior college in the San Fernando Valley: Drafting, Life Drawing, Painting, Astronomy, and Philosophy.

During that time, I worked through a series of part-time jobs: on the graveyard shift bonding aircraft parts; as a short-order cook at A&W Root Beer; and delivering furniture. I was also the guy in the front window at Divino's Pizza in Toluca Lake, tossing and spinning pizza into the air. I had some crazy acrobatic pizza skills.

After seven weeks on the waiting list, I received a call from Universal Studios. They fazed the program out a week before I was supposed to start.

I didn't have a lot of options and didn't know what else I wanted to do. I'd never thought about being a stuntman. I decided to talk to my father about it. He was thrilled.

What the hell? I jumped in.

I quickly realized how hard it was going to be, following my father into the industry. It came with a lot of excess baggage. Back in the day, being really successful brought a lot of envy; you found you had a lot of friends and a lot of enemies. The politics of the motion picture business can be complicated.

That was over forty-five years ago – before cell phones, computers, and FaceTime. My life has been a journey that has provided me with a treasure chest of memories. What I've learned on that journey can't be taught. It can only be experienced. The inescapable truth of the real experience cannot be taken for granted. I have a profound appreciation for having lived, experienced, and shared the golden years of action in the motion picture business.

As I reflect on those years, I realize I am the luckiest man who ever lived in that golden era. What follows is my story of that stuntman. That stunt coordinator. That second unit director. That director.

# CHAPTER 1

## A Lucky Man

Growing up, one of my favorite people in the world was my grandfather, Russell E. Craig. For sixteen years, he was the Harbor Master of Newport and Balboa, California. He lived in Corona del Mar, in China Cove, directly across the channel from the Wedge on Balboa Island.

It was a different time in Southern California back then. You never locked your car. People actually said, "Hello, how are you?" and meant it. There was no traffic. Nobody knew what smog was. Corona del Mar and Balboa were just sleepy beach communities. We used to sail and water ski in the back bay when it was just a wide expanse of mud flats. Today, it's been completely developed with $20-30 million mega-mansions on the water.

When my grandfather was sixteen, he fought in World War I on the battlefields of France. He lost half a lung to mustard gas burns. Mustard gas was named for its mustard-like odor; it was an oily liquid only used during the First World War. It has a blistering, disabling effect.

He became Harbor Master in the late forties; in the fifties, he wrote all the charters for the harbors up and down the West Coast, from Newport to Seattle. He was a waterman man's man, a man's man, a lady's man. He could be stubborn and a bit reclusive, but he had a great sense of humor. I loved that man.

That's where I remember growing up. Where I discovered how much I loved the ocean. When I was eleven years old, my dad bought me my first surfboard. That's when I started surfing. I would stay in the water for hours. Like any kid, I loved to explore, walk over the

**Craig Baxley 16 yrs. old, 1965**

bluff on my way to the big beach, climb down the cliff into Pirates Cove, walk through the caves and dive back into the ocean. I used to take off on the Schwinn one-speed bicycle and ride for miles, usually not back until after dark.

I didn't have any desire for things; I still don't.

A couple of years later, I remember riding a sixteen-foot wave off the end of the jetty at the big beach in Corona del Mar; it was probably a pretty insane thing to do for a fifteen-year-old - probably kind of a fearless thing to do for a kid that age.

We used to sail to Catalina Island. Just the sound of the ocean and the sails flapping in the wind was mesmerizing. We'd tie up in Avalon or the isthmus, usually Avalon. I'd dive for abalone. In the fifties and sixties, there was abalone everywhere along the rocky shore of Catalina. They were so fresh, just out of the ocean. He'd pound them, egg and dredge'em, then fry the pieces in butter with a little squeeze of lemon. Probably the best thing I ever ate in my entire life.

My grandfather was an incredible man; we had some of the most amazing experiences I've ever had on the water. We used to all go over to the big beach, light a fire in one of the concrete fire pits, throw some burgers and dogs on the grill, and just listen to the waves as they cooked. I loved the ocean more than anything when I was a kid. Sometimes, everyone would run down the beach in the moonlight and jump into the surf: the laughing, the innocence. I loved how simple life was then.

Where have those times gone?

My mother was her father's daughter, also an incredible human being. A champion swimmer. A champion yachtsman. In her teens, she was a life guard at the big beach in Corona del Mar. The three of us shared some great times; I'll never forget our time together in and on the water.

* * * * *

High school droned on. My father couldn't understand why I didn't want to play football. He and the football coach tried to get me to go out for the team every year. They both thought I'd make a great wide receiver. It was hard for either of them to understand what surfing and competitive swimming meant to me. My mother never missed a meet. It didn't matter where it was; she was always there for me.

**1966 Varsity Championship Swimming Team certificate**

My first car was a van, a used '61 VW van - every surfer's first choice. Gasoline was thirty cents a gallon then.

In 1967, I had just turned seventeen and graduated from high school. Like every other kid, I thought I had and knew it all. After all, I'd seen The Rolling Stones first L.A. concert in '66, Big Brother and the Holding Company with Janis Joplin, The Doors, Jimi Hendrix, and The Cream - their last L.A. concert in early '68.

I was the youngest surfer in Pidas Surfing Association. We were all trying to ride for as many surf shops as we could. Free boards. If you won a contest back then and were really lucky, you got the good-looking chick. What else was there in life?

All anyone could talk about in those days was Vietnam and when they would be going.

During World War II, my father fought in the Pacific as a Marine, scout, and sniper in the 4th Division. He fought on Kwajalein (Roi-Namur), Iwo Jima, Saipan, and Titian. He received two Purple Hearts, a Bronze Star, and a letter of commendation from the President of the United States. He taught Sniper school on Paris Island briefly after the war.

In 1968, on my eighteenth birthday, I stepped on a plane at LAX bound for Lackland Air Force Base in San Antonio. After completing eight weeks of basic training, eighty-three airmen were selected from hundreds on the base as part of an experiment. But nobody was told why. All were good athletes.

Unlike the other airmen, who were sent to the air force tech schools all over the country, we eighty-three were sent to Fort Lee - an Army Fort in Richmond, Virginia. None of us were happy about it. It seemed like a one-way ticket to Nam.

For the next eight weeks, we were sent through four Army tech schools. We were dropped into Ranger school, Defense Information school, Pathfinder school, and Cook's school. Cook's school? None of it made any sense to me. I never signed up for any of them.

We all stayed in one building and only displayed the Air Force insignia on our uniforms. No names. Nothing else. Most of the Army personnel wondered who we were. Our commanding officer was a second lieutenant who didn't seem to be present, always kind of spaced; he never told us why we were there or what was going on. All we were given was the time and location of our classes.

On the weekends, he usually spent his time upstairs behind a locked door with a hooker from Petersberg, totally coked out. One weekend when he was going out, I asked him, "What's up?" He said he was going to a concert at the community hall. I asked him who it was.

"Ike and Tina Turner," he said.

"Got any extra tickets?" I asked.

"Tickets? I don't need any ticket," he answered and walked out.

I knew he was going to bullshit his way in. I looked at my friend Dean and said, "C-mon."

When we got to the Fort Lee concert hall, I glanced past the soldier at the door; it looked like the interior held about five hundred people. It was packed. The soldier asked me for our tickets. I leaned in and saw our commanding officer sitting in prime seats with the Army officers. I looked back at the soldier and said, "We're with him; sorry we're late."

He nodded and let us in; we walked in and sat down next to our commanding officer, who looked at us and just shook his head.

The lights went down, out came the Ike and Tina Revue. Ike and Tina were backed up by the "Ikettes," three vocalists and backup dancers wearing the same red wig and red dress that Tina did. The show was unbelievable, Tina and the girls were high octane. The only thing that moved on Ike was his fingers while he was playing or taking a drag on the cigarette that was stuck on the end of his guitar. What a night.

After we completed the eight weeks, we were sent to various Air Force bases. Two of us were sent to March Air Force base in Riverside, California - SAC, Strategic Air Command. I had no idea what was going on.

It was a strange time in the United States; Vietnam was raging. I remember the two of us were on our way back to California on a commercial flight. We had a six-hour layover in Baltimore. While walking through the airport in our dress blues, people seemed to get off on heckling us; two even spit at us. As an eighteen-year-old, I had a hard time dealing with it, but we just continued to our gate. Six hours later, we boarded our flight.

Once we got to March, nobody seemed to know what to do with us, or why we had been sent to an Army Fort. After three weeks, the last of which they had me drawing cartoons for the Air Force magazine, the commanding officer sent us home. He said the Air Force would reach out in a couple of weeks, and we'd be given our next assignment. It never came. Six years later, during which I received three promotions and pay grades, I finally received my honorable discharge.

Seven months after we were sent home, life had changed; I had long hair and a beard. I was in one of the hottest surf clubs in California, racing motocross, and in a band called Mother Ball. What more could there be in life?

We were a garage band, primal and spontaneous, kind of a cross between Santana and Blue Cheer. We had three lead guitarists, John Brown, a great surfer, and I were two of them. John always bugged me, he was a couple of years older, and I thought maybe a better surfer. He always gave me "that look," like I know what you're thinking. We had a guy on a Hammond B3 organ. I can't remember his name, he never looked up from the keyboard, but he was great.

One of the guys I do remember was my dear friend Howard Kaneg. He was a great bassist and could play *Train Time* better than Jack Bruce of the Cream. Howard was also a world-class surfer with whom I spent many summers. I always thought it was strange that he was terrified of driving. I drove us everywhere in my Volkswagen van until his eighteenth birthday.

Another bandmate was Steve Leshner on the congas. Steve, also a great surfer, later went on to play congas for Neil Sedaka and many other music superstars. Honorable mention was our amazing drummer playing a double set of drums.

I can't get our first gig out of my mind; it was on Santa Monica Blvd. It was the opening of one of the hottest clubs in West Hollywood.

We started the set with *Whole Lotta Love* by Led Zeppelin, then onto *Summertime Blues* by Blue Cheer. I'm not sure they got us. We were awful.

It was 1970; I was a surfer, a skier. By then, I'd had enough of Junior College; I was bouncing from one part-time job to the next. The future was unclear until I met Valerie.

My family was a mix of predominately Welsh and German ancestry, Valerie's French and German with a little Castilian Spanish thrown in. She was a gorgeous, long-haired, blue-eyed, tan blonde. A gymnast. A 4.0 grade point average. I was the guy that barely got out of high school.

This wasn't part of my master plan. I was loving life. The next thing I knew, I was loving Valerie.

Six months later, in 1971, I sold two surfboards, my Gibson SG guitar, a Fender Dual Reverb amp, drove my VW bug to Las Vegas, and married her.

# CHAPTER 2

## The Seventies

After I finished my first job in the motion picture industry, *Diamonds Are Forever;* I went straight on to *What's Up, Doc?* for the next four months. The film starred Barbara Streisand and Ryan O'Neal. It had a major chase sequence through the streets of San Francisco, ending with all four vehicles racing onto a pier, jumping off the end into the San Francisco Bay.

My father, Paul Baxley, was the stunt coordinator.

Loren Janes was the stuntman doubling Mr. Jones, played by Philip Roth, who was seated in the back of a Cadillac convertible. As the four vehicles approached the end of the pier, Loren stood up, and he was suddenly knocked unconscious by the awning on the dock just before the convertible went off the end of the pier.

Two safety boats were standing by. I looked down and realized they were still tied up. Nobody was moving. The 1st Assistant Director was screaming at them through his bullhorn. I didn't wait; I dove off the pier and swam out to Loren; he was floating face down. I rolled him over as the first boat arrived.

As we loaded Loren into the boat, he started spitting up water; thank god he was alright. I'll never forget when his eyes opened; he just stared at me with disbelief. He never forgot either; every time I saw him, he would tell the story to anyone that would listen.

*What's Up, Doc?* also had a lot of sight gags. A friend of mine, Jack Verbois, was the guy who swung down from a light pole as he arched across the street, exploding through the giant plate glass window that was being carried across the intersection by two other stuntmen.

Craig Baxley diving into the moving truck on *Search*

I was the guy that ran from the garbage cans that suddenly came rolling around the corner down the hill out of nowhere. To get out of the way, I vaulted over the six-foot fence, landing ten feet down on a table surrounded by a half dozen people eating ice cream.

Sylvester Stallone was an extra on *What's Up, Doc?*

\* \* \* \* \*

I finished the year with an acting stunt part on the TV series *Bearcats,* starring Rod Taylor, Dennis Cole, and a $90,000 1914 Stutz Bearcat replica.

I was working in New Mexico with one of the best horsemen in the business, Billy Burton. We were both playing calvary soldiers at the turn of the century.

On the second day of filming, I got shot and did a saddle fall, got dragged down a riverbed, and did a horse jump over a fence alongside Billy. I still have Sgt. Spears' hat.

\* \* \* \* \*

1972 was a full slate, starting with *Conquest of the Planet of the Apes, Trouble Man, The Poseidon Adventure, The Outside Man, Ben,* and a number of TV series. I finished off the year working on a TV series, *Search,* doubling the star Doug McClure for the entire series.

Loren Janes was the stunt coordinator, and he was still telling the rescue story from *What's Up, Doc?*

I'll never forget a stunt I did on the back lot at Warner's on Halloween night. Doug's character was supposed to climb out of a third-story window onto the ledge, then dive off into the empty street as a stake bed truck drove into view, passing under him as he landed in the back.

Doug brought out a priest with him that night. The two just stood there staring at me. It was kind of creepy. At first, I thought it was a joke, but as Doug introduced him, I realized he was just a good friend that wanted to see the stunt.

I was out on the ledge getting a line-up on the truck, driven by another stuntman, Orwin Harvey. The timing was tricky; the speed of the truck had to be constant. Suddenly, Art Levinson, the first assistant, started yelling and waving his hands; I quickly realized it wasn't at me.

I glanced at Doug standing next to me; he had climbed out on the ledge. The set was dead silent except for Art pleading with Doug to come down. Doug was a great guy and a good athlete; he was always kidding around. I coaxed him back inside and told him to go back downstairs. We did the stunt once.

\* \* \* \* \*

Another time on the series, Valerie was eight months pregnant, standing at the sink of our rental home in the Hollywood Hills. She was washing dishes at the kitchen sink, listening to Elton John's *Tiny Dancer*. She looked out the window, across the Hollywood Freeway, wondering who the guy was climbing down the outside of the Universal Sheraton Hotel.

I wasn't always forthcoming with what I was doing back then because, in some cases, the stunt coordinators didn't let me know what I was doing until I arrived on set that day. Plus, I didn't want to worry her. We were both so young.

I climbed down ten stories on the outside of the building with no safety wire. Loren, who was a world-class gymnast, told the director I didn't need it.

The idea was, Doug's character was climbing down the outside of the building, trying to catch two people inside riding down in the elevator. It was crazy! Today, without question, they'd put a safety wire on the stuntman. I just looked at Loren and shook my head. We did the stunt once.

After the stunt was done, the next part of the sequence was for Doug to catch the two people as they left the hotel. I dove off the portico of the main entrance, eighteen feet off the ground, down onto Max Kleven and Patty Elder, who were basically my moving catchers on the sidewalk. They were doubling John Vernon and another actress. As I sailed down with my feet over my head, Max started to move, basically duck. In the business, we call it an "ole." But I caught him on the shoulder as we all tumbled down the sidewalk.

I stood up and looked at Max; he was totally embarrassed. He knew I knew.

Loren said, "Oh my god, guys, that looked incredible! Craig, you should thank Max."

* * * * *

**Walter Matthau holding Kristin, 18 days old**

It was a very busy year; Valerie and I had our first baby - Kristin Marie Baxley.

Caro Jones, the casting director on *Bearcats,* had spoken to Mike Connors, the star of *Manix.* She convinced him that I should be the quest star on his series. It was what I hoped was the beginning and the ending of my acting career.

I played a German hit man who terrorized Los Angeles. Before the episode was over, I had killed five people. The third victim, I fought and threw out a six-story window in downtown L.A. Dick Ziker, the stunt coordinator, did the sixty-foot fall. I think it was the actor's second job in the industry; his name was Sam Elliot.

Then onto *Battle for Planet of the Apes.*

I finished the year working the last three and a half months on *Charley Varrick,* a film directed by Don Siegel. Don was fresh off the Clint Eastwood film *Dirty Harry. Charley Varrick* starred Walter Matthau, Joe Don Baker, and Andrew Robinson (the killer in *Dirty Harry*).

Working on *Charley Varrick* was the first time our family was on location together. I still have the picture of Walter Matthau holding Kristin when she was eighteen days old. I always thought he was a very cool guy, not to mention an incredible actor.

\* \* \* \* \*

That year I was asked to join The Stuntman's Association. A couple of months later, we were invited to the Annual Stuntman's Ball. It was a black-tie event at the Ambassador Hotel in Los Angeles held in the Coconut Grove Nightclub.

When I told Valerie about it, she was very excited; I wasn't really into black-tie back then. I was told the headliner was Andy Williams. Strike two. I told her it might as well be Perry Como; my parents would love it. I was not going. Period.

When we got there, the room was packed. Not just stuntmen, but actors, directors, producers — it was quite the scene back then.

As we were eating dinner, the opening act came out onto the stage. It was one man, dressed in wool pants, a long underwear T-shirt, and a black papakha - a Russian Cossack hat. He just stood there for a moment, starring out at the audience, then pulled out a joint and lit it up.

He started to speak in a stilted Russian-American dialect of some kind. People didn't know what to make of him. It was Robin Williams' first appearance in Los Angeles. By the time he was done, everyone in the room was exhausted from laughing so hard. Poor Andy Williams had to follow that act.

\* \* \* \* \*

I was one of five or six stuntmen doing all the major car chases and stunts during the early and mid-seventies - the jumps, cannon rolls, pipe ramp turnovers, etc.

The chases with Alan Gibbs (*Smokey and the Bandit*), Gary "Wiz" McLarty, (*Beverly Hills Cop, The Blues Brothers*), Bill Hickman (*Bullitt, The French Connection*), Carey Loftin (*Bullitt, Duel*), and later Bobby "O" Orrison and Henry Kingi, who were both my soul brothers from another mother, are some of the fondest memories I have.

In 1973, Hal Needham and I did the first major car jumps in the industry. Hal did his on *White Lightning*, doubling Burt Reynolds. I did mine on *The Parallax View*, doubling Warren Beatty. I always looked forward to doing a chase with Alan Gibbs and Bill Hickman; there was none better. We could read each other and challenge the other to do better.

Gary McLarty did the first cannon roll in the motion picture industry on *McQ*, a John Wayne film; it was probably the most innovative car stunt done to date. Eight times wheel to wheel. It was the most amazing vehicle stunt I've ever seen.

A cannon is a three-foot-long, thirty-three-inch-wide metal cylinder welded to the vehicle's roll cage. Usually, it was located behind the passenger seat, although sometimes it was mounted in front where the passenger seat was. Six ounces of black powder were loaded into the cylinder, followed by a three-foot-long telephone pole, which pushed the black powder to the top of the cylinder.

To execute the stunt, the driver would come in between sixty and sixty-five miles per hour, throw the vehicle sideways, and fire the cannon. The charge would blow the pole into the ground, flipping the vehicle. There weren't many stuntmen back then that were even asked to do them.

I did the next three after Gary on various films. My last was on the television show *Harry O*, six times wheel to wheel.

I was brought in for twelve episodes of *Harry O* as the stunt coordinator and second unit director by producer Jerry Thorpe, who also produced *Kung Fu*. Jerry wanted to add more action to the show. The jump I did on the first episode ended up on the cover of TV Guide.

**Craig Baxley, *Harry O* car jump**

My father and Alan Gibbs probably had the biggest impact on my career in the early days. Matching egos. Matching talents. Both incredible all-around stuntmen. There couldn't have been more polar opposites.

# CHAPTER 3

## Warren Beatty, Part 1

In April of '73, I got a call to be at Paramount studios at 10 a.m. the following day. I was told it was to work on a movie called *Parallax View.* When I got there, I was ushered into an office where nine other stuntmen were standing in a line. Nine 6'1" stuntmen. One of them, Mickey Gilbert, flashed me a million-dollar grin and snapped his profile at me and said, "Don't worry, kid, I got this," and turned back as the door opened.

Warren Beatty and his life-long personal assistant, Helen Feibelmann, walked in, followed by the director, Alan Pakula. Warren Beatty of *Bonnie and Clyde, Splendor in the Grass, McCabe and Mrs. Miller.*

This was a big deal. Warren was a major movie star.

Warren continued down the row of stuntmen, studying them like insects under a magnifying glass. He stopped in front of Mickey, leaned in to look at Mickey's nose, turned back, and smiled at Helen. Then he moved on.

He finally stopped at the end of the line, in front of me. He stood there for what seemed like an eternity. Finally, he said, "This is the guy," then was gone.

Helen stepped up, smiled, and softly said, "Yeah." She turned and left, followed by Alan - who just winked at me.

We all just stood there, then somewhere down the line, Mickey muttered, "What the fuck?"

That was the beginning of one of the most important chapters in my career. I became Warren Beatty's stunt double, stunt coordinator, and second unit director for the next twenty years. Because of the longevity of our relationship, we had a chance to develop a good strong friendship that was more than just an acquaintance. We had some great times working together. The best.

* * * * *

One day during filming, I was standing in the parking lot at the base of the Space Needle in Seattle. I had long hair like Warren and Warren's wardrobe. Warren wanted me to wear a beige trench coat so nobody would think I was him.

Suddenly, somebody walked up behind me and threw their arms around me. I spun around, face-to-face with the blue eyes of Julie Christie, from *Doctor Zhivago*.

She instantly realized I wasn't Warren. "Oh my god, I'm so sorry," she said.

I was speechless.

She and Warren first worked together on *McCabe and Mrs. Miller.* I always thought they were the perfect Hollywood couple, if there was such a thing. I worked with her a couple of times after that on *Shampoo* and *Heaven Can Wait.* She was always such a beautiful woman and such a class act.

*Parallax View* was a political thriller. It was directed by Alan Pakula, who produced *To Kill a Mockingbird.* He also directed *Sophie's Choice, Klute, Comes a Horseman, All the President's Men,* and a dozen more.

The director of photography was Gordon Willis, who shot *Klute, Comes a Horseman, All the President's Men,* and many other classics like *Annie Hall* and *The Godfather,* to name a few.

The film began with a senator being assassinated; three C.I.A. agents chased the killer up onto the top of the Space Needle - six hundred and five feet above the ground. The agents were played by my father, Fred Scheiwiller, and myself.

As the killer struggled to escape, the C.I.A. agents closed in from opposing sides. In the film, the killer either slipped or was thrown off the Space Needle by the agents, a story point left intentionally unclear.

It was a crazy location; the roof was sloped almost forty-five degrees and had just been painted with slick white enamel paint;

**Top of Space Needle**

the wind was blowing about sixty miles an hour. Before the stunt was done, we checked and rechecked the six pieces of plywood that we rigged in place inside the restaurant below. We secured them to the safety platform outside the restaurant. They stuck out into space below the roofline, not visible to the camera. Rigging it was a stunt itself.

I looked at Chuck Waters, the stuntman playing the killer, and asked him if he was ready. He nodded, then I looked at my father and gave him a thumbs-up. He glanced at the camera crew and Howard Koch Jr., the first assistant (who were all tied off with safety lines around the open hatch to the roof), and shouted, "We're ready."

Seconds later, Chuck was tumbling down the roof and off out into space – six hundred and five feet off the ground - appearing to fall to his death as the agents stopped just short of the edge.

What the audience didn't see was that when Chuck left the roof and dropped out of sight, he actually dropped eight feet, hit the plywood, and bounced back up into the air, back inside the restaurant.

As I look back on it, it was probably one of the strangest gags I've been involved with.

The major car sequences were filmed in Burlington, Washington, Los Angeles, and Pico Rivera. I doubled Warren for the entire movie. The driving sequence started at a house in Topanga Canyon in Woodland Hills. The next location was in a logging yard in Washington. Then I did the car jump in Woodland Hills, from Mulholland Drive down to Topanga Boulevard.

The sequence ended with the car weaving through traffic in Woodland Hills, then crashing through the front of a supermarket in Pico Rivera.

**Car jump,** *Parallax View*

**Police car crashing into market**

When I arrived at the location in Pico Rivera, the special effects man approached me and said the location had an issue. The front entrance was three inches narrower than the car, and on each side, there was a metal I-beam inside the brick and concrete. The only option I could see was to shoot down a set of 2x12's on each side of the entrance, creating a funnel outside the glass doors. If I was off by inches, it would deflect me back to the center.

The idea was to come in hot and stomp the breaks at the point of impact. When I did the stunt, the car seemed to stop for a split second at the point of impact; then popped through the glass doors like a champagne cork into the market. Stunt people dove clear as glass exploded and rained down.

"Cut!" was called; the medic came and checked everyone. The stunt went exactly as planned.

Suddenly there was a commotion at the back of the market. Four crew members were moving toward me, carrying Warren Beatty. As they passed me, I could see that the top of his head and face were covered in blood. Warren looked up at me and muttered, "Good job."

The next day it appeared in *Variety*, in Amy Archer's column: Warren had been upstairs in the manager's office watching the stunt; he was so startled by the car bursting through the entrance that he jumped up and hit his head on the top of the window frame in the office.

Ten stitches - the only injury on the film.

Everyone working on the film were the best in the industry. I always felt like I went to film school on that film.

* * * * *

After *Parallax View*, I went to work on one of Philip Kaufman's earlier films, *The White Dawn*, starring Warren Oates, Timothy Bottoms, and Louis Gossett Jr. I doubled Timothy Bottoms.

*The White Dawn* was an Eskimo saga, similar to *A Man Called Horse*. The next three months were spent on Baffin Island in the Northwest Territories, above the Arctic Circle. We stayed in Frobisher Bay, in a small Inuit community. The entire movie was filmed there, on the rolling tundra and ice flows.

The movie was set in the late 1800s. Dispatched from the fleet, a small twenty-foot whaling boat, rowed by a dozen whalers, continued the search for whales. The climax of the hunt came when a harpoon attached to a heavy rope was thrown into a giant whale. The situation suddenly became one of life and death. As the whale picked up speed, the small boat was towed at a high rate of speed - bouncing off ice flows - finally slamming into a large flow where it capsized, spitting the men off onto the flow and into the icy water. Three survived.

To simulate the capsizing of the small boat, we were towed in by an offstage powerboat. We maintained a steady speed of thirty knots, which is about thirty-five miles per hour.

I was in the bow, doubling Timothy. Upon hitting an ice flow, the boat stood up almost vertically and began to flip, spitting the twelve stuntmen out onto the ice flows, most skidding off and into the freezing water. The water was about twenty-five degrees. (The reason it wasn't frozen was because of the high salt content).

Every day was a learning experience in the Northwest Territories.

One day we went to get fuel we had dropped off that morning on a small piece of tundra. We quickly discovered we had a minor problem. In Frobisher Bay, the Island had a ninety-foot tide; when we arrived, it was low tide, our gas cans were thirty-five feet in the air sitting on top of a thirty-five-foot rocky peak. Being the youngest stuntman on the show, I was sent up, climbing the slimy rock to get the gas cans.

Baffin Island is in "The Land of the Midnight Sun," it was continuous daylight for the entire time we were there, the coldest I think I've been in my life. I couldn't wait to get back home to my family.

Philip Kaufman went on to direct *The Right Stuff, Rising Sun,* and *The Unbearable Lightness of Being.*

**Craig Baxley on** *The White Dawn*

# CHAPTER 4

## Another Great Year

In 1973 I spent the beginning of the year on the Charles Bronson film *Mr. Majestyk*. Some say this was his best film. It was directed by Richard Fleischer, who had directed *The Vikings, 20,000 Leagues Under the Sea, Fantastic Voyage,* and *Tora! Tora! Tora!,* among dozens of other classics.

*Mr. Majestyk* was written by novelist Elmore Leonard, who also wrote *Get Shorty* and *Hombre,* among others. It was filmed in La Junta and Canon City, Colorado.

The chase sequence with the 1968 Ford F-100 became one of the most famous chase sequences of the period, following *Bullitt* and *The French Connection.* The Ford motor company used clips from the movie in television commercials to demonstrate how tough their trucks are built.

When Valerie arrived on location in Colorado with our daughter, I realized some of the stuntmen were upset. Locations were party time for stuntmen. Back then, they didn't bring their wives or family. Guess I never got the memo. It was a different time, a time long before the #MeToo movement.

Valerie and I had to make the thirty-dollar per diem work for the three of us. She brought a footlocker on location with her. It had an electric hot plate, toaster oven, and a couple of pans to cook in. She would make these incredible meals in our hotel room with money to spare. Beef bourguignon, coq au vin, pasta, grilled cheese — we ate like kings.

Charlie's daughter, Katrina, was a couple of years older than Kristin; he stopped by our room one day and introduced her. The two just stood there laughing; then they were off to the races. She and Kristin had a great time playing together.

**Charles Bronson, Kristin, and Katrina**

\* \* \* \* \*

After *Mr. Majestyk*, I got a call to be the stunt coordinator on *The Nickel Ride*, a film directed by Robert Mulligan, who directed *To Kill a Mockingbird* and *The Summer of '42*. The producers were David Foster and Larry Turman, who produced *The Graduate*. Jordon Cronenweth was the director of photography on films such as *Blade Runner, Altered States*, and *Garden of Stone*. Here I was working with some of the best filmmakers the business has ever known. I was a very lucky man.

Then onto *99 and 44/100% Dead!*, starring Richard Harris and directed by John Frankenheimer. I was working nights on the film and days on another movie, *Cry Rape*. I was able to pull it off because both locations were in Long Beach, California.

One day I got a call to fly into Atlanta, Georgia, to do a gag on a film. It was a three-day contract, two days of traveling, one day to do the gag. I landed in Atlanta in the middle of a snowstorm. When I got to the production office, the production secretary told me she didn't want to go out in the storm that night; she had tickets to see a local comedian that was outrageous. Great seats, row six in the pit, dead center.

I knew walking in it was a local crowd; as I sat down, I realized I was the only white guy in the pit - maybe in the entire place. A couple of seconds later, the lights went down, and out came Richard Pryor.

I'd never seen anyone like him. It was like he was having a conversation with you - so emotional, so real. I loved it until he suddenly stopped directly in front of me. He snapped, "What'cha do'in here?" The crowd loved it. So did I.

He spent a couple of minutes singling me out; I've never laughed so hard, then he moved on. He was the funniest man I've ever seen in my life. Every so often, he would stop in front of me again. He didn't have to say a word; the crowd would just go nuts.

If you haven't heard his 1974 album, *The Nigga's Crazy,* pick it up. Raw genius . . . so ahead of his time.

I finished off the year working on *Battle for Planet of the Apes, The Outside Man,* and *Earthquake* on the back lot at Universal.

There were also multiple episodes of *Chase* and *The F.B.I.* Davey Sharpe was the stunt coordinator on *The F.B.I.;* he also doubled the lead, Efrem Zimbalist Jr. When Davey found out I was available, he brought me on for a run of four episodes; the first two were shot on location in Arizona. The second two were back in Los Angeles.

I spent the next few weeks doing high falls, car chases, and fights. It was nice hanging out with Davey in Arizona. He was a true gourmet, wine connoisseur, and a true aficionado of the world's finest cigars. And the stories were incredible. He doubled Douglas Fairbanks in *Robin Hood,* and he appeared in over 4,500 films. He was a true gentleman and one of the greatest stuntmen the business has ever known.

**Craig - Motocross**

# CHAPTER 5

## Motocross

Husky and CZ riders dominated the Motocross World Championships through the sixties and seventies. Husqvarna was Swedish and CZ Jawa was Czechoslovakian. I rode a 250 CZ. Honda kind of missed the boat; they came into the game a little late.

In 1972 Honda sent their R&D (research and development) department to the United States and Europe to purchase one of every type of motocross bike - Greeves, Maico, Husky, CZ, Bultaco, Puch, KTM, ATK, Penton, and Hodaka. Upon returning to Japan, with the help of 1972 AMA Champion Gary Jones, prototypes of the CR125 and CR250 Elsinore were built in a very short time.

In late '73, Honda issued a press release on their 125 and 250 Elsinore. Compared to the European bikes, the Elsinore was superior in user-friendliness, ergonomics, carburation, and durability. It was bad news for some smaller companies like Penton, Bultaco, KTM, and Hodaka.

That month I was called for an interview by a commercial house in Burbank, California. When I walked in, there were five of the best motocross/stuntmen in the business. It was like old home week; we all knew each other. It really didn't matter who got the gig; it was just good to see each other. Usually, the only time we saw each other was at work or Indian Dunes, racing on either the International Course or Shadow Glens.

The interview was to choose a rider to be in their first commercial and on every month of the Elsinore Calendar. I guess I was lucky; they chose me. I was told it was going to shoot in Zion and Bryce National Parks in Utah.

The next week I flew to Las Vegas and met up with the Japanese production team. There were two box vans, one filled with a dozen CR250 Elsinore's; the other was filled with camera and grip equipment. I threw my gear into the back of the box van with the motorcycles. I climbed into the station wagon with the director, producer, and interpreter. The producer drove. I quickly realized nobody spoke English but the interpreter, barely.

Zion and Bryce were a two-and-a-half-hour drive from Vegas. The producer was one of those guys who would accelerate, then let off the gas and accelerate again. They never stopped talking - rising and falling like loud banshees. I didn't know if they were having a friendly conversation or were about to kill each other.

The interpreter kept nodding at me, "Everything's going to be okay." Accelerating and off, accelerating and off, accelerating and off... It was one of the longest drives I've ever been on.

Halfway through the day, I was pleasantly surprised. The crew was very fast. We would do a couple of takes at each location, then move on. I was also very impressed with the Elsinore.

The sun was setting as we finished. Everybody seemed very happy. I had no idea, though, I just smiled, and I climbed back into the station wagon.

The drive back was not so uneventful. It was pitch black when it started to rain, and I mean rain. The downpour quickly became a monsoon. Accelerating and off...on and off. A full-blown argument erupted over how to drive in the storm.

It became dead silent when we all realized that the windshield wipers had broken. As the producer became more angry, he seemed to be accelerating faster.

This was like a bad movie until I realized he was about to completely miss a turn. The car was suddenly filled with bright white light; a truck horn shrieked as we crossed directly in front of the tractor-trailer, and the station wagon left the highway. They were all screaming as we came to a stop in the middle of a muddy field.

The rain seemed to be getting even heavier, if that was possible. It took everybody from all three vehicles to get the station wagon out of the mud and back onto the highway. A half-hour later, we were back on the road.

We all sat in silence as I drove the rest of the way back to Las

Vegas. As we pulled into Caesar's Palace, the interpreter explained they had booked a suite for me and wanted to have dinner together.

I said, "Thank you very much. I really appreciate it, but I just want to go home. Could you please just book me on the next flight?"

A couple of my friends saw the commercial, said it looked great. I never did see it. Everyone seemed to be talking about the advertisement Steve McQueen had just done on the Elsinore. I still have the calendar.

# CHAPTER 6

## Rollerball

In 1974, the word went out about *Rollerball,* a new film directed by Norman Jewison that starred James Caan, John Houseman, Maud Adams, Moses Gunn, and John Beck. Tryouts had just begun. They were looking for ten of the best all-around stuntmen in the world. Nine were chosen from the United States, one from England. I was the youngest from the States. There were also a dozen Cockney Roller Hockey players, six American Roller Derby Skaters, a German Speed Skater, and six Asian extras, three of which were trying to work as stuntmen in the States.

**Track with riders and skaters**

*Rollerball* was filmed in the Olympic basketball stadium in Munich, Germany, over the next four months. The production company built a massive wooden banked circular track in the stadium.

Skaters on two opposing teams were pulled around the track by three motorcycles jockeying to score, with a rollerball at an opposing goal. The company brought in thousands of extras for two or three days of each game.

During filming, James Caan told me a story about working with my father on *The Godfather.* James was playing Sonny Corleone.

He told me how my father, the stunt coordinator and second unit director, shot the sequence where Corleone was ambushed at a toll booth on the Long Island Causeway - violently shot to death by carloads of hitmen firing sub-machine guns.

James laughed and said Coppola was over an hour and a half late; the crew was just standing around waiting.

Gordie Willis, the cinematographer, looked at my father and said, "This is bullshit; where is he? Let's do it." So my father directed the entire sequence.

When Coppola finally showed up, the assistant director explained to him what happened. He looked at my father and simply asked, "How did it look?"

My father looked at Gordie; they both looked at Caan, who said, "It looked fuckin' great."

James Caan surprised all of us on *Rollerball.* He really stepped up for the role; he was actually in better shape and a better skater than his stunt double. I did a gag with him where I locked off my skates, hit a spot tramp, and flipped over him. I never touched him. He and Norman loved the gag when they watched the dailies.

\* \* \* \* \*

Chuck "Cappy" Parkinson Jr. and I did the two major motorcycle stunts in the film. I did the gag over the wall through the screen into the seats in the Tokyo game. I snapped a handstand on the handlebars as I hit a knock bolted to the track. As the bike flipped, I kicked into the air, let go, and was launched backward over the wall, through the soft lead breakaway fence into an offstage catcher in the seats as the bike slammed into the wall. Chuck did the final one in the Houston

Craig Baxley and James Caan

**Craig Baxley and Chuck "Cappy" Parkinson**

vs. New York game. He also hit a knock bolted to the track. He was able to go faster, so the motorcycle spit him further and higher into an offstage catcher. Then he overlapped the landing off an air ramp to the hardwood floor.

There were several injuries on the film. My dear friend Tony Brubaker broke his leg, and several American Roller Derby guys and the Cockney Roller Hockey players sustained minor injuries. I had one minor one. One of the American stuntmen, who played a part on the Houston team throughout the film, was finally asked to do a stunt, which he refused. He asked the stunt coordinator, Max Kleven, to have one of the other stuntmen double him.

When Max asked me to do it, I thought he was shitting me. Dar Robinson, the legendary stuntman, wanted to be doubled?

Snatch of Skater - *Rollerball*

The stunt was in the Houston vs. New York game. The character Dar played on skates was supposed to be released from a motorcycle, race down the track, snatch another skater's skate (who had been knocked down) and drag him around the stadium as the crowd cheered him on.

When Max explained it to me, I suggested we do it in cuts. An insert of a hand grabbing a skate, snatching it out of frame. Then I'd rig myself a vest with a cable that ran down my arm, under the wardrobe, and attach it to the skate. Then overlap the snatch, and drag him around the stadium. It seemed to make sense to me.

He said, "Kid, you're the stunt guy. You don't tell me how to rig it. Okay?"

I nodded, "You got it, Max."

We did the stunt his way. It went well, except I partially separated my shoulder.

Two weeks later, I did the motorcycle stunt in the Tokyo game.

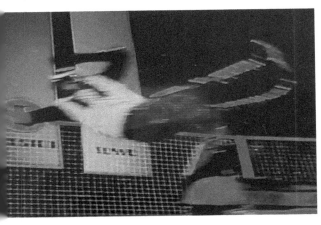

**Craig Baxley, Tokyo motorcycle stunt**

This movie was one of the most physically demanding films I think any of us had ever worked. The last week, the Second Unit stayed behind to film some of the final stunts, and we actually played the game for a couple of days.

*Rollerball* was the first film to give stuntmen credit in the end credits. Quite an achievement for the stunt world.

When I got home, I was asked to become a member of a new

group, Stunts Unlimited. Stunts Unlimited was founded in 1970 by Hal Needham, Ronnie Rondell Jr., and Glenn Wilder.

I grew up around the corner from the Rondell's; Ronnie's father was a very successful production manager in the industry.

Glenn was amazing - I'd worked with him earlier on *Parallax View,* and he'd hired me a couple of times after that.

Hal and my father were never on the same page. My father thought Hal was full of shit. I think the feeling was mutual.

Stunts Unlimited was an elite organization comprised of the top A-list stunt performers. If you wanted to hire the best, you used Stunts Unlimited. It was the cream of the crop. I became the youngest member of Stunts Unlimited in 1974. In 1978, I was elected president of the group.

That same year, I got my D.G.A. (Director's Guild of America) card on a Movie of the Week, *Search for the Gods.* It was directed by Jud Taylor and starred Kurt Russell, Stephen McHattie, Raymond St. Jacques, and Ralph Bellamy.

I first met Kurt when we were both fourteen years old. My father had taken me to work with him on a TV series he was doing at MGM. He was the stunt coordinator on *The Travels of Jaimie McPheeters.* It starred Dan O'Herlihy, Charles Bronson, and Kurt as Jaimie. I remember it so vividly because it was the same year President John F. Kennedy was assassinated.

The first day we arrived on location, about three miles north of Taos, at the Taos Pueblo. When we arrived, I noticed a mint white 1969 Cadillac convertible, sitting in the ditch beside the road with its top down. The location manager looked back at us and said, "It's Dennis Hopper's; he probably walked back to his ranch."

"His ranch?" I asked.

"Yeah, The Mud Palace." (Dennis lived there for several years during his wild, drug-fueled days.)

Taos, New Mexico, was one of the most beautiful locations I have ever been to. It is estimated that The Pueblo was built between 1000 and 1450 A.D., and it is considered one of the oldest continuously inhabited communities in the United States.

*Search for the Gods* had a lot of action on it for a Movie of the Week: a car chase with a cannon roll, fights, and a three hundred-foot rappelling sequence into the Rio Grande Gorge. And working with

**Kurt Russell, Craig Baxley, and Stephen McHattie**

Kurt Russell was as much fun as you'd think it would be. He's one of the nicest actors I've ever worked with and a great athlete.

Life was good. As the stunt coordinator and second unit director on the project, I was one of the youngest second unit directors in the business.

\* \* \* \* \*

Hipgnosis was the premier Art Design group based in London that specialized in creating cover art and dust covers for the biggest rock bands in the world: The Rolling Stones, Black Sabbath, Led Zeppelin, Bad Company, Wings, Wishbone Ash, Genesis, the Scorpions, AC/DC, and The Beatles, to name a few.

In late 1974, they contacted Stunts Unlimited looking for three stuntmen for the cover for the Pink Floyd album, *Wish You Were Here.*

The concept for the front cover was to have two businessmen shaking hands, one of them on fire. Ronnie Rondell, Jr. was the man on fire shaking hands with Danny Rogers. Ronnie wore a fire-retardant suit covered in a business suit. A fire-retardant hood protected his head under a wig. It was filmed between two sound stages on the Warner Brothers lot.

The dust cover and poster concept were to have a splashless diver partially sticking out of Mono Lake, which is south of Mammoth Mountain, California. The lake is hauntingly beautiful, reflecting the snow-capped Sierra Nevadas in its blue water. Unusual shapes of eerie Tufa towers, which are columns of limestone, rise above the surface. The high levels of salt make the lake water alkaline. The clarity is clouded by thousands and thousands of brine shrimp.

I did a yoga handstand on the bottom of a shallow part, remaining submerged, holding my breath as long as possible to let the ripples and bubbles die away. It was a very cool shot; I guess Hipgnosis liked it. They put it on the cover of their book, *The Work of Hipgnosis, Walk Away Rene.*

**Pink Floyd album sleeve and poster**

**High fall on** *Lepke*

# CHAPTER 7

## Still on a Roll

In early '75, I worked on *Logan's Run*. After which, I left for New York to work on the film, *Report to the Commissioner*, starring Michael Moriarty, Susan Blakley, and Yaphet Kotto. I was doubling Michael, who had just won a Tony for *Find Your Way Home* and an Emmy for *The Glass Menagerie*. It was also Richard Gere's first film.

One of the action sequences in the film was a foot chase with Bo Lockey (Michael's character) chasing Thomas "Stick" Henderson, played by Tony King. Tony played professional football for the Buffalo Bills and required no stunt double. There we were, six stories up, jumping from one building to another, going from rooftop to rooftop, climbing, falling down the front of the Winter Gardens Theater, leaping off onto a moving truck, and running through traffic on 42nd Street. Tony was a machine; I was a mere mortal. That was the day I discovered what I was made of.

After that, I did *Lepke*, a gangster film starring Tony Curtis. I was in and out; I did a forty-foot-high fall and a jerk-off with thirty body hits that sent me straight back through the screen in a movie house.

\* \* \* \* \*

Alan Gibbs was the stunt coordinator on *Jigsaw John* – a series Jack Warden starred in. Alan, Gary McLarty, and I were doing most of the car chases on the show. Tommy Huff and Jim Connors would occasionally come in as additional drivers. *Jigsaw John* and *Police Story* seemed to have a car chase every episode.

When Valerie was eight months pregnant, I walked into our home after work one day. She ran up and threw her arms around me, "Oh honey, they're so beautiful. Thank you."

I looked past her at the two dozen long stem roses that sat in the middle of our dining room table. "Sure, you know I love you."

I walked over to the table and just stared at the flowers. There was a minor problem; I didn't send her flowers. I reached down and opened the little envelope. It read: "From your secret admirer." I looked back at my pregnant wife, "Nice, huh?"

Just then, the phone rang; on the other end, there was that very distinctive laugh, that Alan Gibbs laugh. "Ha! Gotcha, Bax! That's for last week."

**Motorcycle wheelie on *Switch***

I had no idea what he was talking about, but that was Alan. I'm not sure he did either; he just kept laughing. I pulled the phone away from my ear so Valerie could hear him. Understanding occurred; she glanced at the flowers and just shook her head.

Alan was a unique guy, a good friend, and one of the best all-around stuntmen I've ever worked with through the years.

But the most important thing that happened that year was Valerie and I had our son, Craig Paul Baxley.

The rest of the year, I wanted to stay in town with my family. I worked on several TV series and mini-series: I was the stunt driver on multiple episodes of *Police Story*, *Jigsaw John*, and *Switch*.

* * * * *

I always loved working on *The Rockford Files*. After doing *Grand Prix* with John Frankenheimer, James Garner became a part-time racer himself.

I remember the first time I worked on the show, James saw me and told his double to go sit down. "How's your Dad? Come on, kid, let's do this."

He was such a great guy, so likable and laid back. He and I did the chase; I had James Garner chasing me. He stuck with me through every turn.

When we got back to base camp, my passenger, Bear "Ace" Hudkins, looked at me and said, "The guy can drive, huh?" Then he shouted at Garner's stunt double, "How's it going, Roydon, you pussy?"

I also worked on seven episodes of *Kolchak: The Night Stalker* that year. It was probably one of the coolest and creepiest shows on television. I was actually a guest star on a couple of episodes playing Mr. Ring and the Black Knight.

TV was busy then; I did sixteen episodes of *Swat*, doubling two of the leads, Robert Forster and Robert Urich.

I also worked on *Sherlock Holmes in New York*, a two-hour Movie of the Week, doubling Roger Moore. I actually got to play backgammon with Roger and John Houston between set-ups. Houston played Moriarty. The stories he told were mesmerizing. John was a true treasure. It was a time when performances meant more than just the pretty faces.

Then there were the mini-series like *Rich Man, Poor Man, Captains and the Kings,* and multiple episodes of *Cannon, Starsky and Hutch, The Rookies,* and *Kung Fu.*

I also worked on *The Killing of a Chinese Bookie,* a feature film directed by John Cassavetes and Drum. The show starred Warren Oates, Pam Grier, Yaphet Kotto, and Paula Kelly.

\* \* \* \* \*

In those days, stuntmen thought working on a feature film was more prestigious. Only the best usually did.

But I quickly realized the money was in television due to the residuals. You received a residual every time the episode, Movie of the Week, or mini-series ran. The second run earned one hundred percent of what you originally made. After that, it would tier down. But back then, it wouldn't go below a certain ceiling, making it possible for stuntmen and actors to live on their residuals. You didn't receive a residual on a feature film until it ran on television. And, if you were lucky, it ran twice.

I'd come home from working on a feature film, and I would have a stack of over a hundred television residuals waiting for me. I still receive a residual on a feature I did in 1987 for *Predator.* Because of how the S.A.G. (Screen Actors Guild) contract was structured back then, I still get a residual every quarter of $750 to $1000, depending on how many runs and platforms it plays on. It can't go below that ceiling, and I will receive that forever for *Predator.* When I look at how many jobs I did in the seventies and eighties, it's a nice nest egg.

That doesn't happen today. When corporations took over the studios, the Screen Actors Guild and Directors Guild of America gave up the pay scales and ceilings. They basically sold out everything that had been hard won in the sixties, seventies, and eighties. Now the unions have new sliding scales, which means your residual is down to almost nothing after a couple of runs. The days of actors and stuntmen living on their residuals are gone forever.

\* \* \* \* \*

I got a call to work on a Warren Miller film. It was part of a ski film shot on Mammoth Mountain, California. I played a ski patrol member that witnessed a skier smoking a joint on the top of Run 1, the shutes called "Oh Shit." As I confronted the skier, he took off. The chase quickly transitioned out of bounds into the powder and through the trees. Once I caught and stopped him, the scene turned into an explosive fight on top of the cornice. The fight ended with the two of us falling off the overhang of the cornice, tumbling down the mountain.

**Fall at Mammoth Mountain, California - Warren Miller film**

\* \* \* \* \*

1976 started off the way 1975 ended. I was working non-stop. I was coordinating and directing the second unit on pilots, Movies of the Week, and television series.

*Gemini Man* was supposed to be a hot new series at Universal, starring Ben Murphy. Ben had starred in the series *Alias Smith and Jones*. He looked like a young Paul Newman. Everyone thought the show was going to be a big hit. I was the stunt coordinator, second unit director, and I also doubled Ben. Unfortunately, it only lasted one season.

\* \* \* \* \*

There were several sad times in my career amidst the great times. One was in November of 1976. I got a call to work on a film up in Seattle; Tommy Huff was the stunt coordinator. Tommy was a good friend and also a member of Stunts Unlimited. It was playing a part, hanging out of a vehicle Tommy was driving, shooting at the car we were pursuing. I was too busy, so I had "Cappy" Parkinson replace me. Handing off a gag to someone was a chance for them to work if available.

Cappy was a good friend; I'd known him since I got in the business. Aside from being a great athlete, he was a world-class gymnast. He worked for me on several episodes of *Gemini Man*. We also worked together on over a dozen shows: *Rollerball, Swat, Beretta,* among others.

A couple of nights later, I got a call from Ronnie Rondell Jr., one of the founding members of Stunts Unlimited. He said, "I hope you're sitting down." After a couple of seconds, "Cappy's dead. He was killed tonight."

I was speechless as he continued, "He was hanging out of a car as it went sideways, a tire blew, it turned over and landed on him."

I just stared at Valerie. "What is it?" she asked.

"Cappy's dead," I whispered. We were both too stunned to say anything else.

Ronnie continued, "You have to go over to their home and tell Michelle... I can't do it."

Car jump, *Gemini Man*

That was one of the toughest things Valerie and I have ever had to do in our lives. Cappy's death was one of the most gut-wrenching moments in my life.

I never questioned the ability of Tommy Huff or Cappy because they were two of Stunts Unlimited's best. The terrible accident was a flaw in the execution and the rigging - no tubes in the tires. When Tommy threw the car sideways, the tire rolled off the rim; basically, it blew, the rim dug into the ground, and the car flipped.

Cappy and his wife, Michelle, had just had a new baby boy around the same time we did. That made the tragic death of Cappy so very personal.

\* \* \* \* \*

In December of 1976, I was doing two shows simultaneously - coordinating and directing the second unit on both.

I worked with the director and the producer, Jerry Thorpe, at night in the San Fernando Valley on *All God's Children.* It had a great cast: Richard Widmark, Ned Beatty, Ossie Davis, and his wife, Ruby Dee. Jerry was the executive producer on *Kung Fu* and *Harry O.* I loved Jerry. He was smart - a true filmmaker.

The second show was in Long Beach during the day. Back then, you could drive from the Valley to Long Beach in forty-five minutes. Now it takes anywhere from two to two-and-a-half hours.

In the middle of the week, I got a call from the producer on *Close Encounters of the Third Kind.* Production was winding down; they had just come back from Georgia and had a couple more weeks of filming in L.A.

He explained that the stunt coordinator he carried for the last nine months to perform the car jump in the movie was suddenly unavailable. Two days before he was to do the jump, he called the producer and said he had the flu and wouldn't be able to do it. The stunt coordinator, Buddy Joe Hooker, suggested they call me.

So there I was, doing two shows, with a sudden chance to work with Steven Spielberg. But I knew I couldn't break away to do it; Jerry was really leaning on me for the action sequences in *All God's Children.*

The producer called me back the next day and asked me if there was any night I was available the following week; he said the company would rearrange the schedule to accommodate me. I checked the schedule; I was off Wednesday, December 1st. I agreed to do it. The fact that I was shooting in Long Beach was a plus; the location was a couple of miles away at White Point in San Pedro.

The location, chosen months before, was completely wrong. The spot was in a turn; I was told the director of photography, Vilmos Zsigmond, wanted to light the jump from the road. The only option was the turn; the fact that Zsigmond wanted to put the lights on the far side of the turn didn't allow any avenue to abort if something went wrong. I was curious why they couldn't change the location; night is night. I was told Steven and the DP didn't want to scout on the weekend and that this was the location, period.

Because I was shooting in the valley, I checked out the car at Warner Bros. Studios. I was curious if it was set up right and what kind of ramps had been chosen. The cage had been made for Buddy Joe, who is maybe 5'6". I'm 6'1". When I climbed inside, I realized the lack of leg and head room; the seat was welded to the horizontal roll tubing behind it. Moving it was not an option at that point in time. Regardless, I felt I could make it work.

The driver asked me what kind of ramp I was going to use.

"What was built for the jump?" I asked.

He told me they were waiting for Joe to give them specs. I told him I would just bring in a kick ramp, considering the jump was off an extremely steep hillside.

Nothing had been done to the suspension either. I had the driver captain stiffen the front-end torsion bars and add helper springs to accommodate the weight I was going to add to the rear end. He told me it was a 440 and could use a tune-up. I asked him to have the mechanic go through it completely. Then I went back to work.

That afternoon I told Valerie about accepting the job. She was extremely upset - not about having the night off, but about doing the stunt. She didn't care about working with Steven Spielberg. She knew I was burning the candle at both ends. She just had a bad feeling about the whole situation.

When I arrived at White Point, the sun was setting, and the crew was setting up. I wanted to check on the car and place the ramps, but the 1st Assistant Director ushered me over to meet Spielberg and the two producers, Michael and Julia Phillips.

It was a circus; they were giving interviews to the press and holding court as the crew was setting up. After a few minutes, I slipped away. After placing the ramps, I went to check on the car. The driver captain was very apologetic; the mechanic was just starting to tune up the police car.

A couple of hours later, Vilmos let production know he was ready. They had five cameras in place, and night was basically turned into day for the shoot. It was surreal; it looked like a moonscape ending in complete darkness.

By the time I had my gear on and climbed into the vehicle, I realized it was even tighter than I thought. I had Henry Kingi and a couple of other stunt guys do everything we could to rig me in safely.

As the 440 Mopar Big Block roared to life, I could tell it was missing – not the best scenario for a car stunt. I waved the mechanic over and asked him to adjust the four-barrel carburetor and set the timing up, which he did.

With a kick ramp (which in this case was ten by ten by two feet high), if the car was set up and weighted properly, you could jump a car over a hundred feet, ten to fifteen feet high. Those specs would allow for an easy landing with the ass end dragging as it landed.

The key with a kick ramp is to come in at a steady speed, then stab the accelerator as you hit the ramp. For this jump, I thought approaching at forty miles per hour, then accelerating to fifty-five would be perfect, as they were hoping for what Joe told them would be a seventy-five-foot jump, ten to fifteen feet off the ground.

From day one, I had two concerns about the location Joe picked. Aside from the fact that there was no way to abort the jump, another embankment went up the opposite side of the canyon a hundred feet out from the first.

As the engine idled, I waited for action. When it was finally given, I eased out, accelerating to fifty-five. About three-quarters of the way to the ramp, the engine coughed. I knew this could be a disaster. With no out, I had only one option; I accelerated, the big engine roared to life, and suddenly I was traveling about sixty-five miles per hour. I was still twenty feet from the ramp and knew I still had to stab it or the weight transfer wouldn't work. When I left the ramp, I was traveling between seventy-five and eighty miles per hour.

At the apex of the jump, I knew I was in trouble; I looked out the side window, and everything seemed to be moving in slow motion. I was twenty-five to thirty feet up - three stories off the ground.

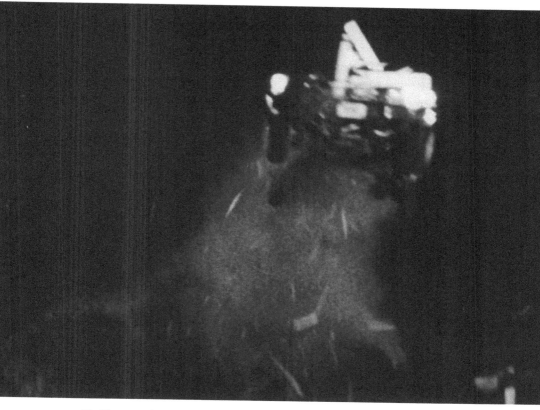

**Police car jump,** *Close Encounters of the Third Kind*

The police car traveled over one hundred and fifty feet at the right altitude, but cleared the entire canyon and hit flat on the uphill side of the opposing embankment. In a bone-jarring sudden stop, all the side windows were blown out. The car was driven back the way it came by the massive force of the impact.

I never lost consciousness; all I remember was hearing people screaming, "He's dead!" "Oh my God, he's dead!" "Bring in the ambulance!" I just sat there motionless, thinking, "What the fuck?"

As the crew arrived, I realized it was bad. As they pulled me out onto the ground, Julia Phillips knelt down crying; she had taken off her white mink and covered me up, thinking I was dead. The medic pulled the mink off as the ambulance moved closer.

That was the first and only time I ever had a major injury in the industry. All I could think about was Valerie and the kids.

My ribs were a mess. I broke my leg and shattered my right ankle and heel - both compound breaks from the floorboard being driven up by the impact. My career also came to a sudden, jarring stop.

The first month, I was in three different hospitals. I finally ended up at Valley Presbyterian Hospital in Van Nuys. After the orthopedic work was completed, they discovered there was another problem. Part of my right foot was dying.

Under massive amounts of morphine and a couple of operations later, it was decided I needed a major skin graft to protect the bone. They brought in a specialist who did the procedure. I laid flat on my back for the next two months with my right foot sewn to my left calf. Nobody was sure if it was going to work.

Valerie was there every night. It was heartbreaking to watch her.

Tommy Huff used to come by three or four days a week to play chess. Sometimes it would become a marathon competition. Tommy hated to lose; who doesn't? He would always complain as he was leaving that he had a migraine headache.

Our friend, Henry Kingi, and his wife always checked in on my family during that time.

Four and a half months after the accident, I left the hospital. They told me if I was lucky, I might walk again in a year or two. I had a wife and two little kids; that was unacceptable.

Five months later, Jim Arnett, a member of Stunts Unlimited, called. He was the stunt coordinator and second unit director on a film that would start in October. "Three months of doubling the star and car chases in San Francisco. You're my first call," he said. I was thrilled.

The next week, in April, I went back to work, but on a different film.

# CHAPTER 8

## Warren Beatty, Part 2

Helen Feibelmann, Warren's assistant, called and told me Warren wanted to see if I was available to work on his new film, *Heaven Can Wait*. He wanted me to be the stunt coordinator and second unit director. It was a comedy, not a major action film, and was going to be shot in Los Angeles - the perfect job for me to ease back into the business.

It featured Warren Beatty, Julie Christie, James Mason, Jack Warden, Charles Grodin, Dyan Cannon, and Buck Henry – what a cast. It was nice to be working with Warren again. *Heaven Can Wait* was a fun shoot; Warren was co-directing the film with Buck Henry.

I brought Davey Sharpe onto the shoot; it was his last job in the motion picture industry. Davey contracted ALS, also known as Lou Gehrig's Disease, in 1978; he passed away in 1980. It was an honor to have known and worked with him.

Warren became the first person to be Oscar-nominated for Best Picture, Best Director, and Best Actor on the same film for *Heaven Can Wait*.

\* \* \* \* \*

*Foul Play* starred Goldie Hawn, Chevy Chase (his first movie), and Dudley Moore. It was a very funny film, in the vein of *What's Up, Doc?* It had three major car sequences through the streets of San Francisco. Chevy's character kept stealing vehicle after vehicle, racing to beat a ticking clock. Jim had me doubling Chevy, doing all the driving, including the Lincoln crash into the pizza parlor, sliding three different vehicles through the city, and ending with a major limousine jump.

We had some of the best stuntmen in the business doing N.D. driving in the sequences, including Hal Needham.

I'll never forget, Valerie and I were lying in bed in the Holiday Inn after a long day, watching Johnny Carson. I found out later Hal had gone back to L.A. to be a guest on the show. When Hal came on, we were surprised; we thought it might be a pre-recorded show. But when Hal continued talking with Johnny about a new show he was working on, he mentioned *Foul Play*. He was explaining to Johnny that he was doing all the stunt driving for Chevy Chase.

My phone rang, it was Jim. He said, "Did you see that asshole?"

I said, "Yeah, but I'm in bed with my lady. See you in the morning, brother."

The next morning, Hal was back on the set. He never said a word about it.

**Limousine jump on *Foul Play***

# CHAPTER 9

## Back in the Game

The week I returned home from San Francisco, I was asked to do a five-part mini-series at Universal Studios. *Wheels*, written by Arthur Hailey, is based on the birth of the Pontiac GTO. It was directed by Jerry London and starred Rock Hudson, Lee Remick, Blair Brown, Ralph Bellamy, and John Beck, whom I'd worked with on *Rollerball*.

Rock Hudson's character was based on John DeLorean.

I was the stunt coordinator for the racing sequences filmed at Riverside International Raceway, as well as the other driving sequences in town.

Mario Andretti brought in two dozen vintage 1969 Formula 1 race cars. I drove a 1969 Bosworth, doubling John Beck, surrounded by some of the best drivers on the circuit.

Mario reminded everyone of the differences between race cars in 1969 and now. "The fuel used in 1969 was methanol; when it burned, it burned clear. Invisible," he stressed, "Don't inhale the fumes."

I looked at the other drivers. "What the hell was he talking about?

The cars also had twin radiators, one on each side of the driver, and much wider tires.

We set up for a couple of practice laps; my car had three cameras mounted on it, shooting back on me. With the full-face helmet, all you could see were my eyes. Jerry wanted to shoot all the race footage with John's character, then move on while we did the racing coverage.

Everything was going smoothly, and we were getting all the coverage Jerry wanted. We were doing the last piece when John's character started moving up through the pack. I worked my way through the other cars, going through turns six and seven. As I approached turn eight, I started to notice every time I downshifted and accelerated, the interior of my cockpit got hotter and hotter.

I accelerated out of turn eight, along the downhill back straightaway, and suddenly both sides of my ass felt like they were on fire. A slight mist began to rise and fog my face shield. I looked from driver to driver on each side of me, and they could tell something was wrong. The cockpit filled with mist, and the fog got heavier as the heat became unbearable.

I downshifted, and the burn hit my ass again; it felt like the seat was on fire. I swerved clear through the other cars and spun off the track into the infield. I leaped out of the car, trying to get my helmet off. Other cars roared into the infield. As the cloud continued to rise from the cockpit, drivers and crew members screamed at me, "Down, get down!"

Firemen and crew members ran to the car, trying to extinguish it. Then without explanation, they stopped.

I stood up as one of the crew chiefs walked up to me, "That wasn't fire; it was steam. Both hoses on the radiators came loose, and every time you accelerated or downshifted, scalding water hit you in the ass."

I wish I could say finishing that sequence was a great experience. If anything, it was humbling. After they fixed the hoses, I gingerly climbed back into the car and spent the rest of the day driving - sitting on my burned ass. I look at myself as the luckiest man that ever lived.

The Riverside International Raceway had six different variants, including two ovals and a four-road course, the longest of which was 2.3 miles. The final Formula 1 US Grand Prix was the last race of the season.

In 1983, the track closed. It was bought by a developer who built a shopping center and a mall on the location.

Years later, I drove NASCAR on a film, Buddy Baker's #1 UNO Buick, at the Atlanta Motor Raceway. I coordinated the second unit on the film. I brought five other stunt drivers with me to do the major stunts on the film.

We all spent the first day on the track building up to the speed the second director, Mickey Moore, wanted the crashes done at. I had a lap average of 187 mph.

**Craig Baxley, UNO Buick at Atlanta Motor Speedway**

Then we started filming with the actual NASCAR drivers. When it came time for the stunts, the filming was isolated to the six of us with the NASCAR drivers in the foreground and background. The NASCAR drivers thought we were crazy; the object was not to wreck a NASCAR at over 150 mph.

# CHAPTER 10

## Come Out to Play-ay

I got a call from Bobby Bass, a good friend who was also a member of Stunts Unlimited. He had been asked to be the stunt coordinator and direct all the fight scenes on a film called *The Warriors*. The film was directed by Walter Hill and produced by Larry Gordon (the two would later make *48 Hours* with Eddie Murphy and Nick Nolte). Bobby was working non-stop and didn't want to leave town to spend the next three-and-a-half months filming in New York. He told me he had spoken with Walter and Larry and had been asked to check my availability.

When I arrived in New York, I realized Bobby left out a few important points. The budget for the action film was only $4-5 million in New York City. The production man explained that they couldn't afford to bring back any stuntmen from California. And as I started to prep the film, I soon discovered most of the stuntmen in New York back then were a little long in the tooth. They had lots and lots of stories about all the incredible stunts they'd done; a couple even asked me what they had to do, hit the ground?

Guess what? This was a film about young gang members.

When Walter told me I had to teach the cast how to do a picture fight because he didn't want to double them, I got an idea. I put out a call to interview some of the best gymnasts and athletes in the city, and I was a little surprised by how many showed up for the weekend call. After weeding through them, I came away with seven and a guy who didn't have a S.A.G. card; his thing was giving hot air balloon rides. But there was something about him; he just struck me as a natural.

**Andrew Lazlo, Walter Hill, and Craig Baxley**

As I started to work with the cast and the eight guys, I was amazed by the talent of the balloon guy. Jery Hewitt was a great athlete and turned out to be the best local fight guy I had on the film. He was as good as any I ever worked with. He later became the stunt coordinator and second unit director on a dozen Coen Brother films.

I pitched Walter an idea for the death of Cyrus at the conclave in the opening. The conclave was attended by over a thousand actual gang members. In the scene, Cyrus was standing on top of a platform addressing the gang members. I suggested that when he was shot, he would be blown backward off the platform, fall fifteen feet, and crash through a breakaway platform below into a six-inch pad offstage.

Walter loved the idea. The problem was there wasn't a black stuntman in New York who would do it.

I wanted to bring Alan Oliney, a member of Stunts Unlimited, to double Cyrus. Alan doubled Eddie Murphy hanging off the back of the semi tractor-trailer in *Beverly Hills Cop*. He was an all-around gymnast. Then, a couple of days before Alan was to get on a plane, the production man said the company couldn't afford it.

I thought that was kinda chicken-shit to wait so late to cancel. Alan had already turned down jobs in L.A. to work with me. I told him Walter wanted the gag, "You tell Walter."

"It was your idea, you tell him."

After the pissing contest was over, I did.

Walter said, "You pitched me the gag; get someone to do it."

That night I put on the wardrobe, the make-up, and the afro sheen, then walked out in front of the crowd of over a thousand real gang members. I just kept my head down as I walked past Roger Hill, who was playing Cyrus. Roger high-fived me and whispered in his very deep voice, "Good luck, brother."

I walked past him and climbed up onto the tower. Everyone was chanting, "Cyrus, Cyrus, Cyrus." It was kind of surreal. I looked at Walter. He smiled, slowly shook his head, and called action.

The next hiccup came about seven or eight weeks into filming. Everyone knew that Walter and Thomas Waites (the original star playing Fox) weren't getting along.

One night I sat down next to Walter, and he said, "I want to kill him."

I didn't know what to say.

He looked over at me and said, "You do it?"

I gave him a "What?" look.

He said, "Figure it out; I don't want to be involved."

I jokingly said, "Got any ideas?"

"Yeah, have two cops approach him in the subway; Fox takes one out with a bat as the other one throws him onto the tracks as a subway train screams by and hits him."

I looked at Walter and nodded, "I don't have any more stuntmen."

He asked me if I would interview the extras and see if I could find someone to be the first cop and find a double for Fox.

I found a guy who said he'd done some work in the business, but he didn't have a S.A.G card; his name was Sonny Landham. He said he would do anything to get his card.

Once we took Sonny out with the bat, which I threw from off stage, under the camera, we set up for the end of Fox. There was no double for Fox.

I tried to explain it to Walter, "You might have to come up with a plan B."

That didn't go very well. "I don't care, find one," he said.

I looked at the first camera assistant; he was young and looked like he was in pretty good shape. I asked him if he had a S.A.G. card. That night he got one.

I had the third rail turned off to film the stunt and put a pad below the platform on the tracks. As we panned the second policeman, he took the Fox double and threw him off the platform (into the offstage pad). As the Fox double left frame, I had the operator lock the camera off. Then we cleared the tracks, turned the power back on, and had the subway race past. With a jump cut, it looked like Fox was impaled on the front end of the car.

Sonny Landham and James Remar, who was Ajax in *The Warriors,* went on to work with Walter on *48 Hours* playing the two Indians in the opening sequence.

**Craig directing the Furies on *The Warriors***

**The Punks on *The Warriors***

I later worked with Sonny on *Predator* and *Action Jackson.*

Working with Walter and Larry on the film was a great experience. The executive producer was Frank Marshall, who later directed a dozen films himself.

The best line in the movie came from David Patrick Kelly. It was totally improvised. He picked up three bottles and started clinking them together, then looked out the window of the hearse, saying, "Warriors, come out to play-ay," over and over. I thought it was brilliant.

I wrote all the fights for Walter in script form as well as shot-listed them for him. The cast did a great job, doing all their own fights. Vermin was the only one doubled for the throw into the mirrors in the Punks restroom fight. My eight stuntmen played the Furies and the Punks.

Walter wanted a couple of new faces in the Punk subway restroom fight. I played one of the Punks and brought in three more stuntmen from California.

It was four months of night work, six days a week. On the last week of filming, I got a call from my father. He told me he was going to do a new series in Georgia. He wanted to know if I could come down and work on the first five episodes with him.

When I got there, he asked me to talk to the special effects foreman and have him build a set of kick ramps per my specs. There was a crazy energy down there; everybody was talking about the star of the show being a Dodge Charger named "The General Lee."

The first jump for *The Dukes of Hazzard* was done in Conyers, Georgia. My father, the stunt coordinator and second unit director, told the producers that the first jump would be about six to eight feet off the ground.

**The first jump,** *The Dukes of Hazzard*

When I actually did it, I was fifteen to twenty feet in the air from ramp to ground.

For the record, the location of that first jump was in the street at a railroad crossing in Conyers.

There's been a lot of misinformation stating the first jump was at the college. The second jump was done at Oxford College. For that one, I was eighteen feet in the air over a police car.

My father had me in a great spot; I did all the chases, mounts, and jumps. I doubled actor John Schneider as his character "Bo" on the show's first five episodes, which were all done in Georgia. I felt like

a rock star; crowds were starting to follow the company everywhere.

When *The Dukes of Hazard* resumed filming in California, I received a call to work on a very high-profile mini-series: *Shogun,* based on a novel by James Clavell. I had taught his daughter how to surf back in the early seventies.

The production manager, Ben Chapman, wanted to get me on the phone with the director, Jerry London, who was scouting locations in Japan. I had worked with Jerry earlier on *Wheels.* When Jerry

**The second jump, *The Dukes of Hazzard***

**Craig Baxley driving mount car in downtown Atlanta**

explained what he wanted me to do for the next year on the mini-series, I was very flattered and very excited. I told him I needed to talk about it with my wife and get back to him the next day to discuss it further.

The next morning, I received a call from David Sosna. David had been the 1st Assistant Director on *The Warriors*. He and I were kind of partners-in-arms on the movie. He was prepping *The Blues Brothers*. He and the director, John Landis, were concerned about the stunt coordinator and second unit director they were about to hire. David asked if I would consider coming on board to do the film.

I asked who the other guy was, and he said it was Gary McLarty. That was a name I didn't need to hear; Gary was a friend of mine. I was caught off guard; I needed to regroup and call them back.

An hour later, I got another call from Walter Hill's producer

**Craig Baxley, another jump on** *The Dukes of Hazzard*

on *The Long Riders.* Walter wanted me to do the film with him. It wasn't really a question.

It was a stuntman's worst nightmare. I'd just been offered three shows any stuntman would've killed for. I sat down with Valerie; she was in disbelief.

*Shogun* starring Richard Chamberlain and Toshiro Mifune.

*The Blues Brothers* starring John Belushi and Dan Aykroyd.

And *The Long Riders.*

"What are you going to do?" she asked.

We talked about it, and soon I knew exactly what to do. I called David back and told him Gary was their man – that he was the perfect choice for the show. I reassured David that Gary would do a great job and bring in the top stuntmen in the industry. I think the fact that David and I had a history might've helped. Gary went on to do an amazing job. *The Blues Brothers* is a classic to this day.

Next, I called Ben Chapman in Japan; I'd worked with Ben more than a dozen times in the past. He got me on the phone with Jerry. Jerry told me he and his director of photography were very excited to have me on the project. I asked him who the DP was. "Andrew Laszlo," he said.

Andy was the DP on *The Warriors.* They both knew I had just finished working with Walter.

I felt like following up with Walter on *The Long Riders* was the right thing to do.

Jerry more than understood. I suggested a friend of mine, Glenn Wilder - one of the founding members of Stunts Unlimited. He was the stunt coordinator and second unit director on *Terminator* and *True Lies,* among so many others. I loved Glen. He was the real deal.

Jerry and Ben were thrilled to have him. I also got Bob Dawson, a special effects coordinator I'd been working with the last couple of years, on with Glen.

The following week I left for Georgia.

**Craig Baxley, high fall**

# CHAPTER 11

## The Long Riders, 1979

Over the next eight months, *The Long Riders* was filmed in Clayton, Leary, and Parrot, Georgia, as well as Tyler, Texas, Sonora, California, and on the Columbia Ranch in Burbank, California. The film starred four sets of actual brothers: The Carradines, the Keaches, the Quaids, and the Guests. It was good to be working with Walter again as his stunt coordinator and second unit director.

Craig Baxley and Walter Hill

During the filming in Georgia, I got a call from Bobby Bass; he was putting together the Stunts Unlimited Competition Special back in California. He wanted to know if I could get off for a couple of days. He had two major stunts he wanted to film and show with the competition when it aired.

"I want you to do a car jump through a billboard which reads '1979 Stunts Unlimited Competition.' As you come through it, we'll set off a series of explosions."

"Sounds pretty interesting," I said. "What's the other one?"

"I'm going to have Ronnie Rondell slide a car to a stop and blow it up in a series of fireballs, then reset and have him come out doing a full burn."

"Let me check with production this morning; I'll call you back."

Walter said there was one day, Sunday, my usual day off. It didn't look good. On top of that, I had Valerie and the kids on location with me.

**Kristin and Craig Jr. in Parrot, Georgia**

When I explained the situation to Bobby, he said, "We can do this. I'll book tickets on the red-eye Saturday night, then have a helicopter pick you and Valerie up at LAX and fly you out to the location at Indian Dunes in Santa Clarita. You do the jump, and we fly you back to LAX in time to make the last flight back to Georgia."

I hesitated, then he continued, "First Class, both of you."

I gave him the specs for the ramp and how I wanted the car set up; he said, "It'll be done by the time you get here."

One of my stuntmen, Cliff Happy, and his wife Margarette, said they'd love to watch our kids.

As I climbed out of the car, Bobby said, "The pilot is waiting to take you and Valerie back to LAX, but CBS wants you to do an interview with Brent Musburger."

As we started the interview, Hal Needham walked up and joined us. As Brent asked me about the stunt, Hal immediately joined the interview and mentioned he had done the first major jump in the

**Jump at CBS Stunts Unlimited Competition**

**Second Angle - Jump at CBS Stunts Unlimited Competition**

industry on *White Lightning,* then went on and on about how he had directed *Smokey and the Bandit.* I knew it was time to go.

Valerie and I both kinda pinched ourselves on the way back to LAX and then back to Georgia.

The special aired on CBS.

\* \* \* \* \*

*The Long Riders* had a number of action set pieces, the major one being the Northfield Raid, which we filmed in Parrot, Georgia. It was epic.

This sequence was a bank robbery gone wrong, and it was basically the end of the James gang and the Youngers. Amidst a barrage of bullet hits, horse falls, saddle falls, a saddle fall into a drag, a jerk-off, horse jumps, and high falls highlighted by six horsemen jumping through plate glass windows (candy glass) in and out of a building.

The McCorkindale pig farm sequence was also a very visual piece. The shootout with the Pinkertons and the James gang was intense. Walter decided he wanted to start the sequence with McCorkindale feeding his pigs, as scripted. But instead of killing him with the first shot, Walter wanted to kill one of his pigs, then McCorkindale.

We weren't prepared for that. Walter jokingly said, "For Crisssakes, just shoot the pig."

The special effects coordinator looked at me. I had two jerk-off ratchets on the show and jokingly suggested we put a bullet hit on the pig and snatch it off in the air. That's exactly what we did.

My second unit shot the opening train sequence in Sonora, California, when the James gang converged and transferred to the train. Originally it was to be filmed in Tyler, Texas, but there wasn't enough room between the trees and the train.

I'd always loved *The Wild Bunch,* written by stuntman Roy Sickner and directed by Sam Peckinpah. I thought our Northfield was right up there with it.

**Craig & Valerie Interview with Brent Musburger**

# CHAPTER 12

## Death Car on the What?

Two days after I got home from filming *The Long Riders,* I got a call from Hal Needham.

He was still going on about how he directed *Smokey and the Bandit* and what an amazing blockbuster it was. I wasn't sure what he wanted; he told me he wanted me to be the stunt coordinator and second unit director on his new project, *Death Car on the Freeway.*

I kinda thought it was a joke at first. Death Car on what? But then he started his pitch.

It was all about a black van, driven by "The Fiddler," who was killing women on the freeways of Los Angeles. A nice family film. He told me it was non-stop action and that I would be shooting most of it. I was in.

I hired some of the best stuntmen in Hollywood from Stunts Unlimited: Bobby Bass, Alan Gibbs, Buddy Joe Hooker, Danny Rogers, Steve Chambers, Glenn Wilder, Jim Connors (one of the funniest men I've ever known), Walter Wyatt, and Tommy Huff as The Fiddler, driving the black van.

Hal was not an easy man to work for. I remember, one day, he said he wanted to have a car come screaming into a used car lot, spin 180 degrees, and continue backward into a parking space between two other new parked cars.

I looked at my guys. It was dead silent. Tommy said, "It's all yours, boss."

I came in hot, snapped it, and slid straight back into the parking spot between the two cars. The camera operator looked up surprised and said, "Perfect, got it." I was more surprised than anyone.

Hal, just to fuck with me, said, "Got lucky, Bax. Do it again."

I looked at Glen and Tommy with a "What the fuck?" look.

"Come on!" he yelled. "I've got a lot to shoot; let's do it!"

So, I did it. I came in hot again, snapped it, and totaled three brand new cars.

"Perfect, that's what I wanted," he said as he walked away.

Tommy looked at me and muttered, "What a dick-ass mother fucker, huh?"

Gibbs said, "C'mon, let it go; you've got a lot to do."

# CHAPTER 13

## Fiat vs. Le Car

When I finished the project with Hal, I got a call from Stunts Unlimited. A French production company was coming to the United States to film a fifteen-minute Marlboro Cigarette commercial to be shown in theaters in Europe. It was to be a duel between Fiat and Le Car. Remy Julienne (some say the greatest European stunt driver that has ever lived) and his team would handle the Fiat side. They wanted to know if I would accept the challenge for Le Car and represent the United States.

It was to be filmed in San Francisco. We could design the course together. The only stipulation was we had to utilize Taylor Street, the famous *Bullitt* chase location. The idea was that each driver could rig any location to enhance or fit his needs. The second driver would drive the same course as the first. The French production crew would film the entire commercial. I asked Remy, "Would you like to go first?" and of course, he graciously accepted.

He had a couple of his family members, who were also some of the best stunt drivers in Europe, prepare the two police cars that would be chasing him.

I knew the Le Car didn't have axles; the wheels were independently slung. I had the rigger wrap the car in a mini cage and reinforce the undercarriage. I also had him put on a larger set of tires with tubes inside. Then I had the effects man start building me three sets of my kick ramps. I brought up two stuntmen from L.A., Steve Chambers and my cousin, Gary Baxley, to drive the two police cars that would chase me.

I had no idea what was about to happen next; it seemed like

everyone in San Francisco had heard about the challenge. As we arrived, the crowds started to grow. Even though the police hired to control the streets were doing their job, extra police had to be brought in for crowd control.

As we began to film, I realized I was working with one of the greatest stunt drivers of all time. I was sling-shotting through turns, trying to emulate his driving style, but more importantly, trying to stay in the game as my guys tried to stay with me. Drifting through turn after turn sideways was a challenge because this was years before specialists in shifter cars.

The French crew was going nuts; I think they loved us both.

I had an idea, watching Remy do Taylor Street. He was amazing. I think he was six feet off the ground on each of the jumps. His family knew he had it. I had my guys drag three kick ramps into position, hidden from the camera, at the top of each hill. Remy looked at me with an "Oh no, you didn't" look. I gave him my best "Oh yes, I did" look.

I hit the series of ramps at sixty miles per hour. I didn't realize until the last jump that all four wheels had blown off on the landing as I exited the frame. The little Le Car went screaming sideways down the hill on the undercarriage, sparks streaming out behind it. I held on as it left the street.

As the smoke cleared, I realized I was sitting in the middle of someone's living room. Suddenly, this Chinese guy came running down the stairs as Steve and Gary pulled me out of the remains of the Le Car. The guy was screaming like a woman on speed. As I hobbled out with my guys (I really felt bad about the man's house), I saw Remy and his guys outside standing on the sidewalk clapping. At that point, I wasn't sure if I wanted me to win or him.

We both knew we had to finish. Two tractor-trailer semis were incorporated into the ending. Remy had the two tractor-trailers crisscross, squeaking through at the last second as the gap closed behind him. It ended with a close-up of him smiling.

Okay, here we go... I had my guys set up my kick ramp. Then I had them get the two semis in position. As I started my approach, they began to crisscross in opposite directions. The gap between the two box trailers continued closing as I sailed over both cabs, the gap closing completely as I cleared. As the Le Car slammed down, it was a cut.

I explained to the French Producer that I wanted to overlap the landing. I had the French camera crew start on an extreme close-up of the license plate that read Le Car. On action, I backed up as fast as I could, as did the two semis. Then in post, I had the editor reverse print and jump-cut it. Which meant the end of the jump would end on an extreme close-up of the front license plate and the words "Le Car."

Remy came up and hugged me. Although we didn't speak the same language, we both knew how much respect we had for each other. He and Davey Sharp are two of the classiest stuntmen I've ever worked with.

**Bobsled stunt,** *Top of the Hill*

# CHAPTER 14

## Top of the Hill, 1980

A producer at Paramount, John Cutts, called me about my availability for a four-hour mini-series, *Top of the Hill.* It was going to be shot in Lake Placid, New York, and Mont Tremblant, Quebec, Canada. John told me he wanted me to shoot all the action sequences, but the first unit director didn't want anyone to receive screen credit as the second unit director. He told me who the director was: Walter Grauman.

I thought it was kind of strange because I had worked with Walter dozens of times in the past. John told me this was a big jump for Walter - to direct a four-hour mini-series. He wanted the sole credit. Walter had his dream cast: Wayne Rogers, Mel Ferrer, Peter Brown, Gary Lockwood, Paula Prentiss, Adrienne Barbeau, Elke Sommer, Rae Dawn Chong, and Sonny Bono. This was Walter's big chance to step up in the game.

I more than understood; I asked John who recommended me. He told me Walter's director of photography, Andrew Laszlo, asked for me. We had worked together on *The Warriors.*

My second unit shot all the action in Lake Placid and Quebec. The bobsled sequences were shot in Lake Placid. One of my favorite sequences had a rider fallout the back of the sled, catch a boot, and get dragged behind the sled as it raced down the entire Olympic bobsled run.

The major stunt in the bobsled sequence was shot in Mont Tremblant, Quebec. With the bobsled about to break the world record, it crashed through the wall of a turn, arched through the air twenty feet off the ground, and sent the riders pin-wheeling. Steve

Boyum and I did the stunt.

It was a challenge to get a two-man, eight-hundred-and-fifty-pound bobsled to crash through the top of the turn wall twenty feet off the ground and fly forty feet through the air. It needed to hit the top of the set piece traveling between thirty to forty miles an hour.

The production designer and his construction crew built a seventy-meter ski jump, basically a ramp on a hillside behind the set piece of the last turn. Then I had them place blocks of ice on the entire run. My stuntmen built a catcher of cardboard boxes forty feet wide and sixty feet long, starting about ten feet from the wall. Then we covered it with a couple of inches of snow.

I was in the front of the sled. I remember looking back at Steve at the top of the run; the sled was sitting on the blocks of ice a hundred feet away. His eyes were as big as saucers; he just shook his head and muttered, "What are we doing, Bax?" I waved my arm to signal the camera crews to roll the cameras. A couple of seconds later, we were on our way.

This was a unique gag; it's not often you do a stunt with a bobsled. My estimate was a little off; we sailed through the top of the wall traveling closer to fifty mph. I did a handstand off the front of the sled, flipping through the air as Steve was fired straight up in the air. We both continued pin-wheeling through the air and landed in the far end of the catcher, dead center.

The studio loved the stunt; the entire first unit was buzzing about it when we walked onto their set. I guess we pulled it off.

I thought another sequence was very visual; I had a Turbo Porche racing across a frozen lake at over a hundred miles an hour. I had multiple camera set-ups covering it. My favorite shot was from a helicopter camera ship. We dropped down, about five feet off the ice, following directly behind the Porche, inside the fifty-foot rooster tail of snow the spit up past us on both sides of the camera ship. I think that angle was one of the most surreal shots I've ever done.

All the ski sequences were shot in Quebec at Tremblant. I had an amazing crew, and we had over a dozen snowmobiles, with local support from a great ski team.

We came up with a rig similar to a Steadicam, a bit more basic, but it was stabilized. We did some insane tracking shots with the skiers racing down the mountain.

A highlight in the ski sequence was when I had one of my stuntmen, John Meier, do a sixty-foot-high fall with rubber skis. It was to depict a skier that had gone out of bounds and off the mountain. The day we shot it, it was about twenty below. As John flew off the cliff, everyone on the crew held their breath until John hit the catcher below, dead center. It was the end of a great sequence.

# CHAPTER 15

## A Guy's Gotta Work

In 1981, the industry was rocked by the Writer Guild of America strike. It was twenty-two weeks, the longest in the history of the Guild.

There was only one movie starting up, *The Seduction.* It was the film debut of Morgan Fairchild. *The Seduction* was a 1980s thriller with a voyeuristic stalking feel, like *The Fan, Body Double,* or *Eyes of a Stranger.*

I was hired as the stunt coordinator. I'd hired my cousin, Gary Baxley, to double the co-star Andrew Stevens. On the second day of filming, Gary came to me and said, "Dude, are you blind? She's hitting on you."

"Yeah, I know, I'm married," I flatly said.

"Okay, I'll take care of it," he said.

He proceeded to walk over to Morgan and basically said, "Craig's married. I'm his cousin; I'm not."

I'm not sure it went the way he expected.

Morgan walked over to me and said, "What the hell was that about?" She had already told me she was an extra on *Bonnie and Clyde* and knew I was Warren's guy. I wasn't sure where this was going.

As the shooting went on, it became increasingly more awkward. She kept on wanting to get together. One night, it came to a head when Morgan told me she wanted me to escort her to an Awards show. I repeatedly told her I was married. She said she didn't care. I did. And I said, "no." It remained awkward until we finished filming.

\* \* \* \* \*

When I think about some of the filmmakers on this little independent film, I realize the crew list was pretty amazing: Frank Darabont was the transportation captain. He went on to direct *The Shawshank Redemption, The Green Mile,* and *The Majestic;* Chuck Russell was the executive producer, and he went on to direct *The Mask, The Blob,* and *Eraser.* (Two of which he was fired from before the completion of each film).

I know that for a fact, because one night I got a call from Arnold's assistant. They were working on *Eraser,* he said, "Arnold hates Russell; he can't stand the guy and wants to replace him. He wanted me to call you and see if you are available."

Unfortunately, I wasn't. You'd think the studios would check a director out before they hired him again and again.

David Householter was the production assistant on *The Seduction.* He went on to be the executive producer on both *Jumanji* films, *Venom,* and *Inferno.*

Michael Cottrell was the production manager. He produced four of the *Fast and the Furious* movies.

Charles Newirth was the location manager. He went on to produce *Forest Gump, Ghosts of Mississippi, Ant-Man and the Wasp,* and *Iron Man 3.*

# CHAPTER 16

## Warren Beatty, Part 3

After working with Warren on *Shampoo* and *Heaven Can Wait,* I got a call from Simon Relph, the executive producer on *Reds.* He explained that Warren needed me to come over to Europe and clean up three or four sequences with a second unit. I told him that I had just been hired to shoot a second unit at the end of next month in the States. He said the shoot would only take a couple of weeks.

So I got on a plane and met with Simon in London; he assured me I would be done in time to start the job back in the States. The next morning, I flew to Paris to meet with Warren and Elaine May at the Hotel Plaza Athenee on Avenue Montaigne. That night I met with them in Warren's room. After four and a half hours, I realized it wasn't going to be a couple of weeks.

Warren convinced Elaine, who was doing the rewrites with Robert Towne, that I was the guy to write the major battle sequence between the Red and White Armies. He also told her I would draw a schematic of the battlefield and provide a shot list of the entire battle sequence, which involved a fully armored train and four hundred horsemen.

Warren failed to tell me that night that I would shoot it in Guadix, Spain, an hour and a half outside Granada.

After the meeting, I flew to Madrid to write the sequence. Warren said he would meet me there at the end of the week.

Obviously, my wife wasn't happy, I think during that time she wallpapered our entire house.

Madrid turned into quite an experience. As I completed the sequence and finalized a rough shot list, Warren called me and asked me to come up to his room. I gathered what I had at that point and went up. It turned out to be something other than the meeting I expected.

Jack Nicholson had joined Warren during the week. When Warren answered the door, he ushered me inside. I saw Jack and a couple of young, very young ladies. "Hey kid, how's it hangin'?" he asked as they disappeared into another room.

As the door closed, Warren said, "She's on her way up; you gotta take her downstairs. I'll join you in about ten minutes." As I was about to ask him who, there was a knock at the door, and he was gone.

I set my briefcase down and answered the door; there stood Diane Keaton, wearing a pair of Ben Franklin glasses with burgundy prisms mounted inside the frames.

She was pissed. "Where is he?" she snapped.

I said, "He's at a meeting; he told me to meet you here and wait downstairs. He shouldn't be long."

"Bullshit," she said.

We rode down the elevator in silence. I felt like I was guilty of something by association.

As we sat down in the restaurant, Diane continued to glare at me and finally said, "You know, don't you?"

I had no idea what she was talking about. That was the longest hour and a half I ever spent in my life. I only know one word to explain it: "wacky." She was all over the place. When Warren finally showed up, it was on. Warren and I exchanged a look. And I was gone.

Over the next month, as we started prepping the sequence, I brought over ten of the best stunt horsemen from the States and a lead special effects man, Bob Dawson. We started to put together a group of Spanish stuntmen and horsemen. Even though our Spanish horse wrangler was one of the best in Spain, one of my stuntmen was also a head wrangler, Jimmy Medearis. He worked for me on *The Long Riders*.

Between the two wranglers, we assembled over two hundred horses and acclimated them to the madness of a movie set - the gunfire and explosions. Other horses were trained for falling and jumping (a major plus was our Spanish wrangler owned a half dozen trained falling horses).

Five weeks later, we started filming. Warren played John Reed, an American journalist who traveled to Russia during the Bolshevik Revolution.

The sequence I wrote began during a scene on the train where Reed was arguing with his comrades. During his speech, which I directed, an incoming artillery shell hits and blows off the rear of the car. We had six massive mortars mounted, hanging outside the breakaway backend of the car. Bob and another effects man rode outside next to the mortars, waiting for the cue to blow them - a line near the end of Warren's speech. Warren kept cutting it a line or two before the cue. After each cut, we would have to back the train up. Bob and three other special effects men were still hanging outside the car waiting for the cue.

When Warren cut it on take forty, I'd had enough. We were starting to lose light. When the train moved out, I knew Warren would do it again, cut the scene, but I saw it coming and jumped his

**Second Unit, charging White army**

cue. All six mortars were set off; the back of the car was gone. Smoke and debris blew past him. Warren was so shocked and surprised that he landed on the center of the table; it was so real, so good. Warren just looked at me and shook his head, then nodded and smiled.

We shot the battle over the next two weeks. It was a massive undertaking: dozens of horses jumping out of boxcars to the ground, carriages with mounted machine guns rolling down ramps off the train, two hundred Red and White army horsemen converging on each other from opposite directions. There were over a hundred explosions. We blew up two carriages sending their crews pinwheeling into the air. There were more than fifty horse falls, ending with us blowing up half of the train. Warren wanted the most epic battle done to date; I thought we did it, and so did he.

I finished working on the film six months later. The schedule for principal filming was fifteen to sixteen weeks, one hundred and twenty days. *Reds* took two hundred and forty days. Over one hundred and thirty hours of footage was shot.

**Second Unit, second angle of charging White army**

Paramount told Warren he had to come in under the running time of *Doctor Zhivago* - one hundred and ninety-seven minutes. He had shot twice that.

A couple of weeks before the premiere, I got a call from Warren. He explained how much he loved the battle sequence, that it was everything he hoped for. But he had to make tough choices; he had to cut over an hour of his footage. Over three-quarters of the battle footage was cut.

*Reds* was delivered at one hundred ninety-five minutes and nominated for thirteen Academy Awards. It won three, including Warren Beatty for Best Director.

One of the perks of working with Warren on *Reds* was when I finished; he booked me into his suite at the Dorchester Hotel in London for a week. I called my wife and told her to meet me there. But I got a little surprise. When I walked into the room, the butler told me there was somebody in the bathroom waiting for me. When I opened the door, there she was in a bubble bath.

For the next week, we had the time of our lives. We explored London and everything it had to offer. Warren set up a six-course meal for us at the Dorchester. Another night we went to Langan's Brasserie, a hot spot on Statton Street in Piccadilly. Halfway through our meal, a man, who turned out to be one of the owners, walked up to our table and asked how our meal was; it was Michael Cain.

One of the most incredible meals we've ever had in our lives was at the Mirabelle Restaurant in Mayfair – the queen of Mayfair's restaurants: French haute cuisine presented in Art Deco surroundings. What an amazing evening. A week was enough though; I wanted to go home and see my kids.

On the flight home, Valerie and I sat in first class behind Lindsey Buckingham and Stevie Nicks. Mick Fleetwood, along with John and Christine McVie, sat across the aisle. Later in the flight, Lindsey looked back at me, "Do I know you?" Doppelganger came to mind.

We went upstairs with the band and hung out drinking martinis for the rest of the flight — what a wonderful way to end a long location and an incredible London holiday.

**Craig Baxley, Second Unit**

# CHAPTER 17

## Back in the States

The day after I returned home from filming *Reds,* I got two calls for job interviews the following morning. The first was on *Breathless,* a film directed by Phillip Kaufman. We had previously worked together on *The White Dawn.*

When I arrived, two stuntmen were waiting outside the building - Everett Creach and Terry Leonard. Terry was one of the two stuntmen who doubled Harrison Ford on *Indiana Jones.*

As I approached them, Terry said, "What are you doing here, kid? The interview is over."

The last time I'd seen Terry, I'd hired him for a day on *The Long Riders.* (My father actually got Terry his S.A.G. card and gave him his first job in the business).

I laughed and told them I just stopped by to say hello to Phil.

While I waited in the outer office, Richard Gere walked by wearing jeans tucked into cowboy boots, a mink vest, and nothing else. He had just finished *An Officer and a Gentleman.* As I watched him disappear into Phil's office, the secretary motioned me inside. Twenty minutes later, I walked out with the job.

Everett and Terry were still waiting outside. As I walked by, I just smiled; nobody said a word.

Even though I had a job, I felt I had to go to the other interview. It was at Raleigh Studios in Hollywood. When I walked into the office, something was off. Two or three people seemed to be packing everything.

The secretary walked me into the production man's office. I'd worked with Mike Maschio on *Zero to Sixty* in 1978. He explained that the company was about to shut down. The project was a pilot called *The A-Team.* Mike said the meeting was with the executive producer and creator, Stephen J. Cannell.

At that meeting, Stephen explained what *The A-Team* was about and that Rod Holcomb would direct it. It would be filmed in Los Angeles and Mexico on a twenty-one-day shoot - most of it to be done in Mexico.

I thanked him for considering me but explained that I'd just returned home from overseas and wanted to stay in town and spend time with my family. I also mentioned I was just offered the stunt coordinator and second unit director on *Breathless* in Los Angeles.

That's when I was blindsided; Stephen told me he wanted me to do this show. I could write all the action sequences and do anything I wanted as long as nobody died. He explained that I would be the stunt coordinator and second unit director, with twenty-one days to shoot all the action.

We sat there for a couple of minutes, just looking at each other. Then he continued, "Okay, I'll pay travel and per diem for your family." He paused again, I think for effect, and then said, "All first class."

I just sat there; I was kind of blown away. Then I told him I had to call my wife and Phillip Kaufman. Stephen just smiled. That was the beginning of a long and very special relationship.

Stephen neglected to tell me that the job was stipulated on a meeting with the star, George Peppard. The next day, I went to the Polo Lounge in Beverly Hills. George was in his usual booth, and as the maitre'd seated me, he gave me that million-dollar smirk. "So, you're Baxley's kid, huh?"

It didn't make me all warm and fuzzy; there was clearly an issue. He continued, "Does your dad know you're meeting with me?"

I told him, "Not that I am aware of."

He explained how he had worked on a couple of films with my father, the last being *Tobruk,* a World War II film. I felt like I was being set up as he continued. He told me how they used to play Hearts while waiting to be called to the set, and that my father accused him of cheating.

There was an awkward moment as our food came, then he continued. "Your father really pissed me off; he called me 'Joe Joe the dog face boy.'"

I was sitting there with George Peppard; this wasn't going the way I hoped. He just sat there in silence eating, then, "But he's a very talented man." Then he smiled. "I hear the apple didn't fall very far from the tree. Give him my best, huh?"

\* \* \* \* \*

**Craig and Henry Kingi,** *The A-Team*

Before sharing my experiences during five seasons on *The A-Team,* I want to clear something up that has always bothered me. When I first met with Stephen, he told me he came up with the idea for *The A-Team* when he was in college. After the pilot, Frank Lupo told people he came up with the idea and was the co-creator.

Truth be told, a year before the pilot was written, Brandon Tartikoff, who was the president of NBC for eleven years, had an idea. He wanted to do a series based on the *Magnificent Seven.* When Stephen pitched his idea for *The A-Team* to NBC, the executives told him they wanted to go with Brandon's idea, and *The A-Team* was born.

I had a nucleus of six stuntmen for the entire series. Henry Kingi, Bob Orrison, and Tony Brubaker were my core. They did the majority of the pipe ramp turnovers and car jumps on the series. We were doing bigger and more innovative gags than most features. Henry did all the major jumps in *The A-Team* van.

I was always amazed how they would take a gag I rigged and make it look better, always higher and always further. I paid them an adjustment, money paid over and above the stuntman's daily for the stunt. Deep down, I always thought they should've been paid more. If I could have, I would have.

I think it was the first time anyone had seen a jeep or car hit a pipe ramp and rotate three hundred and sixty degrees fifteen to twenty-five feet off the ground, traveling over seventy to eighty feet through the air. On the pilot, Henry did two, and Bobby did one.

### *The A-Team* Pilot: Henry Kingi, Second Unit Turnover

### *The A-Team* Pilot: Bob Orrison, Second Unit Turnover

The pilot appeared after *Super Bowl XVII* and was number one in the ratings that week, and continued to be number one in the ratings through most of the five seasons it ran.

On the pilot, I hired a special effects coordinator, Bob Dawson. We had worked together on *Reds*. He did a fantastic job on the pilot.

When *The A-Team* was picked up, Stephen Cannell said he wanted me to use his special effects coordinator from his last series, *The Greatest American Hero*. I met Al DiSarro on the first episode. We were like fire and water. I told the 1st Assistant Director that it was either me or this little Italian fireplug.

Sometimes things are just meant to be.

Al DiSarro turned out to be the best special effects man I have ever worked with. We became the Yin and Yang of *The A-Team*. Al quickly became part of our core. Henry, Bobby, and Tony - the five of us always seemed to be in total sync. I honestly feel Al was just as responsible as I was for the success of *The A-Team*.

There was another stuntman that joined our core during the first season, Al Leong. I first met Al in the late seventies. We've all seen Al in a number of films. He played Minh, the henchman fighting

Brandon Lee in the explosive climax of *Rapid Fire*. He was the guy who electrocuted Mel Gibson in *Lethal Weapon*. You'd also recognize him from *Die Hard*. He played Genghis Khan in *Bill and Ted's Excellent Adventure*. Among the other films he played in during that era were *Big Trouble in Little China, Action Jackson, Escape From L.A.,* and *I Come in Peace*.

During the first season of *The A-Team*, I wanted to have visually explosive martial arts, not the flat-footed Steven Seagal and Chuck Norris shtick. I met with Al and had him bring in a couple of guys he thought were two of the best. He introduced me to James Lew and Jeff Imada. James was world-class. Jeff was solid, although when I first met him, he had a pompadour like Elvis Presley.

Al was the best in the business; James was a close second. I just put a long wig on Jeff, and I suddenly had my three guys. All were adept in Tae Kwon Do and Sil Lum Kung Fu and several other forms of Kung Fu.

As the first season was winding down, I was asked to direct my first episode of *The A-Team*. During the run of the series, I directed nine more episodes. It was kind of a tricky situation because Cannell also wanted me to be the stunt coordinator and second unit director on every episode.

As I finished directing my first episode in Venice Beach, California, I looked at my 1st Assistant Director, then across the street and said, "Book it." It was a sushi bar on Washington Boulevard, which happened to be the hottest spot in the neighborhood. Valerie and I had eaten there several times.

"I want to book it as my way of saying thanks to the cast and crew," Unbeknownst to me, the word had gone out at the Cannell building in Hollywood.

Valerie showed up and said, "Oh my god. You did what!"

In my mind, I heard, "I'm so proud of you; the crew is going to love it."

Department heads and staff from all of Stephen's shows – over a hundred people - showed up. Some even brought their spouses.

Valerie tapped me on the shoulder as Stephen Cannell and his wife, Marcia, walked in. Stephen smiled and waved at us.

Aldo looked at me and said, "Dude, are you crazy?"

As they continued to descend on Washington Boulevard, I

realized it was going to be a long night. Eaten out of all his sushi, the owner and sushi chef started cooking cheeseburgers. The guy looked at me and said, "What a night; I love you."

\* \* \* \* \*

My favorite episode was "Quarterback Sneak." I had Joe Namath, Jim Brown, and John Matuszak in my cast. Yeah, Joe Namath, Jim Brown, and John Matuszak - I idolized these guys growing up.

**Craig Baxley and Joe Namath**

\* \* \* \* \*

We became friends with the producer John Ashley and his wife, Jan, during the filming of the show. Valerie and I went to dinner with them at Mr. Chow's in Beverly Hills one evening. (John was also the voice heard during the opening credits of *The A-Team*). John happened to be wearing his sunglasses at dinner. As we joined them, Valerie softly sang, "I wear my sunglasses at night...."

Jan sort of snapped, "Are you dissing John?"

Valerie was taken aback, "No, it's a very popular song, Jan. Why would I dis John?"

Just then, John watched as a couple walked toward us from the back of the restaurant. "Bax, it's Brandon Tartikoff."

Brandon waved at us, and as he approached our table, John stood up. "Hey, here's the reason *The A-Team* is number one on TV," he said as he walked right past John and shook my hand; I introduced Valerie, and Brandon introduced his wife to us. Then he looked at John and Jan and said, "Hey guys." He looked back at us: "You guys have a great evening," Then he was gone.

Awkward doesn't even begin to cover the rest of our meal.

Another evening John and Jan invited us to the opening of Chinois in Santa Monica. The food was amazing. During our meal, John spotted Wolfgang Puck, who had just left the kitchen, and was walking toward our table. As John stood up to greet him, Wolfgang walked right past John and hugged me as I stood up.

"My god, it's good to see you," he said. "Thank you for coming."

I was kind of in shock, I'd never met him before, but I went with it and introduced Valerie and the Ashleys. After he left the table, John just glared at me. I told him I'd never met Wolfgang Puck before, but the damage was done. Valerie thought it was hilarious, but never let on.

I must have a doppelganger out there.

One of the perks of my job was Valerie and I traveled a lot. Many times I've been mistaken for someone other than myself. Oliver Stone cornered us for fifteen minutes in Santa Fe, New Mexico, telling me how much he missed me. I glanced at Valerie; she knew I'd never met him. I just went with it. I knew his producer was Alex Ho, the location manager on *The Warriors*. I asked him how Alex was.

Oliver told us his new girlfriend just opened a clothing boutique at the end of the street. Then he said I should take Valerie there and pick out anything she wanted. Then he was gone.

The best incident was one in New York. Valerie and I were having dinner in a beautiful restaurant. The couple across from us stared at us the entire meal. When they were finished, they approached our table and apologized. The husband said, "I am sorry to interrupt your meal, but you've been my idol for years; you and 'White Shoes'

Johnson. My god..." As he continued, I realized he thought I was Steve Bartkowski, the quarterback of the Atlanta Falcons. When he finished, he asked me for my autograph; I said sure and signed Steve Bartkowski.

As they walked away, Valerie said to me, "Are you serious?"

I just shrugged and continued eating. It was the late seventies, what can I say.

\* \* \* \* \*

The eighties continued, and I was working fourteen to fifteen-hour days on *The A-Team.* I wrote the action and shot list at night, which left little time for my girl and my kids. Valerie went pro-active, probably because she felt like she was being ignored.

In the eighties, L.A. was inundated with the hottest restaurants in the country: Roy Yamaguchi's 385 North, Jean-Francois Meteigner's L'Orangerie, Michel Blancet's L'Ermitage, Wolfgang Puck's Spago, Joachim Splichal's 7th Street Bisto, Michael McCarty's Michael's in Santa Monica, Patrick Terrail's Ma Maison, Chianti's Au Petit Cafe, La Petit Chaya in Silver Lake, Leonard Schwartz's 72 Market Street in Venice, and Trader Vic's. Two of our favorites were Ken Frank's La Toque and Patrick Jamon's Les Anges on Pacific Coast Highway.

I had no idea where I was going on any Saturday night, but I always knew Valerie had booked us into the best and hottest restaurant in L.A. She even had me taking cooking classes at Ma Maison: a lobster class, a caviar class with Mr. Z, among a dozen others with Patrick Terrail and Wolfgang Puck. The classes she loved the most were from our favorite chef Ken Frank at La Toque.

Ken, Mark Peel, and Jonathan Waxman were among the first chefs to come out of Michael's in 1979. La Toque was definitely our favorite. We usually ate there every Thursday night after work. Thursday night was known as musician's night. It was the best-kept secret in Los Angeles; some of the biggest stars in the music industry came in to eat and sit at the piano and play. We were actually going to invest in Ken's new restaurant, but it didn't work out. Ken and his wife Nancy got divorced soon after, and he closed La Toque on Sunset.

Through the years, we've stayed in touch. Ken always described himself as a French Chef in a Californian's body. Today he's re-married and owns The Michelin Star restaurant La Toque in Napa Valley, California.

It was a great time to be a foodie in L.A.; you never knew who would be having dinner in those restaurants. One night Valerie and I were having dinner in L'Orangerie. At a table next to us was Johnny Carson; on the other side was Joan Rivers. Valerie loved it; it was so much more exciting than seeing an actor.

* * * * *

We were approaching the end of the second season of *The A-Team;* the second unit was filming on the industrial streets of Hollywood - Orange Street, to be exact. We'd just set up the ramp for a motorcycle jump, getting ready to hold traffic, when an old beat-up white Ford Econoline van came roaring past our set police and screeched to a stop just short of the ramp.

The entire crew watched as the driver jumped out, yelling, *"The A-Team, I love The A-Team!"*

It was Jonathan Winters. For the next fifteen minutes, he was improvising, metamorphosing, transforming from character to character. I'd never seen anyone like him. He just kept going on and on. It was exhausting; he was hilarious. It wasn't like he was telling jokes; he was telling stories with the different characters talking to us through them. He seemed like he just wanted everybody to like him. When he was done, he just started shaking everyone's hand; then, he was gone. I don't think anybody could describe what they had just seen. It was a stand-up comedy show in the middle of our workday.

* * * * *

Unlike *The Dukes of Hazard,* who had a full-time second unit and filmed six days on every episode, we had one day of second unit per episode. If we were lucky, we got two. On a couple of episodes, when the director fell behind, we got three to help him finish his show.

I usually cross-drove the POV's in a car chase. Cross-driving was when the operator sat in the driver's seat, and I sat next to him in the middle of the vehicle. I basically drove from that position. The second unit DP, Bud Botham, thought I was crazy the first time I suggested it. But it gave us the driver's true POV, unlike what other shows were doing with the camera sitting close to the driver.

I always thought I had the greatest second unit crew ever put together. Buddy was my second unit DP throughout the series. They always kept themselves available for me, only working one or two days a week, with a day of prep. We usually had three or four major stunts every episode, averaging over forty-five set-ups a day.

One of the ways I showed my appreciation was to always take them out to lunch on our prep day. I'd take them to some of the best restaurants in Los Angeles. As I said, the eighties were the best for a foodie in L.A. I always made sure our location manager picked up the tab.

Once every two or three episodes, I would be called in by the VP of Cannell Productions, Joe Swirling. The meeting usually started off with, "Booby, why do you keep doing this to me?"

I'd reply, "We don't carry these guys; I told them this was your way of saying thanks." And it worked. Until the next time, then I'd just make up another reason.

Then it happened, halfway through season three, Cannell called me in. As I sat down in front of him, he just shook his head, "Why do you do this to Joe? You're driving him crazy."

I explained to him what I'd said to Joe, he just shook his head again. "Okay, I get it. Just try to maybe take the boys to a four or three-star instead of the hottest five-star in town, huh? I'm not sure how much more Joe can take."

I said, "Absolutely."

As I walked out, he said, "The stuff looks great, Bax."

I'm very proud of what we accomplished during those years. I was the stunt coordinator and second unit director for all ninety-seven episodes. And as I mentioned, I also directed nine episodes. Henry Kingi became my assistant coordinator on the second season of the episode I directed.

* * * * *

During *The A-Team*, Stephen also had me coordinate stunts and direct the second unit on several of his pilots: *Hunter* and *The*

**Craig and George Peppard**

*Rousters.* He also had me re-shoot all the action on the two-part pilot for *Hardcastle and McCormick.*

To this day, I still run into people who grew up watching *The A-Team* and *The Dukes of Hazard.* Those shows are truly some of the greatest memories I have.

\* \* \* \* \*

Six years after *Reds,* I got a call from Warren Beatty. He was going to star with Dustin Hoffman and produce the film. It was to be shot in Morocco and New York. Warren felt that he owed Elaine May for the uncredited writing she had done for *Reds* and *Heaven Can Wait.* He convinced Warner Brothers to let her direct a film she wrote, *Ishtar.* (Elaine also wrote *The Birdcage,* which Mike Nichols directed, and starred Nathan Lane and Robin Williams).

Warren told me he wanted Vittorio Storaro to shoot it and would love to have me come aboard as the stunt coordinator and second unit director. After meeting in Paris with Elaine and Warren on *Reds*, I knew it would be a bumpy ride. I gracefully passed, explaining I was in the middle of *The A-Team* and was just about to direct my fourth episode. I recommended a second unit director I'd worked for a couple of years earlier; his name was Mickey Moore.

Mickey was one of the best in the business; he did *Indiana Jones*, among many others.

Let's just say I dodged the bullet on that one.

Mickey called me when he got home and told me some horrific stories about the shoot. Morocco was a volatile country in those days. Between the government and the locals, there was a lot of uncertainty. What was "yes" one day was "no" the next. One issue was when they chose the principal camel, a rare blue-eyed camel. Upon returning to pick it up, they discovered the owner had eaten him.

I made a mistake once and asked Warren about the shoot. We never discussed it again.

Second unit action, *Predator*

# CHAPTER 18

## Stick Around

After four seasons of *The A-Team,* we broke for hiatus. I got a call to work on a film at Twentieth Century Fox Studios. As a stunt coordinator and second unit director, *Predator* was probably one of my favorite films to work on.

A lot of stories have been told about the filming of *Predator.* Some have become the stuff urban legends are made of. This is what I know:

The day I was hired, I was sitting in Gene Levy's office. He was the Head of Production at Fox, and I'd worked with him when he was the production manager on *The Long Riders.* He told me who I was going to have as my special effects coordinator. I knew his guy and had worked with him, and I knew he had seniority in the effects department at Fox Studios. I also knew he was wrong for the job. I went to the producer, Joel Silver. I'd met Joel when he was Larry Gordon's assistant on *The Warriors.* I told him what the problem was and that I had the guy.

"Who is it?" he asked.

"His name is Al DiSarro, one of the best I ever worked with."

"What has he done?"

"Al hasn't done a feature film yet, but he was my effects coordinator on *The A-Team* and *The Greatest American Hero.*"

"Two TV shows? *The A-Team,* huh?" I knew Joel loved *The A-Team.* He smiled and said, "Okay, let's bring this Al DiSarro in and meet him."

The next day I brought Aldo in. Joel liked him immediately. Joel said, "I can see you two doing this together; let's do it."

Al didn't miss a beat; he asked him who the director was, Joel told him it was John McTiernan. Al pressed on, "Never heard of him; I thought this was a big movie. What's the guy done?"

I just closed my eyes. This was true Aldo.

Joel told us that John had just directed his first feature film, *Nomads.*

I jumped in, "Okay, I'm going to take Al to Gene's office and introduce him to his new effects man."

The next day Al and I went to a theater on Ventura Boulevard in Encino. It was the opening day of *Nomads.* We were the only two people in the theater. A few minutes into it, Al looked over at me and said, "What is this crap? It looks like a fuckin' student film. What have you gotten me into?"

A few months later, we were in Puerto Vallarta in the middle of summer. *Predator* was a film that took place in the jungle. This time of year, everything was brown in Puerto Vallarta. Further south, in the rain forest, everything was green. When we asked why we were here, we were told that John and Joel had leased their villas there for the summer. Somebody neglected the tell them it was the wrong time of the year.

There were a couple of bumps along the way. During the last week of prep in Mexico, I walked into the Camino Real Hotel, where the cast and crew stayed. As I walked through the lobby, I noticed John McTiernan, Don McAlpine, the Australian director of photography, and another man sitting together. They all looked up at me, and a couple of seconds later, the man walked up to me and said, "Mr. Baxley, I'm David Eggby, your DP."

"On what?" I asked.

"The second unit, mate."

"Mr. Eggby, I always thought the director hired the cameraman. Mine is arriving next week."

He kinda puffed up his chest. "This is a big film, mate. I think you've been overruled."

After we got that straightened out, David Eggby was the DP on the third unit shooting all the VFX thermal heat vision.

Another issue was when they scheduled four days for the Huey Gunships. I had my aerial coordinator and helicopter pilot, Chuck Tamburro, and hired two other pilots: his brother, Michael, and Peter McKernan. We had scheduled two and a half days for the second unit to shoot all the aerial work and the rappelling sequence. The first unit had one and a half days to shoot the opening at the command post in the coastal fishing village.

On day three, the first unit still had the helicopters sitting on the pads at the beach. That night I went to Beau Marks, the 1st Assistant Director, and stressed how important it was for us to get the helicopters. He just shook his head. "I know, John promised to shoot them out, but he still wants to hang onto them in case we see them in any more coverage," he explained. We finally got them after lunch on day four.

Another issue was I didn't have my usual second unit DP, Buddy Botham, who worked with me on *The A-Team*. Buddy had promised his wife he'd take her on a cruise he had booked six months earlier, so I hired Frank Johnson, the DP on the first unit of *The A-Team*. What Frank neglected to tell me was he didn't do aerial work.

In six hours, we shot all the aerials and the rappelling sequence. My operator from *The A-Team*, John Oteri, did all the Tyler Mount work and fifty percent of the handheld; I did the rest.

I originally had one day to shoot all the rappelling coverage, and now we were losing light. I grabbed everyone and explained the situation. I didn't need to say another word. My stunt guys quickly rigged the rappelling lines and got into the Huey. I grabbed a handheld camera and shot the angle over the gunner onto the other ship with the stuntmen rappelling out. John shot the ground camera coverage, grabbing all the pieces he could.

I had budgeted four takes on the rappelling sequence to get the various coverage I wanted. I thought we could do it in three; we did it in one. Although we didn't get all the coverage I wanted, I thought it looked pretty good.

During every shot filmed in Puerto Vallarta, the first unit had to be dressed with greens. I always thought Don McAlpine took John McTiernan to film school on the *Predator*. I also thought the Editor, Mark Helfrich, did an amazing job. The production hired an army of five hundred workers to dress and redress every first unit location. On some days, John would change his mind after he saw the way it was dressed, and he would have them redress the location in the opposite direction.

The first unit averaged a half dozen set-ups a day, on some days three or four. John became increasingly unhappy with the Mexican keys and crew; he thought they were slow. He would fire them, and I would pick them up for my second unit. I suddenly had one of the best second unit crews in the world.

*Predator* had fifty-six days scheduled for the first unit. After thirty-five days, Joel was becoming increasingly concerned. He was dealing with the studio protecting John, which any good producer would do. But the wheels were falling off the wagon.

The man scheduled to play the *Predator* had just arrived. Joel and I walked down the hotel corridor as Jean-Claude Van Damme and his entourage approached us.

Joel nodded, "Here he comes."

Jean-Claude stopped in front of us; he looked at Joel and asked if he was Silver. Joel nodded, and Jean-Claude, flat-footed, leaped straight up and did the splits with his crotch eye level to me. I wasn't sure where this was going.

After forty-three days, half the film had been shot. Joel knew the studio needed to see some eye candy. The studio hadn't seen any footage of the *Predator* or very much of the action. Three to four weeks had been scheduled for the first unit to shoot the firefight with the guerrillas in the Palapa, including incorporating the cast into the sequence with all the special effects. Joel asked me to rewrite it and shoot it with my second unit in seven days, including the cast. I told him I needed to talk with Jim and John Thomas, who had written *Predator,* and discuss it with them. They both said they were cool with it. So I went to work.

Over the weekend, while the company was off, Al and his effects men and my stuntmen prepped the sequence. We had transportation relocate the chopper wreck to the Palapa location - a Huey 212 hanging in the tree in an earlier sequence. We used foam core, paint, and 1x6's to simulate the chopper blades. (Al hooked them up to a drill motor to simulate the blades turning.) After it was put back together, it actually looked like a mint Huey 212.

We started the sequence on Monday and finished it seven days later with the cast. We averaged forty-five set-ups a day. Near the end of the sequence, I remember where Arnold threw the knife into the guerrilla (he actually held onto the knife as I whip-panned off to the guerrilla, who already had another knife in him). Arnold stopped the take and looked at me, and said, "Bax, I gotta say something here."

From behind me, a voice from the back of the set said, "Stick around, asshole."

Arnold smiled and said, "Thank you, Valerie."

She always amazed me, coming up with great one-liners.

**Second unit director, Craig Baxley, and Arnold Schwarzenegger**

I think all of us knew we had accomplished something pretty special that week. It was one of the sequences I'm most proud of to this day.

There was one buzz kill during our shoot. We (my second unit keys) were watching dailies with Joel, John, and the first unit keys. When the second unit dailies came on, it was dead silent as we continued watching them; suddenly, John McTiernan jumped up in front of the screen and shouted at me, "What the fuck are you doing?

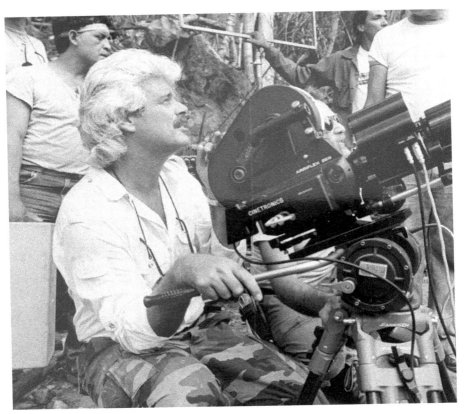

**Craig Baxley operating camera**

This is not a goddam war movie! You're ruining my fucking film!"

Joel shouted back, "Shut the fuck up and sit down, John, or I'll fucking fire you." Then he looked over at me and said, "The stuff is fantastic."

John never said a word after that.

I always thought it was very important to show how good Arnold and his men were before they went up against the Predator. I guess John kind of had his way in the end. He cut the fuel dump blowing up on his director's cut, even though it was a story point. In it, we blew up over two dozen fifty-gallon gas drums, fireballs mushrooming a hundred feet in the air, burning drums pinwheeling into the air as four stuntmen doing full burns ran from it. Another half dozen did partial burns with fire gel.

John also cut one of my favorite sequences. I had Bobby Bass doing a full burn with fire gel, banging on the windscreen of the Huey with both hands - yelling at the pilot and co-pilot while it was revving up for take-off. The scene was shot over both pilots onto him. You could see Bobby's face through the fire as he continued pounding on the windscreen - the fire licking up around his face and body. The second angle was a low angle behind him, up onto the helicopter as he fell backward, landing in the foreground. All in all, John cut over thirty-five seconds of action set pieces from the sequence.

Later it was clear Jean-Claude was not going to work out. Jean-Claude thought the Predator should be a kick-boxer, but that was decided when John finally got around to filming him as the Predator. It was day fifty. Unbeknownst to us, John-Claude was claustrophobic. When he put on the $10,000 head, designed by Boss Films, he suddenly snatched it off and slammed it down on the ground, shattering it.

**Arnold Schwarzenegger, Carl Weathers, and Craig Baxley**

Joel went crazy, firing him on the spot, yelling, "You fuck, you're done! You'll never work in this business again! Get the fuck out of here!" As we all know, Jean-Claude Van Damme's fate was not sealed that day by Joel's outburst.

Two days later, the studio shut the film down. Al and I went back for the final season of *The A-Team*. Three months later, after completing half of the shooting schedule, *Predator* was gearing up with a new Predator, designed by Stan Winston's company.

I first worked with Stan on the pilot for *Get Christie Love* in 1974. Stan was Teresa Graves' personal make-up man. He had put together an amazing team of designers and special effects make-up artists to form Stan Winston Studio. To my knowledge, Shane Mahan and John Rosengrant were instrumental in the design of the new Predator.

The new Predator was played by 7'2" Peter Kevin Hall. Peter also played the creature in *Harry and the Hendersons*. He brought the personality, the rage of the Predator, to life. He was a very talented and amazing human being.

The new location was in Palenque, Chiapas, Mexico - a tropical rainforest. The first time I saw it, I thought this is where the entire movie should have been shot. The shoot was only meant to be with the Predator and Arnold. I brought two stuntmen with me for the sequences: Henry Kingi and Tony Brubaker - both were in the Predator suit for the stunt sequences. On a shoestring budget for the remainder of the film, the company decided they couldn't afford Al and his crew. The Mexican keys Al hired for the shoot finished the shoot.

I think the film is still a classic to this day.

Eleven years later, my son called me one night after he got off work. He had just worked all day doing re-shoots on a film, "Dad, I just worked with a director, he said to say 'hi,' that you're one of his dearest friends."

"What's his name?" I asked.

"John McTiernan," he said.

The film my son was working on was called *13th Warrior*. It was filmed in 1997, in British Columbia. Apparently, after extensive re-editing by the studio and a couple of test screenings, the film was deemed unwatchable. It was based on the Michael Crichton novel, *Eaters of the Dead*.

Craig Jr. was told he would do all the re-shoots of the hand-to-hand fights with the star, Antonio Banderas, plus all the coverage of Antonio fighting the Mist Monsters (these were warriors wearing various animal heads). Craig did every fight with Banderas, changing heads for each.

"Didn't I meet him on *Predator*?" he asked.

"Yeah, you met him"

"I'm back tomorrow; what do you want me to tell him?'

Regardless of what I said, Michael Crichton was so upset with the film that he took over as director the next day.

**Craig Baxley and Carl Weathers,** *Action Jackson*

# CHAPTER 19

## How Do You Like Your Ribs?

There have been many stories about who came up with the idea for *Action Jackson.* It was Carl Weathers while he was working on *Predator.*

I had just directed the last one of the nine episodes I directed on *The A-Team* when I got the call from Joel. I was surprised and blown away that he wanted me to direct *Action Jackson.* Word on the street was Lorimar had already hired a director, Thomas Wright.

Joel told the president of Lorimar, "Bullshit, Carl and I want Craig Baxley." Joel and Carl were so happy with my work on *Predator* that there was not going to be any discussion.

The next day I was at Joel Silver's house in a production meeting. Joel lived in a Frank Lloyd Wright house above Sunset Boulevard. Yes, an original Frank Lloyd Wright house.

*Action Jackson* had a great cast: Carl Weathers, Craig T. Nelson, Sharon Stone, Vanity, Thomas Wilson, and Bill Duke.

Carl and I became friends on *Predator,* and after *Action Jackson,* he was practically a member of the family. He'd come to our house, or we'd go to his when either of us was available on the 4th of July. So many great times. To this day, he, Valerie, and I have remained very close. He's really such a class act and a talented man; I'm blessed to call him my friend.

*Action Jackson* was my first feature film. The budget was $7 million. The production manager, Steve Perry, thought it was at least a $12-15 million movie based on the script.

I told him, "Then I guess we'd better be very creative, especially when it comes to the action sequences."

He pressed on, "We can't afford to blow up a ninety-foot motor yacht."

I told him I'd already discussed it with Al DiSarro and the production designer. We had a plan! I explained that I wanted to take a picture of the yacht and then blow it up to the actual size. Then we could mount the photograph like a billboard on a barge. To this day, I still can't believe how well it worked.

Al laced the billboard with over one thousand feet of primer cord, a highly explosive material in a flexible case. After that, Al and his team rigged the barge using over three hundred gallons of gasoline. They then set over two dozen mortars to push the gas and debris through the photo as the primer cord cut and ripped it apart.

That night when Al set it off, it created a nonstop arc of fireballs as they ripped through and consumed the photograph, sending billowing fireballs up into the night.

I originally wanted Henry Kingi to be my stunt coordinator, but Henry was working for my father in Vancouver, British Columbia. He had a co-starring role in the film and couldn't break away. So I hired my second choice, Jophery Brown. I got Henry back on *Action*

## Joel Silver, Craig Baxley, and Carl Weathers

Carl Weathers and Craig Baxley, taxi sequence

*Jackson* in time for the car sequences. Henry doubled stuntman Bob Minor, driving with Carl on the roof of the taxi cab, and also for Carl during his driving sequences.

The first day of that sequence didn't go quite as planned. The Los Angeles Lakers had just won the world championship a couple of days before, and there were thousands of people in the streets of downtown Los Angeles. They were like ants swarming all over the locations we had scouted. I called an audible and took part of the chase up onto the sidewalk to avoid the crowd.

Then we moved to an alley for a different sequence to finish the day. And there, something magical happened. Henry was doing the driving again, doubling Carl. Between one of the takes, we saw three ladies walking toward us across a field, waving their hands. They were dressed like something out of a bad, over-the-top, Sci-fi movie: big wings on their shoulders, giant head-pieces, it was kinda crazy, but this was Los Angeles.

Suddenly they started shouting, "Henry, Henry, Henry Kingi! Henry!"

**Taxi sequence - Jophery Brown, pipe ramp turnover**

It was the Pointer Sisters; they were filming their new music video around the corner and heard Henry was on set. Henry was one of the stars in *Car Wash* in 1976, and that was when he met the sisters. He played one of the main characters, Goody. I guess Henry was the man.

Fifteen minutes later, I had the Pointer Sisters committed for our theme song, "He Turns Me Out."

We were back on track the following day.

We filmed all over Los Angeles, San Pedro, and Pasadena. A few moments during filming were quite forgettable, like when Paula Abdul was brought on as the dance coordinator. I'm not sure why we needed a dance coordinator; Vanity was just singing. But that was Joel's call. When Paula tried to tell me where to set the cameras for Vanity's sequences, the entire set went dead silent. I simply looked at her as she stood there surrounded by her entourage. To say she was a piece of work might be a bit of an understatement.

The film was loaded with action. We completed it on time and on budget. I even took a five-man crew to Detroit for three days to film the opening titles and a couple of other sequences. I was very proud to be part of the project and proud of everyone involved. We shot *Action Jackson* in thirty-five days. Thirty days of first unit and five of a paired down second unit, which I also directed.

Not to be outdone by my first episode of *The A-Team,* I thought it was time to thank the cast and crew. On the last day of filming in downtown Los Angeles, I had transportation make a run to Philippe the Original on Alameda. Philippe's has been around since 1908 and is considered the best sandwich in L.A. Roast pork, beef, leg of lamb, turkey, pastrami, or ham with your choice of cheese. All that goodness on a french roll, dipped in the gravy of the roast, and Philippe's famous hot mustard. Three hundred assorted dips showed up at the end of the day. Everyone loved it; it was the end of an amazing shoot.

My editor, Mark Helfrich, who I met on *Predator,* did a great job; he and I had a great time cutting the film; I don't think I've ever laughed so much in my life. He's truly one of a kind - a very dear man. We did have one issue; he is an ardent Beatles fan. I was more of a Stones, Doors, Cream guy, but somehow we made it work.

The saving grace was when Michael Kamen came on. Michael had done all the orchestration for all the Pink Floyd albums. He'd written the music for *Die Hard* 1, 2, and 3, the series of *Lethal Weapon* movies, *Robin Hood, Prince of Thieves, X-Men,* and so many others.

We were kind of blown away when Joel brought Herbie Hancock on. The deal was Herbie would have billing over Michael.

Mark and I walked onto the sound stage, Joel made the intros, Herbie sat down and tickled the ivories on and off for about fifteen minutes, then he was gone.

I looked at Mark, "What just happened?"

Then we looked at Michael, who was just standing there smiling, shaking his head to himself. I looked at Joel; he just shrugged it off. The only thing Herbie wrote was a little riff - something he'd taken from *The French Connection* for our car chase. Michael built on it later and wrote the entire score.

**Craig Baxley with handheld camera**

*Action Jackson* was a $7 million IA union picture in Los Angeles. I was very proud of the cast and crew. I felt like it was quite an accomplishment.

Al DiSarro went on to do *Die Hard, Die Hard 2, The Hunt for Red October, Sum of All Fears, The Last Boy Scout, Crimson Tide,* and *Transformers,* among a dozen other major blockbuster films. He was a dear friend. It broke my heart when he passed away in 2011. He was only sixty years old. I still can't believe he's gone.

# CHAPTER 20

## Man to Man

After I finished filming *Action Jackson,* Joel Silver and Larry Gordon approached me to direct *Man to Man* at Fox. It was a joint project between Fox and Lorimar.

*Man to Man* was a $20 million action sci-fi comedy about an alien crashing on earth. While in the middle of the Nevada desert, he hitches a ride with a repo man. The screenplay was written by Randy Feldman, who had written *Nowhere to Run, Metro,* and *Tango and Cash.*

Merv Adelson and Lee Rich founded Lorimar Studios. In those days, Merv owned The Golden Nugget downtown, and word had it, half of downtown Vegas. At the time, he was married to Barbara Walters.

A meeting was set up, and Joel and I met him in his office at Lorimar. He told me I could use any location I wanted, any location, including filming locations that had been off-limits in Vegas for years - that he would fix it.

After the meeting, Joel wanted me to make a pass at the script - he wanted me to write and add more action sequences. I piled it on and wrote car chases in and around downtown Las Vegas. In one chase, I had six police cars chasing our leads, crashing in and out of casinos, through plate glass windows,  through one casino after another, causing havoc, adding another police car with each casino - ending with over a dozen in the chase. Joel read the pages and just said, "Keep writing; I love it."

Schwarzenegger was going to play the alien role, but after *Predator* turned out to be such a huge hit, he became too expensive, so Dolph

Lundgren was hired.

A few days before production began, I was told to fly back to Los Angeles for a meeting with Larry Gordon and Joel Silver. I remember sitting in Larry's office; Larry was the president of Fox studios at the time. We were on a conference call with Bernie Brillstein, the new president of Lorimar, one of the industry's biggest managers. He wanted one of his clients from Saturday Night Live to be the repo man.

I'd already filmed dozens of screen tests on most of them; Joel wasn't buying any of them. He was yelling, demanding Anthony Michael Hall play the role. "I'm the fucking producer," he said. "You're not going to tell me or my director who to hire!"

The argument escalated into a screaming match until there was nothing else to say. For a couple of seconds, it was dead silent. Then Bernie calmly said, "Okay, Joel, here's your answer."

Click.

Larry and I looked at each other.

Joel muttered, "What the fuck was that? Did that asshole just hang up on me?!"

We had all of our locations locked. Sets were being built. Three dozen stunt cars were being rigged. Over thirty stuntmen were traveling to Las Vegas. Local casting was complete. I had an entire crew waiting for me to return to Las Vegas.

The production was canceled. The entire cast and crew came home.

Everyone got paid off except Joel.

# CHAPTER 21

## New Agent

My family and I were waiting at the gate at Burbank Airport. We were on our way to our second home in Welches, Oregon, on the Salmon River. It was located about fifteen minutes from Mount Hood.

Our friend, Henry, had a place there. He had told me about this little house on a point that was for sale, just 450 square feet. But, he said it was a good investment at twenty-five thousand dollars. You could see the sunrise on the river in the morning, and in the other direction, the sun set across the river in the afternoon. We bought it, razed it, and built a 3400 square foot cabin on the Salmon River.

Henry was married to Lindsay Wagner at the time, The Bionic Woman. Her mother, Marilyn Ball, was with Duke, who became our new contractor. Henry met Lindsey when he was the stunt coordinator of *The Bionic Woman.*

Duke was amazing, we designed the cabin, and he built it. Three levels, reclaimed barn wood inside and out, and a rusted, corrugated metal roof. He found three six-foot bear-claw bathtubs that were over a hundred years old and put one in each of the bathrooms. We built a state-of-the-art kitchen for Valerie. The best part was a sixteen-foot river stone fireplace in the living room overlooking the river through four large nine-by-three-foot windows, which we found in a thrift store in Portland. The bottom floor was a wine cellar with six more of the nine-foot windows overlooking the river. Thanksgiving in the snow was beautiful.

We spent many fun summers and evenings barbecuing on the deck overlooking the river. Valerie watched the kids and me go floating by on the river in inner tubes. It became our Oregon paradise.

On this day, Valerie and the kids couldn't wait to get there. Valerie tapped me on the shoulder; I looked back. There was my new agent, Jim Berkus, moving toward us through the airport, waving his arms. After a brief exchange, he handed me two scripts: *Nothing Lasts Forever,* written by Jeb Stuart, and *Johnny Utah,* written by Peter Iliff. "Read them and let me know what you think."

I read them in Oregon, and both were great screenplays. When I called Jim, I told him I loved *Johnny Utah.* It had it all, loaded with action and surfing. He explained that Ridley Scott was the first choice to direct it, but he had left the project to direct *Thelma and Louise.*

I later found out that wasn't the case. Ridley had already done tests on Val Kilmer, Charlie Sheen, Matthew Broderick, Willem Dafoe, and Michael Biehn. And the director was circling Mark Harmon, a quarterback at UCLA. But it was actually a combination of Mark's injury (he'd separated his shoulder playing touch football with a friend) and the fact that the producers just lost the rights to the project, which caused Ridley to step off.

Berkus told me that Warner Bros. was interested in having me come aboard and direct it. As the negotiations began, he told me they were interested in an actor starring in a television series for Stephen Cannell. He set up a meet with the actor the next day.

At the meeting, we both looked at each other. He asked me, "Do I know you? Have we worked together?"

I smiled at Johnny Depp and said, "Yeah, I did the car chase on the pilot of your show (*21 Jump Street*)."

"Cool, I thought I knew you. This is a great script. So, you're a surfer, huh?"

Two days later, Jim called me. "I've got good news and bad news; which do you want first?"

"The good news," I said.

"Johnny loves you."

"And...?"

"The studio doesn't think he can open a movie."

"Then why did they bring up his name?"

"Doesn't matter. Between that and it being a surfing movie, there's no longer any interest; they pulled the plug on it this morning."

I later found out *Nothing Lasts Forever* already had a director. The title had been changed to *Die Hard;* Fox paid Shane Black a million dollars to use the title. It was originally the title of a script Shane wrote, later called *The Last Boy Scout.*

*Johnny Utah* came back four or five years later as *Point Break,* with Kathryn Bigelow directing. It was her second film; I'd heard that her then husband, James Cameron, talked Fox into hiring her. *Point Break* starred Patrick Swayze, Keanu Reeves, and Lori Petty.

I had taught Patrick how to do a picture fight on a two-hour backdoor pilot called *The Renegades,* loosely based on *The Warriors.* It was Patrick Swayze's first job in the industry.

My friend, Dennis Jarvis, who owns Spyder Surfboards in Hermosa Beach, is a world-class pro surfer and one of the hottest shapers in the surfing world. He was also the surfing advisor on *Point Break,* a director in his own right. He taught all three of the actors how to surf in Kauai, Hawaii. He also brought in Matt Archibald as a surfing double for Patrick. Another friend of mine, Glenn Wilder, was the second unit director and stunt coordinator. I loved the film.

# CHAPTER 22

## On Top of the World

The week after *Action Jackson* opened, I had two meetings in one day. The first was with partners Guber and Peters at Columbia. Peter Guber and John Peters were one of the hottest producing duos in the industry in the eighties and nineties. The second was with Mark Canton, the President of Warner Bros.

I was joined by my agent, Jim Burkus, and my attorney, Jake Bloom, who also repped Stallone and Schwarzenegger. Jim owned Leading Artist agency and later founded the UTA agency.

We walked into a conference room at Columbia on Warner's lot and joined Peter Guber. It seemed like a love fest to me; Peter loved *Action Jackson* and wanted to be in business together. Until his partner, John Peters, walked in.

John went from being Barbra Streisand's hairdresser to one of the biggest producers in Hollywood. He just stood there and looked around the room before he locked eyes with me.

"You Baxley?"

Jim said, "Yes, this is my client, Craig Baxley."

John didn't miss a beat. "Well, I fucking hate Joel Silver." Then he flatly said, "This meeting is over," and walked out.

I looked at Peter and Jim and just said, "Well, that went well."

Twenty minutes later, we were led by Lisa Henson (Jim Henson's daughter) into Mark Canton's office. Mark was the President of Warner Bros. Studios. Lisa was his VP. Mark was sitting behind his desk talking on the phone. He gave us one of those, "I'll be right with you" nods.

A half-hour later, he hung up the phone and stood up. "You're

Craig Baxley; I love your stuff. I gotta run. Got a meeting I'm running late for. Tell Lisa here what kind of material you're interested in." A couple of seconds later, he was gone.

I looked at Jim and Jake. I wanted to say, "What the fuck?"

Jim looked at me and said, "Don't say it."

Lisa looked at Jim and Jake and said, "I'm sorry." Then at me, "Maybe we can set something up for next week."

A couple of days later, Jim set up a meeting with the English executive producer on *Needles*. It was about three black heroin addicts who robbed a half dozen banks before they were finally caught. The meeting was on a sound stage at A&M Studios in Hollywood. His secretary led me in; it was pitch black. In the center of the empty stage, a single light was shining down on a card table with two chairs.

She motioned me toward them, "He'll be right with you, Mr. Baxley."

It seemed like something out of a bad movie. I walked over and sat down. Ten minutes later, I heard the door open behind me and listened to footsteps as someone approached. He passed me and sat down directly across from me. He had an incredulous look on his face; after a couple of seconds, he said, "You're Craig Baxley?"

"Yeah," I replied.

Flatly, "You're not black."

I just stared at this tight-ass Brit. I thought to myself, "No shit!"

"No, I'm not," I said.

Incredulously he said, "You directed *Action Jackson?*" The meeting was over a couple minutes later.

The next week, I met with Lawrence Turman. I had worked with him on *Nickle Ride*. He said I was his first choice to direct an action film he had called *The Rookie*. He had Gene Hackman and Matthew Modine set in the starring roles. The meeting went great; I told him I would love to read the script.

It was a solid piece of material, except I felt like I'd seen the action a hundred times before. It was about a group of car thieves boosting high-end cars. I suggested we make it fresh, give the audience something they hadn't seen before. I thought the group of thieves would systematically converge on a moving car carrier, then one after another begin loading the high-end cars up onto it. Then in the final sequence, when they were finally caught, they would dump a half-dozen cars off the carrier one after another - directly in the path of the pursuing police car that had our leads in it.

He loved it.

Then it happened. The Writers Guild of America strike of 1988. The entire motion picture industry shut down overnight. If you weren't already on a film in production, you were unemployed.

I got a call from a friend named Tim Matheson. He was producing a film called *Blind Fury,* starring Rutger Hauer. It was based on Zatoichi, the blind Samurai. They were four weeks into prep, and he wanted to fire the director and have me replace him. I told him I was involved with *The Rookie.*

"Forget *The Rookie,*" he said. "This strike is going to last for months. Come with me, and we'll be working together for the next three to four months in Vegas, Utah, and Hawaii."

I told him I had to speak with Larry, that I'd call him back in a couple of hours.

Larry told me this strike wasn't going to last more than two weeks. He stressed that this was the movie that was going to define my career.

I called my agent Jim Berkus and filled him in; he agreed with Larry. I called Tim back and told him I couldn't do it. Tim couldn't believe it. "I think you're making a mistake," he said.

The strike lasted three and a half months. The director, Phillip Noyce, stayed on the film and stayed employed the entire strike. He later went on to direct *Patriot Games, Clear and Present Danger,* and *The Bone Collector.*

I was not so lucky. *The Rookie* went away. So did Larry and I.

The film was finally made ten years later with Clint Eastwood and Charlie Sheen with Eastwood directing. Although I don't feel they did the sequences justice, the car carrier sequences were filmed exactly as I had written them. They didn't do half the coverage I would have done, and most the gags looked old, like I'd seen them a thousand times.

No. It's not sour grapes. It's just the truth.

# CHAPTER 23

## I Come in Peace

The day after the writer's strike ended, I got a call from Jim. He said one of Jake Bloom's clients had just been signed for the first film to go into production after the strike: Dolph Lundgren.

"The Russian from Rocky?" I asked.

"Yeah," he said. "He's playing the alien. The studio feels he could be the next Terminator."

I didn't say anything.

Jim continued, "Jake says he only speaks the phrase 'I Come in Peace.'"

"What's the budget?"

"It's an independent, $8 million. They want to shoot it in Houston."

"I'd love to read it," I said.

"It's written by David Koepp. It was originally titled *Lethal Contact,* a sci-fi action film. The meeting is set for lunch tomorrow; you're their first choice." (David went on to write *Carlito's Way,* three *Jurassic Park* films, *Mission Impossible, Spiderman, Indiana Jones: The Crystal Skull,* and many more).

"Get me the script," I said.

The next day I walked into the Saint James Club on Sunset Boulevard. Dolph was sitting at a table with Jake Bloom and Mark Damon, the president of Vision International. Dolph appeared very excited; he said he loved the script and looked forward to working with me. Then he asked me, "Do you have any ideas who should play the alien?"

I felt like time stood still for a moment; I glanced at Jake, who looked like he just swallowed a canary.

Then Mark spoke up, "This is a chance for Dolph to really stretch and show his chops; Detective Jack Caine is such a terrific character."

I looked at Dolph again; he was waiting for me to speak. I looked at Jake, who just closed his eyes. That was the moment I realized neither he nor my agent had read the screenplay.

Once the meeting and lunch were over, we all stood up and shook hands.

I looked at Dolph as he smiled and said, "See you in a couple of weeks, Mr. Director."

That night I got a call from Helen, Warren Beatty's assistant. Warren was working with Bo Goldman on an extensive rewrite of *Dick Tracy*. Goldman was probably one of the greatest screenwriters of all time. He wrote *One Flew Over the Cuckoo's Nest, The Rose,* and *Scent of a Woman.* Helen said Warren wanted to know if I was available tomorrow.

When I walked into Warren's house up on Mulholland Drive, Warren was sitting in the living room with Madonna on his lap. It was kinda hard to take the whole situation seriously, but then again, it was Warren. He explained that he was pissed at Bo because he was moving on to another project with Penny Marshall. And he had an issue with a couple of sequences Bo had written for *Dick Tracy.* One was the shoot-out in the nightclub and another a shoot-out in the street out front. He and Bo couldn't agree on either sequence; he wanted me to write and shot list them as I had done on *Reds.* And he also wanted me to direct them with the first unit.

I explained I was leaving in two weeks for Houston to direct my second film.

He pressed on; it was almost comical with Madonna sitting there smiling on his lap.

I told him I would write and shot list it for him; maybe we could get together before I left and go to Universal Studios and walk through the sequences on the back lot.

He said, "Perfect, that works."

I left the two love birds together and went home to work on both projects.

A week later, I met Warren up in Beverly Glen at a little restaurant by his office. But he wasn't alone. He had Bo Goldman, Vittorio Storaro, his cinematographer, and Richard Sylbert, his production designer (both of whom I had worked with on Warren's films many times) with him.

After a brief exchange with the guys, Warren introduced me to Bo. I just stared at him for a moment; the guy was a living legend. Then Warren spoke up, "Let's see what you've got."

I handed him the sequences and caught up with the guys as he read them. Afterward, Warren passed them to Bo. "I love them, exactly what I was looking for," he said.

A couple of minutes later, Bo looked up and smiled, "Good job, very exciting, Mr. Baxley."

An hour later, all four of us were on the back lot at Universal Studios. As we walked through the sequences, Warren asked me again if I could break away and direct them for him.

I told him I couldn't, but I could recommend a good second unit director that I thought would work well with him; Billy Burton was the choice.

Warren hired Billy, but he directed the sequences himself from my shot list. I always thought it was strange that he gave the original writers, Jim Cash and Jack Epps Jr. (who were taken off the film), screen credit and didn't give Bo any credit when Bo completely rewrote the script. And yet Warren gave me "A Special Thanks" in the end credits, which I thought was pretty cool.

The next week, Karen Rea, my casting director, and I went to work on *Dark Angel*. We had to find the bad alien and Jack Caine's partner. We got lucky early on. We found our bad alien - a 6'5" German bodybuilder, Matthias Hues. Matthias was an amazing athlete - a German pentathlon champion and a black belt Martial artist.

Finding Caine's partner, however, was not so easy. After four weeks of reading over fifty established actors, Karen told me she found someone she loved that I had to meet. She also said he hadn't done much, but she thought he would make Dolph shine: Brian Benben.

The day I met Brian, I knew he was a major talent, and we set him as special agent Atwood "Larry" Smith that day. Brian went on to star in HBO's *Dream On*.

I met with Moshe Diamant, the majority partner at Trans World Entertainment and executive producer on the film. I mentioned that I had some structural and dialogue changes I wanted to make to adjust for Dolph playing Jack Caine; Moshe said the writer had been paid for the screenplay, so I would have to make the changes. He also mentioned that he and Mark had changed the title to *I Come in Peace.*

It just kept getting better and better; I was waiting for the other shoe to drop. What next? As I went to work on the script, I made a dialogue pass; then, I started addressing the rest of the script. I felt I needed to surround Dolph with a great cast and bigger, more exciting action set pieces. We didn't have the budget for either.

**Craig Baxley and Dolph Lundgren**

I also needed to add a "B" plot to the movie. I came up with the idea of a good alien, an intergalactic cop coming to earth to chase the bad alien. I got lucky again; we found our good alien the next week. Jay Bilas, a basketball star at Duke University that helped lead the

Blue Devil's to an NVAA championship, fit the part. The fact that he was 6'8" didn't hurt either. He's now a broadcaster at ESPN and considered one of the foremost experts on college basketball.

Our cast also included Jim Haynie, Betsy Brantley, David Ackroyd, Sherman Howard, Sam Anderson, and Michael J. Pollard.

I remember thinking about an earlier film that I really liked, *Robocop*. The film had a weapon I thought was visually interesting.

I made a couple of calls and contacted Randy Moore, the weapons master on the film. I asked him what that weapon was. "A modified Calico M950," he said.

I asked him if he would like to work on our film. He came on board the next day. I told him I wanted him to build two, but I wanted the report (the flames) out of the barrel to extend further. I also asked if the weapon could fire longer. He said he could do it, but we would probably melt the firing pin every time we fired it. I told him, "That's no problem. Let's do it."

He made two, one for each alien. I also told my effects coordinator (one of Al DiSarro's team) that I wanted each round to explode in a fireball.

Like *Action Jackson*, we had a few hurdles to overcome. By the time I'd finished the rewrite, the action alone had a major impact on our budget. When the producer read the opening, he said, "We can't afford to blow up a brand new Mercedes 500. Are you crazy?"

It was time to be very creative again. I had the production designer take a photograph of a brand new Mercedes. Yes, we did it again. We blew the photo up life size. I had the effects coordinator do what he and Al had done on *Action Jackson*. Screaming down from the sky, the bad alien impacted the Mercedes; a split second later, the Mercedes was gone in a non-stop arc of fireballs and debris as they ripped through the photograph – fireballs billowing up into the night.

Then the location manager came to me and said we had a problem. I wrote a sequence where the good alien cornered the bad alien in a supermarket, and a brief firefight ensued. The location manager told me the city wouldn't let us use gasoline for the explosions inside the market. I discussed it with my effects coordinator, and we came up with another concept - balloons filled with propane and one igniter.

The first time we set it up, it was in the produce section. The visual was amazing when the good cop fired, a series of fireballs rolling toward the camera. A split second later, when the fire was gone, there was no residue. Mission accomplished.

As the bad alien ran from the market, the good alien cop fired again. We cannoned the car directly behind him, spitting it up into the air, spinning in a massive fireball ten feet off the ground.

I had hired my father as my stunt coordinator. It was good to be working together again.

One of my favorite sequences that I wrote in the film was when the good alien cop cornered the bad alien in a parking garage. As the good alien opened fire, the bad alien leaped onto the hood of a parked car and ran the length of two dozen parked cars from hood to hood. As he ran, the good alien continued to fire his weapon; as the bad alien cleared each hood, we blew the car up, literally. The image was a tidal wave of massive explosions and fireballs chasing him down the row of parked cars, ending in him leaping off the last one through a plate glass window, dropping fifty feet to the ground.

Matthias did the stunt himself, leaping from car to car with the explosions. We blew the front ends of each car as his foot left it. Standing next to the cameras, I could feel the heat approaching us.

**Matthias with explosions**

After we completed the run, we were set for the window gag. Then I had a stuntman overlap the leap off the last parked car through the plate glass window down into the offstage catcher.

We did things on this film (before CGI) that many of my friends, directors, and stuntmen couldn't believe we did for $8 million.

**Cast, Director of Photography, and Craig Baxley**

In the final fight between Dolph and the bad alien, Dolph side-kicks the alien backward, impaling him on a four-inch pipe. As the bad alien hung there on the pipe, he croaked out, "I come in peace."

Dolph was then going to use the alien's weapon to blow him up.

Before we rolled cameras, Dolph held up his hand. "Bax, shouldn't I say something here?"

A voice from the back of the set spoke up, "And you go in pieces, asshole."

Dolph said, "Thank you, Valerie."

Then we rolled the cameras.

I always knew Valerie was a much more intuitive writer than I was. I must say, a lot of writers and producers have tried to take credit for her great catchphrases in the movies I've worked on, but they all know who wrote them.

I thought Dolph did a great job on the film.

# CHAPTER 24

## Screwface

*Screwface* was the original title for *Market for Death.* My agent, Jim Berkus, called me and told me about the project. It was to be Steven Seagal's second film. He told me Riley Ellis, a studio executive at Lorimar when I did *Action Jackson,* was now a studio executive at 20th Century Fox and wanted me to do it. She had gotten the studio to sign off on me to direct it. End of story.

"The studio just made you an offer, Craig."

The next day at a little restaurant in Brentwood, I met with the writers, Michael Grais and Mark Victor. Together they wrote *Poltergeist.* Both these guys were smart. I liked them immediately.

I'd seen *Above the Law,* Seagal's first film directed by Andy Davis. I thought it was pretty good. I told them I couldn't put their script down; I especially liked the character Screwface, the Jamaican drug kingpin. Word on the street was he had two heads and four eyes. Later, when his severed head was found, it was revealed he had a twin brother. Very cool.

I pitched them the idea of using a Jamaican singer I'd seen. He was a six-foot four-inch, hundred-and twenty-pound Rasta Albino. He had long white dreads to his waist, light white skin with light blue, almost white eyes; he was my choice to play the twins. You couldn't take your eyes off him. He also had an amazing voice.

They loved the idea. I pitched them a couple more ideas, pushing the action to another level. I felt the meeting couldn't have gone better.

Next up was the meeting with Steven Seagal. I drove up to his house in Beverly Hills. He answered the door, completely dressed in black. He smiled. "Craig Baxley, come on in."

As he sat down, I sat down directly across from him.

He just stared at me for a couple of seconds, "Nice to meet'cha. What do the stunt guys call you?"

"Craig," I answered.

"Come on; stunt guys always have a nickname."

"Craig works."

"C'mon, dude, I've talked to my guys."

"My friends call me Bax."

He looked up past me; I turned and saw Kelly LeBrock. Yeah, The Lady in Red, walking down the stairs toward us. Kelly had met Steven on *Hard to Kill*. Steven snapped, "What are you fucking doing? I'm having a meeting goin' on here!" I could see she was embarrassed as she turned away and disappeared upstairs. I had just gotten a glimpse of the man he really was.

He proceeded to say, "So, Bax, I love your work. This is going to be a good fit." After a couple of beats, "Fuck'in great, huh? I think it's really going to be a good fit. But I gotta have a couple'a things; I gotta have my stunt coordinator, my stunt guys, and my DP. You cool with that?"

I wasn't a fan of Steven's martial arts style; it was all inside, kind of flat-footed. I also knew his stunt coordinator; the guy was just a talking head. I knew that wasn't going to work; I was not a fan of his DP either. I just smiled, "Maybe we should discuss the material first; we can discuss the crew later."

He just stared at me. "Heard your dad was a pal of Brando's? Luv the guy." Then he slowly turned and gave me his profile, "A lot of people say I look like Brando; what do you think?"

I knew then and there I couldn't do this movie, not with this guy. On my way home, I called Valerie first and explained how the meeting went. She understood. Then I called Jim and tried to talk him through what happened, why I didn't want to do the film.

He went ballistic, "What are you talking about? Seagal's agent already called the studio; Seagal loves you! Riley put her ass on the line for you; you can't do this! She's gonna fuckin' shit."

Dwight Little directed the movie. He found an actor to play Screwface. He gave him a black dread wig and a pair of white contacts. The actor played both roles, as I was going to do with my

Rasta Albino, but Dwight's Screwface didn't ring true to me.

I thought about what it could have been, but then again, it was the choice I made.

At the end of the year, I got a call from Gary McLarty, "Hey Bax; you want to come out and play with the boys?"

Gary was the stunt coordinator on *Days of Thunder*. There was something nostalgic about the call. Something that gave me a moment to think of "the good old days" - no pressure, just doing what I loved to do. I think Gary knew I couldn't do it, but it was nice to get the call.

# CHAPTER 25

## God Forgives, The Brotherhood Doesn't

Sometimes you have no control over your destiny. It just reveals itself.

A new company, Stone Group Pictures, had just shut down their first two co-productions with Columbia Studios.

Stone Group Pictures was founded by Michael Douglas, who was the executive producer of both films. One was called *Radio Flyer;* the other was *The Brotherhood.* Both had been in production. David Mickey Evans wrote and was directing *Radio Flyer.* Bruce Malmuth was directing *The Brotherhood.*

Columbia and Stone Group were dissatisfied with the dailies on both. *The Brotherhood* had been in production for six weeks and already spent between $5 and $6 million of the $17 million budget. *Radio Flyer* was shut down during the first week.

My agent was negotiating a new deal for me with Universal when I got a call. He said, "You have a meeting in an hour at Columbia with Michael Douglas."

I asked him what the film was; he said, "It's one of two. They're both major motion pictures; they just called about you. I think you should take the meeting."

When I got to Columbia on the Warner Bros. lot, I walked into the office. Five other A-list directors were sitting in the outer office. I knew two of them; it was awkward, to say the least. This was a first for me; it seemed like a cattle call for directors. I'm not sure if my agent knew, but it seemed very odd. I quietly told the secretary that I thought there had been a mistake, that I was negotiating on a project at Universal. She asked me to have a seat; then she disappeared inside the office.

You could hear a pin drop. All five of the other directors just stared at me. A couple of seconds later, she came out and said, "They'll see you now, Mr. Baxley." I slowly stood up and shrugged at the other guys, then walked inside.

I looked at Michael Douglas as I walked in; the guy was pure class. Seated next to him was Moshe Diamant, the ex-Israeli tank commander who was president of Vision when I directed *I Come in Peace*. There were three other executives seated in the office as well.

"Thank you for coming," Michael said as he introduced the other executives in the room. Moshe just smiled at me. Michael explained what had happened with both films and what *The Brotherhood* was about. He also mentioned that the director of photography, John Leonetti, was on location and that he and most of his crew had worked with me previously.

I told him that John was a camera operator on *Action Jackson* for his brother Matt Leonetti, my DP on the film. I fielded a dozen more questions from the other executives, after which Michael asked me if I could wait in the other room.

I opened the door; it was a closet.

I looked back at Michael and the room full of executives, who were as surprised as I was.

"Are you serious?" I said.

Michael was kind of embarrassed, "Sorry, it's not my office."

He looked over at Moshe and nodded. Moshe looked at me and smiled, "I think we have our director."

*The Brotherhood* was a film designed to make Brian Bosworth an action star. Columbia, Michael, and Moshe believed he could be.

The next day I was on a plane to Mississippi. *Radio Flyer* had been shut down for two months of prep. The Brotherhood was shut down for three days. I read the script on the plane. I suddenly realized the magnitude of the undertaking - I needed to rewrite and re-shoot the first six weeks of the schedule.

After I landed, production informed me that I wouldn't get those four weeks or the $4 million back. I had what was left of the budget and schedule to make it work.

I was told the editor hired by Bruce Malmuth wanted to remain on the film. I stopped in to introduce myself. He seemed agitated and angry. Before I could say a word, he said, "You know I'm Bruce's guy. I'm not familiar with your work... stunt guy, huh?" He caught himself; it was awkward, to say the least. He muttered a sullen, half-assed apology.

What the fuck? I didn't want to believe he was that naïve. Did he think I'd take it as an insult? Even if it was his intention, he should've kept it to himself.

Two days later, he was gone, and Mark Helfrich was my editor.

I've never understood why there is so much disrespect in Hollywood for the stuntmen when everyday people fantasize about their lives. You can start out in the mailroom at the William Morris Agency, as Michael Ovitz did, join four other agents to form Creative Artists Agency (CAA), and still always be thought of as the president of CAA. But if you start as a stuntman and become a director, you're still always just a stuntman. Having over thirty directing credits, I can't tell you how many times a crew member has come up to me and said, "Oh yeah, you're the stunt guy."

\* \* \* \* \*

After reading the script, I realized I couldn't shoot the end of the movie as scripted. *The Brotherhood* was about an undercover cop who infiltrates a violent Mississippi outlaw motorcycle gang. The one-percenters. The writer, Walter Doniger, wrote the end of the movie as a violent action set piece that took place on the lawns of the capitol building. A biker gang descended like locusts on a country jubilee attended by friends and families.

It didn't make much sense with the existing storyline.

I called Michael and said I didn't want to be involved with a sequence involving families, especially children. He totally agreed and gave me the green light to come up with something else.

Around that time, Brian had an epiphany; he and his agent wanted to change the name of the movie to *Stone Cold*. That and his mullet were the two worst things I've ever experienced in my life.

I wrote the last thirty minutes of the film at night after I wrapped shooting for the day. It took about a week to write and polish it. That meant only three to four hours of sleep a night; thank god Valerie

Motorcycle and helicopter gag

was there. She always had snacks and wine set up and waiting for me the minute I walked in. She'd take notes for my editor, Mark, as we watched the dailies, then I'd spend the next couple of hours shot listing for the next day. After a glass or two of wine, I spend some more time working on the ending.

For the final sequence, I came up with the idea of a Harley jumping out a third-story window of the Arkansas capitol building. The idea was to hit the mock-up of a hovering Huey 212 (which was hanging from a crane) and explode it into a massive fireball that dropped into a parking lot onto six rigged cannon cars. The scene ended in an explosion of fireballs that shot as high as the dome on the capitol building.

I realized I didn't have the budget to write any more action. But Michael loved the new sequence. So, I knew it was time to stop writing and start prepping. He more than understood.

I hired my father as stunt coordinator and second unit director. I also brought on a special effects coordinator, Russ Hessy, to help coordinate the effects. When we shot the final sequence, Chuck Tamburro flew the Huey 212 up the main street, two feet off the ground at fifty miles an hour. The blades just fit between the light posts on each side, a foot under the lights at the top. As he arched up over the capitol building, I knew we had something special. Chuck was and always has been the best pilot in the industry.

I still marvel at the fact we got permission to do any of it. A couple of weeks earlier, we sat in the governor of Arkansas's office to meet with the governor and his secretary of state. I explained everything I wanted to do inside with the Harleys roaring up the stairs, through the building, as well as everything outside. The governor just kept saying, "Wow, that's cool; I can dig it. Wow, that sounds wild, amazing."

After about twenty minutes into the meeting, he said with a big smile, "Listen, my man Bill McCuen, secretary of state, will finish up the meeting with you boys; I got to run." He stood up, shook hands with everyone, and walked out. We watched Bill Clinton disappear as we finished the meeting with the other Bill.

I was blessed to have two incredible actors on the film, Lance Henriksen, who played Chains, and William Forsythe, who played Ice. When I explained what was on my plate, I couldn't have had two more collaborative partners and filmmakers to work with. While I was making a pass on the script, Lance was making a pass on his dialogue. Working with him was one of the best experiences I've ever had working with an actor on any film I've done.

The first two weeks of filming couldn't have gone better. Suddenly production was halted due to an IA union dispute. John Leonetti came to me with some bad news. Although he had told production he wouldn't leave if the IA stepped in, he and his crew left the film the next day.

Most of his crew had to eat the four-month leases they had on their housing.

The next day we had an entirely new crew with a new director of photography, Alexander Gruszynski. Without missing a beat, we resumed filming. Alexander was a rock star; he did an amazing job regardless of the lack of prep.

I might have pushed the envelope a little too far on the courtroom sequence, Chains gunning down a half dozen judges, but Lance loved it.

The fact that I had my editor, Mark, on location was a huge plus for me, having worked with him on *Predator, Action Jackson, I Come in Peace,* and *The Avenging Angel.* It allowed us to almost have a final cut at the end of our principal shooting schedule.

In my opinion, the film suffered cuts to gain an R rating after the MPAA rated it an NC-17 after seeing the first cut. The fact that we finished on time and on budget, with what remained of the original schedule and budget, is a testament to how good all the crews were. We were able to return to California, film the opening sequence, and enhance the chase with Ice, even within the confines of those restraints.

*Stone Cold's* original budget was $17 million. We shot our entire movie for $11-12 million.

# CHAPTER 26

## Hard Target, 1992

My agent got a call from Tom Pollock at Universal Studios. He wanted to know if I would take a meeting with Jim Jacks and Sean Daniel. They were producing a film called *Hard Target,* along with Moshe Diamant, with whom I had done *I Come in Peace* and *Stone Cold.*

I was reluctant to take the meeting. In 1988 I met with Jim and Sean on *Shadow Company,* written by Shane Black and Fred Dekker. It was a very cool script about a group of special forces soldiers who died in the Vietnam War. They were part of a dark top-secret military experiment - rising from the grave, attacking the town where they were buried, killing everyone during Christmas night.

The meeting couldn't have gone better; they mentioned the budget was between $10 and $15 million and that they had Kurt Russell for the lead. Unfortunately, after the meeting that afternoon, I got a call from my agent. Pollock told him they loved my take on the material. Then Jim apologetically explained it had been set up with John Carpenter directing, with Walter Hill as executive producer, budgeted at $40 million.

"Why was I interviewed then?" I asked.

"The studio felt *Shadow Company* was in the $10 to $15 million range and that they wanted to go forward with you," he said.

Walter, the executive producer, felt bad and said that the studio should never have contacted me. John was his chosen director, and Walter held his ground on that point. Eventually, Pollock pulled the plug on the whole deal, and the project went away.

So there I was again, sitting in Sean's office with Jim Jacks. I was engaged in a conversation that triggered a sort of deja vu. As the meeting concluded, I thought, "It couldn't have gone better. But if it seems too good to be true, it probably is."

I found out later that Universal had already made a deal with John Woo. I was a huge fan of John's; I loved *The Killers* and *A Better Tomorrow*, two of his Hong Kong ultra-violent gangster films. Apparently, John balked at the studio's refusal to bring his crew from Hong Kong to the United States. Unbeknownst to me, I was interviewed to be on stand-by in case John held his ground. Since this was his first mainstream Hollywood film, he didn't.

A couple of years later, at William Forsythe's wedding, Valerie and I were sitting at Billy's table with his new bride, Miguel Ferrer, Andrew Divoff, Dennis Haden, and a couple of other friends.

A voice rang out: "Do you mind if I join you?"

I glanced up at Jim Jacks. He sat down next to me - continuing to listen to Billy, who was just finishing a story about how Michael Douglas had interviewed directors to stand by if he wanted to replace the two directors on both of the films he was producing.

Jim spoke up: "I've got one better than that; I interviewed the same director twice to stand by on two films I was producing."

Billy just stared at him; the table went dead silent.

After a couple of seconds, I said, "Jim, I was that director."

He slowly turned toward me; he had an "Oh, fuck" look on his face. Everyone at the table just sat there staring at him. "Yeah," he apologetically muttered as he slowly stood up and walked away. That's Hollywood for you, no thin skin here.

# CHAPTER 27

## The Nineties

*Dreadnought* was the original title for *Under Siege.* I was sitting outside the commissary at Warner Bros. with my editor Mark. We had just started the final mix on *Stone Cold.* As we ate our lunch, I noticed a big guy in a caftan walking toward us. It was Steven Seagal.

As he walked up to our table, I stood up to introduce Mark; Steven stepped up and gave me a big hug and said, "Bax, how are you, man?"

"I'm good," I said.

"I was pissed it didn't work out on *Marked for Death;* we got the word from your agent you weren't available."

As I introduced Mark, Steven asked me what I was up to. He said he had a big movie coming up at Warner's, and he would love to have me on it. He pitched the storyline; it sounded like *Die Hard* on a battleship. "I'm going to have my producer, Jack Bernstein, call your agent. Is it still Jim Berkus?"

A couple of days later, I got a call on the mixing stage. Jim said, "Warner's just made you an offer for *Dreadnought;* it's a $30-35 million movie starring Steven Seagal."

"Jim…"

"Let me finish, Craig. They want you to co-direct it with Steven. They won't greenlight it unless you agree to do it with him."

"Jim, I passed on *Marked for Death,* remember?"

"Seagal doesn't know that; I told his agent you weren't available. Craig, this is a major studio picture."

Having just completed *Stone Cold,* the idea of doing a Steven Seagal movie just didn't make sense to me at all. I passed.

Warner Bros. wanted to make the movie. They finally agreed to bring Andy Davis on board - he directed Seagal's first movie, *Above the Law*. Then the production hit another snag; Andy wouldn't co-direct it with Steven. It was a firm no. The studio finally agreed that Andy would direct alone, and the movie was made.

* * * * *

The nineties were crazy. Unlike the seventies and eighties, the action seemed to have become dated in the eye of a new generation once again. Now it was becoming stunts on steroids, forget reality. It was the dawn of CGI action.

Everyone was jumping into the TV arena. In some cases, you could make more directing a pilot or a two-hour Movie of the Week than you could by directing a feature film.

So I jumped in. During those years, I directed two pilots, twelve two-hour Movies of the Week, and two six-hour mini-series. My father came on board during that time as my stunt coordinator.

Right after *Stone Cold*, I got called to do a pilot for CBS in Honolulu, Hawaii. It was called *Raven*; it was about the Yakuza and loaded with real action, not CGI.

On my first day of prep, the producer walked into my office and said he thought I should see the director's list from United Talent Agency (UTA). The directors were listed in the order my agent, Jim, thought should be the first choice. I was number five on the list. The list was dated two days after the producer had called me directly at home to ask me to do *Raven*.

Jim became too spread out with the new agency; it almost seemed like he became absent-minded, unfocused. He didn't remember that the producer he sent the list to was also my producer on *The A-Team*. That was the year I left Jim Berkus and UTA.

The pilot for *Raven* starred Jeffrey Meek, who had just starred in a movie called *Winter People*. When I came on board, the most pressing issue before I left to scout locations in Hawaii was to find his co-star, an ex-U.S. Special Forces vet, now a drunken private investigator named Ski.

After reading the script, I came up with two names that felt right - Peter Boyle, who starred in *Joe, Young Frankenstein, Taxi Driver*, and

*The Candidate.* And Badja  Djola, who was in *Mississippi Burning, A Rage in Harlem, The Hurricane,* and *The Last Boy Scout.* Jeff Sagansky, the president of CBS, didn't like Peter Boyle; he wasn't a big fan of his acting. But Jeff was willing to test Badja, even though he had no idea who he was.

I went with Badja for the reading in The Green Room at CBS; I had no idea why they called it that - it was kind of silly. But when we showed up, there was Jeff, with six of his lackeys in black suits, white shirts, and black ties. Badja nailed the reading; I thought he took it to another level.

After he left, Jeff said, "I'm not sure he's right for this."

The meaning was clear to me; he didn't want a black actor in the pilot.

A couple of seconds later, he spoke up again: "I know who we should have in the show." When he mentioned the actor's name, his lackeys chimed in: "That was a brilliant idea Jeff, bla, bla, bla."

I was kind of pissed at the way he treated Badja, so I didn't hold back. "Jeff, I don't know how to tell you this, but the guy you want has been dead for over five years." You could've heard a pin drop.

Jeff just stared at me, then smirked. "Well then, I guess, Mr. Director, we'd better keep looking, huh?" Then he walked out, followed by his lackeys.

It was a pretty cool script; I had John Leonetti as my director of photography. He was the original DP on *Stone Cold.* My take on *Raven* was to make it look and feel like *Black Rain* - very atmospheric.

Valerie and I took the producer, John Ashley, and his wife to see *Black Rain* at Grauman's Chinese Theatre in Hollywood. After watching it, he couldn't have agreed more.

I cast Cary-Hiroyuki Tagawa, who was in *Rising Sun* and *Snow Falling on Cedars,* and Clyde Kusatsu, who was also in *Rising Sun,* as well as *In the Line of Fire,* and many more. I also brought on several great Martial artists to elevate the action sequences: Al Leong, James Lew, and Jeff Imada.

A week before we started filming, CBS finally cast the co-star: Lee Majors. It suddenly became a different show. Jeff and I regrouped, trying to figure out what the tone was going to be. We and the producers thought that it was going to be a darker, edgier piece. Regardless, it was obviously a beautiful location. We shot it in Honolulu and the North Shore. We finished the pilot, it sold, and went right to series. I guess Mr. Sagansky was right.

\* \* \* \* \*

I signed with one of the hottest agents in town, Paul Yamamoto with Favored Artist. We were both surprised to learn that we shared the exact same birthday, right down to the year: October 20th. He was also a surfer.

A couple of weeks after I signed with Paul, I got a call. He told me that he wanted to meet with me, but I could tell something was wrong. At lunch, he told me, "I can't do this anymore. I'm sorry, Craig; I hate this business. I can't do the agent thing anymore. I can't continue to be a bullshit artist. There's got to be something more in life for me out there. I'm out."

I sat there, stunned. I had finally met an agent I liked.

"Would you consider having my assistant rep you?" he asked.

"Are you serious? I just left UTA. You're my guy Paul."

"I'm sorry, Craig."

"I understand." After a couple of seconds, I said, "Scott Henderson? Really?"

"Yes. Scott."

I didn't know what to say.

"Just give him a chance. He's a sharp kid. I've tried to teach him what I know about the business. He'll take care of you; I think he'll be fiercely loyal."

When I met with Scott, he looked like a deer caught in the headlights.

\* \* \* \* \*

I was approached to direct a pet project of Ted Turner's at TNT Classics, *The Avenging Angel*. It was a period piece about the Danites and the Mormon Church. The Danites were the Mormon secret police, vigilantes, who were basically cold-blooded killers. They were called Avenging Angels. The inner core were John Smith's bodyguards. The Danites would do anything for John Smith or Brigham Young.

The executive producers, Esparza-Katz, told my agent that Tom

Berenger had director approval. Esparza-Katz produced *The Milagro Beanfield War*, starring Robert Redford, and *Selena*, starring Jennifer Lopez.

So, the next day I got on a plane with Robert Katz and flew to Cuernavaca, Morelos, Mexico, where Tom was filming *Last of the Dogmen*. We had dinner that night with Tom and discussed *The Avenging Angel*. When we finished, Tom looked at Katz and me and simply said, "Let's do it."

**Craig Baxley, Charlton Heston, and Tom Berenger**

I was working with my favorite casting director, Karen Rea, and my producer, Jay Benson, again. We assembled an amazing cast with Fay Masterson, Jeffrey Jones from *Beetlejuice,* Kevin Tighe, Leslie Hope, Tom Bower, Lisa Banes, James Coburn as Porter Rockwell, and Charlton Heston as Brigham Young.

Charlton Heston, shit, I remember working with him on one of my first jobs in the industry, *Omega Man,* in 1971. How lucky was I to have this opportunity to work with some of the acclaimed actors I grew up watching?

Jay told me Ted (Turner) loved the action in *The Long Riders* and wanted me to put a comparable major action piece in it. Structurally, I thought the beginning of act three was the best place for it. I added a horse chase through the trees, which were about four to five feet apart - I wanted the audience to feel like they were part of the chase, not just watching it. I designed a sequence with ten horsemen pursuing Tom Berenger and Fay Masterson, firing their weapons. Tom's character continued to fire back, taking them out, one by one.

It was a very challenging shoot. We were filming in Utah on some of the actual locations of that period. Now and then, I would notice several men in suits standing in the shadows watching us. Not moving, just watching us - Mormons, members of the Latter-Day Saints church.

After the project was complete, Tom came out to spend a weekend with us in Cali. He loves authentic Mexican food. He was up for Mexican and margaritas, so we took him to our local spot, Los Toros. Our friend Nick, the restaurant owner, and the locals loved seeing Tom Berenger; it was quite a night.

Gary Chang composed an incredible feature film score, similar to *Dances with Wolves.*

\* \* \* \* \*

*Shadow-Ops* was a one-hour backdoor pilot, which was to be filmed in Puerto Vallarta, Mexico. It was written by Peter Barsocchini, who wrote *Drop Zone.* When my agent told me the executive producer was Wallis Nicita, I wasn't sure if it was the same Wally Nicita I knew as one of the biggest casting directors in Hollywood. Wally cast *Silverado, Body Heat, The Witches of Eastwick, The Big Chill,* and

*Caddyshack,* among others.

She had been married to Ric Nicita, one of the founders and a managing partner of CAA. After their divorce, Ric helped orchestrate a deal with Paramount for Wally to become an executive producer. Her first project was *Shadow-Ops.*

During the first week of prep, in the midst of casting, Wallis came rushing into my office; she was very excited. "We got one of the Baldwins to play Dalt!" Dalt was our lead.

"Which one?" I asked. I didn't know what to say as she disappeared into the producer's office to share the news. It wasn't Alec, Billy, Daniel, or Stephen. It was Adam Baldwin; he wasn't one of the Baldwins. Maybe she thought he was a cousin. We never discussed it again. Two days later, we set Adam, who was in *Full Metal Jacket.* I got lucky.

Casting continued as I began to scout locations in Mexico. I chose another actor from his audition tape. The day he showed up on location, he wore a fur coat and had just shaved his head, sporting a cane for style. His name was Terrence Howard. If there was any human being that should shave his head, it was Terrence. He was perfect for the role. Then I added John Ortiz and Leslie Hope to the cast.

On day one of principal filming, we lost Wallis. She was stung by a bee and rushed to the hospital with a potentially life-threatening allergic reaction. It was a helluva way to start production. She returned to the shoot a couple of days later.

*Shadow-Ops* was the first time I worked with David Connell, a brilliant Australian director of photography. He was someone I wanted to work with, and when I found out he was available, I jumped on it. He's one of the most gifted lighting DP's I've ever worked with. He was actually on standby to replace Vittorio Storaro on another film. But I think he enjoyed the way we worked together as much as I did. He loved getting a shot list so he could concentrate on his craft. It was the beginning of a long-lasting friendship and an amazing working relationship.

After *Shadow-Ops,* I worked non-stop, jumping from Movie of the Week to Movie of the Week. And the salary I quoted climbed for each one. Sometimes, I made more than I had on my first feature film, *Action Jackson.*

* * * * *

*Overdrive* was originally written for Clint Eastwood by Dennis Shryack, who wrote *Pale Rider* and *The Gauntlet*. Because of scheduling issues, it never went into production. Eventually, it came back as an action-laden two-hour Movie of the Week, starring Stacy Keach.

Once again, Jay Benson told the studio they'd better get somebody like Craig Baxley to shoot action for *Overdrive*. That day my agent got a call. The deal closed just hours later.

The Vice President of Movies and Mini-series for NBC, Ruth Slawson, couldn't make up her mind if she liked the title or not. She felt it needed to change. I never understood the reasoning. It went from *Overdrive* to *Silent Thunder* to my least favorite - *Revenge on the Highway*. Aside from great performances, it was loaded with major action sequences.

I had a semi-tractor-trailer plow through parked cars (rigged with cannons). They flipped into the air like toys, engulfed in massive fireballs, as the semi continued on. The semi hit another semi-tractor (also rigged with a cannon). It flipped over, rolling three times wheel to wheel as the big rig continued to push it down the highway.

It was not your usual TV movie fare.

After we finished filming, while in post-production, I got a call about another Movie of the Week: *A Family Torn Apart,* starring Neil Patrick Harris and Johnny Galecki. It was written by Matthew Bombeck (Erma Bombeck's son), based on the book *Sudden Fury*. It was a very heavy dramatic piece based on tough love. No action. Not even a slap or punch.

Scott Henderson told me to forget it; ICM had three directors the network was considering.

I said, "Scott, get me in the room. I can nail this."

"Craig, there's no way. It's an ICM package."

"Just get me in the room, Scott!"

We filmed it in Atlanta, Georgia. I had a wonderful director of photography from Brazil, Joao Fernandes, and we put together an incredible local crew for the shoot. The cherry trees were in bloom throughout the city that time of year, and Atlanta was beautiful. And at night, so were the no-see-ums.

* * * * *

As I think back on working with Joao, I remember a funny story he told me.

One night in 2002, Joao and I were having dinner together in Toronto. We were doing *The Glow,* a two-hour Movie of the Week filming in Toronto, which starred Portia de Rossi, now Ellen DeGeneres' wife.

After working together on six Movies of the Week, two cable movies, and a couple of martini's, I guess he thought it was time to confide in me.

He looked at me and said, "You know who I am, don't you?"

"Yeah, Joao, I know who you are," I said.

He started to chuckle to himself. "No, I'm not sure you do; I'm Harry Flecks."

"Who's Harry Flecks?"

"The name was the alias a director gave me. He named me after the Arriflex camera we used on the film we were doing."

"What was the film, Harry?"

"*Deep Throat.*"

"What are you talking about?"

"When I came to this country, it was the only way I could get into the film business."

Here I was looking at this older distinguished man, whom everyone loved. I didn't realize until that moment I was sitting in the presence of greatness.

* * * * *

My agent got a call from Barbara Fisher's office. She was President of Universal Network programing. She and a producer, Dave Bell, were setting up the Sci-fi Network's first in-house movie: *Deep Red.* He was told that I was their first choice.

After reading the script, I was in her office the next day with Dave and the writer, D. Brent Mote. I realized it was kind of a done deal. Barbara asked me who I had in mind for Joe Keyes, the main character. I looked at everyone and said, "Michael Biehn."

Michael had starred in *Terminator, The Abyss,* and *Aliens.*

She laughed, "Dream on. He's doing *Tombstone* with Kurt Russell, Val Kilmer, Sam Elliot, and Bill Paxton."

"Yeah, I know," I said. "But he's perfect for this."

"He'll never do it for the money; this is a cable movie," she said.

That night I called him at his hotel on location. Forty-five minutes later, he committed to do it.

The next morning when I called Barbara, she was in a state of disbelief. "And he'll do it for the money?"

"He'll do it for the money."

I'd been warned - Michael could be trouble. He was hard on directors, and he liked to party. Really party. I found he was like any good actor; he just wanted to work with good filmmakers. If directors weren't prepared or were inexperienced, he would chew them up. We had a great time making *Deep Red;* Michael did an amazing job. He was a perfect Joe Keyes.

Joao Fernandes was my director of photography again, and I wanted to give the film a very noir look and feel. Joao delivered, as usual, it looked amazing. I also cast Joanna Pacula, who was also in *Tombstone,* and Tobin Bell, who worked on *Mississippi Burning* and as Jigsaw in the *Saw* series.

We got a call from Barbara Fisher's office again. Universal was going to handle the production side of the Starz Encore Movie group. *Twilight Man* was to be their first in-house production. After I read it, I could see why; it was a great script. Barbara wanted me to fly to Parker, Colorado, that weekend to meet the founder of Starz. John Malone, one of the richest men in the United States, was going to have a little get-together and wanted a few people to meet his director.

A limo picked me up at the airport in Denver and drove me to his estate. There were over a hundred people there, names and faces I recognized. It was surreal. John Malone certainly wasn't like any executive I'd ever met. And this wasn't like any barbecue I'd ever attended. It was amazing, and so was he.

The next morning I flew back to L.A. to start casting. I found out David Connell was available to shoot it and booked him. *Twilight Man* was the first time I worked with Sonny Baskin. He was the editor on *Overboard* with Kurt Russell and Goldie Hawn, *Purple Rain* with Prince, and *Officer and a Gentleman* with Richard Gere. It was the beginning of a great friendship, and he has edited all of my projects since. He and his wife, Liza, have remained our dearest friends to this day.

We cast my friend, Tim Matheson, as the lead, and were lucky enough to get Dean Stockwell as the co-star. It was kind of a riff on *The Fugitive* that took place over five states. But we filmed the entire thing in Wilmington.

We had a scene in a train station. However, there were no trains or train stations in Wilmington. I found a cafeteria on a college campus where one entire side of the building was a series of giant glass windows. I had the production designer take a couple of photographs of passenger train cars, blow them up and mount them on dollies. As the scene started, I had them pushed into frame, as if the train was coming to a stop outside. Flawless. It looked great.

So did *Twilight Man*. The cable movie looked like a feature film. David Connell as Sonny did a great job.

When my agent mentioned the quote for my salary would be going up on this one, I was shocked when he told me the amount. I asked him, "How high can it go for a cable movie or a Movie of the Week?"

He told me he thought this was it. "Your right up there with Larry," he said.

I asked him, "Who's Larry?"

He said, "Are you kidding? Larry Elikann, the king of Movies of the Week." He went on to tell me Larry makes more than most feature film directors.

Making a Cable Movie or a Movie of the Week was always intense. It could get pretty stressful. Usually, you had twenty days to film it. There was never enough time or money. And they always wanted it to look like a feature film.

If you were at the top of the game, like Larry, you could make a lot of money. He died of a heart attack in 2003.

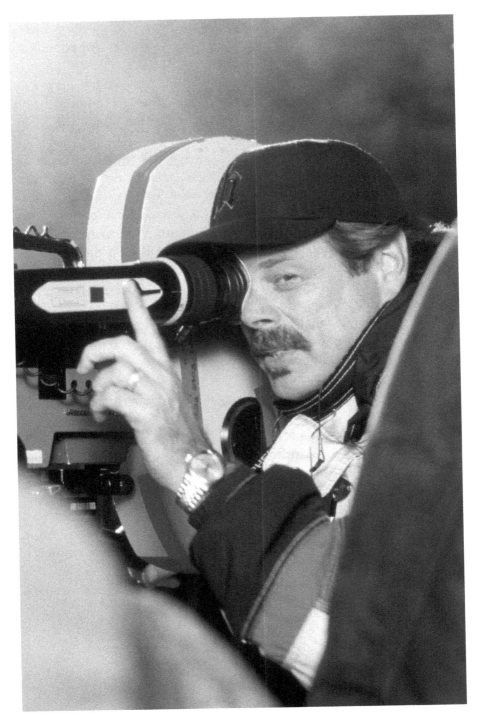

**Craig Baxley**

# CHAPTER 28

## 1997 Should've Had a Happy Ending

Largo Entertainment was founded by Larry Gordon, who later became president of 20th Century Fox Studios. I had worked with Larry several times in the past. I think he was one of the last filmmakers to actually run a studio.

My agent sent me a script Largo had sent over. It was for a feature called *Bad Day on the Block*. The film was about a dysfunctional fireman, similar to the character Michael Douglas played in *Falling Down*. I liked the script, but I thought it needed some work. Before

**Craig Baxley and Director of Photography, David Connell**

I could mention that, he told me I had to meet with the star if I was interested. I asked him who it was, and he said, "Charlie Sheen."

The next day I met with Charlie at a restaurant on Robertson Boulevard in Beverly Hills. Charlie had just come out of rehab, in great shape, and had that sparkle in his eyes. We clicked right away. I think both of us really enjoyed the meeting; Charlie was totally on. He was smart, funny, and very cool.

After my deal was made, I brought on my guys: David Connell, Sonny Baskin, Gary Chang, Karen Rea, my casting director, and my Canadian 1st Assistant Director, Andrew Shea, who I later worked with on *Storm of the Century.*

We cast Mare Winningham and David Andrews as the husband and wife that lived next door to Charlie. Then added John Ratzenberger and Keone Young to the cast.

*Bad Day on the Block* **Cast and Craig Baxley**

I was told by the producers we had $7-8 million to make the film. I thought it was doable, as it was basically a character study of Charlie. Overall, a fairly simple concept: a fireman terrorizing the family next door. One of my concerns was that the film needed to be opened up; it was very claustrophobic as written. The obvious place was the ending.

When I discussed it with one of the producers, he said, "That sounds good, write it."

"What about the writer?" I asked.

"I think we've got her best shot; it's yours now. If you want to fix it, write it."

I pitched the idea to Charlie. He liked it and agreed. So, I wrote a sequence that ended on the freeway with Charlie's character chasing the family, who were fleeing in their family station wagon. I thought the sequence was pretty cool; I came up with an ending that was a complete surprise for the audience.

To save time, I thought I would budget it and shot list part of it during prep. I was pretty happy with it and felt it was the right conclusion. We filmed in Toronto, Canada, in the dead of winter. You have to laugh because the film took place in the San Fernando Valley during a heatwave. The producers had convinced the executives at Largo Pictures there was no problem doubling the San Fernando Valley in Toronto - despite the fact that the houses didn't look anything like the homes in the San Fernando Valley.

Another challenge was a sequence that took place at rush hour, during gridlock on the 118 freeway in the Valley. Anyone who has worked in Toronto knows there isn't anything that remotely looks like the 118 in the Valley. We found a long highway that was the approach to Woodbine Racetrack and dressed it with a center median and lots of signage.

I also had my friend Dennis Jarvis send me a dozen Spyder team surfboards and racks. We dressed the prominent cars in the foreground of the sequence with them. Even I was surprised by how good it looked.

My Canadian special effects coordinator, Michael Kavanagh, did an incredible job with the two major fire sequences. I think they rival any fire sequence ever done.

As we approached the end of production, the unit manager came to me and told me I had to rewrite the ending again. I was kind of blown away; I asked him why.

"We don't have the money to do the freeway sequence."

I said, "What are you talking about? I was told to write the sequence. We're on schedule; I haven't added anything." I was pissed, to say the least.

"I'm sorry. I know how you feel, but the producers just told me to wrap it up in the house. The money just isn't there to do the freeway sequence."

So Charlie and I came up with another concept - the Russian Roulette sequence with the family, where Charlie died in their home.

Charlie was on the entire shoot. It was a great collaboration. The cast and the crew all loved working with him. I thought he gave an amazing performance. He was very generous with the cast and crew. Charlie gave everybody a Mont Blanc pen, and he even had Valerie's and mine engraved.

Months later, after we mixed and previewed the film in Las Vegas, I heard that one or both of the producers were being investigated by Largo for embezzling almost $2 million of our budget.

# CHAPTER 29

## Give Me What I Want, and I'll Go Away

In 1998 I was about to meet on another project when my agent got a call. "Stephen King wants to meet you." I thought he was full of shit; why would Stephen King want to meet me?

"I'm serious," he said. "He saw *Twilight Man* and loved it. He's written a six-hour Mini-Series; it's called *Storm of the Century.*"

"And…" I waited for him to continue.

"And the director that worked with him on *The Stand*, Mick Garris, told him it was impossible to make."

"And…"

"Stephen wants to fly you to Bangor, Maine, and discuss it."

The next day I was on a plane to Boston. I flew with Mark Carliner, the executive producer on *The Stand*. Mark spent the entire flight telling me how much Stephen loved him. It was a long flight.

We landed in Boston during a massive snowstorm. We were the last flight they allowed to land as the airport closed down. It was a three-and-a-half-hour drive from Boston to Bangor. In a storm, it could take twice that. Carliner asked me to drive; he said, "I don't do snow."

When Mark called Stephen, Steve knew what was happening and said he'd drive halfway to meet us in Portland, Maine, at his daughter's restaurant.

A couple of minutes after we got there, an old pick-up pulled up out front, and in walked Stephen King.

I liked him the second I met him; I think we both felt like kindred-spirits.

Mark was also from the east coast; he told Steve I was a west coast guy, born and raised in Southern California, that I was a water guy.

Steve smiled and said, "So, what do I call you? Surfer Joe?"

"No, my friends call me Bax."

The meeting went better than I ever could've imagined. Most importantly, we discussed everything and why I didn't see any problem making *Storm of the Century.*

"It's certainly challenging," I said, "but I've always loved a good challenge."

Steve just smiled and looked at Mark. "Bax is my guy."

Once I started prep, I was told ABC was thinking about Tom Berenger or Gabriel Byrne for the lead. I knew what the casting budget was; I knew we had a problem. *Storm of the Century* had over sixty speaking roles, thirty-five of which were basically co-starring roles. We also had eight children, ages five to six, who were featured as well.

**Craig Baxley and Stephen King**

We needed to find Linoge, a mysterious stranger who came to Little Tall Island, off the coast of Maine, during the heaviest snowstorm in the last hundred years. Linoge's name is a corruption of the French word for snow, "La Neige."

I called Steve and told him what I was thinking. Instead of blowing a major portion of our casting budget on the lead, I thought finding a great ensemble cast made more sense. He agreed and told ABC what we wanted to do.

The next week I flew to New York with Mark Carliner and met with our casting director, Lynn Kressel, to begin casting. We started there because of the incredible talent pool, not only from the industry but also from the stage.

One day, as I walked down the hall to her office, I heard a familiar voice as I passed a smaller office. I stopped in front of the open door, and a woman, the only person in the office, turned back. It was Ruth Slawson, the former Vice President of Movies and Mini-Series for NBC - the executive that changed the title of *Overdrive* to *Revenge on the Highway*.

"Are you going to Lynn's?" she asked.

I told her we were here to cast *Storm of the Century* for ABC. "They're lucky to have you; maybe we could do something together."

I said, "Sounds good, let's catch up later."

Lynn told me Ruth's fall from grace wasn't pretty. Her new headquarters was now that tiny office.

As *Storm of the Century* began to come together, I had a thought for the character Robbie Beals, the Mayor of Little Tall Island. A couple of years earlier, I'd seen an actor in *Citizen X* - Jeffrey DeMunn - he played a Russian serial killer who never spoke a word. He was brilliant.

Lynn said, "Forget it; he'll never do it. He's doing features now. We don't have his money either."

I told her, "Just get me in a room with him. Contact his agent and tell him I loved him in *Citizen X* and that I'd love to meet him."

Jeffrey was also in *The Shawshank Redemption*, *The Green Mile*, and *The Mist*.

The next day after lunch, he came in wearing jeans, a T-shirt, Converse tennis shoes, and a backward baseball hat. A half-hour later, he was set. As we worked together, I soon discovered Jeffrey is one of the smartest and nicest actors I've ever had the pleasure of working with.

And so it went with our casting. ABC kept throwing well-known television actors at us for Linoge. Collaboration is very important to me; I was beginning to second guess myself. But none of them felt right. I thought we needed a completely unknown actor for the role—an actor with no excess baggage.

I'd seen a dramatic Canadian documentary about the eccentric Canadian pianist Glenn Gould, called *Thirty Short Films about Glenn Gould*. It starred Colm Feore, a classically trained actor and a thirteen-year veteran of the Stratford Film Festival in Ontario, Canada - North America's largest classical repertory theater. I sent a tape of the *Glenn Gould* movie to Steve, and he agreed we had our Linoge.

We had an amazing cast, actors from all over the country—Boston, New York, Los Angeles, Toronto, and Nova Scotia. Tim Daly, Casey Siemaszko, Debrah Farentino, Julianne Nicholson, Kathleen Chalfant (an incredible stage actress), Becky Ann Baker, Steve Rankin, and many other gifted actors.

As it turned out, *Storm of the Century* was the most demanding job to date that I've ever done—both mentally and physically. Steve had written a piece in which a snowstorm raged for over five and a half hours of a six-hour mini-series. Aside from my director of photography, David Connell, I was lucky to be working with one of the smartest and most creative producers in the industry, Robert Phillips. I also had my editor, Sonny Baskin, and my composer, Gary Chang, working with me. As we assembled our crew, I realized that most of our keys from Toronto were the best in Canada.

David and I decided we wanted to desaturate the film for the exterior shots and take the silver out of the development process, which would give everything a colder look. ABC didn't want to because once it's done, there's no going back. With Steve's support, we went forward with it.

In pre-production, during the dead of winter, Bob, David, and I took a six-man crew to film Peggy's Cove Lighthouse in Nova Scotia. The temperature was 30 to 35 degrees below.

We utilized real, man-made, and synthetic snow throughout shooting to simulate the storm. We filmed the interiors and sixty percent of the town exteriors in Toronto, Canada.

**Dolly track down the main street during a snowstorm, Southwest Harbor**

We built a double for the main street of Little Tall in a giant beet factory in Mississauga, a forty-five-minute drive from Toronto. The actual location for Little Tall was located in Southwest Harbor, Maine. It was a long five-month shoot.

My first assistant, Andrew Shea, said we should stay in a hotel in Mississauga instead of driving an hour and a half each way every day. We were shooting nights; at the end of the first day, I went to bed at 6:30 a.m. A couple of seconds later, I thought there was an earthquake.

The rumbling kept growing louder and louder. Then there was a pounding on my hotel door. I leaped up and opened the door. There stood a dozen five- and six-year-old Pee Wee Ice hockey players. It was the Canadian Pee Wee championships for the next two weeks. I looked out into the hallway; dozens and dozens of other Pee Wee's were streaming down the corridor. They looked crazed.

I decided the forty-five-minute drive was worth it.

The majority of the interiors were designed by our production designer, Craig Stearns. They were built on a number of sound stages and warehouses throughout the city.

While working in the city, Valerie and I had a standing diner reservation every Saturday night at Sarkis on Richmond, next to Golden Thai. It was a tiny twelve-table restaurant. The executive chef, Greg Couillard, was an incredible, notorious Canadian Chef who rarely lasted over a year at any restaurant. He had a well-deserved bad-boy reputation, but he was one of the best chefs in North America. He ran a small, high-intensity kitchen that rivaled Susur Lee's Lotus, which was undoubtedly the most innovative restaurant in Toronto or North America. It was always something to look forward to during the grueling shoot.

Throughout the shooting schedule, we made three trips to Maine. The company chartered a DC3 for the cast and crew. The first time

**Director Craig Baxley on camera**

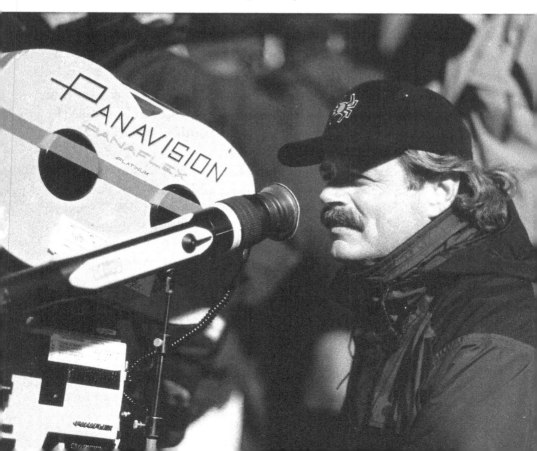

was in the dead of winter. The day we landed, it was the worst ice storm in over eighty years. Our company had the only power on Mount Pleasant Island. As our generators hummed, we continued filming into the night. It was almost thirty below.

While standing in video village, I finally pulled the plug on the first night of filming around 2 a.m. when I looked down and realized David's shoes were frozen to the plywood floor.

The last two trips were in spring and summer.

In the mini-series, the spring thaw was just beginning, and the problem was that when we arrived in Maine, there was no snow. Our special effects crew went right to work making synthetic snow. It started snowing halfway through the second day; we had exactly what we wanted - we couldn't have been luckier.

The next week we shot next to Beal's on the pier in Southwest Harbor. The restaurant was a local favorite and had dozens of lobster trucks floating in the bay. Valerie and I befriended the owner during our filming there; a couple of days a week, he would give us a few three-pound lobsters minus one claw. Valerie would throw them in a pot, and I'd make a homemade Ceasar salad with a little crusty bread. If there was heaven on earth, this was it.

Although, a couple of weekends, we went to Geddy's in Bar Harbor. They were known for taking a large lobster, cutting it in half with a cleaver, basting it with garlic butter, and putting it under the broiler. Then they put it in a basket with fries. That might've been a close second.

\* \* \* \* \*

CGI was really starting to creep into the industry. We did a lot of sky replacements that I thought were very effective. And we also used it for a flying sequence with the children and a couple of transitions with Linoge. Both screamed of CGI; I wasn't a fan. We also had a miniature unit that dealt with the lighthouse, using plates we shot in pre-production and the dock sequence. But for the most part, *Storm of the Century* was shot in camera. Nearing the end of our principal filming, we were all set to do the aerials one weekend. They were the establishing shots of the ferry to Little Tall Island and the opening shots.

I had three producers on the mini-series: Executive producer, Mark Carliner, who basically sat in the production office and came to the set for lunch; Bob Phillips, who really did all the producing and heavy lifting; and Tom Brodek, the network guy.

David and I were preparing to go up in the camera ship when Tom walked up and said, "We've got a report of thunder clouds moving into the area; it doesn't look good."

"Do you want to push it to tomorrow?" I asked.

"Not going to happen, we only have David and the helicopter for one day this weekend - today."

David spoke up: "Mate, I don't mind. We can do it tomorrow; I'm not even charging the company for today."

Tom just shook his head. "It's today or never."

I looked up at the sky; it was getting dark.

"Mate, I can't do it - not with the weather report. Let's see if Bob can find the money to do it another time."

I knew where we were with the budget; it wasn't going to happen. I looked at the pilot, "What do you think?"

"I think we can beat the front." I nodded okay.

He shook his head, smiled, "If you want to do it, let's do it."

He and I went up and completed everything. As we flew back to the airport, it started to pour.

After principal was completed, I took a small second unit with David Connell, Bob Phillips, and a half dozen crew members to San Francisco and then onto the Mojave Desert to complete the series. Gary Chang once again wrote an incredible score, reminiscent of *The Shawshank Redemption.*

Making *Storm of the Century* was one of the most gratifying experiences I've ever had in the motion picture business. Steve told me that he loved it, that it was his favorite television special based on his material.

*Storm of the Century* won a Saturn Award and a KHG (International Horror Guild) Award for Best Television Presentation in 2000. It also won a primetime Emmy for Sound Editing. It was nominated for a primetime Emmy in Outstanding Visual Effects and by the Casting Society of America for an "Artios" - Best Casting.

After *Storm of the Century* aired, I got a call from Steve. He was ecstatic; he wanted me to fly to Bangor to discuss our next project together. The next day I got on a plane with Mark Carliner and flew to meet with him.

At lunch, he gave me a 1500-page manuscript. It was titled *Dreamcatcher*. It was about four childhood friends who saved Duddits, an older boy with Down syndrome, from a sadistic group of bullies. They began to share his unusual powers, including telepathy, shared dreams, and seeing "The Line" - a psychic trace left by the movement of human beings.

Steve told us, "This one is going to be a major mini-series, bigger than *Storm of the Century*."

I read it on the plane flying back to L.A. The following morning, when we landed, I called my agent and told him the news about *Dreamcatcher*; he said, "Haven't you read the trades this morning?"

"What are you talking about?"

He continued, "Castle Rock just optioned *Dreamcatcher* for Lawrence Kasdan." Kasdan had directed *The Big Chill, Silverado, Wyatt Earp,* and *Grand Canyon.*

Stephen called me that morning and told me the news. He said he was sorry - that his agent, Rand Holston at Creative Artists Agency (CAA), had given the option to Castle Rock. But, he said, "I've got something else in mind for you, Bax."

# CHAPTER 30

## Serendipity

Coming off *Storm of the Century,* I received a call from my agent. I think Scott was becoming overwhelmed. ABC and the two executive producers of a ten-part mini-series wanted me to alternate with another director already onboard as a producer. The executive producers were Sidney Poitier and Harry Belafonte. They owned the rights to *Parting the Waters,* written by the Pulitzer Prize winner Taylor Branch.

It was a masterful account of the American Civil Rights Movement from 1954-63. The fact that I had just become available put me in the mix.

After ABC interviewed almost every director in town, I was honored to be considered. The only problem was that it was Friday and the decision had to be made on Monday.

I was asked to meet with the director, Jon Avnet, on Sunday at his home in Topanga Canyon. John was a good filmmaker; he directed *Fried Green Tomatoes* and *Red Corner* with Richard Gere. I was familiar with *Parting the Waters,* but obviously, I couldn't read the entire book (1088 pages) in one day. I still took the meeting though.

Jon took me on a tour of his entire house; he was very proud of it. We ended up in his screening room and met with Harry and Sidney's reps. Sidney smiled at me, and after he left, we got into the material. We discussed it in depth. I really enjoyed the meeting. The two reps definitely responded to my take on the material. Jon is a very smart filmmaker. I felt the collaboration could work; we were absolutely on the same page.

After the meeting, as we walked back to my car, Jon was very cordial. I remember his last words as he smiled, "Do you believe in serendipity?"

As I drove away, I thought about that moment. It seemed disingenuous, a bit odd. What the fuck? Of course I believe in it. Although different levels outweigh others, it's just a part of life. We all make choices.

Unbeknownst to me, ABC, Sidney, Harry, and Jon had already made a choice a couple of days earlier. He had chosen a friend of his, another TV director, to alternate on *Parting the Waters* with him. I never spoke to Jon after that, but I always thought it was kind of chicken-shit of him to waste my time that weekend.

Later I heard that Sidney and Harry had pulled the project from ABC. I got a call from one of Sidney's reps; she said, "Sidney was pissed and wanted you to say hello to your father for him."

My father had worked with Sidney on *All the Young Men*, playing a part alongside Sidney and Alan Ladd. So much for serendipity.

\* \* \* \* \*

Stephen King had written the first draft of *The Haunting* for DreamWorks. It was based on the novel, *The Haunting of Hill House*. When Steven Spielberg didn't respond to it, he and Stephen parted ways. Steve re-worked it into *Rose Red*, a six-hour mini-series for ABC.

DreamWorks went on to make *The Haunting* with Jan de Bont directing. The tagline for The Haunting was: "Some Houses are born bad," which Stephen King wrote.

Unlike *Storm of the Century*, which Stephen and I cast, ABC was now under a new regime. Maura Dunbar had replaced Barbara Lieberman, whom we had dealt with on *Storm of the Century*. Maura was Barbara's secretary at that time. And Maura was now in charge of mini-series and special projects. She insisted on being more involved in the casting process.

Once again, we were working with the same casting director, Lynn Kressel. In the beginning, none of us were happy with most of the names that Maura and ABC mentioned. Eventually, we worked through it, and it came together.

I've made it a point not to dis anyone in this book. However,

I have to make one exception. Two days before we were to start production, Maura demanded we cast an actor in the co-starring role of Steve Rimbauer. It was clear from the day he stepped on the set he was completely wrong for the role. It was the first time I'd worked with such an unpleasant actor. It wasn't so much that he had to let everyone, cast and crew, know that he went to Juilliard; he just made everyone's life miserable, a total nightmare. He refused to hit a mark, which made us adjust how we filmed his scenes. In the end, his persona came across on the screen as well.

When Steve saw his dailies for the first time, he said, "This guy's an asshole; you have to make him more likable, Bax."

I said, "Steve, I don't think he's capable of it; he's just playing himself. The cast and crew can't stand him."

"Make him likable, Bax. That's why you get the big bucks."

Steve was right. I did what I could, but it was what it was; I never heard much about him after that.

Thank God it was a great ensemble cast. I had Nancy Travis, and people probably don't realize what a great actress she is. She definitely elevated the material. I also had Julian Sands, David Dukes, Kimberly Brown, Judith Ivey, Kevin Tighe, Matt Ross, Tsidii Leloka, Melanie Lynskey, and Emily Deschanel.

*Rose Red* was the first time Steve had me doing the re-writes on set. I'd make a pass and send it on to Steve for his approval. It was a great experience getting inside his head. He's an absolute genius. I learned so much from him about writing and developing a character arc.

Once again, I worked with the same team I had on *Storm of the Century:* Producer Robert Phillips, DP David Connell, Production Designer Craig Stearns, Editor Sonny Baskin, Composer Gary Chang, and my son, Craig Baxley Jr. as the stunt coordinator. We created the illusion of the sprawling Rose Red mansion in the heart of downtown Seattle, Washington. The main part of the Manor was actually Thornewood Castle in Tacoma, Washington, about forty-five minutes south of downtown Seattle.

To create the illusion of it being in downtown Seattle, we relocated the main gate we built at Thornewood. After completing the coverage in Tacoma, we moved the main gate set piece to downtown Seattle where we did the reverse coverage of all the scenes. The aerials were done with CGI and a miniature build. The interiors were built on sound stages outside Seattle at Sand Point Naval Base. Sand Point is located about five miles northeast of downtown Seattle.

We tried to ground the CGI/Visual Effects in reality. I was also very lucky to have Stuart Robinson as my visual effects supervisor. Stuart won an Academy Award for *What Dreams May Come.*

There were truly some amazing sequences in the mini-series. One of my favorites was when the boulders started raining from the sky on a house in the opening. And then again on Rose Red in the final sequence.

It was second nature the way we all worked together. The creativity, the respect we all had for each other. It was a great team. They all made me look good. In the end, I think we elevated the material. Steve was very happy with the result.

After filming, the producers were contacted by Tim McGraw and Faith Hill's representative. They were interested in buying Rose Red. Even though they were told it didn't exist, they continued to inquire about the purchase for months.

*Rose Red* was nominated in several categories in 2002:
- A Saturn Award for Best Television Presentation.
- An IHG Award for Best Television Presentation.
- Best Visual Effects in a mini-series.
- Best Production Design for a mini-series.

# CHAPTER 31

## 9-11-2001

Like the rest of the world, the motion picture business came to a halt on September 11, 2001. Like everyone else, I became unemployed.

One of the first films to start production after that fateful day was *Sniper 2*. My agent told me I had a meeting at Screen Gems; the picture was actually being made for Columbia Pictures. He said it had the same budget as *Sniper,* $20 million. And the star, Tom Berenger, had already signed off on me.

When I took the meeting at Screen Gems, the executive told me that the budget was not $20 million; it was only $5 million. Tom was to get a million and a half; five hundred thousand would cover the salaries for the rest of the cast. I would have $3 million to make the movie, and it was to be shot in Budapest, Hungary.

Hungarian and Finish are probably two of the most difficult languages to learn. It made learning Japanese from my Berlitz tapes back in the day look easy.

The next agenda was trying to get inside the heads of the two writers. *Sniper 2* was written by Ron Mita and Jim McClain. They also wrote the feature film *S.W.A.T.,* which made the television series from the seventies look brilliant. Not only did I have a concern about the budget, but I also had a bigger concern about the action; it read like a bad Chuck Norris movie. The Sniper, Tom Berenger, killed hundreds of soldiers to get from point A to point B.

The executive at Screen Gems agreed with me and told me to address it with the writers. The next day I had the writers come to my home. As we discussed my concerns, I quickly realized it wasn't in their wheelhouse to solve the problem. The corny ideas kept coming.

I suggested that we come up with something better. Rather than try to make a movie that we couldn't afford, I suggested a concept that we could do within our budgetary constraints.

Basically, I pitched the idea of another sniper and his elite team tracking our sniper and his spotter. They loved the idea, so I wrote the sequences.

I brought on David Connell, Sonny Baskin, an American 1st Assistant Director, and my son as the stunt coordinator and second unit director.

Filming in Budapest was challenging to say the least. The language was a very tough thing to overcome with our resources. Another was the Buda bureaucracy.

One of the sequences I wrote involved a streetcar that our two leads tried to escape in. They commandeered it and roared down the tracks, only to find two police cars had been pulled onto the tracks directly in front of them. Both police cars were rigged with cannons and loaded with gas bombs. My son doubled Berenger, and he crashed the streetcar into the two vehicles, which were meant to be blown out of the way on impact.

Everything was going great until two different municipal cars arrived. A half-dozen government officials in suits stepped onto the set. It seemed each one of the two tracks was in a different district. Our location manager had gotten the permit from one district, but not the other. And he was clearly not happy with us being there.

We sat there for over an hour as they yelled and argued with each other. We had no idea what they were saying or what was going to happen. In the end, it was just about a pay-off.

Another time, while moving through the heart of the city, I noticed our police escort suddenly pulled over. I cut the camera as the two motorcycle officers ran past our van.

When we opened the rear doors, Tom stepped out with the sniper rifle, and that's when two other police officers drew down on Tom. It was some serious shit. These guys looked like they weren't fucking around. Our two officers were screaming and waving their arms at them. Nobody was moving. Tom continued holding the rifle over his head; it seemed like a moment frozen in time. We had no idea what anyone was saying. And then... everyone stopped talking. It was a bizarre standoff.

A couple of minutes later, our production support vehicle pulled up. After more yelling and more arm waving, we were allowed to get back into the van and return to basecamp. To live another day.

We completed the film on time and on budget. I think we were all surprised at how good it looked. After the screening at Columbia Studios in Culver City, the President of Columbia stood up and asked where I was in the room. He looked at me and said, "It looks great. If it weren't Tom Berenger, I would give this film a major theatrical release. Well done." Then he began to congratulate the executives at Screen Gems and their president, Clint Culpepper.

Valerie leaned over and whispered, "That's a buzz kill; I love you."

While in post-production on *Sniper 2*, a script arrived in the editing room. Stephen had just finished writing a screenplay with Ridley Pearson, titled *The Diary of Ellen Rimbauer*. It was a stand-alone two-hour prequel to *Rose Red*. ABC wanted to go right into production.

While finishing up the mix on *Sniper 2*, we began the casting process. We cast Lisa Brenner as Ellen Rimbauer, Lisa co-starred in *The Patriot* with Mel Gibson, and Steven Brand, who had just co-starred with Dwayne "The Rock" Johnson in *The Scorpion King*.

When I met Steven, he mentioned he had just worked with a friend of mine - Al Leong, the sword fighting coordinator on *The Scorpion King*. He loved Al. Who doesn't?

We filmed *The Diary of Ellen Rimbauer* in some of the same locations that we had *Rose Red* - in Seattle and at Thornewood Castle in Tacoma. We shot it in twenty days. It was nominated for a Saturn Award in 2004 for Best Television Presentation.

* * * * *

I got a call from Stephen. He had just finished writing a new series based on Lars von Trier's *The Kingdom*, an eight-hour Danish mini-series based on Riget. Riget means The Realm or The Kingdom. Although it was based on *The Kingdom*, Steve had definitely made it his own.

His *Kingdom Hospital* was a fifteen-hour series, made up of thirteen stand-alone episodes, which opened with a two-hour premiere and closed with a two-hour finale. I couldn't put it down. After I read it,

I called him.

"So, you liked it, huh?" Steve said.

"What do you think?"

"Good, because you're going to direct the whole series."

I didn't know what to say; I was literally at a loss for words.

"Steve, this is a juggernaut. It's incredible. But how about I direct the opening two-hour and the finale two-hour?" The line was silent, so I went on, "And all the action and the visual effects?"

He laughed, "If you can do all that, you can direct the whole series. You're my guy."

\* \* \* \* \*

In March of 2003, Valerie and I were invited to the premiere of *Dreamcatcher* in Westwood. We were seated next to Steve's accountant and his wife. As the movie was about to start, the accountant looked over and asked, "So, you're Craig and Valerie?" I nodded yes and introduced him and his wife to Valerie. Somewhere behind us, a voice rang out. I mean rang out.

"Craig Baxley? Where is Craig Baxley?"

Valerie and I turned back. I looked at the faces of Frank Marshall, Lawrence Kasdan, Frank Darabont, and several other major players in the industry – they were all watching Stephen King walk down the aisle.

"Craig Baxley. Where is my director? Craig, stand up!"

Frank looked at me with a "What the fuck is going on?" look.

"Stand up, Craig!"

Valerie nudged me and whispered, "Stand up."

I slowly stood up. Everyone in the entire theater was staring at me as Steve walked up and put his arm around me. "I just wanted to introduce everybody to my director; he's going to direct my entire new series, *Kingdom Hospital*. He's a helluva guy."

I didn't know what to say; I just stood there. Then he smiled at me and said, "Okay, now you can sit down, Bax." Which I did as Stephen walked up to the front of the theater. "Isn't he a great guy?" he questioned before he introduced *Dreamcatcher* to the audience.

The screenplay for *Dreamcatcher* was written by Lawrence Kasdan (*The Big Chill*) and William Goldman (*Butch Cassidy and the Sundance*

*Kid* and *All the President's Men*). How could they get it so wrong? It became a movie about shit weasels, some kind of creature coming out of one's ass. Nothing but visual effects and Morgan Freeman looking like Don King. Those eyebrows almost poked my eyes out. I thought Steve deserved better.

The next week I was at ABC. Understandably, Sony and ABC wanted thirteen different directors to do the series.

When Disney and ABC hired Susan Lyne as the president of ABC Entertainment, it was a whole new era at ABC. Susan was a filmmaker's friend. She loved Steve and told the heads at Sony that they would meet at ABC and hear "how and why Craig Baxley thinks he can do the whole series."

A couple of days later, I was in a conference room with the heads of ABC, Sony, and their executives, giving my take on *Kingdom Hospital*. I think I hooked them when I suggested block-shooting locations out. In some cases, the reverses would be shot a month or two later, which meant we wouldn't need to return to the same locations for each episode repeatedly. I'm not sure all of them got it; a couple of executives tried to second guess how that was possible.

I explained, "I shot list everything and would also have schematics of every scene and video playback to refresh the actor's memory." I also suggested doing it in two blocks of six months each.

At the end of the meeting, I looked up at Susan; she smiled and just nodded.

When I arrived on location in Vancouver, British Columbia, I was feeling pretty good. I had the team together again. I also found the perfect place for Valerie and George, our Rottweiler, to make me feel at home.

I learned a lot about my producers during Stephen King's three previous projects. All I can say is I'm glad I had Robert Phillips on board; he truly produced all three of them. He's one of the few filmmakers I've worked with through the years that I can say is really a producer. He's smarter than any other producer I've worked with.

Mark Carliner found his groove. Basically, he would show up for lunch, then be gone until the next day at lunchtime.

*The third Producer, Tom Brodek, only lasted through the prep of Kingdom Hospital.* Apparently, the scope of the production was too much for him. One day during prep, he just disappeared and went back to California. It was very strange; he never said why or goodbye to anyone.

Sony Pictures wanted the series to be shot on HD video. With their HD cameras. This was during the infancy of HD in the motion picture industry, before the video revolution found its way. My DP, David Connell, and I wanted to shoot on 35mm film. Back then, you basically had to shoot everything on Prime lens - there was no depth of field. How do you make a thriller with no depth of field? Everything shot on HD had the look of a bad soap, sometimes worse. There was only one reason Sony wanted to shoot on HD; it was cheaper. It was clear they didn't care what it looked like. Steve agreed and paid for the additional expenses to shoot on film out of his own pocket.

This was years before the Alexi, Red, Panavision Genesis, Sony Cinealta F65, and the Arricam, which changed the face of filmmaking forever. With a good lighting DP, like David, it can look amazing, and now I love to use it.

Shooting *Kingdom Hospital* made *Storm of the Century* look like a Movie of the Week. Every episode was almost a movie on its own. Once again, we had one of the best crews in Canada. Everyone was very excited to be working on *Kingdom Hospital.*

During the first few weeks of filming, the guy on our coffee truck brought me a coffee. He said, "A friend of yours, Mick Garris, is directing *Riding the Bullet* and said to say hello. He wanted to buy you a coffee." (*Riding the Bullet* was based on a Stephen King short story.)

I smiled, "Mick Garris? How long's the shoot."

"Twenty-one days," he said. "In and out."

I told him, "Tell Mick thanks for everything." (What I actually meant was, "Thank you for telling Stephen King *Storm of the Century* was impossible to make.") I bought Mick a coffee every day for the remainder of his shoot.

I'm not sure I want to know where Steve went in his mind to write this one. It was the densest piece of material I've ever read. The most bizarre character was the Antibus, a giant telepathic anteater, which was actually the Egyptian deity Anubis. Anteaters are toothless insect-eating mammals. They have a long tubular muzzle and a worm-like tongue to lap up ants and insects. Antibus, as written, was a mysterious, threatening creature. I felt I had the dramatic license to come up with something more visual that would support that.

I decided to pitch Steve an idea. I illustrated the anteater with a mouth positioned under the long muzzle. When the Antibus opened its mouth, razor sharp teeth (similar to shark's teeth) would splay forward into a threatening position. He liked the idea, so we moved forward and created the creature.

While filming, Valerie and I lived in a house on Ogden in Kitsilano Beach. The house faced out onto English Bay and had panoramic views of the North Shore Mountains. For the next year, it was our home away from home.

Our cast came together as we continued to prep: Andrew McCarthy, Bruce Davison, Ed Begley Jr., Jamie Harrold, Jack Coleman, Julian Richings, and Diane Ladd (Laura Dern's mother). I sat down with producer Bob Phillips, my first assistant Steve Webb, David Connell, and our Canadian unit manager, Mary Anne Waterhouse (who was amazing). We came up with a game plan of how to block shoot the hospital.

We had two hospitals: the modern-day hospital and the dead hospital. Where Steve came up with that, I don't know. We block shot each one out. We shot the good hospital out for every episode it was in, then re-dressed the entire hospital, and shot the dead hospital out.

Every episode had something very unique in it. One had a character named Headless Frank running around Kingdom Hospital carrying his head in his hands. *The Young and the Headless, Hook's Kingdom, Butter Fingers, Black Noise* - it was never-ending. There were mysterious earthquakes, and a cast of some of the most bizarre characters that I've ever read or seen.

Speaking of bizarre, Valerie and I planned a birthday dinner for our friend David Connell. Valerie asked David what he wanted for dinner; he told Valerie, "Craig's ribs, fries, and martinis."

Diane Ladd overheard the conversation and said, "I'd love to come, but I don't eat meat or drink."

That weekend the four of us got together; David was in heaven. The man can eat. Diane was in heaven too. She ate four racks of ribs and drank three martinis. So much for abstaining from meat and alcohol.

\* \* \* \* \*

Sonny Baskin and I would cut the dailies every day at lunch, so we could finish each episode. Then we would Skype Gary Chang back in California and spot the music with him. Gary is one of the most brilliant composers I've ever worked with; he always brings something beyond my vision and elevates the material.

I wasn't getting much sleep those days, but it sure was a great ride. When Steve wasn't on the set, we'd send him the cut sequences for his approval. As the series budget increased to avoid Sony's interference, Steve paid for all the overages himself. I've never worked with a more collaborative and supportive filmmaker in my life than Stephen King. There's nobody like him. God, I love the guy.

As we finished production, I was given the bible for the second season. Steve said, "We're going Voodoo on this one; it's going to be freaky, Bax."

When Valerie and I read it, we just looked at each other. How the fuck does this guy keep coming up with such fresh ideas? It was Stephen King at his best.

I couldn't wait to start the new season; I was all in. Once again, he wanted me to direct the entire season. My mind went into overdrive.

When Susan Lyne saw the end product of *Kingdom Hospital,* she let Steve know how much she loved it. She really loved it. Susan was responsible for other successful shows, such as *Lost* and *Desperate Housewives.*

She was turning the network around, making it number one again. And Steve was part of it. She told him she really wanted to push the envelope and do a programming stunt like Fox did with the *X-Files* – she wanted to run the same episode twice a week.

Steve loved the idea and went to work. He paid for a media blitz out of his own pocket, and he took out full-page ads in major newspapers across the country.

But unbeknownst to Steve, Susan had just been blindsided. Disney fired her and brought in Stephen McPherson. McPherson liked *Kingdom Hospital* but felt it wasn't under his tenure. He decided not only would he not air it twice a week, but he would move it from the great time slot we had to another slot - up against the number one show in television, *CSI.*

When we all tuned in on the nights it was scheduled, there was no *Kingdom Hospital.* Steve was devastated, or more to the point, pissed.

Number one, about Susan Lyne being fired. He genuinely liked her; that was a first for Steve with any network executive. He didn't like many of them. Two, about what a fucked-up move McPherson made. Steve had just told all his fans how proud he was of *Kingdom Hospital* – about the media blitz and the double airings. McPherson just buried it.

Steve is a stand-up guy; he didn't deserve it.

We didn't make the second season.

I still have the bible.

*Kingdom Hospital* won a Visual Effects Society Award. It was also nominated for an IHG Award for Best Television Presentation and a Primetime Emmy for Outstanding Visual Effects in 2004-2005.

# CHAPTER 32

## Home in Time for Dinner

Valerie and I were just about to start dinner when I got a call from Stephen. He was in Los Angeles for the movie premiere of *The Manchurian Candidate*. He stayed at the Hotel Bel-Air in Stone Canyon, and he wanted to invite us to the premiere. He asked us to join him for dinner at the hotel, then ride with him to the theater.

When we arrived, he gave Valerie a big hug and said, "I've ordered dinner; we have to be at the screening in a couple of hours. Valerie, you look great. Craig, okay, not so bad."

The meal was amazing; after eating and catching up, we climbed into his limo. He just smiled at us, "You guys are beautiful; let's have some fun tonight, huh?"

When we arrived at the Samuel Goldwyn Theater on Wilshire Boulevard, I realized it was a black-tie affair. People were walking the red carpet.

Steve was wearing an athletic jacket and jeans; I had on a Tommy Bahama shirt and jeans, as usual. And Valerie looked great. As Steve climbed out, I looked at Valerie and shrugged, "Let's go."

He motioned us along as he was ushered down the red carpet. He stopped in front of the Foreign Press, cameras clicking like machine guns. Steve answered a question, then turned to us and introduced us to the press. Valerie and I knew they didn't give a shit about us, but that was Steve. He was refreshingly down to earth.

As we arrived in the lobby, Steve introduced us to the director. He had a cabin in Lovell, Maine, across from Steve's cabin. It was Jonathan Demme, the director of *Silence of the Lambs*.

He gave me a "Do I know you?" look, and I heard Valerie

whisper, "Oh no." But it wasn't another Doppelgänger moment; I actually knew him.

I just smiled and said, "Jonathan, I worked with you on *Citizen Band*." That was one he directed in 1977, which starred Paul LeMat (he also starred in *American Graffiti*).

\* \* \* \* \*

My father had been hired as the stunt coordinator on *Citizen Band*, but he wasn't available when it was time for him to do the film. So, my father made a deal on his fee and the stunt adjustments with Ben Chapman, a friend of his who was the production manager.

I got a call from Ben, telling me I had a pre-paid ticket at Burbank Airport. I had no idea what he was talking about. Somebody forgot to tell the stunt guy.

When I arrived in Sacramento, Roy Hollis, the transportation coordinator, picked me up. I had worked with Roy on *Diamonds are Forever*. On the way to the location, Roy asked how I wanted the vehicle rigged for the stunt, since he only had the morning to get it done. I had no idea what he was talking about.

Somebody forgot to tell the stunt guy.

When we arrived on location, Ben walked up to me smiling. I'd worked with Ben a dozen times through the years. "This is a quick one. You should be back on the plane later this afternoon."

"Okay, sounds good. So, what's up, Ben?" I glanced at Roy, who was standing nearby.

Ben told me I needed to drive down the two-lane road as a bi-plane flew overhead. The plane would loop and land on the road directly in front of me; then, it would continue to taxi directly toward me. At the last second, as it lifted off, I needed to throw a 180 and race back after it as it dropped back down onto the road.

I looked at the road; it had a levee on each side about six to eight feet down, each filled with water.

"That's the car over there," Ben said, pointing at a 1957 Chevy Nomad sitting on the side of the road.

I had a bad feeling, and I was right. The Nomad was a six-cylinder, three-speed on the column with a hand brake. I looked back at Roy. "Tubes?"

"Knew you'd want it done, did it," he said.

"Hand break?"

"Cable is as tight as I could make it. It's old; I didn't want to snap it."

"How's it running?" I asked.

He smiled. "Did all we could."

Bob Dawson, the special effect coordinator, walked up, "Where's your Dad, kid?"

I just looked at him.

"Did it again, huh?" he said.

I looked back at Ben. "Who's the pilot?"

"Local guy; owns his own crop duster," he pointed up at the sky. "Here he is now."

Ben was a fighter pilot in World War II; I figured he would have at least checked the guy out. The bi-plane landed on the road and taxied toward us – its prop spinning as it rolled to a stop. The pilot climbed out and pulled up his goggles. The guy was about eighty years old. Maybe eighty-five.

As he approached us, he smiled. I could see he was missing half his teeth.

I looked at Ben. Ben whispered, "It's gonna be fine, pappy."

Later, I asked Jonathan and Jordan Cronenweth, the DPs, where the camera positions were located. There wasn't room for a camera position on either side of the road. So, my main concern was for the safety of the camera crews, not so much what the coverage was.

Jordan said, "We're going to have five cameras on it. They are all mounted on the Nomad, and they focus on the bi-plane in front of you as well as behind you."

"I guess we're going to shoot the rehearsal," I said.

"Great, let's mount the cameras and get a line-up," Jonathan said.

I told Ben I wanted to see the pilot make a practice pass. I put a cone on the highway where he would lift off and another where he would touch down again.

He did the pass; it was perfect. As he taxied past us, he spun a 180 and stopped, facing us. He just sat there looking at me. A half-hour later, he took off.

It was kind of strange sitting in the middle of the road waiting for the bi-plane to get in position. I knew the timing wasn't completely up to me. I had to count on this guy pulling up in time. The entire crew was down the road; they had ducked down out of sight. I looked down at the switches for the five cameras. As the bi-plane arched into view, I realized I was calling "action" for myself.

A couple of seconds later, I rolled the cameras and eased out. I continued to pick up speed as the plane began to drop down. He was coming fast. His wheels touched down, and he continued to taxi directly at me as we quickly closed in on each other.

For a second, I thought he was getting too close. All I could see was the prop growing bigger and bigger in front of me. Then, at the very last second, he started to pull up. I grabbed the hand brake and snapped the 180. As he touched down again, I raced back after him. He continued to taxi down the road. As we both came to a stop, he spun around, facing me.

The crew members began to appear on the road. Jonathan and Jordan ran toward me, "How did it look?" Jonathan shouted.

"It looked pretty good from my view; I think you've got it."

Jonathan was thrilled. Bob Dawson walked up to me and pointed at the top of The Nomad; the top above the windshield had two big concave indentations in the roof, both from the landing gear.

The pilot walked up and looked at Ben, then at me. "Sorry about that. Do you want to do it again?"

I got home in time for dinner that day.

# CHAPTER 33

## What the Hell is a Show Runner?

In television, it started in the early nineties. Giant corporations started buying studios and networks. Lawyers and executives who knew nothing about filmmaking were in charge of the business instead of filmmakers running the studios. After all the years of negotiating with the studios to bring industry wages up, three of the strongest unions in the industry, The Directors Guild, The Screen Actors Guild, and The Writers Guild, all caved.

It was the beginning of the end of quotes.

A director could no longer work using their credits to raise their quote. Before the change up, if someone did a good job directing a project and it was well received, their quote would go up. It was the same system for SAG members.

No longer. "Scale" became the new norm. And it was a hard pill to swallow. At the time, I had the highest D.G.A. quote for a Movie of the Week and a mini-series in the industry. Then the term "Show Runner" began to appear. For years, the director and the producer had creative control over a project once it went into physical production. The writer was given writer's credit or executive producer credit; that was it. Before it became a writer's medium, it was a studio medium.

Writers are just that – writers. And often, they are not suited for managerial roles. They're really two different parts of the brain. Sometimes what's on the written page doesn't always translate visually to the screen - that is where the filmmaker came in.

I've always thought that making movies was such a collaborative medium. The system that had been in place for forty years seemed to work pretty well. The director used to have the final word during production. He or she was hired to bring their vision to life. Now the show runner would oversee that and have the final word.

In this new era, a show runner is often a head writer that the studio has chosen. In most cases, this person didn't write the original material. But they become responsible for all creative aspects of the show and are only accountable to the Network.

Regardless of what I think, it is now the new norm.

# CHAPTER 34

## The Mother City

In early 2005 I was doing a project with David Connell in Toronto, Canada. My agent wanted to know if I could call Dean Devlin in L.A. Dean had produced *Independence Day, The Patriot,* and *Stargate.* When I spoke with him, he asked if he could fly up from L.A. and meet with me in the morning. I asked him what it was about; he told me he had a six-hour mini-series that he and his partner, Bryan Singer, wanted me to direct. Bryan had directed *Usual Suspects, X-Men, Valkerie,* and was currently in Australia directing *Superman.*

I said sure; when I got back to the hotel that night, the script was there waiting for me. It was *The Triangle,* a very high profile mini-series for the Sci-Fi Network.

I had met Dean briefly on *The Diary of Ellen Rimbauer;* his girlfriend Lisa Brenner, whom he later married, starred in it.

That morning I met with him in the restaurant at the Sutton Place Hotel in Toronto before I went to work. He seemed very excited about me being involved. He did mention I had to give him an answer because there was a ticking clock. The Sci-Fi Network had an offer out to director Michael Watkins. They were going to close his deal that afternoon.

I asked Dean how he could get out of it, and he said Bryan told him, "If Baxley says yes, I'll take care of it." Dean didn't mention I had to leave for Cape Town, South Africa, two days after I completed the project I was doing. That meant the following week.

He also failed to mention the budget was a third less than *Storm of the Century,* and that my salary was half of what I was paid for that series. Not only was *The Triangle* more ambitious than *Storm of the*

*Century*, it had over eight hundred visual effects that I also had to shoot all the elements for.

But the business was continually changing. If I wanted to stay current, I needed to be flexible and change with it.

There was one sticking point Dean fought me on. When I told him I wanted to bring on my DP, David Connell, and my editor, Sonny Baskin, he said that wouldn't work. It was a firm no. He wanted the Director of Photography he had on *Eight Legged Freaks* and his brother-in-law as the editor.

The day before I left, he finally agreed how important it was for me to have both of them, and we made their deals. I also brought on my son as my stunt coordinator and second unit director. Then I was on my way to South Africa.

Working in South Africa was an amazing experience. The crew had an incredible work ethic, like the Australians. Cape Town, "The Mother City," turned out to be one of my all-time favorite locations. We had an amazing cast led by Eric Stoltz and Sam Neill. We also had Charlie Martin Smith, Lou Diamond Phillips, Catherine Bell, Bruce Davison, and Lisa Brenner.

Dean and Bryan were never on location. Dean was doing *Flyboys* in London, and Bryan was shooting *Superman* in Australia. I was lucky to have a great producer on location with me, Alex Garcia. He was there every day, twenty-four-seven - a very sharp and savvy filmmaker.

We built a full-scale replica of the Santa Maria and placed it on a platform device. The device was a massive forty-foot hydraulic multi-axis gimbal, and it was capable of doing a twenty to thirty degree front to back, side to side movement. We surrounded the ship with huge dump tanks and special effects men with fire hoses that would cover the entire ship. The massive amount of water created the illusion of a raging storm while giant waves from all sides pummeled the ship. Stuntmen were hit and thrown to the decks by the water from the dump tanks.

We also put a sixty-foot cigarette boat, also known as a go-fast boat, on the gimbal. We then created the raging storm again, and chased the cigarette boat with three V-22 Osprey tilt-rotor aircrafts firing rockets from their APKWA systems (Advanced Precision Kill Weapons System). The cast was amazing; they never complained even though we did multiple takes.

One of my favorite sequences involved the head-on confrontation between a 747 airliner and eight World War II fighter planes. As the fighters closed head-on and screamed past the 747, the 747 went into an evasive steep dive. To create the illusion of weightlessness inside, we rigged cables through the ceiling of the set to pick points throughout the stage. Then, on cue, dozens of passengers (stunt people) were sucked straight up into the ceiling, others spinning across the cabin through the air. Complete chaos. It was visually amazing; you couldn't stop watching the playback. We filmed it in two days.

Alex Garcia got a call from Bryan Singer. He watched our dailies and loved the sequence. Alex said Bryan had just shot the interior of his 747 to create the same illusion. He'd spent seven days shooting it. Alex told me Bryan had just scheduled a re-shoot and would completely re-do his sequence to mimic ours.

In our mini-series, the 747 had disappeared into the Bermuda Triangle, only to be located by divers years later at the bottom of the ocean. After we finished filming the 747 set, it was sealed and became a giant tank for the underwater sequence in which we filmed divers going through the cabin, past the rows of empty seats. All the passengers had vanished.

We filmed 90 percent of the mini-series in Cape Town, then finished up shooting in Miami and on the Seven Mile Bridge in the Florida Keys.

The Sci-Fi Network was extremely happy with the end result. They had a gala premiere at the Design Center on Melrose in West Hollywood. After the screening of Part 1, they held an amazing cocktail reception. Bonnie Hammer, the president of the network, and Brian Singer walked up to Valerie and me. Bonnie was beaming, "We loved it, Craig."

Brian shook my hand, "Blew me away, Baxley. Great job."

*The Triangle* Won a Saturn Award in 2006 for Best Television Presentation and a Primetime Emmy for Outstanding Visual Effects.

# CHAPTER 35

## Talking Head

In 2006, on the last day of the mix on *The Triangle,* I got a call on the mixing stage. It was stuntman David Barrett, the son of stuntman Stan Barrett. Stan was married to Patty McCoy, and her family owned the Mammoth Mountain Ski Resort in California.

David explained that Bruckheimer Television had shut the *E-Ring* series down after fourteen episodes. Taylor Hackford had directed the pilot. The show wasn't canceled; it was a reorganizing period. They were ready to start filming again, and they wanted me to direct the first episode.

David told me he was the director-producer on the series. I'd never heard that term used before on a series. I wasn't sure what it was.

I asked him, "When would you need me?"

"When do you finish the mix on *The Triangle?*"

"Today is our last day."

"Tomorrow then," he said

On my first day of prep, he walked into my office and sat a thick binder on my desk. Without missing a beat, he said, "This is the bible."

"The bible?" I asked.

"I wrote it. It tells you what you can do and can't do on the *E-Ring* series."

I thought he was joking; he explained to me that it was his job to make sure all the directors followed it - that it defined the new look of *E-Ring.* After he walked out, I opened it and looked at it briefly. It told me when and where I could or couldn't use handheld: never in the main *E-Ring* set. It also explained when I could utilize Steadicam, but only if approved by him. Furthermore, any changes in an action sequence had to be run past him for his approval.

I knew then what a director-producer was.

I tossed the bible in the drawer and started prepping.

On my last day of prep, the director of the next episode walked into my office and introduced himself, David Anspaugh. David had directed *Rudy, Hoosiers,* and multiple episodes of *Miami Vice, Hill Street Blues,* and *St. Elsewhere.*

He was really upset; he asked me, "Who the hell is David Barrett?"

"You mean our director-producer?"

"Yeah, what the hell is that anyway? He said I had to shoot 'the bible.' If I didn't, he was going to fire me on the spot."

I knew ageism had been creeping into our business for the past decade, but David was only in his early sixties, and a fine director. I told him to do what he always did; nobody was going to fire anyone.

He sat down, and we started to discuss the show. I knew he had directed Dennis Hopper on *Hoosiers.*

I told him how my father had doubled Dennis on *Gunfight at the O.K. Corral.* Then I explained the last time I saw Dennis was in 1981. I was on a flight to Acapulco, Mexico, sitting between Marty Feldman and Kenneth Mars. Both were there to start filming *Yellowbeard,* and I was there for *The A-Team* pilot. As our plane taxied to a stop, we watched the Federales carry a man wearing nothing but his underwear off another plane on the tarmac. That man was Dennis Hopper, who was out of his mind, screaming incoherently.

David loved hearing the story. If there ever should have been a director-producer on a series, I thought it should have been David Anspaugh. He was a truly great filmmaker.

And now here I was to direct Dennis Hopper and his amazing cast: Benjamin Bratt and Aunjanue Ellis. When I met with Dennis, it was in the main *E-Ring* set. I was going to utilize the Steadicam for a two-and-a-half-page scene. I noticed the crew rolling three teleprompters onto the set. I asked the first assistant, "What are those for?"

"Dennis," he said. "He uses them all the time."

Nobody mentioned that during prep—no one, not even our director-producer. I planned to do a "walk and talk," working through a 360-degree blocking sequence so that we could see the entire set.

As Dennis walked up to me, he asked, "Are you Paul's kid?"

"Yes," I replied.

"You know he doubled me on *Gunfight at the O.K. Corral.* How is he?"

"He's great." I looked at the three teleprompters and smiled. "Yeah, he's great; he wouldn't need to use these."

"Funny, kid, let's do the rehearsal, huh?"

As we ran through it, I blocked the move for the camera operator; I knew it would be tough. But I thought I could still do it without seeing the teleprompters. After rehearsal, the crew began to light the set. When we came back to shoot the scene, the teleprompters were gone.

I looked at the first assistant as Dennis walked back onto the set.

Dennis looked at me and smiled. "Tell Pops hello for me."

He and Benjamin Bratt nailed it on the first take.

The schedule was pretty intense, six days on stage and one day out. My exterior locations had three moves in and around Los Angeles; then one last move back across town at the lot in Culver City. The last location was meant to be in the Middle East. I had the production designer dress an alley between two stages like Afghanistan.

I remember what my favorite director, Ridley Scott, had done on one of my favorite films: *Black Hawk Down* (another was *Black Rain;* both in my top ten). He desaturated the film and varied the shutter speed on the action, which gave the illusion of staccato flashes of gunfire and pieces of the explosions hanging in the air. When we played it back, our footage was very cool.

Then I realized David, my director-producer, and his executives were standing directly behind me. The DP had called David to tell him what I was doing.

"What do you think you're doing, man? Marv called me."

I looked at Marv; he looked like he just swallowed the canary. I just said, "Take a look at it."

We played it back. Mr. Director-Producer wasn't happy. But his executives sure were. It became the look for the exteriors for the rest of the series.

My episode was called "Five Pillars," which featured Aunjanue. I got lucky — she was magic, an absolutely incredible actress. She blew me away with her performance.

When the executive producer and CEO of Jerry Bruckheimer Television, Jonathan Littman, saw the episode, he called my agent. He told him "Five Pillars" was his wet dream. When the season ended, "Five Pillars" and "Fallen Angels," the episode David Anspaugh directed, were his two favorites.

# CHAPTER 36

## The Lost Room

My agent told me Lionsgate Television had an eight-part mini-series, *The Lost Room,* and they wanted to alternate two directors. It was a co-production with Lionsgate and the Sci-Fi Network. I asked him who the other director was; it was Michael Watkins. He told me he would send me the script so I could read it before my meeting.

The next day I was sitting in the office of the Chairman of Lionsgate Television, Kevin Beggs. He was flanked on each side by six of his executives. Through the years, I realized the shortest tenure of anybody in the industry was that of a television executive. It always seemed like they had a short learning curve, then they were gone. Out with the old in with the new. I didn't recognize anyone in the room.

After we discussed the material, I asked him what the budget was. When he told me, I told him I didn't think they had the budget for a six-part, let alone an eight-part, mini-series. If they made it a six-part, I thought it made more sense to have one director do it.

He told me they'd already made a deal with Michael Watkins. I told him, "No harm, no foul. Michael's a fine director, and he'll do a great job."

The room was dead silent for a couple of seconds, then he said, "Okay, great. We'll be in touch." End of meeting.

The next day I got a call; Kevin Beggs wanted to meet with me again. This time the tone of the meeting was completely different. Kevin said he had discussed it with his execs, and they agreed with me about the budget. He said he'd like to have me involved. The idea was to scale it back to a three-part mini-series.

I asked him, "You've already made a deal with Michael; what am I doing here?" Something didn't feel right.

Kevin decided to have me direct the first part, Michael the second, and me the third.

He went on to explain, "Michael is okay with it; he's got something else he's been offered." The problem was that they could only offer me scale for the first and third parts.

The room was dead silent. I realized everybody was staring at me. Waiting for my answer. This was another example of the new norm. It really didn't matter to me. I liked the material, so I accepted the deal.

Later, when I met Michael, I liked him immediately. He told me Lionsgate basically paid him off. They paid him for directing two parts when he was only going to direct one. He said, "I guess we're even for *The Triangle*, huh?" We both laughed.

Next stop? New Mexico. I had David Connell, Sonny Baskin, and my son with me on the project. As we scouted locations in Albuquerque and Santa Fe, we assembled another great local crew for the shoot. After the first part, which was actually the pilot, I handed the crew to Michael for the second episode.

During prep, I realized it was going to be an interesting journey. The three first-time writers were given executive producer credit as well as their writing credit: Laura Harkim, Christopher Leone, and Paul Workman. The producers also informed me that the three were going to be on the set as well. This was something new; it was like having three wannabe show runners on set. The three writers were there twenty-four-seven; they knew nothing about physical production or on-set protocol. A writer telling an actor how to interpret or play their character is not the most productive thing to do. I tried to stress how important it was for the cast to have one voice during production. They didn't have a clue.

I asked them if I could see the script for the third episode; I was told they were doing a final polish.

Once again, the saving grace was we had a great cast: Peter Krause, Julianna Margulies, Elle Fanning, Peter Jacobson, Dennis Christopher, and Kevin Pollak, among others.

Julianna's first day started off a bit awkward. When she was introduced to me, she asked, "So, you were a stuntman, huh?"

Not sure where this was going, I simply said, "Yes, I was."

"Well," she continued, "I just worked with a director who was a stuntman. It was the worst experience of my life."

"What was that on?" I asked.

"*Snakes on a Plane.*"

I knew who the director was. Was the question rhetorical? Suggesting a similarity or a difference? It seemed unimportant and petty. In my mind, there's no comparison between two stuntmen or two directors, whether one is better than the other. I just shrugged and said, "Well, let's hope you have a better experience on this one, huh?"

We filmed it in Albuquerque, Estancia, Santa Fe, the New Mexico State Prison, Moriarty, and the Zia Pueblo. The pilot went well; I was very happy with it. I handed it off to Michael and went back to L.A. to discuss the third episode with the network executives.

When I went to Lionsgate for the meeting, I sat there with Kevin and his executives; there was no script for the third episode. No outline. Nothing. Kevin told me he just spoke with the writers, and they assured him when I returned, I would have the script to prep.

This was a first for me; I'd never heard of a studio green lighting, let alone buying a mini-series without seeing the finished material. There were always adjustments to make, but at least you could figure out the best way to budget and schedule it. Nobody at Lionsgate or the Sci-Fi Network seemed to care; I was told they loved the dailies.

When I arrived back in Albuquerque on the second day of my prep, the production manager told me there was still no script. I asked, "Where are the writers? Let's sit down and figure it out."

"They're out on location with Michael," he said.

We had a location breakdown, nothing more. I knew *The Lost Room* needed closure at the end of the third episode, yet it had to be left open for a series. I was very lucky to have Eric Grenaudier as our visual effects supervisor. He and I sat down and started discussing concepts with our production designer, Keith Neely. At the end of the third day, we got the first five acts, but we still didn't have an ending.

Eric, Keith, and I pitched our idea to the writers. Chris liked it, Laura and Paul weren't sure they understood it. They said they needed more time to explore the show's resolution. But they never could figure out how *The Lost Room* would end visually. I convinced the producers to pitch our concept to Lionsgate and Sci-Fi Network. We ended up filming the concept that Eric, Keith, and I developed. It was pretty cool. And it left it open for a possible series.

Regardless, we finished the show on time and on budget. The ratings were better than anyone expected. Lionsgate and the Sci-Fi Network wanted to go straight to series, but each wanted a bigger stake in the show. The head of the Sci-Fi Network wouldn't give in. So it went away, only to be re-invented a few years later by the Sci-Fi Network as *Warehouse 13*.

The Lost Room was nominated for several awards:

- 2007 Saturn Award for Best Television Presentation
- Best Direction
- Best Production Design
- Best Visual Effects
- Best Casting in a Mini-series
- Best Lead Actor for Peter Krause
- Young Artist Award for Elle Fanning

# CHAPTER 37

## Want to Stay in the Game?

Long gone were the days of the big-budget TNT westerns. When Ted Turner sold the network, the era of Turner Classics was over.

*Aces 'N' Eights* was written by Dennis Shryack, who wrote *Pale Rider* and *The Gauntlet.* He also wrote the Movie of the Week I had directed earlier, *Revenge on the Highway.* Aces and eights are known as the "dead man's hand." It was the hand held by Wild Bill Hickok when he was shot in the back of the head at the poker table.

There I was, sitting across from Nick Lombardo. Nick was the head of production at TNT when I did *Avenging Angel.* Now he was head of production at RHI/Hallmark. My agent had already told me what the budget was, less than seventy-five percent of what I had on *Avenging Angel. Aces 'N' Eights* was also a period western.

Nick said, "You realize what you've gotten yourself into?"

If you wanted to stay relevant, you had to play the game. I told him, "Yeah, it's a good script; I'll push the envelope, get it done. Maybe we can get a decent cast."

The cast was solid: Casper Van Dien, Bruce Boxleitner, Jeff Kober, Jack Noseworthy, and Ernest Borgnine. I also had my son on as my stunt coordinator. With such a low budget, he ended up doing most of the major stunts on the film himself.

We filmed it in twenty days. After I delivered my cut, I got a call from Nick. He said he loved it, but he wasn't sure if they would get it. It might be too stylized for RHI.

* * * * *

I got a call from Dean Devlin; I'd directed *The Triangle* mini-series for him. He wanted me to come in and direct the third episode of his new series, *Leverage*. I found it kind of funny; he had my DP, David Connell, and my editor, Sonny Baskin, on the series - the two he'd fought me on when I wanted to bring them on *The Triangle*. This time I was a hired gun, in and out. Dean just wanted it filmed. Creativity and freshness was not a priority, as it had been on *The Triangle*.

After that, I wasn't sure if the episodic world was a world I wanted to live in.

In 2009, I was off to Vancouver, British Columbia, for an episode of *Harper's Island*. It was nice to be back, having spent a year and a half there on *Kingdom Hospital*. Vancouver is a beautiful city.

I got a call in 2011 from the director-producer on *Human Target*, a series on Fox which was also being filmed in Vancouver. After my experience with the director-producer on the *E-Ring*, I was hesitant to take the job. But the fact that he was somebody I'd gotten into the business when I signed for his SAG card and his DGA card? I thought it might be fun to do. And he was a member of Stunts Unlimited.

When he called me, he told me I'd be following him in the rotation - that I would have eight days of first unit and one day of second unit. It sounded great; I was in. He asked me if I could write a more exciting conclusion to my episode. I came up with a Parkour, a free-running sequence with explosions weaved in and more exciting fights.

I got lucky again; my episode featured Jackie Earle Haley. It was titled "Cool Hand Guerrero." I really enjoyed working with him. He's such a talented and smart actor. I suggested James Remar for the part of the Prison Warden. The show runner and my director-producer said we would never get him; he doesn't do episodic. I called James directly, then called them back and told them we had him for the money.

When I got to Vancouver, the production manager explained that the director-producer's episode was running over and he needed more time to finish it. He told her to take one day of first unit and my only day of second unit from my episode. I tried to explain that I had been asked to expand the action in the last act on my episode.

She said, "He said you would be fine, and you'd understand."

I shot the script as written. When we got to the final sequence, I tried to do the free-running scene I wrote justice. We did one shot where I had a stunt double leap across from one beam to another, then down twelve feet to another beam, then down onto one of the running heavies amidst explosions. For the first piece, we rigged a cable overhead so I could have a cameraman (my stunt coordinator) in a harness with a wire hooked to the overhead cable. Then he slid down it, maintaining the distance behind the stunt double. It was a very cool shot.

We finished the episode in seven days, but the last day was over eighteen hours. So much for it being okay. My director-producer friend just turned out to be another talking head. After I finished the episode, I wasn't surprised to learn that he was a friend of David Barrett, the director-producer of the *E-Ring*.

# CHAPTER 38

## Nirvana

Nirvana appears when we let go - when we live in the reality of the present. It refers to profound peace of mind or enlightenment, synonymous with rebirth.

I started in the motion picture industry fifty years ago. It wasn't always an easy career. Long, tough hours sometimes. I've lived and worked through the three greatest decades of the motion picture business - before the corporations, CGI, and comic book characters/ action. I was front and center when it was about filmmaking.

Through the years, I've watched people like my father become bitter about the changes, yet he couldn't walk away after an incredible career. Others like him couldn't leave the business or Los Angeles. They just couldn't let go; it was in their blood. It became their persona; it was what defined them. "Oh, my god, you're a stuntman," or "Oh, my god, you're a motion picture director." It seemed like a professional athlete; their ego needed the recognition.

The magical people that I was lucky to have in my life were the friends that stayed with me through the years. Through the hard times and the good times. They are the ones that defined who I became in the industry. My friends were also part of my family: Henry Kingi, Bobby 'O', and Tony Brubaker. They also knew I was completely committed to them.

My family understood that if I worked overtime and couldn't make it home for a birthday or dinner date, it was my job. They understood the business. My job never defined who I was. I was a husband and a father. It was just my job.

In 1987 Valerie and I designed and built our "Dream Home" on two acres in a gated community called Indian Springs. Fifty-two, two-acre lots in Southern California, Indian Springs was developed on the Iverson movie ranch by Gene Kilmer, Val Kilmer's father. It's actually where Val and his two brothers grew up. The community was surrounded by beautiful massive rock formations similar to the rock formations in Santa Fe, New Mexico. It was the best kept secret in L.A. It is where they filmed the *Lone Ranger* and hundreds of other classic Westerns.

The home we built was a two-story Mediterranean 6500 square foot villa. The property had eighteen mature oak trees on it when we purchased it. We landscaped it like Hawaii, with over two dozen thirty-foot palm trees. We also had a grove of twenty fruit trees, a beautiful pool with a Baja shelf, and fountains. It was our beautiful oasis tucked away from Los Angeles.

**The front of the house in California**

**The rear of the house in California**

Life was good; Smokey Robinson lived two lots down from us for over twenty years. We'd watched the neighborhood grow; it became an incredible development. Cedric the Entertainer moved in down the street about ten years ago.

I always thought this was where Valerie and I were going to spend the rest of our lives. Then one day, she heard me talking with our friend Henry Kingi about how the business had changed, and how hundreds of guys were calling themselves stuntmen. Most of them had no idea what it meant to really be a stuntman. Most of their work came from doing background, basically extra work for major CGI action sequences.

She had an epiphany. Valerie said, "This has been a wonderful home. I've loved living here. We've raised both our kids here. But it's just too much for two people, honey. It's over 6500 square feet. When we grew up in California, what took thirty minutes to drive to, now takes almost three hours. There are homeless camps everywhere; our water is now $3500 for two months. The traffic. The smog. What are we doing?"

A couple of months later, I got a call from our son; he had just returned from doing a job in Hawaii. And he couldn't believe some of the people he was asked to work with. He said, "Dad, I look in their eyes, and they know I know they haven't a clue. They have no business calling themselves stuntmen."

When I told Valerie what he said, she looked away for a couple of seconds and just shook her head. "You know I've been thinking a lot about this lately." Then she looked back at me. "I don't want to live here anymore. Let's do something new. We both love Hawaii and Mexico; how about Florida?"

I thought she was kidding; two weeks later, we put our home on the market. I knew it was time; I was done.

What is really important? What matters? Maintaining one's integrity, and physical and mental health is what matters. George Bernard Shaw once said, "We don't stop playing because we grow old; we grow old because we stop playing."

During the last fifty years, the business had taken us all over the world. So many amazing locations. So many incredible experiences together. Directing over thirty-three projects. The motion pictures, the mini-series, the Movies of the Week, and the episodic television. Not to mention the stunts. I'm very proud of those stunts.

I've always lived my life moving forward, growing every day. Memoirs are about looking back. I want to thank Valerie for sharing her recollections of our ride together and helping me piece together all the memories.

It was time to begin the next chapter of our life.

I knew it would be Hawaii or Florida; we both love a warm climate and warm water. Not to mention Valerie grew up in Hawaii. It was going to be a tough decision.

Our son lives in California with our three grandchildren. Our daughter, her husband, and two grandchildren live in Florida.

Quality of life, beautiful white sandy beaches, palm trees everywhere, crystal clear blue water, fresh local fish. No state tax.

Florida it was.

**Valerie in Jupiter, Florida**

We now live in Jupiter, Florida. We love how simple life feels now. On the water. Our Nirvana. But two nights ago, our new security guard pulled up to me while I was walking Sammy D, our black-faced caramel-colored pug.

His window slid down.

I said, "Hi, I'm Craig."

"Oh yeah, I know who you are; you're the stunt guy."

I thought to myself, what a lucky man I am.

Top: **Grandson, Cash Baxley, First Place. Los Angeles, 2017 Junior Karting Championship Series**

Bottom & Left: **Son, Craig Baxley Jr., car jumps**

# EPILOGUE

*Tiger father begets tiger son.*
CHINESE PROVERB

It's funny how future generations sometimes follow in the footsteps of their fathers: like father, like son. It's not always easy to follow in your father's footsteps, which some say is the embodiment of the American Dream.

Our son Craig and his son, Cash, are just that. When it comes to our family, we are our father's sons. Both Craig and Cash have carved out their path and destiny in the motion picture industry. I couldn't be more proud of both of them.

**Paul Baxley (1923-2011)**

# IN MEMORY

## Paul Baxley

Thanks for starting it all; what a ride, huh?
I love and miss you, Dad.

## PAUL BAXLEY FILM CREDITS

A Place in the Sun
Adventures of Don Juan
All the Young Men
Around the World in 80 Days
Baby Face Nelson
Black Shield of Fallworth
Boy on the Dolphin
Captain Nice
Captains and the Kings
Cast of 1999
Catch 22
Charlie Chan & the Curse of the Dragon Queen
Charlie Varrick

Comanche Territory
Coogan's Bluff
Death Hunt
Deep Red
Deep Valley
Desert Legion
Diamonds are Forever
Elmer Gantry
Exorcist III
Fun with Dick & Jane
Gemini Man
Get Christie Love
Getting Even
Giant

Man in the Grey Flannel Suit
Man with the Golden Arm
Mr. Majestyk
Mutiny on the Bounty
One Eyed Jacks
Pee-Wee's Big Adventure
Pirates of Monterey
Pontiac Moon
Rebel Without a Cause
Red Badge of Courage
Red Beret
Report to the Commissioner
Revenge on the Highway
Rich Man, Poor Man
Riverboat
Rob Roy
Shadow-Ops
Shane
Shy People
Son of Alibaba
Son of Dr. Jeckle
Spartacus
Star Trek
Stone Cold
Storm of the Century
Strangers on a Train
Sunburn
Switch
T109
Telefon
T.H.E. Cat
The Appaloosa
The Avenging Angel

Goin' Coconuts
Gunfight at the OK Corral
Harper
Harum Scarum
Hell Below Zero
Hell on Frisco Bay
I Come in Peace
In God We Trust
Knock on Any Door
Kolchak: The Night Stalker
Lady from Shanghai
Left Handed Gun
Mad Bull

The Badlanders
The Black Knight
The Boy Who Cried Werewolf
The Carpetbaggers
The Crimson Pirate
The Deep Six
The Dukes of Hazard
The Godfather
The Great Bank Robbery
The Great Race
The Greatest Story Ever Told
The Helicopter Spies
The Iron Mistress
The Killing of a Chinese Bookie
The Late Show
The Mambo Kings
The Man from U.N.C.L.E.
The Parallax View
The Prize
The Proud Rebel

The Split
The Travels of Jamie McPheeters
The Ugly American
The Untouchables
The West Point Story
The White Dawn
Third Day
Twlight Man
Vagabond King
Viva Las Vegas
Wagon Train
What's Up Doc?
Whiplash

**PAUL BAXLEY**

As

Lieutenant Cotter

**Paul Baxley (1923-2011)**

# ACKNOWLEDGMENTS

The author would like to thank the people who made this journey possible: Paul Baxley, Stephen King, Warren Beatty, Henry Kingi, Tony Brubaker, Bob Orrison, and all my brothers and sisters at Stunts Unlimited. And to all the other incredible filmmakers I had the pleasure of working with through the years.

A special thanks to Ken W. Hanley, who provided an insightful foreword and penned *FANTASTICA presents Inside the cult of Craig R. Baxley. The Prophet of Action Cinema.* Originally published on FANGORIA.com, July 14, 2015.

My sincere appreciation to Michele Dalton, my editor.

And to my wife Valerie, who took the ride with me from day one.

# A GIFT FROM CRAIG

### Excerpt from "FIVE HOURS"

## PROLOGUE

*"Life is more or less a lie, but then again,
that's exactly the way we want it to be."*

— BOB DYLAN

An arid plain.

A mind-blowing landscape.

Living Clouds.

The wind slowly snaked through golden grass, undulating like an irresistible siren's hips.

Locust made a steady, unnerving sound as an orange ball was slowly swallowed by the horizon - the other worldly light continuing to seep away across the vast expanse of the Zuni Pueblo reservation in Grants County, 150 miles south of Black Rock, New Mexico.

The breeze whistled and moaned as an American flag flapped above an ancient airstream trailer – its busted screen door slowly creaking on tired hinges. The wind snapped a sheet of plastic in a window.

Somewhere a dog barked, and a rhythmic rumble grew louder.

Inside, a lamp illuminated a motionless silhouette. A pair of black eyes watched, and his rough hand ran over the top of a pack of cigarettes like a blind man reading braille.

Outside, a pick-up rolled into view and stopped. Polarized aviator sunglasses shielded the driver's eyes from the sun. For five hours, he had raced across the flatlands of New Mexico.

The driver climbed out; his eyes fixed on the silhouette in the window. He reached inside the pick-up and pulled out a briefcase.

As he moved away from the vehicle with the briefcase in one hand and a Glock-19 pistol in the other, a diamond back rattler coiled out, rattling and hissing. He fired once; the gunshot echoed through the valley like the aftermath of dynamite as the flaming sun extinguished itself on the horizon.

* * * * *

## CHAPTER 1
*Five Hours Earlier*

A white band cracked the pre-dawn horizon of the barren Mexican desert. The sun was barely beginning to appear.

Somewhere on Route 81 in the Chihuahua Desert, a dark shape continued to grow through a collage of shimmering heat waves, slowly resolving into a Jeep Cherokee. Camping equipment was strapped to the roof.

Inside it was silent, except for the steady hum of the road. The driver, Jack Mathews, looked up at his reflection in the rearview mirror then back toward the highway. The stubble that darkened his jawline and crow's feet around his eyes suggested his twenties were well behind him.

Eyes hidden by sunglasses, he rumbled, "Did I do anything last night I should know about?" Jack quickly glanced over at his passenger, Samantha Collins.

Her eyes refocused and blinked to attention. She brushed the hair back from her face and wiped the perspiration from her forehead.

"You okay, Sam?"

"I couldn't get to sleep last night; I think the trouble started with the shots," she replied.

"We said we'd come down here and give it a chance."

She turned and looked into his eyes. A silence hung between them; she just stared at him as he continued.

"I'm trying. You still on board?"

She nodded her head, then leaned in and kissed him softly. "Of course I am. You dream about me last night?"

"Yeah."

"Have a good time?" she suggestively asked.

"Yeah… So'd you," he said.

She smiled and settled back, her eyes focused on a sign on the shoulder that announced: "Antelope Wells Border Inspection Station, 3 miles."

In the distance, a building with a corrugated metal roof squatted in the sweltering heat. A man wearing a wife-beater t-shirt and ball cap stood, leaning against the side of a pick-up. Polarized aviator-style sunglasses shielded his eyes from the bright morning sun. He watched the Cherokee as it pulled into the parking lot of the run down gas station and rolled to a stop in front of a small market.

A couple of bikers sat revving their engines, waiting to take off. As the couple climbed out of the Cherokee, Jack's eyes flicked past Sam to one of the bikers; the biker looked back. For an instant, their eyes locked. The biker nodded, sharing a hint of a smile. One of those nods like, "I know you." Jack warily acknowledged the stranger.

The man leaning against the pick-up continued to watch them with an impassive face. Sam looked up at him. A moment passed between them, then she looked back at Jack. "I'll see ya in a minute," she said before she continued around the side of the market and disappeared from view.

Jack opened the screen door to the market and walked inside. The place was empty and blistering hot. He got his bearings as he made his way through the small store. A ceiling fan slowly turned above him, circulating the suffocating heat.

The Ed Sullivan show with "Topo Gigio" droned from a TV. A man sat behind the register eating a burrito, speaking into the phone in Spanish, watching Jack approach.

Jack caught an old woman looking at him, waving herself with a hand fan, trying to stay cool. He looked at her with a good-natured smile. "Morning."

The woman glared at him; she didn't understand English and didn't like Gabachos either.

A few minutes later, Jack paid for two coffees, exchanging pleasantries with the man in broken Spanish.

He looked around the room. Something was bothering him, but he didn't know what it was. He looked back, out the front window

at the Cherokee. Sam wasn't back yet. Jack pushed open the screen
door, moving toward the Cherokee, looking around; the bikers were
gone, so was the pick-up. The only other vehicle in the parking lot
was a black, late model Chrysler 300.

Jack set the coffees on the hood of the Cherokee, then glanced
back at the market. A dim light shined from a dirty window inside
a small, rundown, disgusting restroom. Jack's voice rang out, "Sam,
are you okay?"

A beat later, the door swung open. Light spilled in from outside
as Jack leaned in, "Sam?" His eyes did a fast scan of the tiny room.
There was a brutal silence. The only sounds were the water-torture-
like noise of a slow drip in the rust stained sink and the muffled echo
of the Mexican music playing in the market.

He stood there trying to process the scene. He seemed to have
trouble breathing, and he found his image staring back at him from
the mirror. A beat later, he was gone. On a dead run toward the
Cherokee, looking in every direction, he shouted, "Samantha?!"

Still, no Sam. He started to panic and moved back toward the
market when suddenly a cell phone rang. He recognized it; it was
Sam's. He ran back to the Cherokee, reached inside, and picked it up,
"Where are you?"

A man's voice answered, "Some vacation, huh?"

"Who is this?! You listen to me, if…"

The voice interrupted, "If you ever want to see her again, don't
talk. Listen."

Jack tried to remain calm as the voice continued, "Are you
listening to me, Jack?"

"How do you know my name?"

"Keys are in the ignition. You've got five hours to drive to Gallup."

Jack started to lose it, "What are you talking about?! I'm not
leaving Sam!"

"You have nothing to worry about as long as you do what you're
told."

Jack hesitated, then said, "Gallup is an eight hour drive."

"I love New Mexico… where else can you travel 1,000 miles in
just under eight hours. You've got five. Do we understand each other,
Jack?"

The line went dead. Jack stood motionless, his head spinning, feeling like the most helpless man alive. Then he looked back at the Chrysler.

* * * * *

**Get the rest of Craig's new novella, "5 Hours"
when you join his mailing list at:
www.CraigBaxley.com**

# BOOK PREVIEW

## Excerpt from "Last Exit to Hell"

It had been 2,027 days since a massive technological failure brought the entire planet to a standstill. The population became consumed by images of what people thought they wanted to be, never realizing that those images were slowly taking over and assimilating their world.

Nobody could remember the exact moment when they lost control of their lives. But it happened; and, there wasn't anything they could do about it.

Man's entire existence had been cataloged into bytes of information – every shred of humanity – all passed into a melting pot of deleted programs. Glitches. Viruses and updates. It was a wave of information that defined everything about the human race.

Meanwhile, quantum computers explored a parallel universe with shared memory and distributed it with memory virtualization that caused a split. The quantum gateway completed a circuit between reality and the parallel world – a world built on a reflection of people as they truly are: all the good, the bad, the evil, and the ugly. In essence, life became a virtual bridge between heaven and hell.

Those that still knew the truth fought to take back what remained of their world. Borders were overrun. The suffering and loss grew to an epic scale. Then came the Plague. Suddenly there was nothing left, just the few that survived.

Those who remained called themselves Clans, and these ravaged creatures were starving. Cannibalism was a rampant necessity that ensured survival since only human blood could guide them to the portal. The lost souls who had gone to the other side were waiting. Those caught in the between, the "Glitches," were their only hope. Only they could free them. It was their blood that would end their pain.

\* \* \* \* \*

"Last Exit to Hell"
**Coming in 2022**
by Craig R. Baxley

# ABOUT THE AUTHOR

Craig Baxley is a third-generation filmmaker. After starting his career in front of the camera, Craig worked his way up as a successful stunt coordinator and second unit director on films like *Predator, Reds, The Long Riders,* and *The Warriors* with such talented directors as Don Siegel, Alan Pakula, Warren Beatty, Norman Jewison, Walter Hill, and Steven Spielberg, after which he transitioned – making his directorial debut on the acclaimed hit series, *The A-Team*.

His first feature film, *Action Jackson,* for Joel Silver, was the beginning of a very diverse career working in many genres. Craig later went on to direct a number of mini-series, including Stephen King's *Storm of the Century* and *Rose Red,* along with the entire television series, *Kingdom Hospital*. Craig also directed Bryan Singer's *The Triangle* and *The Lost Room*.

Craig and his wife, Valerie, live on the water in Jupiter, Florida.

Lightning Source UK Ltd.
Milton Keynes UK
UKHW021331270123
416064UK00014B/845

9 798985 195224